Handbook of War Studies II

Handbook of War Studies II

EDITED BY

Manus I. Midlarsky

Ann Arbor

The University of Michigan Press

Published in the United States of America by
The University of Michigan Press
Manufactured in the United States of America
⊗ Printed on acid-free paper

2003 2002 2001 2000 4 3 2 1

A CIP catalog record for this book is available from the British Library.

Library of Congress Cataloging-in-Publication Data

Handbook of war studies II / edited by Manus I. Midlarsky.
p. cm.
Includes bibliographical references and index.
ISBN 0-472-09724-5 (cloth : alk. paper) —
ISBN 0-472-06724-9 (pbk. : alk. paper)
1. War. 2. International relations. 3. World politics.
I. Midlarsky, Manus I.

U21.2 .H35 2000
355.02—dc21 00-037734

Contents

Part III. Structure-Based Theories of War

Part IV. Summary Approaches

Contributors

Michael Brecher is the R. B. Angus Professor of Political Science at McGill University. He was the founder of the Shastri Indo-Canadian Institute (1968) and is president of the International Studies Association in 1999–2000. He has held visiting professorships at the University of Chicago, the Hebrew University of Jerusalem, Berkeley, and Stanford. Among his 17 books, the most recent are *Crises in World Politics* (1993) and *A Study of Crisis* (1997), coauthored with Jonathan Wilkenfeld, which is also available in a paperback/CD-ROM version (2000).

Claudio Cioffi-Revilla is Professor of Political Science and Director of the Long-Range Analysis of War (LORANOW) Project at the University of Colorado, Boulder. He has published more than 30 works on the causes of war in journals such as the *American Political Science Review, American Journal of Political Science, Cross-Cultural Research, Journal of Conflict Resolution, International Studies Quarterly, Synthese*, and *Mathematical and Computer Modeling*. He is the author or coauthor of *Mathematical Models in International Relations, Communication and Interaction in the Global System* (with R. L. Merritt and D. A. Zinnes), *The Scientific Measurement of International Conflict*, and most recent, *Politics and Uncertainty: Theory, Models and Applications* (1998). He has received national and international grants from the National Science Foundation, NATO Science Committee, Italian National Research Council, and others.

Martha Crenshaw is John E. Andrus Professor of Government at Wesleyan University in Middletown, Connecticut. She is the editor of *Terrorism in Context*, a collection of case studies of terrorism ranging from the nineteenth century to the present.

Paul F. Diehl is Professor of Political Science and University "Distinguished Teacher/Scholar" at the University of Illinois at Urbana-Champaign. His recent books include *War and Peace in International Rivalry* (2000), *A Road Map to War: Territorial Dimensions of International Conflict* (1999), *The*

Dynamics of Enduring Rivalries (1998), *International Peacekeeping* (1994), and *Territorial Changes and International Conflict* (1992). He is the editor of seven other books and the author of more than 80 articles on international security matters. His areas of expertise include the causes of war, UN peacekeeping, and international law.

Charles F. Doran is the Andrew W. Mellon Professor of International Relations, Johns Hopkins University, School of Advanced International Studies (SAIS), Washington, D.C., directing both the International Relations Program (Theory and History subfield) and the Center of Canadian Studies. In addition to power cycle theory and its policy implications, his research encompasses security policy and commercial, environmental, and energy resource issues in international politics. Director of a number of research projects on NAFTA and international political economy, Doran also led a major study for the Middle East Institute on Persian Gulf energy security and pioneered work in political risk analysis. Doran is a member of the Council on Foreign Relations, the North American Committee, and the Western Hemisphere Committee of the Atlantic Council. A regular adviser to government and business officials, he has provided congressional briefings and testimony on trade, security, and energy policy.

Daniel S. Geller is Professor of Political Science at the University of Mississippi. In 1998–99, he was William C. Foster Fellow at the U.S. Arms Control and Disarmament Agency and subsequently with the U.S. Department of State. His principal research focus is the quantitative analysis of international conflict, and his theoretical and data-based work involving the effects of military and economic power balances on the probability of interstate wars has been published in such journals as *International Studies Quarterly, Journal of Conflict Resolution, International Interactions,* and the *International Political Science Review.* He is the author of *Domestic Factors in Foreign Policy* (1985) and coauthor (with J. David Singer) of *Nations at War: A Scientific Study of International Conflict* (1998).

Gary Goertz teaches political science at the University of Arizona. His books include *Contexts of International Politics*, and with Paul Diehl *Territorial Change and International Conflict*, and *War and Peace in International Rivalry*. His current research projects include the analysis of conflict management and resolution, the theory and methodology of necessary conditions, and a book on international norms.

Jacek Kugler is the Elisabeth Helms Rosecrans Professor of International Relations at the School of Politics and Economics, Claremont Graduate University, where he has also served as director and chairman. He is the cofounder of Decision Insights Inc. His publications in world politics and political economy are widely available in scholarly journals. He is the coauthor of *The War Ledger, Births, Deaths, and Taxes,* and *Power Transitions* as well as the coeditor of *Parity and War, Exploring the Stability of Deterrence,* and *Political Capacity and Economic Behavior.*

Douglas Lemke is an assistant professor of political science at the University of Michigan and an associate in the Institute for Social Research's Center for Political Studies. He is coeditor of *Parity and War: Evaluations and Extensions of the War Ledger*, coauthor of *Power Transitions: Strategies for the 21st Century*, and the author of articles appearing in various journals.

Jack S. Levy is Board of Governors Professor of Political Science at Rutgers University. He is author of *War in the Modern Great Power System, 1495–1975* and numerous articles and chapters on the causes of war and decision making in foreign policy. His current research interests include the role of loss aversion and problem framing in foreign policy, politically motivated opposition to war, the militarization of commercial rivalries, the phenomenon of trading with the enemy in wartime, and the conditions under which democracies fight "preventive wars."

Manus I. Midlarsky is Moses and Annuta Back Professor of International Peace and Conflict Resolution at Rutgers University. He is the founding past president of the Conflict Processes Section of the American Political Science Association and a past vice president of the International Studies Association. He is the author of *The Evolution of Inequality: War, State Survival, and Democracy in Comparative Perspective* (1999), *The Onset of World War* (1988), *The Disintegration of Political Systems: War and Revolution in Comparative Perspective* (1986), and *On War: Political Violence in the International System* (1975). Midlarsky is also the editor of *Inequality, Democracy, and Economic Development* (1997), *From Rivalry to Cooperation: Russian and American Perspectives on the Post–Cold War Era* (with J. Vasquez and P. Gladkov, 1994), *The Internationalization of Communal Strife* (1992), *Handbook of War Studies* (1989, 1993), and *Inequality and Contemporary Revolutions* (1986). His most recent articles have appeared in the *American Political Science Review, International Studies Quarterly, Journal of Conflict Resolution,* and *Journal of Peace Research.*

James D. Morrow is Professor of Political Science at the University of Michigan. He is the author of *Game Theory for Political Scientists* (1994), and his research applies game theory to explicate theories of international politics. He has published extensively on war and crises, alliances, the domestic politics of foreign policy, and international relations theory in the top journals in political science. In 1994, Morrow received the Karl Deutsch

Award in recognition of his contributions to the scientific study of international politics.

Karen Rasler is Professor of Political Science at Indiana University. Her publications are *The Great Powers and Global Struggle, 1490–1990* and *War and State Making: The Shaping of the Global Powers* (both with William R. Thompson). She has also published a variety of articles in the *American Sociological Review, American Political Science Review, American Journal of Political Science, Journal of Conflict Resolution,* and *International Studies Quarterly.* She is currently working on a research project dealing with the de-escalation of rivalries and the termination of protracted conflicts.

Bruce M. Russett is Dean Acheson Professor of International Relations and Political Science and Director of United Nations Studies at Yale University. He has served as editor of the *Journal of Conflict Resolution* since 1972 and has held visiting appointments at Columbia University, the University of Michigan, the Free University of Brussels, the University of North Carolina, the Richardson Institute in London, the Netherlands Institute for Advanced Studies, and Tel Aviv University. Most recently he was Visiting Professor of International Markets Law at Tokyo University. He has published nearly 200 articles and 21 books, of which the most recent are *Grasping the Democratic Peace: Principles for a Post–Cold War World, The Once and Future Security Council,* and the sixth edition of *World Politics: The Menu for Choice* (with Harvey Starr and David Kinsella). *Triangulating Peace: Democracy, Interdependence, and International Organizations* (with John Oneal) will appear early in 2001.

Harvey Starr is the Dag Hammarskjold Professor in International Affairs and Chair of the Department of Government and International Studies at the University of South Carolina. He specializes in international relations theory and method, international conflict, geopolitics, and foreign policy analysis. He has been vice president of the American Political Science Association, and editor of *International Interactions*. His most recent books are *Anarchy, Order, and Integration: How to Manage Interdependence* (1997), *Agency, Structure, and International Politics* (1997 with Gil Friedman), and the edited volume, *The Understanding and Management of Global Violence* (1999).

William R. Thompson is Professor of Political Science at Indiana University. Recent books include *Great Power Rivalries* (1999) and *The Emergence of the Global Political Economy* (2000). He is currently engaged in projects on the democratic peace, strategic interstate rivalries, evolutionary IR theory, and North-South developmental divergence.

John A. Vasquez is Professor of Political Science at Vanderbilt University specializing in international relations and peace research. His recent books include *The Power of Power Politics: From Classical Realism to Neotraditionalism* (1998), *The War Puzzle* (1993), *In Search of Theory* (with Richard Mansbach; 1981), and *The Scientific Study of Peace and War: A Text-Reader* (coedited with Marie T. Henehan; Lexington Books, 1992, 1999). He has also published articles in *World Politics, International Studies Quarterly, American Political Science Review, International Organization, Journal of Peace Research, Journal of Politics, International Political Science Review, British Journal of Political Science,* and *Millennium*, among others. He is a former president of the Peace Science Society.

Jonathan Wilkenfeld is Professor and Chair in the Department of Government and Politics at the University of Maryland. He is past editor of *International Studies Quarterly* and has been a visiting professor at the Johns Hopkins School for Advanced International Studies and the Hebrew University. He also serves as director of Project ICONS, an Internet-based foreign policy simulation. His most recent book is *Negotiating a Complex World* (with Brigid Starkey and Mike Boyer, 1999).

Introduction

Eleven years ago the *Handbook of War Studies* was published as a summary of empirically based research on the causes of interstate war. Approximately 700 works were cited. A measure of this field's progress is the continuing vigorous concern with the causes of interstate war, but also an emerging strong interest now in the etiology of additional types of warfare and the causes of peace. The temporal dimension of the inquiry also has been expanded considerably. And instead of the roughly 700 references in the earlier handbook, the second one contains approximately 1,300.

Chapters in this new version reflect the political sea changes that have occurred during this past decade. Interest in the arms race, emblematic of the cold war, has abated, to be replaced with newer concerns in uncharted fields of interstate warfare or identity conflict. A new focus like the democratic peace has become virtually a cottage industry for large numbers of international relations scholars captivated by the simultaneous parsimony and substantial explanatory power of the theory. Polarity and other systemic foci, although still important as explanatory variables, have given way now to emphases on dyadic forms of exploration.

These changing emphases are reflected in both the contents of this volume and its organization. Gone are the articles on arms races, although those that appear in the earlier version may still be very useful to scholars. Gone also are the explicit studies of polarity, although, here again, the earlier volume may still be useful, as are certain chapters in this volume that review the earlier studies. Emphases missing from the earlier work such as studies of international crises and game-theoretical concerns are represented here.

Organization of this volume is designed to highlight the newer contributions while recognizing the importance of certain older emphases. To this extent, the book opens with three topical approaches entirely absent from the previous book. Terrorism, identity conflict, and ancient warfare have either demonstrated a tenacious presence over time (terrorism), emerged recently to the forefront as a ubiquitous form of conflict (identity), or demonstrated importance as a research enterprise (ancient warfare).

Terrorism, analyzed by Martha Crenshaw, is seen by her to be a limitation on sovereignty. Its contemporary relevance for international conflict harks back at least to the assassination of the archduke Franz Ferdinand at Sarajevo and extends to the very recent bombings of the U.S. embassies in Kenya and Tanzania. Crenshaw's approach to causation, not surprisingly, follows three levels of analysis: structural conditions at the societal level, strategic calculations of groups, and psychological concerns at the individual or group level. Permissive causes, or background conditions such as geopolitical location and type of political system, are distinguished from precipitants like grievances or social, cultural, and historical facilitation. Interestingly, political parties, the stalwarts of political institutionalization and development can, under certain conditions, give rise to terrorist offshoots. Perhaps the ability to respond effectively to terrorism depends in part on the utilization of the association between terrorists and a political party, as in the negotiations with Sinn Fein leading to a possible future abatement of terrorism and a normalization of politics in Northern Ireland. The presence of international cooperation also is found to be effective, again in the instance of Northern Ireland; the important role of the United States in recent negotiations is a case in point. Yet despite its importance, Crenshaw finds no unifying theory of terrorism, and cumulativeness is weak. This may be a consequence of the absence of common agreed-upon definitions among researchers or simply that terrorism is frequently a random phenomenon admitting of no ready simple explanation. Crenshaw concludes with a provocative list of research questions to be addressed by the international relations scholarly community.

My own chapter on identity and international conflict also is divided into three levels of analysis: the structural systemic roots of such conflict, minimally dyadic ones, and the unit or group level. Because the most devastating (thus far) conflicts of this type have emerged from collapsing state structures, as in the former Yugoslavia, structural causes receive a considerable share of attention. The security dilemma and systemic causes of war are twin foci. The former is expanded beyond its initial formulation and application to identity conflict; the latter is applied directly to the Yugoslav imbroglio, with one prediction concerning its trajectory confirmed by later events. Systemic conflicts of great intensity may have consequences for other societies, if the conditions are right for the diffusion of violence as apparently was the case in the Bosnian genocide's influence on the Hutu extremists in Rwanda. Yet dyadic identity conflict may hold the seeds of future mass destruction. Although a spreading democratic peace between dyads may augur well for a peaceful future, the democratization process, at least in India, has led to intensified internal identity conflicts between Hindus and Muslims and a jingoism that greatly facilitated the recent nuclear tests by India and then Pakistan. The unit or group level is important for understanding the rise of nationalist leaders who may have done much to foment recent identity conflict, particularly in the former Yugoslavia. A synthesis of explanations at all three levels is proposed by a prominent institution dedicated to policy analysis.

As befitting an introductory section on international violence, the next chapter thoroughly reviews the extant literature on ancient warfare. Its purpose, among others, is to provide the political scientist with a temporal dimension in depth, sorely missing from studies of war that on the whole tend to emphasize the past two centuries. Claudio Cioffi-Revilla focuses on both the chronological attributes of such warfare—that they occurred a long time ago and how long ago is an interesting question—and the behavioral dimension. How *was* warfare practiced in the distant past? Indicators of warfare including forensic, locational, structural, artifactual, iconographic, and epigraphic evidence are reviewed and applied to nine areas of the world where warfare arose in relatively pristine form. Some of these are the Levant, Southern Mesopotamia, Egypt, China, and the Andes. Chronologies of the first appearance and later development of warfare are presented. Perhaps most salient for our concerns is the complex relationship between warfare and political development. Although reasonably well understood in the contemporary period, this relationship, which is intimately connected with the origins of war and state formation, cries out for systematic research. Cioffi-Revilla has provided an admirable start in this direction.

When we turn to the minimally dyadic theories of war—those that require at least two conflict units—we find ourselves in the research domain that has demonstrated the greatest progress in recent years. Older theories have been even more firmly grounded empirically, and newer ones have demonstrated considerable empirical validity in a surprisingly short time.

Fittingly, we begin with the democratic peace as the exemplar of the latter category. The number of references alone, and very recent ones, attest to the vitality of this research program. Bruce M. Russett and Harvey Starr provide a densely argued, nuanced view of the democratic peace. Perhaps most important from the perspective of scientific development is the existence of significant integrative cumulation within a relatively short period. Not only is there now strong evidence for the democratic peace between dyads, but also that even the escalation of low-level militarized disputes between democracies to higher levels is rare. Moreover, using multivariate analyses, evidence continues to accumulate for the monadic peace. Interestingly, the second most peaceful dyadic relationship is that between autocracies. Russett and Starr are carefully attentive to the necessity for convincing theory needed to explain those findings. Theories range from those based on culture and structure to rent-seeking, provision of public goods, maintenance of legitimacy, domestic winning coalitions, and density of intergovernmental organization (IGO) linkages. Here, in the last instance, the research program already extends beyond the democratic peace alone to elements of a broader Kantian peace. Linkages to other research programs, such as the tendency for democracies to be status quo powers within a power transition framework, are presented. Counterarguments to the democratic peace also are given, including the possibility of a reversal of the causal arrow from democracy leading to peace, to peace leading to democracy. A richness of both theory and evidence is palpable here.

The power transition is another integrated research program that has demonstrated considerable empirical validity. Jacek Kugler and Douglas Lemke first review basic elements of the theory: internal growth of the state, a focus on international hierarchy, the importance of relative power, and evaluation of the international status quo. They contrast the power transition's emphasis on hierarchy with the anarchy inherent in much of realist thought. Empirical studies overwhelmingly confirm the pacifying effect of power preponderance in comparison with power parity, a key proposition of the theory. The status quo has increasingly appeared as a variable in this research program as has the existence of multiple local hierarchies subordinate to the global hierarchy. Indicative of the power transition's success is its incorporation into formal models that examine, for example, the speed of a challenger's overtaking of the dominant power and the timing of that overtaking relative to the onset of war. A number of fascinating and occasionally counterintuitive findings emerge from these analyses. The consequences of war, the strategic implications of the power transition's research findings, policy implications, comparison with cognate theories, and a future research agenda are detailed. In their concluding section, the authors are candid in their estimation of both the strengths and weaknesses of the theory, but it is clear from the confirmatory evidence that the former clearly outweigh the latter in any objective evaluation. The power transition appears now in another setting, the applicability of game theory to understanding international conflict.

Game theory is a theoretical approach that has made great strides in recent years. James D. Morrow reprises elements of noncooperative game theory relevant for the understanding of war: Credible commitment (reviewed briefly in the Midlarsky chapter) is important here, as is the role of limited information. These and other ideas are applied to four theories of war: deterrence, balance of power, power transition, and the democratic peace. Morrow first demonstrates that "rational" deterrence theory (RDT), which is reliant on the clear communication of threats and the credibility of those threats, cannot work in a rational choice model. Uncertainty inherent in crises as well as other factors, like signaling costs, undermine the logical foundations of RDT. Turning next to the balance of power, Morrow finds an uncertainty also inherent in this theory and especially that a wide range of capability distributions and many unequal ones appear to support balancing. A focus on the power transition reveals a gap in the theory. Whereas the power transition typically focuses on shifts in power between the challenger and dominant power, a game-theoretic perspective reveals the importance of concessions needed to accommodate the challenger peacefully. The value of war and the value of concessions need to be compared by all parties to a dispute, yet power transition theory specifies only the former. Finally, Morrow examines the role of credible signaling and the insecurity of leaders in democracies relative to the workings of the democratic peace. These perspectives add to our repertory of theoretical insights into the operation of this especially well grounded regularity. Rigorous development of the logic of a theory is a hallmark of the game-theoretic approach, as demonstrated convincingly in this chapter.

But game theory, in its relentless rationality, may suffer from precisely this set of logical blinders. Human beings simply may not behave in the manner predicted by the rational choice–expected utility calculus; game theory is very good at identifying a set of *possible* outcomes, but not necessarily the *actual* ones. Enter prospect theory as an experimentally based set of correctives. Jack S. Levy reviews the contributions of prospect theory to our understanding of international conflict with applications to, among others, the Falklands/Malvinas crisis, the Cuban missile crisis, the Iraqi invasion of Kuwait, and the Japanese attack on Pearl Harbor. In each instance, he shows that prospect theory, with its emphasis on framing, reference points, and loss aversion, lends considerable explanatory power to the actors' decision-making processes. Our understanding of the bargaining process generally is enhanced by prospect theory. Concession aversion is a phenomenon observed in bargaining behavior that helps us understand the frequency of nonagreement in negotiations. The success of a negotiated settlement may well depend on whether the participants view the compromise agreement as a gain from an adversary's initial offer, or as a loss from their own. If the latter, then agreement may be more difficult to achieve. Despite the theoretical advantages conferred by prospect theory, Levy clearly points to the limitations of the theory and especially to the areas requiring additional empirical research. In this way, not only is the sterile debate between rational choice and prospect theorists bypassed, but also our understanding of decision making in international conflict settings may be considerably enhanced.

As a final perspective on minimally dyadic conflicts, Gary Goertz and Paul F. Diehl present a review of rivalries (enduring and otherwise) in international conflict. This is the first treatment to introduce an explicitly temporal dimension; later we will encounter such time dependence in structure-based theories of war. (Perhaps in some sense we might say that the rivalry itself constitutes a conflict structure that can endure over time.) The idea of rivalry here is based on repeated militarized conflict between two states, which immediately distinguishes such dyads from others without those characteristics. Rivalries do not merely denote a past history of repeated disputes but also the expectation of future ones. Conceptualizations and types of rivalries are reviewed, followed by an in-depth examination of the problem of operationalization. This, of course, is an extremely important question here because of the explicit need to distinguish conflicting dyads that make the cut for inclusion from those that do not. Goertz and Diehl find that standards for operationalization have tightened substantially in recent years. The remainder of their chapter explores the implications for international conflict research of changing the traditional unit of analysis from a "war" or a "dispute" to a "rivalry." This is an extremely important change in research practice that could yield substantial explanatory dividends, especially concerning our understanding of conflict dynamics as they evolve over time. Entire bodies of literature such as that of the arms race may be reinterpreted in light of understanding the arms race as a species of enduring rivalry.

The empirical findings, as Goertz and Diehl amply demonstrate, are extremely rich. In their agenda for future research, they outline both theoretical and empirical requirements for their research program, including especially the identification of conditions that lead some rivalries to persist and others to simply peter out.

Enduring rivalries, or in their terminology, protracted conflicts, also appear in the chapter by Jonathan Wilkenfeld and Michael Brecher on international crises, but as part of a larger treatment. Here, for the first time, system structure looms large in an explanatory framework. International crises, especially those involving many actors, are inextricably linked to system structure and have some probability (greater than zero) of ending in systemic war. Their chapter concentrates on the nexus between crisis and war, especially conditions facilitating or inhibiting the escalation of crises to wars. Six themes are emphasized. In their order of presentation, these are: polarity and violence, geography/territory and violence, protracted conflict and war, ethnicity and violence, regime type/democracy and war, and third-party intervention. Interestingly, although polarity and violence as a category subsumes the earliest research (the first reference dates back to 1948), the number of references cited actually is second to regime type/democracy and war, despite its recency in international relations research. This is one more indication of the phenomenal growth of this research program. Among their findings are the greater instability of polycentric and multipolar systems in comparison with bipolarity (contrast this finding with that predicted by game theory in Morrow's chapter), the role of ethnicity and protracted conflict in facilitating violent triggers in polycentrism, again in comparison with the greater stability of bipolarity, and the pacifying role of democracy in inhibiting the likelihood of violence. Not only is the probability of violence examined carefully and in great detail, but also factors that lead to the termination of crises and wars are considered. In the scope of their analyses and the evidentiary foundation upon which they are based, this is an extraordinarily comprehensive treatment.

System structure appears even more forcefully in the next contribution, that by Karen Rasler and William R. Thompson on global war and structural change. Here we are presented with a macro view of both global politics and the time span of analysis. In an important sense, this chapter and the one preceding it are mirror images of each other. Whereas Brecher and Wilkenfeld concentrate on 152 variables (of which 11 are selected for emphasis here) within a fairly short time period (1918–94), Rasler and Thompson focus on a much smaller number of variables, approximately 30, over a much longer period of systematic analysis (1490–1990). Yet both approaches are equally valid, because of the large number of crises (412) and crisis actors (895) to be compared with the 500 years as time units represented here. Additionally, as in the preceding chapter, illustrations are provided outside of the framework of systematic analysis.

Rasler and Thompson focus on the economic and political factors that contribute to the concentration and deconcentration of global reach capabilities. The basic assumptions are that global concentration makes a difference as to how things work, that such concentrations cycle over time, and that uneven long-term economic growth drives the cyclical momentum. Global war is a function of these long-term economic growth processes. The lead economy and its associated global reach are critical in this process, as are technological innovation and diffusion. Five global wars are examined for their antecedent processes, which include, importantly, the interaction between global and regional structure/change. Greater concentration at the regional level leads to a greater likelihood of intensive conflict, but greater concentration at the global level leads to a decreased likelihood of such conflict. This dissynchronization is an important ingredient in the onset of global war. Possible scenarios for future global war are outlined in great detail, thus yielding a predictive dimension to the analysis not typically found in international relations research.

Cycles appear again in the following chapter by Charles F. Doran. Here, it is the power cycle of the state that is invoked within the context of the international system, for it is the absolute power of the state relative to the absolute power of the system that is the key variable. It is a holistic theory of power that is developed here which suggests that the embeddedness of the state within the system is critically important. A disjunction between the power of the state and its role in the system is a key element of the theory. Typically, major powers pass through a power cycle consisting of turning points and infection points that are dangerously unsettling to the decision maker. Inversion in the trend of expectations creates possibilities for disastrous outcomes in the form of major power war. An important element is the nonlinearity, even at times discontinuity, of change, which can make secure predictions of even the most responsible world leaders virtually impossible. Doran provides evidence from the histories of 11 major powers. He effectively compares his power cycle theory to other cognate approaches such as status inconsistency or the power transition and suggests the very important policy implications of the theory as well as its explanatory power.

The final section is devoted to summary studies of the evidence disclosed by systematic research on the causes of war. John A. Vasquez presents his understanding of the steps to war, including initially the raising of territorial issues, followed by alliance formation, military buildups, and repeated crises that can end in war. Each step taken increases the probability of war. Variables analyzed in the preceding chapters or elsewhere are now combined in this sequential process. For each of these stages, Vasquez presents evidence for its importance with an emphasis on territorial issues as not only empirically compelling but also having nonobvious theoretical importance. Evidence for the importance of certain types of alliance also is compelling, as is the evidence for arms races increasing the probability of war. Here, as elsewhere in this volume, the conclusions are framed in terms of the probabilities of certain outcomes, thus veering away from implications of determinacy. This is one more indication of the increased sophistication of research on international conflict during the past decade.

Just as Vasquez provides a summary processual approach to the causes of war, Daniel S. Geller gives us an overview of causation, touching on many themes developed in the preceding chapters. As in certain of these chapters, Geller divides these studies into those located in the levels of analysis of state, dyad, region, and system. Not all levels receive equal attention, reflecting, for example, the greater emphasis on the dyadic level of analysis in recent years. Moreover, not all of Geller's judgments on these studies necessarily agree with those of the earlier chapters. (Nor do all of these chapters agree among themselves, as in the somewhat different consequences projected for democratization as a process in the Midlarsky chapter and the Russett and Starr chapter.) One approach might be placed within the state level of analysis in this chapter, whereas the author of another chapter might place it within the systemic level of analysis. Nevertheless, this "birds-eye" view of empirical research on the causes of war gives a needed "second opinion" on how these studies relate to each other and their respective contributions to the cumulation of knowledge. Additionally, some studies not reviewed in the preceding chapters make an appearance here. Power, polarity, alliances, regime type, borders, and territory, among other variables, reappear here with a consistency that suggests their signal importance in the explanation of war. But the way they appear, not in a simpleminded laundry listing of possible factors, but as empirical findings embedded within a network of relationships, suggests the distance this field has traversed since publication of the earlier *Handbook.*

There is much to be learned from the chapters in this book. They not only reprise important elements from the earlier volume but also explore new research frontiers not even considered in the earlier work. This perhaps is the most important sign of a maturing discipline: the maintenance of strongly contributing elements of the old, while pushing open the frontiers of the new. Yet, despite these substantial successes, there is some cause for concern stemming from the still limited nature of our tools of exploration. Such limitation is indicated by a lingering emphasis on linear models, even as many of the chapters in this volume have demonstrated the importance of the nonlinearity of key relationships. If a linear association between two or more variables (such as polarity and war) is not disclosed, then the relationship often is assumed not to exist. Further exploration is deemed to be unnecessary. Yet we know that some of the earliest and most enduring relationships have been curvilinear (the inverse square law of attraction between physical bodies or the inverted U-curve relationship between government repression and mass political violence). To some extent, as researchers, we may be hostages to the statistical programs readily available and most user-friendly. These often tend to be linear. Yet new horizons in both theory and research tools are opening that may bypass our traditional research dependencies. I hope that the next version of this *Handbook* will exhibit the theoretical and empirical fecundity of this book and the opening of still new analytic horizons.

MANUS I. MIDLARSKY

PART I

Topical Approaches to the Study of War

Terrorism and International Violence

MARTHA CRENSHAW

The significance of terrorism as a problem for global security lies in its qualities of extraterritorial violence. The use of terrorism by any actor violates the formal rules and informal norms of the contemporary state-dominated international system. Terrorism undermines the centralized and hierarchical organization of global violence. Not only does it represent a private use of violence that the state is determined to monopolize, but it also represents a merger of the private safety of individual citizens and the public security of the state. Most important, terrorism is a violent challenge to the institution of sovereignty, one of the mechanisms by which states impose their control over the international system (see Thomson 1994).

Terrorism can be interpreted as an anachronistic remnant of the pre-1900 era, when violence was more democratic, mercenary, and international than it came to be in the twentieth century. Laqueur (1996, 27), for example, compares the importance of contemporary Sudan for international terrorism to that of the Barbary Coast for piracy in the early nineteenth century. However, more than an archaic throwback to an earlier age, terrorism is a constant reminder of the conditionality of sovereignty. Despite the end of the cold war and the low likelihood of great power conflict in the modern international system, nonstate violence has not been eliminated from global politics, nor have states desisted from the clandestine authorization or even direction of conspiratorial violence outside their borders. Furthermore, state responses to terrorism, particularly the use of military force, can further erode the principles of territorial sovereignty.

If one's conception of global security is based solely on material power rather than perceptions of power, terrorism is insignificant.

Terrorism has little direct effect on the distribution of capabilities in the international system. Nor do the conventional hallmarks of power guarantee invulnerability from terrorism; to the contrary, the most powerful states constitute the most attractive targets precisely because of the scope and complexity of their external interests and involvement. Nevertheless, targeted states respond with military force to minor threats because their leaders feel the need to demonstrate resolve. For most states, terrorism is perceived as a threat to reputation and credibility, not material power. However, much more is at stake for states divided internally along ethnic or religious lines. If foreign adversaries support domestic separatists in their use of terrorism, both internal order and regional stability are threatened.

This chapter reviews a selected literature linking terrorism to conflict among states. (A review of earlier relevant literature can be found in Crenshaw 1989a. See also Crenshaw 1992, Lakos 1991, and Ross 1991.) Approaches to the study of terrorism are interdisciplinary and heterogeneous. The subject lacks a unifying theory to integrate disparate empirical findings and middle-range hypotheses. Accordingly, the cumulativeness of knowledge is weak. This review begins with a discussion of the problem of defining terrorism. It then examines theories of the causes, processes, and outcomes of both nonstate- and state-sponsored extraterritorial terrorism. (This review is thus not centrally concerned with state repression.) Projections of the future of terrorism, especially the possibility of escalating destructiveness through the use of chemical, biological, nuclear, or radiological weapons, are treated as part of the dynamics of the process. In addition, much analysis has focused on why and how states have responded, particularly the effectiveness of counterterrorism policies and the relationship between democracy and terrorism. Last, this review assesses methodological and epistemological perspectives, focusing on recent econometric and critical or constructivist approaches to terrorism.

Definitions

It is impossible to examine the relationship between terrorism and international conflict without acknowledging the difficulty of defining the phenomenon, although the subject has been discussed at such length (e.g., in Schmid and Jongman 1988) that reopening the controversy might seem both unnecessary and pointless. Terrorism is a "contested concept," the use of which is taken by some to imply a pejorative connotation, thus making its neutral or objective analytical function problematic (see Crenshaw 1994). Recognizing this issue, Alex Schmid (1992) outlines four "arenas of discourse" on terrorism: academic, official or state, public, and internal (the proponents of terrorism). He rejects academic definitions as too complex and detailed to be adopted by governments or publics and dismisses the definitions of those who defend terrorism as biased. Instead he proposes a legal definition as a compromise. If terrorism is considered a peacetime equivalent of war crimes, then any attack on noncombatants or resort to nonmilitary violence such as hostage-taking is prohibited, regardless of ideological justification. Badey (1998) also argues for a pragmatic approach to defining international terrorism. He proposes a definition that is neither "politically convenient nor academically aloof" (105). Terrorism is distinguished from other types of violence by the repetition of the activity, its political motivation and coercive intent, the involvement of nonstate actors, and its effect on more than one state. Another practical conception of terrorism is found in Laqueur (1996, 24), who argues simply that terrorism is "the substate application of violence or threatened violence intended to sow panic in a society, to weaken or even overthrow the incumbents, and to bring about political change." If one regards the phenomenon of terrorism as a continuum, at one end it may merge into guerrilla warfare, while at the other it may become a substitute for interstate warfare. Nevertheless, either form of warfare has a territorial dimension that terrorism lacks.

Taking a more theoretical approach, Gibbs (1989) identifies a set of common attributes that all examples of terrorism must possess. He argues that control is the factor that links all properties of terrorism into a coherent concept. He proposes first that terrorism is necessarily criminal or illegal in the jurisdictional context in which it occurs. Illegality is not a moral or normative judgment, but a statement of the relationship between terrorism and domestic or international society. Terrorism is meant to alter or uphold a norm or set of norms in a particular social order. It is, furthermore, secretive or clandestine violence or the threat thereof, since the actors using terrorism seek to conceal their identities and locations. Terrorism is distinctive because it is perceived as linked to its normative goal via the creation of fear in groups or communities other than the immediate targets of violence. Furthermore, Gibbs suggests,

"Describing and thinking about terrorism require recognition more of what terrorists attempt to control than what they actually control" (336). Thus terrorism is illegal because it challenges the state's control of violence. The public (or publics) and/or state officials perceive the political goals of terrorism as unacceptable and unrealizable, which means that terrorists may lack popular support and/or face determined official opposition from the state—hence the necessity of a strategy that is economical: terrorism requires few participants, maximizes limited resources by manipulating popular attitudes, and relies on secrecy so as to preclude retaliation and punishment.

Another way of defining terrorism is to consider it as a form of communication. Schmid and de Graaf (1982) originated the argument that terrorism is violence that is intended to convey a message. This view is similar to the traditional idea underlying nineteenth century anarchist terrorism, that terrorism is "propaganda of the deed" (see also Crelinsten 1991). In this perspective, terrorism is a representation of ideas through symbolic political action. As such it resembles a dramatic performance or narrative script. Interpreting terrorism as drama implies that any single act of terrorism engages multiple audiences, some of whom may identify with the victims, some of whom may identify with the perpetrators, and some of whom will be indifferent. It will thus elicit a range of emotions, from fear and outrage to enthusiasm.

It should be clear from these definitions that the concept of terrorism is not tied to any specific ideology. The method can be used to uphold the status quo as much as to challenge it. It may be a tactic, one method among many employed in the service of a political cause, or a strategy to which an organization is exclusively devoted. Terrorism can serve grand ambitions such as national independence or revolution, or further more limited or prosaic goals such as protest against a particular government policy or action, extortion of specific policy concessions, intimidation of a class of people, or advertisement of a cause. Terrorists often seek to provoke government repression in order to gain popular support. In doing so, they intend to persuade by gaining a moral advantage over the incumbent, to arouse desires for revenge, or simply to force a community to fight to defend itself against government persecution.

The practice of contemporary terrorism is heterogeneous, ranging from selective assassinations of individual political leaders (e.g., the archduke Franz Ferdinand by Serbian nationalists in 1914, or Rajiv Gandhi by the Liberation Tigers of Tamil Eelam in 1991) to bombs of massive proportions causing numerous random casualties in public spaces. It may be a form of bargaining rather than direct attack. All forms of hostage seizures, including kidnappings and hijackings as well as barricade-type incidents, are attempts to bargain with governments. The targets may be civilians chosen at random from a selected class, passengers on a hijacked or bombed airliner, for example, or individuals chosen deliberately for their symbolic value, such as diplomats or heads of state. Bombings remain a favored method, but levels of destructiveness vary widely. The actors who use terrorism include both substate groups acting outside the boundaries of a home state, perhaps without the state's knowledge or consent, and states employing terrorism as a form of surreptitious coercion or retaliation against other states.

A thoughtful and concise historical overview of terrorism can be found in Rapoport (1992). For comprehensive descriptions of the range of contemporary international terrorist activities, the U.S. Department of State's annual publication, *Patterns of Global Terrorism,* is a convenient and accessible source. In the official American view, adopted in 1983, "international" terrorism means simply actions involving the citizens or territory of more than one country.

Causes and Processes of Terrorism

The question of the causes of terrorism continues to perplex researchers. Answers typically focus on one of three levels of analysis: structural conditions at the societal level, strategic calculations of groups as collective actors, and psychological causes at the level of the individual or the group (see Crenshaw 1981; della Porta 1995; Reich 1990). A review of psychological theories (Ross 1994) notes some of the problems inherent in the literature on causality. First, Ross cautions that an attempt at understanding causality does not imply or assume that knowledge of causes will produce better "treatment" or control of terrorism. Second, it is often unclear whether explanations apply specifically to terrorism or to all persons or groups engaging generally in violence, radical opposition, deviance, or criminality. Analysts must take care to distinguish terrorism from other forms of political violence. Furthermore, few attempts at explanation succeed in integrating different levels of analysis. Accordingly Ross (1994, 162–63) suggests the following psychological model of causality for substate terrorism:

> Early childhood and adolescent experiences will condition individuals to develop personality traits which predispose them to engage in terrorism. . . . These traits motivate individuals to either commit terrorism alone, form bonds with other individuals who are predisposed to engage in terrorism, or sometimes develop or join terrorist organizations. Engaging in terrorism and the existence of terrorist groups satisfies a number of psychological needs of those predisposed to use terrorism. In the organization, members are exposed to a variety of learning experiences and adopt different roles which mold their behavior. All of these processes are connected to audiences, victims, other terrorists, and government organizations. Ultimately, the final decision to use terrorism is a rational choice.

Ross (1993) has also proposed a preliminary model of structural causes. He follows Crenshaw (1981) in distinguishing permissive causes from precipitants. In his as yet untested model, the key permissive conditions or systemic causes are geographical location, type of political system, and level of modernization. The precipitants, or immediate causes, are social, cultural, and historical facilitation; organizational development or splits; presence of other forms of political unrest; support from popular constituencies or states; failure of the counterterrorist response; availability of weapons and explosives; and, most important, grievances, which may be political, economic, ethnic, racial, legal, religious, or social.

Della Porta (1995) also links levels of analysis in a domestic context. She focuses at the outset on political opportunity structures, defined as the environmental opportunities and constraints available to actors. Within this category, she singles out state actions, in particular the state's reactions to protest and the differential responses of opposition movements. She stresses the organizational dynamics and the resource potentials, especially recruitment possibilities, that lead individual factions of social movements to adopt different methods, including terrorism. "Violent entrepreneurs" compete with other radical organizations to mobilize resources. In doing so they form collective identities and develop intense commitments that isolate them from the reality of the struggle. Her analysis compares Italy and Germany.

A compatible structural theory is based on a comparative sociological analysis of groups in Italy, Spain, Peru, and the Middle East. Wieviorka (1993) argues that terrorism is the antithesis of a social movement. Terrorism results when social actors are isolated or disconnected from the popular movement they claim to represent. They substitute violence for representation. The relationship to a popular constituency is imagined or artificial. According to Wieviorka's analysis, terrorism appears on the international scene when the interests of states and substate actors coincide. It is misguided to interpret international terrorism simply as state behavior that reflects changing distributions of power. One has to examine the motivations and rationales of substate actors, who have in effect become doubly disconnected from their origins. They are the driving force behind terrorism. He thus explains local and international terrorism in the same terms.

Sprinzak's approach (1991) also traces the processes by which terrorism emerges from general social conflict. He describes a series of stages of delegitimization, the result of a radicalization of the interaction between government and opposition. His view is that terrorism is the extension of initially nonviolent opposition; it emerges slowly among a minority and is likely to be transitory.

Weinberg's (1991) work on the relationship between terrorism and political parties complements these analyses. Weinberg found that the political parties most likely to stimulate the formation of adjunct or offshoot terrorist groups (e.g., Hezbollah in Lebanon) have grandiose political ambitions, almost inevitably frustrated given the level of aspiration, and a doctrine that emphasizes the illegitimacy of the prevailing political order. If the incumbent regime (or the state that the party opposes on ideological grounds) appears weak, the likelihood of terrorism is further enhanced.

However, Ross (1993, also 1991) contends that causal models should not attempt to be universal; instead they should distinguish between different types of oppositional terrorism. (On the subject of typologies, see Flemming and Stohl 1988; see also Sprinzak 1991.) It cannot be assumed that all terrorism has local roots, and thus international, transnational, or state-sponsored terrorism is likely to require a different explanation from domestic violence. O'Brien (1996) makes a similar point. He notes that "although terrorism is a presumably complex and multicausal phenomenon lying between the nexus of war and peace, scholarly research on the causes of international terrorism has all but escaped rigorous empirical analysis" (320). Accordingly he focuses on state interests in an analysis of the relationship between superpower state sponsorship of international crises and the incidence of terrorism. O'Brien argues that during the cold war the Soviet Union and other communist states were more likely than the United States and other liberal democracies to employ terrorism to advance their interests. He suggests that the incentives to use terrorism are strengthened when states are militarily weak, defeated, or marginalized in a crisis. For states that have suffered temporary setbacks, terrorism can level the playing field while providing convenient deniability. He finds that losers in a crisis are most likely to find terrorism useful. When the Soviet Union and other authoritarian regimes were defeated by a democracy in a foreign policy crisis, terrorism increased, but if they were advantaged by the crisis, terrorism decreased.

Along the same lines, Hager (1990) analyzed the Soviet connection to terrorism in Latin America during the cold war. He examined the view held by several scholars and journalists during the late 1970s and 1980s, endorsed by the Reagan administration, that the Soviet Union sponsored terrorism as a means of low-intensity conflict against the noncommunist world. He concluded that Soviet assistance to radical left groups during this period was usually indirect and limited. In fact, the Soviet Union was often hostile to the unorthodox Marxism these groups espoused. In Hager's view, Soviet leaders provided assistance to local leftist groups because they feared losing support in the ideological competition for leadership of the third world communist movement. As China's status as a rival diminished, and as the Soviet Union sought to appear more "respectable," support for far left groups decreased. Furthermore, although the Soviet Union was often seen as the instigator behind Cuban support for Latin American revolutionary groups (e.g., M-19 in Colombia), Cuba actually had its own independent agenda. In a general sense one could say that the Soviet Union bore some responsibility for terrorist acts that were committed in the name of revolutionary causes, but the Soviet Union was not linked to specific actions. Mickolus (1989) also emphasizes that the question of what constitutes state support for terrorism is complex. "Support" may range from acts by "intimidated" governments, who are not ideologically sympathetic and passively submit to terrorist demands, to direct material assistance.

Falk (1988) takes a normative stance. He argues for an enlarged conception of terrorism that condemns its use by states and nonstates alike. He is as critical of the behavior of the United States as of the Soviet Union, noting that "opportunistic support of terrorist activity is an ingredient of geopolitical rivalry" regardless of ideological orientation (7). (On the subject of generalized state responsibility and questions of blame, see also Stohl 1988a.)

Singh (1995) also focuses on terrorism as a form of surrogate warfare by states. Emphasizing that the superpowers were not alone in employing international terrorism against their enemies, he cites Pakistan, Iran, and Libya. He emphasizes that in developing countries the close links between foreign policy and domestic conditions (ethnicity, religion, ideology, repression, or economic discontent) create incentives for states to exploit the internal divisions of their enemies. Terrorism becomes an expression of regional animosities and a powerful tool of destabilization. It is also facilitated by the ready accessibility of weaponry in regions where armed interstate conflicts flourish. In the third world, furthermore, the legacy of the postwar struggle against colonialism legitimizes the use of violence by nonstate actors (Singh 1995, 126–27). Thus any international or regional conflict creates a "noncooperative environment" or permissive condition for terrorism, as does the spillover of civil conflict.

Similarly Ranstorp and Xhudo (1994) warn of linkages between Iran and Islamic movements in the Balkans. They consider state-sponsored terrorism a source of irredentist claims that threaten both democratization and regional stability. (On the relationship between Iran and terrorism, see also Green 1995, and Karmon 1998.) In addition, Hoffman (1989) has analyzed Palestinian terrorism against Israeli targets in Latin America.

The complexity of international terrorism has led researchers to try to explain specific practices rather than general patterns. As noted earlier in this chapter, there are important distinctions in terrorist behavior. Much terrorism consists of tactics such as bombings or armed attacks that are meant to intimidate, shock, demoralize, or otherwise alter the strategic calculus of an enemy. However, when hostages are seized and held for ransom, terrorists are engaged in short-term blackmail or extortion. Kidnappings, especially of diplomats, business executives, and foreigners; aircraft hijackings; and seizures of embassies all fall in this category of attempts to coerce governments into negotiations and concessions to terrorist demands. Terrorist actors also exercise latitude in choice of targets, location, and level of destructiveness of their actions. Explanations of preference in terrorism are typically based on differences in motivations, resources, and opportunities.

A key question is the selection of targets for terrorism. Sandler and Lapan (1988) analyze the choice of targets in nonbargaining situations. Assuming that terrorists are rational individuals, operating under resource constraints, they can attack only one country. If that potential target increases its defensive measures, terrorism will only shift to another target state. On the basis of formal modeling, Sandler and Lapan predict a displacement effect. That is, effective unilateral countermeasures by one state will increase the vulnerability of other states who do not take such measures. Thus terrorists' choices are sensitive primarily to what governments do to protect themselves. Enders, Sandler, and Cauley (1990) also suggest that a substitution effect exists: when new technologies or policies are applied to prevent specific kinds of terrorist events, terrorists transfer their efforts to new but related targets. Further support for the substitution effect is presented in Enders and Sandler (1993) and in Cauley and Im (1988). Installing metal detectors in airports, for example, apparently led to a decrease in hijackings but to an increase in other forms of hostage seizures, such as kidnappings, and in assassinations.

Hoffman (1993, 1997) has also analyzed terrorist targeting. He found that in the 1970s and 1980s terrorists were consistent in their targeting, weapons, and tactics. They tended to repeat the same limited operational repertoire. Terrorism was largely a matter of routine, and the past was a good predictor of the future. Bombings, for example, account for about half of all terrorist attacks, and in general the most frequent terrorist attacks are those that are the least complex and sophisticated. Yet terrorists have shown some operational ingenuity, which enables them to defeat government counterterrorism security measures, particularly in concealing, delivering, and detonating bombs (e.g., in the bombing of Pan Am 103 in 1988). Hoffman notes, however, a contemporary trend toward increasingly lethal terrorism, which he attributes to changes in both motivation and competence. More groups are motivated by a religious imperative, which lessens restraints on violence; more "amateurs," such as the bombers of the World Trade Center, are active now that the means of and knowledge about using terrorism are widely available; and "professional" terrorists are becoming more sophisticated as well as ruthless. Hoffman also argues that groups are less likely to claim credit for their actions than they were in the past. The choice of target, then, is linked to both opportunity and intent.

Both these claims—that terrorism is becoming more lethal in terms of mass civilian casualties and that actions are increasingly unclaimed—have been disputed (see, e.g., Hoffman, Pluchinsky, and Rapoport 1997), but data are available to test them. In addition to the Department of State annual report, the RAND Corporation has produced a database of incidents since 1968. (The database was maintained at St. Andrews University from 1994 to 1998.) Since 1994 an annual chronology and statistical breakdown of international terrorist incidents has been published in the journal *Terrorism and Political Violence* (for details on this and other databases including the ITERATE [International Terrorism: Attributes of Terrorist Events] data available through the Inter-University Consortium for Political and Social Research at the University of Michigan, see Hoffman and Hoffman 1995; see also Gordon 1995, Mickolus and Simmons 1997, and Ross 1991). However, Jongman (1992) assesses the problems associated with trend analysis of terrorism and concludes that the results are inconclusive. Each database includes different types of events. There is no common definition or coding protocol and thus almost no compatibility. Since the data are inconsistent, one cannot say in general that terrorism is increasing in frequency or becoming more lethal.

These caveats about the utility of quantitative data notwithstanding, Enders and Sandler (1999) argue on the basis of data collected for 1970–96 that international terrorism has been reduced since the end of the cold war. They use time-series and vector autoregression analysis to identify a "terrorism-reduction dividend" beginning in 1994. This reduction is apparent in both hostage-takings and bombings, although most importantly in the latter. At the same time, Enders and Sandler find that terrorism follows cyclical patterns that appear to be unrelated to the political events (such as the end of state support from the former Soviet bloc) and enhanced security measures of the 1990s that probably caused the reduction in overall terrorism. They conclude that the underlying dynamic process of terrorism has not changed greatly despite these shifts in post–cold war international politics.

Another question about the patterns of international terrorism is whether incidents or types of incident are characterized by processes of transnational contagion (see Midlarsky, Crenshaw, and Yoshida 1980). If the diffusion of terrorism has a structure based on attributes of the international system, such as hierarchy or geographical contiguity, then it becomes much more predictable. Proceeding with similar assumptions, Ross (1992, 163) analyzes "the possibility that previous acts of terrorism can serve as catalysts for the initiation and succession of more terrorist actions," facilitated by news media coverage that furnishes a means of communication. Although the results of his analysis of the Canadian situation are inconclusive, he poses important questions about the transition from domestic to international terrorism.

Questions about the role of the news media in the process of terrorism have provoked extensive debates among researchers (see Alali and

Eke 1991; Nacos 1994; Paletz and Schmid 1992; Picard 1993). Without publicity, would terrorism have become internationalized in the 1970s and 1980s? For example, Picard (1993) argues that media coverage is not necessary for the diffusion of terrorism. He also contends that media coverage generally distorts both the scope and nature of terrorism, although on some occasions it does provide important information about previously unknown international conditions to both the public and policymakers. Rather than promoting the cause of the terrorists, news coverage tends to support the status quo. However, Nacos (1994) argues that terrorists successfully use the media to manipulate mass and elite opinion. She blames American mass media coverage for allowing terrorists to influence public sentiment. Media coverage, in her view, is the "heartbeat" (154) of international terrorism. She claims that "those who have committed anti-American terrorist spectaculars abroad have been stunningly successful in provoking and manipulating press reporting" to gain attention and recognition (13).

In terms of predicting future change in terrorism, one of the newest issues for research is the prospect of "super" or "catastrophic" terrorism using weapons of mass destruction (WMD). The Aum Shinrikyo poison gas attack on the Tokyo subway system in 1995, which killed 10 and injured thousands of people, was an ominous sign that future terrorists might use nuclear, chemical, biological, or radiological weapons. Although concern about possible nuclear terrorism dated from the 1970s, the collapse of the Soviet Union and the new salience of threats of chemical and biological warfare renewed interest. Apprehension about terrorist use of WMD was enhanced by the discovery of the extent of the Iraqi program in developing chemical and biological weapons, as well as by other indications of the proliferation of WMD to states suspected of sponsoring terrorism, such as Iran. The preemptive strike by the United States against a pharmaceuticals plant in the Sudan in 1998 signaled the importance of such threats to American interests. In the 1990s academic attention to the subject also grew. The questions at issue revolve principally around the likelihood and potential cost of "bioterrorism" or chemical terrorism. The possibility of "cyberterrorism" or information warfare has also attracted attention. Falkenrath et al. (1998) analyze the technical possibilities for different forms of terrorism using weapons of mass destruction, outline the limited historical precedents for such use, and prescribe detailed policy responses. Stern (1999) argues that constraints against the terrorist use of WMD are eroding, largely due to changes in terrorist motivation as well as expanded opportunity, and that the United States is especially vulnerable. However, she concludes that such terrorism is likely to be rare and that prudent government policies can minimize the danger. Other contributors to the literature include Roberts (1997) and Laqueur (1999). Additional participants in the debate over the future include Sprinzak (1998), Betts (1998), Carter et al. (1998), and Lesser et al. (1999). Sprinzak, for example, finds the threat exaggerated and sensationalized.

Responses to International Terrorism

If there is a displacement or substitution effect in terrorism, then a government's response matters not only to the government's reputation and the safety of its citizens but to all other states in the international system. A variant of the security dilemma operates, since efforts by one state to improve its security inadvertently decrease the security of others. However, despite the importance of governments' policy choices, polemical and descriptive accounts abound while explanatory theories are scarce. The democratic peace proposition may hold for relations among states, and democracy may be spreading around the world, but liberal states may still be disproportionately prone or vulnerable to terrorism, and democratic policymakers are still searching for an effective response.

Eubank and Weinberg (1994), building on the work of Schmid (1992), found that terrorist groups of domestic origin are more prevalent in democracies than in nondemocracies. They suggest that "it is democracy that attracts terrorist groups and that this tendency persists across time" (429). They also point to rapid economic growth and high economic discrimination in conjunction with social mobilization as conditions that promote domestic terrorism. Other analysts, however, disagree (see, e.g., the initial responses by Miller [1994] and Hewitt [1994] to Eubank and Weinberg [1994]). Sandler (1995) also raised methodological concerns. He argued that data on terrorist events rather than the presence of terrorist groups would be a more reliable indicator of the relationship between democracy and terrorism. Using events data would allow researchers to measure the intensity of terrorism by the number of incidents and account for extraterritorial terrorism—those actions perpetrated by foreign rather than domestic groups. "Spillover" and state-sponsored terrorism are omitted if one focuses only on countries that are "home bases" for terrorist groups. Possibly terrorism that occurs in democracies is actually "exported" from authoritarian regimes.

In further research, Weinberg and Eubank (1998) replied that using events data confirmed their earlier finding that international terrorism was more common in democratic countries. They also found that countries that had recently gone through political transitions, whether toward or away from democratization, were most likely to experience terrorism.

Turning to the question of response, what are the merits of different alternatives and why do states make the choices they do? Single country studies of national responses are numerous, but they are not always comparative, either across policies or across countries, and they do not always distinguish between policies against domestic and international terrorism if attacks occur within the country's borders (e.g., Janke 1992; Rubin 1990; and Schmid and Crelinsten 1992; see also Levitt 1988). An exception is a volume edited by Charters (1994). This collection of case studies systematically analyzes attempts by Western democracies to strike a balance between effective countermeasures against international terrorism and the protection of democratic practices and civil liberties. Each case study (of Great Britain, Germany, Italy, France, Israel, and the United States, respectively) examines the nature of the threat, the context in which responses were developed, the policies adopted and their effectiveness, and the impact of the response on democracy at home. Charters concludes that international terrorism did not seriously threaten the stability and functioning of Western democracies; although most states were willing at least privately to deal with international terrorists, their publics supported strong countermeasures. Most security legislation that affected civil liberties was directed against domestic terrorism. Overall, liberal states did not rush to restrict democratic freedoms for the sake of greater security from international terrorism.

In terms of policy effectiveness, the case studies found that unilateral negotiations and "deals" with terrorists were largely ineffective, but that international cooperation produced positive results. Direct functional collaboration between subnational bureaucracies such as intelligence agencies or police forces produced the most successful outcomes. Furthermore, countries that maintained permanent crisis management institutions handled incident responses most effectively. Charters (1994) criticized American policy as based on a biased analysis that overestimated the threat to the state. He was also critical of the policy of reprisals, a practice followed not only by the United States but also France and Israel. In his view, the use of military force to retaliate against terrorist incidents produced no visible deterrence: "the political and moral costs of reprisals were usually greater than their deterrent or attrition effects" (220). The most productive role for military force was the rescue of hostages.

As his conclusion implies, a particularly contentious aspect of counter-terrorism policy is the use of military force. For example, Brophy-Baermann and Conybeare (1994) generally support the findings of the case studies. Through the use of rational expectations theory, they conclude that retaliation has no long-term deterrent *or* escalation effect. Their propositions were tested on Israeli data: "Whatever effect reprisals may have in deterring future attacks or causing a 'spiral' of counterattacks is but a short term phenomenon lasting no more than nine months, in the case of Israel" (209). Enders, Sandler, and Cauley (1990) also found that retaliatory raids impose short-run costs with no long-term benefits. The subsequent research of Enders and Sandler (1993) supported this proposition, especially in the case of the Reagan administration. However, Shaikh (1992) argues that deterrence could work if a government were unhindered by the interference of third parties, but that retaliation is effective only if based on subsequent apprehension and prosecution of terrorists. He generally supports a policy of punishment rather than retaliation through the use of military force. See also Schmid and Crelinsten (1992, 315–22) and Smith (1989), whose conclusions are also critical of the retaliatory use of military force. On the specific issue of deterrence, see also Purkitt (1984) and Schelling (1991).

Singer (1989) considers the legitimacy as opposed to the effectiveness of the use of force against terrorist bases abroad. The resort to force can be considered self-defense and thus legally permissible under the terms of the UN Charter if it meets a test of necessity. Such a test would require "(1) a previous and ongoing series of terrorist attacks, and demonstrated responsibility for those attacks by the actors, state or non-state, against whom force is used; (2) immediately expected or imminent terrorist attacks endangering human life; and (3) the absence of non-forcible remedies effective in terminating the terrorist threat" (456). Furthermore, the use of force should be proportional to the danger. (With respect to international law, the firsthand account of the Achille Lauro affair by the Italian jurist Antonio Cassese [1989] is also informative.)

A second major issue in evaluating counterterrorism policy is whether governments do or should negotiate with hostage-takers. Zartman (1990) presents a conceptual framework of the dynamics of hostage-taking, arguing that the key to successful resolution is reducing expectations on both sides. The government has to change the terrorists' expectation of concessions, while the terrorists try to induce the government to yield. Schelling (1991) also considers negotiation to be inherent in any hostage seizure, although he regards the accomplishments of international terrorism as inconsequential. From a different point of view, that of moral philosophy, Hughes (1990) specifically criticizes the claim that governments should never negotiate with terrorists. He denies that negotiations confer legitimacy on the opponent or imply submission to dictation. In his view, there is no domino effect: ransoming some victims does not endanger others. Lapan and Sandler (1988) agree that the conventional wisdom that states should not negotiate does not withstand theoretical scrutiny. They use a game-theoretic approach to analyze whether states should commit themselves in advance to a no-negotiation strategy. Their findings suggest that "when governmental declarations are not completely credible and uncertainty characterizes the government's costs of not negotiating, then never negotiating is likely to be time inconsistent and not a plausible policy" (16). (On bargaining, see also Atkinson and Sandler 1987.) On the other hand, Clutterbuck (1992) argues for a domino theory. Concessions to terrorist demands make a government vulnerable to future terrorism, although he admits that this relationship does not always hold true. Shaikh (1992) also supports a "credible" no-concessions policy.

Looking at government practice, Reuben Miller's (1986) empirical research on the period 1968–77 concluded that governments were reluctant to comply with the demand that prisoners be released but that they acceded to less-threatening demands such as ransom or publicity. Governments also tended to compromise or negotiate rather than comply directly. He found that governments were willing to practice hard-line policies but not to declare them publicly. (In the United States, however, the Iran-Contra affair seems to suggest the opposite. Rhetorical policy was firm while operational policy was conciliatory.)

International cooperation, whether bilateral or multilateral, regional or global, has been a centerpiece of American counterterrorism policy since the early 1970s. Although less visible, the pursuit of cooperation in international politics has been much more common than the unilateral resort to military force. Cooperation has taken place under the auspices of a variety of international institutions, including the UN, the Group of Seven, the European Union, and NATO. The issue is constantly on the agenda of summit conferences. Numerous treaties prohibit terrorism in general and behaviors such as hijackings and attacks on diplomats in particular. Bilateral cooperation is extensive, for example, in negotiating extradition treaties or providing antiterrorism assistance. (Much analysis of this subject is situated in the field of international law; this essay will not review legal approaches specifically, but for further reference see Higgins and Flory 1997. On extradition specifically, see also Mani 1995.)

There is general agreement that cooperation is necessary and desirable in combating terrorism. Theories of a displacement effect help support this conclusion. However, questions remain as to whether cooperation goes beyond lip service to concrete implementation of antiterrorist principles (see Crenshaw 1989b and Allan 1990). Thus even with the end of the cold war and Soviet-American rivalry, a central focus of analysis is still explaining the lack of cooperation in the struggle against terrorism (e.g., see Shaikh 1992). Free riding is a particular problem (Lee 1988). Why would states put themselves at risk by supporting punitive measures or extraditing suspects? How to penalize noncompliance or defection, implement enforcement mechanisms, and reduce the costs of compliance remain unsolved problems. For example, Enders, Sandler, and Cauley (1990) found the results of UN conventions against terrorism disappointing. Their findings are supported by Valentin Romanov's account (1990), which provides a practitioner's critical perspective on the UN. The former director of the International Law Division of the UN Office of Legal Affairs cites a lack of enforcement mechanisms for existing conventions, their nonbinding character, limited applicability to the full range of international terrorism, lack of universality in terms of signatories, and weak coordination with regional arrangements. On the other hand, Cauley and Sandler (1988) were sufficiently optimistic about the future of international cooperation among Western democracies to advocate the formation of a transnational antiterrorist commando unit in order to "win World War III."

Since one obstacle to cooperation is a large number of actors, it is not surprising that cooperation is most successful among long-standing allies. Winkates (1991) found substantial policy consensus on all actions short of the use of military force in the Group of Seven (G-7), since both institutional and normative circumstances favored cooperation. Another active regional forum for cooperation is the European Union (see Chalk 1994; Jackson 1994; and Schmid and Crelinsten 1992, Part III). The 1992 Maastricht Treaty, which established a single unified market, provided for extensive cooperation in matters of security against terrorism.

It is natural that American policy against international terrorism would be a central theme in many treatments of response. The retaliatory use of military force in the 1986 U.S. raid on Libya is a frequent topic (e.g., Celmer 1987, Gold-Biss 1994, and Sloan 1993). Theories of coercion and coercive diplomacy, applied to the American case, generally produce negative assessments. Zimmermann (1994) concludes that the Reagan administration's policy of coercion against Libya suffered from an almost exclusive reliance on military force rather than other coercive instruments, a limitation imposed in part by the lack of international cooperation in implementing political and economic sanctions. Nor did the administration's objective of ending Libyan support for international terrorism permit a tangible and definitive resolution. Lepgold (1998) asks whether coercion is effective against new transnational security threats that do not fit within the traditional state-oriented international relations paradigm, such as terrorism or drug trafficking. He argues that "transstate outlaws" are less susceptible to coercion than states but that coercive responses to such threats may be important in terms of domestic legitimacy. Byman, Waxman, and Larson (1999) analyze the use of air power to coerce nonstate actors in a variety of situations, including the 1998 American bombing of targets in the Sudan and Afghanistan in retaliation for an attack on embassies in Kenya and Tanzania. The United States experiences significant difficulties in coercing nonstate actors directly: lack of identifiable and targetable assets (particularly problems in distinguishing military from civilian targets), inaccurate intelligence, nonstate actors' frequent lack of internal control, and their ability to exploit the state's countermeasures, especially through the manipulation of public opinion. They conclude that "Despite an extremely favorable balance of conventional military power, the United States is likely to face huge obstacles in securing escalation dominance over or denying the strategic objectives of these adversaries" (125). Similarly, in a study also commissioned for the U.S. Air Force, Lesser (1999) advocates a multidimensional approach to the threat of future terrorism, as well as the integration of policy toward terrorism into broader national security planning. In this view, the appearance of a "new" more lethal terrorism that lacks hierarchical organization, clear political goals, or state sponsorship necessitates a reorientation of policy.

Other questions concern the determinants of American policy toward international terrorism and its relationship to American foreign relations in general. From the perspective of diplomatic history, Kumamoto (1999) argues that the United States has always allowed larger global concerns to influence policy toward terrorism, due primarily to public opinion. Even terrorism against non-American targets influenced policymakers, who often found hard-line policies precluded by domestic political sympathies. Nacos (1994) also interprets official attention to terrorism in terms of domestic factors, particularly the news media. She describes a policy dilemma in which "terrorist incidents, especially those involving hostages, are nightmares for presidents, who are often forced to choose between protecting Americans' lives . . . or acting in the overall national interest by not dealing with terrorists, so as not to encourage further hostage takings" (15). Studies of the bureaucratic framework for policymaking also include Tucker (1997) and Simon (1994), who analyze the organization of the government for the conduct of policy as well as the choice of strategies. Hermann and Hermann (1990) and Sick (1990) focus explicitly on American decision-making processes. In addition, Wilson (1994) provides a succinct historical overview of past American policy.

Issues of Methodology and Approach

This chapter has referred to the specific findings of formal modeling, game theory, and econometric analyses of terrorism, as well as to historical and conceptual accounts. An excellent overview of game-theoretic and choice-theoretic methodologies is found in Enders and Sandler (1995). These approaches include time-series analyses involving vector-autoregression intervention procedures. As Enders and Sandler summarize the literature, studies have investigated negotiation strategies in hostage seizures, terrorist targeting, military retaliation, the general effectiveness of antiterrorist policies, and international cooperation. Enders and Sandler (1999) also add to this literature by analyzing the problem of whether the incidence of terrorism is increasing or decreasing in the 1990s. In 1995, they predicted that recent developments in economic methods and game theory, such as games involving asymmetric information, would be particularly suited to the study of terrorism. They also advocated more empirical applications of formal models.

From a different perspective, critical studies approach "terrorism" as a construction of Western governments who need national security threats to maintain domestic cohesion. The idea of an explanatory theory of the empirical phenomenon of terrorism is dismissed out of hand. For example, Adrian Guelke (1995) argues that the concept of terrorism is so elastic as to be without boundary. The use of the term, in his view, is entirely subjective, since conceptions of terrorism are rooted in a specifically Western worldview and are meant to assert the supremacy of Western values and deny the worth of competing perspectives. He anticipates a thorough disintegration of the concept by the end of the century, since the "age of terrorism" was part of the postcolonial era, when anomic and marginal groups using violence employed an anti-imperialistic rhetoric that gave the deceptive appearance of a collective will. Zulaika and Douglass (1996) also reject causal analysis to focus on "the use and abuse of terrorist discourse." "Terrorism" is considered a label that substitutes for genuine political debate. It is not possible to define it or to give an account of the "facts" that presumably constitute the phenomenon. Der Derian (1992, 73–126) offers a compatible "poststructuralist" argument about terrorism and the "security culture." Through a "cultural reading of terrorism," which in this instance is identified with the Iran-Contra scandal, he means to "descript" its history. Der Derian argues that "international terrorism is not a symptom nor a cause nor an effect of this systemic crisis: it has become a spectacular, micro-cosmic simulation" (81). The spectacle itself distracts the public from the reality of international disorder. Thus "much of what is read and written of terrorism displays a superficiality of reasoning and a corruption of language which effects truths about terrorism without any sense of how these truths are produced by and help to sustain official discourses of international relations" (81). "Terrorism" is staged not by terrorists but by governments and the "terrorism industry."

Conclusion: Questions to Be Asked

Although terrorism has attracted academic interest since the early 1970s, its relevance to theories of international conflict and war or to conceptions of global security has rarely been addressed directly. The key questions in this area of inquiry concern not only how the process of terrorism becomes international, but whether or not the roots of terrorism lie in international or regional conflict and what effect terrorism has on patterns of conflict and cooperation. Although the economic consequences of terrorism have been analyzed (see Enders and Sandler 1996 and Enders, Sandler, and Parise 1992), its political consequences have received less attention. Rigorous and systematic inquiry into questions of both cause and effect is still needed.

For example, terrorism may serve as a convenient and economical form of surrogate warfare between rivals, a "spoiler" in peace processes and impediment to conflict resolution, or a precipitant of crisis and escalation in an already hostile relationship. As an indirect source of conflict, it may undermine international norms of civility and trust. It diminishes the transparency and trust that are essential for international cooperation. Sustained terrorism may destabilize states internally, thus altering the distribution of power in the international system. It can form a bridge between civil and international conflict, as violence "spills over" from localized discontent to foreign targets and locations. It is a popular tool of ethnonationalist movements, a prominent source of disorder in the post–cold war era. Terrorism can make it difficult to distinguish between state and nonstate actors and to ascertain responsibility for disruptive behavior. It increases uncertainty. It blurs the distinction between what is "international" and what is "domestic."

Furthermore, rather than assuming that terrorism is meant to accomplish international objectives, we should ask whether the international consequences of terrorism are intended or unintended. That is, we should avoid reasoning from effect to cause. For example, Lustick (1995) suggests that terrorism may actually be "solipsistic," meant to unify a constituency rather than alter an enemy's decision-making calculus. The strategic effect on the adversary and on patterns of conflict may be incidental to the real goal of mobilizing popular support.

Another set of questions focuses on the effects of counterterrorist policy, both on terrorism itself—its targets, frequency, diffusion, and destructiveness—and on the international system. Further study is needed of specific coercive and noncoercive responses, including the use of military force, labeling states as sponsors of terrorism, application of sanctions, and concessions or resistance to terrorist demands. The direct effects of international terrorism may well have been inconsequential so far, as Schelling (1991) believes, but government responses to terrorism, especially military retaliation against perceived state sponsors, can lead to more serious disorder. If future terrorists do resort to technologies of mass destruction, it is difficult to imagine that terrorism and the response to terrorism could still be seen as inconsequential.

Moreover, as Enders and Sandler (1995) emphasize, the field could profit by more empirical research, both to answer new questions and to test the informal hypotheses and formal models that already exist. Critical theories that define terrorism as merely the construction, representation, or simulation of governments who wish to distract their publics or rally support cannot answer these questions, but they provide a useful warning against hyperbole and exaggeration of the threat. Since conceptions of terrorism do matter, analysts should look at how the threat is framed or represented by governments as well as how policy toward terrorism is determined. For example, although the role of ideas in constructing policy toward domestic terrorism has received some attention (e.g., Katzenstein 1993), comparable treatment of policy toward international terrorism is lacking. Counterterrorism policy should be considered as an outcome of both domestic and international factors.

Although analysts disagree about the future—whether incidents of terrorism are increasing or decreasing, whether terrorism is becoming more destructive or more lethal, and whether governments should prepare for "catastrophic" or "super" terrorism—clearly terrorism will remain a problem for global security into the twenty-first century. It persists despite changes in the international configuration of power and in the nature of the units that compose the international system. It will continue to be a problem for governments, scholars, and the public.

Identity and International Conflict

MANUS I. MIDLARSKY

This chapter explores the often complex relationships between international and identity conflicts. It is not intended to be a complete review of the sources of identity conflicts, including ethnic, revolutionary, and civil war variants, nor is it intended to comprehensively review the etiology of international conflict. Instead, I shall concentrate on the nexus between identity and international conflicts. Where necessary and appropriate, the sources of identity conflict will be examined.

The material is presented according to the levels of analysis commonly used in analyzing international conflict: system structure, dyad, and unit (the identity group, sometimes coterminous with a nation-state). These are not mutually exclusive categories, for certain approaches can fall into one or another category, depending on the perspective of the researcher. Nevertheless, they represent an analytic convenience that can be used to organize and hopefully render plausible a large quantity of sometimes inchoate information. First, some definitional matters require attention.

International conflict is commonly and straightforwardly understood as conflict up to and including violence between states, or more broadly conceptualized as armed conflict occurring in the international system defined as all areas outside of the boundaries of a given unit. To fix ideas more precisely, this type of conflict can be understood as hostile activity directed by the government or members of one unit against the government or members of another, or alternatively, as the influence of violence, its threat, or its cessation occurring in one portion of the system on that occurring in other international loci. At times, the systemic locus of the violence can be situated within one unit, which then may influence the violence occurring in another. On other occasions, the source of the conflict or violence may originate in the system and affect identity conflicts within a unit.

Because the meaning of the term *international* is necessarily somewhat variable in this context as identity groups sometimes become nation-states virtually overnight, a liberal use of the term is found here. Not surprisingly, theories of international conflict such as the security dilemma or the origins of structural systemic war will prove to be useful. And because the preponderance of deaths in identity conflicts have occurred in connection with the collapse or radical transformation of state structures and their influence on other conflicts, these instances will be emphasized.

The matter of identity also is complex, and many scholars have written on this topic in recent years.[1] Yet for purposes of this chapter, identity will be taken to mean something very close to ethnicity, with one important exception to be noted shortly. Smith (1993, 28), in particular, establishes this equivalency in arguing that "to grasp the nature and power of ethnic nationalism today, one must focus primarily on the collective level of identity and community. The particular collective cultural identity of concern here is the *ethnie,* or ethnic community."

People with collective identities or ethnies typically share common proper names, a myth of common ancestry that denotes a common origin in time and place (Horowitz 1985), shared historical memories in the form of shared memories of a common past, elements of a common culture that tend to include religion, customs, and language, a link with a homeland, either imagined or real (Anderson 1991), and a sense of solidarity (Hutchinson and Smith 1996; Smith 1993).

Several of these elements of collective identity deserve comment. First, it is not the reality of a common genetic heritage, physical descent, or some other scientifically verifiable evidence of commonality that is important, although at times it may be supportive. Instead it is the myth or collective storytelling handed down from generation to generation that is critical in forming and sustaining the collective identity.[2] To this extent, historical memories, real or imagined, are important, for they contain the essentials of the collective mythology. They not only reflect the people's common past experience, but suggest their common destiny as well.

Second, language is important, but not critical. Certainly, knowledge of Serbo-Croatian is crucial for Serbian identity, but it also is critical for Croatian and Bosnian Muslim identity. Other, and from their perspective, far more important identity markers distinguish among these peoples. Obversely, despite the absence of knowledge of Hebrew, Yiddish, or Ladino (a Sephardic Diaspora language), an American Jew and a French Jew may be quite able to identify with each other.

Third, attachment to a territory follows from the common history/ folk myth. There may even have occurred an exile from the common homeland. Yet perhaps even more in its imagined state, the territories of real or presumed common ancestry exert a hold on the sentiments of exiles. Although commonly associated with long-standing exilic communities such as those of Armenians or Jews, these attachments to homelands also were found until very recently among the Irish and even somewhat surprisingly among Norwegians. These sentiments were held despite a common economic success in the diaspora experience or in their homelands. Perhaps a common experience of subjugation or persecution at the hands of more powerful entities—Armenians (Turkey), Jews (Christian Europe), Irish (England), Norwegians (Sweden)—supersedes any immediate sense of economic well-being.

Fourth, one must distinguish between the ethnic or collective identity category and the ethnic community (Smith 1993). The ethnic community revels in a sense of solidarity built around the themes of common history, destiny, and the like. The ethnic category simply exists denotatively without any sense of belonging, which really arose only during the modern period. Historically, only a small elite consisting generally of a monarch, landed nobility, and religious leadership shared any sense of collective identity. With the advent of increased literacy, communication, and transportation in the modern period, the elite worked to transform the ethnic category into the ethnic community, thus initiating the period of modern nationalism.

Finally, although largely coterminous, the ethnic community and a common religion reveal one important distinction between them. Whereas the ethnic community simply exists, the religion is programmatic for the present and future. As Hobsbawm (1996, 357) puts it, "The call of ethnicity or language provides no guidance to the future at all. It is merely a protest against the status quo or, more precisely, against 'the others' who threaten the ethnically defined group. For, unlike fundamentalism which, however narrow and sectarian in its actual appeal, draws its strength from the claim to universal truth, theoretically applicable to all, nationalism by definition excludes from its purview all who do not belong to its own 'nation,' i.e. the vast majority of the human race."

It is no accident that perhaps the most prominent exponent of identity conflicts in international relations (Huntington 1996), focuses not on ethnicity per se, but principally on the religious component of identity, namely Islam, Confucianism, or Eastern Orthodoxy. More on that later.

Structural Systemic Conflicts

It is clear that the recent violence in the former Yugoslavia among Serbs, Croats, Bosnian Muslims, and others (e.g., Slovenians) represents a structural systemic conflict in that region. Treating it as such allows at least two theoretical perspectives to be brought to bear on the conflict. The first is that of the security dilemma emergent from realist theory and applied now to identity conflicts.

In a situation of ethnic rivalry, made far worse by the collapse of a unifying structure such as a state or empire, ethnic groups must now vie among themselves. Posen (1993) argues that this is the precise condition for the applicability of the security dilemma.[3] Every effort by one or another group to legitimately, in its own view, enhance its security yields an increment in insecurity as a rival group proceeds to match whatever security increment (say armaments or strategic position) was achieved by the first. It is easy to see how such an uncontrolled rivalry can spiral out of control into a systemic conflict.

An aggravating factor, according to Posen (1993), is the inability to distinguish between offense and defense. At the relatively primitive armaments levels of national militias, most any type of weaponry could be used both offensively and defensively. Therefore, any increment in such weaponry can be threatening to the other side. Further, as a consequence of the geographic dispersion of large numbers of one ethnie in the environment of another, both feel equally vulnerable. Each of the villages feels surrounded by a hostile environment that requires immediate defensive measures, which could easily be interpreted as offensive by the rival group. Anarchy and systemic conflict can be the result of this process.

Posen (1993) argues that the history of Serbo-Croat relations provides a conflictual backdrop to the more recent hostilities. First, the entire region has experienced much war during the past several hundred years. The area was a frontier of the Habsburg and Ottoman Empires, with Croatia securely part of the Habsburg military apparatus. During the late nineteenth century, both Croats and Serbs experienced harsh political and military conditions, with the former coming under Hungarian rule (within the Austro-Hungarian Empire) in 1868 and the latter emerging from Ottoman rule in 1878. More specifically, the political and military domination of Yugoslavia by Serbia after World War I, the deaths of more than 500,000 Serbs during World War II, many of them killed by the fascist Croatian Ustase, made matters far worse, as did the deaths of many of the 200,000 Croats killed at the hands of the Serbian nationalist Chetniks. The military domination of post–World War II Yugoslavia by the Serbs, especially its officer corps, did not help matters when the collapse of the former Yugoslavia came about in 1991.

An argument similar to the security dilemma had been applied by Schmookler (1984) to rivalries among states and can be applied directly to ethnic conflict. This model is derived from the parable of the tribes. Consider a set of tribes living in fairly close proximity to each other. Even if only one of them takes it upon itself to behave aggressively, for whatever reason, the outcome can be a persisting warlike system. A potential victim of the aggressor can (1) withdraw from the region, (2) allow itself to be destroyed, (3) surrender to the aggressor and become a tributary vassal tribe, or (4) be absorbed culturally and politically into the aggressor tribe. If it wants to survive in its pristine state, on the other hand, it has no choice but to fight. Over time, the surviving tribes are those that chose to fight, either initially in response to the aggressive behavior, or in a later rebellion after an early capitulation and resulting tributary status. The fate of many now extinct biblical peoples, such as Ammon, Moab, or Edom, followed one version or another of this trajectory, as did the indigenous Baltic Prussians and Livonians more recently. The fate of the Jews as a small people vulnerable to conquest and/or assimilation, especially in the post-Holocaust period, might have been similar, except for the Zionist fighting response and the very different response of a demographic resurgence of ultra-Orthodox Jewry (forbidden to use birth control) as an alternate coping mechanism in response to the threat of demographic extinction.

The security dilemma as developed by Posen (1993) relies very much on the concept of state collapse exemplified by the case of Yugoslavia. Although less heinous in its consequences, the breakup of the Soviet Union engendered severe identity-based violence in Chechnya, Armenia, Azerbaijan, Georgia, and elsewhere. Containment of fear by a functioning state apparatus (Lake and Rothchild 1996) is no longer possible, and information failures as well as problems of credible commitment arise (Fearon 1998).[4] Generalizing the model, one can understand the collapse of the state as but a special (and extreme) case of state (in)security, which can be defined as the relative freedom of the state from threats to its existence emanating either from its domestic or its international environment. The term *relative* is important because state security often is assessed by policymakers relative to some recent period in national history, or in some instances relative to other states. Later, in the more formal exposition, the variable *change* in state security will be examined.

Although state collapse clearly is a spectacular case in point, it is not the only instance of state insecurity. At the height of the cold war, for example, the United States experienced considerable fear of nuclear war, despite its status as the world's leading superpower. A state that recently has emerged from defeat in a major war also may experience a sense of insecurity. Of course, the ultimate condition of state insecurity is found during major war itself when the state could be torn asunder as the result of defeat, as in fact happened to Nazi Germany at the end of World War II. And it was during wars that boded extremely ill for the state that Turkey during World War I and Germany during World War II engaged in the most destructive form of identity conflict, genocide, respectively against the Armenians and the Jews.

A renewed determination and an acceleration of the killing can stem from a perceived threat to state security. Hitler apparently recognized as early as November 1941 that the war could not be won as the Germans bogged down in their advance toward Moscow.[5] After the first major German defeat of the European land war before Moscow in December, and the virtually simultaneous entry of the United States into the war after the Japanese attack on Pearl Harbor, this conclusion must have been reinforced.[6] Yet the formal process beginning the industrialized mass murder of European Jewry took place shortly thereafter on January 20, 1942, at Wannsee (Epstein and Rosen 1997, 331). Despite hindering the German war effort by the large number of transports and personnel needed to carry out the plan, it continued even into 1945, as the war clearly was lost. One can infer that the increased danger to state security by the stiffening resistance to the Nazis and the expanding coalition against them allowed this extreme anti-Semitic policy to be enacted. "If we have to pay, then they will pay" appears to have been their reasoning.[7] It is possible that the same reasoning was found in the Turkish decision making of World War I concerning the Armenians. And a serious threat to the Rwandan state appeared in the form of the Rwandese Patriotic Front (RPF), which threatened to overthrow the Hutu-dominated state, leading to the 1994 genocide against the Tutsi. More on that will be presented later.

Consider now the condition of state security, or more accurately, a change in state security in a positive direction. Here there are no clear indicators such as warfare or state collapse. Nevertheless, historic events like the ending of the cold war can be seen as increasing state security, especially for states affiliated with one of the cold war alliances. Newfound security implies that societies can now begin to grapple with issues that heretofore had either been deferred (by consensus) or had simply not been addressed because of pressing security concerns. The decline or disappearance of an external threat allows segments of a society to now address issues that in their view had been put off far too long. A severe external threat can act to unify a society at least temporarily as long as the threat is still manifest (Coser 1956; Simmel 1955). But when it diminishes or disappears, then muted antagonisms or grievances can surface abruptly. Even the United States as the strongest world power found itself at the end of the most intense cold war period dealing with the issue of civil rights and the associated urban disorders as a form of ethnic or identity-based conflict. It is no accident that the major civil rights legislative enactments of the 1960s began two years after the successful conclusion of the Cuban missile crisis and the somewhat earlier resolution of the Berlin crisis of 1961. A period of more attenuated hostilities between the United States and the Soviet Union was ushered in. The earlier preoccupation with foreign policy of the Eisenhower and Kennedy administrations gave way now to a concentration on domestic concerns that facilitated a simultaneous eruption of urban racial conflict, partly as a consequence of recognition by the government that long-term wrongs needed to be corrected. A kind of quasi legitimacy was lent to the disorders.[8]

The attenuation or end of the cold war would influence other countries as well. In the Middle East, the demise of the Soviet Union and disappearance of their one superpower ally led Arab states such as Syria and Jordan to recognize that they must deal directly with Israel or at least not strongly oppose the peace process. As a consequence, Israel experienced a sense of security almost entirely absent from its 50-year history. Turkey is also experiencing a state security that has been enhanced considerably by the disappearance of the superpower to the north, one that had in earlier imperial guise defeated the Turks repeatedly, especially at the end of the nineteenth century. Both Israel and Turkey have been wrestling with serious identity problems in the post–cold war era. The rise of the Islamist Turkish Welfare Party (Refah), even to the point of briefly capturing the seat of government, brought the question of Turkish identity into sharp focus, namely the existential relationship between what constitutes a Turk and Islam, a connection that had been severed at the governmental level in favor of a secular and more European-oriented identity since the rule of Kemal Ataturk.

Another predominantly Muslim country, Egypt, also has experienced considerable identity conflict after the outbreak of peace with both Israel and Libya, its two principal military opponents in recent years. The rise of Islamist terrorist organizations in Egypt led to one of the bloodiest identity conflicts in the Middle East. Indeed, the spread of Islamism in this region, with varying degrees of success, has been one of the more important systemic phenomena in recent years (Bronson 1996).

Salient identity issues have been raised in Israel since the signing of the Oslo Accords and the existence now of formal peace treaties with both Egypt and Jordan. The assassination of Yitzchak Rabin by an Orthodox Jewish opponent of the Accords is symptomatic of the growing divide between secular and observant Israeli Jews. For the first time, the vexing longtime question of who is a Jew is being addressed in open forums, even including international repercussions in the American debate between Orthodox Jews, on the one hand, and Reform and Conservative Jews, on the other. Even within the Orthodox community there are divisions between the ultra-Orthodox (sometimes called *Haredim,* or those who tremble before God) and modern Orthodox who are more assimilated in their work and social lives but are fully observant Jews (Lustick 1988). As if that were not enough, long-standing feelings of inequality nurtured by the Sephardim or Eastern Jews have begun to be more visible and embodied in one of the newest and most powerful political parties, Shas, which caters mostly to observant Sephardim (Garfinkle 1997).

These arguments may be summarized in figure 1, which suggests a curvilinear U-curve relationship between change in state security and the probability of identity conflict. This function is more appropriate than others such as a V-curve, because beyond the first impact of a change in state security (rapidly changing portion near the origin), societal variables such as inequalities of various types[9] assume importance. Hence, for portions of the curve far from the origin, the probability of identity conflict becomes essentially independent of changes in state security. Given two or more salient identities for significant proportions of the

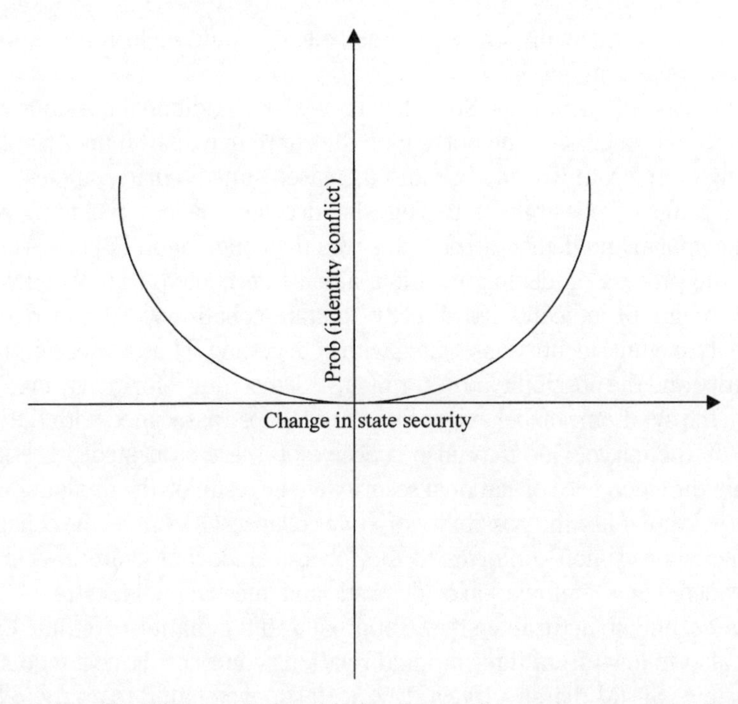

FIGURE 1. Curvilinear relationship between change in state security and the probability of identity conflict

population, the probability of identity conflict is high at both extremes of the curve. A change in the negative direction of decreasing state security on the left side of the curve yields a greater probability of identity conflict. Similarly, a change in the positive direction of increasing state security on the right side of the curve also gives rise to an increased probability of identity conflict (Midlarsky and Aronoff 1999).

Although the *probability* of identity conflicts is high at both extremes, this does not mean that the *intensity* or severity of such conflict is the same for both. Extreme state insecurities exemplified by major wars or state collapse create possibilities for violence on a much larger scale than those found in increasing state security. World Wars I and II or the collapse of the former Yugoslavia and the Soviet Union are cases in point. Nevertheless, one should not minimize the more long-term dangers inherent in the lower intensity identity conflicts found on the right side of the curve. The rise of Islamism in important Middle Eastern countries, such as Turkey or Egypt, or the potential scuttling of the Oslo and Wye

Accords by right-wing forces in Israel, clearly could yield future severe international conflict.

The case of the former Yugoslavia reveals an additional possibility. A process that begins in one portion of the curve may end in another. The ending of the cold war in 1989 and increased state security, suggested a broad range of possibilities to Yugoslav decision makers, including economic reform and democratization as was then ongoing in Poland. And it was the process of democratization, albeit interrupted, that Woodward (1995, chap. 5) indicates led directly to state collapse via the increased appeals to ethnic identity associated with vote-getting. Thus, increased state security and the possibility now for intense democratic reform may eventuate in the syndrome of behaviors like state collapse associated with the left side of the curve. One may also conceive of these as nested processes; within the emergence of national security as the result of the diminution of external threat lies the possibility of state collapse. Of course, the collapse of the Soviet Union conforms to the "classic" model of state insecurity engendered by a combination of domestic and international factors.

A second structural systemic approach to the matter of ethnic conflict also follows from international relations concerns. Here a model of systemic war (Midlarsky 1988a, 1992a, 1997a) was found to apply to the spread of ethnic conflict in the former Yugoslavia. Additionally, a specific prediction was borne out by subsequent events. The model emphasizes multipolarity leading to resource inequality that in turn affects alliance formation and alliance memory. An overlap or conjunction between conflict structures then occurs leading to a change in the balance of power followed by systemic war, either of a global or regional variety. The model, with minor variations, was found to apply equally to both global and regional systemic conflicts. Thus:

> Multipolarity ➜ Resource inequality ➜ Alliance formation ➜ Alliance memory ➜ Overlap in conflict structures ➜ Change in the balance of power ➜ Systemic war

The first of these relationships was suggested by a probabilistic analysis that showed multipolarity to be associated with resource inequality, and bipolarity to be associated with equality (Midlarsky 1989a). The greater the scarcity of resources in a multipolar setting, the greater the inequality of resource distribution between most- and least-favored actors. Such inequalities can lead less-favored actors to seek allies as a way to redress the apparent inequality.

Within a society, equalities among the members are more likely than inequalities to yield stability in the long run. Envy and political intrigue can be a consequence within a multipolar system, thus leading to the deterioration of intergroup or interstate relations. This outcome is suggested by theories based on relative deprivation, rapidly declining economic circumstances, and scarcities of valued commodities.[10] In the modern period the most stable societies by far are those with industrialized economies and their associated equalities; in contrast, severe inequalities are found in largely agrarian countries that are prone to instability.

Old conflicts can persist as the result of memory among alliances, especially the memory of conflicts with other groups, and these memories can have implications for later warfare. This memory, in turn, can lead to the overlap in conflict domains; when these two sets of conflict behaviors overlap, nations or ethnic groups are well on the way to systemic war.

In the former Yugoslavia, a precipitous economic decline (Woodward 1995) yielded the scarcity that would aggravate inequality in a multipolar structure. During the 1980s, Slovenia enjoyed full employment, Croatian unemployment was single digit while "unemployment reached 50 percent in Kosovo, 27 percent in Macedonia, 23 percent in Bosnia-Herzegovina, and over 20 percent in Serbia. Inflation soared, climbing to 50 percent in the early 1980s and then sky-rocketing to 1,200 percent in the late 1980s. Per capita income dropped by almost 50 percent between 1979 and 1988" (Daalder 1996, 42). Clearly this is a condition of strong scarcity and inequality among the republics, loosely coterminous with ethnies in the former Yugoslavia.

The incipient emerging alliance with Germany by Slovenia and Croatia, albeit informal, next exacerbated this process. Slovenia and Croatia increasingly sought European (especially German) protection from the Serb-dominated Yugoslav army as the disintegration of Yugoslavia proceeded. Here, the richest republics feared the military activism of one of the poorer ones. It was Germany, in the vanguard of the European Community (EC)—possibly because of its earlier alliance with Croatia during World War II or because Croatia was for so long a province of the Austrian (later Austro-Hungarian) Empire—that hastened European recognition of independent Slovenia and Croatia and fostered increased Serbian hostility. Germans had long vacationed along the Dalmatian Coast, which increased their affinity with the Croats. Another possible determinant of this hasty recognition of Slovenia and Croatia may have been a desire to impose a fait accompli on the former Yugoslavia, in the mistaken hope that the existence of these newly recognized, sovereign entities would preclude the possibility of civil war. One consequence of such widespread warfare might have been increased Balkan immigration into Germany at a time of increased ethnic tensions within Germany itself. Thus alliance formation, in an informal if not formal sense, strongly influenced the Serbs to proceed as they did.

It is probable that the renewed association between Germany and Croatia intensified the Serbian memories of the fascist Croatian Ustase slaughter of Serbs (and Jews) during World War II. Some Muslims also participated in the killing. An intensification of memory could have resulted, making Serbs far more willing to fight, and to fight more brutally, than would otherwise have been the case.[11]

The latent hostilities between Serbs and Muslims, especially in rural environs, now overlapped with the ongoing Serbo-Croatian conflict. Hence, two conflict structures overlapped: enmity between Serbs and Croats and between Serbs and Muslims. This almost exactly parallels the overlap between Balkan conflicts—involving Austria-Hungary on the one hand (mainly concerning Slavic minorities in the Empire) and European great power disputes on the other—that was found to be a necessary condition for the onset of World War I.[12] The Serbo-Croatian War not only facilitated the Bosnian conflict, it raised issues of the balance of power in the Balkans that led each of the protagonists, especially the Serbs, to seize as much territory as possible. (This is one possible reason for the willingness of the Serb-dominated Yugoslav federal army to withdraw from Slovenia after only 10 days of war, and for the demonstration by the Slovenian militia of their willingness to fight. Given the geographic distance of Slovenia from Serbia, possibilities for the permanent conquest and annexation of territory were remote, especially when compared with Serbia's proximity to Croatia and Bosnia.) Calculations of the balance of power between Serbs and Croats appeared to strongly influence both groups to seize as much Bosnian territory as possible. Systemic conflict was the result. Thus, if we replace the term *alliance memory* with *intensification of alliance memory* and use the term *regional systemic war* instead of *systemic war,* the causal sequence detailed in the theoretical framework can just as easily explain the violence occurring in the former Yugoslavia.

Why was this regional systemic war not externalized beyond the confines of the former Yugoslavia? Precisely because this was a systemic war of great intensity, there was a reluctance on the part of other European powers and the United States to intervene. Regional systemic conflicts of great intensity but limited externalization potential—civil wars, for instance—tend to discourage direct intervention. The nineteenth-century experience of the United States, or more recently that of China and Nigeria, come to mind. External actors tend to avoid such involvement not only because of their own potential losses, but also because the self-absorption of the immediate protagonists in the war makes them appear less threatening internationally, at least in the short run.

There were other reasons for the absence of an immediate externalization of the conflict. The absence of a European multipolar system as it existed in the early twentieth century strongly diminished the probability of an immediate externalization. Great powers have much less incentive to intervene when they have few if any potential antagonists to be concerned about, lest their opponents gain from the conflict. Russia and Turkey have stakes in the conflict, but in contrast to the period preceding World War I, they are more symbolic than driven by *realpolitik*. Russia extends its support to the Serbs partly as the result of a common Orthodox faith and historic national connections, but the outcome of the Bosnian conflict in no way affects a Balkan balance of power relevant to Russia, as was the case prior to 1914 in the Balkan disputes between Austria-Hungary and Russia. Turkey also no longer has a direct power interest in the Balkans; its borders now end well east of the recent Balkan violence, whatever religious affinities may exist between Turks and the Slavic Muslims in Bosnia. Resource inequality has been minimized by certain redistributive policies of the EC (now EU), and, of course, the older styles of alliance formation endemic to Europe historically no longer apply to the EU and NATO settings. As a result, conflict among the European powers has been minimized, and they had less desire to be involved in the violence that has occurred recently in the Balkans.

When did the Bosnian violence become virtually inevitable—that is, when was there no turning back from the path to systemic war within much of the former Yugoslavia? In prior research, I asked this question in regard to eight systemic wars, and the answer appeared to be clear-cut. The causal pathway to systemic war appeared to be irreversible only after the overlap in conflict structures occurred (Midlarsky 1988a, 204–6). Prior to that time, these wars could have been averted through strenuous efforts of diplomacy. Multipolarities and resource inequalities are found throughout the international arena, and even alliances differentially favoring one side, as Germany did in Slovenia and especially Croatia, do not necessarily lead to systemic war. But when alliance formation, even of the informal variety, facilitates the overlap in conflict structures, the conflict process enters the irreversible stage. When Germany openly tilted toward Croatia, thus encouraging independence, with the further (correct) implication that the remainder of the EC would be brought along, and with the promise of support from the recently unified economic giant of Western Europe, this informal alliance obviously encouraged Croatian sovereignty. There was a further important implication for the Serbs. If Croatia and Slovenia were to be recognized by the EC, why should not Bosnia also be enveloped within the German embrace? Hence, when the EC officially recognized Croatian independence on January 15, 1992, the Serbs initiated the Bosnian conflict. Alliance formation facilitated both the Serbo-Croat and Muslim-Serb conflict, which overlapped in this now virtually unavoidable systemic war.

Why did this regional systemic war, though severe, avoid the truly horrendous loss of life involved in global systemic wars such as World Wars I and II? As in other regional conflicts of this type, the system in question simply did not have the autonomy required to persist unfettered on its path to massive destruction. There were few if any outside influences to limit the destruction in the two world wars, until one or another principal actor was defeated. Here, on the other hand, the Western powers and especially the United States later took an active and ultimately successful role in limiting the extent of the violence. Threats of intervention, even if only from the air, against exposed Serbian artillery positions were effective in reining in the most extreme ambitions of the Serb politicians, which could have included immediate action against the ethnic Albanians in Kosovo and against the Macedonians, as well as continued action against the relatively defenseless Muslims. Other regional systemic conflicts that could have proceeded much farther along the path of destruction, such as the Arab-Israeli War of 1967 and especially that of 1973, were limited by the active involvement of the superpowers, the United States and the Soviet Union.

One finding of the earlier analysis had implications for the more recent Yugoslav situation. This was the almost certain occurrence of a mobilization war subsequent to the structural systemic war outlined in the causal sequence. I made this prediction in December 1993 at the first of two conferences leading to publication of the edited volume *Wars in the Midst of Peace* (Carment and James 1997b; also containing Midlarsky

1997a); the actual successful Croatian mobilization effort leading to the capture of the Serb-held Krajina region occurred in August 1995. After each structural systemic conflict, such as the French revolutionary wars or World War I, there followed mobilization wars that entailed the strong mobilization efforts at conquest on the part of at least one protagonist in the earlier war. France in the Napoleonic Wars and Germany in World War II are cases in point. One reason for the occurrence of the later war is the relatively inconclusive outcome of the first, structural war. In the French revolutionary wars, a kind of stalemate resulted that could be overcome only by Napoleon's mobilization efforts against France's enemies. Germany was not so defeated in World War I that it could not rise again as a formidable great power after significant mobilization efforts leading up to World War II.

At the regional level, the Yom Kippur War of 1973 can be understood as a mobilization war following upon the structural war of 1967 (Midlarsky 1988a, 210–12). Although the Israeli victory in the earlier war was clear-cut (as was the Allied victory in WWI), nevertheless the enormous geographic size and demographic imbalance between Arabs and Israelis made it conceivable that a future Arab mobilization, if organized effectively, could at least partially reverse the consequences of the 1967 war.

Similarly, a new and heavy round in the fighting among Serbs, Croats, and Muslims became likely as a result of the residual anger among Croats and Muslims after the first war, and in the absence of complete destruction of their communities that would have ruled out a future mobilization effort. Alternatively, the Serbs could have mobilized more fully, as did the French in the first decade of the nineteenth century, and attempted a complete obliteration of the Muslim communities, also including as many Croats as possible. Only the slow decay, or "cleansing" of the remaining Muslim communities, or an internationally guaranteed settlement, could prevent the onset of a new mobilization effort on the part of the Croats, Muslims, or Serbs. The successful Croatian mobilization effort of August 1995 was the result in this instance.

Systemic wars are conflict phenomena that may have consequences that go beyond the war itself. By this I mean that more salient features of the conflict could be imitated by ethnies that are not party to the original conflict. In this sense, there is spillover beyond the region of the conflict.

Consider the 1994 genocide of the Hutu by the Tutsi in Rwanda. It is difficult to understand the magnitude and savagery of the killing of approximately 500,000 to 800,000 people within several weeks, without viewing it within the context of prior events. Even within the context of a vastly troubled relationship between Hutu and Tutsi in the twentieth century, the extent of the killing was extraordinary. Its status as the most rapidly (although not the most extensively) executed genocide in the modern period renders it unique. As Prunier (1995, 261) put it, "The hurricane of death had crushed 80 per cent of its victims in about six weeks between the second week of April and the third week of May. If we consider that probably around 800,000 people were slaughtered during that short period . . . the daily killing rate was at least five times that of the Nazi death camps."

Such rapidity required considerable advance planning, as writers such as Des Forges (1999), Destexhe (1995), and Prunier (1995) clearly show. These plans date from the first awareness of the relatively unopposed genocidal and ethnic cleansing activities of the Serbs against the Muslims in Bosnia. "It is probably during those late months of 1992 that the general notion of 'solving' the power-sharing question by a large-scale slaughter of most Tutsi and of all the known Hutu opposition supporters, began to look to the hardline *akazu* [Hutu political elite] circles like both an attractive and a feasible proposition" (Prunier 1995, 169).[13] And we know that the Serb massacres and ethnic cleansing began in March of 1992, and in earnest, at the latest in April 1992 (Daalder 1996; Danner 1997). It would be difficult to imagine that the hard-line Hutu extremists would be unaware of such a signal event in post–World War II European history even as the Arusha (in Tanzania) negotiations on power sharing between the Tutsi-dominated rebel Rwandese Patriotic Front (RPF) and the Hutu-dominated government were ongoing. "A clearer demonstration of the global village that modern communications have created . . . would be difficult to imagine" (Apple 1993, A1). Although not written in connection with the Bosnia-Rwanda nexus, this statement could easily apply here.[14] And there are six additional reasons for the salience of the Bosnian model.

First, theoretically we would expect European political behavior to be a model for the Hutu extremists, especially when it meshes with their goals. The status of the model has been found to predict the behavior of an imitator, at least in the instance of Latin American military coups (Midlarsky 1970). Assuming that this modeling of instability extends to genocide as well, if Europe as a former colonial metropole that gave its Roman Catholic religion and French language to so many Rwandans could be home to such political violence, then Africans also could allow themselves this sort of license. French military and diplomatic support of President Habyarimana's regime and refusal to criticize it openly even up to the onset of the genocide (Callamard 1999, 169; Jones 1999, 141) must have reinforced this modeling effect.

Second, the fact that the emerging genocide of at least 200,000 persons in Bosnia (Daalder 1996) went unopposed, at least militarily in the opening, most influential stages of the conflict, made it appear that genocidal activities could be accomplished without serious external constraint in the post–cold war climate of the 1990s. In other words, "if they can get away with it, so can we."

Third, certain of the tactics used by the Hutu extremists appear to have been drawn directly from the Bosnian experience. Specifically, rape as a tactic of humiliation and ultimately dehumanization appears to have been consciously implemented in Rwanda, much as had been done earlier in Bosnia.[15] This stands in contrast to the typical historical pattern of rape as a random adjunct of war in which rape was an opportunistic crime, often committed by invading victorious troops.

Fourth, it does not even require a large-scale societal awareness of external events to initiate such a well-planned and rapidly executed process. It is clear that the genocide was organized from the top or as Prunier (1995, 241–42) put it, "The actual organizers of the genocide were a small tight group, belonging to the regime's political, military and economic elite, who had decided through a mixture of ideological and material motivation radically to resist political change which they perceived as threatening." If such an elite, presumably keenly aware of events in other countries, could be persuaded of the feasibility of such a genocide in Central Africa, then it could be organized effectively from the top down.

Regarding another African conflict, "I call it the copycat syndrome," said Dame Margaret Anstee, who was the Secretary General's special envoy in Angola in the early 1990s. She said that in 1992, when the rebel leader Jonas Savimbi "chose bullets over ballots," he had been watching the Bosnian Serb leader Radovan Karadzic "getting away with murder" (quoted in Crossette 1999, 16). This interpretation accords with the finding of Hill and Rothchild (1986) that receptivity to outside political violence is conditional upon a recent history of domestic strife, amply found in both Angola and Rwanda. The fighting between Hutu and Tutsi in 1959–61, the sporadic persecutions after independence (especially in 1973), and the ongoing strife after the RPF invasion of 1990 amply satisfy this condition. Further, the importance of the media in disseminating information that can augment a contagion effect also is confirmed by Hill and Rothchild (1992).

Fifth, it may not even require a close proximity in time, or modeling of presumably higher-status prototypes, for genocidal behavior in one location to influence that occurring in another. We know that when the constraints on German behavior were lifted by the onset of World War II, the unopposed massacre of Armenians by the Turks during World War I became a model for the Nazi genocide of European Jewry. Prior to the September 1939 invasion of Poland, in a speech to his chief commanders, Hitler is said to have justified the killing of Polish civilians by referring to this earlier instance. "Only thus shall we gain the living space [*Lebensraum*] which we need. Who, after all, speaks today of the annihilation of the Armenians?" (quoted in Fein 1979, 4). And the Rwandan president Habyarimana who most likely was involved in the planning of the genocide was known to have in his possession copies of films about Hitler and Nazism (Des Forges 1999, 80).

Finally, the Rwandan genocide took place after one antecedent of major hostilities—threat to state security—was already occurring in the form of the RPF military advances that ultimately would prove to be successful in toppling the Hutu-dominated regime. The earlier Bosnian genocide provided the model for an exit from the dilemma of extreme state insecurity by breaking the demographic base of the RPF opposition.

There can even exist tertiary effects of genocidal systemic conflict beyond that of the initial imitative behavior. Much of the recent violence in Congo is attributable to the presence in that country of Rwandan refugees, either the Banyamulenge of Tutsi descent, or the more recent arrival of as many as two million Hutu following their extermination campaign against the Tutsi and now fleeing the newly installed Tutsi-dominated RPF regime. Hit-and-run military activities by Hutu exiles in Congo attacking locations in western Rwanda led to a barely disguised Rwandan (RPF) invasion of Zaire, as it was then called. This resulted in the fall of Zaire's longtime dictator Mobutu Sese Seko and the installation of President Laurent Kabila in 1997. The expulsion of Tutsi military advisers to the Kabila government, combined with the even more important failure of Congo to prevent the Hutu incursions into Rwanda, led the Rwandan regime to oppose the Kabila government, apparently sponsoring the insurrection against Kabila. As one observer put it: "For anyone setting out to write a history of recent strife in Central Africa, few opening lines could be more tempting these days than: In the beginning there was Rwanda" (French 1998, 3).

Now, if one were setting out to write a history of recent genocide-related strife worldwide, it would be tempting to write: "In the beginning there was Bosnia."

Dyadic Effects

Moving away now from large-scale structural systemic conflicts and their consequences, dyadic conflict involving ethnic groups has become relatively common. Various systematic studies of ethnic strife have pointed to the importance of affinities between minority populations in one country and populations of similar ethnicity in a neighboring country (Carment and James 1997a, 1997b; Davis, Jaggers, and Moore 1997; Huth 1996a; Moore and Davis 1998). The Indian intervention in the Sri Lankan conflict or Syria in the Lebanese civil wars are illustrations that come to mind.

Which dynamics account for these dyadic interventions? First, most generally, we know that territorial contiguities (or proximities), alliances, rivalries, contagion, and the breakdown of a political order (Vasquez 1992) affect the spillover from one state to another. Goertz and Diehl (see their chapter in this volume) analyze the conditions under which enduring rivalries begin and persist, with contiguity an important originating condition. Johnson (1992) demonstrates how the cultural revival and religious, as well as ethnic commonality between Tamil-speaking Hindus in both South India and in Sri Lanka ultimately generated pressure on the Indian government to intervene in the domestic conflict between the Tamil Tigers and the Sinhalese Buddhist–dominated government in Colombo. Clearly, geographic proximity, with only a relatively small body of water separating the South Indian state of Tamil Nadu from the heavily Tamil-speaking Jaffna peninsula in Sri Lanka, facilitated this intervention.

Proximity in the form of contiguity also facilitated the Syrian intervention in the 1976 Lebanese domestic strife. Rasler (1992) details the Syrian feelings of vulnerability to a potential Israeli attack through southern Lebanon, as well as a desire to control the PLO activities in order to be uniquely positioned in the Arab world as a sponsor of the Palestinian cause. Thus, balance-of-power considerations vis-à-vis Israel and neighboring Arab countries such as Iraq and Jordan dominated Syrian motivations, not terribly different from those of Serbs, Croats, and Muslims in their systemic conflict in the former Yugoslavia. Here, however, narrower considerations may motivate the actions of one party, in this case Syria, in contrast to the larger structural contours of the etiology of the systemic conflict.

As important as these considerations are, perhaps even more salient for the etiology of future dyadic identity conflicts are issues of democracy and democratization. If democratic peace theory is valid, then not only would dyadic identity conflicts be minimized in their consequences for international violence, but also regional democratization would lead to fairly widespread peaceful relations (Maoz 1997b).

In treating this topic even only briefly, two distinctions are immediately necessary. The first is that between democracy as a fully realized political condition and democratization as an ongoing process. Little dispute exists now on the validity of the proposition that democracies do not war against each other, at least in the post–World War II period (see Russett and Starr's chapter in this volume). But democratization as a process has engendered debate on its consequences for war or peace (Mansfield and Snyder 1995). And Gurr (1994) has identified regime transition, including democratization, as a principal source of ethnopolitical conflict. An awareness has emerged that nationalism as the large-scale politicization of ethnicity is not necessarily incompatible with democratization. Nodia (1994, 7) in particular suggests that an intimate connection exists between nationalism and democratization: "Democracy has always emerged in distinct communities; there is no record anywhere of free, unconnected, and calculating individuals coming together spontaneously to form a democratic social contract *ex nihilo* [*sic*]. Whether we like it or not, nationalism is the historical force that has provided the political units for democratic government. 'Nation' is another name for 'We the People.' "

This connection is particularly strong when democratization is occurring and the people are being asked for their vote. In doing so, elites are either consciously or unwittingly creating a political consciousness. Historically in France, such a process took place subsequent to the French Revolution in creating a single French nation where only separate groups existed without any sense of common nationality or even without a common knowledge of the French language (Weber 1976). Currently, such a process may be occurring in the former communist states of Eastern Europe, but at a quicker pace. Therefore, democratization and a heightened sense of ethnicity may go hand in hand, unless the type of nationalism that Meinecke (1970) and Kohn (1967) referred to as a kind of "political nationalism" displaces a cultural identity-based nationalism. (This distinction is also referred to as that between civic and ethnic nationalism [Breton 1988].) In that instance of displacement, particular ethnic feeling within a larger nation-state may be subordinated to a larger sense of encompassing political nationality associated with the founding of a polity. To some extent, this process has occurred in the United States. Yet as Castells (1997, 11) suggests, identities "if and when constructed, are not built any longer on the basis of civil societies, that are in the process of disintegration, but as prolongation of communal resistance."

A particularly dangerous process of this type has occurred recently in South Asia. Beginning with the growing success of democratic institutions in India, ethnoreligious discord and political violence have increased. Ganguly (1996, 144) details the mechanism: "Increased access to education, growing media exposure, and the growth of grass-roots power through local and state elections have all contributed to an extraordinary level of political mobilization in India. Long-disenfranchised groups, most notably Muslims and 'untouchables,' have become increasingly assertive in Indian politics. This assertiveness, in turn, has generated a tremendous backlash from sections of the Hindu community, many of whose leaders have exploited the growing sense of unease about the erosion of the majority's privileged status."

The accession to political power of the Hindu nationalist Bharatiya Janata Party (BJP), and its tenuous hold on the reins of government, probably facilitated the recent round of extremely popular (domestically) Indian nuclear tests and the Pakistani response in kind.[16] Since the conflict over the future of Kashmir is not yet settled, the ongoing democratization in India could, in the end, have extraordinarily destructive consequences. And the probability of major hostilities is increased because here we have a long-standing dispute between a democracy (albeit an imperfect one) and a nondemocracy, the most dangerous condition for regime-type disputes, according to the findings reported in Russett and Starr's chapter in this volume. Whether nuclear deterrence would work at the relatively undeveloped levels of Indo-Pakistani operational deployments, is, of course, another question.

De Nevers (1993) nevertheless asserts that under certain conditions, democratization can reduce the prospects of ethnic conflict. Among these are the direct addressing of ethnic issues early in the transition process, the relative equality in size of the ethnic groups that would make one group unable to dominate the other readily and therefore both seek some sort of accommodation (note the contrast with power transition theory reviewed in Kugler and Lemke's chapter in this volume), unity of ethnic groups in their prior opposition to the *ancien regime,* the moderation of ethnic tendencies, and the absence of an external ethnic ally that might embolden one group to confront another (e.g., Tamils in Sri Lanka and India, and Croats in the former Yugoslavia via their relationship with Germany, even without the ethnic link).

Conditions to be avoided in the democratization process are the identification of the regime with a specific ethnic group, the reference to historical grievance by one ethnic group versus another and the manipulation of the ethnic mix in subordinated areas as was done in the Baltic states by the Soviet government. Yet, in the final analysis, it may be the generation of appropriate democratic institutions, particularly of the federal variety that may be critical to the success of the democratization process. Either a working democratic federalism on the Indian model (Hardgrave 1994; Horowitz 1994) with its own dangers, as we just saw, or the more difficult development of norms of ethnic inclusiveness as in Malaysia or the Indian state of Kerala would be required to successfully democratize under conditions of intense ethnic divisions.

Introducing the second distinction between democracy and liberal democracy makes matters a bit more complex, although possibly more hopeful. Democracy alone in the form of voting rights can heighten both ethnic feeling and nationalism if it is not accompanied by liberalism in the form of freedom of speech, press, religion, and other liberties associated with liberal democracy. Indeed, Zartman (1998, 328) suggests that democracy which reinforces majority domination is not the best solution to ethnic conflict. However, much of nineteenth-century nationalism, especially in the universalistic Mazzini mode (Avineri 1994) was associated with liberalism. The idea of freedom meant especially freedom from foreign domination, both Austrian and French, with all its restrictions on the individual. Nationalism in this view was a liberating force where the ultimate purpose was the institutionalization of a form of liberalism, hopefully liberal democracy. The distinction between democracy and liberal democracy will be treated later empirically in the context of Huntington's (1996) prediction of civilizational conflict.

Turning to the empirical findings on ethnicity and democracy, the view is less sanguine. According to Horowitz (1994), when societies are divided ethnically, democracy suffers. "Democracy is about inclusion and exclusion, about access to power, about the privileges that go with inclusion and the penalties that accompany exclusion. In severely divided societies, ethnic identity provides clear lines to determine who will be included and who will be excluded. Since the lines appear unalterable, being in and being out may quickly come to look permanent." Rabushka and Shepsle (1972) find that democracy is not viable in an atmosphere of strong ethnic identification. Powell (1982) finds that ethnic divisions intensify the tendency toward political violence, which in turn hinders democratic development.

Finally, we consider primordialism as an explanation of ethnic strife. Although seemingly unit-centered, primordialism generally is invoked as an explanation of dyadic conflict. Probably the best-known example in recent years is the work of Kaplan (1993). Here, the primitive ancient hatreds between peoples weighted by the baggage of history flare up at a given historical moment in uncontrolled fury. The communal riots between Hindus and Muslims in 1947–48 in the Indian subcontinent, leading to at least half a million deaths and upwards of 11 million refugees of both groups (Hardgrave 1994), constitute a case in point. But Kaplan's major concern, of course, is the former Yugoslavia with its seemingly endless outpouring of murderous rage during the 1991–94 period. Other recent writings on Bosnia also acknowledge the important role of primordialism, among other perspectives, in the origination and continuation of this conflict (e.g., Danner 1998a, 1998b).

What is primordialism? Probably the classic definition is given by Geertz (1996, 41–42): "By a primordial attachment is meant one that stems from the 'givens'—or, more precisely, as culture is inevitably involved in such matters, the assumed 'givens'—of social existence: immediate contiguity and kin connection mainly, but beyond them the givenness that stems from being born into a particular religious community, speaking a particular language, or even a dialect of a language, and following particular social practices. These congruities of blood, speech, custom, and so on, are seen to have an ineffable, *and at times overpowering, coerciveness in and of themselves*" (emphasis added). It is the last, emphasized phrase in the quotation that is important for our purposes here. An "overpowering coerciveness" is attributed to primordial ties. Later Geertz (1996, 42) speaks of an "unaccountable absolute import attributed to the very tie itself." Others, such as Eller and Coughlan (1996), challenge the concepts of "ineffability" and "absolute import," but such deterministic notions still lie at the heart of primordial theory. Connor (1996) suggests that the primordial tie lies "beyond reason." All that is required is the spark of state disintegration (Yugoslavia) or national independence conjoined with territorial partition (India, Pakistan) to set these primordial sentiments on their predetermined path. Another dyadic variable is differential demographic growth. Here, as in the power transition (see Kugler and Lemke's chapter), one group's population grows more rapidly than another within a particular unit—country or region. One group's former dominance is exchanged now for secondary status. A prime example is Bosnia during the past three decades. In 1961, Muslims constituted only 26 percent of the population of Bosnia-Herzegovina, with the Serbs comprising 43 percent. By 1991, virtually a complete reversal had occurred with the Muslims rising to 44 percent and the Serbs dropping to 31 percent (Huntington 1996, 261).

Even more compelling in its international consequences has been the displacement of the Serbs as the dominant population in the Yugoslav province of Kosovo. The high birthrate of ethnic Albanians (mostly Muslim) led Kosovo to increase its share of the former Yugoslav population from 3.5 percent in 1921 to 7.1 percent in 1981, by far the largest increase for any ethnic group in that country (Vojnić 1995). Under these circumstances, the displaced dominant group may feel especially threatened. If there is a neighboring affine ethnic population, especially a local majority that can come to the aid of the dispossessed dominant, then it may do so, as in the instances of Serbian intervention in Bosnia and Kosovo, and the consequent recent NATO military activity. Even only a threatened future local dominance, as the result of a high birthrate, may fuel ethnic hatreds with potentially murderous consequences. Such apparently was the case in parts of eastern Poland, Lithuania, and the Ukraine during World War II where elements of the local population became participants with the Nazis in the mass murder of the local Jewish population (Fein 1979).

A neighboring affine population can aid in the attack on a minority population, as in the case of Serbia helping the Bosnian Serbs in their destruction of Muslim communities, but only if there is no neighboring large additional affine population to protect the minority. Turkey and other Muslim states have no common border with either Serbia or Bosnia, and in any event the largely Slavic Bosnian Muslims have no ethnic affinity with any other sizable Muslim populations that could come to their aid (Glenny 1996; Woodward 1995).

More generally, the presence of a large and/or powerful affine population within close proximity of a threatened local population can make the difference between the outcome of a protracted conflict or a shorter genocidal one.[17] Consider the case of the Tamils in Sri Lanka. Although only a minority of the population in Sri Lanka, the presence of the vastly greater Tamil population in the Indian state of Tamil Nadu just across the Palk Straits probably did much to prevent serious thoughts of genocidal activity by the majority Sinhalese. A populous state containing an affine population nested within a much more powerful country (India) must have been a source of considerable discouragement to the local Sri Lankan majority. A protracted conflict, not yet settled, has been ongoing. Or consider the relatively benign Israeli policy toward Palestinian insurrection since 1987. Instead of rubber bullets, metallic ones supplemented by the use of tanks could have been employed against the Intifada with genocidal implications. The avoidance of even the appearance of such an intention is probably due at least in part to the presence of large affine Arab populations in neighboring countries that even only passively constitute a protective umbrella for the Palestinians. The settlement of this protracted conflict has been notoriously difficult to achieve.

The recognition of a status reversal can fuel the protracted conflict. A member of a minority Tamil community in Sri Lanka exposed to discriminatory provisions by the majority Sinhalese knows that in Tamil Nadu he or she would be a member of the majority and enjoy, if anything, a favored status.[18] Muslim Arabs under Israeli rule know that in neighboring Muslim majority states, they would enjoy a privileged status especially relative to Jews or Christians. These resentments can yield additional fodder to protract the conflict and not yield to the temptation of political settlement. Protracted conflicts therefore have been found in Sri Lanka and in Israel. Genocide has not been on the political agenda, in contrast to Bosnia and Rwanda with their absence of large powerful neighboring affine populations serving to protect the threatened minority.

The Unit Level

In stark contrast to primordial feelings stands the unit-level explanation of elite-generated ethnic strife. Here, instead of ancient hatreds roiling beneath the surface of ethnic populations, elites create a domestic political climate in which ethnicity is the only politically relevant identity.

Prior to elite intervention, there is considerable mixing of different ethnic populations, including the prevalence of intermarriage. It is only after elite manipulation that ethnic violence begins. Probably the most prominent exponent of this view is Gagnon (1994, 1995). Essentially, in his view it was the challenge of the reformists to the conservative dominance of the Communist Party that precipitated events of the 1980s that were to culminate in the recent violence.

After the economic crisis of the late 1970s precipitated by the global recession, rising oil prices, and mismanagement of the Yugoslav economy, it was Marshall Tito's death in 1980 that was to set these events in motion. Once-dormant talk of economic reform was heard again in elite circles. In the interests of reform, cross-republic alliances among intellectuals were being formed, albeit loosely, and it was in the face of their threat to conservative dominance that the individual leaderships of the Yugoslav republics turned to extreme nationalism and the fomenting of ethnic hatred. For example, Slobodan Milosevic's tenure as head of the Belgrade Communist Party was notable for its nationalist campaign among Party members. The issue of Kosovo and its ethnic Albanian majority, despite its incorporation within the Serbian republic, was especially useful to the nationalist conservatives because of Kosovo's history as a presumed site of historical Serbian resistance to the Turkish invaders. As the breakup of the former Yugoslavia appeared to be inevitable early in the 1990s, ethnic hatreds were directed by the Milosevic cadre against Croats and Bosnian Muslims as well. In all of this nationalistic ferment, issues of radical reform were shunted aside. A similar, although certainly not identical, process took place in Croatia with the use of Ustase symbols from the fascist puppet regime of World War II as a virtual legitimation of the new regime of Franjo Tudjman (Glenny 1996). Here, in place of the hatreds of ancient ethnic enemies, the domestic needs of newly ascendant leaders become the driving force behind interethnic mass destruction.

Yet, before we mistakenly simplify the causes of East European ethnic violence and pigeonhole them as elite driven, one must recall the case of Moldova. Here, as Kaufman (1996, 122) convincingly demonstrates, "The initial ethnic mobilization in Moldova was a classic example of mass insurgency—it was a bottom-up movement, not one manufactured by government leaders."

Further, elite manipulation may not be independent of communal norms, a potentially close kin of primordialism. It is no accident that two of the most manipulative and brutal Serb leaders—both indicted war criminals—Radovan Karadzic and Ratko Mladic, hailed from small mountain communities. Thus, despite an urban education in both cases, Karadzic the psychiatrist and Mladic the general behaved according to the most primitive communal norms of exclusion and potential violence (Anderson 1999, 30). This essentially urban-rural divide and the imperatives of local communities[19] in the Balkans help explain why the cosmopolitan centers of Sarajevo and Belgrade with high rates of intermarriage could coexist with the brutalities of ethnic cleansing and worse.

Finally, we examine the last group-level variable, namely that of culture. Although clearly susceptible to external influences, nevertheless the principal variables affecting culture appear to be generated internal to the unit in question. (Consider the contrast in societal and political responses to Islamism between Egypt and Algeria, on the one hand, and Tunisia and Morocco, on the other.) Anthropologists such as Renfrew (1972), while acknowledging that some cultural elements can diffuse, nevertheless opt for the sui generis origins of the basic elements of a society.

Generally, the formation and maintenance of cultural identities is a dynamic process that may, in fact, be endless. As Koshar (1994, 216–17) asserts, "there is no end to the process of appropriating things that demonstrate the identity of the possessor. Perpetual motion is needed to assert the unique and inviolable core of identity. . . . Nationalist discourse, or any cognate collective discourse, is constantly insecure." It is this insecurity that can fuel the dynamism, which in turn can spill over into political violence.

Consider now a basic cultural-religious identity, namely Islam. Huntington's (1993, 35) remark that "Islam has bloody borders" reflects the conflicts that Muslim populations have had with, among others, Hindus in India, Orthodox Serbs in Bosnia, and Jews in Israel. Is the Islamic identity determinate in its consequences or are there other influences on behavior of equal or greater impact? Because of the importance of democracy in generating pacific relations, as we saw in the preceding section, the relationship between democracy and Islam is of great importance. If Islamic societies can emerge as democracies, then it is likely that whatever other elements of Islam are practiced, Muslim groups and larger societies will tend to have peaceful relationships with others.

The cultural compatibility between democracy and Islam has been seriously questioned. Bernard Lewis (1987), for one, asserts that a fusion exists between religion and state in Muslim societies that makes Western-style liberal democracies difficult to institutionalize. More recently, he affirms the unity of Islam as a civilization, for as he puts it, "It is a political identity and allegiance, transcending all others" (Lewis 1993, 4–5). While Islamic fundamentalists generally espouse authoritarian solutions to the problems of Muslim societies (e.g., the chapters in Sidahmed and Ehteshami 1996), even sympathetic Western observers such as Esposito and Voll (1996, 30) question the willingness of Muslims to accept Western democratic models, opting instead for "authentically Islamic democratic systems."

A test of compatibility between democracy and Islam was carried out (Midlarsky 1998c). Three versions of democracy were used as dependent variables. A measure of Islam—percentage of the population that is Muslim—as well as other theoretically suggested variables were used as independent variables. The three dependent variables are Gastil's (1988) political rights index, Bollen's (1993) index of liberal democracy, and the Polity III index (Jaggers and Gurr, 1995). Independent variables include cultural variables such as the measure of Islam, British colonial heritage, and European location. Environmental variables previously examined for their impact on democracy (Midlarsky 1995), such as the number of sea borders (a measure of the minimization of the threat of war) and precipitation (in its absence associated with autocracy because of the necessity for bureaucratized irrigation works), were included.[20] Land inequality was included, again because of its theoretical and empirical association with democracy found in the previously cited works.[21] Using the Athenian experience as a prototype, the Solonic reforms effectively established land inequality as the basis for a primitive democracy that allowed some with more land and a greater agricultural yield to break through and overcome the hereditary entitlement of others to govern in traditional tribal settings. Remaining variables, such as economic development (GDP/CAP) with a long history of analytic association with democracy (e.g., Lipset [1959] and Dahl [1971]), or age of the polity, were essentially used as controls.

The findings suggest the conditional nature of cultural influence. Whereas the two measures of democracy that reflect the cultural influence of liberalism—Bollen's liberal democracy index and Polity III—demonstrated significant negative associations with Islam even after all the theoretically suggested and control variables were introduced, this was not true of the political rights index. Based principally on the presence or absence of the right to vote, the political rights index was uniformly nonsignificant in its negative association with Islam after the additional variables were included. This outcome suggests that although Western-style liberal democracy may be incompatible with Islam, this is not true of voting rights. More rudimentary forms of democracy could be successfully introduced in Islamic countries, with liberal forms possibly gradually developing at a later time. Indeed, the analysis revealed that democracies may evolve in a sequence beginning first with voting rights, later institutional development, followed by the introduction of liberal reforms. However, as we have seen, the democratization process itself could present some very rough patches for newly democratizing Islamic countries, especially those with multiple ethnicities within their borders.

Environmental variables such as sea borders and precipitation, or economic variables like GDP/CAP and land inequality, turn out to have much stronger positive partial correlations with the political rights index than does the variable, Islam, in a negative direction. This general finding suggests that we should be very careful before specifying culture as a cause of identity conflict. If it is not determinative in regard to an important conflict-related variable such as democracy, then it likely also is not a direct cause of domestic or international violence. On the other hand, if there are cultural elements that could lend themselves directly to political violence, say xenophobia, or there exists an absence of direct violence inhibitors such as liberalism (or liberal democracy), then elements of the culture may be manipulated to serve violent ends. Perhaps this is a principal lesson of the collapse of the former Yugoslavia and its consequences.

Conclusion

Our analysis has traversed the three levels of analysis in the explanation of identity conflict with implications for international violence. At the present time, none of the three levels appears to be superior in explanatory power. Indeed, combining explanations at two or more levels may be the most productive way to proceed. For example, as we have just seen, understanding the sources of a unit-level variable like democracy may be critical for the operation of a violence inhibitor such as liberal democracy that can operate dyadically in the democratic peace. At the same time, the balance of power, when viewed either within a dyadic or, alternatively, a systemic context such as the successor states to the former

Yugoslavia, may be related to the onset of systemic war at the regional level. A flexible analytic approach to understanding the relationship between identity and international conflicts is required, as in most other research enterprises.

Indeed, just such an approach[22] was adopted recently by a policy-oriented summary of approaches to understanding and anticipating identity conflicts (Tellis, Szayna, and Winnefeld 1997, 12–13). Given a situation of "closure" (to mobility) and deprivation—essentially the economic and/or political subordination of one or more identity groups to another—then five factors are enumerated as bases for the transformation of potential into likely ethnic strife: (1) an incipient or actual change in the balance of power among ethnic groups, (2) the occurrence of a "tipping" event as a conspicuous public event that can galvanize ethnic sentiments, (3) leadership or "identity entrepreneurs" who can act to mobilize ethnic populations, (4) access to resources and the development of organizations to channel these resources into the conflict arenas, and (5) the strong possibility of foreign assistance that can support the mobilization efforts of one or more committed ethnies. All of these are structural systemic (subordination, balance of power among three or more groups generally requiring some structural arrangement, foreign assistance), dyadic (subordination, balance of power between two groups, foreign assistance), or group level (identity entrepreneurs, group resources and organization).[23] Even the tipping event can be dyadic or systemic in origin, as was seen earlier in the probable influence of the Bosnian genocidal activities on the Hutu extremists. Together, those individual approaches make for a comprehensive explanation. Future research may indicate which of these contributes more powerfully to the variance in identity conflict and in which contexts.

Finally, consider the relative absence of recent identity conflicts in a region, East-Central Europe, where two potential causes of such conflict—democratization and increased state security (or at least reduction of foreign domination)—have been manifest. It is clear that the presence of NATO and the EU as promoters of democratization coupled with guarantees of minority rights has been extraordinarily influential in keeping such conflicts to a minimum both within and between states (Vachudová 1996). The impact of large, successful international organizations in close proximity to the loci of potential identity conflicts perhaps suggests a model for the future minimization of those conflicts.[24]

Notes

1. One of the earliest warnings (late 1970s) of the importance of ethnicity in world politics, especially in connection with the impending dissolution of the Soviet Union, is recounted in Moynihan (1993, 35). Overarching treatments of ethnic groups in international polities are found in Gurr and Harff (1994) and in Brown (1996). An interesting conjoining of the concepts of identity and the international system is found in Wendt (1994). Giddens (1991, 1, 5) explores this connection in the following way:

   > One of the distinctive features of modernity is an increasing interconnection between the two extremes of extensionality and intentionality: globalizing influences on the one hand and personal dispositions on the other. . . . The more tradition loses its hold, and the more daily life is reconstituted in terms of the dialectical interplay of the local and the global, the more individuals are forced to negotiate lifestyle choices among a diversity of options. . . . Reflexively organized life-planning . . . becomes a central feature of the structuring of self identity.

2. Identity certainly is not invariant over time. It can be transformed, negotiated, and changed in various ways. For the mutability of identity, see, among others, Clifford (1988), Hobsbawm and Ranger (1983), Handler (1994), Buckley and Kenney (1995), Olick and Levy (1997), and Ross (1997).
3. For the initial statements of the security dilemma applied to international politics, see Herz (1951) and Jervis (1978). For a distinction between perceptual and structural security dilemmas, see Snyder (1985).
4. Although this is a convincing game-theoretic model of credibility (or noncredibility) of commitments, there are general limitations on such use of game theory or other rational choice perspectives. For some of these limitations, see Midlarsky (1996).
5. On November 29, 1941, Dr. Fritz Todt, Minister for Armaments and War Production of the Nazi government, after returning to Berlin from the Russian front, reported to Hitler: "Given the arms and industrial supremacy of the Anglo-Saxon powers, we can no longer militarily win this war" (quoted in Gilbert 1989, 265).

   On December 30, Colonel General Franz Halder, army chief of staff, recorded in his diary, "total losses on the eastern front (not counting sick) 743,112, ie [*sic*] 23.12 per cent of the average total strength of 3.2 million. . . . On the Eastern Front [*sic*] the Army is short of 340,000 men, ie 50 per cent of the fighting strength of the infantry. Companies have a fighting strength of 50–60 men. At home there are only 33,000 men available. Only at most 50 per cent of load-carrying vehicles are runners" (quoted in Warlimont 1964, 207).
6. As early as January 9, 1941, Hitler said to his military leaders that if Germany should have to face the combined forces of Great Britain, the United

States, and the USSR, then she would find herself "in a very difficult situation" (Burrin 1994, 83).

7. Both Burrin (1994) and Friedländer (1994) reach this conclusion based on substantial evidence of Hitler's awareness as early as the late summer or early autumn of 1941 that there would be considerable German bloodletting even in the event of victory, but even more so in the case of a more probable defeat.
8. Put somewhat differently, "it is significant . . . that rioting blacks in urban ghettos demand not a separate state but a share of the pie promised by their status as Americans" (Ferguson and Mansbach 1996, 38). The effect of the cold war on the civil rights of American minorities is complex. In one sense, it supported them through the competition with the Soviet Union for world opinion; the United States could not be seen as oblivious to the rights of people of color. Nevertheless, the only serious *overt* governmental activity in support of those rights was initiated only after the most serious confrontations of the cold war already had taken place. Earlier court actions in favor of minorities, especially African-Americans, of course originated through legal actions initiated by private organizations such as the NAACP. For additional treatments of these issues, see Rosenberg (1991) and Skrentny (1998).
9. For a discussion of the role of inequality in both state dissolution and the onset of political violence, see *The Evolution of Inequality* (Midlarsky 1999). Also see the various chapters in Midlarsky (1997b).
10. For analyses of these related approaches to political instability, see, for example, Gurr (1970) and Midlarsky (1988b, 1999).
11. For treatments of the Bosnian conflict and its origins, see, among others, Glenny (1996), Woodward (1995), Silber and Little (1996), Judah (1997), Rieff (1995), and Sells (1996).
12. This systematic finding was first reported in Midlarsky (1984) but finds parallels in earlier research such as that of Bernadotte Schmitt (1958, 6–7), who stated that in regard to the origins of World War I, "the primary cause of the war was a conflict between political frontiers and the distribution of peoples, the denial of . . . the right of [national] self-determination. . . . More than any other circumstances, this conflict between existing governments and their unhappy minorities was responsible for the catastrophe of 1914" (quoted in Moynihan 1993, 10).
13. In particular, two events, among others, indicate the hardening of genocidal resolve among the *akazu*. First, on September 21, 1992, Colonel Déogratias Nsabimana, chief of staff, sent a secret memorandum to his commanders identifying "the enemy" as "the Tutsi inside or outside the country, extremist and nostalgic for power, who have NEVER [*sic*] recognized and will NEVER [*sic*] recognize the realities of the 1959 social revolution and who wish to reconquer power by all means necessary, including arms." Further, the memorandum went on to state that "You will distribute this document widely, insisting especially on the sections relating to the definition of the

enemy, identification of the enemy, as well as the groups within which the enemy is recruited. You will inform me of the impact made by the contents of this document on the men under your orders" (Des Forges 1999, 62).

The second event is a speech delivered on November 22, 1992, by Léon Mugesera at a meeting of the Mouvement Révolutionnaire National pour le Développement (MRND), the party of President Juvénal Habyarimana. In a wide-ranging speech he attacked the Tutsi as essentially foreigners and traitors to Rwanda. Referring to the distant Hamitic origins of many Tutsi, he stated that "I am telling you that your home is in Ethiopia, that we are going to send you back there quickly, by the Nyabarongo [River]" (Des Forges 1999, 85). In the context of his speech, transportation along this river must have meant the mass slaughter of Tutsi and dumping their bodies in the river, a usual practice in earlier massacres of the Tutsi. He also called them "vermin" that must be liquidated. Excerpts of the speech were broadcast on the radio and one newspaper reported it in its entirety. Coming one week after a speech by President Habyarimana in which he disavowed the Arusha Accords and promised to employ the MRND militia, its significance cannot be doubted.

14. This statement was made in connection with the influence of ongoing events in Somalia on those occurring in Haiti. A small gang of Haitian toughs threatened to create "another Somalia" for the United States if American troops landed in Port-au-Prince. The transport ship *Harlan County* carrying American troops then left Haitian waters. The subtitle of the *New York Times* article reads "As Peacekeeping Falters in Somalia, Foes of the U.S. Effort in Haiti Are Emboldened" (Apple 1993, A1).

15. Widney Brown, a women's rights advocate with Human Rights Watch has stated: "In Yugoslavia rape was a part of ethnic cleansing, because the message that you got was if you stayed, the men would be murdered and the women would be raped. That was followed very quickly by what happened in Rwanda, where we have similar widespread allegations of rape and mutilation. In fact, part of the preliminary campaign that created the atmosphere that allowed the genocide to happen was the demonization of Tutsi women as oversexualized creatures who were seductresses. It's not surprising that during the conflict they were subjected to rape, and a lot of sexual mutilation. Mutilation is another way of saying, 'We don't perceive of this person as a human being'" (Crossette 1998, 6).

16. Mishra (1998, 55) asserts that "the response [to the nuclear tests] in India makes it clear that it was more a local than an international audience that the BJP had in mind. The nuclear tests have been extremely popular, particularly among the urban middle class, the BJP's prime constituency; initial opinion polls showed an approval rating of 91 percent."

17. This idea was first presented in a keynote address to a conference on intrastate conflict (Midlarsky 1998a).

18. This "geographic" status reversal is supplemented by a temporal one wherein prior to Ceylonese independence, Tamils were favored by the British colonial civil service over the Sinhalese. This preference of course was reversed after independence and the institution of discriminatory legislation favoring the Sinhalese population and their language.
19. Perhaps for this reason it is more appropriate to use the term "communal strife" in place of ethnic or identity conflict when examining the more violent forms (Midlarsky 1992d).
20. The impact of the minimization of the threat of war on democracy was first developed in Midlarsky (1992b, 1995). Here the causal arrow underlying the democratic peace is reversed. Instead of democracy yielding peace, historically the evidence suggests that it was the minimization of the threat of war that facilitated the development of early democracy in island nations such as Iceland or Britain, or in peninsular settings like Athenian Attica. At the same time, wherever its failings, the democratic peace has been identified along with the power transition as one of the mature theories of contemporary international political analysis (Midlarsky 2000), implying a considerable degree of empirical validity.
21. See especially Midlarsky (1988a, 1992c).
22. Brown (1996) also includes a particularly valuable summary.
23. Note that culture as a variable is not specifically mentioned in their summary.
24. For the role played by international organizations in recent ethnic strife, see Esman and Telhami (1995), and Lindley (1996).

Ancient Warfare

Origins and Systems

CLAUDIO CIOFFI-REVILLA

Warfare is an ancient and virtually universal social phenomenon, the origins of which are found in antiquity, thousands of years ago, when warfare became a distinct pattern of social behavior in several regions of the world. When and where did ancient warfare first originate as an identifiable form of social behavior? How did it first emerge? What are the main properties of early warfare? How did different areas of the world first experience warfare? What role did political development play in the rise of warfare? How does ancient warfare compare with modern warfare? Some tentative answers to these and related questions are addressed in this chapter, with the caveat that scholarly advances in the disciplines that study ancient warfare—archaeology, political science, international relations, sociology, epigraphy, ethnology, military history—will eventually improve upon our current understanding of this complex puzzle.

This chapter provides a brief survey of present-day scholarly investigations on ancient warfare, covering various disciplines, different approaches, as well as Old World and New World origins of ancient warfare. Given the broad scope and the necessity to decide among several perspectives, I shall emphasize the origins of warfare as given by the extant empirical evidence, as opposed to its later development. After a brief introduction, I discuss the following dimensions of ancient warfare: conceptual dimensions (what do we mean by the term "ancient warfare"?), chronological dimensions (what are the key time periods for the origins of war in various polity systems?), and empirical dimensions (where and how did warfare originate in each system?). While an in-depth treatment of each of these aspects of ancient warfare is not possible in one chapter (each could occupy a monograph), I hope at least to provide some foundations for readers who encounter this topic for the first time in a systematic way, as well as for those who may wish to investigate more specialized or interdisciplinary aspects.

The chapter is divided into five sections, each dedicated to the preceding dimensions of ancient warfare. The last section provides a summary with some tentative conclusions, including a preliminary model of the punctuated interaction between warfare and political development, based on the empirical evidence presented earlier (see the section entitled "Empirical Dimensions").

Introduction: Why Study Ancient Warfare?

The modern "progressive" mentality underestimates the value of studying the remote past, often trivializing antiquity as remote, obscure, archaic, unsophisticated, and—most of all—completely irrelevant for understanding society today. With few exceptions (archaeology), the social sciences have all but abandoned the study of antiquity. Political science as a discipline, including the field of international relations, largely ignores the past as if governance and political systems had emerged only a few decades or at most a few centuries ago. This shallow and biased mentality—not merely the so-called Western bias but, what is worse, a chronological "longitudinal" bias almost exclusively focused on the present—has done an immense disservice to the advancement of scientific knowledge about human society in virtually every area of civilized life, including warfare and politics. The cost has been high: today we know far less than we could about fundamental puzzles and properties of political life because political science has ignored the past.

Warfare—purposive homicide among organized groups using specialized weapons and coordinated behavior—is an ancient phenomenon that began thousands of years ago and continues today in many regions of the international system. The study of ancient warfare should begin by addressing the question of how and why warfare began and developed in the history of human society. Many scholarly approaches are required in this important investigation, including the contribution of most social sciences (anthropology, international relations, linguistics, political science, sociology, economics) and humanities (military history, art history, philosophy). Political science can contribute many new insights to the understanding of ancient warfare, and, conversely, as a discipline it stands to gain a great deal from the study of ancient warfare.

The study of ancient warfare should rank high on the agenda of contemporary social science research—including that of political science—for multiple important reasons: pursuing pure research, conducting comparative analysis, developing international theories, understanding political behavior, practicing interdisciplinary methods, understanding modernity. A better understanding of ancient warfare and how, why, and where it originated can help in designing better, more robust policies of conflict resolution.[1]

Conceptual Dimensions: What Is Ancient Warfare?

In the previous section, consistent with earlier work, I defined warfare as "purposive homicide among organized groups (armies) using specialized weapons and behavior coordinated by a leader" (Cioffi-Revilla 1991, 1996). Empirically this includes conflict events such as raiding, burning, theft, and other chiefdom-level forms, as well as the higher-level forms of states and empires. I shall now explore this concept further, clarifying its meaning for purposes of empirical observation, measurement, and subsequent theoretical development.

Meaning of Ancient Warfare

The term *ancient warfare* contains at least two conceptual dimensions that should be highlighted in the interest of clarity. I call these temporal and behavioral dimensions. From a *temporal* dimension, the term *ancient warfare* denotes conflicts that took place "a long time ago," in "premodern" times, among people that are presumably "no longer around." Interestingly, how far back in history one goes is itself an intriguing puzzle and an important issue discussed in this chapter (e.g., homicide antedates warfare). In this first sense, ancient warfare refers essentially to warfare that took place in times that today are seen as quite "remote," "distant," or even "removed" from today's reality. By this criterion, ancient warfare refers to the warfare that originated in the Old World thousands of years ago and in the New World thousands of years before the European conquest. Ancient warfare in this sense was practiced by Sumerians, Chinese, Xiong-nu, and their descendants in the Old World, and by Moché, Olmec, Zapotec, and their descendants in the New World, as I explain later.

From a behavioral perspective, the term *ancient warfare* denotes conflicts that are seen as somehow being socially "primitive," technologically "backward," or organizationally "archaic," regardless of the temporal perspective. In this sense, some ancient warfare is also practiced by people who are still around today. Warfare against aboriginal groups in colonial times was also of this type (Ferguson and Whitehead 1992). In this second sense, ancient warfare is putatively unsophisticated as judged by the complexity of modern warfare (Ember and Ember 1996). By this second criterion, it refers to conflict in extant ethnographic societies, such as the Zulus, Ashantes, Yanomanö, Jívaros, and others.

In this chapter I shall consider only the first perspective, so by the term ancient warfare I mean the organized lethal group conflict that took place in antiquity—a temporal connotation. An important aspect of my analysis of ancient warfare is to consider both the ancient Old World and the ancient New World, unlike most extant work on ancient warfare that considers only the former (Dupuy and Dupuy 1993; Ferrill 1997; Kagan 1995), ignoring the increasing volume of evidence on indigenous Amerindian warfare in the preconquest New World.

Actors of Ancient Warfare

Ancient warfare is also characterized by the nature of the belligerents who practiced it, particularly by those belligerents who practiced it for the first time in a given region. These are polities—the first sedentary political communities ("villages," as they are called in archaeology) that also exhibit the emergence of public life—that have leadership and have learned how to solve some collective action problems, including conquest and defense. As such, there is a significant qualitative difference between the first belligerents that practiced warfare and other contemporary societies where warfare did not originate but later developed. Politically, the key difference lies in the original solution to numerous collective action problems that arise—and must somehow be solved—in connection with warfare—in preparations as well as in actual conduct. Some of these include leadership formation and maintenance, resource extraction and harnessing, strategic and tactical planning, and implementation of defensive and offensive requirements. Empirically identifying and understanding how the first human communities attained these quantum thresholds of political development—and the broader political systems that they gave rise to—are central objectives in the study of ancient warfare.

In relation to the level of political development of belligerents, most of the ancient warfare that I identify in this study refers to warfare among what are called "chiefdoms" in political anthropology (Earle 1991, 1997; Stein and Rothman 1994), because states developed but did not invent warfare. Some indicators of ancient warfare are more suitable for detecting warfare among belligerents that are below or above this threshold. A succinct characterization of warfare among chiefdoms is as follows:

> Chiefdoms may occasionally clash over resources like good land. Unlike states, however, most chiefdoms do not have the manpower or political structure to conquer and hold onto others' lands. They may therefore content themselves with burning a rival village, destroying its temple or Men's House, killing its chief, then returning home to torture or sacrifice a few prisoners. (Marcus and Flannery 1996, 124)

Thus, ancient warfare at the political level of chiefdoms (prestate societies) already contains many of the later characteristics (political motives, incipient warrior classes, specialized weapons, basic military engineering) that warfare will develop and enhance with increased political complexity. The agents of earlier ancient warfare (prechiefdom societies, outside the scope of this study) manifested only an archaic form of warfare that was not distinguishable from basic homicidal and hunting skills (coordinated killing of other humans; Taçon and Chippindale 1994).

Time Line of Ancient Warfare

Conceptually, it is also important to distinguish between two qualitatively distinct stages in the process of ancient warfare: origins and development. By *origins* I mean the process whereby warfare emerged as a separate and distinct form of behavior, different from other forms of behavior during ancient times (viz., hunting and homicide).

To focus on origins—as opposed to its later development—raises empirical and theoretical issues. Empirically, we need to describe (measure) when, where, and how ancient warfare first originated as a distinct form of social behavior. Theoretically, a focus on origins involves explaining why warfare first emerged, based on some specifiable causal mechanism with testable hypotheses. For example, as we shall see, the focus on origins examines the emergence of war among political communities in ancient Palestine, Mesopotamia, China, Peru, and Mexico—areas where the first regional political systems formed thousands of years ago.

By the *development* of ancient warfare—the second stage in the time line of war—I mean the subsequent process of conflict that continued to take place among political communities (belligerents) after they had already formed (organized) for the first time. In general, the development of ancient warfare involved states (no longer chiefdoms), and this higher level of political complexity set and enhanced most features of warfare that are still observable today (conscription, standing armies, logistics, engineering, fortifications, militarized rivalries, arms races). Thus, Babylonian, Greek, Roman, Inca, Aztec, or Medieval warfare all belong to this subsequent stage, because none of these belligerents invented warfare ex novo; rather, each developed or enhanced warfare from patterns first set by their predecessors.

I deal primarily with the former of these topics—ancient origins and empirical aspects—in the various regions of the world where warfare first emerged.

Indicators of Ancient Warfare

Given the preceding discussion on concepts, actors, and stages of ancient warfare, the next question is: how do we measure its origin(s)? How can we establish when, where, and who first originated warfare?

Since warfare—ancient or present—is a form of collective action involving multiple behavioral manifestations (planning, implementation, consequences, etc.), it follows that its measurement must be based on multiple empirical indicators (Leege and Francis 1974), or what archaeologists call "multiple lines of evidence" (Renfrew and Bahn 1996). In the case of ancient warfare, this redundant measurement strategy is indispensable, because unfortunately all indicators do not have the same survivability in the extant record. Castles and cannons—powerful indicators of ancient warfare—have a much higher survival probability than painted murals, fragile scrolls, or wooden spears that may tell of equally significant warfare. Moreover, other features of warfare—for example, perishable weapons, troop movements, battle actions, and others—are archaeologically invisible (Vencl 1984).[2]

Given a multiple-indicator strategy, the following six indicators are used as evidence to detect or measure the emergence of warfare for a given region: forensic, locational, structural, artifactual, iconographic, and epigraphic.

Forensic. Forensic evidence of warfare is contained in human skeletal remains, including but not exclusively violent traumatic wounds (Molleson 1991; Roper 1969). Embedded projectile points, parry fractures, perforated or fractured skulls, decapitated or dismembered skeletons, and other similarly deadly lesions imparted by force constitute forensic evidence that may indicate the presence of warfare, particularly when such remains are present in large numbers in a small area (high density of skeletal trauma) having some military significance. Sometimes the original trauma by violence may not cause immediate death, but instead cause a severe wound that eventually causes death (Bachechi, Fabbri, and Malegni 1997). Although in some cases forensic evidence may provide a stronger and more reliable indicator of warfare than mere locational evidence, caution must be exercised in the evaluation of forensic evidence because alternative explanations for its presence—for example, religious sacrificial practices unrelated to warfare, or cannibalism without actual warfare—may also account for the extant forensic evidence. Where forensic evidence potentially indicative of warfare is found, it is therefore essential to also have an understanding of the other social practices of that political community. Forensic remains may indicate warfare, conditional upon the co-occurrence of other such practices. Unfortunately, the most unambiguous osteological evidence of warfare emerges well after warfare originated (Molleson 1991).

Evidence of trauma in skeletal remains is not the sole type of evidence of warfare found with forensic (osteological) material. Skeletal remains of warriors buried with artifactual evidence of warfare—viz., weapons, armor, or other—also proves the existence of warfare. An early Old World example is the royal cemetery of Ur (Tell al Muqayyar), Lower Mesopotamia, Iraq, which contained weapons buried with their warrior owners (British Museum, London; University Museum of the University of Pennsylvania, Philadelphia; and Iraq Museum, Baghdad; illustrations in Pritchard 1958; Woolley 1963).

Locational. Locational evidence of warfare refers to the defensible location of a given site in a surrounding physical environment. The positioning of a site on (1) a high ridge, (2) a sloping terrain, (3) an island, or (4) a peninsula may constitute locational evidence of warfare. This is often among the oldest evidence, because it may not require much technology (a community's decision to locate on a defensible site still requires collective action problem solving). As J. Topic and T. Topic (1987) point out, however, locational evidence is a weak or often ambiguous indicator of warfare, because an arguably "defensible" location may have been chosen on grounds other than threat of conflict—for example, for its religious significance, trade or communication links, access to natural resources, or other nonmilitary advantage. Locational evidence at an individual isolated site is generally not a sufficient indicator of warfare, but a regional widespread pattern of several defensible locations is a stronger basis for inferring warfare (Haas 1989). Often locational evidence (e.g., a hilltop) combines with structural evidence (enclosing walls, even without parapet) to indicate warfare (e.g., Quebec, Canada; Habuba Kabira, Iraq; Monte Albán, Mexico).

Structural. Forensic and locational information sometimes constitutes weak or soft evidence of warfare. Structural evidence, in the form of purposively planned and executed military engineering works, constitutes hard evidence of warfare (sufficient conditions for the existence of at least a threat of warfare) and is also a common indicator of significant political complexity. As opposed to a decision on location alone, structural works involve a significant level of planning and execution, involving a nontrivial proportion of able labor in the community. The polity responsible for military works will often have reached state-level complexity (with internally differentiated institutions, specialized elites, and other stable features that go beyond the mere centralization of power [chiefdom]; Spencer 1990; Wright 1977). Chiefdoms can achieve some of these engineering goals (e.g., moats, palisades), but not all of them (more extensive or territorial wall systems).

In turn, structural evidence of warfare can assume diverse forms, such as fortifications, moats, towers, bastions, ramparts, baffled gates, and guard houses. In terms of measuring the origins of warfare, these often constitute substitutable forms (Cioffi-Revilla and Starr 1995; Most and Starr 1989). A palisade is an early form of fortification, erected around the perimeter of a local polity (chiefdom; e.g., Palisade I, Cahokia, Illinois; Emerson and Lewis 1990). Palisades often include baffled gates for controlled entry (e.g., Banpo [Pan-p'o], China; Chang 1986, 116), and sometimes they represent just the first stage of what will eventually become a more formidable wall that can include bastions as well (Palisades II–IV, Cahokia, Illinois). A palisade is erected primarily for purposes of exclusion and protection against limited-range projectile weapons.

A *wall*—built of stones, bricks, stamped-earth, or plastered stockade—is a more substantial fortification than a palisade and sometimes also marks the transition from chiefdom to statehood, because of the greater specialization and coordination required. In Palestine, the earliest defensive walls were built of stone, at Jericho, during the so-called Pre-Pottery Neolithic A (PPNA) period, sometime in the eighth millennium B.C., or soon after 8000 B.C. (*terminus post quem;* Kenyon 1979, 26). In China, on the other hand, the earliest massive walls indicative of warfare were built with a layered, stamped-earth construction technology during the Longshan [Lung-shan] period, East Henan phase, in the third millennium B.C. (Chang 1986, 262–67; Chi 1956; Underhill 1989, 1994). J. Topic and T. Topic (1987) note that a wall with *parapet*—a vertical structure to protect defenders—is an unambiguous indictor of warfare, but without a parapet a wall may simply have other functions, such as social separation, privacy, or traffic control. However, some walled sites that contain other evidence of warfare (e.g., weapons deposited on the immediate outside proximity) lack parapets, so a parapet can be interpreted as a sufficient but not necessary condition for warfare.

A *tower* can be another form of fortification. Most commonly, towers are integrated with walls, as in a castle, sometimes located in frontier regions (Peru), or as part of a more extensive wall system (the famous Great Wall of China built during the Zhou and Qin dynasties; Hadrian's Wall between Northumberland and Scotland, far more modern). In somewhat later times—during the later development of ancient warfare (Yadin 1963)—wooden towers and other protected structures became mobile siege engines and were used to encase and carry other large-scale specialized weapons (e.g., battering rams, catapults) and assault troops for attacking a fortified site (e.g., siege of Lachish, Nineveh [now in British Museum]; Ferrill 1997, 75–76; Pritchard 1958, 372–73, fig. 101; Yadin 1963). There is no evidence for the existence of siege engines in the New World—although most components (beams, ropes, walls) would have been highly perishable.

Besides walls and towers, other military structures occur individually or in combination, depending on local needs and capabilities (opportunity-willingness conditions; Cioffi-Revilla and Starr 1995). A *moat* is a deep and wide excavated trench, usually filled with water, most frequently located outside a fortified perimeter. Like walls and towers, moats were built both in the Old World (e.g., Tell es-Sawwan, Iraq; Banpo, China) and in the New World (e.g., Becán, Mexico; Webster 1976). Moats—more specifically, the layers of sedimentary deposits found in a moat—also often contain additional evidence of ancient warfare (e.g., artifactual or forensic). A *rampart* is a broad embankment or artificial ridge raised as fortification. It is sometimes surrounded by a moat, with bridges across to control access (Becán, Mexico). A *baffled gate* is a protected or concealed entry, the purpose of which is to control access through a flow point (LeBlanc 1999, 255, fig. 6.21; and Fletcher 1995, 135–36). Finally, a *guard house* is often part of a baffled gate, or it may occur separately. Originally, most of these structures occurred individually, consistent with a chiefdom level of political development, as with most of the evidence I examine in the next section. However, as warfare developed in later times, as state-level political complexity emerged, many of these structures occurred jointly—as in a walled city with baffled and guarded gates, moated ramparts, and fortified with protruding towers and parapets designed to provide overlapping fields of fire against attackers.[3]

Artifactual. The primary form of artifactual evidence for ancient warfare consists of weapons. Two types can be distinguished: *specialized* (used for combat only) and *generic* (also used for hunting). The mace is arguably the oldest specialized weapon (O'Connell 1991; Rollefson, Kafafi, and Simmons 1990), having been developed for the primary purpose of causing a lethal cranial injury. Maces are also found in the earliest iconography of ancient warfare throughout the ancient Near East (e.g., Narmer Palette and Hierakonpolis murals, Egypt; Stela of Vultures, Iraq; stelae of Ugarit, Syria; Pritchard 1958; Yadin 1963, 40–41). In addition, other specialized weapons include axes and swords, as well as protective bodily gear, such as helmets, shields, and body armor. Siege engines and other machines built by the first military engineers (battering rams, assault towers, mobile catapults) are large-scale artifacts (Hogg 1993, 63–96). The chariot played a notorious role in ancient warfare, although much more so during the subsequent development of war than during its origins.[4]

Among generic weapons, those first developed for hunting include projectiles, bows, spears, bifaces, atlatls, slings, and knives.[5] Although each of these weapons was used for hunting animals during the Paleolithic and Mesolithic and, therefore, appeared in the archaeological record prior to the emergence of ancient warfare, these weapons were also commonly used in warfare. Some generic weapons disappeared soon after the appearance of specialized weapons (e.g., the sword replaced cruder forms of knives and bifaces), whereas others continued to be used for thousands of years after the appearance of specialized weapons (e.g., spear, bow and arrow).

Another common—but I would argue less useful—distinction is between short-range and long-range weapons (Yadin 1963), which misses the sociopolitical dimension that is captured by the specialized/generic distinction. Short-range weapons can be specialized (e.g., a mace) or generic (a knife), as can long-range weapons. In state-level societies the production of weapons for use in warfare was specialized and kept separate from the production of other artifacts, a pattern consistent with the more specialized and differentiated nature of institutions and elites.

Iconographic. Iconographic or pictorial representations of ancient warfare are another source of evidence. The most frequent occurrences of battle scenes are in murals and in stone, including warriors with weapons engaged in combat (e.g., stone bas-relief of fortified cities under siege in the Near East); or domination scenes of conquest in a postwar context (e.g., Maya stelae depicting a ruler standing on top of defeated enemies; or Egyptian palettes representing the pharaoh smiting the vanquished).[6] Some of the earliest rock art in European Paleolithic caves, particularly in Spain, is also of this form, although the scenes depicted sometimes include hunting as well as warfare (Ferrill 1997, 16–22). At present the earliest depictions of "battle scenes, skirmishes and hand-to-hand combat" are those found in the Arnhem Land region, Northern Territory, Australia, dated at ca. 8000 B.C. Iconographic evidence sometimes appears simultaneously with epigraphic evidence in the same record (e.g., Stela of Vultures, Girsu [Telloh], Iraq [Demange et al. 1994, 54]; Monument 3, San José Mogote, Oaxaca, Mexico [Marcus 1992a, 39]). The iconography of warfare is abundant for both the Old World and the New World. It also developed considerable artistic quality (from sketchy engraved art to rich colorful murals) as part-time artisans became full-time artisans in the transition from simple (chiefdom) to more complex (state) political systems. Many artistic masterpieces of antiquity consist of iconographic representations of warfare. Besides their obvious aesthetic value, they also provide valuable information for scientific research.

Epigraphic. Evidence of warfare comes also from written records. Until recently, the presence of written records marked the beginning of truly "historical" warfare. Today, however, most scholars of antiquity acknowledge that the true history of warfare begins much earlier than the appearance of written records. Moreover, since written records may provide unreliable accounts—for example, in the Old World, the boastful claims of Mesopotamian kings; or, in the New World, the equally doubtful exaggerations of Maya rulers—in some instances "prehistoric" data based on, say, fortifications, are more reliable and valid indicators of warfare. Thus, "more recent" or "more historical" does not necessarily mean "more reliable" or "more valid." Nonetheless, in general, epigraphic records are the most detailed and useful sources for constructing precise data sets of past wars (Cioffi-Revilla and Lai 1995, 1999)—particularly when validated by other alternative indicators or lines of evidence, such as forensic, structural, or iconographic.

Other. Marcus (1994, vi), Roper (1975), and other scholars often identify additional kinds of evidence that I omit here—for example, boundary or other territorial markers, changes in settlement patterns (i.e., all valley-floor sites move to hilltop locations), burned sites, abrupt cultural changes. Here I consider only the preceding six indicators because I view them as less ambiguous, not because other indicators are irrelevant. Unfortunately, a systematic study of multiple indicators has not been conducted, although one is clearly overdue.

Chronological Dimensions: What Else Was Happening When Ancient Warfare Began?

Antiquity—containing the time periods during which warfare originated and underwent its first developments—is marked by chronological periods that are region-specific. I shall now describe the time periods that are relevant for the origins and early development of warfare in each region.

The study of ancient warfare requires an understanding of the various regional chronological frameworks that are used by specialized area scholars for each region of the ancient world. From a political science perspective, *absolute* (calenderical, ratio-level scale) chronologies are preferred over *relative* (sequential, ordinal-level scale) chronologies, because of the greater measurement precision of the former. In addition, it is important to distinguish *protobellic* and *protopolitical* periods or phases in each chronology or time line, referring to the earliest time in which organized warfare and complex political life originated in a given region of time and space. In general, I find that *the protobellic period precedes the protopolitical period,* but often not by much. In turn, as I discuss later in greater detail (see the last section), each of these formative periods consists of a *prehistoric* and a *historic* phase, corresponding to the earliest visibility of warfare from material archaeological evidence (e.g., forensic, structural, artifactual) and from written records (epigraphic data), respectively. For example, in west Asia the protobellic origins of warfare are dated to ca. 7500 B.C. (PPNA level at the ancient site of Jericho, Palestine; Kenyon 1960, 1965, 1979; Roper 1975), whereas the historic period reveals the protobellic origins of warfare in west Asia that date to ca. 2800 B.C. (Sumerian texts of the Early Dynastic I period). Clearly, the "historical" standard is behaviorally deficient and conceptually invalid, so the "prehistoric" standard must be used instead.

To facilitate the combined diachronic and synchronic comparative analyses, figure 1 illustrates the chronological framework for each of the regions of space-time that I am discussing in this chapter. Each chronology begins with the period when warfare began in that region; earlier chronological periods exist but are omitted here. In most cases, the first chronological periods contain the material archaeological or "prehistoric" evidence for the origin of warfare (locational, forensic, or structural indicators of warfare), whereas subsequent periods contain further development of warfare, including epigraphic or "historical" evidence when available (i.e., in all regions except the Andes, where no writing system existed). In each case the material evidence precedes the written evidence, often by thousands of years.

Old World Chronologies

The earliest war-related chronology for the Old World starts in west Asia, where two distinct protobellic regions gave rise to warfare: the Le-vant and Mesopotamia. The second-oldest Old World protobellic region is in east Asia.

Levantine chronology. The west Asia chronology for ancient warfare begins with the PPNA period in Palestine and the Levant (8500–7500 B.C.; Mazar 1992, 30; see also Rothman 2000, 5, table 1; Falconer

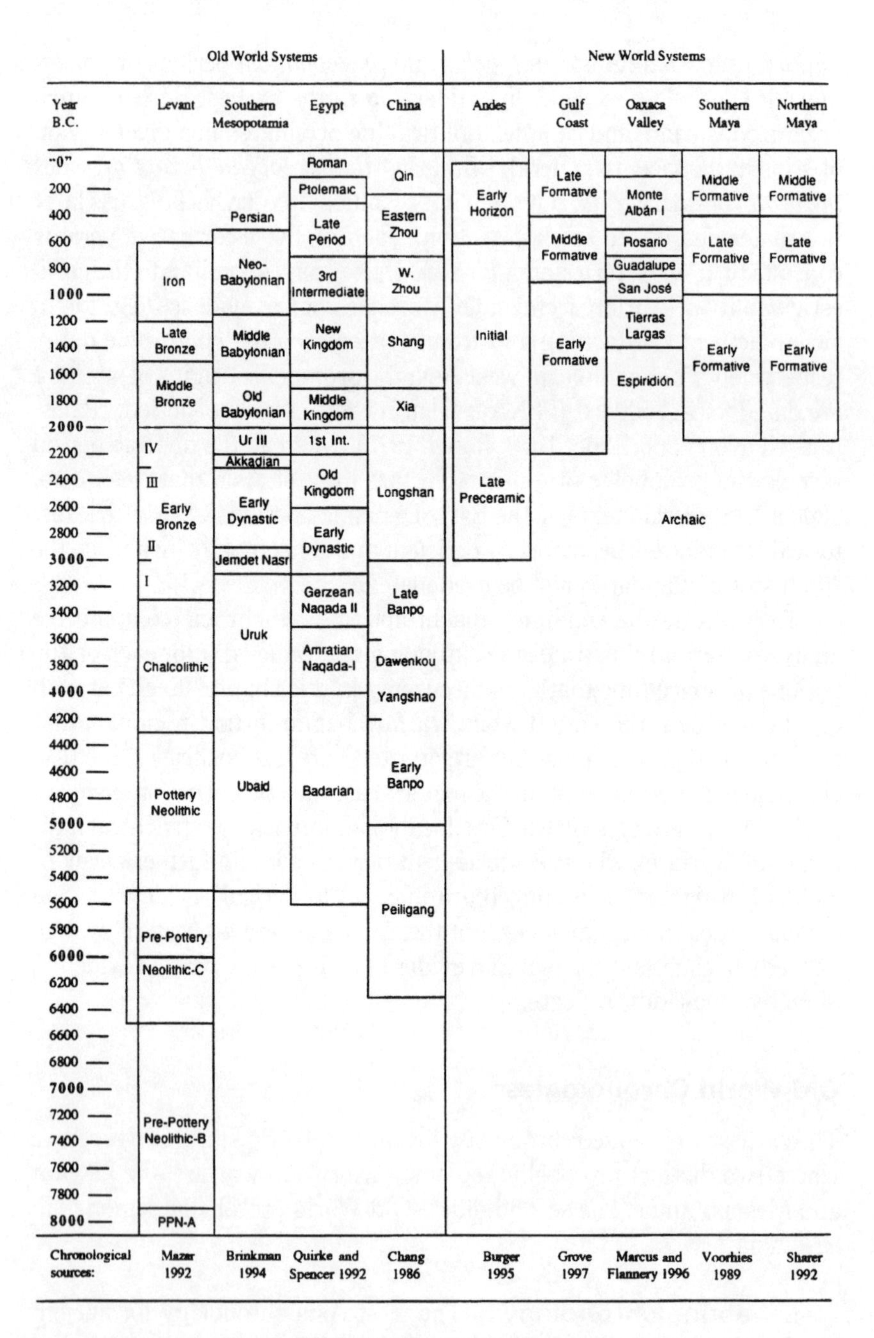

FIGURE 1. Periodization in Old World and New World chronologies (Prepared by the author. Copyright © 1998 Claudio Cioffi-Revilla.)

and Savage 1995), a vast region in the area presently occupied by southeast Turkey, Syria, Lebanon, Israel, and Jordan. Caubet (1994, 166) defines this area somewhat more narrowly, as "la façade méditerranée de l'Asie qui comprend les pays actuels de la Syrie, du Liban et d'Israël, plus d'île de Chypre." I include Jordan, southeastern Turkey, and western Syria as well. This is also the earliest protopolitical region of the world, marked by the rise of a complex political community at Jericho, Palestine, a society complex enough to have solved significant collective action problems posed by the construction of the most ancient fortified city in the world (Kenyon 1960, 1965, 1979). States formed in this region by the Chalcolithic period (4300–3300 B.C.), accompanied by abundant evidence of warfare (Frangipane 1996; Stein and Rothman 1994). Throughout much of its later history, this region was within the sphere of influence—or was actually occupied by—the neighboring hegemonic empires of Akkad, Egypt, Assyria, Babylon, and Hatti.

Mesopotamian chronology. The southern Mesopotamian chronology of warfare begins toward the end of the Neolithic period, during the 'Ubaid period (5500–4000 B.C.), which is the time when the first agricultural settlements and chiefdom-level polities were established in the lower and middle Tigris-Euphrates Valley (Brinkman 1994; Ehrich 1992; Falconer and Savage 1995; Jasim 1985; Stein and Rothman 1994). This is followed by the Uruk period, which experienced the formation of the first states, and is divided into three phases: early (4000–3750 B.C.), middle (3750–3500 B.C.), and late (3500–3100 B.C.). Following the brief Jemdet Nasr period (3100–2900 B.C.), the Early Dynastic period of Sumerian city-states lasted almost six centuries (2900–2335 B.C.), during which time warfare was already fully developed. The periods that followed (i.e., Akkadian, Third Dynasty of Ur, and Babylonian periods) saw the continued escalation of warfare and political complexity, up to the level of empire (multi-ethnolinguistic territorial polity).

Chinese chronology. In east Asia the protobellic and protopolitical phase have very long duration (Chang 1986), covering the final phases of the Peiligang [P'ei-li-kang] period (6500–5000 B.C.), the Banpo period (5000–3000 B.C.), until the terminal phases of the Longshan period (3000–2000 B.C.). All three periods are predynastic. Within the Banpo period, the Yangshao [Yang-shao] and Dawenkou [Ta-wen-k'ou] (4200–3600 B.C.) are important for the earliest rise of political complexity.

During the Yangshao phase the first fortifications were erected, followed by extensive and more-sophisticated structures, weapons, and forensic evidence during the Longshan period (Liu 1996). By 2000 B.C., at the start of the Three Dynasties period, warfare was already common and well developed throughout the Central Plains in northern China. The first dynastic period in China is the Xia [Hsia] (ca. 2000–1200 B.C.), whose terminal cultural phase overlaps with the start of the Shang culture (ca. 1700–1000 B.C.), which culturally also overlaps with the subsequent Western Zhou [Chou] (ca. 1300–700 B.C.). Culturally speaking, therefore, the Three Dynasties were coeval for a brief time span (ca. 1300–1200 B.C.), a period of cultural (albeit not political) "tripolarity." From a political dynastic perspective, however, the following chronology is standard: Xia (ca. 2100–1700 B.C.), Shang (ca. 1700–1100 B.C.), and Zhou (ca. 1100–256 B.C.). The Shang was arguably the first state to form in China (Chang 1986; Keightley 1983), although considerable political complexity had already been achieved by earlier polities (Liu 1996). By the Qin [Ch'in] dynasty (222 B.C.), when China is unified under a strong state (arguably the first true hegemon in east Asia), warfare and politics are already fully developed, remaining basically un-changed for the next 2,000 years. Nivison's (1998) new chronology will have substantial impact for measuring warfare and political development (Cioffi-Revilla and Lai 1995).

New World Chronologies

In the New World the earliest war-related chronology starts in South America, followed much later by a complex network of protobellic and protopolitical areas in Mesoamerica. In turn, Mesoamerican chronology is localized for the Gulf Coast and the Oaxaca Valley. All Mesoamerican areas begin their chronology with an Archaic period (hunter-gatherer, nonsedentary communities) that lasts until ca. 1800 B.C.

Andean chronology. Following Topic (1989), Andean chronology for warfare begins by 3500 B.C. *(terminus ante quem)* or, following Burger (1995) and earlier Pozorski and Pozorski (1987), with the Late Preceramic period (ca. 3000–2000 B.C.). Warfare was present by the Initial period (ca. 2000–600 B.C.) and the Early Horizon period (ca. 600–1 B.C.). The earliest forms of politically complex societies (chiefdoms) emerged during the Late Preceramic period in the Peruvian coastal area (e.g., Aspero, Peru; Feldman 1987). The first Andean states formed some time between the Initial Period *(terminus post quem)* and the Early Intermediate period *(terminus ante quem)* in several coastal valleys, such as the Casma, the Santa, the Moche, and the Nepeña—areas where warfare and other conditions played a significant causal role in political development (Carneiro 1970; Haas, Pozorski, and Pozorski 1987; Pozorski 1987). Note that these developments in Peru and nearby Andean areas in South America occurred not hundreds, but approximately 2,000 years prior to the rise of the Inca Empire (ca. A.D. 1400–1533), which was conquered by the Spaniards.

Gulf Coast chronology. The Olmec chronology that covers the protobellic and protopolitical stages consists of three periods, each lasting several centuries (Grove 1997): the Early Formative (2200–900 B.C.), the Middle Formative (900–400 B.C.), and the Late Formative (400 B.C.–A.D. 100). In turn, these three periods of general Mesoamerican chronology contain more specific archaeological phases at the sites of San Lorenzo and La Venta. Chiefly warfare may have originated during the San Lorenzo phase late in the Early Formative period (1150–900 B.C.), followed by warfare in the La Venta phases. Given the relatively minor extent of excavations in the Olmec area, however, the political complexity attained by Olmec society during its protobellic stage is still unresolved—some (Coe 1968, 1981; Coe and Diehl 1980) claim it reached the state level; others claim it was just a chiefdom, not as sophisticated as the Cahokia “maximal chiefdom” (Marcus 1989 and personal communications).

Oaxaca Valley chronology. Following Marcus and Flannery (1996, 25), five periods of Zapotec chronology cover the entire protobellic and proto-political stage of development in the Oaxaca Valley: Tierras Largas (1400–1150 B.C.), San José (1150–850 B.C.), Guadalupe (850–700 B.C.), Rosario (700–500 B.C.), and Monte Albán I (500–ca. 150 or 100 B.C.). During this time, Zapotec society formed the first chiefdoms (San José Mogote, Huitzo, and others in the Etla subvalley of the Valley of Oaxaca, beginning during the San José phase) and later the first state (the powerful Monte Albán regional state, which formed during the Monte Albán Ic period, 300 to ca. 150 or 100 B.C.). As I discuss later in greater detail, warfare originated during the early chiefly periods (San José, Guadalupe, and Rosario phases) and became fully developed during the Monte Albán periods. The Spaniards conquered Oaxaca in the sixteenth century A.D., more than 2,000 years after the rise of warfare in this exceptionally important region of ancient Mesoamerica.

Empirical Dimensions: What Do We Know About the Origins of Warfare?

Our present knowledge about the precise origins and early development of warfare in the various regions of the ancient world is still incomplete. However, a tentative pattern is beginning to emerge—a pattern that is different and far more precise than that which was imagined even just a few years ago. Based on the concepts and chronologies already discussed, I shall now provide a tentative synthesis of the main empirical findings for measuring as precisely as possible the protobellic (and in some cases the protopolitical) stages. As a whole, these data begin to provide some tentative answers to the basic questions of when, where, and how warfare first originated in each area of the world.

From an empirical perspective there are several aspects involved in the identification (measurement) of the rise of warfare in each region. The first I call *evidential* and concerns the set of indicators (forensic, structural, iconographic, etc.) that are observable in the extant record. The second aspect is *chronological* and concerns the temporal identification associated with the evidence being used to determine the presence of warfare. Even in the best of circumstances both sets of data are "fuzzy," even in a formal sense (Cioffi-Revilla 1981; Viertl 1996), which is why redundant indicators are necessary. However, increases in redundancy produce diminishing marginal gains in information (Cioffi-Revilla 1998a), so a few indicators are generally sufficient; not all are necessary.

Table 1 presents a summary of some of the earliest evidence available according to each empirical indicator discussed earlier (see the section entitled "Conceptual Dimensions") for each protobellic region. To keep my discussion as succinct as possible, and in the interest of space, I shall omit all sources or details already referenced in table 1. The reader should attempt to follow my discussion of each origin with the additional information contained in the table.

Ancient Warfare in the Old World

Levantine origin. The earliest plausible evidence of warfare in the Levant—arguably the oldest in the world—comes from Natufian human remains, at ca. 10,000–7500 B.C., from Nahal Oren, Israel, quite possibly cannibalized. Cannibalism often accompanied warfare in all six regions of the Old World and the New World examined in this study (west Asia, east Asia, South America, Mesoamerica). Soon after, during

TABLE 1.

Early Evidence of Ancient Warfare: Protobellic Systems and Multiple Indicators (lines of evidence)

	SOURCE OF EVIDENCE (INDICATORS)					
Protobellic Area	**Forensic[a]**	**Locational**	**Structural**	**Artifactual**	**Iconographic**	**Epigraphic**
			I. Old World: Afro-Eurasia, Eastern Hemisphere			
1. West Asia: Levant Palestine-Syria, Israel, Jordan, Lebanon, Syria, south central and south-eastern Turkey.[b]	10,000–7,500 B.C.: Natufian remains possibly cannibalized, Nahal Oren, Mt. Carmel, Israel[c] 5600–5000 B.C.: Burial no. (v) at Mersin (Yümük Tepe) level–XIX, S. Anatolia, Turkey, probably caused by Halafian attack.	7000–6000 B.C.: Ugarit (Ras Shamra), Syria, basal level–Vc, and Byblos (Gebal), Lebanon, are established on coastal high defensive ground.	ca. 7500 B.C.: PPN-A Tell es-Sultan fortification at Jericho, Palestine, with ditch, wall and tower. Wall rebuilt twice during PPN-B 7000–6000 B.C.: Fortification of Beidah, S. Palestine, near Petra, Jordan 6000–5000 B.C.: Level–Ia, Haçilar, Anatolia, fortified and numerous Halafian fortifications.	ca. 6000 B.C. Mace heads, 'Ain Ghazal, Jordan. 5600–5000 B.C.: Cache of clay sling pellets at Mersin fort (Yümük Tepe), S. Anatolia, Turkey. 4300–3300 B.C.: Mace heads, Nahal Mishmar, Israel.	ca. 2000 B.C.: Stela of Baal, Ugarit (Ras Shamra), Syria, with god Baal brandishing a mace.	ca. 2000 B.C.: Mention of swords, smiting, maces, threats and battles, in the epic of Baal; tablets translated from Ugaritic cuneiform.

(continued)

Table 1.

Continued

Protobellic Area	Source of Evidence (indicators)					
	Forensic[a]	Locational	Structural	Artifactual	Iconographic	Epigraphic
			I. Old World: Afro-Eurasia, Eastern Hemisphere			
2. West Asia: Mesopotamia Sumer Iraq and western Iran.[d]	No evidence available prior to the Early Dynastic period, <2900 B.C.	ca. 6000 B.C.: Tell es-Sawwan level–I, Hassuna phase, built on a cliff over Tigris R., Iraq. ca. 4000 B.C.: Uruk-dominated peripheral cities located on high ground, Iraq.	ca. 5600 B.C.: Tell es-Sawwan, Iraq, level–III fortified with moat, wall, baffled entrances. ca. 4000 B.C.: Uruk-period cities fortified, Iraq.	ca. 5600 B.C.: Slingballs deposited in Tell es-Sawwan's moat.[e] ca. 5500–4000 B.C.: Ubaid-period mace heads, Abu [c]Ilba, Iraq.[f] ca. 3500–2900 B.C.: Mace heads, Girsu (Tello), Iraq, and Susa, Iran, Late Uruk period.	ca. 3500 B.C.: Cylinder seals, Susa, Iran, and Uruk, Iraq. ca. 2450 B.C.: Stela of Vultures, Early Dynastic, Lagash, Iraq.	2685 B.C.: Sumerian-Elamite warfare from Sumerian King List, Iraq. ca. 2450 B.C.: Stela of Vultures, Early Dynastic, Lagash, Iraq.
3. East Asia: North China Central Plains region: Huang He [Huang Ho] Yellow River basin, Shaanxi, Shanxi, Hebei, Henan, Beijing,	ca. 3000 B.C.: Longshan period scalped skulls in Jianguo [Chien-kou], Hopei; Haojiatai [Hao-chia-t'ai], Yancheng; and other Longshan period sites	ca. 5000 B.C.: Banpo [Pan-p'o] founded on terrace 9 m. above Chan [Ch'an] River bed.[h] 4100–2600 B.C., Dawenkou [Ta-wen-	5000–3000 B.C., Yangshao: Banpo ditch 5–6 m. deep and wide; Jiangzhai [Chiang-chai] erects palisade with surrounding defensive moat and baffled entries.	3000–2000 B.C.: Bow and arrow and spears used at Yaoguanzhunag [Yao-kuan-chuang] and other Longshan culture sites.	1200–1180 B.C.: *Che* (chariot) graphs in Shang oracle-bones, late Wu Ding's reign.	1200–1045 B.C.: Shang epoch oracle bone inscriptions, turtle shell. ca. 500 B.C.: First military treatises written.

Shandong, northeastern and eastern provinces.[g]	in the Central Plains region.	k'ou] period: Pingliantai founded on elevated flat mound.	3300–2800 B.C., late Yangshao: Xishan erects wall. 3000–2000 B.C.: Chengziyai [Ch'eng-tzu-yai], Shandong, erects massive 6 m. high and 9 m. wide walls, and other Longshan fortifications.	ca. 2000 B.C.: Blades and axes from Shixia [Shih-hsia], followed by Erlitou weapons, Xia period. 1700–1200 B.C.: Bronze weapons, Shang period. 1240± 145 B.C.: Chariots from Anyang.		
II New World: Americas, Western Hemisphere						
4. Andes: Pacific Coast of Peru and central Andes region.[i]	ca. 3000 B.C.: Headless skeletons and mutilated skulls, Asia, Peru.	ca. 3500 B.C.: Ostra site, Salinas de Santa, Peru, established on an "old uplifted bay" protected by a ridge.	ca. 3500 B.C.: System of two parallel linear arrays of slingstone piles are deployed at Ostra site, Salinas de Santa, Peru. ca. 500 B.C.: Early Horizon fortifications in the Casma, Nepeña, and Santa valleys, Peru.	ca. 3500 B.C.: Slingstone piles are located along crest of ridge at Ostra site, Salinas de Santa, Peru. 3000–2000 B.C.: Weapons at Asia, Peru, Late Preceramic.	ca. 1500 B.C.: Warriors with shields in early atrium, Pyramid A, Garagay, Peru; armed warriors and captives carvings, Cerro Sechín, Peru. Pre-500 B.C.: Warriors, Alto Magdalena, Columbia.	Not applicable.

(continued)

TABLE 1.

Continued

Protobellic Area	Source of Evidence (indicators)					
	Forensic[a]	Locational	Structural	Artifactual	Iconographic	Epigraphic
II. New World: Americas, Western Hemisphere						
5. Mesoamerica: Gulf Coast Olmec Tabasco and southern Veracruz.[j]	ca. 1200 B.C.: Cannibalized human remains at San Lorenzo.	ca. 1400 B.C.: San Lorenzo Tenochtitlán founded on the highest area in 10 km radius, surrounded by two branches of Coatzacoalcos R.; artificial mound.[k]	ca. 900 B.C.: "Destruction" of San Lorenzo, Mexico.	No specialized weapons or artifactual evidence found.	ca. 1500–900 B.C.: Early Formative "knuckle-duster" in Mounument 10, San Lorenzo. ca. 900–500 B.C.: Bas reliefs on stone stelae and altars at La Venta.	None available.
6. Mesoamerica: Oaxaca Valley Zapotec (Mexican state of Oaxaca).[l]	ca. 600–500 B.C.: Burial 55, sacrificial adult victim, under Str. 26, Rosario phase, San José Mogote, and possibly in Str. 2, Huitzo, both in Oaxaca Valley.	1900–1400 B.C.: San José Mogote (SJM), Oaxaca, on "a piedmont spur" overlooking the Atoyac R., Espiridión phase. 1150–850 B.C.: Huitzo founded during San José phase, rival of SJM, derives fr. Zapotec *Güijazoo* "military watchtower."	700–500 B.C.: Rosario phase villages, Etla sub-valley, Oaxaca, become fortified. Extensive burnt remains in this period.	700–500 B.C.: Eleven obsidian projectile points, Tomb 10, San José Mogote, Oaxaca.	ca. 700–500 B.C.: Monument 3, San José Mogote, Oaxaca, during the Rosario phase.	ca. 500–400 B.C.: Monument 3, San José Mogote, Oaxaca, during the Rosario phase.

700–500 B.C.:
Rosario phase
villages, Etla Valley,
Oaxaca, on defensible
locations (hills).

Source: Prepared by the author based on the sources cited for each region. Additional sources, not included here due to space limitations but recorded in the LORANOW Project documentary database, can be obtained from the author.

[a]However, cf. Richards (1975, 343–42) argues against the validity of forensic evidence for warfare.

[b]Bar-Adon 1962; Caubet 1994; Garstang 1953; Ginsberg 1958; Huot, Thalman, and Valbelle 1990; Kenyon 1979; Levy 1995; Mazar 1992; Mellaart 1960; Pritchard 1958; Rollefson, Kafafi, and Simmons 1990; Roper 1975.

[c]Rather surprisingly, Mazar (1992) is silent about the forensic evidence at Nahal Oren, Mount Carmel, Israel.

[d]Adams and Nissen 1972; Algaze 1993; Brandes 1979; el-Wailly and Abu es-Soof 1965; Emberling 1998, personal communication; Huot, Thalman, and Valbelle 1990; Jacobsen 1939; Liverani 1988; Molleson 1997, personal communication; Nissen 1990; Yasin 1970; Yoffee 1997, personal communication.

[e]The sling was in use by Neolithic times (Mellaart 1960), perhaps for hunting purposes, but at Tell es-Sawwan the sling-balls deposited in the moat outside the city's defensive wall establish a direct link to warfare.

[f]Similar mace heads to these from Abu [c]Ilba, Iraq, described by Adams and Nissen (1972, 211) are displayed at the Louvre Museum, Paris (Cioffi-Revilla 1994, 15, 159; Demange et al. 1994, 18, Louvre cat. no. AO-14099).

[g]An 1994; Chang 1986; Chi 1956; Keightley 1978, 1996; Liu 1996; Loehr 1956; Sawyer 1993; Shaughnessy 1988; Underhill 1989, 1994; Yates 1988.

[h]This and other locational events on elevated grounds may have been motivated by ensuring against flooding, not necessarily against threats of aggression.

[i]Burger 1995; Drennan 1991; Haas, Pozorski, and Pozorski 1987; Pozorski 1987; Topic 1989; Topic and Topic 1987, 1997; Wilson 1988.

[j]Andrews 1987; Coe 1968, 1981; Coe and Diehl 1980; Cyphers 1996, 1997; Gillespie 1997 and 1998, personal communications, Grove 1997; Ortiz and Cyphers in press; Sharer and Grove 1989; Stark and Arnold 1997.

[k]Later, at ca. 900 B.C., La Venta was built on an island surrounded by swamps. Both situations are admittedly ambivalent, given the necessity to locate on well-drained soil or nonflooded area (Gillespie 1998, personal communication; Marcus 1998, personal communication).

[l]Flannery and Marcus 1983; Marcus 1983, 1992b; Marcus and Flannery 1996; Postgate, Wang, and Wilkinson 1995.

the PPNA period, at ca. 7500 B.C., the first fortifications were erected at Jericho, Palestine, including the oldest known massive walls and a tower. Other key centers follow soon after Jericho, including Beidah, Jordan, and Haçilar, Turkey. Simultaneously, Ugarit and Byblos on the Mediterranean coast are settled on high defensible locations, and mace heads begin to appear in Jordan, followed by stocks of sling pellets at the Mersin fort, southern Turkey. By the sixth millennium B.C. numerous fortifications already exist in the eastern Levant and northern Mesopotamia, by which time these regions form one large "Crescent system." Warfare is fully developed in the Levant by at least 4300 B.C., based on the garrison at Mersin fort and other centers. By ca. 2000 B.C., the Ugaritic text of the epic of Baal is completely fluent in the language of warfare.

Mesopotamian origin. In the area of Mesopotamia warfare appears first in the northern part of the Tigris-Euphrates Valley, with mace heads already present at Jarmo by 7000–6000 B.C., which is somewhat earlier than the earliest maces in the nearby Levant region at 'Ain Ghazal, Jordan. Locational evidence at ca. 6000 B.C. also shows Tell es-Sawwan being built on a cliff over the Tigris River, and soon after, at ca. 5600 B.C., being fortified with a system of moat, wall, and baffled entrances. In the southern part of Mesopotamia, the first 'Ubaid-period agricultural settlements, starting at ca. 5500 B.C., are being defensively located on islands—arguably the only defensible locations in the southern alluvial plain—and mace heads are also already common throughout the area (e.g., at Abu ᶜ Ilba, Iraq). During the Uruk period, from ca. 4000 B.C. the most important cities in Mes-opotamia are fortified, including many in the periphery, at which time cylinder seals also begin to display a clear array of warfare scenes, including prisoners of war being smitten by their captors. Warfare is already fully developed well before the rise of the first Sumerian city-state system that followed soon after ca. 3000 B.C. By the time writing is invented in Mesopotamia, it is ready to record the continuation of stately warfare (Sumerian) and, not much later, the first imperial warfare (Akkadian).

Chinese origin. In the Chinese protobellic area of the Yellow River, in the northern part of the country known as the Central Plains, warfare is first evidenced soon after ca. 5000 B.C. by locational (higher elevations) and by structural (moats, palisades, baffled gates) indicators at Banpo (possibly) and Jiangzhai (certainly). Clearly, these early chiefdoms must have been seeking security from some neighboring or outside aggressors, although their identity remains unknown (not unlike the first fortified chiefdom sites in west Asia and the New World). This first stage in the rise of warfare in China occurred during or soon after the first successful settlements were established (Yangshao village chiefdoms), similar to the 'Ubaid settlements in southern Mesopotamia. Later (Longshan chiefdoms in the Central Plains region), starting at ca. 3000 B.C., plenty of structural (massive walls) and artifactual (first weapons) evidence exists with increasing frequency, followed by further increases in the period that saw the rise of the first states during the Bronze Age and the Three Dynasties. In China, as elsewhere in the world, warfare is fully developed before the time the first states form and begin to interact.

Ancient Warfare in the New World

Andean origin. The first evidence of warfare in the Andean region occurs along the Peruvian coast during the Late Preceramic Period, through mutilated human remains and weapons at Asia (ca. 3000 B.C.) and an assemblage of locational, structural, and artifactual evidence at the Ostra site (aka Salinas de Santa, ca. 3500 B.C., *terminus post quem*). The early nature of these first indications of Andean warfare at Asia and Ostra during this early stage of political development (prechiefdom?) is reminiscent of the similarly isolated cases of Jericho or Çatal Hüyük in the Levantine system. Unequivocal indicators of warfare begin occurring consistently about 2,000 years later. Although written records never appeared in this region, by ca. 2000–1500 B.C. the iconography of armed warriors and captives at Cerro Sechín (Casma Valley) and elsewhere leaves no doubt that warfare has emerged from its protobellic stage and is entering a more developed stage. Warfare is fully developed with the appearance of numerous hilltop fortifications during the Early Horizon Period, a pattern that continues and reaches maturity by the time of Chavín de Huantar's supremacy, ca. 500–250 B.C., by which time complex chiefdoms—perhaps states—had formed. Thus, the Inca imperial warfare that followed much later was preceded by chiefly and state warfare thousands of years earlier.

Gulf origin. At the main Olmec political centers of San Lorenzo (founded on high defensible ground at ca. 1400 B.C.) and La Venta near the coast of the Gulf of Mexico, there is some plausible locational and iconographic evidence of warfare (helmets, clubs, knuckle-dusters, blade axes depicted on stone), as well as generic weapons. However, Olmec iconography is arguably ambiguous as evidence of warfare. For example, "helmets can be simply headdresses. The association of the ballgame with warfare is not a direct one" (Gillespie 1997, 1998, personal communications). The earliest large political center that attained at least the chiefdom level of development, San Lorenzo, contains locational evidence, as well as structural and forensic remains that some interpret as valid indicators of warfare. Figurines and statues of ballplayers may also provide some evidence, because elsewhere in Mesoamerica the ball game was associated with warfare, albeit at a later time. What was once thought to be the violent and systematic destruction of San Lorenzo, ca. 950 B.C.—which could have been the first concretely dated occurrence of warfare for this area of Mesoamerica—is no longer viewed with such certainty. Warfare at the subsequent Olmec polity of La Venta, on the other hand, is not debated, given the numerous iconographic indicators present after ca. 900 B.C. (depictions of warriors, weapons, armor, captives, and others).

Oaxaca origin. Using locational evidence alone, the protobellic origins in the Oaxaca Valley could date back to the founding of San José Mogote, on high ground ("a piedmont spur"), overlooking the Atoyac River, during the egalitarian (prechiefdom) political stage of the Tierras Largas phase, ca. 1400 B.C. However, high ground may have been chosen to avoid flooding of the nearby river, not necessarily as a defensible location. Soon after, at ca. 1100 B.C., another community was founded in the northern area of the Etla subvalley, called Huitzo, which means "military lookout" in Zapotec. By the Rosario phase, 700–500 B.C., warfare is already clearly shown by the defensible position and fortification of many communities in the Etla subvalley, by weapons buried with chiefs, and by the iconography showing nude prisoners and war captives. For example, more than 300 prisoners were set up in a gallery just before state formation at the regional capital of Monte Albán. This pattern of increasing sociopolitical complexity continues to evolve until warfare reaches an imperial (albeit brief) stage during the period of the Monte Albán state—arguably the first state in Mesoamerica. Again, as in the Inca case, the warfare that the Spaniards encountered in Mesoamerica in the A.D. 1500s was the result of a protobellic process that had begun thousands of years earlier, at a chiefly stage of political development.

Summary and Conclusions

This chapter provided a broad, albeit tentative, analysis of ancient warfare, particularly from a political science perspective that draws on some parallel efforts taking place in allied disciplines. In particular, I focused on conceptual, chronological, and empirical dimensions of ancient warfare, all of them minimally necessary for advancing our scientific understanding of this puzzle. The following are some of the main preliminary conclusions that may be drawn by way of summary. As research continues in this rapidly evolving field, and along each of the research dimensions discussed in this chapter, most of these ideas will undoubtedly require revision.

I began by highlighting the fact that the study of ancient warfare represents a vast field that covers many complex puzzles (when, where, and how did warfare first occur?), a field that is largely untapped by political science and other social sciences that study war (besides archaeology). I also pointed out that modernity—the same intellectual revolution that produced contemporary social science—is largely responsible for trivializing ancient warfare, thereby ignoring this fundamental aspect of social behavior. I argued for the importance of studying ancient warfare through rigorous social scientific procedures, based on a set of important needs, including conducting pure research and comparative analysis, developing better and testable theories, understanding political behavior, developing interdisciplinary methods, and others.

In the section entitled "Conceptual Dimensions," I addressed the basic question: what is ancient warfare? In particular, I focused on two distinct meanings of the term "ancient warfare," one temporal and the other behavioral. My emphasis here has been on ancient warfare in the former sense. I then focused on the actors of ancient warfare, an issue closely related to fundamental and enduring puzzles of political development—the rise and early evolution of political complexity in social groups. Following this identification of actors, I then distinguished between the origins of warfare (the main emphasis in this chapter) and its subsequent development. Given the identification of actors and time periods, I then discussed the various indicators (what archaeologists call "lines of evidence") of the multiple-indicators approach that I apply later: forensic, locational, structural, artifactual, iconographic, and epigraphic. Such an approach is necessary, given the partial and imprecise nature of the individual data.

In the section entitled "Chronological Dimensions," I outlined and briefly compared the separate chronologies for each region of protobellic activity, for the Old World (Levant, Mesopotamia, China), and the New World (Andean, Olmec, Zapotec). These periodizations (figure 1) combine relative and absolute chronologies, based on the findings for each region. These time periods were used later for determining and interpreting the main empirical findings.

Empirically, in the section "Empirical Dimensions," I presented and briefly discussed the extant evidence on the origins of ancient warfare produced in each region of the Old World and New World. Warfare ignited independently in several places in ancient times, both in the Old World (west Asia and east Asia) and New World (South America and Mesoamerica).

Moreover, in each case warfare (1) in its earliest form (organized raiding and group warfare) originated prior to, or at the latest was contemporary with, the earliest political systems (chiefdoms); and (2) was already well-developed by the time that the first states formed. The state did not produce war, but it did enhance it with unprecedented organization and lethality. State systems in each area experienced fully developed warfare. Very probably, as outlined in figure 2, the causal mechanism that accounts for the origin of warfare in antiquity is based on the further specialization, growth, and refinement of a set of background behavioral skills acquired by humans during the Paleolithic period: (a) *homicidal skills* on how to kill other humans; and (b) *hunting skills* on how to coordinate a group for killing animals. Each of these primitive (prebellic and prepolitical) activities produced a set of transmittable skills (cross-culturally and intergenerationally), including homicidal know-how and the know-how necessary for successful group hunting (i.e., authoritative command, coordination of movements, basic tactical formations, minimal supplies, intelligence, stealth and concealment). The negligible level of political organization that existed during the Paleolithic and early Neolithic explains why at most only "protowarfare" was produced by these nonspecialized skills (fig. 2, stage 0). Protowarfare—not yet war-fare as defined earlier—was essentially indistinguishable from humans-hunting-humans, leaving behind only ambiguous forensic and locational information (e.g., projectile points embedded in skeletal remains, cannibalism, plausibly defensible locations, etc.) and no other evidence of warfare (i.e., no defensive structures or specialized weapons; certainly no writing this early).

The chiefdom, the state, and eventually the empire were forms of political organization that acted as catalysts, reinforcing and magnifying the initial background conditions through a complex interactive process—back

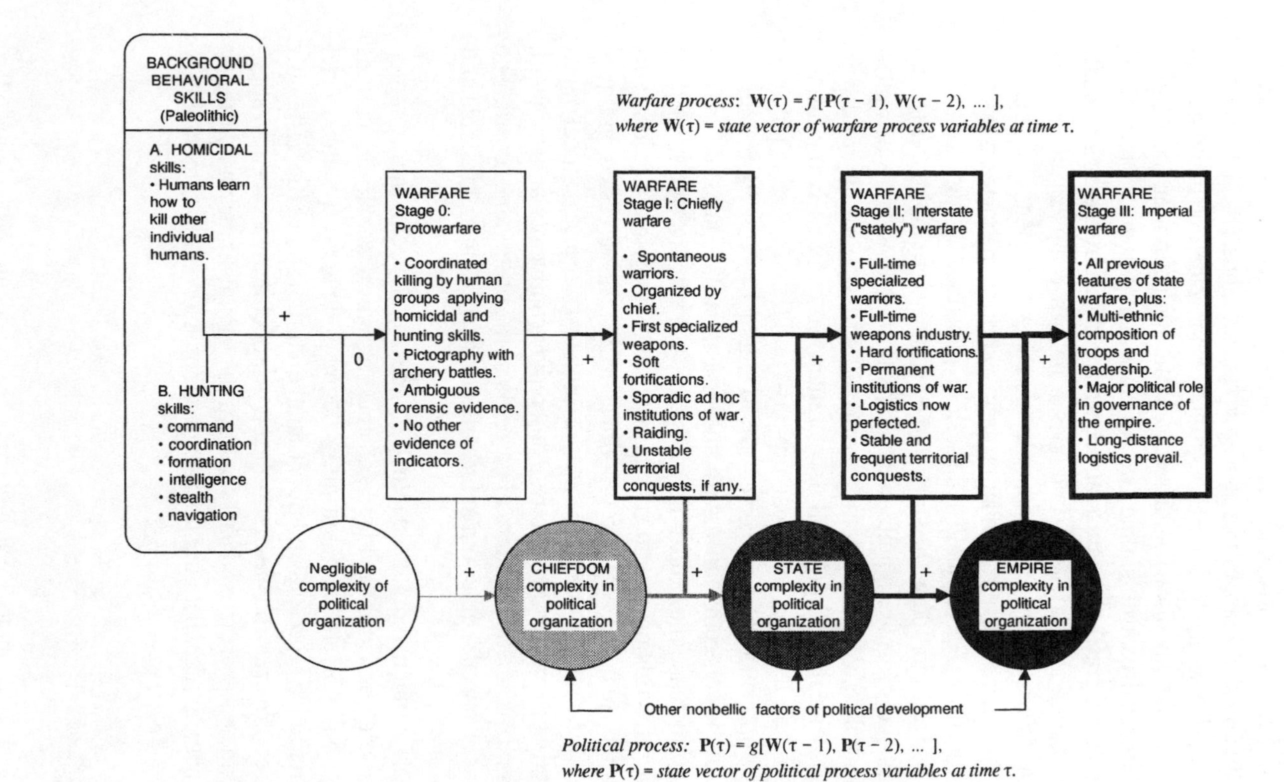

FIGURE 2. Warfare and political development: An interactive punctuated model with quantum complexity (© Copyright 1998. Claudio Cioffi-Revilla. All rights reserved.)

and forth between politics and warfare—that produced punctuated stages (quantum levels) of both, warfare and government. Thus, (1) chiefly warfare (fig. 2, stage I) emerged from the background of homicidal and hunting skills, boosted by chiefly political complexity (centralization of power, social ranks, weak territorial control, simple two- to three- tier settlement hierarchy); (2) interstate or stately warfare (stage II) was produced by the earlier chiefly patterns, boosted by state-level conditions of political complexity (hereditary rulership, internal bureaucratic specialization, writing system, multi-tier settlement hierarchy); and (3) a similar process holds for imperial warfare (stage III), the most complex on this ordinal scale of punctuated phases.

In turn, the chiefdom, the state, and eventually the empire were themselves partially formed, maintained, and reinforced by warfare (as well as by other collective action factors connected with opportunity and willingness). Warfare and political development were mutually reinforcing processes because (1) warfare can produce conditions favorable for political development (e.g., a perceived group emergency condition, centralization of power, compliance with authority); and (2) political development can increase the probability of success in waging war. It was not necessary for this process to spiral everywhere, only in a few locations (protobellic areas and some protopolitical areas). As suggested by figure 2, this model predicts quantum levels of both warfare and political development (not a continuum of states), ordered by complexity and each with its own mix of distinct empirical patterns in the observable record. The ordering of specific quantum stages also makes this model testable and nontautological.

Clearly, much more needs to be understood about this complex process, but the extant evidence on the origins of warfare in various regional polity systems of antiquity begins to suggest a viable model with interactive processes and punctuated quantum stages (fig. 2). Such a model requires rigorous testing in each protobellic area. The investigation of ancient warfare and early political development may hold the key to enduring and challenging puzzles in social science and contemporary world politics.

Notes

I thank Richard L. Burger, Geoff Emberling, Susan Gillespie, David N. Keightley, Joyce Marcus, William McNeill, Manus I. Midlarsky, Theya Molleson, Roger Moorey, David S. Nivison, Donald Ortner, Charlotte Roberts, William R. Thompson, John R. Topic, Barbara Voorhies, and Norman Yoffee for comments or advise in preparing this study. Any errors are my responsibility. Funding for the Long-Range Analysis of War (LORANOW) Project has been provided by the University of Colorado, the Conflict Resolution Consortium of the William and Flora Hewlett Foundation, the Center for International Relations, the Department of Political Science, and the President's Fund for Advanced Information Technologies under a grant from the Apple Computer Foundation. The goal of the LORANOW Project is to investigate the origins and early development of warfare and world politics through the application of interdisciplinary social science methods and information technologies.

1. For a recent and encouraging perspective on the methodological and theoretical advantages of long-term research in political science, not just world politics, see Aldrich (1997).
2. Vencl's (1984) incisive discussion of the systematic biases of archaeological data—biased in favor of surviving material evidence, against immaterial features of warfare—is reminiscent of Achen's (1983) and Aldrich's (1997) discussion of missing data and related problems in political science research.
3. An impressive New World example of a fortified site with towers that offered overlapping fields of fire against attacking infantry was Cahokia, Illinois (Emerson and Lewis 1990; Fowler 1989; Iseminger 1996). Ruling out a long siege or some covert infiltration, such a site could only be successfully taken with large-scale assault engines that offer protection to assault groups, such as towering and mobile battering rams or catapults, none of which was available to the Mississippians. The walls of Cahokia (Str. IV) were probably never penetrated, assuming they were defended from within.
4. Cf. Anthony and Vinogradov (1995), Kierman and Fairbank (1974), Littauer and Crouwel (1979), Moorey (1986), Piggott (1983 and earlier works), and Shaughnessy (1988).
5. The precise antiquity of the bow has not yet been established (Bachechi, Fabbri, and Mallegni 1997, 135–36), but most scholars agree that it was already in use by the Upper Paleolithic (*terminus ante quem;* ca. 30,000–15,000 B.C.) and already widely diffused in the Old World by Mesolithic times. Powerful crossbows were extant in China by the middle of the first millennium B.C.
6. The recently computer-restored murals of the Maya southern Lowland city of Bonampak (Structure 1), Mexico (M. Miller 1986; Miller, Ferorelli, and Stern 1995), provide one of the most magnificent examples of iconographic evidence for the presence of warfare in the ancient New World (ca. A.D. 790).

PART II

Minimally Dyadic Theories of War

From Democratic Peace to Kantian Peace

Democracy and Conflict in the International System

BRUCE M. RUSSETT and HARVEY STARR

Introduction

We begin from the basic empirical observation that democracies very rarely—if at all—make war on each other. Understood as a strong probabilistic observation, rather than an absolute "law," the finding is now generally though not universally accepted. This is the conclusion reached by three recent and extensive review articles (Chan 1997; Ray 1997b, 1998). Book-length studies supporting it include Bueno de Mesquita and Lalman (1992), Russett (1993), Singer and Wildavsky (1993), Ray (1995), Risse-Kappen (1995), Maoz (1996), Weede (1996), Owen (1997), Rummel (1997), and Weart (1998). Different procedures for coding political system types (especially over long time spans as in: the Freedom House annual beginning 1973; Doyle 1986; Jaggers and Gurr 1995; Vanhanen 1984, 1990) produce somewhat different rankings of states by their degree of democracy. This is to be expected, especially where democracy is a continuous rather than dichotomous variable. Nevertheless, the basic finding of a virtual absence of war between democracies emerges with every rating scheme employed.

Also now generally accepted is the corollary that pairs of democracies are much less likely than other pairs of states to fight or threaten each other even at low levels of coercive violence. This extension has survived very sophisticated methodological scrutiny intact (e.g., Beck, Katz, and Tucker 1998), especially for the post–World War II era.[1] By surviving such investigation, the statements about lower-level violence within democratic dyads provide greater confidence to the statements about war between democracies. That is particularly important as wars are relatively rare events in international history and thus present greater difficulty for establishing strong generalizations. Therefore, in this chapter we are concerned with the broad range of conflict between democracies. We address a variety of issues raised in the numerous articles written on the democratic peace. We do not, however, review yet again what is now a fairly stale debate over the existence of the democratic peace, nor do we attempt a complete review of all the work on the basic empirical finding that democracies very rarely fight each other.[2]

Rather, this chapter is a progress report on extensions of the democratic peace proposition, concentrating on the more recent contributions. We embed them in an elaboration of theory in order to extend it as a "progressive" research project (Lakatos 1978) that exhibits integrative cumulation. Deductive logic produces a range of auxiliary puzzles or hypotheses that, in empirical investigation, can lead to findings not anticipated in the original formulation. We begin by discussing monadic effects, based on analyses that were developed only after scholars had begun to investigate theoretical explanations of the dyadic democratic peace. Subsequently, we merge dyadic and monadic analyses as well as synthesize cultural and structural theoretical explanations, in our attention to models of strategic decision making for understanding the democratic peace. These decision-making models are also useful, and different, in their attention to two-level games and an agent-structure framework. We not only bring together various strands of evidence (as do several of the other review articles) but also respecify pieces of this literature in terms either of new independent variables or of similar liberal propositions. Finally, we explicitly put the democratic peace within a broader theoretical perspective, one that includes integration, community, legitimacy, and a special "liberal" relationship between governments and societies.

Two Dimensions of the Democratic Peace: Dyadic and Monadic

The most widely accepted part of the democratic peace project is its assertion about the behavior of pairs of states, or dyads. It is sometimes defended as an absolute statement about wars; for example, Ray (1995,

125) says that none of the many proposed exceptions "is appropriately categorized as an international war between democratic states." And it is worth noting that whereas virtually none of the systematic quantitative analyses so far have extended beyond 1992, there have—to this writing—been no new interstate events clearly characterized as wars between democracies by the customary standard (1,000 or more deaths) despite the continued expansion of the international system and the spread of democracy within that system. Such a war could, of course, yet happen. Most proponents of the democratic peace both expand the range of phenomena and more cautiously express their proposition as a probabilistic statement that democracies rarely fight each other even at subwar levels of violence. At the level of wars, however, and allowing for some ambiguity of perception or measurement error in a very few cases, joint democracy in effect does appear to constitute a sufficient condition for peace between two countries (Braumoeller and Goertz 1997; Chan 1997; Gleditsch 1995; Russett 1996; Starr 1997b, chap. 7).

This does not, of course, mean that joint democracy is a necessary condition for the absence of war. Many pairs of states, particularly small ones physically distant from each other, have neither the opportunity nor the willingness (issues in conflict) to fight each other. Many others that might have the opportunity *or* willingness are dissuaded by well-understood realist influences such as great imbalances of power (the weak know better than to make war, the strong know they can get their way without it) and alliance configurations, by the absence of sufficient expected utility for war (Bueno de Mesquita 1981b), which reflects a combination of state power and alliance portfolios, or even, perhaps, by domestic or international normative constraints not directly related to democracy. Even two democracies may appear to be restrained from fighting each other primarily by power considerations when some popular movements are clamoring for a fight.

The empirical result, nevertheless, is there are few if any clear violations of the "sufficiency" expectation for wars. Additionally, we can now make a strong probability statement that escalation of low-level militarized disputes between democracies to higher levels of violence is rare. In part to increase the number of cases that could be studied, and in part to look at militarized conflict that existed below the level of war but had the potential to escalate to war, many scholars have investigated militarized interstate disputes. They usually find that joint democracy diminishes many elements of militarized disputes, in their initiation as well as their escalation (Bremer 1993; Maoz 1993; Rousseau et al. 1996; Russett 1993).[3] In multistate crises, escalation to violence is less common when one or more parties on both sides is democratic (Hewitt and Wilkenfeld 1996).

The general pattern is that the dyads most likely to be at peace, whether for wars or lower-level military disputes, are those composed of two democracies. Dyads composed of two autocracies are much more war and dispute prone, as are dyads containing a democracy and an autocracy. Precisely because democracy is a continuous variable rather than a dichotomous one, peoples' perceptions of one another can sometimes vary or be mistaken, and disputes are more likely when one state is only marginally democratic than when both are very democratic.[4] When one state is democratic, the farther apart the two states are in political distance on a democratic to autocratic spectrum, the greater is the probability of violence. Democracies and autocracies get along like cats and dogs (Oneal and Ray 1997; Oneal and Russett 1997).

Perhaps the most prominent and still vexing puzzle of the democratic peace literature pivots on the so-called monadic-dyadic distinction. There has long been skepticism about the monadic proposition in the social scientific community. Richardson (1960b), for example, found many democracies high on the list of frequent war participants. The authors of another early empirical investigation (Small and Singer 1976) are well known for asserting that democracies in general are as war prone as other states as well as for mistakenly dismissing their finding that democracies rarely if ever made war on each other as spurious.

At the dyadic level of analysis the suggestion that the statistical relationship is spurious has since been largely refuted by elaborate multivariate analyses, most clearly for the post–World War II era (Maoz and Russett 1993; Oneal and Russett 1999a; Russett, Oneal, and Davis 1998), but extending back well into the nineteenth century also (Bremer 1992, 1993; Henderson 1998; Oneal and Russett 1999b, 1999c). Singer and Small's other conclusion, that democracies are no more peaceful in general than are other states, has been much more widely accepted even though there too their reasoning was badly flawed (Rummel 1997, 75–76). Most scholars to date, believing the dyadic form of the proposition but not the monadic one, have searched for a theoretical explanation. Even one of the authors of this review leaned toward acceptance of what then was a near consensus: "Though there are elements of plausibility in the argument that democracies are inherently peaceful, it contains too many holes, and is accompanied by too many exceptions, to be usable as a major theoretical building block" (Russett 1993, 30–31). The previous near-consensus was, however, not complete; in several earlier articles summed up in his recent book, Rummel (1997) was conspicuous for insisting that democracies were more peaceful in general, a position subsequently propounded by Ray (1995) and further argued by Benoit (1996).

We take this counterattack seriously, on theoretical as well as empirical grounds. The emerging majority view now seems to be that the monadic effect of democracy is real, and discernible in most of the evidence when one looks carefully—especially in the relatively low frequency with which democracies, in general, *initiate* militarized disputes (Rioux 1998; Rousseau 1996; Rousseau et al. 1996). This monadic result is masked by selection effects when one looks only at existing crises. While a clear effect by the usual standards of social science, this monadic effect is not nearly as strong or robust as the dyadic effect that emerges in the interactions between two democracies. This is one reason for the initial lack of attention to the monadic effect. We discern at least three other reasons why the monadic evidence was initially ignored or widely underappreciated.

1. Too few analysts really thought multivariately. Although in simple bivariate counting the monadic relationship between democracy and conflict is rather weak, bivariate results fail to consider the other influences on conflict, notably the challenges states face in global and especially regional systems. Since geographical proximity by itself makes conflict more likely, it is important to know what types of regimes democratizing states have as neighbors; one would expect those with many autocratic neighbors to have more conflicts than those largely surrounded by democracies (see, e.g., Simon and Starr 1995; Starr 1995). For example, throughout the nineteenth century, and much of the twentieth, democracies were relatively rare. Most democracies then were more likely to have autocratic neighbors, so we would expect them to be involved in disputes more often (the cats and dogs effect) than they would later, in regional zones of democratic peace. As democracies come to be numerically predominant in a system, the more peaceful in general the average democracy would be, and the more dispute prone the average autocracy would then appear (Gleditsch and Hegre 1997).

   Maoz has done several analyses (1996, 1998) directed to this point, using concepts of democratic networks and a state's "politically relevant international environment" (PRIE). He finds that democracies have lower military expenditures, and experience far less international conflict, when their PRIEs are predominantly democratic (see also Garfinkel 1994). This addresses a level of analysis phenomenon that is illuminated by the ecological fallacy problem (Robinson 1950); namely, that whereas at the dyadic level democracies are peaceful, when democracies are a large minority in the international system in general—but not necessarily in localized democratic PRIEs—the system may experience more militarized disputes (Maoz and Abdolali 1989).

Thinking multivariately helps us understand the implications of a "progressive" extension of the democratic peace research program. This extension addresses the question whether the process of democratization, resulting in perhaps initially unstable regimes, may increase the short-term likelihood of conflict even though established democratic regimes might be more peaceful. Russett (1993, 133–34) raised this possibility, and Mansfield and Snyder (1995), while explicitly not disputing the basic democratic peace result, make a strong theoretical argument, with empirical support, that democratizing regimes are indeed more war prone than are stable political systems; (on Eastern Europe, see also Kozhemiakin 1998).

Efforts to replicate Mansfield and Snyder's results, however, have not been very successful. Their findings are not robust with different data sets, indicators, and analytical procedures. It is not at all clear the democratizing states are typically the initiators, rather than the victims, of interstate violence. Moreover, regime instability in general appears to be the problem, not democratization: processes of autocratization (from democratic to authoritarian regimes) seem as conflict-inducing as democratization may be, or more so (Enterline 1996, 1998a; Mansfield and Snyder 1996a, 1997a, 1997b; Maoz 1998; Thompson and Tucker 1997a, 1997b; Ward and Gleditsch 1998). In addition, these analyses are typically monadic and bivariate. Analyses taking into account the characteristics of states' neighbors, with a good multivariate set of controls, find no effect of democratization on the probability of conflict (Enterline 1998b; Oneal and Russett 1997; Rousseau 1997). Braumoeller's (1997) survey results in Eastern Europe and Russia suggest that the degree to which democrats in democratizing states *perceive* their neighbors as democratizing helps to reduce conflict.

2. Failure to recognize a monadic effect for democracy and war also arose from a neglect of thinking strategically. This is a perspective that became prominent only after the initial dyadic empirical observation (democratic dyads appeared to be quite peaceful) was established, and thereby impelled a search for theoretical explanations of that observation.
3. Therefore, a strategic perspective impels one to consider the direction of relationships; that is, what kinds of states are likely to be targets rather than initiators of disputes and war. These theoretical innovations, which in turn required fresh looks at the empirical evidence, illustrate the integrative cumulation achieved in the democratic peace perspective. We turn now to these developments.

Theories of Dyadic Democratic Peace

Initial Explanations: Culture or Structure?

Renewed interest in the dyadic peace proposition drove the necessity of understanding why such a relationship should exist; without a good theoretical explanation the empirical result might yet turn out to be spurious. Such explanations were placed initially into two categories: cultural explanations based on shared democratic norms and expectations of behavior, and structural explanations based on institutional constraints on decision makers (Maoz and Russett 1993; Russett 1993; Starr 1992a). The two need not be antithetic: culture conditions institutions, and institutions shape culture. Immanuel Kant, in *Perpetual Peace,* regarded them as complementary and in some degree sequential: a good constitution for representative government would, over time, generate a good moral culture (Heldt 1997b).

A dichotomous approach to theories of the democratic peace generates several related difficulties. The chief problem derives from treating them as "contending" approaches—where one has to be correct and the other incorrect. Even avoiding that extreme, it was common in early empirical studies to ask which approach (through various operationalizations) worked "better."[5] This "contending" approach delayed scholarly investigation into how the two explanations were related, and how they interacted to generate peace within pairs of democracies. It is not unreasonable to postulate that peace among democracies is an overdetermined phenomenon, explainable by several related but nonetheless distinct, perhaps sequential, and reinforcing causal mechanisms. The culture-structure debate obscured the likelihood that multiple and overlapping dynamics lead to peace between democracies. Just as Bremer (1996) argues there are multiple paths to war, there are multiple, "substitutable," paths to peace. Moreover, the culture-structure debate omitted (and delayed acceptance of) an important synthetic set of explanations that looked at the strategic decision making of governmental leaders. Some creative recent efforts (Bueno de Mesquita et al. 1999; Reiter and Stam 1998c) have produced deductive models designed to explain several empirical democratic peace results. These efforts are promising, though we are unsure whether any single deductive structure can ever satisfactorily cover the empirical diversity.

Both the cultural and structural arguments can be seen as contextual theories; theories that consider conditions existing within democracies to constrain and enable behavioral outcomes (see, e.g., Goertz 1994; Most and Starr 1989). As such, it is relatively easy to bring them together to help see how they affect the opportunity and willingness of decision makers to choose among conflictual and cooperative options that exist under different conditions (such as the nature or type of the other party). Various studies now do integrate these two broad theories by focusing on how decision makers weigh the costs and benefits of different policy options, calculate expected utility, and make choices. The effort is worthwhile, even though it will not satisfy proponents of extreme theoretical parsimony.

One of the earliest works that explicitly directs analytic models of purposive choice toward explanation of the dyadic democratic peace proposition is that of Bueno de Mesquita and Lalman (1992). Their international interaction game is specifically designed to take domestic factors into account within a general agent-structure notion of decision makers playing two-level games. They place states' decisions regarding the expected utility of war and peace in a strategic context, adopting a game-theoretic approach. From this, they deduce the conditions that are logically associated with various outcomes of the interactions of two states. Further, they contend that the demands that states make of one another do not reflect solely a desire for more power vis-à-vis potential rivals. Rather, the magnitude of their demands is determined by internal political processes, norms, and considerations.

Internal politics affects the likelihood of military conflict because the domestic political costs associated with the use of force differ for democracies and nondemocracies. The high political costs of war typically experienced by the leaders of democracies make the use of force less attractive to them. Whereas decision makers in the real world can never be sure whether an opponent is averse to the use of force, there is fairly common knowledge whether or not the opponent is a liberal democracy. If a state is a liberal democracy, then decision makers know that its leaders will be more likely to bear heavier costs than the leaders of nondemocracies—that the leaders will be under greater constraints, and more likely to be averse to the use of force. All of this is known because of the free movement of information in liberal democracies, the existence of opposition groups, and knowledge of internal politics, institutions, and debates (democratic transparency).

Thus the international interaction game provides an informational or signaling explanation of the democratic peace. The strategic logic of the game also could account for the widely held belief that democracies are as inclined to violence as nondemocracies. An autocracy, relatively unconstrained by domestic politics, may believe it can force a constrained democratic rival to capitulate; but even a democracy prefers to defend itself when attacked. Ironically, given reasonable assumptions about the cost of losing the military initiative and the domestic costs of capitulating to a demand backed by force, a possible scenario is that a democracy will anticipate the consequences of delay and choose to preempt the attack it expects from its nondemocratic rival. In short, democratic constraints on the use of force can make democracies "vulnerable to threats of war or exploitation" and possibly liable to launch preemptive attacks against presumed aggressors (Bueno de Mesquita and Lalman 1992, 159).[6] Although preemptive attacks are rare (Reiter 1995a), these analyses may explain some conditions both of dyadic democratic peace and some democratic belligerence against autocracies.

As Starr (1992b, 211) summarizes Bueno de Mesquita and Lalman's argument, the assumption that democracies are more likely to be "doves" is based on both cultural and structural arguments. This separation of opponents into hawks and doves affects the expected utility of war and the choice of options. The general logic supporting utility-based models of the dyadic democratic peace relates the political survivability of decision makers to war participation, war outcome, and conflict behavior in general. Key is the nature of the constituencies to which decision makers are responsible and the institutional context within which the leader-constituency relationship is situated. Bueno de Mesquita, Siverson, and Woller (1992, 644) conclude:

> The evidence presented here can be taken as an evaluation of the claim that the political welfare of foreign policy makers is intimately tied to national performance in conflicts that pose a potential threat to sovereignty and that the preferences of such leaders are constrained so as to give highest priority to maximizing the state's overall welfare. . . . Leaders can anticipate that they will be held accountable for failed foreign policy adventures. Consequently, the choice of war-related behavior is likely to be dampened by the fear that the regime will be punished if things go awry.

Leaders are punished for policy failures—they do not survive as leaders. Democratic leaders are particularly subject to this effect; thus, leaders of democracies tend to choose wars with a lower risk of defeat (Bueno de Mesquita and Siverson 1995).[7]

Strategic Interaction

Bueno de Mesquita and Siverson (1997) develop the argument further. To satisfy the "selectorate" and maintain a domestic winning coalition, leaders have both policy objectives and rent-seeking objectives. Leaders were assumed to be motivated to retain their hold over office. To do so they were assumed to distribute private goods to their supporters as well as to pursue collective goods—public policies consumed by all. Elsewhere, Olson (1993) shows in an elegant argument how the leaders of democracies are driven both to lower rent-seeking and to raise their commitment to the provision of collective goods that benefit all of society. These dynamics are related to the range and depth of the interests that leaders and elites have in a society, or the breadth of the stake they have in society.

Olson concludes, as do Lake (1992) and Brawley (1993), that such leadership will have greater legitimacy and support from society. This would both make them "powerful," as Lake suggests, and forge a utility calculus for leaders based firmly within the domestic setting. Bueno de Mesquita and Siverson (1997) outline domestic or endogenous institutional constraints based on the nature of the selectorate and the size of the winning coalition (somewhat akin to Putnam's 1988 argument concerning two-level games and the domestic "win set"). In sum, given the nature of the overall set of relationships between leaders and rent-seeking, the provision of public goods, the creation and maintenance of legitimacy, the care and feeding of the selectorate and the domestic winning coalition, policymakers in democracies *must* pay particular attention to the overall expected utility of getting involved in conflict. In a state with a wide voting franchise, leaders cannot readily seek rents for themselves while spreading the costs of military action among the populace (Verdier 1994).

The analysis of democracies as countries satisfied with the status quo is yet another variant on strategic decision making, also based on the examination of the utility of war (or the use of force more broadly). Although the status quo has been approached from several different theoretical perspectives, the main point is the same: states that are satisfied with the status quo will be less likely to make demands to change the status quo, and thus less likely to generate conflict that could escalate to war (as found in various system change theories such as those of Doran 1991; Gilpin 1981; or Organski and Kugler 1980). States that are satisfied with the status quo are, in essence, deterred from challenging or attacking other states. Deterrence—not initiating or engaging in activities one is currently not doing—is based on the calculation of cost and benefit. The calculation may be affected either by increasing the costs of undertaking some activity (the threat of punishment, which is how analysts usually think of deterrence), or by increasing the benefits of abstaining from some activity. For example, Oneal and Russett (1997) show that bilateral trade (looking at the bilateral trade-to-GDP ratio) reduces the likelihood of conflict. Dyads with high bilateral trade derive major benefits from the economic status quo, benefits that would be disrupted by militarized conflict.

Democracies may also be more easily satisfied with the status quo due to greater legitimacy and economic well-being through low rents and high provision of public goods. Democratic societies receive political, social, and economic benefits within systems where government extraction is relatively low compared with bandits or autocrats, and where governments see it in their interest to provide high levels of public goods. Such domestic satisfaction may easily translate into satisfaction with the territorial status quo of the international system. Kacowicz (1998), for instance, supports the idea that democracies are indeed more satisfied with the status quo in an analysis of the territorial demands of democracies. If so, then peace among pairs of democracies as status quo states would also be consistent with power transition theory, as demonstrated by Lemke and Reed (1996). Rousseau et al. (1996), investigating crisis initiation and escalation, find both dyadic and monadic effects for democracy, through their examination of satisfaction with the status quo.

The dyadic argument goes something like this: If two democracies evaluate the status quo similarly, and both are satisfied with the status quo, there is no incentive to challenge each other—with the possibility of escalation to the use of force with all the costs that such an escalation would entail—over demands that they would expect (through both the cultural and structural arguments) to be reconciled in a peaceful manner. As we shall show later, this corresponds to the Deutschian notion of responsiveness that is required for the zones of peace found within security communities.

The monadic argument is based on incentives to expand, make demands, and fight—incentives that appear to pose a higher threshold for democracies in many cases, and an almost impossible barrier when facing other democracies. Lake (1992, 29) asserts, "Democracies will expand only when the initial costs of conquest and ongoing costs of rule are less than the discounted present value of future economic benefits" from peace. Very simply, Oneal and Russett (1997, 18), in analyzing not only war but militarized disputes as well, continue to find evidence for the liberal peace while controlling for a measure of the expected utility of conflict. Thus various models of strategic decision making combine cultural and structural explanations of the democratic peace. They place our investigation of the democratic peace argument within an agent-structure framework. This framework forces us to consider both the opportunity and the willingness of leaders to fight.

"Consilience": Converging Findings and Expanding Applicability

We have shown how models of strategic decision making have built on previous theories of the democratic peace, explained the same phenomena, and then gone beyond to expand the domain of explanation—all in the Lakatosian (1978) sense of developing "better" theory. We can also demonstrate how the democratic peace, through integrative cumulation, has evolved as a research program to cover a broader range of phenomena and incorporate a wider range of explanatory models. Indeed, rather than a simple descriptive statement about the world—"pairs of democracies do not fight wars with each other"—the democratic peace inquiry illustrates Lakatos's (1970) notion of a "progressive" research program (see also Moon 1975).

> The basic, descriptive dyadic democratic peace proposition served as a platform for the development of a variety of theories which could usefully explain why we should observe such a phenomenon. The generation of theories, and then the comparison of theories, forced scholars to look closely at the processes by which any alternative explanation would lead to the result of democracies not going to war against other democracies, and under what conditions. Each theory or model should be looked at as a "story" which not only produces some particular outcome (peace in democratic dyads), but, under certain conditions, other outcomes as well. Can any of these explanations help us understand other phenomena, help us go beyond the dyadic democratic peace proposition? To do so would suggest stronger theory and explanation.

Such an approach follows the Lave and March (1975, 19–20) procedure for the development of disciplined speculation in the social sciences:

1. Observe some facts.
2. Look at the facts as though they were the end result of some unknown process (model). Then speculate about processes that might have produced such a result.
3. Deduce other results (implications-consequences-predictions) from the model.
4. Then ask whether these other implications are true and produce new models if necessary.

Therefore, if some explanation is set forward for the dyadic democratic peace proposition, what else should we expect to follow from that explanation or model? And does empirical research support such expectations? Here, the concept of "consilience" (Wilson 1998), the unity of knowledge, allows us to move beyond simply the occurrence of "war" between two democracies. The term was coined for a theory that explains facts of very diverse kinds by William Whewell, a nineteenth-century writer on scientific method. Consilience can be seen as an important component in the theoretical specification of why democratic peace occurs (Chan 1997, 61).

Remember two points, however. First, consilience studies are about comparing and refining the theories that can account for the democratic peace, and not about the empirical fact that war is absent between pairs of democracies. Thus, consilience studies do not typically "test" the democratic peace (as is often misunderstood by critics). Second, the nature of consilience studies is analogous especially to the monadic studies noted—the results represent tendencies and probabilities. While many of these results are robust in comparison to social science findings in general, they again cannot compare with the strong, sufficient nature of the basic dyadic democratic peace finding. We should not expect all democracies to behave the "right" way all the time.

As scholars have tried to explain the dyadic democratic peace they have investigated how some of the theories have broader applicability. These exercises of expanding applicability and converging findings have taken two forms, looking at either different dependent variables or different independent variables. We begin by exploring new dependent variables, what other cooperative or conflictual behavior we might see democracies engaged in.

Common Interests

If democracies have greater expected utility for avoiding conflict with each other because they share common interests, we should expect those common interests also to show up in cooperative behavior. And they do. Democracies are more likely to collaborate with each other at the start of militarized disputes (Mousseau 1997), and to ally with one another (Siverson and Emmons 1991), especially in war (Ragnerud and Hegre 1997). Werner and Lemke (1997) corroborate this, suggesting that institutional differences among states lead to perceptions of threats. They also find that whereas autocracies tend to bandwagon with stronger states whose power is growing, democracies' alliance decisions are not very sensitive to power changes. Some of this may be a result of ideological preferences during the cold war era (Simon and Gartzke 1996). Nevertheless, analyses consistently show that alliances between democracies are more durable, apparently because democracies are able to make more credible long-term commitments due to the public way in which those commitments are produced (Bennett 1997b; Gaubatz 1996; Reed 1997).

Perhaps the most cogent realist critique of the democratic peace findings about wars and militarized disputes is Farber and Gowa's (1995, 1997a; also Henderson 1999) assertion that the result is misleading—a consequence of shared interests between democracies, especially as manifested in alliance patterns during the cold war era. If alliances are treated as a measure of interests, and both disputes and alliances are a consequence of other interstate actions, then the customary inclusion of a simple statistical control for alliances along with democracy in a multivariate equation explaining disputes may not solve this problem. Farber and Gowa's results are sharply disputed and not readily replicated (see Farber and Gowa 1997b; Maoz 1997a; Rousseau et al. 1996, 523; Thompson and Tucker 1997a, 1997b).

Farber and Gowa (1997a) recognize that the use of alliances as a proxy for common interests is problematic. A full resolution of this matter may have to await testing of a larger model of simultaneous equations that considers the triangular and indirect effects of democracy, alliance, and conflict on one another. Shared interests of similar political types (e.g., democracies) may well affect preferences for alliance partnerships, providing an additional, indirect reduction in conflict between democracies. Thus alliances cannot be treated as a privileged indicator of interests. Shared interests also may arise from high levels of trade or be reflected in the kinds of policy preferences that produce UN voting patterns. Gartzke (1998) finds the latter eliminates the effect of alliances on disputes, and it weakens the effect of joint democracy (using a specification by Oneal et al. [1996] that is superseded by Oneal and Russett [1997]). But this also does not satisfactorily untangle the causal relations among democracy, alliances, and preferences. Arguably democracy and alliances have a causal impact on conflict, but presumably no one would assert that states fight *because* they vote differently in the UN. Rather, democracy, trade patterns, and alliances affect disputes both directly and indirectly, the latter by shaping the shared preferences that are represented by UN voting and that in turn influence conflict decisions (Oneal and Russett 1999c).

An ingenious twist to this question arises by changing the dependent variable (Gelpi and Griesdorf 1997). If both shared democracy and common security interests, as measured by alliances, could impel democracies to settle disputes among themselves peacefully, one can ask which of the two states in a dispute is likely to prevail. The mere existence of an alliance offers no prediction about this, though a realist perspective would predict that the more powerful state would usually prevail. A democratic peace perspective, however, would predict that in disputes between democracies shared norms and institutional procedures for peaceful conflict resolution would temper the dominance of power. Gelpi and Griesdorf therefore examine which side won or lost in all disputes over most of the twentieth century. The realist prediction that relative power matters holds true in general. But among democracies, relative power has no such effect; actually, the weaker side is more likely to get its way.

Interventions

If democracies rarely fight each other overtly, and share many common interests, then why have democracies sometimes intervened in the internal affairs of other democracies? One form of intervention is covert action. Several critiques of the dyadic democratic peace are based on studies of the use of covert intervention operations against other democracies (Forsythe 1992; James and Mitchell 1995). Using structural arguments and the greater accountability within democracies, the analysis of covert operations should actually be seen as evidence in support of the democratic peace, not a critique. The fact that covert operations against democracies would be widely denounced, perhaps across the political spectrum, would lead democratic leaders to hide such activities. Fear of criticism in a free press increases the incentives to keep any intervention covert (Van Belle 1997). In terms of Putnam's (1988) two-level games, covert action against another democracy would not be included in the domestic win-set: such a policy would lose because it would be perceived as illegitimate. Thus the use of covert activities against other democracies can be seen as confirming the conclusions of Mintz and Geva (1993; see also Geva, DeRouen, and Mintz 1993), as well as those of Bueno de Mesquita and Lalman (1992). Such activities are covert because they would generate high levels of opposition. Policymakers keep such operations low key—at low levels of violence and low levels of forces employed—because higher levels (as they escalate toward war) will bring major societal and political opposition. In large part policymakers attempt to keep covert operations secret because the public does not support the costs of such inherently antidemocratic activity (see also Russett 1993, 122–24).

Moving up to overt interventions, the data more clearly and directly support democratic peace expectations. Systematic empirical analyses are now concluding that, while powerful democratic states have sometimes intervened against weaker democratic or semidemocratic governments, this is not especially common. At first, Kegley and Hermann (1995) reported democracies were more likely to intervene in other democratic or partly free states than in autocracies. When they analyzed a different database, however, this was not true (Kegley and Hermann 1997). Moreover, further analysis discovered that the majority of "interventions" were either to protect the intervenor's citizens or property, or actually were in support of the "target" democratic government; only a minority were hostile acts of coercive diplomacy (Hermann and Kegley 1996, 440).

Moreover, their analysis (Hermann and Kegley 1996) of interventions only as acts of coercive diplomacy found democracy to provide a degree of inoculation: democracies were less likely to be the victims of such interventions, by democracies or autocracies. This picks up arguments concerning the strength of democracies. Dixon (1997) shows that interventions by democracies are more likely to be "legitimate" in that they occur with endorsement or authorization. Nincic and Nincic (1995) present democracy as a factor in the ending of armed interventions. Other analyses report that, whereas there are obvious counterexamples, states subject to U.S. military intervention during the cold war generally became more democratic than did states where the United States did not intervene—and especially so in instances when the U.S. president declared its goal to be the promotion of democracy (Hermann and Kegley 1998; Meernik 1996). A further analysis, of a century-long era of U.S. interventions (Peceny 1999), concludes that although intervention itself produced no generalized positive impact on democracy, when the United States provided active support for "free and fair" elections, the result was often profound and positive. Thus open interventions, especially those where the intervenor felt the need to proclaim democracy as the goal, have not generally been antidemocratic in their consequences.

Conflict Management

The ability of the public to observe open policy-making and implementation rests on the key element of transparency that permeates the political and economic systems of democracies (see Starr 1997a). The transparency of political processes, along with the mechanisms required for both transparency and the regularized competition for the control of government, also help democracies signal their interests more clearly and credibly (Fearon 1994b) and, when resolved, to project that resolve more effectively (Eyerman and Hart 1996). If a democracy is highly resolved and the political opposition supports the state, it is able to communicate this resolve and thus to prevail without war. But if the opposition does not support the government's wish to confront a foreign adversary, the government will be in a weak position versus the adversary and so not likely to initiate a dispute. The adversary is more likely to interpret such an initiation as a bluff. So democracies are more likely than autocracies to settle disputes peacefully, less likely to initiate disputes, and less likely to use force when they do (Schultz 1998).

Indeed, numerous studies have extended theories of the democratic peace to investigate conflict management and cooperation among democracies. Bennett (1997a, 1998) shows that states engaged in enduring interstate rivalries are more likely to end those rivalries at times when both states happen to be democratic. Disputes between democratic rivals are both shorter (nearly half last less than a day) and less severe than between other rivals (Mitchell and Prins 1999). Leeds and Davis (1999) find that democratic dyads engage much more than other dyads in a wide range of cooperative behaviors. Stressing institutional theories, several studies have moved to investigate how the conflict management techniques utilized by pairs of democracies might differ from other types of dyads. Dixon (1993, 1994, 1998) shows how democracies settle conflicts peacefully through mutual concession and compromise (see also Mousseau 1998), and by the use of third parties for mediation or other means of dispute resolution. When, however, Raymond (1994, 1996) focuses on third parties with "judicial competence," that is, powers of arbitration or adjudication to impose binding settlements, the picture becomes murkier. He does find that pairs of democracies have a greater propensity to submit their disputes to arbitration: but the conflict-resolving effects of arbitration were not necessarily more durable than for nondemocratic pairs (Raymond 1996). Very possibly, selection bias is operating. Because nondemocratic pairs are generally reluctant to use binding third-party mechanisms, on the issues for which they do find it desirable to use them they may be more disposed to abide by the imposed solution. As in other kinds of analyses of international conflict, scrutiny of existing studies for potential selection-bias contamination is required, as is building in better techniques to control for selection bias in the future.

What constitutes "a legitimate casus belli" for democracies is best explained by the democratic culture/democratic norms argument. People in democracies who themselves manage conflict peacefully and within legitimized institutions and procedures, and who know that people in other democracies do the same, will expect their governments to act similarly regarding interstate conflict. People who share norms of self-government, governmental constraint, civil liberties, and the workings of democratic transparency know that people in other democracies do the same and will expect their governments to find appropriate modes of nonviolent conflict resolution. Thus the range of legitimate casus belli is greatly restricted in democratic dyads. The transparency of democracies, along with shared democratic norms and procedures, makes it nearly impossible for policymakers to dehumanize the people of another democracy through the manipulation of images of the other as the "enemy." In contrast, authoritarian and totalitarian states are both less transparent to others and limit their own people's access to information, facilitating the development of enemy images in both directions (Boulding 1956; Regan 1994; White 1970).

This argument is supported by the experimental work of Alex Mintz and associates, which tests a "political incentive" explanation for the dyadic democratic peace (e.g., Mintz and Geva 1993). They argue that the leaders of democracies do not pursue war against other democracies because they have no political incentive to do so. The results of their experiments indicate that the use of force by one democracy against another is perceived by the public as incompetent leadership—incompetent in part because the use of force or war is not seen as being worth the costs or risks, especially in interactions with states where peaceful conflict resolution is expected. Mintz's experimental results are also consistent with the structure and preference orderings of states in Bueno de Mesquita and Lalman's arguments about pairs of international "doves." The leader of a democracy/dove, after performing a cost-benefit analysis of the war option against another democracy/dove, sees there is no advantage or profit to that course of action. Decision makers leading democracies could expect different levels of domestic opposition and support for the use of force against different types of targets.

While we began with the strong result of the dyadic democratic peace phenomenon, we have also indicated a variety of related analyses that generally link democracy—both dyadically and monadically—to less violence and more cooperative behaviors. If the origins of war are to be placed within "process models" (Bremer 1996), then we need to be concerned with the onset of disputes, their escalation and de-escalation, and the dynamics of conflict management that move conflicts away from violent outcomes. Again, beginning with general theories to explain the dyadic democratic peace, scholars have linked democracy in dyads, and the democratic nature of single states, with de-escalatory behaviors. We do know, however, that democracies are not "pacifists"; they do participate in violent conflict, and frequently do initiate violent conflict. Yet using tools for analyzing strategic interaction we are becoming better at understanding which conditions (i.e., types of opponents and situations) are most likely to eventuate in democracies threatening to use and actually employing force.

Why Do Democracies Win Their Wars?

Another example of how the democratic peace research program has expanded is as part of a wider extension emphasizing liberalism under the same principles of individual liberty that apply to political expression and to economic behavior in a market economy. The logic and empirical evidence support each other nicely. Democracies are more likely than are autocracies to win the wars in which they engage (Bennett and Stam 1996; Bueno de Mesquita, Siverson, and Woller 1992; Stam 1996). Why? Lake (1992) opened the discussion with the hypothesis that democracies would be better able to generate wealth and military capability, leaving them more likely to prevail in wars. Schultz and Weingast (1997) find that democracies, by their ability to limit the scope of government, make themselves more attractive to international capital lenders and hence better able to raise the resources they may need to compete with authoritarian powers for dominance in international politics. Russett (1993, 137) suggests that democracies both better motivate their citizens and make better-informed policy choices. Democracies do seem to choose to fight wars that they are likely to win, a selection effect perhaps attributable to the greater political costs democratic leaders incur in fighting. The argument for selection effects is strengthened by the fact that democracies are particularly likely to win only those wars they initiate, rather than those in which they are targets and do not make the choice for war. They do not seem to fare better by mobilizing greater material capabilities (Reiter and Stam 1998a).

Democracies generally suffer fewer casualties in war than do autocracies (Siverson 1995). But if democracies continue wars for very long, civilian support and military morale decline, largely as a result of mounting casualties (Gartner and Segura 1998; Mueller 1973). The decline is faster in democracies than in autocracies, and the longer the war goes on, the less likely democracies are to triumph. So democratic leaders must win their wars quickly (Bennett and Stam 1998). And why are they able to do so? Again, part of the answer is in selection—they choose to initiate wars they are not only likely to win, but wars they can win within a year or two. Once in wars, democracies do seem to exhibit superior organizational effectiveness and leadership—though the logistical competence and morale of democratic armies worsens over time (Reiter and Stam 1998b). Democratic leaders are more likely to choose maneuver strategies in wartime, and those strategies can win with lower human costs (which are important to democracies). Such strategies, however, require granting considerable autonomy to field commanders—which autocratic governments are usually less willing to do (Reiter and Meek 1999).

More important, the greater legitimacy of the democratic state motivates superior performance on the battlefield. Here we have a microlevel (individual soldiers' decisions whether to fight or surrender) explanation, consistent with a normative and cultural perspective, of macrolevel phenomena (states' behavior in choosing and winning wars). Remember that democracies' wars are virtually always with autocracies. Autocracies treat prisoners of war much more brutally than do democracies, regularly violating the Geneva Convention. Soldiers know this. In wars with democracies, soldiers of autocratic states frequently defect, voting with their feet to become POWs; democratic soldiers, however, rarely voluntarily become prisoners of autocratic states (Reiter and Stam 1997). This helps to explain why democracies usually win, and perhaps, in expectation, how they decide which wars to fight.

The Domestic Conflict/Foreign Conflict Puzzle

A long-standing perspective on the relation between internal politics and external relations is the hypothesis that leaders of governments may pursue diversionary policies; that is, in the face of moderate domestic political unrest leaders may try to invoke a "rally 'round the flag" effect by diverting their people's attentions toward foreign "enemies." Such actions may be especially likely to happen in democracies, where the government must present itself periodically for elections, and in elections its popularity may hinge heavily on whether the people are prosperous or are suffering from inflation and/or economic recession. If so, such a finding would pose a serious challenge to the idea that, monadically, democratic peoples and their governments are relatively peaceful. Alternatively, in the face of serious and large-scale domestic upheaval, leaders may not wish to compound the threat to their hold on office with an external war.

Heldt (1997a) nicely reviews most of the recent literature on these topics; Levy (1989b) provides the standard earlier survey. Even the more recent examples of this long-standing inquiry have produced rather mixed results. Lian and Oneal (1993), Oneal and Bryan (1995), and James and Rioux (1998) find only modest support for the rally effect in the United States. Studies investigating a basis for inferring that American leaders have consciously sought to invoke a rally at politically convenient times are more negative. Miller (1995) and Leeds and Davis (1997), for example, fail to uncover any systematic evidence that other democracies experience international conflict particularly tied to internal political or economic cycles. Meernik (1994) finds international influences have a greater impact on American decisions to use or threaten to use force than do domestic conditions, and Meernik and Waterman (1996) suggest that a failure to control for selection bias, in the form of crises in which no force was used, leads to erroneous support for the diversionary hypothesis. Wang (1996) produces evidence of both internal and external influences—but force is invoked less frequently when elections are proximate (perhaps the rally effect is too unreliable), and more frequently to avoid a high negative expected utility of a foreign policy defeat. And as noted, Oneal, Lian, and Joyner (1996) similarly find that American leaders have been more likely to use force to resist aggression than to engineer internal changes in other countries. (This also has some relevance to the intervention question addressed earlier.)

What begins to emerge is the need to take a more theoretically sophisticated view of this problem. If the use or threat of force is associated more with international conditions, then one must consider the effect of particularly dispute-prone relationships as embodied in long-term rivalries or the dyadic conditions studied in analyses of the democratic peace. Democratic leaders who do not respond as "realists" to challenges may be vulnerable at home (Huth 1996a). More complex possibilities of strategic interaction must be examined (Smith 1996a). For example, if democratic governments are prone to exercise diversionary actions in response to domestic economic or political difficulty, their potential antagonists may anticipate that and thus be especially careful not to provoke democratic leaders at such times (Leeds and Davis 1997; Miller 1999)! In effect, their antagonists (chiefly autocrats) will produce another kind of selection effect. Thinking in a multivariate, dyadic, strategic frame of reference thus has great promise for untangling this otherwise confused and troublesome puzzle.

Civil Wars

Analyzing monadic conditions within democracies suggests some other elements of consilience. Perhaps because of higher levels of legitimacy and responsiveness, or because democratic governance presents leaders with the greatest range of interests in society (as suggested by Olson), democracies experience much lower levels of civil war than do other forms of government (Hegre et al. 1997; Krain and Myers 1997). Highly democratic and effective states have the least violence within their borders (Benson and Kugler 1998). The finding about civil wars, while rather weak by comparison with the dyadic relationship between two democracies, is yet strong by the normal standards of social science. It also may be obscured by a curvilinear relationship between political system and civil war (Ellingsen and Gleditsch 1996; Goemans 1997; Muller and Weede 1990). During the period 1955–96, partial democracies more often experienced violent state failures than did either full democracies or autocracies; countries open to international trade had fewer failures, as did those with below-median infant mortality rates (Esty et al. 1998). The vast majority of civil wars in the twentieth century have occurred neither in democracies nor in effective totalitarian states able to repress opposition vigorously. Rather, they have appeared mostly in mixed regimes or in decaying very autocratic regimes in the process of losing their grip and thus becoming more overtly violent. Transitional regimes may engage in substantial repression of newly released dissent.

The American Civil War (1861–65) is often cited as an exception to the paucity of civil wars in democracies. So it is. It also illustrates the necessity of remembering that democracy is a continuous variable, producing probabilistic expectations about behavior and an emphasis, from the work on international conflicts, on the importance of political distance. In this case the continuous variable exhibits considerable political distance between the Union and the Confederacy. Although the voting franchise was limited to males, at the time the North arguably represented the most democratic large political system in the world. In the South not only did females have no vote but one-third of the total population, in addition to lacking the franchise, was legally no more than property. Weart (1998) plausibly labels the South as an oligarchic republic. Thus while the political distance between North and South was less than between, say, the North and Imperial Russia, it was so great that it is hardly surprising that the two systems were unable to coexist within the same state.

In turn, civil war is a strong predictor of state-sponsored mass murder (Krain 1997). Drawing on both culture and institutional constraints (and linking economics and politics as well), the corpus of Rummel's work (e.g., 1985, 1994, 1995a, 1995b) demonstrates that democracy is related to lower levels of violence in general, especially in regard to "democide," or the killing of a government's own people. Rummel (1997) therefore characterizes democracy as a general "method of non-violence." In this sense, peace within democratic polities becomes logically prior to the democratic peace in international relations.

Beyond "Democratic" Peace Alone

The Kantian Peace

The first dimension of consilience discussed in the preceding looked at additional, related phenomena that might explain peace. We start now to ask a key question about democracy: Of what is democracy an example? What broader phenomena does democracy represent? How far back must we step?

Many scholars have begun to work within the tradition of Kantian arguments that peace is the result of multiple and overlapping liberal behaviors (democracy, economic interdependence, and international law and organizations). This approach entails analyses that specify what other independent variables can be theorized to lead to peace.[8] Russett and colleagues have engaged in the study of the triad of factors underlying the Kantian peace (and their multiple indicators). Kant's full prescription rested on three complementary influences: (1) "Republican constitutions" (in modern parlance, representative democracy rather than direct democracy) would constrain autocratic caprice in waging war, (2) "cosmopolitan law" (economic interdependence) would reinforce structural constraints and liberal norms by creating transnational ties that encourage accommodation rather than conflict, and (3) international law and "federations" of independent states (in the contemporary era, international organizations), building on an understanding of the legitimate rights of all citizens and all republics, would provide the moral and legal edifice for peaceful conflict resolution. In Kant's view all three are conceptually related, and it is not simply that each is useful—democracy may be the keystone, but trade and international organizations contribute importantly to maintaining the full structure of stable peace and nonviolent conflict resolution (Doyle 1997; Heldt 1997b; Huntley 1996; see also the dialectical learning model of Cederman 1998).

The proposition that trade should reduce interstate conflict derives from two arguments. One is that trade and other elements of economic exchange provide states with strong interests in maintaining peaceful relations. To use or threaten to use military violence against an important trading partner is likely to disrupt commercial intercourse, or at the least raise its costs. Military conflict would endanger an importer's regular and cheapest supply of goods and services, and an exporter's markets. If one state's nationals have invested heavily in the other, war could mean the destruction of the very facilities they own there. A complementary perspective emphasizes that trade and investment also serve as media for communicating interests, preferences, and needs on a broad range of matters beyond the immediate commercial exchange. These communications form potentially important channels for averting militarized conflict.

Evidence supports the basic proposition, though without being able to distinguish between these two hypothesized effects. The more heavily any two states trade with each other (mutual trade as a proportion of their GDPs), the less likely they are to experience wars or militarized disputes. Like the Kantian results for democracy, this is a probabilistic statement, made in the context of the same control variables (relative power, distance, etc.) as in the quantitative analysis of democracy and conflict. And it also applies when democracy is controlled for; that is, economic interdependence provides an additional pacifying effect on relationships (Domke 1988; Oneal and Russett 1997; Polachek 1997).

This finding is not yet as extensively established as that about democracy, but support is growing. Methodological problems in the analysis of large cross-sectional and cross-temporal data sets remain unresolved, and the effects of time dependence on trade may be more serious than those on democracy; econometric methods do not yet provide agreed answers. Whereas Beck, Katz, and Tucker (1998) judge the democracy and peace finding to be extremely robust, the effect of trade on the probability of disputes weakens markedly in many of their specifications. Yet other analyses, using Beck, Katz, and Tucker's methods as well as alternative tests for time dependence, find the conflict-reducing effect of trade to be robust (Oneal and Russett 1999a, 1999b).

Most of the large-scale empirical work to date applies to the post–World War II period. While Way's (1997) analysis and new work by Oneal and Russett (1999b, 1999c) support this finding back into the nineteenth century, Barbieri (1996a, 1996b) provides a dissent for that era. Controlling for distance—which is known to be positively related to trade and to conflict—however, seems to allow the pacifying effect of trade to emerge in those years. It is even clearer with a measure of the economic importance of trade-bilateral trade as a proportion of GDP (Oneal and Russett 1999a). Democracies are much more likely to conclude preferential trade agreements (Mansfield, Milner, and Rosendorff 1998). Power transitions turn into major power war only if at least one power is authoritarian or totalitarian and follows an autarchic economic policy (Houweling and Siccama 1993). A recent review of the full literature, while cautioning that "outstanding empirical and theoretical questions" make "elevating this hypothesis to the status of a social scientific 'law' . . . premature," concludes that "the position advocated by liberalism is strongly supported by the existing literature" (McMillan 1997, 34). Moreover, the benefits of trade remain significant even when the reciprocal effect of conflict in reducing trade is estimated simultaneously (Kim 1998; Mansfield 1994; Reuveny and Kang 1996).

The liberal perspective is further strengthened by considering the relationship between democracy and trade. After allowing for the influences typically employed by economists to predict trade patterns (size of economy, distance, relative costs, and comparative advantage), democracies still trade more with one another than with autocracies (Bliss and Russett 1998; Morrow, Siverson, and Tabares 1998). Because of the democratic peace phenomenon, a democratic trading partner will feel its security less threatened by another democratic state than by many autocracies. Democratic leaders need be less concerned that a democratic trading partner will use gains from trade to threaten their security; thus they can pursue absolute gains without as much concern for who gains most relatively. Political leaders may encourage their private economic actors to direct trade accordingly.

In turn, private actors will prefer, where possible, to trade with those in states with whom relations are reliably peaceful. They also can be more confident in the business practices and laws of another democracy than of an autocracy where such capricious acts as expropriations may threaten their interests (Olson 1993). Weede (1996, chap. 7) contends that free trade increases prosperity, which in turn promotes democracy (and thus peace). Some evidence on the experience of industrialized countries (Volgy and Schwarz 1997) poses a possible long-term concern for Weede's argument; that is, free trade can magnify income inequality, which may ultimately endanger democracy. The matter of possible causal relationships between democracy and economic development is hotly contested and beyond full review here. In general, the position that high levels of economic development facilitate or promote democracy is generally accepted. Adam Przeworski and his colleagues (Przeworski et al. 1996; Przeworski and Limongi 1997), who have arguably done the most comprehensive work, confirm at least a strong correlation. They submit that wealthy democracies survive: no state that has achieved both democracy and a moderately high level of prosperity (at the level of Argentina in 1975) has subsequently become undemocratic. In less affluent countries, democracy is more likely to survive if the economy is growing, inflation is moderate, and economic inequality is narrowing. Some recent work (Feng 1997; Leblang 1997) also suggests that democracy, when it has become institutionalized and stable, in turn promotes and stabilizes economic growth.

The role and impact of international organizations and international law provide analogous arguments to those made for cultural or norm-based explanations of the dyadic democratic peace. Expectations of peace between democracies have been based on the view that democracies externalize their domestic processes of conflict management and resolution (building peace from within and below, as elaborated by Russett 1993). We have discussed some of the evidence that they do indeed employ "democratic" means when dealing with other democracies. These processes, as we argue later, are also manifestations of community, responsiveness, and legitimacy.

Organizations, norms, and formal rules are created within societies to reduce decision costs, to provide buffers against costly mistakes, and to enhance efficiency (as well as "rationality") in the creation and implementation of policy. Democratic societies have created not only laws but also procedures for how such laws are to be created, interpreted, applied, appealed, and changed. Legislatures, courts, instruments of mediation or arbitration, as well as the whole range of political and social organizations, serve these functions. Organizations exist not only to facilitate the use of law in conflict management and resolution but also to facilitate societal responsiveness—the willingness to comply with the demands of others and to reconcile conflicting demands that occur within society. (This includes the use of political and social organizations of all types.) They socialize members to common norms and generate narratives of mutual identification. Thus, within democratic societies, organizations and rules are core components of complex systems that ease interactions among individuals and groups, facilitate the recognition and pursuit of common interests, and manage conflict—systems similar to the webs of governance that many international relations scholars study as "regimes."

In accordance with both cultural explanations and models of strategic decision making, the leaders of democracies would expect to use organizations and law similarly in their interactions with other states, especially other democracies. They do so, in part, because the people who live in democracies also expect that their leaders will use organizations and law—elements of international civil society—in their relations with other democracies the same way such phenomena occur within society. And, following the work of Mintz, not to do so will be perceived as failure or incompetence on the part of leaders.

International organizations are often regarded as weak and ineffectual, particularly on matters that critically affect states' security interests. It is true that in most circumstances international organizations lack the effective coercive power that nation-states have over their constituent actors. But international organizations—global, regional, and functional—can and do fulfill many of the same functions among nation-states as domestic organizations do within nation-states. Therefore, it is reasonable to ask whether pairs of states that together belong to many of the same international organizations are less likely to engage in militarized disputes with one another.

Russett, Oneal, and Davis (1998) have done this, extending the previous aggregate analyses of democracy and trade on conflict to test this third Kantian leg. They find that in the post–World War II era, dense links of international organization (IGO) membership reduce the initiation of conflict in dyads by about 23 percent from a "baseline" of links of merely average density. This is in addition to the independent and statistically significant effects of democracy, economic interdependence, and the power and alliance variables represented in their term for expected utility. Together, high values for the three Kantian variables reduce the likelihood of militarized disputes by about 72 percent. Furthermore, an equation to explain IGO members suggests that disputes do reduce states' readiness to join or remain in international organizations with each other; this effect is not strong enough to reverse the causal interpretation that IGOs in fact reduce conflict. In effect, a "virtuous circle" operates whereby peace and IGOs strengthen each other. The equation to predict IGO membership also shows that democracies and economically interdependent states are more likely than others to join international organizations with one another, bringing together the three elements of the Kantian peace. Not all these results should yet be treated as conclusive; they need to withstand tough methodological critiques and their validity for other historical eras must be assessed. Nevertheless, they begin to provide powerful evidence that a Kantian system of feedback loops or virtuous circles operates within at least a major portion of the international system.

One more virtuous circle may be the influence of peace on democracy. Threats to national security in the shape of war or danger of war often inhibit freedom of information and expression. Conversely, the expectation of peace is likely to promote and strengthen democratic government, which in turn further improves the prospects for peace (Crescenzi and Enterline 1999; Midlarsky 1995, 1998a; Russett 1993, 137; 1998). Although peace may encourage democracy (James, Soleberg, and Wolfson 1999), any such effect operates in addition to and not instead of the causal arrow from democracy to peace (Oneal and Russett 2000). Indeed, since democracies most often win their wars against authoritarian states, and leaders who lose wars are often deposed from office, democratic-authoritarian wars may even expand the proportion of democracies in the international system (Mitchell, Gates, and Hegre 1999).

Democracy and Integration

Starr's (1992a, 1992b, 1997a, 1997b) analysis locates the dyadic democratic peace as a subset of the processes and results of integration, especially of Deutschian models of social communication. He argues that the international interaction game of Bueno de Mesquita and Lalman (1992) can help explain how Deutsch et al. (1957) get from a social communication process that explains the development of responsiveness (Russett 1963b) and community to the outcome of that process, namely a security community. The Deutschian model of a security community has begun to attract renewed interest, as expressed in a collaborative enterprise stimulated by Adler and Barnett (1998 and chapters therein, such as Russett 1998; also Wendt 1994). The security-community model presents a process of integration based on a wide array of intersocietal transactions that are of mutual benefit to the people involved. The process is based on learning—learning that such transactions provide benefits, that such benefits outweigh the costs involved, and that there are positive payoffs to continue such interactions and even expand them. As such interactions expand and become institutionalized, the peoples involved become more and more interdependent, and thus raise the costs of stopping such interactions. Indeed, for these reasons as well as the greater sensitivity of democratic leadership to the broadest selectorate, democracies appear to be able to "learn" from past experience more effectively (Reiter 1995b).

As peaceful interactions occur and increase, peoples develop greater responsiveness to one another, the expectation that wants and needs will be responded to positively. At some point this produces the "we feeling," trust and mutual consideration that Deutsch et al. (1957) call community. It is a matter of mutual sympathy, trust, and loyalties; of partial identification in terms of self-images and interests; and of mutually successful predictions of behavior. It operates as a perpetual dynamic process of mutual attention, communication, perception of needs, and responsiveness in decision making.

Responsiveness and community arise out of a continuing and growing set of social transactions by which people learn they can benefit, and through which they come to respect and trust others, and expect such respect and trust in return. Putnam (1993) refers to this as "dense networks of social exchange." He contends that networks of civic engagement are an essential form of social capital: the denser such networks in a community, the more likely that citizens will be able to cooperate for mutual benefit. Similarly, Taylor and Singleton (1993) argue that community can act to reduce uncertainty, and thus lower the transaction costs of solving collective action problems.

This process of integration is at the heart of Deutsch's social communication model. The most tangible outcome of that process is the security community. This refers to a group that, because of responsiveness and community, has given up the military option in regard to their mutual interactions, replacing it with "dependable expectations of 'peaceful change'" (Deutsch et al. 1957, 5). There need not be the creation of a single entity (amalgamation) to have a security community; rather, states may retain their sovereign independence, forming a pluralistic security community but with a degree of shared identity (Risse-Kappen 1996).

If leaders are to incur the significant costs of breaking the bonds of interdependence, then they will have to present compelling reasons for the expected utility of force or war. But they cannot do so within a security community. Bonds of mutually rewarding transactions and feelings of community raise the costs of using force to a prohibitive level. If simply identifying a state as a democracy significantly raises the odds of correctly identifying a dove, having a state with whom one has developed mutual responsiveness, high degrees of community, and interdependence creates virtual certainty of its dovelike nature.

Decision makers must learn what behavior is relevant to distinguishing between types of states. The social integration process provides decision makers with overwhelming information and transparency, which allows them to have full confidence in how they separate states. Those states with whom they form a security community are doves, averse to the use of force. As such, the Bueno de Mesquita and Lalman proof that two doves with common knowledge must negotiate or stay at the status quo applies. War will not occur. This is the Deutschian definition of the security community, and it also characterizes the dynamics of the dyadic democratic peace. The Adler and Barnett (1998, 3) volume "thinks the unthinkable: that community exists at the international level, that security politics is profoundly shaped by it, and that those states dwelling within an international community might develop a pacific disposition" toward one another.[9]

Legitimacy, Liberalism, and the "Good Society"

Many writers stress Kant's attention to republicanism as the core of liberalism; others stress private property and the free market as the basis for economic relationships. Interactions can be seen as stemming from the rational self-interest of economic actors in expanding markets and profits. Rational actor models often provide powerful explanations of the phenomena we are trying to understand in the expanded democratic peace research program. The liberal state, then, supports the pluralism necessary for the popular selection and replacement of governmental leaders, and the workings of a market economy. Yet while these are part of the core relationship between state and society, they do not capture all the important norms of societal integration and legitimacy.

We conclude, then, with an admittedly speculative attempt at integrating previous themes, in the hope of stimulating new theory and research. Democracy works through three central relationships: (1) among individuals and groups within society; (2) from society as a whole (and its various components) to government—how society perceives and reacts to government; and (3) from government to society—how government perceives and reacts to society.

The first relationship is rather straightforward. Models of social community work at a variety of societal levels; they describe "nationalism" (Deutsch 1953), and how humans form community at any level of aggregation. Also consider Taylor's (1982) three elements of community: shared values, beliefs, identities, and meaning; multiple and multifaceted direct relationships; recognition of long-term interests, reciprocity, and even "altruism." Democracies have not only community, but a community based on special values, such as legal equality, democratic process for governance, and belief in civil and political liberties. Individuals within societies sharing democratic values based on community and responsiveness would expect their governments to behave in the same manner toward the governments of other such societies.

For democracies the second relationship, that between society and government, must be characterized by legitimacy. Both political culture and institutional structure contribute to the legitimacy of the political system, a legitimacy that rests on the same conditions that undergird security communities. Jackman (1993, 98) defines a regime as "legitimate to the extent that it can induce a measure of compliance from most people without resort to the use of physical force. The compliance need not be total, but it does need to be extensive." Or consider Nie et al.'s (1996, 2) somewhat idealized description of legitimacy as the "cement of society": "Democracy requires relatively little punitive or physical coercion for legitimacy; there are no secret police, domestic passports, or national lists of citizens in American democracy. The method of social governance for the majority of citizens is, in essence, noncoercive, voluntary, and compliant." Just as norms and procedures for dealing with each other within democratic society are externalized, so are the norms and procedures by which citizens in democracies (individually or in groups) see their governments. The community, responsiveness, and legitimacy of these relationships are assumed for other democracies as well and fashion relations between democracies.

The third key relationship concerns how government sees and reacts to society, a relationship represented by the notion of the "liberal" state (Onuf and Johnson 1995). Doyle (1995, 84) calls liberalism "a family portrait of principles and institutions" recognizable by "a commitment to individual freedom, government through democratic representation, rights of private property, and equality of opportunity" (see also Moravcsik 1997 and McMillan's 1997 discussion of "sophisticated liberalism"). Polanyi (1944) emphasized not pure laissez faire but the importance of social protection to the stability of an open international economy. Ruggie (1982) adds, with his concept of "embedded liberalism," the idea of a shared social purpose. Garrett (1998) contends, against contrary interpretations, that the experience of the Organization for Economic Cooperation and Development (OECD) countries is consistent with interdependence, growth, and social democracy.

This shared social purpose can be expressed in economic terms, as providing domestic stability by ensuring economic improvement overall while maintaining a minimum standard of social welfare for the poorest. Leaders in Olson's (1993) analysis also share broad interests in society and act to provide stability, low rents, and high levels of public goods. But that is not enough. Consider Nie et al.'s (1996, 19) discussion of democratic citizenship: "Just as formal education is important to political engagement by enabling citizens to recognize and pursue political interests, education, in its effect of democratic enlightenment, also limits the harmful pursuit of self-interest. In the absence of democratic values and norms, and with democratic citizenship as political engagement only, the practice of democracy would be more akin to unbridled freedom" (see also Ostrom 1997, chap. 11).

When governments recognize the first two relationships—societal integration that orders behavior among individuals and groups, and democratic legitimacy that lies at the core of societal behavior toward government—this recognition generates a set of norms about how government ought to behave toward society. Democratic governments are expected to care about people and society in a normative way that goes beyond Olson's economic utility arguments. Evidence for this is perhaps found in studies that suggest that democracies are more respectful of the international law of human rights (Arat 1991; Poe and Tate 1994). Major twentieth-century famines have occurred only in authoritarian states (Sen 1981). Democracies may also be more likely to resist forces causing environmental degradation

(Gleditsch 1997). Midlarsky's (1998b) multivariate analyses dispute this; however, his data set does not include the communist countries.

Many such norms derive from "natural law" (rather than utilitarian) foundations of reciprocity. In Lippmann's (1943, 363) "good society," a key element is the recognition that all humans are "persons" and not "things." "There must be a strong desire to be just. There must be a growing capacity to be just. There must be discernment and sympathy in estimating the particular claims of divergent interests. There must be moral standards which discourage the quest of privilege and the exercise of arbitrary power. . . . There must be patience and tolerance and kindness in hearing claims, in argument, in negotiation, and in reconciliation."

Integration, legitimacy, and the good society together are represented by cultural and structural theories of the democratic peace. Solingen (1996, 84) neatly summarizes the basic conceptual links between democracy and conflict and cooperation: (1) domestic legitimacy and accountability; (2) institutional checks and balances; (3) democratic transparency, communication and the costs of regime creation; (4) democratic process, credibility, and ratification; and (5) sensitivity to the human and material costs of war. To the degree these forces actually come together in democracies, they help account for the preference orderings of democratic leaders, and thus for the purposive choices of those leaders. Similar elements of a liberal international system may also provide elements for a more just international society (Brilmayer 1994; MacMillan 1998).

Notes

We are grateful to John Oneal, James Lee Ray, and Randolph Siverson for comments, and to the Carnegie Corporation of New York, the Ford Foundation, the National Science Foundation and the World Society Foundation of Switzerland for financial support.

1. Beck, Katz, and Tucker's methods of controlling for the effects of time dependence, as well as their suggestions for estimating statistical significance using robust standard errors that take into account the clustering of data by dyads, remove previous concerns (e.g., Spiro 1994) that the democratic peace result was not statistically significant due to noninterdependence of observations.
2. Russett (1995, 1996) addresses some of the early objections raised by critics of the democratic peace. The most thorough analysis and response to the quantitative critiques is by Maoz (1997a, 1998). A new edited collection (Elman 1997) employs a comparative case-study method to reach mixed con-

clusions and suggest some modifications, but it is marred by conceptual inconsistencies and the absence of any clear research design to guide case selection. A proper framework for case studies must avoid selection bias and address the mystery of the dogs that do not bark. Focusing just on crises between democracies to determine whether their political regime type was critical to avoiding war ignores, for example, the question of why militarized disputes between them are so rare. The existence of a dispute is a dependent variable as well as an independent variable in the chain of events leading from peace to war. One might address this question by comparing crisis behavior in enduring rivalries that are at some times but not others identified as jointly democratic, or by systematically comparing cases of crisis bargaining and management between democracies to such behavior between otherwise comparable autocracies or democratic-autocratic pairs.

3. The low frequency of democratic-democratic escalations is important, since some game-theoretic perspectives suggest that a strong and well-known aversion to the initiation of wars between democracies could lead them, for bargaining purposes, to initiate or escalate crises between themselves knowing that the process would stop short of full-scale war. One recent study (Senese 1997a) claims evidence for within-crisis escalation between democracies, but uses a more problematic escalation scale than do Rousseau et al. (1996).
4. Peceny (1997) makes this point about the Spanish-American War in the context of a constructivist argument. Oren (1995) and Bachteler (1997) carry the constructivist perspective further. We believe it more useful simply to recognize the probability that to some degree perceptions will vary concerning political regimes that are marginal in terms of the standard categories of analyses—and the categories themselves will vary over some historical contexts.
5. Such a "contending" approach is antithetical to the Most and Starr (1989) admonition that rather than asking which theory is right and which is wrong, we need to ask how both could be right—that is, under what conditions each would be more likely to hold. Thus, each could have relevance under different conditions, and each could have important interactive effects with the other.
6. Schweller (1992) reports that dominant democracies, when declining in power relative to a challenger, do not initiate preventive wars. Democracies' tendency to be satisfied with the status quo, even a somewhat decaying one (see later) would account for this. Preventive wars, however, typically are deliberately planned and initiated to meet a growing threat, whereas preemptive wars arise out of crisis conditions favoring the side that makes a first strike.
7. This assumes that voters are "rational," stable in their opinions, and reasonably well informed on foreign policy questions. Almond (1950) contended they were not, but more recent work supports the affirmative. See Graham (1988), Nincic (1992), Page and Shapiro (1992), and Russett (1990).

8. Another example is the research project of Hermann and Kegley (1995), focusing on the effect of governmental leadership and the social-psychological factors that influence the choices of leaders.
9. When we look closely at the components of the Deutschian social-communication model of the integration process as well as the neofunctional process model of Haas (1958), we find all the primary components of the two main theories used to explain the dyadic democratic peace. The structural constraints model involves the constraints of interdependence, organizations, and formal laws or constitutions; the democratic culture argument involves the presence of community, responsiveness, shared values, and norms. Thus, key components of the two basic explanations of how the democratic peace works are found in the two basic theories of integration.

The Power Transition Research Program

Assessing Theoretical and Empirical Advances

JACEK KUGLER and DOUGLAS LEMKE

Introduction

Ten years ago Kugler and Organski (1989) summarized the theoretical and empirical advances offered by the research tradition spawned by Organski's power transition theory. Since then a great deal of cumulative work has been added by a variety of scholars employing a wide range of analytic tools. Our task here is to revisit Kugler and Organski's "retrospective and prospective evaluation" by describing these subsequent contributions. Such a revisiting is especially appropriate in the case of the power transition research program, because the past decade has seen a dramatic increase in attention given to it, demonstrated by the number of books and articles as well as by the increasing acceptance of the importance of the work's central components within international conflict studies.

What follows is not simply a laundry list of disparate empirical findings or disconnected conceptual musings. Rather, it is an account of the progress of an intellectually integrated research program. The empirical and theoretical extensions discussed in this chapter are interconnected; they inform and build cumulatively upon each other. In this way, power transition research offers an explanation of international relations generally, rather than a more limited account of international war. It allows us to understand seemingly diverse phenomena, while simultaneously indicating what it cannot help us understand, where future elaboration is necessary, and what subsidiary hypotheses must be true if the basic arguments are valid.

To describe these advances fully, we must start by summarizing power transition itself. After providing a short description, we discuss in some detail the impressive empirical evidence that has been produced in its support. We review past and ongoing research on the power transition, highlighting both theoretical and empirical progress. We then compare power transition to a number of similar theories in international relations research, noting where these other theories converge or diverge, in order to indicate clearly where in the extant literature power transition falls. We also explore implications of power transition research for the nuclear environment as well as for the possible future course of international relations. We close with a brief discussion of how power transition arguments address or even subsume a number of existing strands of international relations inquiry generally seen as unconnected to the power transition research program, and we describe some of the implications of this work for policy-making.

We make, and attempt to substantiate, some rather grand claims about the explanatory capabilities of power transition research. We look forward to continued debate about these claims and anticipate continued interest in this research program. At a minimum, we believe power transition should be considered a major contender for explanations of international phenomena by any serious researcher.

Fundamental Elements of Power Transition Research

Power transition arguments have been part of the scholarly debate about international relations for more than 40 years now. Originally advanced as a competitor to balance-of-power theories by Organski (1958), some of its propositions were first explicitly evaluated empirically by Organski and Kugler in *The War Ledger* (1980). Over the years many scholars have commented on power transition at some length (see, inter alia, Claude 1962, 57–58; Levy 1985b, 353–54; Vasquez 1993, 98–107), providing productive critiques but occasionally obscuring various components. To be clear about what we mean by power transition, we provide a brief review of what we think it is and is not. In short, the fundamental elements uniting all power transition research are concerns with the importance of *internal* growth for *international* politics, a focus on international *hierarchy* rather than *anarchy,* and the importance of *relative power* and *evaluations of the international status quo* in anticipation of interstate war.

The international system described by power transition research involves an international hierarchy of power and privilege. Organski (1958, 326–33) provides great detail about the international "power pyramid" with a dominant power at the apex, below which are the rest of the great powers: the major powers, the middle powers, and then the minor powers. Relations within this hierarchical international system are not anarchical in spite of the fact that formal rules and enforced international laws are nonexistent. Rather, there are established "patterns" or "international orders" (Organski 1958, 315–16) to international interactions, labeled "the status quo" (Organski 1958, 325). This status quo concerns economic, political, and military relations. It reflects the distribution of value (Kugler and Organski 1989, 173) within international relations such that to be advantaged by the status quo means one's state will be richer, more prestigious, more secure than it otherwise would be. According to power transition theory, the dominant power establishes the status quo when it ascends to its premier position. This is usually in the wake of a global war from which the dominant power emerged victorious.

The dominant power creates and maintains the international status quo in order to further its own long-term interests. According to power transition the motivation for state behavior is the maximization of net gains (Kugler and Organski 1989, 172). To secure more net gains, more value, from its international interactions, the dominant power creates self-serving patterns of interaction. Thus, a wealthy free-market dominant power will likely create a liberal economic order, a democratic dominant power will most likely create democratically operating international political institutions. Given its favored position in the international system, a dominant power of any stripe should be expected to create defensive military alliances. Such established orders together compose the status quo. Once established, the dominant power preserves these orders, preserves stability, because it expects to profit in the long run by doing so. The more other states are similar in domestic composition and international outlook to the dominant power, the more they too will benefit from the status quo. These states that also benefit are "satisfied with the status quo" (Organski 1958, 326–33).

Unfortunately for international peace, there are always some members of the international system who do not benefit from the status quo. Generally they were weak when the existing status quo was established.

And as their internal organization differs widely from that of the dominant power, they are disadvantaged by the status quo. These states are the "dissatisfied," and their dissatisfaction makes them desire to alter the prevailing international order. So long as the dominant power remains preponderant it can preserve the status quo. However, when a dominant power declines relative to a dissatisfied state so that they are roughly equal in power, it may no longer be able to preserve the status quo by threats, coercion, and deterrence. At parity the dissatisfied challenger can press its demands for change with the expectation of being able to substantiate these demands militarily. At such times major war is anticipated between the dominant power and the newly risen challenger. The war is fought for nothing less than control of the international status quo, and is thus costly.

Given the story told by power transition, one might reasonably ask how a dominant power could ever lose its leading position? How could parity ever be reached given that the dominant power has a head start and establishes international patterns in a self-benefiting way? The response to the objection highlights an oft-ignored aspect of power transition, the emphasis on domestic growth as *the* source of national power. Domestic growth is so central that initially the term *power transition* referred to the process by which a country develops domestically (it undergoes a transition from underdeveloped to developed; see Organski 1958, 300–306; for related arguments from economics, see Lucas 1988; Romer 1986). Thus, the dominant power begins its reign advantaged and receives benefits from its position, but it cannot prevent the internal development of dissatisfied states. The demographic transition (Davis 1948, chap. 21; Organski and Organski 1961; Organski et al. 1984) describes the internal process by which population changes drive development, which in turn increases national power. To prevent a dissatisfied state from rising in power, the dominant power would have to subvert its domestic demographic and economic transition.

Power transition maintains that even though benefits are to be had from international interaction, national power is, at base, determined by domestic processes. If the international status quo does not help a country develop, it can still develop in isolation. This requires ingenuity from domestic leaders and resilience from followers, but it is possible. Arguably this is exactly the situation faced by Germany between the world wars, or by the Soviet Union in the 1930s through the 1950s. In spite of a status quo that was economically, politically, and militarily contrary to German and Soviet interests, both managed to develop. Their experiences provide a concrete example of why there can be rich and powerful dissatisfied states: they became rich and powerful *in spite of* the status quo. Even when such a state becomes as rich and powerful as the dominant state, it remains dissatisfied because it would have had an easier time developing had the status quo been different. Further, it would still benefit more from a revision to the international status quo.[1]

Some scholars characterize power transition as simply another realist account of international relations (e.g., Lebow 1994a). Given the emphasis on relative power relations, such mislabeling is understandable. However, power transition is fundamentally different from realist thought. Specifically, realists believe that the international system is anarchic, and that all actors react identically to a given stimuli. In contrast, power transition posits that states will not react to international imperatives in the same ways unless they share similar evaluations of the status quo. Satisfied states agree that the status quo should be maintained. They thus have nothing over which to fight. Should a satisfied state undergo a power transition and catch up with the dominant power, there is little or no expectation of war.[2] However, should a dissatisfied state undergo a power transition and catch up, the expectation is that war will likely occur. In both instances the international stimuli is the same (a power transition leading to parity), but the expected behavior is very different. This important emphasis on status quo evaluations clearly distinguishes power transition from realism, and it links domestic and international politics within a single perspective.

In sum, power transition research provides an account of international relations that allows us to anticipate when peace will occur as well as when major wars are expected.[3] It offers an alternative to realist arguments because satisfied states are argued to behave fundamentally differently with each other than they do with dissatisfied states. The research also describes how the international system comes to have the international orders or status quo that it does, as well as how this can change. This is a lot to expect from any single theoretical school, and yet there is still much that power transition has not yet illuminated. For example, power transition research has only perfunctorily explored when wars between any states other than the dominant power and the main dissatisfied challenger might occur (although the multiple hierarchy extensions described later have greatly expanded such exploration). It has said little or nothing about interactions among dissatisfied states and has been generally mute about relations that do not concern the dominant power. In spite of these limitations, this research tradition has much value. There is also much empirical evidence in its support. We turn to a discussion of this evidence.

Early Power Transition Research

Power transition posits a hypothetical international system and then tells a story to explain behavior therein. To be of value, the hypothetical system it describes must be similar enough to the real world that the propositions advanced are consistent with historical experience. The main propositions of interest to most scholars have been those that specify when war is likely to occur. Thus, status quo evaluations and the presence or absence of power parity are the critical predictor variables identified by past research.

A review of the extant empirical literature on international conflict turns up many articles and books that include either relative power relationships or status quo evaluations as the central independent variables or include them as control variables in other analyses of conflict.[4] Many of these studies are not directly relevant to evaluations of power transition because they include all dyads, or all great power dyads. Technically, power transition research only makes predictions about dyads that include the dominant power, and thus true tests of power transition's war hypotheses have a very limited empirical domain indeed. However, these other dyadic studies are reviewed because they establish how important power parity or status quo evaluations are generally. Further, recent extensions of power transition arguments to minor power regional systems suggest power transition's empirical domain might be larger than originally specified, and thus we might be able to anticipate a more general relationship between parity and war, or between status quo dissatisfaction and war, beyond merely those dyads that include the dominant power.[5]

A number of studies comparing various dyadic power distributions and the incidence of international conflict have been conducted. Weede (1976) reports that overwhelming power preponderance (a ratio of 10-to-1 or more) is a pacifying condition among contiguous Asian dyads, at least over the years 1950–69. In a pair of studies, Garnham (1976a, 1976b) reverses Weede's focus by asking whether neighboring states that war on each other are more nearly equal in power than are neighbors that do not war on each other. Garnham's conclusion is that power parity characterizes warring neighbors much more than it does peaceful neighbors. These three studies were the first to evaluate dyadic power and conflict propositions empirically. They suggest, in their limited spatial and temporal domains, that parity is associated with war while preponderance is associated with peace. The three studies thus provide, admittedly limited, support for power transition.

Another piece of evidence in favor of power transition expectations is offered by Bremer (1980), who empirically investigates the war propensity of nations at various power ranks. For example, if it is true that great powers are involved in more wars than minor powers, is it the case that the most powerful state is the most war prone? Of specific interest to power transition proponents is Bremer's finding that the number two nation, what power transition identifies as the challenger, has the highest relative frequency of war initiations (1980, 69). Since power transition identifies the challenger as the initiator of the war with the dominant power (Organski 1958, 325; Organski and Kugler 1980, 19), Bremer's finding provides some measure of support for the empirical veracity of the story power transition tells.

A similarly intriguing clue is offered by a pair of studies that evaluate the extent to which the presence of a dominant power or, in the phrase preferred in these studies, a *hegemon* pacifies international relations. Spiezio (1990) reports that as British power declined from 1815 to 1939, war involvement by major powers increased. Similarly, Volgy and Imwalle (1995) find considerable evidence that the greater the support for and power of the hegemon, the less violent the international system was in the post–World War II period. These findings are relevant to power transition because the dominant power behaves like a hegemon in its creation and maintenance of the status quo. If powerful dominant powers/hegemons are better able to keep the peace in the real world, we have increased confidence in power transition.

Yet another clue suggesting that power transition is descriptively accurate of the real world is found in a pair of studies about the duration and costliness of war. Both Cannizzo (1980) and Bennett and Stam (1996) find that wars fought between unequal states are generally shorter and less costly than are wars fought between more equal adversaries. Power transition anticipates wars fought between rough equals to control the international status quo are the most costly of wars (Organski and Kugler 1980, 45–47). Cannizzo's and Bennett and Stam's findings regarding the relationship between relative power and the nature of the subsequent war is thus consistent with power transition expectations.

Aside from these clues and early general findings, numerous direct tests have also been conducted. The first intentional test of power transition, *The War Ledger* (Organski and Kugler 1980), specifically compares power distributions within contender (the very strongest of great powers) dyads to the incidence of great power war and finds that a condition of being "equal and overtaking" is a necessary condition for such wars. All five warring great power dyads in their data set were warring in the presence or immediate aftermath of a power transition. In their evaluation Organski and Kugler also observe five great power dyads undergoing transitions but not going to war.

Following Organski and Kugler's work, Houweling and Siccama (1988), Kim (1989), and Gochman (1990b) evaluate power transition's central claim that a transition which brings a challenger to equality with the dominant state increases the probability of war. These subsequent studies broaden the empirical domain to include all major power dyads. Houweling and Siccama find a stronger relationship between power transitions and wars than Organski and Kugler report;[6] Gochman finds that power parity is associated with war for all major power dyads, and also for Latin American rivals. Kim reports a strong relationship when the expected contributions of potential third-party joiners are included in the calculations of dyadic power relations. These studies are supportive of power transition, but not perfectly congruent because they include dyads in which the dominant power is not a member.

In a more recent effort, Lemke and Werner (1996) compare the dyadic distribution of power and war experience of great power dyads *only if* those dyads include the dominant power. They employ multiple measures of power (Correlates of War [COW] composite capabilities index, Gross Domestic Product) and consider both dynamic power balances (whether or not a transition has occurred) and the static distribution of power. They report that regardless of the measure of power or the specific operationalization of parity, there is a positive relationship between power parity and war in dyads that include the dominant power.[7] By focusing only on dyads including the dominant state, Lemke and Werner limit the number of cases for analysis, but their results are thus most directly relevant to power transition's war hypothesis. They provide the strongest evidence in its favor to date.

This discussion has focused exclusively on empirical evaluations of power transition's expectation of a relationship between power parity and interstate war. However, power transition places equal or greater emphasis on the importance of status quo evaluations in the onset of such conflicts. Only when *dissatisfied* states rise to parity with the dominant state is war anticipated. All of the results discussed in the preceding evaluate power transition without consideration of status quo evaluations. In this way they offer incomplete support. The most likely reason for the failure to include this important variable is that for a long time there was no empirical measure of status quo evaluations. Fortunately, in the last decade a number of creative measures have been developed.

In a detailed analysis of the Seven Weeks War, Bueno de Mesquita (1990) offers a measure that could be used to indicate status quo evaluations. He suggests that changes in money market discount rates (how a nation's currency is valued relative to other currencies) may indicate the level of satisfaction or dissatisfaction the people of that state feel for the international status quo. If a nation's money market discount rate were in decline, the people of that country would be able to buy less with their money, and consequently would be dissatisfied. If, in reverse, the discount rate were climbing and the people could buy more goods, they would be satisfied. Unfortunately for power transition, Bueno de Mesquita reports both Austria and Prussia were satisfied with the status quo when they fought in 1866.

Since Bueno de Mesquita's initial study others have offered measures of status quo evaluations. Kim (1991) correctly interprets power transition to suggest that satisfied states should think about international affairs and act in international matters in ways similar to the dominant power. Specifically, he argues satisfied states should form alliances similar to those formed by the dominant power. If the dominant power feels that protecting country X with a military alliance is important, other satisfied states should be disposed to favor protecting country X with an alliance. Kim measures the degree of alliance similarity between each state and the dominant country by employing Bueno de Mesquita's (1975) "tau b" measure of alliance portfolio similarity. In a series of empirical evaluations Kim (1991, 1992, 1996) demonstrates that status quo evaluations are powerful predictors of wars among major powers. In fact, he concludes that status quo evaluations are more important empirically than is power parity in anticipating major power wars.

In a related attempt, Werner and Kugler (1996) focus on the behavior of rising and declining states, looking for indications that the rising state might be dissatisfied with the status quo. They observe whether or not the rising state is undergoing an extraordinary military buildup. If the rising state increases its military expenditures at a rate greater than it has in the past, and greater than any buildup the dominant state might be undergoing, they designate that challenger as dissatisfied. The absence of a buildup as parity approaches is indicative of acceptance of the status quo by the challenger. In their empirical evaluation they find that Organski and Kugler's power transitions followed by wars involved challengers undergoing extraordinary military buildups, while the transitions not followed by wars generally lacked such arms increases. Subsequently, Lemke and Werner (1996) employ Werner and Kugler's measure in their analysis of dyads including the dominant power and find very strong support for power transition's expectation that parity and dissatisfaction are jointly dangerous correlates of war.

A large body of work has been created to evaluate the empirical claims advanced by the power transition research program. Virtually all of this evidence is supportive, either partially or entirely. However, a large number of studies also employ the central components of power transition (power parity and/or status quo evaluations) as important explanatory variables or as control variables, generally justified with some reference to the work of Organski or Organski and Kugler. We review some of these studies here, because they suggest a growing general acceptance of the importance of power parity and status quo evaluations by scholars of international relations.

In his two articles identifying which characteristics of dyads make them especially disputatious, Bremer (1992, 1993) consistently finds that the presence of preponderance reduces the probability of conflict. This pacifying impact of preponderance is consistent with Weede's much earlier analysis, with power transition's general expectation that parity is associated with war, and holds even in the presence of a large number of additional control variables. Similarly, in their authoritative evaluation of the democratic peace proposition, Maoz and Russett (1993) report that the more unequal two states are, the less likely they will experience a militarized interstate dispute. This result holds in the presence of five or six other known correlates of war. In an analysis of conflict initiation, Huth, Bennett, and Gelpi (1992) consider 14 independent variables. They find that the occurrence of a power transition within a dyad increases the probability of a militarized interstate dispute by almost 10 percent, holding all the other variables constant. Huth and Russett (1993) report that within rivalries, the occurrence of a power transition increases the probability of war by more than 21 percent. In their analysis of ethnopolitical conflict, Davis and Moore (1997) find that overwhelming preponderance (a 10-to-1 ratio or more) has a consistently negative impact on conflict relations. Apparently such overwhelming preponderance can dampen even ethnic conflict. Finally, in their ambitious study of democratic peace and liberal interdependence arguments, Oneal and Russett (1997) include relative power relations as a control variable. They find that as the members of a dyad are increasingly unequal, the probability of a militarized interstate dispute between them decreases. The studies reviewed in this paragraph use a wide range of empirical domains and operational definitions of relative power relationships. They also include a wealth of additional variables that could be argued to account for the relationship power transition proponents claim to have found between parity and war and between preponderance and peace. That these additional studies also find evidence of a pacifying effect of preponderance and bellicose effect of parity strongly suggests how robust the relationship is.

Scholars have also begun to employ status quo evaluations as an important concept in their analyses of international conflict. Ray (1995) claims the Fashoda crisis did not escalate to war because Britain was preponderant over France *and* favored the status quo. By contrast, the newly powerful United States had an advantage over Spain in the late 1890s, favored changes to the status quo, and thus the Spanish-American War occurred. It should be pointed out that Ray is talking about a dyadic status quo, mostly the distribution of peripheral territories between the involved states, and not about the international status quo of power transition. However, in spite of this difference the notion of dissatisfaction being the motivation for international conflict is directly comparable. In other studies, Rousseau, Gelpi, Reiter, and Huth (1996) find that the party to a dispute dissatisfied with the status quo is more likely to initiate the use of force than is a party satisfied with the status quo. Finally, in an analysis of the diversionary hypothesis, Gelpi (1997) reports that states satisfied with the status quo at issue in a crisis are dramatically less likely to give in to domestic pressures to divert attention abroad by initiating the use of force. None of these studies use the term *status quo evaluation* exactly as a power transition researcher would, but they all use the same sorts of underlying conceptualizations of dissatisfaction increasing the likelihood of conflict, and of satisfaction decreasing it.

In short, there is much direct and indirect evidence in favor of power transition's claim that power parity between the dominant power and a dissatisfied challenger is a very dangerous situation. The empirical relationship between parity and war, and between status quo dissatisfaction and war, appear to occur across a wide range of spatial and temporal domains, exist across a large number of different data sets and operational definitions, and persist even in the presence of a wealth of alternate correlates of war. Also indicative of the importance of these variables is the increasingly widespread use of them in so many analyses not specifically geared to evaluation of power transition hypotheses.

Ongoing Power Transition Research

Power transition research initially was limited to a description of great power interactions within an international hierarchy. In this original form it was limited to description of interactions between the very strongest of states with the strongest state. It anticipated wars among the great powers. Consequently, the research program was unable to illuminate a great deal of additional international behavior. Relations between minor powers, or even those within great power dyads not including the dominant state, were largely outside the research program's purview. In terms of war, power transition applied to world wars only.

Great power interactions comprise an important area of international behavior, especially as world wars are generally the most costly and destructive of social events. However, such interactions omit *most* of international relations. To enlarge power transition's empirical relevance, the multiple hierarchy model of power transition has been developed in recent years.

The multiple hierarchy model (Lemke 1993, 1995b, 1996) suggests that minor power regional hierarchical international systems exist and operate much like the overall international system of the original power transition research. Where Organski (1958) and Organski and Kugler (1980) write of an international hierarchy directed by the dominant power, Lemke's emendation envisions multiple local hierarchies subordinate, but directly comparable, to the overall global hierarchy. The multiple hierarchy model suggests that many of these local power hierarchies exist, each with a local dominant power that establishes and defends a local status quo. Over time, differential growth rates change relative power standings within the local hierarchies. If a local challenger dissatisfied with the local status quo achieves power parity with the local dominant state, war between these local contenders is anticipated. Similarities with expectations at the global level are obvious. The multiple hierarchy model suggests that the patterns of relations between great powers are more general than power transition researchers originally recognized.

This simple enlargement of power transition's empirical domain raises a number of difficult subsidiary questions. First, which minor powers interact with which other minor powers sufficiently to qualify as a local hierarchy? Further, what types of interaction are relevant to each local status quo? Finally, if the global dominant power establishes a global status quo, wouldn't each local status quo be influenced by the dominant power as well as by other great powers? Put more generally, would interference by great powers in minor powers' local hierarchies represent a fundamental difference in minor power relations compared with the great power relations described in the original version of power transition?

These questions have been addressed at varying length. Local hierarchies have been defined conceptually and empirically by the ability to interact militarily. Lemke (1993, 1995a, 2000) offers an empirical description of "relevant neighborhoods" within which minor powers can exert military influence. Where these neighborhoods overlap, Lemke defines local hierarchies to exist. He then evaluates whether power parity and dissatisfaction with the status quo increase the probability of war within local hierarchies. The second question, what comprises the local status quo, has been addressed to a much more limited extent. Lemke (1995b) and Lemke and Werner (1996) suggest that a local status quo most likely concerns issues omitted from the international status quo because they are primarily of local interest. Such issues might include access to strategic territory or transit routes, important cultural or religious sites, or the ability to exploit natural resources. Finally, the question of great power interference has only been tangentially addressed and thus remains as an important area for continued research.

Does the multiple hierarchy model have any empirical validity? The preliminary answer appears to be that it does. Evaluation of local hierarchical relations in South America (Lemke 1993, 1996; Lemke and Werner 1996), the Middle East (Lemke 1995c), and the Far East (Lemke 1997b, 2000) suggests that power parity and status quo dissatisfaction are important predictors of war within local hierarchies, just as they are within the global hierarchy. Power parity appears to be less important empirically than does status quo dissatisfaction in accounting for minor power wars, and this too seems to mirror the findings at the global level (at least as reported by Kim 1991, 1992, and by Lemke and Werner 1996). It appears that the underlying logic of the original power transition research might be a great deal more general than its creators anticipated. If so, this is further evidence of the importance of the power transition tradition.[8]

The multiple hierarchy model's effort to generalize power transition beyond the great powers is indicative of only one area of ongoing research within the power transition tradition. A number of other issues provide incentives for continued inquiry. These include questions about the relationship between the specific manner by which parity is obtained and the probability of war (i.e., are faster-growing challengers more likely to be involved in war?), whether wars occur before or after parity is obtained, and why dominant powers do not wage preventive war against rising challengers.

A trio of formalized versions of power transition arguments have not only redemonstrated the logical consistency of the theory (already established by Bueno de Mesquita 1980b, 380, and Bueno de Mesquita and Lalman 1992, 217) but also begun to address these persisting vexing questions.

Abdollahian (1996) and Kadera (1996) utilize differential equation models to explore the dynamics central to power transition. This approach formally specifies the tenets of power transition, showing that the speed of overtaking, the commitment of contenders to preserving or recasting the status quo and the probability of war are all related. Further, the work of Abdollahian and Kadera suggests that the specific ways in which these factors are interrelated determines the timing (relative to actual overtaking), severity, and duration of any war that does occur. Their deductions, consistent with each other, are that faster overtakings should lead to more serious but less likely wars (this differs from Organski's [1958, 335] original anticipation that faster transitions made war *more* likely). Further, they deduce how very important status quo evaluations are. Finally, they both find logical support for the expectation that power parity between the dominant state and a dissatisfied challenger is dangerous. In both of these models, the objective is not simply to anticipate when war will be initiated but also to account for its timing, severity, and duration.

Abdollahian and Kadera's results are consistent with those obtained from a dynamic game-theoretic model offered by Alsharabati (1997). Alsharabati also demonstrates that relative power, status quo evaluations, actors' risk propensities, and the speed of the challenger's growth are directly related to the probability and characteristics of war. Basically, Alsharabati's model depicts a situation in which the dominant state and a challenger consider their utility for waging war now versus some time later in a finite time interval. The two actors discount what they would get if they waged war and won (revision of the status quo) at some point, against what they currently enjoy (peace and the existing status quo). Each actor thus weighs the potential gains and losses from fighting at any given point against the potential gains and losses that would follow from war later in the time interval of interest.

A number of fascinating deductions follow from Alsharabati's model. First, she deduces a counterintuitive relationship between the speed of the challenger's growth and the probability of war. Very fast growth can actually preserve peace, since the challenger may not need to wage war in order to secure changes to the status quo. If it grows fast enough, the dominant power will simply have to give in (the alternative is to fight a war it cannot win). Moderate growth is the most dangerous, because the challenger then anticipates a long delay in satisfying its aspirations. As expected, if the challenger's growth is insufficient to propel it into parity with the dominant state, no war is anticipated because the challenger will forecast that it cannot win. A second fascinating implication concerns the character and probability of war before versus after the actual overtaking. Organski (1958, 325) originally argued wars would occur before the actual overtaking, while Organski and Kugler (1980, 59) report that most wars follow the overtaking. Alsharabati's model suggests both expectations may be right. In brief, she deduces that the probability of war is higher *prior* to the overtaking, but that such wars will be of low severity. Conversely, the probability of war *after* the overtaking is lower than before, but when wars do occur after the overtaking, they are expected to be much more severe.[9] Finally, Alsharabati deduces that the declining state *will not* wage preventive or preemptive war on the rising challenger. The myopic dominant state that waits for the challenger to attack it has long been a problem for power transition proponents. Alsharabati's model dismisses the description of the dominant state as myopic in that she suggests the moment of greatest utility for preempting is at the very beginning of the game's time interval. The dominant state will not enjoy any policy gains from defeating the challenger as the existing status quo will be maintained. So, with no net gain to be had, the only variable the dominant state can consider is its probability of victory. Since the dominant state declines in relative power monotonically through the time interval of her dynamic game model, its probability of victory also declines monotonically. Thus, if it is to attack at all, it should do so at the very first instant. Perhaps the most important contribution of Alsharabati's model is her demonstration that even with complete information and certainty among decision makers, war is possible *even if* it would involve nuclear weapons. Previous models (like Schelling's [1960] and Powell's [1990]) have argued that nuclear war was possible only under uncertainty. Alsharabati's is a chilling deduction.

These formal representations of power transition demonstrate the consistency of the logic of the research program. They also suggest possible routes for continued empirical evaluation. Cumulatively, Abdollahian's, Kadera's, and Alsharabati's work suggest we should pay more attention to the empirical importance of the speed of the challenger's growth, the risk propensities of the actors, and the characteristics of the wars that do occur. These are important and helpful redirections.

A final area of ongoing research within the power transition tradition concerns the importance of the consequences of war not only in understanding international war itself, but also in understanding the character of the international system in the aftermath of wars. Such research is important to power transition for two reasons. First, if it is the case that the international status quo is established by a newly victorious dominant power in the aftermath of war, then how wars end, who wins wars, and how international relations change due to war are all important questions for power transition researchers. Additionally, it is important for power transition researchers to study the consequences of war because if wars stall national growth, then it would be very unlikely that a defeated challenger would be able to recover and challenge again unless a great deal of time passed between the challenges.

Spurred by this second concern, Organski and Kugler (1977) investigate the consequences of war on subsequent growth of great powers. They report the existence of a "phoenix factor"; within 20 years of the conclusion of major wars the participants not only have recovered to prewar levels of power, but have even recovered to levels they would have been expected to have achieved had the war never occurred. Great powers literally rise from the ashes of war, much as the mythological bird from whom the phenomenon draws its name. Subsequent research by Kugler and Arbetman (1989) and by Arbetman (1996) suggests the phoenix factor operates among minor power conflict participants as well.

Although the phoenix factor represents only one analysis of the consequences of war, it has contributed to a more serious study of these consequences than otherwise might have been undertaken. Other analyses of war termination and consequences not only are important to power transition research but also might all be made sense of with respect to power transition expectations. Rasler and Thompson (1985a) demonstrate that great power governments grow larger as a consequence of wars, and that the larger the scale of the war, the greater the growth of the government. This is consistent with power transition's expectation of wars among great powers being severe and requiring tremendous mobilization and is also consistent with notions of power being fundamentally driven by domestic politics and development. Siverson and Starr (1994) report that the alliance portfolios of states change, sometimes dramatically, when they are defeated in war. This is potentially consistent with the reorientation of the international status quo in the aftermath of wars. Finally, Werner (1996) reports that the probability of a foreign-imposed regime change in the wake of war is greater the more domestically dissimilar the victor and vanquished are. When we recall that dissatisfied states are expected to be internally dissimilar to the dominant power, such a finding is consistent with notions of wars between states with disparate status quo evaluations being more severe and internationally consequential. Although power transition research was not the prime motivation for much of this consequences of war literature, it offers a lens within which to connect and interpret these findings.

Strategic Implications of Power Transition Research

Power transition research offers a number of important implications for analysts of international security. A first relevant area concerns the likely near-future of the international system, and more specifically who the likely future challengers and dominant powers will be. In so doing, power transition indicates which states might be involved in a new world war, as well as who might establish the next status quo. A second area in which power transition offers important strategic implications concerns the potential use and proliferation of nuclear weapons.

Power transition identifies the challengers as the most powerful of states, countries conceivably able to challenge the dominant power for control of the international system. To be able to do this, they must have the ability to achieve rough equality with the dominant state. Thus, powerful countries growing even more powerful are the contenders. For most of the post–World War II period, the Soviet Union was the main contender to American dominance. The Soviet population exceeded that of the United States (important since power transition research identifies demographic resources as the ultimate source of power),[10] and Soviet economic growth was very impressive. However, the internal inconsistencies of central planning and the many failings of the Soviet political system have removed Russia from consideration as a contender, at least for the foreseeable future. Should Russia recover and begin to develop rapidly again, it might well reemerge as a potential challenger. More likely the current and near-future challenger to American dominance is the People's Republic of China. With more than one billion people and some of the fastest economic growth on record, China looks certain to achieve parity with the United States early in the next century. Should China evaluate the status quo negatively (a strong possibility given the domestic differences between China's and America's political and economic systems), power transition anticipates war between them. This potential is the most dire implication of power transition research.

After China who are the likely contenders for dominant power status according to power transition? India's enormous population always makes it a potential future contender. Some estimate that India will have a population larger than China's within the next few decades. Should Indian development ever really take off, India will become the most powerful state in the world. When and if it does, it will surely be a contender. Who else might be a contender? A unified Europe could possess enough resources in aggregate to claim the premier international position. Such union would have to be nearly total and is thus unlikely, but remains a possibility. Other potential aggregations of states could create new political entities that might challenge whoever is then the dominant power.[11]

A great deal of work has investigated the implications of power transition arguments within a nuclear environment as well. The same logic suggesting the bellicosity of power parity also implies that under nuclear asymmetry stability and peace can be maintained, but that under nuclear parity a conventional conflict can escalate to nuclear war. Thus, unlike classical deterrence arguments that see ultimate stability following from secure second strike capacities, the implication from power transition theory is that symmetry among nuclear arsenals (even at levels that assure mutual destruction) combined with conventional parity sets the stage for not only war, but also nuclear war (these ideas are developed at more length in Alsharabati 1997; Alsharabati and Kugler 1996; Kugler 1984, 1996; Kugler and Zagare 1987, 1990; Organski 1968; Zagare 1987). These implications are important ones, so we develop them here at some length.

Classical nuclear deterrence theory was advanced by Brodie (1946, 1959) and represented formally by Intriligator and Brito (1984). Figure 1 highlights their arguments. This "weapons plane" is defined by the destructive arsenals of two actors. The further along each axis one goes, the more destructive the arsenal of the corresponding actor. The first set of diagonal lines is often interpreted as the threshold from conventional to nuclear weapons. The second set of diagonal lines represents the threshold from small to large nuclear arsenals. In this representation the structure of deterrence is simply defined by the interaction between two competitors facing potential levels of destruction resulting from military exchanges as the result of conventional or nuclear war.

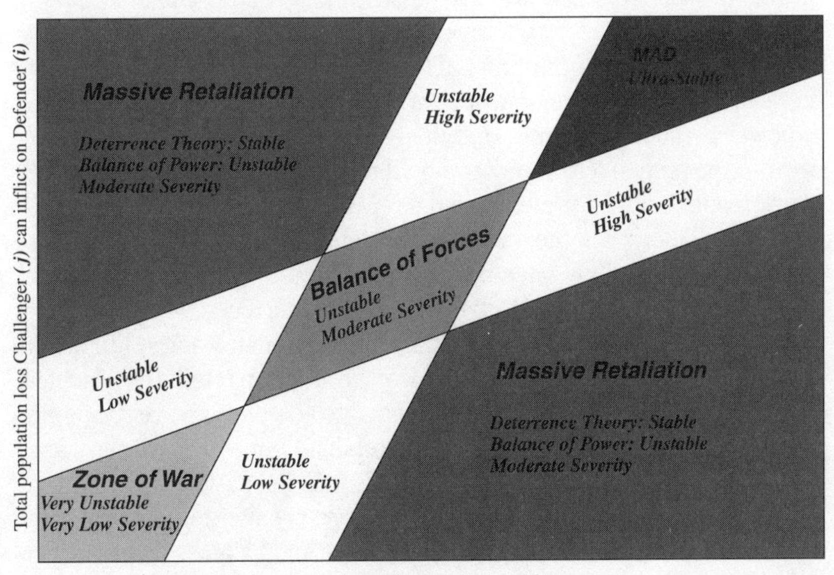

FIGURE 1. The structure of deterrence

Classical nuclear deterrence arguments were derived from balance-of-power theory. Consequently, they suggest stability depends on how high the expected costs of war are. In general, high costs are associated with stability while low costs are associated with war. Thus, the zone of war in the lower left-hand corner of the figure is especially unstable, for conventional war produces relatively low casualties, thereby allowing the possibility of war. In this zone, under strict balance-of-power arguments, war will occur under asymmetry, but nuclear deterrence theory postulates war can be waged regardless of specific power distributions because neither state's arsenal is sufficiently deadly to deter the other. Moving along the line of parity, corresponding to a positively sloping 45° diagonal, as the destructiveness of arsenals increases we find first the "balance of terror" (BOT) and then the "mutual assured destruction" (MAD) zones. They differ fundamentally in their anticipated stability. In the BOT zone nuclear arsenals are limited, and neither side has achieved a secure second strike. Preemption driven by uncertainty is anticipated (Powell 1990; Wohlstetter 1959). In the MAD zone the costs are so high that neither side will initiate or retaliate. Here both nuclear deterrence and balance-of-power theories argue that stability will be maintained as the likelihood of war is minimized by assurances of mutual destruction. Indeed, the zone of MAD is argued to be ultrapeaceful. The two zones of asymmetry are those of "massive retaliation" (MR) where one actor can punish the other with impunity. The MR zones provide some disparity between balance-of-power and nuclear deterrence supporters. The balance-of-power perspective argues that under anarchy, MR should be unstable because the preponderant power would take advantage of its superiority to impose its political preferences (i.e., Waltz 1979). From the perspective of nuclear deterrence theory, however, deterrence would be stable here since nuclear weapons have no use other than to deter war (cf. Brodie 1946). Somewhat counterintuitively, nuclear deterrence theory proposes that any nuclear power under anarchy should not strike first but assure opponents that an aggression will lead to nuclear retaliation. Nuclear deterrence theory, therefore, can be argued to accept the power transition notion that the nuclear nation waits to retaliate but rejects power transition in assuming that the satisfied and dissatisfied nations will act alike. Finally, movement from one zone to another produces uncertainty and could trigger nuclear war. Nuclear deterrence and balance-of-power theories concur that balance is superior to asymmetry since the preponderant nation has the incentive to preempt when an opponent is still weak but threatens to develop nuclear weapons (i.e., Israel vs. Iraq). Likewise, if a nation in nuclear balance were to develop a credible defensive shield, such as the United States proposed to do with the Strategic Defense Initiative, the other nation is expected to preempt to forestall having its destructive potential effectively eliminated.

A fundamentally different picture emerges from power transition. Figure 2 indicates that preponderance in the hands of the status quo defender (what power transition researchers would call the dominant power) is stable, in the hands of the challenger is unstable, and that nuclear parity is dangerous. Thus, from a power transition perspective all of the zones on, above, and to the left of the 45° diagonal are dangerous. Moreover, the farther out along this diagonal we go, the more deadly the resultant war. Power transition does not anticipate that high expected costs deter conflict, thus nuclear deterrence does not offer us the cold comfort of stability even under MAD. It warns that any war that breaks out given the existence of such large arsenals is likely to escalate to nuclear war. According to power transition, stability is found when MR favors the dominant power. When it favors the challenger, demands to change the status quo are expected to be followed by a nuclear war initiated by the challenger. Indeed, had the Soviet Union or Iraq acquired nuclear weapons first in their respective hierarchies, power transition suggests that nuclear war could have been waged. Likewise, the implications under

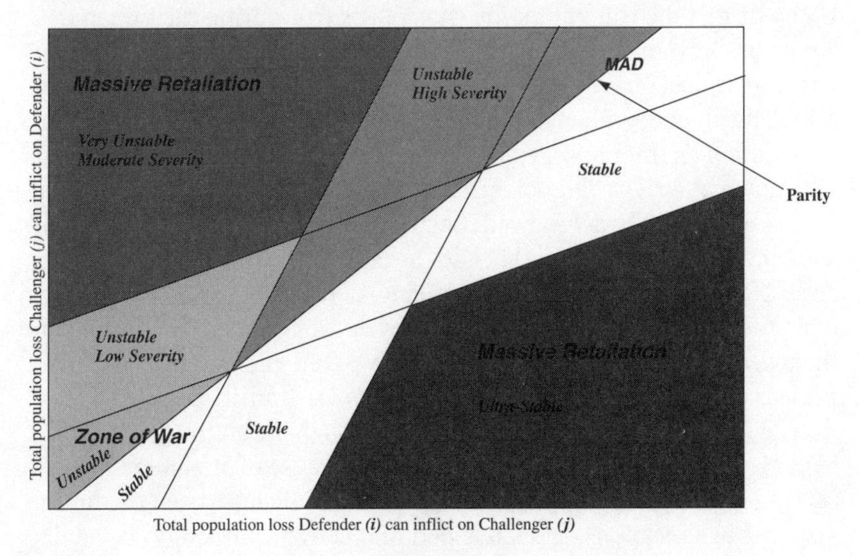

FIGURE 2. Power transistion perspective

MAD are disturbing. A dissatisfied nation that matches the nuclear capacity of the status quo defender is expected to use its capability to advance demands for a new status quo. For this reason, when China reaches power parity with the United States in the next century, the possibility of a nuclear war will rise unless these two nations find a means to reconcile their differences. Similarly, the Middle East with Israel as a nuclear nation and several Arab challengers seeking such capabilities is seen as the most likely region for a potential nuclear war in the coming decades.

Clearly, the implications for nuclear deterrence offered by the nuclear deterrence theory and by power transition could not be more different. Given the likely consequences of a failure to understand whether nuclear deterrence will succeed, knowing which perspective is more accurate becomes extremely important. There is a good bit of indirect evidence, both logical and empirical, to suggest that implications drawn from power transition are consistent with reality. First, some anecdotal empirical evidence: Secure second strike capabilities were not available to both superpowers until the late 1960s or early 1970s. Thus, if the balance-of-power view of nuclear deterrence expectations are correct, crises in this period should have resulted in an American nuclear attack, since the United States had strategic preponderance. Yet the United States did not launch nuclear weapons against China during the Korean War, the Soviet Union during the Hungarian Invasion of 1956 or during the Cuban missile crisis, or against the North Vietnamese during the Vietnam War. Similarly, Israel has for over a decade held nuclear preponderance within the Middle East, and yet has not launched an attack in spite of such strong provocation as Iraqi missile attacks against Israel during the Gulf War. An American or Israeli apologist might be tempted to suggest that the United States and Israel showed constraint because they are "good" countries, presumably imputing that had the tables been turned the Soviets or Arab states would not have shown similar restraint. Such an *apologia* must then confront the fact that the Soviets were similarly restrained in their dealings with China after the Sino-Soviet rift, in spite of Soviet nuclear preponderance over the Chinese. Power transition suggests that in each hierarchy and subhierarchy, even though the status quo defender held nuclear weapons, it did not use them because of its interest in preserving the status quo. In each case, had the challenger been the first to acquire such weapons, the likelihood of nuclear war could not be dismissed.

Perhaps the most troublesome anecdotal evidence confronting classical deterrence proponents is the fact that the superpowers moved *peacefully* from nuclear preponderance to nuclear parity. It is very difficult, based on nuclear deterrence theory arguments, to explain why the United States allowed its nuclear preponderance to be eroded when it could have preserved its superiority via preemption. This scenario has been repeated many times since, and the only exception is Israel's preemptive action against an Iraqi uranium facility in 1982. Additional troubling questions confront nuclear deterrence theory arguments. Once MAD was reached and nuclear war became an impossibility, why did the superpowers take steps consistent with efforts to win a nuclear war? Why did the Soviets develop silos that could be reloaded? Why did the superpowers create strategic triads of land, sea, and air nuclear weapons? Why did both sides develop tactical/theater nuclear weapons? Why did the United States develop a war fighting strategy in Europe? If nuclear deterrence arguments are correct, these were costly policies that wasted time and money. Statistical evidence also challenges arguments of nuclear deterrence theory. If this theory is correct, high expected costs should deter aggression. The highest, surest costs must be those facing a nonnuclear state in a confrontation with a nuclear opponent. In such instances, if high costs deter actions, the nonnuclear state *must* give in. However, Kugler (1984) and Huth and Russett (1984) report that in a rather surprisingly large proportion of crises pitting a nonnuclear state against a nuclear opponent, the nonnuclear state prevailed or else nuclear weapons failed to have the posited deterrent effect. This is even the case when the nuclear state made an overt threat to employ its nuclear capacity.

Perhaps the most damning case against nuclear deterrence theory concerns inferences about nuclear proliferation. In short, nuclear deterrence arguments favor proliferation, power transition arguments oppose it. If the MAD zone is ultrastable, then it should be similarly stabilizing for all putative opponents to achieve a secure second strike. The very clear implication is that if one accepts the nuclear deterrence arguments, one should also accept universal proliferation of nuclear weapons as a common good that leads to ultrastability (some proponents of nuclear deterrence arguments accept this logical connection; e.g., Bueno de Mesquita and Riker 1982; Intriligator and Brito 1984; Rosen 1977; Waltz 1981). If all states had a secure second strike, nuclear war would be impossible. If, in absolute contrast, one accepts the power transition implications for nuclear deterrence, then proliferation to dissatisfied states is extremely dangerous, and all proliferation is destabilizing. Support for selective proliferation to satisfied states must be tempered by the possibility those satisfied states can become dissatisfied, perhaps due to revolution. Indeed, any proliferation of nuclear weapons makes the dissemination of nuclear technology more widespread, and thus increases the chance of indirect proliferation to dissatisfied states. Opposition to nuclear proliferation is so widespread that the Nuclear Non-Proliferation Treaty has been signed and is being implemented particularly against rogue (dissatisfied?) states. Apparently, policymakers intuitively understand that power transition implications for a world with nuclear weapons are plausible. Indeed, since only nuclear asymmetry can prevent nuclear transitions, and since capability shifts continue to occur, the only logical response is that nuclear asymmetry must be maintained by the satisfied nations to ensure peace in the global and regional hierarchies. The achievement of such a condition is a major challenge for this generation during the interlude between overtakings we now enjoy.

Extensions for Future Research

When Kugler and Organski wrote their evaluation of power transition research for the first volume of the *Handbook of War Studies,* perhaps the strongest criticism that could be made of progress within the power transition research tradition was the lack of any effective measures or inclusion of status quo evaluations in empirical examinations of central hypotheses. Further, there was no rigorous discussion of what it might mean to be satisfied rather than dissatisfied with the status quo. In the ensuing years a number of creative measures of status quo evaluations have been offered (Bueno de Mesquita 1990; Kim 1991; Lemke and Werner 1996; Werner and Kugler 1996). But much still remains to be done before status quo evaluations are as thoroughly understood as is relative power (this is one of Oneal, de Soysa, and Park's [1998] main points). The first step in this process might well be refinement of the indicators of status quo evaluations. Such refinement might grow out of recent formal and empirical work and is discussed here as a potential extension of power transition arguments.

Existing measures of status quo evaluations are creative and reliable, but perhaps not completely valid. Specifically, there are potential problems with the three existing measures. Bueno de Mesquita's money market discount rate indicator (which gauges the satisfaction level of a state by observing whether the international value of its currency is rising or declining—rising currency values are "satisfying," declining are "dissatisfying") could identify the dominant power as dissatisfied, since it is conceivable the currency of the dominant state could decline in value. This objection could be overcome by simply always designating the dominant state as satisfied, regardless of the value of its money, but two additional potential problems are not as easily dismissed. First, a state with low levels of trade or foreign investment would not be as sensitive to fluctuations in the international value of its money. The populace of such a state would thus be less dissatisfied by a fall in the value of the currency than would that of a trade-dependent state. Second, if a state's economy is dependent on exports, the decreasing value of its money may make its products more competitive abroad, thereby strengthening the domestic job market and making the people satisfied. Finally, the international value of a state's currency is not likely something upon which regional status quo evaluations depend. Thus, Bueno de Mesquita's measure may be of little or no use in multiple hierarchy extensions of power transition theory.

Kim's alliance portfolio similarity measure is also threatened by potential problems. Recently, Signorino and Ritter (1999) demonstrated that tau-b (Kim's measure of association) measures the linear association of two alliance portfolios; it does not measure their similarity. Instead, they offer a measure, *S,* which does measure similarity. However, one wonders if even *S* would be the best measure of status quo evaluations. Specifically, comparing alliance portfolios assumes that alliances are not only sincere statements of policy preferences in the international system but also the single most important statements of such preferences (Signorino and Ritter point out this limitation, too, 1999, 123). Some states form few or no alliances; others form many. It may not be disparate evaluations of the status quo that account for the difference.

Finally, Werner and Kugler's arms buildup measure of status quo dissatisfaction is limited to only indicating a state is dissatisfied as parity approaches. The absence of such a buildup indicates satisfaction by assumption. This may be valid, but it very likely may not be. It could be that a weak dissatisfied state evaluates its prospects for success as very low, and thus doesn't bother to arm. Further, the presence of a buildup by a vastly weaker state probably cannot be taken to represent dissatisfaction as it would by a state at parity with the dominant power, because the likelihood of war between the dominant power and the vastly weaker state is very small.

A better measure of status quo evaluations might be adapted from recent work by Werner and Lemke (1997, 1998). Werner and Lemke are specifically interested in differentiating between pairs of states that have compatible versus incompatible interests. They argue that states with similar domestic institutional arrangements will tend to have compatible interests, because they will tend to be benefited by the same things. Werner and Lemke (1997) find that similarities in domestic political and economic institutions allow them to correctly classify which sides of disputes states will join. This finding suggests that domestically similar states see each other as worth protecting, as valued, probably as having compatible interests. It might well be possible to create a valid indicator of status quo evaluations by calculating the degree to which states are domestically similar to the dominant state. Recall that the dominant state benefits from the status quo because it externalizes what has worked for it domestically. Similarly organized states would also likely benefit from the status quo. Thus, the degree of domestic similarity between a given state and the dominant power might be the most valid indicator of status quo evaluations possible. The problem lies in identifying what specific domestic institutions matter (this point is discussed at length in Werner and Lemke 1997, 1998). Perhaps one of the most promising future directions for power transition studies lies in such investigations of domestic attribute similarity.

Comparison of Power Transition and Other Arguments

The central ideas and empirical components of power transition research are increasingly common in general international relations research. In addition to the wide range of studies reviewed in the preceding, there are also a number of theoretical traditions that seem to draw from the power transition. These studies rarely make explicit reference to power transition, but since it predates these competitors, and bears so much resemblance, it is hard to dismiss the possibility that the theories are informed by their older cousin.

A first example is offered by leadership long cycle theory (Modelski 1978, 1987; Modelski and Thompson 1996; Rasler and Thompson herein), which posits an international dominant state or "world leader" that rises in the aftermath of a global war, reconstructs international interactions in its favor, and eventually declines only to be replaced by a new world leader. The major difference between leadership long cycle theory and power transition may be the cyclical regularity with which leadership long cycle theorists claim global wars occur and recur (see Thompson 1983a, 1983b, 1996a for studies that specifically link power transition and leadership long cycle theory).

A second example is found in hegemonic stability theory (Keohane 1980, 1984), which argues that international economic and military stability is created by a dominant state or "hegemon" that is so powerful it can be a privileged actor providing the collective good of international stability. Eventually the hegemon declines in power, and the stability it created wanes. Similarities between the hegemon of hegemonic stability theory and power transition's dominant power seem evident.

A third theory very similar in many regards to power transition is hegemonic leadership theory (Gilpin 1981). In Gilpin's theory a dominant state structures international relations to its advantage and challengers rise in power and wage war with the dominant state in an effort to themselves become dominant. Gilpin's theory is very nearly power transition, minus consideration of status quo evaluations. Gilpin has been prominently classified as a proponent of neorealist thought (Ashley 1984), and thus his hegemonic leadership theory might be seen as a later neorealist revision of power transition arguments.

Yet another theoretical tradition similar in many respects to power transition is the research concerned with status inconsistency arguments (Midlarsky 1975; Ray 1974; Wallace 1973b). According to this work, actors in any social/political system can be ranked according to their achieved or objective status (such as the amount of power they have accumulated) as well as according to their ascribed or subjective status (such as the amount of respect they are shown by other members of the system). Actors high on achieved status, but low on ascribed status, are "status inconsistent" and are posited to be frustrated by the inconsistency. The frustration is expected to then lead to aggression, directed at achieving the respect the actor feels is its due. The similarity between status-inconsistent actors and power transition's dissatisfied rising challenger seems rather close, as has been pointed out by Danilovic (1996). Perhaps power transition tells us about a specific status-inconsistent actor, and when to worry that this actor's frustration is likely to turn to aggression.

The various foregoing discussions suggest power transition is the core of a very fertile research program and that its central concepts are increasingly common in international relations theory and research. One of the hallmarks of superior theory and research is its ability to subsume other arguments, to explain excess empirical content. Ample evidence suggests that power transition offers just this kind of "excess empirical content" over additional areas of international relations research.

A first example concerns the democratic peace proposition. This well-known proposition is based on the empirical observation of little or no conflict between democracies for at least the past two centuries (see Russett and Starr's chapter in this volume for a detailed review). The democratic peace has become one of the most-researched issues in the field in recent years. Yet few efforts have been made to account for the democratic peace from the perspective of an existing theory of international relations. Lemke and Reed (1996) argue that the democratic peace can be understood as a subset of a larger "satisfied peace" anticipated by power transition arguments. Specifically, for the past 200 years the dominant power in the international system has been a liberal democracy. If we recall that the dominant power establishes the status quo to benefit itself, and also recall that states similar in domestic arrangement are likely to benefit from the status quo as well, then it is likely the case that, for the past 200 years, democracies are disproportionately likely to be satisfied with the status quo. Since satisfied states are not expected to get into conflicts with each other and since democracies are disproportionately likely to be satisfied, power transition anticipates a democratic peace as a subset of a "satisfied" peace. In the empirical section of their article, Lemke and Reed demonstrate that democracies have been disproportionately likely to be satisfied states, and they provide indications that joint satisfaction may provide a greater pacifying effect than does joint democracy.

Another area of scholarly inquiry that power transition can address concerns the likely course of international relations in the post–cold war world. Scholars are deeply divided over whether the end of the cold war is cause for concern (Mearsheimer 1990) or celebration (Singer and Wildavsky 1993). Lemke (1997a) argues that power transition research suggests the optimists and pessimists are both half-right, but also half-wrong. Power transition predicts that great power wars are likely only when a dissatisfied challenger achieves parity with the dominant power. The power transition explanation for the lack of great power war during the cold war is that the Soviet Union (the premier dissatisfied challenger) did not achieve parity with the United States. That the Soviet Union has now disintegrated and that the successor states largely claim to want to become democratic and capitalistic provides cause for celebration. The satisfied coalition has gotten larger and stronger, or promises to do so in the near future. However, other potential challengers are on the horizon. Should a communist and dissatisfied China achieve parity with the United States, power transition predicts that great power war could occur. This is cause for concern.

A third area of research power transition might illuminate concerns the literature on enduring rivalries (see Goertz and Diehl's chapter in this volume for a comprehensive review). One major problem rivalry theorists have encountered to date has been an inability to predict in advance which pairs of states will become rivals. As a consequence, most rivalry studies compare the behavior of known rivals to known nonrivals, because there is no way a priori to anticipate which states will become rivals. The result is that there are no studies to compare the behavior of predicted rivals to predicted nonrivals (although Hensel's [1996a] evolutionary approach offers preliminary hints about what sorts of state interactions are associated with the development of rivalry). Power transition arguments might be of some help in anticipating which states will become rivals. Rivals have some basic disagreements over which they cannot resolve their differences. Disparate evaluations of the status quo are a quintessential example of a disagreement unlikely to lend itself to easy solution. Thus, it may be that rivalries are much more likely to occur in dyads composed of states with disparate status quo evaluations. If this were found to be true, then power transition might help us anticipate which pairs of states are likely to become rivals, and which are not.[12]

Policy Implications of Power Transition Research

A final way in which power transition research demonstrates its worth concerns policy implications that follow from power transition arguments and findings. These concern the treatment of future challengers and related prospects of great power war, nuclear weapons, alliances, and regional conflict. We review these only briefly here, as they are described in more detail elsewhere (Kugler 1998; Tammen et al. 2000).

First, if China is the next potential challenger to the existing status quo, efforts should be made to ensure that China is satisfied and thereby becomes a supporter of stability. This is especially crucial as China will likely overtake the United States in power sometime in the early twenty-first century. Recognition of China's importance is not enough, however, because only if China becomes an integrated participant in the current international status quo can the looming power transition between the United States and China be anticipated to pass peacefully. Steps that can be taken to ensure a peaceful overtaking include efforts to further liberalize China economically, while simultaneously encouraging political democratization. Inclusion of China in the World Trade Organization is a specific step that could pay large international dividends. Efforts to integrate China into global governance through the UN, by fostering closer ties with the other great powers, or eventually integrating China into Western defense institutions are similarly desirable. It is extremely important that the United States, as the current international dominant power, take whatever steps it can to bring about Chinese satisfaction with the status quo. These steps may be very costly for the United States in the short run. For example, Americans should not reject economic relations that disproportionately profit Chinese, if these relations thereby improve China's evaluation of the status quo. The short-run costs of seeking accommodation with the Chinese may be high, the long-run costs of failing to do so will be considerably higher.

A very clear implication from power transition research is that nuclear weapons are every bit as dangerous as popular perception holds them to be. According to power transition arguments, wars are fought between contenders even though costs are anticipated to be extremely high. Consequently, nuclear weapons are not seen by power transition researchers to foster a fundamental change in international calculations. Nuclear weapons will only raise the costs of war, they will not prevent it. Given this intuitively plausible but chilling implication, whatever effort can be made to constrain the proliferation of nuclear weapons or reduce existing weapons stocks, especially those not closely controlled by status quo defenders, must be undertaken. Given the current premier position occupied by the United States, this is an especially auspicious time to achieve such weapons reductions. Efforts must be continued to reduce nuclear arsenals and to ensure that nuclear technologies not be spread to additional states. This is especially true of states opposed to the status quo.

A third policy area power transition research can illuminate concerns the expansion of NATO. Recent expansion to include Poland, the Czech Republic, and Hungary are controversial. Inclusion in NATO, given the concomitant economic and political coordination often associated with the alliance, is symptomatic of support for the international status quo. Enlarging NATO is thus similar to enlarging the set of satisfied states. The larger this set, the more peaceful the world is likely to be. Those who oppose NATO expansion to Central and Eastern Europe generally oppose it because it might alienate Russia. From the power transition perspective such expansion is to be sought, but only as the stepping-stone to the larger goal of eventually including Russia, and perhaps one day even China, within NATO. Obviously this would alter NATO's basic mission from North Atlantic security to preservation of the international status quo, but it would be desirable nonetheless. An additional impetus for such expansion is offered by Kim's (1991, 1992) research that suggests it is power parity, but specifically parity taking into account anticipated support from allies, that allows us to anticipate when wars will occur. If the United States were able to anticipate support from Russia and perhaps even from China, no other challenger could reasonably achieve parity, and thus war would not be anticipated to occur. At a minimum, Organski and Kugler's (1980, 56) analysis suggests that who emerges victorious in wars between great powers is determined by which side has the stronger coalition. If the coalition in support of the status quo is enlarged so that it remains preponderant, the current status quo is likely to be maintained.

Finally, power transition research also allows us to speculate on potential conflicts within minor power regional settings. To preserve peace among minor powers, efforts should be made to achieve agreement about the local status quo within each region. Further, consideration of relative power relations within minor power local hierarchies will indicate where future wars might occur.[13]

Conclusions

In the foregoing pages we have attempted to describe and integrate a rather large amount of scholarly research. The task is an important one because we honestly believe the power transition research program has been dramatically advanced since the publication of the first volume of the *Handbook of War Studies*. Many empirical studies have added substantive weight to various claims of power transition researchers, either in whole or in part. Theoretical emendations have broadened power transition's empirical domain, addressed persistent puzzles raised by power transition, and used power transition arguments to address other ongoing questions in international relations research. The number of studies that address power transition concerns either directly or indirectly is itself testimony to the increasing importance it has attained within the research community. Even the most strident critics must admit that the research tradition spawned by power transition theory is both productive and healthy.

And yet, we candidly admit that power transition research is incomplete. It does not provide a definitive general explanation for international relations. It suggests that wars are fought (either among the great powers or, with the multiple hierarchy extension, among minor powers) by roughly equal contenders. The historical record provides an embarrassingly large number of counterexamples, wars in which vastly unequal sides contended. The Pacific War during World War II is an example among the world's most powerful states, while any of the Indo-Pakistani wars serve as examples of asymmetric wars among the less powerful. Why dominant states (either global or local) generally do not preempt rising challengers from achieving parity is poorly understood. Further, power transition seems to suggest the dominant state can achieve its aims so long as it remains preponderant. Yet American efforts to achieve various foreign policy goals have not been uniformly successful, even when the United States enjoyed a vast power advantage over all others.

Such inconsistencies between theory and reality do not justify rejecting power transition's explanations. Science progresses by developing less incomplete or less incorrect explanations of reality. We suggest that power transition may offer the least incorrect of existing explanations of international conflict in specific, and of international relations more generally. It seems clear, from the large number of studies that build on power transition's foundation, that this view is increasingly taken by other researchers. In a Lakatosian sense, power transition may be the most productive research program, or paradigm, available for international relations researchers.

According to Lakatos (1978, 32), a scientific research program is superior to alternatives if it accounts for what others address, yet also accounts for new phenomena the alternates fail to explain. The power transition research program is at least as successful empirically as the contenders discussed earlier in this chapter. What is more, it offers explanations for a variety of disparate international phenomena such as the Democratic Peace, the pacificity of the Long Peace, the role of nuclear weapons in deterrence, the likely future course of post–cold war great power relations, conflict relations between minor powers, and perhaps for other areas as well, such as the genesis of international rivalry. Power transition also offers a variety of policy implications. These examples sum to a rather large amount of "excess empirical content," much of which has been corroborated by empirical analysis.

In spite of this impressive track record, there is much that research within the power transition tradition does not explain. The remaining gaps and puzzles provide directions for continuing power transition research. We eagerly anticipate further discussion, debate, and advance.

Notes

1. This argument is advanced by Lemke and Reed (1998), and critiqued by Oneal, de Soysa, and Park (1998). An additional objection might be that dominant powers should militarily preempt their rising potential challengers by waging preventive war. We return to this objection later in the discussion of ongoing research within the power transition research program.
2. This is a critical difference between power transition and work on hegemonic stability (Keohane 1980) or hegemonic leadership (Gilpin 1981) because these other works do not consider the domestic characteristics of states as important for international politics.
3. For recent studies that evaluate how well power transition's focus on parity and status quo evaluations anticipate *domestic* conflict, see Benson and Kugler (1998) and Kugler et al. (1997).
4. A number of studies focusing on the importance of the systemic distribution of power (Bueno de Mesquita 1981a; Mansfield 1992; Singer, Bremer, and Stuckey 1972) are not reviewed here because power transition offers hypotheses about the *dyadic* distribution of capabilities between the dominant power and a potential challenger.
5. These extensions to minor power regional systems are described in detail later.
6. See de Soysa, Oneal, and Park (1997) for a recent, and more cautious, replication and reinterpretation of Houweling and Siccama's study.
7. Lemke and Werner's article accomplishes a number of other tasks as well, such as including status quo evaluations as a variable and widening the empirical domain to include regional minor power international systems. These additional contributions are summarized separately later.

8. The multiple hierarchy model variant of power transition research bears a number of similarities to Midlarsky's (1986) "hierarchical equilibrium theory of systemic war" developed quite a bit earlier. In that work Midlarsky describes an international system composed of various hierarchies. Atop each hierarchy is a great or major power. Each hierarchy is akin to a sphere of influence and is argued to be present whenever an alliance or system of alliances or a loosely knit empire is observed. Midlarsky argues, among other things, that the more powerful the great power atop each hierarchy, the better the systemic prospects for peace. His conceptualization of an international system composed of various hierarchies is similar in this regard to that of the multiple hierarchy model, but it differs from the multiple hierarchy model of power transition most obviously in that the leading states in the local hierarchies of the multiple hierarchy model often are minor powers. Further, Midlarsky is concerned with wars fought *across* his hierarchies, while the multiple hierarchy model is concerned with wars fought *within* its hierarchies. The two models are not mutually exclusive, however, because hierarchies in each are defined quite differently (by alliances or empires in Midlarsky's work, by ability to interact militarily in the multiple hierarchy model).
9. This deduction is far from obvious and thus requires a bit more description. In Alsharabati's model the actor with more to gain from war is the challenger, since the status quo already favors the defender (or dominant power in power transition terms). Prior to the power transition the challenger is weaker than the defender, and thus the defender can expect to win. This makes the defender more willing to fight before the transition than after. If the challenger has sufficiently low evaluations of the status quo, it might be willing to initiate war even if defeat is more likely than victory. Given that it is stronger than the challenger, the defender is likely to resist this initiation, and thus war is more likely. This war is expected to be low cost, however, because the challenger is still a weak state. After the transition the power relationship reverses, making the defender the weaker party. As such it is more likely to concede the challenger's demands. But, if the challenger's demands are extreme enough, the defender will risk war to stave off unacceptable changes to the status quo. Such extreme revisionist demands are unlikely, and thus war is less likely after the transition than before. However, if the various elements do favor the defender resisting, the war that is fought is likely to be high cost, since after the transition both challenger and defender are very powerful states.
10. The importance of demographic potential for power transition arguments is not widely recognized. However, questions of demographic resources were so important in early power transition arguments that Organski and Organski (1961) dedicated an entire volume to their consideration. In sum, states become powerful by undergoing a domestic transition from underdeveloped to developed. This domestic transition is also known as the demographic

transition, in which the population goes from being largely independent of the central government to being integrated into a national political and economic system. In the course of this, birth and death rates both decline and stabilize, and the country's now mobilized and stabilized population generates more wealth. This wealth translates into national power. This growth in power moves the country "up" in the international power pyramid. The larger the population, the more people mobilized after development, the more wealth, the more international power. The various components of this explanation are explicitly presented in Organski and Organski (1961) but are also central to Organski (1965) and Organski, Kugler, Johnson, and Cohen (1984).

11. These implications are not new as they are prominently advanced in both editions of Organski's *World Politics* (1958, 1968) and in the conclusions of *The War Ledger* (Organski and Kugler 1980).
12. The potential importance of power transition for rivalry studies has not been ignored by scholars. Geller (1993), Huth and Russett (1993), and Hensel and McLaughlin (1996) all investigate whether power transitions or power parity make wars within rivalries more likely. Geller and Huth and Russett find that they do; Hensel and McLaughlin find that they do not. However, an important point to bear in mind is that none of these studies consider the role status quo evaluations might play in the development and unfolding of rivalry interactions.
13. Kugler (1995) makes just such speculations about future possible wars within Asia, based on the power transition perspective.

The Ongoing Game-Theoretic Revolution

JAMES D. MORROW

This chapter differs from the other chapters in this volume. The other chapters present coherent theories of war, its causes, and consequences and survey the evidence that supports those theories. This chapter describes the results of research that uses game theory, especially noncooperative game theory, to examine the logic of those and other theories of war. Rather than present a single theory of war, then, this chapter discusses how game theory has been used to explicate four theories of war.

Rigorous assessment of evidence is critical to the scientific enterprise. Such assessments of evidence, as seen in the theories presented in the other chapters of this volume, make it possible for a scientific community to arrive at a consensus on whether reality matches the predictions of a theory. The game-theoretic revolution advances the other dimension of rigor critical for scientific progress, rigorous examination of the logic of a theory. Game theory provides a flexible and useful tool to create formal models of the strategic interactions present in theories of war. It allows us to analyze whether the claims of the argument of a theory can be deduced from its premises. In this sense, this chapter advances the goal of this volume, to survey the status of our scientific progress in the study of war.

I must make four important qualifications about the claims of this chapter before beginning. First, game theory is not the only tool available for formal analysis of the logic of theories. Any number of other mathematical tools—differential equations, control theory, and combinatorics, among others—can and have been applied fruitfully to the explication of theories of war. I claim only that the recent literature has used game theory fruitfully to address a spectrum of theories of international conflict. Second, the application of game theory is not novel to the recent literature; applications of game theory to understand international conflict go back to at least Schelling (1960) and Ellsberg (1960). However, the development of noncooperative game theory in the late 1970s and early 1980s expanded the ability of game theory to address critical questions on war and its causes. Third, although the logical critique of theories is an important part of the scientific enterprise, it alone is not sufficient for scientific progress. I endeavor to show how game-theoretic models have improved our ability to assess the evidence presented for and against different theories of war. Fourth, although I believe and will argue here that noncooperative game theory is changing the study of war, the revolution reported here works through the explication of theories of war rather than presenting a competing theory of war. Game theory is a useful way to examine the logic of theories of war; it by itself is not a theory of war.

The chapter begins with a brief survey of what noncooperative game theory is and why students of war should be interested in it. It then proceeds by examining a number of theories of war, surveying how game theory models contribute to our understanding of those theories. I have tried to use theories also discussed elsewhere in this volume to highlight the contribution of game theory where possible. None of these surveys should be seen as encyclopedic of the contributions of game theory to each theory of war. The literature now is often too large to review all of its contributions in one chapter of this handbook. Instead, I seek to hit the high points of those contributions.

What Is Noncooperative Game Theory?

Game theory is a mathematical theory of strategic interaction.[1] Decision theory analyzes how actors should choose among options to gain their desired ends. Game theory is the branch of decision theory that covers situations where more than one individual's choices can affect the outcome. Each actor must then consider not only what course of action he or she should take but also the likely choices of the other actors who can influence the outcome. Their decisions interact through the strategies that each pursues, hence the term strategic interaction.

Strategic interaction is central to many theories of international conflict, and so game theory is a natural tool to examine the logic of strategic interaction in those theories. For example, deterrence theory argues that the threat made by the deterring power can dissuade the threatening side from its intended course of action. That is, the threat is chosen for its effect on the actions of the threatening state, not because it produces the desired outcome directly. Game theory provides a way to examine the strategic interactions central to many theories of war. Should actors behave as these theories argue they do?

Such assessments require stating the strategic situation of the theory in a game, which can then be solved. To define a game, we must specify who the actors are, what choices they have, the sequence of those choices, the outcomes that can result from the choices, the value each actor attaches to each outcome relative to the other outcomes, and what each actor knows about the game, the other players' motivations, and what moves have already been made for each point where it may have to make a choice. The sequence of possible moves in a game specifies both the course of actions that occur and the possible counterfactuals—alternate courses of action that do not occur—in a situation (Bueno de Mesquita 1996). A game can capture important elements of the strategic situation in a theory of conflict, allowing us to analyze the strategic logic of that theory separate from that theory.

We solve games by searching for their equilibria. An equilibrium requires each player's moves to produce the best possible outcome for that player given the moves of the other players. In equilibrium then, no actor can make itself better off by changing its own actions. Equilibrium does not mean that the best of all possible outcomes results; it could be that all players can be made better off if they all changed their moves in concert. Nor does equilibrium imply that the outcome is balanced, fair, or desirable; after all, war will be an equilibrium outcome in many of the models in which we are interested. Rather, equilibrium merely states that no actors would wish to change its course of action in the situation, given its anticipations about the other players' likely actions.

Game theory as a field dates back to at least 50 years, and there are many branches of game theory that address different sorts of strategic problems. This chapter discusses the application of noncooperative game theory to theories of international conflict. Noncooperative game theory combines two ideas, perfection and incomplete information in game-theoretic terminology, to address strategic problems of commitment, signaling, and bargaining. Because the latter problems recur in theories of war, noncooperative game theory is useful in explicating such theories (Morrow 1999).

Commitment is a problem when an actor wishes to make a threat or promise that others doubt it will carry out if necessary. Commitment can be a problem in deterrence where the threatening state may doubt the willingness of the deterring state to carry out its deterrent threat. Commitment can be a problem in power transition theory where the challenger may be unable to reassure the dominant state that it will not exploit its coming dominance to change the order that the dominant state has constructed. Perfection is the idea that actions taken in a game must be in the acting player's interest at the time the action must be taken; it captures the commitment problem by judging an actor's willingness to carry out a costly action at the time the action must be taken. Often, an actor can benefit if it can precommit itself to a course of action and force others to adjust to the consequences of that course of action. Generally though, states do not have the opportunity to precommit themselves in international politics, and perfection allows us to test the credibility of commitments within a game.

Even though states cannot precommit themselves to actions, they do try to convince other states about what actions they will take under certain conditions in the future. Alliances, for one, are mutual promises among allies to come to one another's aid if a member of the alliance is attacked. For an alliance to deter a threatening state, the allies must convince the latter that they will come to one another's aid if the threatening state attacks one of the allies. This argument about persuasion requires that the threatening state be uncertain about the future actions of the allies, which leads to the second main idea in noncooperative game theory—limited information.

Actors have limited information when they do not know important facts about the game they are playing. Games of limited information provide a way to analyze such uncertainties and their strategic effects. Specifically, such games allow us to model situations where persuasion, signaling, and bluffing are present. Formally, each player may have some information about the game that only it knows; we call such information private. Other actors hold beliefs about that private information. For example, a state may know exactly how committed it is to its ally, but its ally and the threatening state hold beliefs about the first state's degree of commitment. Because an actor chooses its actions in part because of its private information, other actors may be able to infer an actor's private information from its actions.

The combination of perfection and limited information has proven to be fruitful. Perfection allows us to analyze issues of credibility, and limited information addresses questions about how perceptions and actions determine each other. In short, the combination of the two opens up these questions for formal analysis. Because these questions recur throughout theories of war, noncooperative game theory has demonstrated its value as a tool to explicate such theories. The rest of this chapter examines the game-theoretic literature that addresses four specific theories of war—deterrence, balance of power, power transition, and the democratic peace—to show how the game-theoretic revolution changes our understanding of the logic of these theories. I further show how the logical critique also leads to new empirical work when possible.

Deterrence

Rational deterrence theory (henceforth RDT) is one of the best-known theories in the field of war studies. Kaufman (1956) provides one of the earliest and best-known statements of RDT. Briefly, a deterrent threat will work when the deterring state has (1) credible military capabilities, (2) a clearly communicated deterrent threat, and (3) a credible willingness to carry out the threat. This idea of rational deterrence has given rise to an extensive literature of both tests of RDT and criticism of it. Among the most notable examples of the former are Russett (1963a) and Huth (1988a, 1988b). Empirical research on RDT tries to assess the credibility of threats from historical cases by testing possible correlates of such credibility. For example, an alliance between a major power and a small state under threat could be a sign that the former's deterrent threat is credible.

My point in this section is simple; the second and third elements of effective deterrence threats according to RDT are problematic. The nature of a deterrence crisis undermines both the clear communication of threats and the credibility of those threats. Put another way, RDT cannot work in a rational choice model. Further, game models of deterrence imply both the existing pattern of results contrary to RDT and patterns in the historical record not previously observed.

The literature on deterrence using noncooperative game theory is large.[2] Deterrence arguments contain a basic sequence of events that can be captured in a game. First, a state, called the challenger, makes a demand for a change in the status quo. If no demand is made, the status quo holds. Second, the deterring state, often called the defender, either threatens the challenger with force if the challenger moves to change the status quo or acquiesces in the challenger's demand. Third, the challenger must decide whether to press its demand in the face of a deterrent threat or to back down from its demand. If it presses its demand, the defender must make a final decision whether to carry out its threat and go to war. If the defender does not carry out its threat, the challenger gains the stakes in its original demand. This basic sequence can and has been embellished or truncated in different models. However, this basic sequence appears in some form in most models of deterrence.

Some have criticized RDT, claiming that the states in actual crises do not nicely break into challengers and defenders. Both sides see themselves as defending the status quo, according to these claims. Others argue that RDT makes the choices too clear for both actors, and that there are no clear last choices between war and peace. Without commenting either favorably or unfavorably on the validity of these criticisms, the game-theoretic critique takes RDT as a given, tries to capture its premises in models, and then asks if the conclusions of RDT follow in those models. If RDT fails this test of logical consistency, then it must be amended or abandoned before empirical testing.

Returning to the basic sequence of RDT, consider the problem of the credibility of the threat. In the challenger's final choice, the defender's threat is credible if it convinces the challenger to back down rather than press its threat. The defender's willingness to carry out its threat follows directly from the comparison of its payoffs for what happens if it carries out its threat, war, and what happens if it does not, loss of the stakes in the crisis. The difference in the defender's payoffs for war and losing the stakes express its willingness to carry out the threat. If it prefers war to losing the stakes, the defender will carry out its threat.

However, credibility of a deterrent threat lies in the mind of the state to be deterred, not the deterring state. Working backward to the decision of the challenger to press its demand, the deterrent threat is credible if it is sufficient to convince the challenger not to press its demand. If a threat convinces the challenger to back down, then it is credible, even in the case the defender would not carry out the threat if forced to choose between war and the loss of the stakes. Here lies the heart of the problem with RDT, exposed by noncooperative game theory. The defender only wants to carry out its deterrent threat if it prefers war to losing the stakes. The challenger can anticipate the defender's willingness to carry out its threat, and will presumably press its demand only when the challenger knows that the defender will not carry out its threat.[3] This logic is a perfection argument; both sides only make moves that are in their interest at the time of the move, and they both know that the other will do so and can then anticipate the other's future moves.

Why would the challenger make a demand to begin the crisis if it anticipates that the defender will make a credible deterrent threat, that is, a threat sufficient to convince the challenger to back down from its demand? We commonly assume that the challenger prefers the status quo to backing down from a demand. Backing down reaffirms the status quo, and the challenger loses face in the eyes of others. If so, then the challenger should not even make a demand if it anticipates that the defender has a credible deterrent threat.

Similarly, the defender is willing to make deterrent threats only when it knows that threat will succeed. It, like the challenger, loses face if it makes a threat that it does not carry out later. This argument based on perfection concludes that successful deterrence never occurs because challengers will not begin crises if they believe that deterrence will be successful. The only crises that occur have the defender accepting the demands of the challenger without contest, according to this argument. So far, these conclusions do not match what we see in international disputes.

Incomplete information, the second main idea in noncooperative game theory, solves this problem. Assume now that neither side exactly knows the other actor's value for war. Instead, each holds beliefs about the other's value for war, which they use to form their anticipations about the other's future moves. Return to the question of when the deterrent threat is credible. As before, the defender knows whether it prefers carrying out its threat to backing down from it. The challenger, on the other hand, cannot predict whether the defender has the willingness to carry out the deterrent threat. The deterrent threat is credible, that is, it convinces the challenger to back down from its demand, when the certainty of backing down itself with the attendant loss of face is better as the challenger sees it than the chance that the defender will go to war rather than back down from its threat. Credibility of a deterrent threat lies in the eyes of the challenger, not the defender's true willingness to carry out the threat.

When will the defender be willing to make a deterrent threat when it cannot fully anticipate the likely response of the challenger? The challenger's reaction to a deterrent threat depends in part on its value for war, which the defender does not know. The defender must judge how likely the challenger is to press its demand rather than back down. The defender will make a deterrent threat when the chance that the challenger will not press its demand is large enough to offset the risk of having to carry out that threat. The defender's willingness to make such a threat depends in part on its own value for war because there is some chance that it may have to choose between carrying out its threat by going to war and backing down from the threat. Those defenders who are unwilling to fight may not be willing to make a deterrent threat.

The challenger may be able to learn something about the defender's willingness to fight from the act of making a deterrent threat. The challenger is uncertain about the defender's willingness to fight; the defender could have a high value or a low value for war. If the defender makes the deterrent threat when it has the high value for war but not when it has the low value, then the challenger can conclude that the defender has a high value for war if the defender makes a deterrent threat. Further, the challenger can then correctly anticipate that the defender is willing to carry out the deterrent threat. The key to learning about the defender's motivation from its actions is that the different types of defender take different actions. In the parlance of noncooperative game theory, the types separate. Generally, the challenger cannot reduce the defender's willingness to fight to just two possibilities, so it may not be able to determine the defender's precise motivations from its action. Still, if the defender would take different actions for different levels of willingness to fight, then the challenger can learn something about the defender's motivations from its action, and so have a more accurate anticipation of the defender's future actions.

The same logic holds for the challenger's demand that begins the crisis. If some but not all challengers have a sufficiently high value for war that they are willing to take the risk of war, then the defender can learn something about the challenger's willingness to press its demand from the act of making a demand to begin with. Those challengers with a low value for war would rather keep the status quo than make a demand and run the risk of war. The defender learns that the challenger does not have a low value for war, and so is likely to be willing to press its demand if it makes a deterrent threat in response to the demand.

This logic leads to an important point against RDT; a perfect deterrent threat cannot be made. A perfect deterrent threat would cause any challenger to back down rather than press its demand. If such a perfect threat existed, then any defender, regardless of its willingness to fight, would make that threat. But then the challenger would not make the demand to begin with, anticipating the perfect deterrent threat and its own retreat from its demand in the face of that threat. RDT holds out the prospect of perfect deterrent threats; do these things and the challenger will be deterred.

Instead, crises necessarily involve uncertainty by both sides about each other's motivations and actions. Neither side can know that its actions will allow it to prevail. At every move, there are types of challenger testing the resolve of the defender, seeking an easy victory short of war. Similarly, there are defenders at every step doubting their own resolve and hoping that the challenger will back down before they do. Because the deterrent threat might convince the challenger to back down from its demand, even some unmotivated defenders are willing to make a deterrent threat. At every move, neither side is certain about what the other will do in the future. They always face the possibility that the other side will back down if confronted forcefully.

This observation has important implications for the second and third elements of RDT. The third element contends that deterrence requires a credible willingness to carry out the threat. But the credibility of the threat resides in the challenger's perception of the defender, not the defender's mind itself. Some challengers will find a threat credible and other, more highly motivated challengers will not, and the defender does not know which type of challenger it faces. The third element of RDT is correct only in the sense that a threat that convinces the challenger to back off its demand is credible by definition. The second element, a clearly communicated threat, is even more problematic. The efficacy of a threat lies not in how clearly it is communicated, but in how well it convinces the challenger of the defender's willingness to fight. Given that both motivated and some unmotivated defenders make deterrent threats, the challenger cannot determine the exact willingness of the defender to carry out its threat from the statement of the threat itself. The motivations of both sides make clear communication impossible.

What makes deterrence effective then? More precisely, when can a deterrent threat convince the challenger to back down from its demand? The challenger must learn from the threat that the defender has a higher willingness to go to war than before the threat, and so is more likely to fight if the challenger does not back down from its demand. If the defender is not that willing to fight, it does not make the deterrent threat. The key here is that making the threat must be sufficiently costly that not all types of defender are willing to risk war by making the threat. The cost of making the threat convinces the less-motivated defenders to concede the challenger's demand rather than responding with a deterrent threat. This idea is called costly signaling; the cost of making the signal of your intentions makes the signal credible. Here the deterrent threat is the signal that the defender is willing to go to war.

If costs are necessary for credibility, where does the cost come from? Costly consequences could arise endogenously in the process. If the deterrent threat does not dissuade all types of challengers, the defender faces the prospect of either losing face by backing down from its threat or going to war. Either course of action can be costly for the defender, compared with accepting the challenger's demand. A highly motivated defender prefers war to backing down, so making the threat is not costly for it. A defender who prefers granting the challenger's demand to war faces the prospect of a worse outcome when it makes a deterrent threat rather than accepting the challenger's demand. The cost of making the deterrent threat comes from the possibility that the threat may fail to deter the challenger.

Having the possibility of war create the cost needed to make deterrent threats effective faces a problem if there is no externally imposed final choice between war and peace. In the sequence I described earlier, the defender has the final choice between war and peace when it decides whether to carry out its deterrent threat. Some (Fearon 1994a) argue that such externally imposed last clear chances to avoid war do not exist. Rather, states find ways to create such last clear chances through their actions. Leaders can manipulate their position in a crisis to convince relevant domestic and international audiences of the seriousness of the issue. If a leader backs down after raising the importance of the issue, these audiences punish the leader for his or her failure to live up to the position that the leader had his or her state adopt. These audience costs then raise the cost of backing down and so make war more attractive. If one side can raise its cost for backing down high enough that its leader prefers war to backing down, then the onus of avoiding war falls on the other side. The other side faces the last clear chance between war and peace because the first side is now committed not to back down.

In summary, game theory models have led us to rethink RDT. RDT emphasized credible military capabilities, clear threats, and credible willingness to fight as the source of successful deterrence. The revised theory shows that clear threats cannot exist in a crisis because both sides must be uncertain about each other's precise motivation and that the defender cannot be certain that its willingness to fight is credible in the eyes of the challenger. Further, audience costs, particularly those imposed by the domestic audiences of national leaders, are essential to effective signaling of resolve through deterrent threats.

What are the implications of these arguments for empirical work on deterrence? First, the cases that we observe are the product of selection on unobservable variables. This selection bias cannot be corrected, although we can seek appropriate hypotheses to test game theory models of deterrence. Return to the sequence of a deterrence crisis I described earlier. The willingness of each side to fight a war is unobservable to the other and outside observers; that is the definition of private information. The other side and outside observers can attempt to infer a state's value for war from its actions, but they cannot observe the true value. Each holds beliefs about the other's value for war based on factors that are observable before the crisis, such as the size of both sides' military and existing alliance commitments. Whether the challenger makes a demand initially and, if so, whether the defender makes a deterrent threat in response depends in part on both sides' unobservable value for war. Deterrent threats should only be made when both the challenger and defender are more willing to fight than we would expect from looking at the factors that are observable before the crisis begins. The systematic but unobservable selection of cases in favor of more resolute states biases how we understand deterrence.

The bias has several effects. It reduces the effect of important observable variables in the cases that occur. If the defender is strong on an observable indicator of resolve, such as military capabilities, the challenger will make a demand only when the challenger holds unobservable advantages that compensate for its observable disadvantage. Such a highly motivated challenger is difficult to deter, and so deterrence attempted by strong defenders will not appear to be successful very often. For example, Kugler (1984) argues that nuclear weapons do not provide deterrent value because there are a number of crises where nonnuclear states challenge nuclear powers and often prevail. Fearon (1994b) points out that the nonnuclear states only challenge the nuclear powers on issues that are peripheral to the interests of the nuclear powers but central to their own interests. Such challenges are likely to succeed simply because the stakes are very important to the challenger but not to the defender. The consequence is that it appears that nuclear weapons have little deterrent effect if we look at the cases that occur. The real effect of deterrence shows up in the cases that do not occur: those where either the challenger is not strongly motivated or the defender is strongly motivated. In contrast, nuclear powers are willing to challenge nonnuclear powers on issues that are critical to the latter. They are willing to make demands even without unobservable advantages.

This unobservable bias cannot be corrected because the compensating cases do not occur. We cannot oversample on events that never happened (Achen and Snidal 1989). The bias has further implications for how we select cases for systematic study. Because deterrence requires both parties to be uncertain, we must look for broad sets of cases that encompass the range of possible unobservable variables. If we limit ourselves to particular sets of cases, we are likely to get misleading results. For example, Lebow and Stein (1990) criticize the Huth and Russett (1984) study of deterrence success for examining cases where the challenger was not determined to use force before the deterrent threat was made. They argue that deterrence is successful only when it dissuades a challenger intent on war if its demand is not granted. Lebow and Stein's argument, however, does not consider the defender's problem in deterrence; it cannot know whether the challenger is bent on war when it makes a deterrent threat. To limit ourselves just to the cases where the challenger intends to use force, we ignore the strategic problem of the defender. Further, the argument I laid out earlier suggests that any challenger that is bent on using force before the deterrent threat is made probably cannot be deterred because it has a high value for war. Not surprisingly, Lebow and Stein find in their limited set of cases that deterrence is unlikely to succeed; they have defined away the cases where it could work.

Second, we should expect that ex post measures of a state's willingness to fight should predict deterrence success better than ex ante measures. The latter include only factors that are observable to both sides before the crisis, while the former—being the product of a state's unobservable motivation—also reflect the unobservable factors. For example, Maoz (1983) finds that relative resolve, which he measures by actions taken during a crisis, predicts the outcome of disputes better than relative capabilities, which he measures using the Correlates of War (COW) indicator of composite capabilities. This result is not surprising when we consider that the latter is only a reflection of factors that both sides know before the crisis begins, while the former is a record of what each side did in the crisis. As such, Maoz's measure of resolve reflects unobservable values for war.

Finally, how can we tell whether these models and their selection effects are present? Instead of looking at patterns of behavior in deterrence crises, we can look at the sets of crises that occur. These arguments predict that states with observable disadvantages should engage in disputes only when they hold unobservable advantages to compensate. When they do make challenges or deterrent threats, though, they should have a good chance at prevailing in the resulting crisis. Comparing how often minor powers prevail in disputes with major powers, Morrow (1989) finds that minor powers win almost one-half of the time, much more than we should expect given the difference in capabilities. However, Morrow also finds that major powers are about three times as likely to challenge minor powers as minor powers are to challenge major powers. This difference in the likelihood of a challenge is evidence of the selection bias of unobservable variables.

In summary, game theory models have led to key revisions in RDT. The ability to make costly signals is critical to successful deterrence, rather than clear communication and a credible willingness to fight. Further, domestic audiences are central to understanding how states can make costly signals. Uncertainty on the part of both parties is central to deterrence, and so optimal deterrent threats, those that deter any challenger, cannot exist.

Balance of Power

The hypothesis that a balance of power produces peace is perhaps the most famous single idea about the origins of war. But what exactly is "a balance of power"? Many scientific studies have investigated the question of whether an equal distribution of military capabilities makes conflict more or less likely (see Siverson and Sullivan 1983 for a survey of much of this work). Some studies find that conflict is more likely when states are roughly equal in capabilities; others find that inequality in capabilities makes conflict more likely.

These studies, however, may not really address the question of whether a balance of power leads to peace. The problem lies not with the studies but with the idea of a balance of power. Balance-of-power theorists have not always been clear about what a "balance of power" is; for instance, do we measure balance within a dyad or across all states in the system? In the latter case, what distributions of capabilities among five states are balanced? Recent balance-of-power theory (Walt 1987; Waltz 1979) takes the problem further by arguing that balance is not a property of distributions of capabilities, but rather of the behavior of the actors. States form a balance of power when they engage in balancing behavior; that is, when they join efforts against a state that threatens to achieve dominance in the international system. Balance of power then is a property of the behavior of states in the system, not of the distribution of capabilities.

Even if a balance is behavior, we must ask what distributions of capabilities can support balancing behavior. Game-theoretic models can test the logic of recent balance-of-power theory. In particular, this section examines the attempts of Niou and Ordeshook (1990; Niou, Ordeshook, and Rose 1989) to model recent balance-of-power theory.

Niou and Ordeshook's model attempts to capture balance-of-power theory through a series of assumptions. First, a fixed pot of resources is divided among the states in the system. For convenience, I will say there are 300 points of resources, as 300 divides easily by 2, 3, 4, 5, and 6. I denote a distribution of resources by listing the resources of the states in the system in order from strongest to weakest; (100, 100, 100) describes a system of three states where the resources are distributed equally across the three. Any state with 0 resources is eliminated from the system. Second, states want to increase their resources, but fear the threat of elimination. Given two distributions of resources, a state prefers the distribution where it has more resources, unless there is a chance that it might be eliminated in that distribution and its continued existence is certain in the other distribution. Third, resources determine the outcome of wars. Again for convenience, assume that the side with more resources always wins a war. Fourth, the game is continual; the result of one round of the game is the starting point of the next round. States then must consider not only the immediate effects of their actions but also the long-run effects in future rounds.

These basic assumptions capture recent balance-of-power theory well. States do not seek just to maximize their power as measured by their resources. Instead, states care about security, and sometimes more resources produce less security. Security maximization is a long-run problem, and states consider the full effects of their strategies when choosing. The question is when balancing behavior can emerge under these assumptions.

To model this question, we need a sequence of moves. The game is composed of a series of rounds. In each round, one state is chosen at random and given the opportunity to make a threat. A threat gives an attacking coalition, its targets, and how the members of the attacking coalition will divide the resources of the targets among themselves if they win. The other members of the attacking coalition must agree to participate in the threat. The target states then are chosen in random order and each given an opportunity to counter the threat. A counter is either a new threat aimed at some members of the attacking coalition or an offer to transfer resources to some members of the attacking coalition, and so persuade them to drop out of the attacking coalition. A counterthreat leads to another set of counters by the new targets if it is approved by all the members of the counterthreatening coalition. An offer to transfer resources must be accepted by the recipients of the resources. If the counters offered by all the original target states are rejected, then the original threat is implemented. If the members of the threatening coalition have more resources than their targets, the latter are eliminated, and the threatening coalition divides the targets' resources in accord with the threat. A threat that is not approved by the members of the threatening coalition, a threat that is implemented, or a successful transfer of resources ends one round and begins the next with the new distribution.

We wish to see what distributions of resources are stable in this model. However, there are two different concepts of stability here. System stability means that no states are eliminated from the system; that is, all states can ensure their security. Resource stability means that no resources are ever transferred from one state to another; that is, war never occurs and can never be used to extort resources from another state. These two concepts of stability are different. A system could be system stable without being resource stable.

Because states consider the long-run consequences of the threats they make and how they counter threats directed at them, I begin the analysis by looking at a two-state system and proceeding to larger numbers of states. If two members of a three-state system make a threat that eliminates the third, then the next round is a two-state system of the two victors. Each must consider the consequences of the resulting two-state system when they agree to the threat that will eliminate the third state.

A two-state system is stable in either sense only when resources are divided perfectly equally between the two—(150, 150). Otherwise, the state with more resources threatens and eliminates the state with less at its first opportunity. The model then produces a result directly at variance with the arguments of neorealists. For neorealists, bipolar systems are very stable; in the model, such two-state systems are very unstable, requiring a perfect balance for stability. Later in this section, I will consider possible revisions of the model that might address this discrepancy.

A three-actor system produces the possibility of coalitions, and so the possibility of balancing by two against the third. Obviously, a state with more than 150 points of resources can threaten and absorb the other two on its own. In a three-actor system where one state controls exactly 150 points (i.e., half of the resources in the system), the other two must come to each other's aid if it threatens either of them. Otherwise, the state that sits on the sidelines will be eliminated in the next round. If the stronger of the two weaker states threatens the other, the latter can transfer resources to the state with 150 resources, and so doom the threatening state. This behavior looks like balancing; the two weaker states depend on each other for their survival, and so each is willing to come to the aid of the other.

When all three states have less than 150 resources, then all three are at risk of a threat from the other two. Assume the current distribution of resources is (120, 100, 80). How should the third state respond if the first two join together to threaten it? The threat of the first two must agree to split the third state to produce a distribution of (150, 150) in the next round because that is the only stable two-state distribution. If the third state offers a counterthreat by trying to pull off one member of the threatening coalition, the latter member can reject the offer and ensure itself 150 resources and permanent security. Instead, the third state should offer to transfer 30 resources to the largest state, increasing the largest state to 150 resources and creating a system that is both system and resource stable. In general, the target of any threat in a three-actor system should transfer enough resources to the strongest threatening state to lift the latter to 150 resources, and so secure its own existence. Three-actor systems then are generally system stable but not resource stable.

This move is always possible in a three-actor system where none of the three actors has 150 or more resources because any combination of two actors totals more than 150 resources. Put another way, every state is a member of a minimal winning coalition (Riker 1962)—that is, a coalition with more than 150 resources where the coalition will not have 150 resources if any single member is removed. With four or more actors, there can be states that are never a member of a minimal winning coalition. For example, the weakest state in (110, 100, 60, 30) cannot be a member of a minimal winning coalition; any pair of the other states forms a minimal winning coalition, and the weakest state cannot form a winning coalition with any other single state. It cannot secure its position in the system by offering enough to raise another state to 150 resources.

States that are members of some minimal winning coalition will be called essential. Essential states can ensure their continued existence in this model of the balance of power. They can transfer sufficient resources to create a new distribution where they are secure. Nonessential states—those that are not a member of any minimal winning coalition—cannot guarantee their continued existence through their own efforts alone. They may succeed in surviving if some other state becomes the target of a threat first. Distributions of resources where all states are essential are system stable, although not necessarily resource stable. Such distributions can support a balance of power in the behavioral sense of the term. Table 1 summarizes these results. It gives the distributions of power that are system stable, resource stable (and hence also system stable), and neither for two, three, and more states.

What are the empirical implications of the model? First, the only states that are eliminated are inessential at the time of their elimination from the system. This hypothesis is the primary test of balance-of-power theory according to this model. Inessential states may not be eliminated, but essential states can never be eliminated. However, the judgment of which states are inessential may prove to be more difficult than it appears at first glance. Consider the following two distributions of resources: (80, 76, 73, 71) and (80, 77, 74, 69). All four states are essential in the first distribution, while the last state is inessential in the second one. Our measures of national capabilities are rough enough that we might not be able to tell the difference—less than 1 percent of the total capabilities in the system—between the two distributions if they occurred.

Second, a wide range of distributions of resources, including many that do not look balanced, can support a balance of power. The two distributions in the previous paragraph both appear to be balanced at first glance, although the first is and the second is not. Distributions that appear very unbalanced can support a balance of power; for instance, all the states in (140, 80, 60, 20) are essential. The demands of a balance of power on the distribution of capabilities are probably quite weak, although no empirical work has been done on the frequency of distributions that can support a balance of power.

TABLE 1.

Summary of the Stability of International Systems in the Balance-of-Power Model

	STABILITY OF SYSTEM		
Number of States in System	**Resource and System Stable**	**System Stable Only**	**Unstable**
Two	Exactly even division of resources—150, 150	None	Any other division of resources
Three	Any division of resources where one state has exactly half the total—e.g., 150, 100, 50	Any division of resources where no state has more than half the total—e.g., 120, 100, 80	Any division of resources where one state has more than half the total—e.g., 160, 80, 60
More Than Three	Any division of resources where one state has exactly half the total—e.g., 150, 100, 30, 20	Any division of resources where all states are essential—e.g., 120, 80, 60, 40	Any other division of resources—e.g., 100, 80, 80, 40

Note: The examples of systems have a total of 300 resources. A system is resource stable if no resources are ever redistributed either peacefully or through war. A system is system stable if no state is ever eliminated. A system that is resource stable is then system stable by definition.

Third, balancing need not work as the neorealists assume. Neorealists describe balancing as the formation of a coalition to stop a state on the verge of dominating the system, and so preserve all other states in the face of that threat. They oppose balancing with bandwagoning, joining with the threatening state. In the model, balancing does occur to preserve threatened states. However, their existence is preserved by a transfer of resources to the strongest member of the threatening coalition. These transfers look like bandwagoning rather than balancing. If we define balancing more broadly to include all behavior that helps to produce a balance, then large ranges of behavior could be called balancing simply because many distributions of capabilities can support a balance. Any action that helped to produce such a distribution could be construed as balancing.

It may be that these and other differences with neorealism are a consequence of particular features of the model. In the model, multipolar systems are likely to be system stable, while bipolar systems are not. The instability of bipolar systems arises because the side with more resources, even just one point more, always wins in a war. What happens if we make the outcomes of war uncertain, so the stronger cannot be certain it will win when it makes a threat? Uncertainty in war outcomes could be introduced in two ways. First, the outcome could be probabilistic; for instance, each side's chance of winning equals its share of the two sides' resources. Second, sides could hold private information about their own resources with victory still always going to the stronger side. Each side is then uncertain about whether it will win a war because it does not know the other side's resources exactly. Either of these approaches introduces uncertainty about war outcomes.[4]

Uncertain war outcomes immediately raise the issue of what risks states are willing to accept to gain resources. In the original model, states would not accept any risk of elimination to gain resources. Taken literally when war is uncertain and there is some chance of elimination in any war, then every system would be resource stable because no state would accept any risk of elimination no matter how small that risk was. If war is uncertain, we must consider how states vary in their willingness to accept risk. For illustration, consider a bipolar system where each side's chance of winning a war equals its share of the two sides' resources. Attitudes toward risk are reflected in the smallest chance of winning that a state needs to be willing to start a war; the higher this break-even probability, the less willing the state is to take risks. If both states had break-even probabilities of two-thirds, then any bipolar distribution where neither state had more than 200 resources would be system and resource stable. So risk-averse states faced with uncertain wars can stabilize bipolar systems.

At the same time, such chances could destabilize multipolar systems. The ability to create the single, stable, bipolar systems makes tripolar systems stable in the model. When many bipolar systems are stable, then the third state may wish to stay on the sidelines if the strongest state threatens the weakest state. The third state may be able to guarantee its own existence even if the strongest state conquers the weakest state. Further, it might join the strongest state against the weakest state if the strongest state was risk averse and the weakest state was willing to take big risks. The weakest state would be a threat to the third state if it won the war with the strongest state. As of now, there are no clear results if war is uncertain. This discussion shows rather how difficult the problem is. States now cannot be judged simply by their resources; a state's willingness to take risks is just as important to judge the threat it poses to other states. A balance of power may depend as much on what states want as on how power is distributed in the system (Morrow 1988).

A second objection to the model concerns the credibility of the promises that states can make to one another in the model (Wagner 1994). The model assumes that states can commit to how they will divide the resources of the targets when they make a threat and that states can commit to making transfers of resources. In the first case, suppose that the division of resources among a victorious coalition is determined by the relative resources within the coalition. Now the members of a victorious coalition can no longer set the postwar distribution of threats as they wish, which makes some threats less attractive. For example, in three-actor systems, any threat involves the two victors splitting the third state to produce an even postwar distribution of (150, 150). If they cannot control the division, the weaker state will not want to join the coalition because the stronger will end the war with more than 150 resources, and so conquer it in the next round. Similarly, removing the credibility of promises to transfer resources undermines counters to many threats. Targets of threats can no longer freeze the system with a transfer. Both of these changes may have dramatic effects on what distributions of resources can support a balance of power.

In summary, the balance-of-power model questions informal understandings of balance-of-power theory and empirical tests of that theory. A wide range of distributions of capabilities, including many very unequal distributions, appear to support balancing, although what actions constitute balancing is unclear. We are left to puzzle what exactly is a balance of power and how we might know one is operating.

The Power Transition

Power transition opposes balance of power as systemic theories of international politics (see the Kugler and Lemke chapter of this volume). Power transition theory postulates a system dominated by a single state. Another state rises in power as a consequence of its own internal economic and political development to emerge as a challenger to this dominant state. The question is whether this power transition will lead to war.

Can the dominant state and its challenger resolve their political differences peacefully?

The key strategic question here is dynamic; when during the transition is each side willing to fight? The challenger must determine when it is willing to push the dominant state to make concessions in the existing political order in favor of its own interests. The dominant state must ask when it is willing to fight to defend the order it has constructed. Because the military balance is shifting between the two states, each side's chance of winning changes during the transition. The challenger's chance of winning is increasing while the dominant state's chance is declining. The dominant state will presumably make some concessions to the challenger to avoid war, but will those concessions be sufficient to satisfy the demands of the challenger for change in the system?

Neither side can commit itself to future actions when they negotiate over those concessions. The challenger might like to reassure the dominant state that it will not attack in the future when it is even stronger than it is at the time of the negotiations. The dominant state might be willing to concede something to the challenger now, but then commit itself not to make any further concessions in the future. However, neither promise is credible at the time they are made because each side's willingness to live up to its promise will change as the military balance shifts. These credibility problems are at the heart of whether power transitions lead to war.

The challenger seeks to change the status quo created by the dominant state, preferably through peaceful means rather than war. Its willingness to make demands depends on the likely response of the dominant state. If the dominant state will grant a demand for change in the status quo, then the challenger would always demand changes in its favor. The willingness of the dominant state to fight varies as the transition proceeds, which could vary in two ways. First, the dominant state becomes less willing to fight as its power declines through the transition. Second, the dominant state's willingness to make concessions decreases as the transition progresses. The key is the difference in the value of war and the concessions needed to satisfy the challenger, and power transition theory is silent on this issue. Either view is consistent with power transition theory, although they have very different implications for how war arises.

Figure 1 illustrates these two views. In both views, the dominant state's value for war and for making concessions decline as its capabilities decline through the transition. In the view on the left of the figure, the

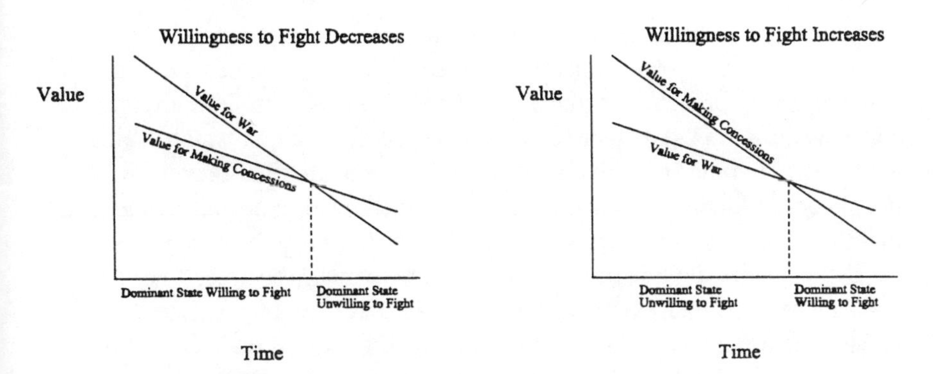

FIGURE 1. Two views of the willingness of the dominant state to make concessions during a power transition

willingness of the dominant state to fight declines because its value for war drops more rapidly than its value for making concessions. In the view on the right, the dominant state becomes more willing to fight because its value for concessions drops more quickly than its value for fighting. Because power transition theory only specifies that both values drop through the transition but not which declines more quickly, both views are possible.

Shifting capabilities drive the dominant state's willingness to fight in the first case. Kim and Morrow (1992) analyze this case. War, according to power transition theory, resolves the differences between the dominant state and the challenger in favor of the victor. The dominant state prefers fighting early in the transition because it has a higher chance of winning now than later. Because it would like to fight late in the transition, the challenger does not demand changes in the status quo. Instead, it waits for its power, and so its chance of winning a war, to rise. The dominant state prefers making concessions to fighting at some point in time. At that time, all challengers will demand changes in the status quo because those demands will be granted. Some challengers may be unwilling to accept the current status until that time, and so make demands before that point. Such premature demands spark war.

The change in the value of the concessions drives the dominant state's willingness to fight in the second case. The first concessions to the challenger do not alter the fundamental nature of the system that the dominant state has created, and so it is willing to grant those concessions to purchase peace. As the transition progresses, those concessions grow in importance, and the dominant state becomes less willing to make continued concessions. At some time, the concessions are large enough that the dominant state prefers war to making further concessions. Although the challenger always wants more concessions from the dominant state, there is a moment in time after which it is no longer willing to fight to gain additional concessions. The status quo has changed enough at that moment that the challenger is no longer willing to fight to change the system.

If the dominant state becomes less willing to make the necessary concessions as the transition progresses, it faces a problem of appeasement. Powell (1996b) analyzes the problem of whether the challenger will be satisfied in the long run with the concessions that the dominant state makes to avoid war. If the dominant state will grant concessions, the challenger always wants to ask for more. If concessions now will buy peace, then the dominant state is willing to grant them. If it believes that it cannot not satisfy the long-run demands of the challenger and so must fight eventually, then the dominant state prefers fighting now to fighting later. However, the dominant state does not know how many concessions will satisfy the challenger. It must judge whether the concessions currently demanded will buy lasting peace or merely a hiatus in the demands of the challenger. The dominant state is vulnerable to "salami tactics"—unending small demands that eventually erode the status quo it has constructed. It prefers granting the immediate demand to fighting now, while preferring war now to the complete string of concessions that salami tactics can extract from it. The dominant state can call a halt to these demands by threatening to go to war when the alternative is a string of future concessions leading to a worse status quo than the outcome of a war now. Those challengers that are satisfied with the changes in the status quo to that time cease their demands; challengers unsatisfied with the scope of concessions to date go to war.

Both sides suffer from the credibility problem here. Both would be better off if they could strike a bargain short of war if the challenger is about to make a demand that will lead to war. However, the challenger cannot commit itself to make no demands later, making the bargain unenforceable. Similarly, the dominant state cannot commit itself to fight in the future, and so deter further demands from the challenger. In either case, the problem of dynamic credibility makes power transitions dangerous.

These game-theoretic models raise an important question for power transition theory. That theory concentrates on the shifts in power, but not the shifts in the status quo. The two preceding cases—when the dominant state becomes less willing to fight versus more willing to fight as the transition progresses—differ in the value of the concessions that must be made to accommodate the demands of the challenger peacefully. Willingness to fight requires a comparison between the value of war and the value of concessions, and the theory specifies only the former. They lead to different conclusions; the speed of the transition is irrelevant to whether war occurs if the dominant state's willingness to fight declines as the transition progresses, while faster transitions are more likely to end in war if the dominant state is more willing to fight as time passes. However, power transition theory has not addressed the question of the nature of the concessions that the dominant state makes to the challenger during the transition, and so cannot answer which case fits its argument better.

The Democratic Peace

The study of the democratic peace begins with the observation that no two modern, liberal democracies have fought a war (see chapter by Russett and Starr in this volume). I discuss only one small part of that large literature, the attempts to use game theory to explain this regularity. These attempts focus on two questions. First, why might pairs of democracies be more likely to reach peaceful settlements than a democracy and an autocracy? The rates of violent conflict in these two types of dyads are quite different and appear to be key to the democratic peace.[5] Second, given that the answer to the first question assumes that democracies are less willing to fight than other types of states, why would that be so? The two questions are related. The answer to the first leads us to ask the second, and the first explains why the answer to the second alone is not sufficient to understand the democratic peace.

The puzzle in the first question concerns the dyadic nature of the democratic peace. If democracies are less inclined to fight than other types of states, why should the chance that they fight with other democracies be so much lower than the chance that they fight with other types of states? Bueno de Mesquita and Lalman (1992) and Fearon (1994a) propose that signaling issues drive the difference.

Wars are almost always preceded by crises where the sides try to pressure each other into giving up the stakes of the crisis without a fight. Each side must judge the other's value for war when it decides whether to continue the crisis, because the other in turn will decide whether to concede the stakes in part on its own value for war. The ultimate coercive step in a crisis is a fait accompli, a use of force that places the other side in a position where it must either surrender the stakes or go to war. Such a step cuts off the possibility of the two sides finding a negotiated settlement in lieu of war.

A state's value for war varies with the issue in dispute. A state's resolve is known only to itself; it is a state's private information. The other side must judge the state's value for war from what it knows about the state before the crisis and its actions in the crisis. Assume that democracies on average have a lower value for war than other states. This assumption does not mean they are less likely to fight, because the decision whether to fight depends on the alternative to war. The alternative to war depends on the possibility of a negotiated settlement with the other side. Whether war occurs then depends on both sides' value for war, what they perceive each other's value for war to be, and how the values and perceptions affect their bargaining strategies in a crisis.

When an autocracy faces a democracy, it has some reason to doubt the resolve of the democracy. As assumed earlier, democracies have a lower value for war than other types of states. Highly coercive strategies, such as a fait accompli, may have a better chance of working against states that are not highly resolved. Autocracies then may engage in very coercive strategies against democracies in the hope of winning the stakes without war. Democracies faced with the prospect of such coercion are likely to adopt highly coercive strategies in response. Offers to negotiate are likely to be read as signals of weakness, and so encourage further escalation by the autocracy. If there is an advantage to striking first, the democracy may be willing to strike first to forestall an attempted fait accompli by the autocracy. The strategic interaction of a democracy and an autocracy is likely to encourage both sides to use coercive strategies that foreclose the opportunity for a negotiated settlement.

When two democracies face each other, each has some confidence that the other has a low value for war simply because they are both democracies. Both can explore negotiated settlements without the fear that the other side is likely to exploit a perceived weakness. The chance that either will try a fait accompli is small, reducing the chance that either will consider such steps to forestall the other's rush to war. Because each democracy believes that the other is unlikely to want to fight, the dynamics of signaling resolve in a crisis are different.

Fearon (1994a) argues a variation of the idea that crises between democracies are less dangerous than those between other types of states. Recall that costly signaling made a state's position credible in a crisis. Fearon argues that escalation is more costly for democracies than for other types of states. The signal of resolve that escalation sends is more credible when a democracy sends it. Then crises between two democracies are more likely to be resolved peacefully because both sides' signals of resolve are more credible. The side that values the stakes less can determine the resolve of the other side and back down short of war. A state facing an autocracy in a crisis must always wonder about the credibility of the autocracy's signal. Does it really intend to go to war or is it escalating because escalation is cheap for an autocracy? Democracy makes international signaling more credible and so more efficient.

This answer leads us back to the second question: why do democracies have a lower value for war, all else equal, or why is escalation more costly for democracies? The position of democratic leaders is less secure than that of autocratic leaders (Bueno de Mesquita and Siverson 1995). War or failure in a crisis is more likely to lead to the ouster of a democratic leader than the ouster of an autocratic leader. Consequently, democratic leaders have to judge carefully the risks they take in international politics, precisely because they are more likely to bear the consequences. Their audience costs are higher because their domestic audience is watching and will hold them accountable.

Why are domestic audiences willing to hold their leader responsible for the consequences of his or her actions? After all, the mistakes are in the past, and presumably the domestic audience cares about what will happen in the future. Why replace a proven, quality leader with an unproven alternative? Smith (1996a) presents a model based on models of retrospective voting (such as Ferejohn 1986). The electorate does not know the competence of their leader and so must judge it from his or her actions. Success in crises and wars depends in part on the leader's competence. Then retrospective judgments of success and failure provide a way for the electorate to judge their leader's competence, and so anticipate likely outcomes in the future. However, the incentives that these judgments produce for leaders also have consequences. Leaders tend to act more aggressively than they would if they made policy solely on its merits. Passivity in the face of a threat signals that a leader is not competent, because a competent leader is confident in his or her ability to prevail in the crisis. At the margin then, leaders of lesser competence escalate crises that they would not on their own merits.

Conclusion

This chapter has surveyed models that use noncooperative game theory in war studies. It is not a comprehensive survey; rather, I have identified how such models have been used to critique the logic of four theories of international conflict. In all four cases, noncooperative game models direct us to consider how problems of signaling and commitment occur in each issue area. How do states signal their resolve in deterrence crises? Why might commitment problems over time make power transition dangerous? In each case, the models present new questions for these theories and expose limitations in their logic. In some cases, the models show that existing empirical tests of those theories are inadequate and propose different tests in their place.

How does one go about using game theory to think about conflict? First, a game or model must be specified. The analyst must identify the relevant actors, what choices they have, the sequence of those choices, the consequences of those choices, how the actors evaluate those consequences, and what the actors know about the game at each choice that must be made. Specifying the model is the most critical step of any game-theoretic analysis because it is the stage where the analyst renders his or her understanding of social science theory into a formal game. For example, the games used in the study of deterrence theory reflect the set of threats and responses that deterrence arguments typically assume that the actors have. Deterrence arguments also limit the range of possible payoffs in such models. Actors then prefer prevailing peacefully to fighting because deterrence theory assumes that they do.

Once the game is specified, the analyst must find the equilibria of the game and consider whether some of those equilibria are implausible in the particular situation. Solving games is the province of textbooks on game theory, and I have nothing to add here. Once the equilibria are found, the resulting behavior can be analyzed using the method of comparative statics. Do the players' actions change with the underlying parameters of the game, and if so, how do those parameters change with observable indicators? In this way, we can arrive at testable hypotheses. For instance, the defender's value for war is likely to increase with its military capabilities.

How does equilibrium behavior change as the defender's capabilities increase? What relationship does the model predict?

In all stages, the process of modeling disciplines the analyst. Complicated games are generally difficult to solve. Often then, the simplest model is the best model. A simple model is easier to solve, and the resulting equilibria are easier to interpret. There is always a creative tension between parsimony and richness. Make a model too simple, and its results are uninteresting. Make it too complex, and it is impenetrable. The best models distill critical strategic problems that recur across many situations.

The use of game theory is revolutionary in that it forces rigorous development of the logic of a theory. Of course, one does not need such models to think rigorously nor is game theory the only tool for the rigorous logical development of theories. Still, game theory has some particular advantages for thinking about war. Conflict has important strategic elements. Both sides think about what the other will do when they escalate a crisis. Many theories of war advance purposive arguments for why war occurs. Game theory is the best-developed tool we have to date for the study of purposive strategy. For example, balance-of-power theorists assume that states seek security and consequently seek to create and maintain a balance of power. Does balancing behavior actually follow from those assumptions? What exactly is a "balance of power"? Are additional, unstated assumptions necessary for balance-of-power theory? Game-theoretic models of the balance of power can help us answer these questions. As we saw in the section on balance of power, the answers are more complicated than one might think at first. The game-theoretic revolution, then, does not propose a new theory of conflict; instead, it forces us to improve our existing theories and helps us to judge which theories explain why wars occur.

Notes

1. Morrow (1994) provides an accessible introduction to game theory and its application to political science.
2. Some notable works are Banks (1990), Bueno de Mesquita and Lalman (1992), Fearon (1994a), Kilgour and Zagare (1991), Morrow (1989), and Powell (1990, 1996a).
3. This conclusion assumes that the challenger prefers backing down from its demand to war. If not, then war could result because both sides prefer war to allowing the other to prevail.

4. The ideas here have not yet been fully developed in the literature. Schweller (1993) starts down this line of argument, but his failure to specify fully his model undermines his argument. See Fink, Humes, and Schwebach (1997) for a trenchant critique of Schweller (1993).
5. I ignore the question of whether democracies are more peaceful in general than other systems to focus on the dyadic question of why democratic dyads are so peaceful. There is a notable literature on the question of whether the democratic peace is monadic or dyadic (e.g., Rousseau et al. 1996).

Loss Aversion, Framing Effects, and International Conflict

Perspectives from Prospect Theory

JACK S. LEVY

The study of international conflict has changed substantially in the decade since the publication of *The Handbook of War Studies* (Midlarsky 1989b), and the result has been an unmistakable improvement in the quality of theory and empirical research (Levy 1998). Some new intellectual trends in the field have originated in response to the end of the cold war, the collapse of the Soviet Union, the rise of ethnonational conflicts, and the spread of global capitalism and democracy. Other new lines of research have grown out of autonomous analytical developments.

One example of the latter is the application of prospect theory to international relations. Developed by social psychologists (Kahneman and Tversky 1979) in an attempt to integrate experimental evidence of descriptive inaccuracies in expected-utility theory into an alternative theory of risky choice, prospect theory has been widely applied in a number of fields, including organizational theory, management science, consumer economics, and insurance and investment behavior. Since the early 1990s it has begun to have an impact on the study of international relations.[1]

Prospect theory suggests a rich set of hypotheses about the foreign policy behavior of states and the strategic interaction between states in the international system. It also raises a number of difficult conceptual and methodological issues that must be overcome before these hypotheses can be validated empirically. I have examined some of these problems elsewhere (Levy 1997), and it is important to read this essay in that context, but here I focus primarily on the theoretical implications of prospect theory for various aspects of international conflict.

I begin with a brief survey of some of the most important behavioral deviations from the predictions of expected-utility theory and describe how prospect theory attempts to integrate these patterns into an alternative theory of choice under conditions of risk. I then turn to a lengthy discussion of the implications of the key prospect theory concepts of reference dependence, framing, loss aversion, and variable risk orientation for state security policies and for interstate bargaining.

Summary of Prospect Theory

Prospect theory is inductive rather than deductive in its origins. The dominance of expected-utility theory as a normative theory of choice under conditions of risk led social psychologists and then experimental economists to undertake a series of experimental tests of the descriptive validity of the theory.[2] These experiments have repeatedly demonstrated a series of violations of the basic axioms of expected-utility theory. This has led scholars to attempt to integrate these findings into a more descriptively accurate theory of risky choice. One of the most prominent of these "behavioral decision theories," and the one that has attracted the most attention in political science, is prospect theory.

The experimental evidence suggests a number of ways in which people do not behave according to the assumptions and predictions of expected-utility theory. First, contrary to the postulate of an individual utility function that is defined over levels of assets, people appear to be more sensitive to changes in assets than to net asset levels, to *gains* and *losses* from a *reference point* rather than to levels of wealth and welfare (Kahneman and Tversky 1979, 277). This *reference dependence* (Tversky and Kahneman 1991, 1039) is the central analytic assumption of prospect theory.

Reference dependence is critically important because of the tendency for people to respond differently to gains and to losses—they overvalue losses relative to comparable gains, so that the pain of losses exceeds the pleasure from gains (Kahneman and Tversky 1979; Tversky and Kahneman 1986, 1991). This is known as *loss aversion.* As Jimmy Connors once said, "I hate to lose more than I like to win" (Levy 1992a, 175).[3]

Because of loss aversion, people tend to value what they have more than comparable things that they do not have, and the psychological cost of relinquishing a good is greater than the psychological benefit of acquiring it. This is the *endowment effect* (Thaler 1980, 43–47). People often refuse to sell an item for a price at which they would not have considered purchasing that item in the first place, so that selling prices tend to exceed buying prices, often by a substantial amount (Knetsch and Sinden 1984; Kahneman, Knetsch, and Thaler 1990, 1336; 1991; Tversky and Kahneman 1991; Camerer 1995, 665–70).

The asymmetry between losses and gains also affects *risk orientation.*[4] People tend to be risk averse in choices among gains but risk acceptant with respect to losses. Given a choice between $40 for certain and a 50/50 chance of getting $0 or $100, over 70 percent of subjects choose the certain $40. But given a choice between a certain loss of $40 and a 50/50 chance of losing $0 or $100, roughly 70 percent take the risky gamble. That is, in choices involving possible losses people will take risks in the hope of avoiding loss, even though the result may be an even greater loss, and even though the expected value of the gamble is worse—and sometimes considerably worse—than the value of the certain loss.

Risk aversion for gains and risk seeking for losses imply that value functions are concave in the domain of gains and convex in the domain of losses, with a *reflection effect* around the reference point (Kahneman and Tversky 1979, 268). This pattern of risk orientation, represented by an S-shaped value function, is repeatedly found for a variety of individuals and situations.

Given the asymmetry of gains and losses around a reference point, how actors define the reference point can have a critical effect on the choices they make. A change in reference point can result in a change in preferences (*preference reversal*) even if the values and probabilities associated with outcomes remain the same (Kahneman and Tversky 1979; Tversky and Kahneman 1986; Roth 1995, 68–75; Camerer 1995, 652–65). The identification of the reference point is known as *framing,* and a change in preference and choice as a result of a change in frame is a *framing effect.*

One striking example of framing effects can be found in the hypothetical medical example offered by Tversky and Kahneman (1986, S260):

> Imagine that the U.S. is preparing for the outbreak of an unusual Asian disease, which is expected to kill 600 people. Two alternative programs to combat the disease have been proposed. Assume

that the exact scientific estimates of the consequences of the programs are as follows:

> (Survival frame)
> If Program A is adopted, 200 people will be saved.
> If Program B is adopted, there is 1/3 probability that 600 people will be saved, and 2/3 probability that no people will be saved.

The identical description of the situation is given to a second group of subjects, but the same information about the alternative treatment programs is framed differently.

> (Mortality frame)
> If Program C is adopted 400 people will die.
> If Program D is adopted there is a 1/3 probability that nobody will die, and 2/3 probability that 600 people will die.

In the survival frame 72 percent ($N = 152$) of the subjects preferred Program A, indicating a risk-averse preference for saving 200 with certainty over a gamble with the same expected value. In the mortality frame ($N = 155$), however, 78 percent preferred Program D, indicating a risk-acceptant preference for a gamble in the hope of preventing 400 people from certain death. The only difference in the choice problems faced by the two groups is the framing of the outcomes in terms of the number of lives saved or lost.

Reference dependence and framing effects are extremely important for prospect theory. Preference reversals induced by changes in frames rather than by changes in subjective utilities or probabilities are difficult to reconcile with expected-utility theory or with rational choice theories more generally because they violate the fundamental assumption that logically identical choice problems should yield identical results. Evidence that behavior varies depending on whether the glass is seen as half-empty or half-full does not easily lend itself to a rational choice explanation (Tversky and Kahneman 1986, S252–57; Levy 1997, 92–93).

In the "Asian flu" example, as in most laboratory studies of framing, the experimenter manipulates the reference point in a way that she can be relatively confident that subjects will not "reframe" the problem they face; consequently, any difference in behavior can be traced to the manipulated framing effects. Similarly, there may be many simple choice problems in the real world in which the framing of the reference point is for all practical purposes determined by the situation.

In static situations that involve a well-defined status quo, for example, actors usually frame choice problems around the status quo. Thus Tversky and Kahneman (1991, 1046–47) argue that "the reference state usually corresponds to the decision maker's current position." They concede that this is not always the case, however, and that expectations, aspiration levels, social norms, and social comparisons quite distinct from the status quo can also influence the framing of the reference point.

Some applications of prospect theory ignore this important qualification and assume that the status quo always serves as the reference point. If this were true, prospect theory would lose much of its distinctiveness, for the primary value-added of prospect theory over expected-utility theory lies in reference dependence and framing effects. Framing is a *variable,* and most important prospect theory hypotheses involve the explanation of variations in outcomes as a function of variations in the framing of the reference point. The tendency to examine cases in which actors frame their reference points around the status quo is a limitation of many applications of prospect theory to international relations (e.g., McDermott 1998).

Framing around a reference point other than the status quo is particularly likely in dynamic situations in which there is no stable status quo to serve as an obvious focal point. In a situation that involves a sequence of successive choices rather than a single choice, for example, it is not clear whether an actor will define her reference point in terms of her asset position at the beginning of the series of choices or with respect to her current asset position after a series of actions, or if this is affected by whether the outcomes of each decision involve gains or losses.

There is substantial experimental evidence that people adjust to gains more rapidly than to losses. They "renormalize" their reference points after gains but not after losses, and they do so very quickly. This *instant endowment effect* (Kahneman, Knetsch, and Thaler 1990, 1342) has extremely important implications. It leads to the prediction that after a series of gains individuals will frame around those gains (the new status quo), regard any subsequent setback as a loss rather than as a foregone gain, overweight that loss, and engage in risk-seeking behavior to maintain their cumulative gains against that loss.

After a series of losses, however, individuals will not adjust to the new situation but rather continue to frame around the old reference point. They will perceive any chance of "improving" their position to a point that still falls short of the original reference point as a loss, and they will

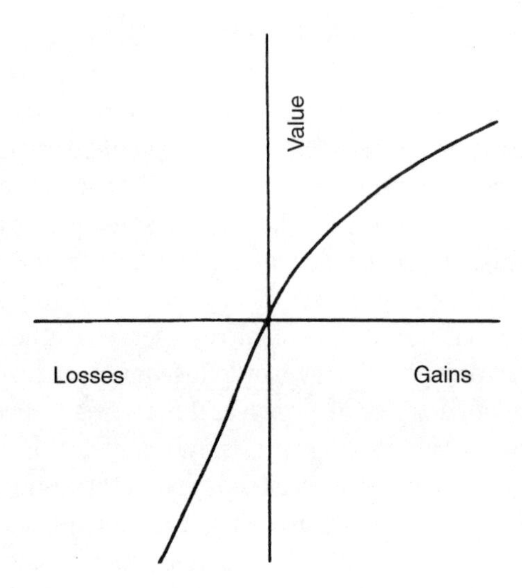

FIGURE 1. A prospect theory value function

engage in risk-seeking behavior to eliminate those losses and return to the reference point.

Most applications of prospect theory to international relations have focused on loss aversion, framing, and the reflection effect. Another important finding is that individual choice behavior demonstrates a *nonlinear response to probabilities,* contrary to the linear combination of utilities and probabilities posited by expected-utility theory. People overweight outcomes that are certain relative to outcomes that are merely probable (the *certainty effect*). They tend to overweight small probabilities and to underweight moderate and high probabilities.[5] In other words, people tend to give more weight to the utility of a possible outcome than to its probability of occurrence as long as probabilities are not small. If probabilities are extremely small, however, people are quite unpredictable in their behavior. Some buy insurance against rare catastrophes, for example, while others do not (Kahneman and Tversky 1979; Camerer 1995, 620–22).

Prospect theory attempts to combine these observed violations of expected-utility theory into a single integrated theory of choice. Toward this end Kahneman and Tversky (1979) distinguish two phases in the choice process. In the *editing phase* the actor identifies the reference point, the available options, the possible outcomes, and the value and

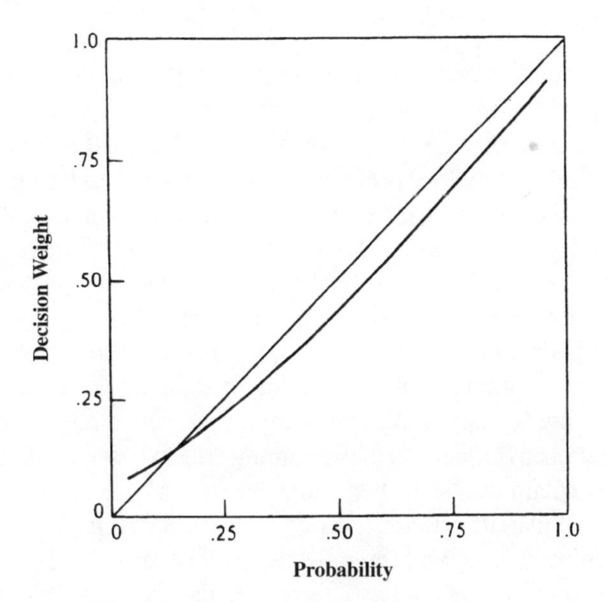

FIGURE 2. A probability weighting function

probability of each of these outcomes. In the *evaluation phase* the actor combines the values of possible outcomes (as reflected in an S-shaped *value function,* illustrated in fig. 1) with their weighted probabilities (as reflected in the *probability weighting function,* illustrated in fig. 2) and then maximizes over the product (the "prospective utility").

It is important to note that attitudes toward risk are determined by the combination of the S-shaped value function and the probability weighting function and not by the value function alone. This combination usually generates risk aversion for gains and risk acceptance for losses, but the overweighting of small probabilities can lead to a reversal of risk propensities under certain conditions, depending on the precise shapes of the two functions (Kahneman and Tversky 1979; Levy 1992a, 183–84). This is illustrated by gambling (risk acceptance for gains) and by the purchase of insurance (which involves taking a certain loss in the form of an insurance premium in order to avoid the risk of a larger loss).

There are some serious conceptual and methodological problems that need to be overcome before we can test these hypotheses against the empirical evidence or utilize prospect theory as a reliable framework for explanation in international politics. I analyze these in detail elsewhere

(Levy 1997; see also Morrow 1997), but a brief summary would be useful here. One analytical problem derives from the fact that prospect theory is a theory of individual choice, whereas international relations involves the strategic interaction of states (and other actors). We need a theory that explains how individual-level preferences and frames get aggregated or transformed into the collective preferences and frames of states. We also need a theory that explains how the choices of two actors interact in a strategic setting—one that subsumes the decision-theoretic propositions of prospect theory into a game-theoretic framework.

At the methodological level, we cannot begin to make progress unless we can identify actors' reference points independently of the behavior that we are trying to explain. We cannot infer an actor's reference point from his or her behavior and then use framing effects based on that reference point to explain that same behavior.[6] It is also necessary to rule out the alternative explanation that actors' choices are determined not by loss aversion, framing effects, and the reflection of risk orientations around the reference point, but instead by actors' calculations that the expected utility of the chosen option was greater than the expected utility of the alternatives.

Implications for Foreign Policy Behavior

Prospect theory and the descriptive findings upon which it is based generate a rich set of hypotheses about the impact of framing effects, loss aversion, and variable risk orientation on state foreign policy behavior.[7] One proposition concerns the greater tendency toward status quo choices than expected-utility theory would predict. This *status quo bias* has been observed in both experimental research and field studies of consumer and investment behavior (Samuelson and Zeckhauser 1988; Knetsch and Sinden 1984; Hartman, Doane, and Woo 1991).

We can explain this pattern in terms of loss aversion and the endowment effect. If an individual frames a choice problem around the existing status quo, she or he will treat the costs of moving away from the status quo as a loss and the benefits of moving away from the status quo as a gain, overweight the former relative to the latter, and consequently demonstrate a bias toward remaining at the status quo.[8]

The status quo bias is reflected in the common observation that states appear to make greater efforts to preserve the status quo against a threatened loss than to improve their position by a comparable amount. They are sometimes willing to fight to defend the same territory that they would not have been willing to fight to acquire in the first place. This is illustrated by Ross's (1984, 247) argument that Soviet leaders were willing to engage in the "use of decisive and perhaps risky action far more readily for *defending* as opposed to *extending* Soviet gains."

These observations are consistent with "defensive realism," which essentially argues that "states maximize security by aiming to preserve the status quo in the international system" (Labs 1997, 9; see also Posen 1984, 69; Snyder 1991). This perspective is the object of Schweller's (1996) critique of "neorealism's status quo bias." Though Schweller (1996, 99, 106) does not explicitly refer to prospect theory, the connection is striking when he argues that "states value what they possess more than what they covet," and that "rational states do not seek relative gains so much as avoid relative losses."

Other variables, including reputational and domestic political considerations, might explain the tendency toward status quo choices in international politics. These explanations are not necessarily inconsistent with prospect theory, however, for reputational and domestic political interests may themselves be influenced by loss aversion. Political leaders may be more concerned to prevent a decline in their country's (or their own) reputation or credibility than to increase it by a comparable amount, and more worried by the costs of falling dominoes than hopeful about the gains from others bandwagoning in their favor (Jervis 1991). It is also conceivable that domestic publics tend to punish their political leaders more for strategic or economic losses than to reward them for comparable gains. The conventional wisdom among students of American politics, for example, is that political candidates are more concerned to avoid alienating key constituencies than to strengthen support among those groups.

Thus there may be loss/gain asymmetries in the impact of both reputational interests and domestic politics on foreign policy behavior. It is important to know, however, where in the causal chain loss aversion has an impact. Are political leaders themselves prone to loss aversion in their evaluation of the reputational or domestic consequences of certain outcomes? Or does loss aversion occur earlier in the causal chain and have a more indirect impact, affecting the reaction of domestic and foreign audiences (as anticipated by political leaders) but not the calculations of political leaders themselves? Or does loss aversion affect both leaders and their audiences and thus have a "double whammy" effect? These causal paths are analytically distinct, but they cannot be empirically differentiated by looking at outcomes alone.

Nincic (1997) provides some evidence for the hypothesized asymmetry in public support for political leaders in his study of the impact of American military interventions abroad on the president's domestic support levels. Nincic focuses on justifications offered by the president for the active use of U.S. military force abroad, which he categorizes as either "protective" of existing interests or "promotive" in the sense of enhancing American interests. Nincic examines a set of 18 American military interventions and measures presidential justifications through a content analysis of public statements. He finds that the increases in presidential popularity are six percentage points greater for interventions framed as protective than for those framed as promotive.

Nincic (1997) also examines the likelihood of congressional support (in the form of a congressional resolution) for military interventions as a function of presidential framing of those interventions as protective or promotive. Again he finds a difference, with the odds of the president securing a resolution in support of a protective intervention being about five times greater than for a promotive intervention. Nincic (1997) concludes that "the U.S. public and Congress are more willing to reward the president for foreign policy actions intended to preserve or restore a situation that had already been attained than for those meant to pursue a new gain or to create a new outcome."[9]

If all states defined their reference point in terms of the status quo and if the status quo were basically acceptable and unchanging, then loss aversion and the status quo bias would lead states to be excessively cautious in attempting to improve their positions. Consequently, there would be fewer challenges to the status quo than we might expect on the basis of expected-value calculations, and the status quo bias would reinforce stability in international politics.[10]

The problem is that political leaders do not always frame around the status quo. They sometimes frame around an expectation or aspiration level. If actors define their reference point above the status quo, they will evaluate the status quo as a loss, recognize that inaction will result in a certain loss, and tend toward risky gambles in the hope of eliminating a certain loss but at the risk of incurring a larger loss.[11]

This suggests that the concept of a status quo bias is technically misspecified. It is really a *reference point bias* (Levy 1996a), a greater tendency to move toward the reference point than is predicted by expected-value calculations. The status quo bias occurs only when actors define the status quo as their reference point. Whereas the hypothesized status quo bias is generally stabilizing in the sense that it reinforces the status quo, the reference point bias may be destabilizing whenever actors frame their reference points above the status quo.

Consider the situation immediately after an actor has suffered a loss—whether territorial, reputational, or domestic political. After suffering losses political leaders have a tendency not to renormalize their reference point but instead to gamble in the hope of eliminating those losses and returning to the reference point, even at the risk of suffering a larger loss.

One illustration is the 1982 Falklands/Malvinas crisis. Argentine military leaders, faced with serious domestic economic and political problems and with a status quo defined by continued British occupation of the Malvinas, adopted a potentially risky strategy of attempting to seize the Malvinas by force rather than continue negotiations with Britain. The hypothesis that Argentine leaders framed their reference point around an aspiration level defined by Argentine control of the Malvinas gains additional credibility from the fact that the junta's deadline for recovering the islands was the end of 1982, which happened to be the very symbolic 150th anniversary of the Argentine loss of the islands (Levy and Vakili 1992).

Another example comes from U.S. decision making in the 1962 Cuban missile crisis. There is substantial evidence that President Kennedy framed his reference point in terms of zero Soviet offensive missiles in Cuba, that he perceived the existence of Soviet missiles in Cuba as a loss from this long-standing expectation level, and that the issue was not whether to remove the missiles but how (Whyte and Levi 1994, 248–51). Kennedy recognized that a strategy of compellence to induce the Soviets to remove the missiles would be risky, but he was willing to take these risks to avoid the certain loss that would follow from inaction.

This interpretation gains added support from the fact that Kennedy apparently believed that the best he could do was break even and that a successful outcome of the crisis would not so much bring gains but restore the situation to the status quo ex ante. As Sorensen (1965, 680; cited in Whyte and Levi 1994, 250) writes, "not one of us at any time believed that any of the choices before us could bring anything but either prolonged danger or fighting. . . ." It is true, however, that in his choice among alternative means of removing the missiles JFK and his advisers opted for a naval blockade strategy that was less risky than alternative strategies.

Risk-acceptant behavior to recover losses also relates to the sunk cost phenomenon. Loss aversion and the failure to renormalize the reference point after losses help to explain the fact that actors frequently incorporate sunk costs into their calculations, contrary to the normative prescriptions of standard microeconomic theory. Sunk costs are perceived as a certain loss in the absence of further action, and attempts to recover sunk costs to eliminate the loss often contributes to entrapment in escalating conflicts (Brockner and Rubin 1985).[12]

Once lives are lost in battle, for example, there are psychological and domestic political pressures (driven by loss aversion) on decision makers to persist in the war to ensure that their soldiers had not died in vain. This might help to explain why states continue to persist in failing policies, as evidenced by the American intervention in Vietnam, the Soviet intervention in Afghanistan, Japanese expansionism leading up to the attack on Pearl Harbor (Taliaferro 1997), and in countless other cases. Given the pervasiveness and importance of this phenomenon, it is rather surprising that international relations theorists have not attempted to explain escalating but costly conflicts in terms of framing, loss aversion, sunk costs, and entrapment.

Another situation in which political leaders are likely to frame their choices as losses is when they find their state undergoing a decline in relative power. They will most likely frame their reference point at (or above) the current status quo, perceive inaction as leading to a certain loss, and see the alternative as a preventive war. This option offers the prospect of eliminating the certain loss by blocking the rising adversary while the opportunity is still available, but also runs the risk of a costly and possibly unsuccessful military action.

Decisions regarding preventive war are quite complex, in that they involve two rather than one risky option (because inaction also involves risks), a comparison of current risks with future risks, and the discounting of value over time (Levy 1992b, 302–3). As a first approximation, however, a straightforward application of prospect theory would predict that if the expected values of inaction and preventive war are at all comparable, leaders may be tempted to fight a preventive war in the hope of avoiding the losses that are the inevitable by-product of continued decline.[13]

One of the additional complications involved in the analysis of preventive war, and a more general problem in empirical applications of prospect theory, is the possibility that a victorious war might go beyond eliminating losses to generate positive gains. Actors who face choices involving a certain outcome and a risky gamble that leads to positive or negative outcomes relative to the reference point are in a "mixed lottery" rather than a domain of pure gains or pure losses. Laboratory tests of behavior in mixed frames demonstrate that standard prospect theory hypotheses still hold but that they are weaker in strength.

Whereas experimental studies of mixed frames are structured in such a way that the expected values of different choices are strictly controlled, this is much harder to do in the empirical study of international relations. One danger of applying prospect theory to mixed frames in the absence of such controls is the possibility that the gain from the positive outcome is sufficiently great that it increases the expected value of the gamble to the point that it exceeds the expected value of doing nothing. As a result, the preference for a risky gamble over a certain loss may follow directly from an expected value calculation rather than from a prospect theory hypothesis based on loss aversion, the certainty effect, and risk acceptance.

Consider, for example, McDermott's (1998, chap. 3) analysis of how the Carter administration framed its decision regarding the Iranian hostage rescue mission. McDermott demonstrates convincingly that Carter perceived that inaction would lead with certainty to the continued deterioration of the U.S. international position and his own domestic support, whereas a risky rescue mission held out the promise of eliminating those losses but ran the risk of even greater losses should the mission fail. McDermott concludes that Carter's choice for the rescue mission was consistent with the prospect theory prediction of risk acceptance in the domain of losses. She also shows that different expectations about the future by Vance, Brzezinski, and Carter led each of them to frame the issue in slightly different ways and consequently to arrive at different policy preferences.

McDermott (1998, 65) concedes that Carter believed that a successful rescue mission might not only allow him to recover his losses but also bring some domestic political gains as well. This raises the possibility that the prospective gain from success sufficiently outweighed the downside risks of failure, particularly in comparison to the costs of doing nothing, so that Carter's decision is easily explained by a straightforward expected-value calculation. McDermott recognizes this potential challenge to her prospect theory explanation and effectively deals with it by demonstrating that the perceived probability of success of the mission was very low. In response to a question from General Jones of the Joint Chiefs of Staff about the probability of success and the risks involved, Charles Beckwith, who eventually led the mission, replied, "Sir, the probability of success is zero and the risks are high" (in McDermott 1998, 69).

Implications for Strategic Interaction and Bargaining

The previously mentioned hypotheses relating to framing, loss aversion, and risk orientation all focus on national-level foreign policy choices of political leaders, but they have some important implications for dyadic-level strategic interaction. There may be some situations in which two adversaries each see themselves in the domain of losses and each is more likely to engage in risk-seeking behavior than we would predict from standard expected-value calculations.

Consider a situation in which state A has just made a tangible gain at state B's expense, say through the seizure of territory. The endowment effect suggests that A will renormalize its reference point and assimilate its gains much more quickly than B will adjust to its losses. Consequently, B will attempt to recover its losses and restore the old status quo, and A will attempt to maintain the new status quo against B's encroachments. Each will be in the domain of losses and accept larger than normal risks in order to maintain its own version of the status quo. One implication of this is that fait accomplis are less likely to succeed than standard theories of deterrence and coercive diplomacy suggest (George and Smoke 1974, 536–40), because they generate both risk-seeking behavior by the target to recover its losses and risk-seeking behavior by the initiator to preserve its gains.

The 1991 Persian Gulf War provides one example. It is clear that President Bush defined his reference point around the status quo ex ante, viewed the Iraqi occupation of Kuwait as a loss, and saw military action as a means of restoring the status quo ex ante.[14] At the same time, the deteriorating Iraqi economy and the risks it created for Saddam Hussein's continued hold on power were important factors behind Saddam's decision to invade Kuwait (Freedman and Karsh 1993). Although more research is necessary to determine precisely how Saddam framed his reference point, it is plausible to argue that after the seizure of Kuwait Saddam renormalized his reference point around his new gains, feared the reputational costs at home and in the Arab world of retreating from the new status quo, and adopted a risk-seeking strategy in his standoff with the United States.

Still another example of two adversaries both operating in the domain of losses was the July 1914 crisis between Austria-Hungary and Serbia. The leadership of the Dual Monarchy almost certainly perceived themselves in the domain of losses because of external decline in relative power, internal problems deriving from ethnic divisions in their multinational empire, and the affront of the assassination. Given the extraordinary demands of the Austrian ultimatum and its infringement on Serbian sovereignty (Joll 1984), it is reasonable to assume that Serbian leaders also saw themselves in the domain of losses. In the absence of additional evidence that these are correct assessments of leaders' reference points in 1914, however, one would have to be very cautious in making inferences linking these frames to subsequent behavior.

Another type of situation in which adversary state leaders may each define their choices in the domain of losses is one in which each side perceives itself to be in relative decline, though possibly for different reasons deriving from different assessments of different components of military power, different time horizons, or different analytic frameworks. Mutual perceptions of decline, whatever their sources, may create temptations for preventive war by both parties.

One example might be the Japanese-American conflict leading up to the Pacific War. By fall 1941 key Japanese decision makers believed that their current position could only deteriorate. Although they recognized that there was little chance of victory in a long war with the United States, they believed that they had a 70 or 80 percent chance of an initial success that might improve their bargaining position for a favorable settlement that would avoid a long war, and that those odds would continue to decline the longer they waited. The only alternative to war would be a return to an American-dominated international system that was intolerable to Japan (Iriye 1987, 161, 173–74; Van Evera 1999, 89–94), in part because Japanese leaders probably framed their reference point around the Co-prosperity Sphere that they hoped to implement (Levi and Whyte 1997).

Thus it is pretty clear that Japanese leaders saw themselves in the domain of losses and that they gambled on a risky preventive war to consolidate their regional hegemony while the opportunity was still available.[15] The United States, meanwhile, never accepted Japanese expansion into China, insisted on a return to the status quo ex ante in Asia, feared the erosion of its global position by a rising and expansionist regional power, and implemented highly coercive economic sanctions against Japan, which only increased Japanese dissatisfaction with the status quo (Iriye 1987).

Most of these illustrative examples involve the failure of deterrence or compellence, and prospect theory has important implications for coercive threats and bargaining. Framing and loss aversion help to provide a theoretical explanation for Schelling's (1966, 69–91) insight that deterrence is easier than compellence. Deterrence entails dissuading actors from taking an action they have not yet taken and thus usually involves denying adversaries a possible gain. Compellence involves threats to persuade others to do something they are not currently doing, to stop doing something they are already doing, or to undo something they have already done, which usually involve the imposition of a loss. Psychological costs of losses are greater than those for gains, so in these situations compellence is harder than deterrence.

It is incorrect to assume, however, that targets in deterrence situations always frame their reference points around the status quo and that deterrence always involves denying gains to the adversary. When a state loses territory, it usually does not quickly renormalize its reference point, and it usually perceives any subsequent attempt by others to deter it from recovering that territory as a reinforcement of losses rather than a denial of gains. French attitudes after the German seizure of Alsace-Lorraine in 1871 are examples of this.

Similarly, if state decision makers perceive that their position of power is threatened by domestic political opposition, they may be tempted to engage in belligerent foreign policies in order to generate rally effects and thus solidify their domestic support. If these decision makers frame their reference point around earlier and more positive support levels, attempts to deter them from using military force abroad will be perceived as the continued imposition of losses rather than the denial of gains and will be less likely to succeed (Lebow and Stein 1987).

The more general proposition about deterrence and compellence is that influence attempts based on coercion are more likely to be successful if the target sees itself in the domain of gains and is contemplating an effort to improve its position. Coercion is less likely to succeed if the target sees itself in the domain of losses and is considering how to prevent its position from deteriorating further or to recover its losses.

Framing and loss aversion also have potentially important implications for standard approaches to the study of immediate deterrence. It is conventional here for researchers to select cases based on a prior threat by a challenger (Huth and Russett 1988).[16] If the target or its protector responds to a challenger's initial threat with a deterrent threat of its own, the challenger must decide whether to defy the deterrent threat and implement its initial threat (or some variation of it) or to withdraw its initial threat.

The challenger recognizes that its initial threat has certain consequences because of the reputational and perhaps domestic political costs involved in making such a threat and then withdrawing it, and how the challenger frames its reference point will influence how it evaluates those costs. If the actor defines its reference point as the status quo ex ante, it will see its failure to implement the threat as a retreat *to* the old status quo, which involves a foregone gain. If, on the other hand, the challenger frames around the situation created by its new demand and associated threat, it will see any withdrawal of the threat as a retreat *from* the new status quo, which involves losses. The second frame is more likely to induce risk-seeking behavior and the escalation of the conflict. Presumably, however, the challenger will anticipate the potential costs of withdrawing a threat in the face of a counterthreat and make the initial threat only if she or he is highly resolved (Fearon 1994b).

Let us now turn to a more direct focus on bargaining in strategic interaction within dyads. I spoke earlier about the status quo bias (or, more accurately, reference point bias) in individual choice. There is a comparable tendency in dyadic bargaining. Bargaining involves making concessions on some issues in return for compensation on others. Loss aversion and the endowment effect imply that actors have a tendency to treat the concessions they give up as losses and the compensation they receive from the other actor as gains, and consequently to overvalue what they give relative to what they get. This leads to a greater tendency on both sides to risk the consequences of a nonagreement or deadlock, and hence a lower probability of a negotiated agreement, than utility-based bargaining theory might predict.

This is often described as a *concession aversion* in bargaining (Kahneman, Knetsch, and Thaler 1990, 1345). Concession aversion applies even when the value of the concessions and acquisitions in bargaining are perceived to be equal by each actor. The implication is that if everything were the same except that the ownership of the specific goods in question were reversed, each actor would still have a concession aversion against a bargain over those goods.

The implicit hypothesis underlying this discussion is that people behave differently when the issue is the distribution of losses rather than the distribution of gains, so that how the bargainers frame the problem in terms of gains and losses is itself a critical variable. Consider a bargaining situation in which each side makes an initial offer and then is given the choice between accepting a compromise agreement halfway between the two offers or accepting an arbitrated solution. We assume for the purposes of this example that actors can achieve a negotiated settlement with certainty if they select it and that arbitration is a risky alternative, in that it can lead to an outcome that is either better or worse than the negotiated outcome. We also assume that the expected value of the arbitrated outcome is lower than that of the negotiated alternative, due to such arbitration costs as time delays, arbitration fees, loss of control over the outcome, and so on (Crawford 1979; Neale and Bazerman 1985, 37).

Hypotheses on framing and loss aversion imply that the likelihood of the negotiated settlement being accepted depends in part on whether the two negotiators frame the compromise agreement as a gain from their adversary's initial offer or a loss from their own initial offer. If they frame the compromise as a retreat from their initial offer, they will define compromise as a certain loss and be more inclined (ceteris paribus) to accept the risky gamble of arbitration in the hope of eliminating their loss but at the risk of incurring a greater loss. If they frame the compromise as a gain from the adversary's initial offer, they will be more inclined to accept that settlement and lock in a certain gain rather than take a risky gamble.

Although less experimental work has been done on the impact of framing on bargaining behavior than on individual choice, the evidence provides some support for this framing hypothesis (Tversky and Kahneman 1986, S262; Bazerman 1983). Neale and Bazerman (1985) conducted an experiment in which subjects were assigned the role of management negotiators. One group of subjects was given a negative frame ("Any concessions beyond those granted will represent serious financial losses to the company") and another was given a positive frame ("Any union concessions from their current position will result in gains for the company"), but the choice problems facing each group were mathematically equivalent.

Neale and Bazerman (1985) find as predicted that individuals in the negative frame (as compared to those in the positive frame) are less likely to settle for the certainty of the negotiated agreement, more likely to accept the riskier gamble of arbitration, and more likely to end up with inferior outcomes. They also find that the likelihood of subjects selecting the riskier arbitrated settlement depends also on their degree of confidence in being able to secure a favorable outcome from arbitration.

These findings have important implications for international conflict, for a comparable situation to the preceding would be a crisis in which two states both define their options as either a negotiated settlement that they have good reason to believe that the other would agree to, or a war that would generate some possibility of a better outcome than the negotiated settlement and some possibility of a worse outcome. In addition, overconfidence in securing a favorable arbitrated outcome parallels the tendency among political leaders to overestimate the probability that their own coercive threats will induce compliance by the adversary or that they can defeat the adversary in war if the crisis escalates.[17]

These behavioral studies of bargaining also have important implications for the study of the conditions for cooperation in international relations. Most of the empirical work on cooperation focuses on international political economy and defines the question in terms of cooperation to distribute the gains of economic interdependence. Hypotheses on framing suggest that international cooperation should be more difficult when the issue involves the distribution of losses rather than of gains (Stein and Pauly 1992).

The psychological asymmetry between actual losses and foregone gains, between out-of-pocket costs and opportunity costs, also has some important implications for judgments of moral responsibility and for social norms regarding fairness. Although the literature on the role of international norms has grown significantly in the last half-decade (Katzenstein 1996), little work has been done on the impact of norms of fairness and how they affect the origins and escalation of international crises and other aspects of international behavior. Evidence from other areas, however, suggests some interesting hypotheses regarding international behavior.

People have a tendency to treat errors of commission or action as more blameworthy than errors of omission or inaction (Ritov and Baron 1990; Camerer 1995, 668). The enactment of a crime is usually judged more harshly than the failure to prevent a crime from occurring. In tort law, judges distinguish between "loss by way of expenditure and failure to make a gain." In contract law, a party that breaches a contract in order to make an unforeseen gain is more likely to be held to the original terms of the contract than if the action were taken to avoid a loss (Kahneman, Knetsch, and Thaler 1991, 204). Similarly, social norms against hurting another are probably more compelling than norms to help another, and there is some evidence that people are more cooperative when they perceive the others to be in a loss frame rather than a gain frame (de Dreu, Emans, and van de Vliert 1992).

Judgments of fairness or injustice can be an important factor in the origins and escalation of international conflicts. They may have a particularly important impact on how actors frame their reference points and how quickly they adjust or renormalize to changes in the status quo. Actors are less likely to renormalize their reference points after the loss of territory—and more likely to adjust to a gain in territory—if they perceive that territory as a long-standing moral entitlement. It is useful to compare the behavior of France and Germany with respect to Alsace-Lorraine in 1871 and 1918. France failed to renormalize its reference point after the loss of Alsace-Lorraine in 1871 but rapidly renormalized to its recovery in 1918, whereas Germany never fully incorporated her gain in 1871 and quickly accepted her loss of Alsace-Lorraine in 1918 (Welch 1993, 24–25).

The status quo bias, concession aversion, and related hypotheses are based on the endowment effect. Experimental evidence suggests that under some conditions the endowment effect is likely to be minimal. One of the most important of these, at least in terms of implications for international bargaining, is the tendency for goods that are acquired for later sale rather than used to generate small endowment effects (Kahneman, Knetsch, and Thaler 1991, 200).

One important implication is that "bargaining chips" are evaluated differently than are other goods. If concessions involve a bargaining chip, and especially if the items or resources involved were acquired or created with that purpose in mind, the asymmetry of value attached to concessions given and compensation received is likely to be much less, which minimizes the concession aversion. The Israeli seizure of the Sinai Peninsula from Egypt in the Six Day War and subsequent return of the Sinai to Egypt as part of the 1979 peace treaty is a good example here. It is clear that Israeli leaders regarded the Sinai as a bargaining chip (Yaniv 1994, 213, 221), though it is not clear whether that was a primary motivation in the initial seizure of the territory.

Another interesting qualification of the endowment effect concerns responses to sudden windfalls. Gamblers who are ahead for the day sometimes refer to "playing with the house money" and gamble rather recklessly as a result, rather than assimilate the windfall into their psychological endowment and renormalize their reference points, as the instant endowment effect would predict. Thaler and Johnson (1990) refer to this as the *house money effect.* This effect diminishes as the size of the potential loss threatens to cut into one's initial stake or endowment (Battalio, Kagel, and Jiranyakul 1990).

It is not clear that the house money effect has any meaningful parallels in international behavior, though Taliaferro (1995) provides an interesting application to the U.S. decision to intervene in Korea in 1950. One possibility is that political leaders who unexpectedly receive a boost in domestic political support may be more willing to take diplomatic (or domestic) actions that carry domestic political risks, given the additional cushion provided by their windfall.

The Strategic Dimensions of Framing

I have emphasized the centrality of framing to prospect theory and the empirical problems associated with identifying the reference point and doing so independently of the behavior we are trying to explain. The assumption, here and in all of the literature, is that framing is exogenous and that causality runs unidirectionally from framing to preference and choice. We must be sensitive to the possibility, however, that under some circumstances framing might be endogenous. That is, one's preference for a certain outcome might influence how one frames the choice problem.

This is particularly important in a group or interactive decision-making context. Individuals may articulate a particular frame or reference point for the primary purpose of influencing another's behavior by attempting to manipulate how they frame their choice problem. What appears to be an actor's exogenously defined reference point may in fact represent strategic behavior. This raises the difficult methodological problem of how to differentiate empirically between genuine frames and strategic frames.

In Japanese policy deliberations leading up to the Pearl Harbor attack, for example, do repeated references to the Co-prosperity Sphere by Japanese decision makers represent genuine framing around an aspiration level, as Levi and Whyte (1997) argue? Or do they represent strategic efforts by some actors to manipulate others' preferences by framing the way they define the situation? In emphasizing the zero-missile reference point in the Cuban missile crisis, was Kennedy expressing his true frame or was he behaving strategically to shape others' reference points in a way that would support Kennedy's policy preferences?

One approach to this problem is to examine both private documents and public documents, on the assumption that the former are more likely to reveal genuine preferences and that any discrepancy between the two may reflect strategic attempts to manipulate frames. This is the rationale behind Levi and Whyte's (1997) comparative content analysis of transcripts from both the Liason Conferences and Imperial Conferences in Japan in 1941. They argue that various factions were freer to voice their dissenting opinions during the deliberations in the Liason Conferences, where decisions were made, than in the Imperial Conferences, where recommendations were presented to the emperor for approval and where there were strong norms against revealing disunity within the decision-making group. This approach helps to control for deference to authority in the Imperial Conferences, for moderates made more references to the Co-prosperity Sphere in the Imperial Conferences than in the Liason Conferences, but the problem of separating genuine from strategic frames in the Liason Conferences remains.

The problem of identifying the direction of causality between frame and preference is even more difficult for individual behavior, where there are fewer written records that might be used to infer a reference point. It is conceivable that an individual's preference or risk orientation may lead him or her to frame a choice problem in a way that reinforces the preferred outcome, strategy, or risk orientation. Actors who prefer a cautious policy for psychological or other reasons, for example, may frame their reference point in a way that renders the status quo an acceptable outcome and thus reinforces their psychological preference to avoid risky gambles. Or, actors who prefer a confrontational policy may frame their own reference point around a higher aspiration level; this would leave the status quo as a loss and reinforce the preexisting tendency toward risk-acceptant choices.

It may be very difficult to distinguish between these alternative explanations and to disentangle what comes first, the frame or the preference. Consider the Cuban missile crisis. Presidential adviser Sorensen (quoted in Blight, Nye, and Welch 1987, 181) states that

> . . . the President drew the line precisely where he thought the Soviets were not and would not be . . . if we had known that the Soviets were putting 40 missiles in Cuba, we might under this hypothesis have drawn the line at 100, and said with great fanfare that we would absolutely not tolerate the presence of more than 100 missiles in Cuba. . . . I am suggesting that one reason the line was drawn at zero was because we simply thought the Soviets weren't going to deploy any there anyway.

This implies that, in Sorensen's view, the causality runs from Kennedy's preference for a cautious response to the Soviet action, in conjunction with his expectations about likely Soviet behavior, to a zero-missiles reference point, not the other way around. Kennedy's public warning to the Soviets not to install offensive missiles in Cuba was an attempt to neutralize political criticism at home without incurring much military risk (Whyte and Levi 1994, 252). Sorensen's account includes the counterfactual hypothesis that had Kennedy expected a certain number of missiles in Cuba he would have drawn his line in the sand above that number so as to minimize the likelihood of any confrontation.

It is not clear, however, that this evidence reflects an individual adjusting his own reference point consistent with a certain level of risk he was willing to accept, or whether it reflects an attempt to manipulate the reference point of public opinion to contain their demands for excessively confrontational policies.

The preceding discussion concerns an actor's attempt to influence the policy preferences of others in a collective decision-making setting by influencing how others frame their reference points. A similar "framing game" occurs in bargaining between adversaries. In a bargaining situation I have an incentive to attempt to influence my adversary's evaluation of the relative costs and benefits of various policy choices, and also the adversary's images of my own preferences, resolve, and expectations. In addition, however, I may also have an incentive to try to influence the adversary's resolve indirectly by shaping the way he or she frames his or her choice problem and the way the adversary perceives that I frame my own choice problem.

The basic hypothesis is that I should try to influence the adversary to treat his or her concessions as foregone gains rather than as losses, and at the same time to convince the adversary that I treat my own concessions as losses rather than as foregone gains. That is, I should induce the adversary to shift her or his reference point to a lower expectation or aspiration level and to believe that my reference point is at a higher expectation or aspiration level. This would decrease the psychological cost to the adversary of making concessions to me, increase my own costs of making concessions (as perceived by the adversary), and consequently shift the bargaining outcome in my favor. Whether these various forms of strategic framing actually go on, and whether the magnitude of their effects are significant, is an important empirical question that scholars have yet to explore.

There are other ways of presenting negative outcomes besides foregone gains, and different frames induce different subjective assessments of value. Most people do not think of insurance premiums as a loss, for example, but rather as a cost of protection, the psychological cost of which is lower. Slovic, Fischoff, and Lichtenstein (1982) find that only 20 percent of their study subjects preferred a sure loss of $50 to a 25 percent chance of losing $200, but 65 percent preferred to pay $50 for insurance against a 25 percent risk of losing $200 (see also Schoemaker and Kunreuther 1979).

These and related patterns lead Kahneman and Tversky (1984, 349) to make a distinction between uncompensated losses (or "dead losses") and costs of protection. The former, but not the latter, are overweighted in risky choice behavior. This has prescriptive implications. If people psychologically frame negative outcomes as costs (e.g., the costs of doing business or costs of insurance) rather than losses, they can reduce the psychological impact of those losses.

The implications for international relations are potentially important but undeveloped. It is intriguing to speculate whether it makes a difference—in terms of the psychology of political decision makers or in terms of public opinion—if certain negative outcomes in international relations are framed as costs of "doing business" and insuring against future losses in a hostile and competitive international system, or if they are framed as losses.

Conclusion

Kahneman and Tversky (1979) developed prospect theory to explain patterns of individual choice that deviate from the predictions of expected-utility theory in systematic and predictable ways. The theory builds on the central analytic assumption of reference dependence and the asymmetry between gains and losses to generate a rich set of hypotheses about individual behavior. In this chapter I have tried to develop the implications of framing and loss aversion for international conflict and bargaining. The resulting hypotheses provide some new perspectives on some old questions in the study of international conflict, and they also put a new set of questions on the agenda for further theoretical and empirical exploration.

The tasks facing the prospect theory research program are both theoretical and empirical. I have discussed some of these elsewhere (Levy 1997), but this chapter suggests some additional points that I should mention. Some of the most important tasks involve the analysis of framing. Reference dependence is the key assumption of prospect theory, but we have few hypotheses on how actors actually identify their reference points and no accepted methodology for empirically measuring where those reference points are and when and how they change. We know that actors renormalize their reference points much more quickly after gains than after losses, but we do not know how much more quickly and whether this varies as a function of issue area, the magnitude of the losses, or personal characteristics. A related question concerns the conditions under which states that have suffered losses finally accept those losses and renormalize to the new status quo. Britain has adjusted to the loss of its North American colonies, but Argentina has yet to accept the loss of the Malvinas and some Israelis and Palestinians frame around reference points that go back millennia.

Another question is whether actors can influence how others define their reference points or induce changes in those reference points. I have suggested that both in group decision making and in bargaining with adversaries actors may have incentives to attempt to influence how others frame their reference points, but these "framing games" have not been developed theoretically or examined empirically or experimentally.

At this stage of the prospect theory research program it would be more useful to pursue these tasks and to develop further the implications of prospect theory for international relations and foreign policy than to engage in more abstract debates with rational choice theorists about the relative merits of the two paradigms. In particular, visions of a paradigmatic war between rational choice and prospect theory are not particularly useful. McDermott's (1998, 14) comment that "prospect theory renders rational choice models descriptively vacuous, empirically static, and normatively bankrupt with respect to understanding risk-taking in international politics," for example, is unproductive and supported neither by theoretical argument nor by empirical evidence. It greatly exaggerates the extent of progress in the empirical verification of key prospect theory hypotheses in international relations. It also fails to recognize that prospect theory and rational choice theory share many of the same assumptions and many of the same limitations.

I have spoken elsewhere about the complex relationship between the two theories and have argued that prospect theory is not easy to classify in terms of the "cognitive-rational" debate (Levy 1997). It is true that the process of framing undoubtedly involves cognitive and affective variables and thus is inherently "psychological" in nature. But most research on prospect theory focuses on the evaluation phase of the theory, which treats preferences and subjective probability judgments as exogenous and which shares much in common with expected-utility theory and other rationalist utility-based models of choice.

As McDermott (1998, 5) correctly notes, "prospect theory is a theory of decision making, not one of judgment." Like utility-based rational choice theories, prospect theory must be combined with a theory of judgment that explains subjective assessments of the likelihood of various outcomes and also with a theory of preferences that explains how actors identify different possible outcomes and evaluate their respective utilities. Neither prospect theory nor rational choice theory alone provides a complete theory of international politics. In many respects they share more similarities and differences, and proponents of both should recognize that they face greater enemies than each other.

Notes

I thank Jon DiCicco and Geoffry Taubman for helpful comments on an earlier draft of this manuscript.

1. See the special issues of the *International Journal* (1992) and *Political Psychology* (1992), which were reprinted as edited books by Stein and Pauly (1992) and Farnham (1994), respectively; the book by McDermott (1998); articles by Peterson and Lawson (1989), Whyte and Levi (1994), Boettcher (1995), Levy (1996a, 1997), Weyland (1996), Nincic (1997), Levi and Whyte (1997), Taubman (1997), and Berejikian (1997); chapters in several books (Geva and Mintz 1997); and a rapidly growing number of convention papers and journal submissions (Geva and Mintz 1994; Levy 1996b; Taliaferro 1994, 1995, 1997; Davis 1997). In addition, much of the increasing interest in risk

behavior in international politics (Vertzberger 1995, 1998; Kowert and Hermann 1997) has been influenced by debates relating to prospect theory. The historian John Lynn (1999, 43–44) uses prospect theory to help explain Louis XIV's motivations in the 1680s and 1690s.

2. The expected-utility principle postulates that actors aim to maximize their expected utility by weighting the utility of each possible outcome of a given strategy by its probability of occurrence, summing over all possible outcomes, and selecting that strategy with the highest expected utility. Expected-utility theory posits that an individual's utility for a particular good is a function of net asset levels of that good. An actor's attitude or orientation toward risk is defined in terms of marginal utility or the shape of the actor's utility function. Actors are risk averse if their utility function is concave, risk neutral if their utility function is linear, and risk acceptant if their utility function is convex. This section builds on Levy (1996a).
3. Similarly, John Elway (*New York Times,* 25 January 1999) remarked that "The fun of going to the Super Bowl in no way compares to the wrath you get for losing one."
4. Loss aversion and risk orientation are analytically distinct. Loss aversion is reflected in the steepness of the value function on the loss side, whereas risk orientation is reflected in the curvature of the value function. The concepts of loss aversion, the endowment effect, and the status quo bias can all be applied to choice behavior under conditions of certainty, where there are no risky gambles, as well as to choices under risk. Tversky and Kahneman (1991), for example, develop a model of loss aversion in riskless choice that has nothing to do with lotteries.
5. Preliminary experimental evidence suggests that overweighting begins when probabilities are below .10 or .15 (Levy 1992a, 183).
6. For example, we cannot infer that because Saddam refused to withdraw from Kuwait in the face of U.S. coercive threats, he must have framed his reference point around his new acquisitions and engaged in risk-acceptant behavior to keep them.
7. The following discussion builds on Levy (1992b, 1996a, 1996b).
8. Similar logic affects compensatory decision rules in multiattribute choice problems. More specifically, actors' trade-offs among competing values are complicated by the fact that a loss on one dimension cannot be compensated for by an "equal" gain on another dimension, for the loss will be overweighted relative to the gain.
9. There is some danger that these findings may be distorted by selection effects and related endogeneity problems. Nincic (1997) selects only cases of intervention and ignores other cases in which presidents may also have preferred intervention but backed off in the presence or anticipation of low levels of public or congressional support. It would be useful to identify such

cases of nonintervention, to explore how these were framed by the public and Congress and president, and to analyze whether framing explains which cases led to intervention and which did not.

With regard to congressional support, Nincic's indicator ("the presence or absence of an affirmative resolution originating within either house of Congress") is affected by whether the president seeks such a resolution, which in turn is affected by the expected probability of winning such a resolution. President Bush sought and received a congressional resolution just prior to taking military action against Iraq in the 1990/91 Persian Gulf War, but had planned to withdraw the request and avoid a vote if anticipated head counts had turned negative (Freedman and Karsh 1993). It is not clear, therefore, whether causality runs from intervention type to support levels or from anticipated support levels to presidential proposals for intervention.

10. An alternative explanation for the observed tendency toward status quo choices is an *inaction bias.* Some experiments show that subjects prefer a default option (which would be selected if no explicit action were taken) over the current status quo when the two are different (Camerer 1995, 669). This could be particularly important in dynamic situations in which the failure to act might leave one worse off than before. This question needs more investigation in the laboratory and in the empirical world of international relations.
11. There has been a great deal of work in management science and organizational behavior on the role of aspiration or target levels, and this has potentially important but undeveloped implications for international relations. The standard hypothesis is that organizations define an aspiration or target level and that this point divides success from failure. Performance above a target level leads to a primary focus on avoiding actions that might drop one below the target, which leads to risk aversion. Below target-level performance, on the other hand, leads to greater risk taking in an attempt to reach the target (March and Shapira 1987).
12. Substantial experimental evidence supports the importance of sunk cost effects (Arkes and Blumer 1985). In one hypothetical experiment, Thaler (1980, 47) finds that people are more likely to drive through a snowstorm to go to a basketball game if they had paid for the tickets than if they had been given the tickets. There is also evidence that betting on long shots at racetracks increases as the day goes on, which suggests that those who play the horses do not adjust to their losses.
13. One might argue, however, that the risks of delay are greater than the risks of war now because the number and magnitude of negative outcomes presumably increases as one's relative power declines. This would create an incentive for a risk-acceptant actor to delay, but for a risk-averse actor to prefer preventive action now (Levy 1992b). This tendency for risk-acceptant dominant states to prefer inaction but for risk-averse states to prefer a pre-

ventive war now follows from Kim and Morrow's (1992) formal theoretical model of war decisions during power transitions, which receives some support from their empirical analysis for the period since 1815.

14. This may have been a mixed frame for Bush, in that he may have seen military action as a means of setting back the Iraqi nuclear program, establishing a precedent for allied cooperation in the "new world order," and increasing (or restoring) his levels of domestic political support.
15. Levi and Whyte (1997) find in their content analysis of Japanese documents that recommendations for war were accompanied mainly by reference point arguments relating to Japan's unsatisfied aspirations and the unacceptable nature of the status quo. Recommendations for diplomatic options, on the other hand, were associated with non–reference point arguments, including probability estimates of success and failure. This is consistent with more general findings that individuals' concerns with the probability of success or failure decline as the status quo becomes more aversive (Cohen, Jaffray, and Said 1987). Note that this runs contrary to the standard assumption (in both expected-utility theory and prospect theory) that actors' subjective utilities and probabilities are formed independently.
16. A prior threat suggests some motivation for military action on the part of the challenger, and thus minimizes the likelihood that the failure of the challenger to undertake military action after a deterrent threat from an adversary is due to the absence of motivation on the part of the challenger, rather than to the hypothesis of successful deterrence by the target.
17. One experimental study in international relations that bears on this is Morgan and Wilson's (1989) test of a spatial model of crisis bargaining. They find that subjects sought agreements when the payoffs were positive but were more likely to risk war when the payoffs were negative; in each case the preferred outcome had a lower expected value than the alternative. See also the experimental work by Geva and Mintz (1994) on Israeli attitudes toward a negotiated agreement with Syria.

(Enduring) Rivalries

GARY GOERTZ and PAUL F. DIEHL

Introduction

Research on the democratic peace starts with a fact: democracies almost never fight wars with one another. Research on (enduring) rivalries begins with a contrasting observation: a small proportion of dyads accounts for a very large percentage of all militarized disputes and wars. A series of results (originally from Goertz and Diehl 1992a, and updated in Diehl and Goertz 2000) indicate that enduring rivalries (only 5.4 percent of all conflictual dyads and even less of all possible dyads) account for almost half of all militarized disputes and war over the past 200 years. Furthermore, enduring rivalries account for a disproportionate fraction of other important interactions including peaceful and violent territorial changes as well as low-level and violent international crises (Hensel 1998).[1]

These findings lead to the general hypothesis that these repeated conflicts between the same dyad are related to one another, and that explaining war requires understanding the relations between these disputes. Intuition supports this basic claim in many cases. For example, India and Pakistan have fought three wars in the last 50 years, with the outcomes of the first two wars arguably having a strong influence on the occurrence and timing of the war that followed. Similarly, Israel and the Arab states have clashed over the same pieces of territory four times since 1948; the Yom Kippur War in 1973 is one that most obviously traces its roots to the circumstances and outcome of the previous war. Even in those competitions that stopped short of war, as with the United States and the Soviet Union during the cold war, leaders relied on "lessons learned" from previous confrontations with the same enemy.

"Rivalry" broadly refers to repeated, militarized conflict between two states: rivalry is a relationship in which both sides deal with issues using the military tools of foreign policy. If such militarized relationships last long enough, the rivalry becomes "enduring." Wars, crises, disputes, and conflict management all occur within the context of rivalry relationships. Sometimes issues are resolved early and the rivalry does not mature into the enduring phase. In other cases, early wars establish the tone, and repeated conflicts and wars keep the rivalry going. This explains our putting "enduring" in parentheses in our chapter title. Although most work has focused on enduring rivalries for a number of key issues, one needs a concept of rivalry that extends from the very short to the very long.

To look at war and militarized conflict in terms of rivalry represents a dramatic shift in theoretical and methodological perspective. Most of the theories and approaches surveyed in this volume use wars and disputes as the basic units of analysis, with the standard dependent variable being the dichotomous war–no war distinction. The analysis usually treats these data in a purely cross-sectional fashion. By putting these events into the rivalry context, scholars introduce a historical and longitudinal dimension into the analysis. The distinctiveness of the study of rivalries follows in many ways directly from these two key changes in standard practice: (1) taking rivalry as the focus of analysis and (2) taking into account the temporal existence of that focus. Instead of examining war with a pile of snapshots, the scholars of rivalries prefer to look at it as a series of short- to full-length movies.

Unlike many other research programs, the focus on rivalries is a relatively recent one and has only just begun to spread beyond a small set of scholars. Yet, even within its short life span, rivalry research has moved beyond a concern with definitional issues to more theoretical concerns. It has also evolved to consider more than simply *enduring* rivalries to those of all length and magnitude, an essential element in asking and answering questions about international conflict behavior. Rivalry research has also developed from exclusive use of rivalries as a background condition within the *causes-of-war* framework to form a central and new way of analyzing international conflict.

This review begins by tracing the conceptual and operational history of the rivalry concept. This is reflective of the early work on rivalries, but such concerns also provide the essential groundwork for empirical research. We then describe what has been called "the rivalry approach to war and peace," which is purported to constitute an alternative theoretical framework for understanding international conflict behavior. Finally, we summarize and integrate the extant empirical research on a wide range of concerns about rivalries, such as their origins, dynamics, and termination.

The Rivalry Concept

The term *rivalry* has formed part of the lexicon of international relations scholars, used casually by many to characterize feelings of enmity between states. Certainly it has attracted nowhere near the conceptual attention, for example, that "power" and "interdependence" have. Nevertheless, concepts similar to rivalry began appearing in the last 20 years, and in the past few years, several works have sought to define carefully the concept of rivalry, enduring rivalry in particular. In this section, we briefly review a number of those efforts (see also Hensel 1996a).

Early work considered the idea of "international enemies" (Feste 1982; Finlay, Holsti, and Fagan 1967), which signified states that exhibited overt or latent hostility that might lead to war. The enemies concept certainly conveyed the militarized element that is characteristic of many rivalry schemes and definitions, yet it provided little sense of the temporal length or degree that such hostility was felt, except to indicate with respect to the latter that war was recognized as a significant possibility. At the other extreme is the concept of "protracted conflict" (Azar, Jureidini, and McLaurin 1978; Brecher 1984; Starr 1999). Protracted conflicts referred to a long series of hostile interactions. Although this concept included the temporal element seemingly absent from the idea of "international enemies," it did not seem to differentiate between different degrees of hostility, potentially mixing protracted trade disputes with little prospect of war with dangerous military competitions that might experience multiple wars over a period of time. Ideas such as international enemies and protracted conflict were largely precursors to the recent attention given to enduring and other rivalries.

At its outset, the scholarly literature joined "rivalry" to "enduring." We suggested in the preceding that rivalries could be short as well as enduring; hence, the concept of an enduring rivalry is less important than that of a rivalry in general. Enduring rivalries do merit special attention, however, because they constitute a serious problem and an enhanced risk of war. The first mentions of the term *enduring rivalry* in the scholarly literature (Diehl 1985a; Gochman and Maoz 1984; Wayman 1982) did not generally include explicit discussions of the concept. Rather, the term was used to describe an empirical set of cases that was characterized by states clashing repeatedly in militarized disputes (Gochman and Maoz, 1984) over some short or long period of time. At the same time, Wayman, Diehl, and others developed operational definitions of rivalry. Although largely a case of "putting the cart before the horse," rivalries did not receive serious and extended conceptual attention until a small critical mass of studies had been conducted. Thus, the concept of rivalry became a topic of interest sometime after various operational definitions were in existence. This odd state of affairs arose because initially those who used the idea were not interested in rivalries per se, but in using rivalries to investigate hypotheses about war and power transition, arms races, and so on (see later). Slowly it became clear that rivalries deserved attention in their own right, and the concept itself began to receive some sustained examination.

Rivalry in virtually all studies means *dyadic* rivalry. Goertz and Diehl (1993) call this criteria spatial consistency: rivalries include a consistent set of states in their domain. Given that most militarized conflict has thus far been dyadic (Jones, Bremer, and Singer 1996), one can anticipate that most rivalries will involve only two states. Nevertheless, it is possible that, by virtue of alliances, for example, more than two states might be involved in a rivalry. It is also possible that a multistate rivalry might overlap with a dyadic rivalry. France and Britain were jointly involved in a series of conflicts with the declining Ottoman Empire during the nineteenth century. One could also envision a rivalry involving more than two states arrayed in opposition to one another in a multilateral fashion.[2] That is, three major powers, for example, may in be in competition with each other over the same issues, but none may be aligned with another major power and each may have its own distinct set of preferences that are incompatible with those of the other two states. An example might be the United States, the Soviet Union, and China in the postwar era (Goldstein and Freeman 1991). Nevertheless, virtually without exception the rivalry literature has treated rivalry as a dyadic phenomenon.

Rivalry has also signified that nations use threats and military force to deal with their conflicts. Nations experience all kinds of conflicts, but only some are conducted regularly with the military tools of foreign policy. Rivalry signifies a hostile relationship, in which the competition is conducted militarily. Thus, most conceptual definitions include some type of militarized component, and as noted later, operational definitions focus on repeated militarized actions. Hensel (1996a) stresses the need for both competition and threat perception. The first component, competition, is almost self-explanatory in that there must be some disagreement over the division of some good, and the assumption seems to be that such competition cannot result in a fully positive sum outcome.

Yet Hensel notes that his focus on militarized interstate rivalries requires the second component, namely that states believe that their rival threatens national security interests. Threat perception then distinguishes a wide variety of competitions (e.g., some trade disputes) from hostile disputes involving the potential use of military force. Goertz and Diehl (1993; Diehl and Goertz 2000) make a similar argument in requiring that rivalries have a competitive element. Having conflicting goals does not necessarily mean that preferences of the competitors are irreconcilable or that the competition is entirely zero-sum (although this may be the case in some rivalries). These goods may be intangible, such as political influence (as in "power politics" conceptions) or ideological/religious dominance. The competition may also be over more tangible goods such as natural resources or territory. In practice, it is likely that individual rivalries reflect varying mixes of these sources of competition.

Rivalries are not just a history of conflict, however, but also the expectation of future conflict. The first dispute or war between a pair of states potentially begins a long-term rivalry. One distinguishing characteristic of rivalries is that the participants anticipate military conflict against each other in the future. They may not know exactly when or where it will occur, but they believe it to be likely and plan for it by acquiring arms, alliances, and the like. Thus, a rivalry relationship consists of a past and a future, and both may be crucial in understanding how rivalries get started and how they are maintained over time (Goertz and Diehl 1993, 1995a).

One can call the approach that relies only on the expectation of future military conflict, and operationally looks only at manifestations of rivalry in terms of disputes and wars, as the "behavioralist" view of rivalry. In this approach, all that matters is that nations use the military tools of foreign policy in the conduct of the rivalry and expect to do so in the future. The commonality is not the issue in contention, but the means of dealing with some issues. By focusing only on the tools of foreign policy, the behavioralist approach may connect unrelated disputes. For example, some lists of rivalries include one between the Britain and Brazil in the mid–nineteenth century. Some of these disputes involved the slave trade, and others concerned territorial issues regarding British colonies, as well as additional issues. Do all these conflicts constitute a single rivalry? According to the behavioral approach they do, because Britain dealt consistently with Brazil using military force and vice versa.

In contrast, a number of students of rivalry have argued that in addition to military means one needs to consider the issues over which rivals fight. What characterizes a rivalry relationship is that military force is used *and* that the rivalry is over one issue or set of issues. Issue consistency over time thus permits one to say that all the competitions in the rivalry belong to the "same" relationship. The advantage of issue conceptions is that it makes one more certain that the various incidents in a rivalry really belong together as part of same relationship. Because the issue remains constant one can link the various disputes of a rivalry.

Bennett (1993) is indicative of this mixed model (behavior and issues) view of rivalries. He conceptualizes enduring rivals as those states that have disagreed over the same issue for an extended period of time. Rather than simply minor disputes or those between allies, Bennett also stipulates that the rivals must have devoted significant resources (military, economic, etc.) to the rivalry, and his operational definition suggests that a willingness (and acting on that willingness) to use or threaten military force against one's rival is also an essential part of the rivalry relationship. Vasquez (1993) claims that states define rivals in terms of what gaining or losing stakes will mean for one's competitors; thus, the concern in rivalries is with relative, rather than exclusively absolute, gains and losses.

The issue dimension raises the question about whether the source of the dispute is necessarily consistent over the life of the rivalry. States may fight over essentially the same issues during a rivalry (e.g., the Arab-Israeli conflict since 1948). Yet, it is also plausible to conceive of a rivalry in which there is some variance in the issues (e.g., Britain and France in the eighteenth century). States may compete over a series of goods and the confrontations may vary according to which goods at the time are in dispute. Rather than talk about issues in dispute, Diehl and Goertz (2000) use the concept of "the expectation of a continued conflict relationship." This expectation can arise in different fashions, some of which fall under the intuitive idea of issue. Unresolved territorial claims are an issue that can produce such expectations, but so too can a history of mistrust and struggle between two states. It can be the case that there are different sources of competition leading to the same rivalry effect, much as different foreign policy choices can produce the same outcome (see idea of "substitutability" in Most and Starr 1989). Nevertheless, adding the issue component can have significant practical effects. This appears most clearly in the case of "interrupted rivalries" (Goertz and Diehl 1993). The pure behavioralist takes a rivalry to have ended operationally after a certain number of nondispute years. By including issue criteria the rivalry can remain alive through long periods of no overt conflict.

Unfortunately, we have no pure issue-based conceptions of or data on enduring and other rivalries. All current work (even that from the mixed view) starts with purely behavioral criteria (as noted later, in practice this means the presence of militarized disputes) and then moves to issue aspects. Yet there may be important conflicts that do not manifest themselves with overt military threats or behaviors, or do so only irregularly over long periods of time. Which of these cases deserve to be included in an issue-based list of rivalries? Thus far the scholarly literature has not addressed this or related questions from an issue-based approach.

The previous attempts at conceptualizing rivalry have been heavily influenced by a research focus on enduring rivalries and more subtly by the operational definitions of rivalry that rely on the occurrence of militarized disputes. Thompson (1995b) complains that the enduring aspect of enduring rivalry has been overemphasized at the expense of the rivalry aspect. Accordingly, he sees most conceptual and operational definitions as overly broad. In his view, a state's rival is more than simply an external threat or continuing source of problems for that state. In place of the typical notion of enduring rivalries, Thompson advocates the adoption of the term *principal rivalries*. Thompson distinguishes competitions that represent some threat to security from those that are primary and fundamental (see also McGinnis and Williams 1989). Thompson, agreeing with Kuenne (1989), rejects the notion that rivalries are mere competitions. Unlike most market competitions, for example, rivalries exhibit nonanonymity in that the competition is focused directly on one competitor. Some level of endurance is implicit in Thompson's idea of principal rivalry, but continuity seems to be a more major concern.

Types of Rivalries

Beyond the general conceptions of rivalries, scholars have sought to differentiate different types of rivalries, with the implicit assumption that different types exhibit different behavioral patterns. Hensel (1996a) suggests the possibilities that rivalries can be nonmilitarized and that rivalries do not have to involve nation-states. Although these remain interesting possibilities, the empirical literature has focused almost exclusively on militarized rivalries between states (in part for reasons of data availability).

The common differentiation among types of rivalries is based on their length. Hensel (1996a) as well as Goertz and Diehl (1993; Diehl and Goertz 2000) introduce a temporal dimension to their conceptions of rivalry: it must last long enough to focus each state/rival's attention on the other. On this dimension, rivalry types vary according to their length, ranging from brief competitions to those that extend over many years, the latter of which are labeled as "enduring." For a rivalry to be enduring, one might suggest that it last longer than a brief period, although the exact time frame has been more a matter for empirical measurement than of conceptual clarity. Goertz and Diehl divide the continuum of rivalry into several parts (Goertz and Diehl 1992a). Isolated rivalries are those of very brief duration, sometimes representing very severe conflict, but whose bases of conflict are resolved in a short period or wither away such that recurring conflict and war are no longer central concerns in the relationship. Enduring rivalries are the longest of the rivalries and have the greatest expectations of an ongoing conflictual relationship. The impact of history in those relationships is also greater given there is more history to affect the relationship. One might think of enduring rivalries as lasting elements in international affairs. Proto-rivalries represent something of a middle ground between the isolated and enduring kind; they persist for a moderate amount of time, but the history of hostility has less of an effect than in enduring rivalries, but more so than in isolated competitions. Indeed, protorivalries can be thought of as potential enduring rivalries that terminate in adolescence before they reach that maturity, whereas isolated rivalries undergo something akin to crib death.

Thompson's (1955) more narrow focus on principal rivalries should not imply that he regards all these as the same. He classifies rivalries according to two dimensions: (1) the type of competition and (2) the locale or scope of that competition. With respect to competition type, he distinguishes spatial rivalries from positional ones. Spatial rivalries are those that are fought over territorial control and tend to be less intense than their positional counterparts. Spatial rivalries are likely to involve minor power states and even involve states with asymmetrical capabilities, although such a condition is thought to make such rivalries end more quickly. In contrast, and more interesting from Thompson's theoretical perspective, are positional rivalries, which are competitions over relative positions in a power hierarchy. These are essentially regional or global power struggles that inherently assume some capability symmetry (a competition over power and influence is unlikely if one state is dramatically stronger than another).

The second dimension, location, indicates where the rivalry is contested, and there are four possibilities: (1) dyadic, (2) regional, (3) global, and (4) regional-global. Dyadic rivalries are competitions confined to a narrow geographic area, and these rivalries are thought to be primarily of the spatial variety. Regional rivalries concentrate on slightly broader areas and are competitions over power in a more defined region, such as the rivalry between Spain and France in the sixteenth century. Global rivalries, such as between Venice and Portugal in the fifteenth century or the United States and the Soviet Union in the twentieth century, are those international competitions for leadership, consistent with the framework of the long cycles literature (Modelski 1987; Modelski and Thompson 1989). The final category combines the previous two and is illustrated by the Netherlands' rivalries with Spain and France in the sixteenth and seventeenth centuries, respectively.

Some scholars argue that militarized competition and therefore rivalries must involve states that can realistically challenge the security positions of each other; in effect, only rivalries between states of approximately equal capabilities are of theoretical interest—major power or minor power rivalries. Mixed major-minor rivalries are thought to have different behavior characteristics (Vasquez 1993). Those who contend that the key rivalries are those conducted between approximate equals believe that a preponderant state does not have to compete with a weaker foe because there is little chance that the weaker state will prevail in the competition.

It may be incorrect to assume that the power distribution necessarily remains constant throughout the rivalry. Furthermore, a rivalry does not end or suddenly begin merely because one side has dramatically increased its strength. Similarly, declaring a series of hostile interactions as a rivalry only after approximate parity is achieved may ignore the roots of the competition and the reason for the shift from preponderance to parity (e.g., the power transition model). Major-minor power rivalries may exhibit different characteristics than other rivalry types, but this is a theoretical and empirical question. It may be best at this juncture not to exclude, a priori, any type of protracted hostile interaction from consideration as a rivalry. Most operational definitions of enduring rivalries include a significant number of major-minor power rivalries, and an important topic of empirical study is how such rivalries differ in behavior as compared with symmetrical rivalries.

Overall, although there is some diversity of approach in conceptualizations of rivalry, there is some consensus that enduring rivalries are those that involve the same set of states clashing in repeated militarized confrontations over a(n) (extended) period of time.[3] In addition, issue criteria may be introduced to prove more links between conflicts. Not surprisingly, the operational definitions of enduring rivalries focus on these elements. Most start with a preliminary list of rivalries generated on purely behavioral criteria, then issue aspects come into play, particularly in determining start and end dates.

Operational Definitions

There has been one attempt to define rivalries of all varieties (Diehl and Goertz 2000; Goertz and Diehl 1992a), but there have been several systematic attempts to develop a population of only enduring rivalries. This is not to say that scholars have not studied rivalries or conflict phenomena that can be labeled as rivalries. The dominant method in defining enduring rivalries has been to use historical judgment. In most of these efforts, a universe of cases is not the goal. These are historical case studies in which no attempt is made to generalize beyond the limited domain of the study. Some cases, such as the Anglo-German conflict at the beginning of the twentieth century or the U.S.-Soviet conflict after World War II, are consistent with conventional wisdom on what constitutes an enduring rivalry. For example, Lieberman (1995) is interested in the Arab-Israeli rivalry, and it is relatively easy to discern the independence of Israel as the event signaling the onset of the rivalry and several wars serving as signposts along the way. In other cases, the particular theoretical questions posed by the researcher inexorably lead to the identification of certain rivalries for study. For example, Kinsella (1995) sought to understand the effects of superpower competition and arms transfers on third world conflict; obviously, he focuses on the U.S.-Soviet rivalry and on four other enduring rivalries (drawn from Huth and Russett 1993) that involve superpower client states. Yet these methods do not result in systematic criteria to develop a universe of cases.

Three main issues dominate all operationalizations of the rivalry concept. All the rivalries must have a beginning and an end. Hence one must develop means for determining the birth and death dates of rivalries. The third issue revolves around establishing the criterion for *enduring* rivalries. How long does it have to last before it becomes enduring?

The Correlates of War (COW) project and its associates have generated most of the operational measures of enduring rivalries. Each of these related efforts share a number of characteristics and empirically produce similar lists of enduring rivalries. Despite the similarities in construction and output, there are minor differences in the definitions; and it is unlikely that there will be one uniform COW definition of enduring rivalries as is the case for militarized disputes (Jones, Bremer, and Singer 1996), for example. Although not identical, the differences between the definitions are relatively minor, usually dealing with auxiliary conditions. We divide these definitional efforts into the first generation, which was mainly concerned with using rivalries to test other hypotheses, and the second generation, which focused on rivalries themselves.

Because most operationalizations have come from the COW Project, not surprisingly most have relied on the COW list of militarized interstate disputes (see Gochman and Maoz 1984 and Jones, Bremer, and Singer 1996) to identify enduring rivalries. Each effort has established some threshold for the frequency of such disputes involving the same pair of states over a given time frame to distinguish short-term conflict from an enduring rivalry. The beginning of the rivalry corresponds roughly to the beginning of the first dispute and termination to the end of the last conflict.

The first generation of definitions used purely behavioral criteria in the form of dispute occurrence. Rivalries began with the first dispute and continued as long as there were disputes, assuming that the interdispute waiting time was not too long. Rivalries terminated sometime in the period after the last dispute, often arbitrarily fixed at 10 to 15 years. For example, Wayman (1982, 1996) designated a dyadic enduring rivalry as any instance in which two states oppose each other in two or more disputes within a 10-year period. He assumes that a militarized dispute has a decade-long impact on a dyadic relationship. If that hostile relationship is reinforced by another dispute, then the two states have extended their hostility and can be considered to be in an enduring rivalry. Thus, a rivalry lasts from the onset of the first dispute until 10 years after the last dispute.

Diehl (1985a, 1985b, 1985c, 1994; Diehl and Kingston 1987) basically extended and refined Wayman's definition, making an enduring rivalry as any situation in which two nations engage in at least three militarized disputes within a period of 15 years. Diehl argues that once established, enduring rivalries need a lesser frequency of dispute occurrence for their maintenance; the competition cannot be considered fully dissipated until the relationship experiences a significant period without military confrontation. Accordingly, the time frame for a given enduring rivalry is extended if a militarized dispute between the rivals occurs within 10 years of the last dispute in the original rivalry sequence. Therefore, there must be a 10-year "dispute-free" interval before a rivalry can be certified as ended. This definition specifically excludes disputes related to ongoing world wars, so as not to confuse their effects with those of the enduring rivalry. Diehl's criteria are more specific than Wayman's, and there is greater sensitivity to the termination as well as the onset of rivalries.

Gochman and Maoz (1984) construct a list of enduring rivalry dyads that include major power, minor power, and mixed types. Their operational criteria, however, are somewhat vague. They consider enduring rivalries as "the pairs . . . of states that most often have engaged in disputes with one another" (1984, 609). In practice, this turns out to be a minimum of seven militarized disputes over the 1816–1980 period. There appears to be no temporal component, as disputes may be years apart and involve wholly unconnected issues; the only things they have in common are the participants.

The second generation of definitions (e.g., Bennett 1996; Diehl and Goertz 2000; Geller 1993; Goertz and Diehl 1992a; Huth, Bennett, and Gelpi, 1992; Huth and Russett 1993; Jones 1989; Maoz and Mor 1996; Wayman and Jones 1991), starting in the late 1980s, took the basic behavioral framework from the first generation, but added more conditions and extended the minimum duration for an enduring rivalry. Here too we see for the first time the inclusion of issue criteria in some definitional schemes. These operationalizations now require an enduring rivalry to contain a minimum of five to seven militarized disputes involving the same two states, and almost all require that there be at least 20 or 25 years between the outbreak of the first dispute and the termination of the last dispute. For any two disputes to be part of the same rivalry, there must be a period of no more than 10 to 15 years between the disputes, or in some conceptions the issues over which the disputes revolve must be the same and unresolved. This is designed to meet the notion that states must consistently be challenging one another either through frequency of conflict within a narrow time frame or over the same issue across a broader time frame.

In addition to these major requirements, some schemes add some additional, minor conditions. In one variation, each dispute must last at least 30 days and include reciprocal threats, displays, or uses of military force (e.g., Jones 1989; Maoz and Mor 1996). The reciprocity requirement is designed to eliminate confrontations in which the use or threat of force did not prompt a reaction from the other party; this ensures that the disputes represent actual competition and hostility by both sides. The duration requirement (about the median for disputes involving the display of force) is apparently designed to eliminate single incidents being classified as rivalry producing disputes. This adds a temporal requirement for the disputes as well as the rivalry as a whole. In addition, several of the individual definitions in the COW group stipulate that the two rivals must be the primary initiator and primary target of the dispute, respectively, or there needs to be direct and prolonged military confrontation between the rivals in a multiparty dispute in which they were not the primary parties. This is designed to eliminate third-party interventions in which one rival is not in direct confrontation with the other.

Looking at militarized disputes is not the only way to generate a list of rivalries, enduring or otherwise. For example, one could clearly use events data in a similar fashion (Hensel 1997). It is the case, however, that no other method or data has been used to develop a universe of cases. Thompson (1995b) perhaps comes the closest in trying to identify a list of principal rivalries; yet he admits that he only presents the "primary" ones over the last five centuries ($N = 12$) and this is largely based on the "long cycles" research framework. It is unclear from his article how one might operationally identify other principal rivalries, although the conceptual scheme seems amenable to operationalization.

All definitions use the same basic data set (various versions of the COW project militarized dispute data set) and rely on the frequency of militarized disputes to identify enduring rivalries. On the one hand, each definition is open to the criticism that militarized disputes are only one manifestation of an enduring rivalry (Thompson 1995b). Yet militarized disputes are a better indicator than arms races and the like because they are better able to meet the conceptual standard for militarized competitiveness, that the use of military force or resort to war is an ever-present danger.

Nevertheless, militarized disputes are not without their problems. All the definitions will pick up on militarized dispute activity only as it reaches above a certain threshold (the threat of military force). In statistical terms, the data may be "truncated" from below, and the beginning and/or the end of conflict in the rivalry may be missed. One aspect of the minor requirements of some COW definitions is to raise the minimum observation level for rivalry. Requirements about reciprocity, duration, and multilateral disputes means that the truncation line is moved upward, which increases the risk of missing a rivalry. This may not be desirable as it reduces the information we have about the rivalry relationship. Truncation from below with dispute data already sets serious observational limits, which these additional conditions exacerbate.

Between the two generations we can see a clear tightening of standards in the operationalization of enduring rivalry. From the first to the second generation, the number of disputes to qualify as an enduring rivalry increases from 2–3 to 5–6 and the duration from 10–15 to 20–25 years. Wayman required only that two disputes occur to establish an enduring rivalry. The other definitions require a varying number of disputes, in part dependent on the time frame established for the rivalry. For example, Diehl sets three disputes for the minimum, but this averages to about one every five years (the same as the Wayman requirement for two disputes in a 10-year period and some of the COW group who look for five disputes in a 25-year time frame), whereas the Gochman and Maoz requirement of seven disputes (the highest among definitions) translates only to one every 23 years over the 1816–1980 period, and there may be little connection between those disputes. Although a serious military threat may be a potentially justifiable minimum level of militarized competitiveness, how long "enduring" should be is not clear. We know of no theoretical arguments for the 20–25 year minimum, but there is an empirical argument for that as a natural breakpoint in the distribution of rivalries. Diehl and Goertz (2000) used the empirical distribution of *all* rivalries according to their lengths and the number of disputes to arrive at their 20-year and six-dispute standards for enduring rivalries. They found significant empirical breaks around those particular points.

Determining the beginning and end points is a crucial aspect of rivalry operationalization, because many important hypotheses focus on these key events. It is often easier to see a rivalry begin, because of a clear set of events, than to understand when it is over. Few definitions really provide termination criteria distinct from those related to the maximum time between disputes. The end of the rivalry occurs sometime after the last dispute. Most definitions do not specify a precise date of termination, only that it occurs sometime between the end of the last dispute and some fixed time thereafter, usually designated as 10 years. The problem with this is that although states might resolve their major differences through war and/or international agreement, operational definitions will not recognize the end of rivalry until at least 10 years after the last dispute. This means that most approaches will only be able to pick up hostile actions and must await the passage of time to make an ex post facto judgment on termination. This is most evident in the recent demise of the cold war, which according to the definitions here may not end until the beginning of the twenty-first century. The use of the COW dispute data set thus implies that all the definitions will have problems accurately determining the exact beginning and end points of rivalries. All definitions consider that a rivalry may continue at least 10 years after the last dispute, but similar consideration suggests that a rivalry could begin 10 years prior to the first dispute (a consideration that all current definitions ignore).

An exception to the reliance on vague or arbitrary post-last-dispute rules for termination points is Bennett (1993, 1996, 1997a, 1997b, 1998). Because he is interested in rivalry termination, he adopts additional and specific criteria for rivalry termination. More than just a cessation of military hostilities, Bennett requires that the issues under dispute also be resolved. This is indicated by the signing of a formal agreement or a public renunciation of claims by the rivals. The choice of criteria for rivalry termination can have a significant effect on pinpointing the end of rivalry and influence the conclusions drawn from empirical analyses about rivalry termination. Bennett (1997c) compared the effect of detecting rivalry termination through (1) the absence of militarized conflict for a sustained period of time versus (2) the timing of the resolution of the issues under contention. He reports that there can be, in some cases, a 25-year difference in determining when a rivalry is over.

For both beginning and end dates, however, it may be unrealistic to try to pinpoint an exact date. Both the beginning and end of rivalries can be drawn out, and we only know post hoc if the rivalry has begun or ended. To determine exact dates is akin to asking when someone was cured of cancer. One only really knows after a certain period of time with no symptoms, and a recurrence becomes less and less likely only after the passage of time. In such cases, one cannot say that the cancer was cured in any particular year. In short, beginning and end dates are important but difficult to observe with exactitude. Formal agreements may apparently signal the end of a rivalry, but later events may prove otherwise.

Nevertheless, one should not exaggerate the problems with post hoc judgments. Viewing things post hoc does not mean that the coding decisions are wrong, but that we only really know post hoc. We may only know that cancer surgery really succeeds some time after it is all over.

The exact number of rivalries identified varies among the COW group according to which definition is adopted and which version of the militarized dispute data is used. Typical of those using the latest available data, Diehl and Goertz (2000) have identified 63 enduring rivalries. The operational measures discussed earlier have all focused on enduring rivalries. Yet for some applications, it is important to include rivalries of all durations. Thus far only Diehl and Goertz have proposed a conceptualization and operationalization of rivalries that runs from the very short, isolated conflicts, to medium-term protorivalries, to enduring rivalries. They use the basic COW behavioral framework already described to construct rivalries using *all* of the militarized dispute data. The shortest rivalry consists of just one dispute; two disputes within 10 years is the next shortest, and so forth. With this procedure and using the MID 2.10 data (militarized dispute data described in Jones, Bremer, and Singer 1996), they identified 223 proto and 880 isolated dyadic rivalries among the 2,000 militarized disputes over the 1816–1992 period (in addition to the 63 enduring rivalries). The utility of these rivalries of different lengths is most apparent in applications of the rivalry approach to war and peace.

The Rivalry Approach to War and Peace

Much of the early enduring rivalry research focused on operational definitions. This was largely because scholars were concerned with identifying those cases that they could analyze in pursuit of studying deterrence, power transitions, and other phenomena. Later research, much of it reviewed in the following, centers on rivalries as central foci in and of themselves. Yet rivalries are not merely a new topic of research—an extension of the logic behind studying "dangerous dyads" (Bremer 1992)—nor are they merely a useful research tool and case selection device. Goertz and Diehl (1995a; Diehl and Goertz 2000) propose that the rivalry approach constitutes a general framework for examining many issues and hypotheses in the conflict literature; it is not just another hypothesis to be added to an already long list, but rather is more like

Most and Starr's (1989) "opportunity and willingness" framework for the study of international conflict. The rivalry approach raises new questions, including new twists on old hypotheses, particularly about the relationship of war to peace. The rivalry approach also suggests some alterations in the typical methodology used to test hypotheses about international conflict. Here, we provide an overview of the rivalry framework, as it increasingly guides the work on (enduring) rivalries and how it relates to common causes-of-war hypotheses.

The rivalry approach focuses attention on issues normally beyond the horizon of the traditional international conflict literature, or what might generically be labeled the causes-of-war approach, in three general ways. The first of these is perhaps the most fundamental because it removes war from center stage. In virtually all analyses of conflict, war is the variable to be explained. In the rivalry approach, the rivalry relationship takes over as the fundamental object of study. This explains our extensive discussion of rivalry and its operationalization. Here we explore some of the methodological and theoretical implications of that concept. The next three sections illustrate how the rivalry approach generates new hypotheses as well as creates new methods to test classic hypotheses.

Changing Foci of Analysis: From War to Rivalry

Research using the traditional causes-of-war framework tries to explain war as the result of certain hypothesized causes typically including events, interactions, or conditions, with some examples being military expenditure patterns, crisis bargaining, or political regime types. Scholars in this tradition search for the presence of the hypothesized causes shortly before or coterminous with the outbreak of war in a set of cases as well as in control groups in which no war occurs. Transferring these sorts of explanatory models into the rivalry framework replaces war with rivalry; one looks for the presence or occurrence of hypothesized events or conditions before the rivalry starts and just before it ends. The former could be called the "causes-of-rivalry" hypotheses and the latter could be called the "causes-of-peace" ones.

Although the causes-of-war literature provides many useful ideas for understanding the causes of rivalry, the causes of peace prove more problematic. The problem with peace is that it has been conceptualized as "not war." How does one explain a nonevent? With rivalry as the unit of analysis, there is a potential event to analyze: the death of the rivalry.

Because of the temporal duration of a rivalry, there are two equally important questions: why rivalry starts and why it ends. An example of the latter application is found in Gibler (1997a), who looks not at how territorial settlement treaties end war, but rather rivalries.

Changing the unit of analysis also expands the horizon of international conflict scholars. They become concerned with the outbreak of peace as well as war, with peace defined as the end of the rivalry relationship rather than simply the end or absence of war. Thus, those who adopt the rivalry approach are able to explore conflict management and resolution, and they do not merely lump all aspects of the absence of a shooting war together. International conflict scholars have long been criticized for their exclusive focus on war, with the accompanying ignorance of cooperative and lower-level conflictual relationships. The rivalry approach addresses this critique, in part, by putting conflict resolution (not just war termination) on the research agenda and by providing some concern for the stability of peace achievements (as the rivalry approach is also concerned with how rivalries begin).

Many of the hypotheses about the causes of war are relevant to explaining the occurrence and severity of rivalries. For example, there has been a debate in the literature over the past several decades about the relative war proneness of bipolar and multipolar systems. By turning our attention away from war to rivalries, fresh questions can be raised and some old controversies addressed. Do certain system structures produce more rivalries that are of greater severity (even short of war) and of longer duration? (Multipolar systems and their allegedly greater fluidity should produce shorter and more numerous rivalries, whereas bipolar systems should produce fewer and more enduring rivalries according to the prevailing logics of each argument.) If major power war is generally avoided in a given system, does this beneficial effect also extend to conflict resolution between the major actors? How does system change affect the conduct of ongoing rivalries? Each of these questions has the potential to provide new insights into old debates as well as to offer some new bases for understanding the impact of system structure on state behavior.

Among the ways the rivalry approach permits a new evaluation of old hypotheses is the simple replacement of dispute by rivalry as the (statistical) unit of analysis. Vasquez (1996) illustrates this by taking his "steps-to-war" framework and testing it using rivalries. In each of his analyses, a rivalry counts as a single case. Gibler (1997a) shows that one can use both rivalry and dispute as the unit of analysis. Although these do not constitute fully independent tests (both rely on COW dispute data), they do examine the robustness of the theory.

Many studies that use rivalries take the cross-sectional time-series approach. Huth and Russett's (1993) work on deterrence provides a good example of this. But one should and can add analyses with rivalry as the focus of analysis. Huth and Russett evaluate their models only in terms of disputes, but they could also see how well it performs at the rivalry level. It may be that such models work well or poorly for certain rivalries, information that does not appear by lumping all the disputes together. A complete rivalry analysis normally should include *both* kinds of statistical tests, dispute and rivalry, as the input to statistical tests. There are a few examples of this in the literature: Gibler (1997a) and Goertz and Diehl (1995b) actually perform both kinds of tests. The general tendency is to privilege the cross-sectional time-series to the detriment of cross sections between individual rivalries.[4]

Longitudinal and Dynamic Implications

Treating rivalry as the focus of analysis generates many new hypotheses and is particularly appropriate when trying to understand the initiation and termination of rivalries. Yet the core of the rivalry approach also stresses the longitudinal and dynamic character of the rivalry relationship; it is an interaction that exists over time. Another series of questions thus arises about the dynamics of rivalries. Certain kinds of expectations are central to understanding rivalries. An enduring rivalry is a hostile and competitive relationship in which each side views the other as posing a significant threat to its own interests. In such a relationship, rivals expect that disputes, crises, and even war will continue into the future. These expectations condition current foreign policy choices, which may then provide feedback to help cause future war (the positive feedback of an arms race model), or prevent it (the negative feedback of deterrence models). Static models based on national attributes or current conditions will not capture this long-range outlook.

If future expectations are significant in rivalries, one might ask where they come from. One obvious response is past interactions. Rivalries have a joint history in addition to a joint future. The concept of "learning" has received a great deal of attention in recent years. In his literature review, Levy (1994b) recommends that one examine learning in the context of one crisis. Yet the rivalry approach argues that learning models can neither be conceptualized nor studied except in a dynamic, longitudinal fashion. If a state has really learned something, then that learning will be evident on many future occasions. If such evidence is not forthcoming, doubt is cast on whether any real learning from the past took place. If it is a trial-and-error or search process, then we can only see that over multiple trials. The rivalry approach provides a framework for examining different models of state learning. An illustration is offered by Maoz and Mor (1998) who attempted to uncover whether certain states in the Middle East exhibited learning in repeated interactions. They find that some adaptive learning does occur within rivalries, but their model is often incorrect in predicting the behavior of the rivals. They cite perceptual shifts about what game is thought to be in play and incomplete information about the process by scholars as possibly responsible for this discrepancy. In any case, there appears to be less learning and its subsequent impact than one might expect, although such processes are often hard to identify and assess (see Levy 1994b).

Another longitudinal aspect of the rivalry approach is a broader consideration beyond a given end point—war. The causes-of-war approach postulates a series of events or states of affairs occurring before war as potential explanations of war. In the rivalry approach, war most often occurs somewhere at the beginning or middle of the rivalry. Hence, scholars are naturally concerned with what happened before the war in the rivalry, but just as often we are concerned with what happens after wars. In a symmetrical fashion, many of the phenomena that occur before a war can take place following it. That is, many of the causes of war can also be the effects of war. For example, does war result in a power transition? in an arms race? in a regime change?

Another focus of the rivalry approach is the dynamics of rivalry evolution. Here the move is away from juxtaposing the rivalry approach with important hypotheses in the war literature. Although the causes-of-war literature can provide us with many hints and suggestive ideas, it cannot respond to the question of the evolution of conflictual relationships. Most of the dynamic hypotheses in the war literature involve escalatory processes, but rivalries escalate and de-escalate (Goertz and Regan 1997); there are periods of calm in addition to the storms that occasionally shake the relationship. We need theories that relate periods of calm to periods of crisis; we need to know if and when crisis, dispute, and war affect the basic parameters of the relationship and when they do not. These are questions that only make sense within the rivalry approach.

The literature on the dynamics of particular rivalries (e.g., Goldstein and Freeman 1991; McGinnis and Williams 1989) offers a useful place to begin. For example, if in rivalries we find that periods of calm are associated with democratic regimes (or democratization) and that periods of greater conflict tend to occur when this is not the case, then this provides direct evidence for the democratic peace hypothesis. Most of the process theories in international relations tend to describe such processes before war, but few connect wars and disputes with each other.

Methodologically, the longitudinal component of rivalries creates new possibilities for testing standard hypotheses and resolving some long-standing problems with previous cross-sectional tests. We would like to mention two possibilities that prove exceptionally useful; one uses rivalries in interrupted time-series analysis, while the other uses nondispute rivalry years as a control group. Huth and Russett's (1993) work on deterrence demonstrates the usefulness of the control group application. Case selection has provoked great debate in the deterrence literature (Achen and Snidal 1989). The problem revolves around finding cases of deterrence success, as deterrence failure is fairly easy to detect. Huth and Russett (1993) solve this problem by considering the nondispute/war years of a rivalry as deterrence successes. Because (enduring) rivalries have both dispute and nondispute periods, they provide a natural set of treatment and control periods. Lieberman (1994) uses the same basic strategy in critiquing Lebow and Stein (1990). He argues that many of the factors they associate with Middle East wars occurred as frequently during nonwar years. Hence there is no significant correlation between these factors and war. In short, one can compare different periods of a rivalry to evaluate various hypotheses.

The interrupted time-series method is a special application of this same idea. Scholars can compare rivalries before and after some critical event to determine the impact of that event on the occurrence of disputes and wars. A particularly interesting application of this methodology investigates the democratic peace hypothesis. One could examine the evolution of a rivalry before or after it makes a transition to or from the joint democratic status. If the democratic peace hypothesis is correct, we would expect to see the rivalry end, or at least a clear reduction in the severity level. Hensel, Goertz, and Diehl (forthcoming) found that militarized disputes were generally much less likely during periods of joint democracy as compared with other periods; the exception is that regime-change dyads that evolved into enduring rivalries continued with their patterns of disputations behavior regardless of the regime types of the rivals. Among rivalries that are transformed to joint democratic status, however, the conflict level tends to be lower when there is a democratic dyad, and the rivalry almost always ends shortly thereafter. Consistent with these findings, Bennett (1997a) finds that joint democracy helps to end a rivalry.

The interrupted time-series technique avoids many of the problems of the standard cross-sectional procedures. One need not define relevant dyads, one need not worry about how to code multiple-year wars, and there is no need to decide about what time frames to use as the basic period of analysis. We do not think that interrupted time-series and control group methodologies exhaust the richness of the longitudinal dimension of rivalry for testing purposes. We suspect that as scholars take the rivalry as a basic unit of analysis more seriously new applications will emerge.

Rivalries as a Contextual Factor

In the previous two subsections we have exposed the methodology and testing possibilities that the rivalry approach creates, but which have been underexploited. Here we start by considering the first major use of rivalries: as a testing and case selection mechanism. We label this use of rivalries as the contextual or background condition. The kinds of questions posed in the background condition literature are quite different from those posed in the rivalry approach. As a background condition, rivalries are only used in an instrumental capacity; they are a case selection mechanism in the research design. The longitudinal component is absent, and often the data analysis consists of purely cross-sectional techniques. Many theories, such as those concerning arms races and power transition, require a condition of underlying hostility or competition. (Enduring) rivalries provide a means of identifying ongoing and prolonged serious conflict between a set of states. Looking at enduring rivalries allows the scholar more valid conclusions than consideration of all dyads or all contiguous dyads (many of which will involve states that have little or no contact with one another).

For example, arms races are thought to be one manifestation of an enduring rivalry. Looking at arms races in enduring rivalries provides some assurance that new weapons acquisition is directed at a specific opponent and that such increases are viewed as threatening (Diehl 1985a; Diehl and Kingston 1987). A similar logic underlies the substitution of alliances and arms races, which often takes place over a broad time frame (Diehl 1994; Sorokin 1994). The most obvious use of enduring rivalries as a background condition is in the study of power transitions (Geller 1993; Wayman 1996). There, enduring rivalries perform the function of specifying the ongoing competition that will be affected by changes in the power distribution between the states. Other dyads might be open to the criticism that the states involved were not directly attuned to the actions of the other state or that the other state was not its primary rival.

Until recently, the primary use of enduring rivalry has been as a case selection device. Huth, Bennett, and Gelpi illustrate this case selection usage: "...the concept of a Great Power rivalry is critical because it identifies the population of cases to be used for testing the model's propositions" (1992, 483). Yet this is a crude way of linking rivalries to phenomena such as deterrence. What these authors are doing is making a theoretical claim about situations in which deterrent threats, for example, are likely to be made; the variables in their models then try to explain why such threats work or not. The rivalry approach suggests that these are related concerns and should be addressed together in the theory, and not relegated to a simple methodological issue.

The logical step is to include rivalry characteristics in the theoretical framework itself. First, this means abandoning the notion that there is necessarily a radical break between enduring and lower-level rivalries (in effect, taking "enduring" out of enduring rivalry research). It also means that the characteristics of the rivalry relationship are thought to influence the process under scrutiny, whether it be deterrence or the escalation of arms races to war. This forces the scholar to identify those characteristics in the model rather than to leave them subsumed under case selection and then forgotten.

In the rivalry as background condition literature, the rivalry concept already exists in the *theory,* yet to hide the theory in case selection distorts both. For example, the classic Richardson (1960a) arms race model includes the grievance term, which *de facto* refers to rivalry but is often ignored in the arms race literature. The power transition (see Kugler and Lemke's chapter in this volume) provides another example. It has two fundamental components, the power transition and competition/dissatisfaction with the status quo. Each is a necessary condition for war; if either is absent, no war is the prediction: "Only when a pair of states are relatively equal in capabilities can both sides in conflict realistically expect to win; only when the challenger is committed to change is there something over which to fight" (Lemke and Werner 1996, 235). Strictly speaking, each component carries the same theoretical weight, but the power transition literature has only really worked on conceptualizing half of the theory. Frequently when rivalries are used for case selection they in fact form key elements of the theory. A better theory and methodology results from explicitly including them in the model to be tested. For example, an appropriate way to theorize about how the rivalry context may affect deterrent threats could be to see the effectiveness of the deterrence variables, as changing according to the underlying rivalry relationship. Credibility may be less effective in a short-term rivalry or an early stage of an enduring rivalry as little opportunity to build reputation has been present.

Empirical Research on (Enduring) Rivalries

In one sense, there has been an abundance of work on rivalries. Yet one would not necessarily see direct evidence of that in examining the scholarly literature. This is because work on rivalries has not carried the rivalry label and has primarily been confined to the analysis of a single prolonged competition between two or more states; most prominently have been those concerned with the United States–Soviet Union rivalry and the Arab-Israeli conflict. There are many primarily descriptive studies that, although insightful on individual events and relationships, do not offer much in the way of a theoretical understanding of how rivalries evolve; there is not much concern with process, as the analysis tends to be static. Furthermore, they offer little in the way of generalizations that extend beyond the single case at hand. Except as excellent sources on the history of individual rivalries, we largely ignore this segment of the literature in our review. More recently, the intrinsic importance of rivalries as a focus of study in their own right has been recognized. In the following sections we more systematically examine the research on the various aspects of the rivalry life cycle: its birth, life, and death as well as outside, exogenous effects on the rivalry dyad. We end with an examination of the outbreak of war in this life cycle.

The Origins of Enduring Rivalries

Various studies look to initial and other conditions to understand how rivalries, especially enduring ones, might develop. Goertz and Diehl (1995b) report that political shocks at the system (e.g., changes in major power distribution) and state (e.g., civil wars) levels are virtual necessary conditions for the onset of enduring rivalries. They found that almost 87 percent of enduring rivalries began coterminous with at least one political shock. Further studies provide some insights about what other conditions might be associated with the beginnings of rivalries.

Levy and Ali (1998) conducted a case study of the Anglo-Dutch rivalry over the period 1609–52. They explored why a purely commercial rivalry remained peaceful for almost a half-century but turned into a militarized rivalry that was soon to experience three wars in relatively short succession. Initially, they point out that the Dutch and the English had diametrically opposed economic interests, which made them logical candidates to clash with each other. Reinforcing this conflict, economic liberalism determined Dutch strategies, while the English pursued a mercantilist strategy. Brummett (1999) also cites commercial interests as the basis for the rivalry between the Ottoman Empire and Venice. We should note that a related argument has been put forward by Friedman and Lebard (1991) with respect to future relations between the United States and Japan. They contend that the cold war held the two states together against a common external enemy (the Soviet Union) and the absence of that threat now will lead the two states to become serious rivals; they also argue that competition over resources will become stiff and almost inevitably involve military confrontation. Based on Levy and Ali's analysis, however, differing economic strategies or market competitions are not enough to turn a trade rivalry violent—several others factors must be at work.

One key factor is the relative power distribution between the two sides. Levy and Ali argue that English naval inferiority until the 1640s prevented them from seriously challenging the Dutch. This suggestion that power imbalance inhibits rivalry conflict is related to the contention of Vasquez (1993) and others that interactions between states of approximately equal capability will be different from other interactions and perhaps more severe. The presence of bipolarity might also make the two leading states more likely to be rivals, as might be argued in the case of the United States and the Soviet Union following World War II (Larson 1999). The logic is similar to the one here—one state cannot plausibly challenge another unless it has sufficient capabilities to make threats credible. Although approximate parity seems to be a vital condition for a militarized rivalry, two caveats are in order, one theoretical and one empirical. Theoretically, parity may not be necessary if the potential rival disadvantaged by the status quo is superior in strength; in that circumstance, preponderance by the revisionist state may be enough to start a rivalry. Empirically, it is evident that not all enduring rivalries between states take place between approximate equals. Although lists of rivals vary across the studies, a significant minority of them involved states with widely disparate capabilities. Thus, approximate parity may be important in many cases, but it is not a necessary condition for militarized rivalry.

Another key factor, noted by Vasquez (1998a) in a case study of the Pacific theater of World War II, is the importance of territorial issues as a basis for enduring rivalries. Rule (1999) also notes that the competition over territory (along with ideology) was an important element in the origins of the France-Spain rivalry of the late fifteenth century. Although there have been a large number of ongoing claims over territory, not all of these have resulted in militarized disputes or the development of longstanding rivalries. Huth (1996b) looks at the role of territorial claims since 1950 in the origins of enduring rivalries. Huth uses a modified realist model, which includes both domestic and international political factors, to explain how states become involved in enduring rivalries over territory. Importantly, he notes that the relative strength of the challenger does not have much of an effect on rivalry involvement, and states also do not frequently challenge allies or extant treaty commitments by resorting to militarized action. Rather, domestic concerns, especially ethnic and linguistic ties between one's own population and those living in the disputed territory, are significantly associated with the recurrence of militarized conflict.

Domestic political pressures are also important factors in other analyses of rivalry origins. Levy and Ali (1998) note that early domestic instability in England inhibited its ability to challenge the Dutch. Later domestic political pressures led that rivalry to heat up, become militarized, and go to war several times early in the militarized phase of the rivalry. Vasquez (1998a) also cites domestic political pressures on Japan, which led to that state's expansionist drive in Asia and ultimately its attack on the United States. Maoz and Mor (1998) importantly affirm that cooperation among rivals is quite possible, but that this does not preclude the beginning or continuation of a rivalry. Rather, the key aspect is that both sides are dissatisfied with some situation leading to the onset and expansion of the rivalry. Yet it may also be that the absence of the ability or incentive for two states to cooperate (to mutually benefit each other in any meaningful way) may be a force in promoting rivalry (see Schroeder's 1999 argument vis-à-vis the Franco-Austrian rivalry), although this alone would seem to be insufficient.

Thus, scant findings indicate that political shocks, parity, territorial issues, and domestic political pressures were associated with the beginning of rivalries, with no strong mitigating effects from some early cooperation between rivals. Some question remains about whether the origins of rivalries, even enduring ones, are any different than international conflict in general.

Dynamics of Enduring Rivalries

We have spoken here in particular of the origins of enduring rivalry. A related question asks why some rivalries become enduring. The literature on enduring rivalries provides some suggestions based on analyses of that group of rivalries, but until we compare enduring rivalries to protorivalries there is little definitive to offer. Only this comparison permits a test of hypotheses about the special early dynamics of enduring rivalry, because it contrasts them with rivalries that do not become enduring rivalry. Cioffi-Revilla (1998b) illustrates the conceptual impact of including all rivalries, not just enduring ones. In his analysis, if one looked only at enduring rivalries, one sees a perhaps counterintuitive decline in stability and life expectancy. But this is like examining the life expectancy of people who are 60 and older; that is, only focusing on the stability of rivalries that have already matured to enduring status. When you examine his results for all types of rivalries, the picture changes dramatically. There is a period of increasing stability before the rivalry hits the enduring stage, at which time it becomes more prone to termination.

More generally, a central disagreement revolves around whether rivalries "evolve" in some sense or whether they "lock in" to basic rivalry patterns at the outset. The debate has been conducted thus far basically between advocates of the "evolutionary" and "basic rivalry level" models. One model of rivalry evolution depends centrally on the concept of a basic rivalry level (BRL) (Goertz and Diehl 1998) and a punctuated equilibrium model (Diehl and Goertz 2000). Azar (1972) proposed that each pair of countries had an average level of hostile or cooperative interaction, which he termed their "normal relations range." Azar's idea of a normal relations range suggests the hypothesis that relations between states vary within certain limits. Goertz and Diehl reformulate this in terms of a BRL around which relations fluctuate. When they speak of pattern in the evolution of rivalries, they refer to change in this basic rivalry level. The unmeasured BRL manifests itself in the severity and duration of disputes that arise between rivals. They propose that this BRL can show different patterns over the course of the rivalry such as increasing, decreasing, concave, or convex. Nevertheless, they argue that a constant, unchanging BRL describes best most rivalries.

The punctuated equilibrium model of rivalries states that periods of conflict and détente are "random" variations around a constant basic rivalry level: there is no secular trend toward more conflictual or more peaceful relations. The conflict level for successive confrontations in an enduring rivalry will be identically distributed, random variations around the unchanging rivalry baseline. In statistical terms, the differences between dispute severity and the BRL are random variables independent of past disputes and wars and constant from one dispute to the next (i.e., the standard assumptions one makes about error terms in linear models).

The punctuated equilibrium model does not suggest that all conflict within a rivalry is exactly the same over time. Indeed they expect some variation in severity and duration across different disputes (and some may be a function of endogenous influences). Furthermore, some large deviations from the basic rivalry level might be expected, namely war events. Furthermore, Goertz and Diehl do not suggest that variations from the BRL (be it constant or changing) cannot be explained and are indeed "random," but rather that there is no systematic factor derived from the previous dispute (beyond that captured by the BRL). They see this basic rivalry level as normally quite stable (except perhaps at the beginning and end of rivalries, or during periods of stress and shock). That is, they expect that patterns in rivalry conflict will "lock in" quickly at the outset of the rivalry relationship and remain that way throughout the rivalry. In effect, hostility does not "fade out" toward the end of rivalry, but the rivalry is likely to end abruptly.

In contrast, Hensel (1996a) offers an evolutionary model of the way that rivalries develop and therefore how conflict events are related over time. The evolutionary model does not assume that structural conditions determine the development of rivalries. Rather, rivalries change over time, and their conflict patterns may vary over the rivalry process and in fact are in part determined by that process. The evolutionary model assumes that rivalries pass through different "phases," each with its own characteristics and conflict patterns. In effect, rivalry context is still important, but it changes over time and contexts are not necessarily unique to specific rivalries. Hensel (1996a) identifies roughly three phases in the evolution of rivalries. In the early phase of rivalry, states have little or no history to affect their current relations; neither is there a strong expectation of future interactions to guide their strategies. He argues therefore that conflict in this phase is less escalatory, involves less coercive bargaining, and is less likely to be followed by future confrontations than conflict in other rivalry phases. The intermediate phase is a transition one in which both the push of the past and the pull of the future begin to have an impact on conflict behavior. The advanced phase of rivalry is characterized by greater threat perception and competition between the rivals. The advanced phase also includes more repeated confrontations and more violence in those confrontations than either of the other two phases.

Both the punctuated equilibrium and evolutionary models postulate that rivalry context affects the likelihood and severity of future conflicts between the same pair of states. Yet they diverge on a number of dimensions. The evolutionary model argues that it is the interactions of states in those early confrontations that help determine if and how rivalries develop into enduring ones (or not). In contrast, the punctuated equilibrium model puts considerably less weight on those interactions, but more on structural factors that determine which will evolve into enduring rivalries. The punctuated equilibrium model postulates that rivalries are born healthy and hence likely to survive until they reach the enduring stage. The evolutionary model argues that events in youth have an important impact on which rivalries make it to old age. The patterns of conflict in rivalries according to the evolutionary model suggest rising hostility over time, either from crisis to crisis or at various inflection points or phases. Thus, the evolutionary model would predict that wars would occur later in enduring rivalries. In contrast, the punctuated equilibrium model states that wars may be just as likely at the outset of such rivalries as in later stages. Finally, the evolutionary model would predict greater variation in the conflict patterns during rivalries than would the punctuated equilibrium approach; the latter would expect such variation to be around the level specified by each rivalry's BRL.

There exists some evidence to support the constant basic rivalry level hypothesis. Goertz and Diehl (1998; Diehl and Goertz 2000) explored whether patterns in the evolution of enduring rivalries followed that predicted by the constant basic rivalry level, the so-called volcano model (a pattern of rising hostility culminating in war and the end of the rivalry), or four other patterns. In terms of basic trends in enduring rivalries, they found that only a small percentage (between 5 and 20 percent depending on the study and indicator used) exhibited volcano-like patterns. In contrast, however, the BRL pattern of no secular trend was the primary one (more than two-thirds of the cases) found in their analyses.

Goertz and Diehl report no systematic relationship between the conflict level of successive disputes and no indication of a gradual escalation of conflict even at the beginning of a rivalry. Despite some results that indicated a constant conflict level throughout a rivalry, there were other indications of significant variation around that level. Structural factors will no doubt account for some variation around the BRL level, but their analysis cannot yet indicate whether the observed patterns are merely the result of structural factors or indicative of several different relationships inconsistent with the constant BRL model. Goertz and Diehl (1998) also note that the basic rivalry level "locks in" at the outset of the rivalry and does not "fade out" at the end; that is, they found no pattern of dispute escalation at the beginning of enduring rivalries or dispute de-escalation at the end. Other findings offer mixed support for the constant basic rivalry level with its quick lock-in and lack of a fade-out pattern. In their game-theoretic analysis of four Middle East rivalries, Maoz and Mor (1996) find that enduring rivalries exhibit acute conflict at the outset with a constant motivation to extend the conflict from the beginning; this suggests that conflicts do not "evolve" into enduring rivalries, but they may exhibit severe rivalry characteristics from their origin.

There is somewhat less empirical evidence directly examining the evolutionary model, although much of it is supportive. Hensel (1996a) finds that as a pair of adversaries engages in more frequent militarized conflict and thus moves along toward an enduring rivalry, their confrontations tend to become more severe and escalatory, more likely to end in stalemates, and more likely to be repeated. Vasquez (1998a) also reports a pattern of rising conflict in recurrent disputes during the U.S.-Japan rivalry that led to World War II, although this is clearly only one case. Other follow-up studies by Hensel also generally, although not universally, support the evolutionary model. Hensel (1998) found that the likelihood of conflict recurrence increased dramatically as one moved into later rivalry phase; the likelihood of recurring conflict doubled in the intermediate rivalry phases and quintupled in the most advanced or enduring rivalry phase. Using events data, Hensel (1997) find that later phases of a rivalry exhibit more intense conflictual (and interestingly enough cooperative as well) interactions. Hensel and McLaughlin (1996) also find that a history of past disputes is associated with greater conflict in a rivalry. Yet, contrary to the evolutionary view, they also find that war is more likely *earlier* in a rivalry.

Also casting some doubt on the evolutionary approach is Maoz and Mor (1998), who found that the games of "Deadlock" and "Bully" were the most common in young rivalries, suggesting that the early stages of enduring rivalries are marked by hostility on both sides with few attempts (at least successful ones) at conciliation, cooperation, and conflict resolution. Cioffi-Revilla (1998b) addresses this debate through his focus on the stability of all—not just enduring—rivalries, where stability was defined as the probability of rivalry continuation into the future. In his analysis, a hazard rate for termination was used to indicate whether rivalries had an increasing or decreasing tendency to end, with the latter signifying a stable relationship. Cioffi-Revilla's results indicated three phases of rivalry stability: initial stability (consistent with a quick lock-in), maturation, and termination. In the initial phase, he discovered that rivalries were very stable and therefore not prone to end in their early phases. The maturation, or midlife, period shows that rivalries become mildly unstable, with an increasing hazard rate for termination; perhaps this indicates that many rivalries never go beyond the proto-rivalry stage and enduring rivalries are special cases that seem to run against the tide. In the termination phase, within the latter stage of rivalries, they have a strong propensity to end. (Bennett [1998] arrives at a similar conclusion.) Overall, both the constant BRL and evolutionary models have empirical support, largely from studies conducted by proponents of each approach.

Beyond the general debate over whether and how rivalries evolve, a series of studies focus on specific endogenous influences on rivalry dynamics. McGinnis and Williams (1989) modeled the U.S.-Soviet rivalry over time with appropriate consideration for how past actions affected contemporary and future decisions; even though the model was only for the superpower dyad, its applicability to other rivalries appears reasonable. More precisely, some scholars have looked at how previous interactions in the rivalry affect future behavior. Wayman and Jones (1991) consider the impact of previous disputes on subsequent disputes in a rivalry; they find that certain outcomes (e.g., capitulations) of those disputes are more likely to produce frequent future disputes or disputes that are more violent (after stalemates). Similarly, Hensel (1996a) reports that decisive or compromise outcomes to disputes lessen the likelihood of future rivalry confrontations. There may also be some evidence of learning over the course of a rivalry; Larson (1999) argues that the United States and the Soviet Union learned conflict management and how to avoid war based on their behaviors during successive crises.

Hensel (1996a) finds that rivalries with a prominent territorial component and those that experience a capability shift among the rivals are more likely to have recurring conflict and have that conflict recur sooner. Yet he acknowledges that the strength of these general findings varies across different phases of rivalries, citing different patterns in the early parts of rivalries versus the middle or latter phases. Ingram (1999) notes a host of factors—technological, ideological, and geographical—as influences on the dynamics of the British-Russian rivalry.

Maoz and Mor (1998) find that the type of game played in enduring rivalries challenges widely held notions. Chicken and Prisoner's Dilemma have dominated the conceptual universe of game-theoretic thinking about international conflict. In contrast, Maoz and Mor find that other games occur as frequently or more than those two classic formulations. Particularly interesting is the importance of Bully and Deadlock in rivalries. Maoz and Mor also challenge common views about the stability of preferences. They found that with some regularity not only did the game change—which could be due to exogenous factors—but also preferences of the states varied. This is consistent with findings about democratization and rivalries that imply new values. Also, Goertz and Diehl (1995b) found that regime change shocks—again indicating new leadership with possibly new ideas—were closely related to both rivalry initiation and termination. Thompson (1995b) also emphasizes preference change at the end of rivalry.

Another conventional factor, democratic regime type, has also been the subject of analysis vis-à-vis conflict dynamics in rivalries. Although subject to some controversy, international conflict research (e.g., Russett 1993) has established that stable democratic states rarely or never fight against each other in a war. Not surprisingly then, some scholars have also found some pacifying effects from democracy in rivalries. Modelski (1999) claims that the rivalry between Portugal and Venice several hundred years ago was more benign than other rivalries because of its "democratic lineage" and that democratic rivalries are more peaceful and more likely to be resolved "on their merits" rather than by military force. Thompson (1999c) also cites mutual democracy as a pacifying condition in the Anglo-American rivalry. The presence of a democratic dyad also apparently has a dampening effect on conflict recurrence in the rivalry (Hensel 1996a). A similar finding is reported by Sommer (1997) in his analysis of southern African rivalries. Nevertheless, Thompson and Tucker (1997a) note that intense rivalries can occur between democratic states and indeed argue that a significant portion of pre–World War II conflict revolved around U.S.-U.K. and U.K.-France rivalries (although they note that direct war was avoided in each case).

Hensel, Goertz, and Diehl (forthcoming) found that the democratic peace effect extends to rivalries, with joint democratic status making participation in rivalries unlikely (and foreclosing participation in the most severe of rivalries) and conflict levels lower; only a few rivalries over the period 1816–1992 involved states who were democratic throughout the entire rivalry and these rivalries generally did not develop beyond the nascent stage. Bennett (1997a) also finds that joint democracy leads to shorter rivalries.

Conflict Management in Rivalries

Hensel's evolutionary model of rivalry dynamics emphasizes the escalatory aspects of rivalry relationships. Nevertheless, rivals do not only fight with each other, but also occasionally try to manage their conflicts. As with the conflictual aspects of rivalries, scholars have implicitly used the rivalry framework to examine conflict management in specific rivalries. For example, Kriesberg (1992) gives much information about the conflict management efforts in the U.S.-Soviet and Middle East rivalries.

Goertz and Regan (1997) have proposed a number of criteria for successful conflict management in the context of enduring rivalries. One proposal takes the BRL level idea and looks for rivalries that have periods with a declining BRL. These are not necessarily common, but examples do exist. They then ask what other kinds of behavioral patterns might indicate successful management activity. They suggest that, in addition, a decline in the level of the most severe conflicts (e.g., avoidance of war) as well as a decline in the volatility of the rivalry might also fit the conflict management concept. They find that some enduring rivalries do appear to succeed in conflict management, but they provide nothing more than a preliminary analysis of different dependent variables.

Bercovitch and Diehl (1997) conducted a study of international mediation attempts that focused on the short- and medium-term effects of mediation in enduring rivalries. They found that mediation had little effect on the next dispute in the rivalry, except a modest lengthening effect on waiting times for the next dispute. Furthermore, the presence or absence of those efforts does not appear to have any impact on significant deviations from those levels, namely the occurrence of war. Bercovitch and Diehl also briefly address the key issue of conflict management in enduring rivalries versus other types of rivalry. Because almost all the mediation literature uses case studies or pure cross-sectional methods, much remains to be investigated (see Bercovitch and Diehl 1997; Bercovitch and Regan 1997).

Undoubtedly the whole issue of conflict management remains one of the most important items on the future rivalry research agenda. Most scholars have approached rivalries because they seem particularly war and conflict prone, but the longitudinal dimension and the noncrisis periods make it a natural framework to investigate theories of security regimes, mediation, and other conflict management techniques.

The Termination of Rivalries

Conflict resolution efforts may contribute to the termination of rivalries, but many other factors may be involved. Hence the termination of rivalries differs significantly from the extensive literature about the termination of war. Wars take place at various junctures of rivalries, at the beginning, middle, and ending phases. Thus, understanding how a particular war ends may offer few or no clues to the end of a rivalry, which may persist for decades after war termination. Cioffi-Revilla (1998b) and Bennett (1998) show that rivalries are more likely to end the longer they persist. Although the hazard rate for rivalries may be increasing, their conflict level shows little sign of abating and the precise time point of rivalry termination cannot largely be predicted by the hazard rate.

There are several possible answers to the puzzle of how rivalries end, something that is not well understood given the sudden and largely unexpected end to the cold war. Bennett (1993, 1996) also adopts a rational choice perspective in attempting to explain rivalry termination. As we suggested earlier, his empirical analysis finds that the occurrence of war in a rivalry does not affect the duration of that rivalry. Neither does the existence of bipolarity or the balance of power between the rivals (in contrast to Levy's [1999] findings, which were based on only one rivalry) seem to enhance the prospects for ending rivalries. Instead, relatively low issue salience at the center of the rivalry contributed to shorter rivalries. Again, territorial issues were thought to be a key example of high salience issues. As we have already noted, the absence of territorial issues made rivalries less likely to start and escalate to war if they did begin; now we also see that the lack of a territorial component to the rivalry may make it end more swiftly. Bennett also notes that common external threats for the rivals makes them less likely to continue their competition. One might assume that common external enemies not only engender greater feelings of amity between the rivals ("the enemy of my enemy is my friend"), but also other rivalries reduce the resources and attention that can be directed to extant rivalries; states must make choices on which enemies to focus upon and this may mean ending one rivalry in order to pursue others.

Two other approaches explore the conditions under which rivalries are terminated. Gibler (1997a) demonstrates that rivalries can end with the signing of an alliance that is in effect a territorial settlement treaty. This finding is largely consistent with research discussed earlier that suggested a strong territorial component to the origins of enduring rivalries. Although Gibler does not investigate whether territorial disputes were important in the origins of the rivalries he considers, he does find that the rivalry ends when the territorial dispute is removed from the relationship. Goertz and Diehl (1995b) argue that political shocks are a necessary condition for the termination of conflict. In particular, they cite dramatic changes at the system level, including world wars and major power distribution shifts, as well as shocks at the state level, including civil war in one of the rivals, as factors associated with the end of rivalries. Although such shocks are coterminous with the end of rivalries, Goertz and Diehl leave unspecified what other factors contribute to the end of rivalry. Shocks are hardly a trivial condition, but neither are they close to sufficient in precipitating rivalry termination. Levy and Ali (1998) point out the importance of political shocks on the stability of rivalry relationships. The Thirty Years War in Germany is cited as a shock that profoundly altered Dutch relationships with its current and potential rivals in the seventeenth century. The death of Frederick Henry also brought a lull to the Dutch-Spanish competition and set in motion events that led to increased competition with the British.

Although political shocks may lead to rivalry termination, a war between rivals does not necessarily constitute such a shock. Wars can signal the beginning of a rivalry, occur during the middle phases, or in some cases constitute the final hostile act in the rivalry. With respect to the latter, it may be that certain kinds of systemic wars may be especially associated with the termination of enduring rivalries. Midlarsky (1988b) identifies "mobilization wars" as those that result from one power's mobilizing resources for war and the change in the salient power dimension is seen as unacceptable by one or more of the protagonists. Enduring rivalries may be particularly susceptible to ending following the conclusion of such mobilization wars; Midlarsky notes that the Franco-Spanish rivalry ended at the time of the war of Spanish succession in the early eighteenth century and the Franco-German rivalry ended after World War II. Even if the rivalry does not end with a mobilization war, that event may signal a diminution of hostilities as can be seen in the Franco-British rivalry after the Napoleonic Wars and the Israeli-Egyptian rivalry following the 1973 Yom Kippur War. Similarly, it may prove that the Serbo-Croat rivalry in the 1990s has been moderated or perhaps ended by the mobilization aspects of the Croat military initiatives (Midlarsky 1997a).

Bennett (1998) attempted to synthesize many of his and other findings on enduring rivalry termination. He concludes that domestic political factors and issue salience seem to be most associated with rivalry termination. He finds distinctly mixed results on security concerns as a driving force behind the end of rivalries. Similarly, he also gets mixed results on the impact of political shocks on rivalry termination. Yet his analysis of political shocks does not properly test the Goertz/Diehl contention that shocks operate only as a necessary condition for rivalry termination (his analysis treats them as necessary *and* sufficient). Furthermore, his analysis assumes that political shocks have an immediate and single year effect on rivalry behavior, a conception at odds with our contention that major political changes are likely to reverberate through the system over the course of several years, rather than at a fixed point.

One of the central problems in the rivalry termination literature is the different specifications of an ending date for rivalries (noted earlier in the discussion of operational definitions). Most definitions of enduring rivalries identify their ends after some period (usually 10 or 15 years) without the occurrence of another militarized dispute between the rivals. The exact date of rivalry termination is often quite ambiguous in these studies. Yet Bennett (1993, 1996, 1997a, 1998) relies on the resolution of the disputed issues and/or a formal agreement to pinpoint the end of a rivalry (although he too is dependent on the absence of subsequent disputes). Differences in identifying the rivalry termination point can be dramatic and, most important, can make a significant difference in testing models of rivalry termination (Bennett 1997b); this makes comparisons across studies difficult and integrative cumulation problematic.

Finally, there is also a plethora of studies that seek to explain the end of the cold war (e.g., Deudney and Ikenberry, 1991–92). Unfortunately, there are several problems with this literature if we are interested in insights on rivalry termination. First, much of the literature is concerned with explaining the collapse of the Soviet Union. The end of the superpower rivalry is then treated as one of many consequences of that collapse. Yet theoretically it is not clear whether a point is being made about domestic political changes and the end of rivalries or whether the end of rivalries is somehow slightly different from the implosion of one of the rivals. Second, it is not clear (whatever the focus) that such studies can or are designed to be generalizable to rivalries other than the U.S.-Soviet one.

Despite these limitations, Lebow (1994b) has attempted to use the cold war case to develop a set of conditions he believes accounts for the thawing of U.S.-Soviet relations under Gorbachev and the winding down of rivalries in general (Lebow 1997). For accommodation to occur, he argues that the presence of the following three conditions for one of the rivals is critical: (1) a leader is committed to domestic reforms, where foreign cooperation is necessary for those reforms, (2) rivalry and confrontation has failed in the past to achieve a rival's goals and will likely fail in the future, and (3) the belief exists that conciliatory gestures will be reciprocated. Thus, Lebow sees the end of rivalries beginning from domestic political considerations.

Exogenous Influences on Enduring Rivalries

One major form of exogenous impact is the linkage *between* rivalries. The dynamics of rivalries are influenced not only by their own pasts but also by their interconnections with other conflicts and rivalries. Muncaster and Zinnes (1993) create a model for an *N*-number of states that is capable of tracking the evolution of rivalries, including how those rivalries influence the relations (and potential rivalries) of other states in the system. A dispute involving two states not only influences their future relations but also affects all other dyadic relations in the system. Also in the formal modeling tradition, McGinnis (1990) offers a model of regional rivalries that identifies optimum points for aid, arms, and alignments in those rivalries; this again provides for exogenous conflicts to influence the dynamics of rivalries.

A number of empirical studies confirm the significance of third-party conflict to the dynamics of rivalries. Ingram (1999) notes that the British-Russian rivalry was influenced by these states' relations with Asian client states. Schroeder (1999) boldly states that the Franco-Austrian rivalry was kept from being resolved by its interconnection with other ongoing European rivalries. According to Levy and Ali (1998), the end of the Dutch revolt against Spain led to the conditions that permitted Dutch economic expansion and the initiation of the rivalry with England. States sometimes have limited carrying capacities in the number of rivalries to which they can devote attention and resources. The Anglo-Dutch rivalry was also linked with the Anglo-French rivalry. England's undeclared war against France resulted in the seizure of Dutch ships that were trading with France, analogous to the contagion model noted by Siverson and Starr (1991) in which a given conflict spills over to encompass neighboring countries. The intersection of these two rivalries had the effect of escalating the competition between the Dutch and the English, who had previously managed their disputes without resort to war. Kinsella (1994a, 1994b, 1995) studied the dynamics of some rivalries in the Middle East with special attention to how the superpower rivalry influenced these minor power rivalries. There is a pattern of action-reaction to superpower arms transfers to that region. He finds that Soviet arms transfers exacerbated rivalry conflicts in several cases, whereas U.S. arms supplies to Israel had no strong positive or negative effects. He also notes that U.S. arms transfer policy may have actually dampened conflict in the Iran-Iraq rivalry. It is clear from Kinsella's studies that the superpower rivalry affected the dynamics of the minor power rivalries in the Middle East, although the reverse was not generally true.

Goertz and Diehl (1997) further confirm that rivalries are closely linked (through alliances, contiguity, common dispute participation, and common rivalry foes), and this has a clear impact on their conflict levels. They found an important impact of major-major enduring rivalries on minor power ones. They confirmed that in general the conflict levels of linked rivalries should be higher than those of unlinked rivalries. The volatility of some linked enduring rivalries was also greater, but the results were not as robust. Their findings were largely the same for the frequency of war as they were for the conflict level. A cross-temporal analysis of rivalries that had prelinked, linked, and delinked periods showed little variation in their basic conflict level, but war was more common during linkage, and less so in the other two periods, especially in the prelinked periods. Bennett's (1996) analysis of rivalry termination also indicated that some rivalries end when the rivals begin to have common external security threats; in effect, the advent of new rivalries with negative links to extant rivalries causes the latter to end.

Various (structural) aspects of the regional or international system form a second key set of exogenous factors. The end of the cold war was an exogenous shock for most minor power rivalries. For example, Maoz and Mor (1998) find that periodically games get redefined as a result of exogenous events. Ideally, they want to have a completely endogenous explanation for the transition between games, but they found they needed to include exogenous shocks and other factors as well.

Systemic effects can take many forms. For example, Cioffi-Revilla (1998b) found twentieth-century rivalries to be more unstable. The twentieth century has significantly more rivalries than its predecessor, owing largely to the relative ease at which states can interact with one another and the larger number of states in the international system; in effect, the "opportunity" (Most and Starr 1989) for rivalries is greater. The greater number of rivalries (of all varieties including enduring ones) may mean that states must divide their attention and resources more broadly than in the past, and it may not be surprising that some rivalries end quickly as states move on to meet other, more pressing challenges. Of course, the declining stability of rivalries in the twentieth century might also be related in part to another trend uncovered by Cioffi-Revilla: bipolar systems produce more unstable rivalries than multipolar ones. The cold war bipolar system may then account for the relatively greater instability than the nineteenth century, which was multipolar throughout.

Systemic conditions are often cited by neorealists and idealists as constraining or enhancing choices for war. According to limited current research, some aspects of the international system were important in affecting the onset of war in rivalries, but generally they were not central. The balance of power at the system level is a classic neorealist factor, but Levy and Ali (1998) note that this made little difference in the rivalry development or war between the British and the Dutch. Nevertheless, Vasquez (1998a) cites another systemic variable largely ignored by realism and its variants: international rules and norms. He notes that the breakdown of the Washington Conference structure, which sought to control military competition (especially in weaponry) between the major powers after World War I, removed the rules and norms necessary to "manage" the competition between the leading Pacific states. In this way, limiting the anarchy of the international system can have a mitigating effect on rivalry competition, and while perhaps international norms and rules may not be enough to prevent or end rivalries, they might assist in restraining the most severe manifestations of rivalries. A similar argument is made by Larson (1999) in her assessment of why the superpower rivalry managed to avoid war.

War in Rivalries

Of course, most international conflict research in general has been concerned with the conditions associated with the outbreak of war. Little of the research directly on rivalries, however, has dealt with war. Those studies that use rivalries as a background condition focus on war, but they answer questions about deterrence, power transitions, arms races, and their relationship to war rather than making direct theoretical contributions about rivalries and war. There are nevertheless a few exceptions to this pattern. Vasquez (1993, 1996) argued that geographic contiguity between rivals was the critical factor in whether a rivalry went to war or not; geographic contiguity between rivals signifies that the conflict between them was a territorial one, and in the view of Vasquez, conflict without this strong territorial dimension will not end in war. Thompson (1999a) makes a similar argument in noting that the Anglo-American rivalry only experienced one war and this early on, in part, because any territory in dispute between the British and the Americans was judged not to be worth fighting over. Vasquez (1996) identifies two paths under which rivalries go to war. In the first path, dyadic war is triggered by a territorial dispute in a process described in his "steps-to-war" model (Vasquez 1993). The other path to war involves rivals without a territorial dispute joining an ongoing war because of what he refers to as contagion factors.

Other conventional factors thought to be associated with war also receive a mixed assessment from current studies. The power distribution is often a centerpiece of models of international conflict, although there is considerable disagreement among scholars whether parity or preponderance is the most dangerous condition. Geller (1998) finds no general relationship between the capability distribution and the identity of the initiator of wars in major power rivalries. Nevertheless, he points out that *unstable* capability distributions are substantively associated with the occurrence of war, although he is quick to acknowledge that they approach a necessary, but not a sufficient, condition for conflict escalation in the rivalry. Changing capability balances in major power dyads have recently been found to be significant in several studies (e.g., Huth, Bennett, and Gelpi 1992). Geller's findings are also consistent with dynamic models of capability change, including the power transition and hegemonic decline models.

Domestic political processes again were found to be critical in the dynamics of enduring rivalries. Vasquez (1998a) notes that domestic hard-liners pushed for war in Japan, preventing that country from making more conciliatory gestures and accepting some peace offers short of war. Levy and Ali (1998) also note strong domestic pressures in England for hard-line policies and external actions. Perhaps this is why the English adopted a hard-line bargaining strategy that prevented effective conflict management. In contrast, Thompson (1999a) argues that domestic political pressures in Britain actually encouraged de-escalation and lessened the chances for war in its relations with the United States.

The conditions for war in rivalries were generally not those at the systemic level according to previous research, although there was a suggestion in one case that international norms and rules might have mitigated the war in the Pacific. Unstable military balances, rather than a particular capability distribution, tended to reinforce or exacerbate the processes leading to war in rivalries. Territorial issues were again most often associated with conflict escalation in enduring rivalries, and democratic dyads are thought to help rivals avoid war.

Future Research Agenda

The rivalry approach has many dimensions. This arises from the two central characteristics we have emphasized throughout: rivalry as a new unit of analysis, and the temporal, longitudinal character of rivalries. Not surprisingly, scholars have applied the same hypotheses to rivalries as they have to war. We have seen studies of power transition, arms race, democratic peace, deterrence, and other phenomena in the rivalry context. The temporal duration of rivalry means a new set of hypotheses regarding patterns of rivalry evolution, both in the conflictual as well as the conflict management sense. Very few of these issues have been studied at great length, so they all easily merit inclusion on a list of future research topics. Nevertheless, we limit our discussion to aspects directly related to rivalries and their life cycle. Although the occurrence and impact of arms races, deterrence, and so forth deserve attention, we leave that to other works devoted specifically to those subjects.

The key item on any research agenda is rivalry dynamics. Not only does this involve the BRL and the evolutionary models, but also the relationship between proto- and enduring rivalries. One test would be to analyze conflict patterns within the population of enduring rivalries. The hypothesis to be tested could be that conflict in early stages of enduring rivalries is less severe than in later stages. A corollary proposition is that there is no significant difference in conflict severity in enduring rivalry early stages and comparable phases in lesser rivalries. The evolutionary model is consistent with each of these hypotheses, and the BRL model would predict the opposite: more severe conflict in enduring rivalries than other rivalries and that severity relatively consistent over the life of rivalries. This would help us answer some questions about the relative importance of issues versus interactions, or structure versus process, in the development of enduring rivalries.

There seem to be at least three other critical areas of research concerning the dynamics of enduring rivalries: their maintenance, variation in the basic rivalry levels across rivalries, and the volatility of conflict within rivalries (including most significantly the outbreak of war). The first concern is with the maintenance of rivalries. Cioffi-Revilla (1998b) and Bennett (1998) indicate that rivalries are unstable in their later phases, suggesting that some process sets in to reverse the effects of rivalry maintenance factors. Yet according to conventional definitions of enduring rivalries, they can last 40+ years (and this is probably a low estimate given that some of the rivalries in these studies have not ended and therefore the end dates are censored and will underestimate the true length of the competitions). Some factors are at work that seem to mitigate the unstable tendencies of rivalries, or there may be "stress" that appears only later, allowing some rivalries to persist well into the future. A valuable line of research might be to identify the conditions that make rivalries persist and conflict to recur repeatedly in the rivalry.

There are some clues to the conditions for rivalry maintenance. One possibility is the kind of issues or stakes under dispute. Vasquez (1996) suggests that territorial disputes are most prone to recurring conflict, given that they relate closely to concerns about national identity and can become linked to other intangible and indivisible stakes; Huth (1996a) makes similar claims in his study of territorial disputes. Hensel (1996a) confirms the importance of territorial disputes in prompting future conflict and doing so more rapidly than other issues. Thus, another consideration is to go beyond the structural aspects of the rivalry relationships and concentrate on the interactions between the rival states. In effect, the past and present dynamics of a rivalry will influence its future dynamics. Maoz and Mor (1998) indicated that only when there is some dissatisfaction among at least one of the rivals does a rivalry continue; some game structures make this all but inevitable (e.g., Bully games will leave the losing side unhappy with the inferior payoff). Yet it also suggests that certain outcomes of disputes are more likely to prompt future conflict. Those outcomes that do not resolve issues in disputes (stalemates) may lead to a return to militarized confrontation; Vasquez refers not only to territorial issues, but *unresolved* ones as instigators of recurring militarized conflict. Similarly, Hensel (1996a) finds compromise dispute outcomes dam-pen the prospects for future conflict.

Another aspect, one even less explored, is the short-term dynamics of rivalries. What is the impact of the last dispute or two on the next one? on the waiting times until the next dispute? Many factors can have both short- and long-term effects. This is another aspect of the contrast between the punctuated equilibrium and evolutionary approaches: the former states that factors fixed early have long-term effects while the evolutionary approach stresses the importance of short-term influences. Maoz and Mor's (1998) along with Thompson's (1999b) case studies show that intensive analyses of individual rivalries can produce insights of great importance. These trace in detail the relations between conflicts that lie at the heart of rivalry approach.

We need much more work that compares *between* rivalries. As we noted earlier most of the rivalry research adopts the cross-sectional time-series approach, which has a tendency to make the differences between rivalries disappear. As much can be gained between comparing rivalries over time within the rivalry as differences between rivalries. This will be key particularly when investigating the system-level factors and their impacts on rivalries. It also permits the investigation of structure of the rivalries themselves. For example, Vasquez (1993) has proposed that the behavior of asymmetric rivalries differs radically from symmetric ones. The empirical investigation of this idea requires between-rivalry comparisons.

Why some rivalries have higher basic rivalry levels than others and some exhibit more variation (volatility) than others relates to between-rivalry comparisons. Another area of fruitful research would be to understand why some rivalries are far more hostile than others—this goes beyond concerns of duration and stability noted earlier to those of conflict intensity. Clues to the preceding puzzle might be found in other traditional correlates of war. One possibility suggested by Geller (1998) is the instability in the power distribution, which prompts greater uncertainty and threat for the rivals. One might also return to the issues in dispute noted in the preceding as an explanation: territorial and other disputes may present higher stakes that lead rivals to adopt more coercive bargaining strategies and respond to challenges with a higher level of force. Of course, certain game structures, suggested by Maoz and Mor (1998), tend to produce more conflictual outcomes (whereas some offer greater incentives for cooperation). It may be useful to compare the game structures across different rivalries to explain the higher levels of conflict in some rivalries. A focus on the game transformation process would help us not only with rivalry dynamics but also in devising strategies to "downshift" especially dangerous rivalries (assuming that game transformation conditions are manipulable by rivals or by external intervention).

Finally, the volatility of rivalries is a prime item for an enduring rivalries research agenda, principally because we share a strong concern for the most dangerous of deviations in the rivalry relationship—war. Understanding volatility and war in enduring rivalries is partly related to understanding differences across rivalries in the basic rivalry level. Those rivalries that regularly operate at high conflict levels need less of a push to cross the war threshold than those rivalries that do not move much beyond the mere threat to use military force. Yet, beyond this, there still lies the concern with what factors make a rivalry more or less hostile at various points. Geller's unstable capability distributions may ratchet a rivalry up the escalation ladder and account for why he finds that instability so important in the outbreak of war among major power rivals. Changes in rivalry conflict levels may also be affected by other challenges or disputes that a given rival may face, beyond those in the immediate rivalry; there even may be a dampening effect on outside conflict and rivalry conflict when the attention and resources of rival states are stretched. These are provocative ideas that enduring rivalry research has barely considered.

We end this survey of the future research agendas with strong support for a closer examination of conflict management and rivalry termination. All too often the study of war has remained divorced, both conceptually and professionally, from the analysis of peace. The study of war was given a tremendous boost when the COW and other projects provided standard data for testing hypotheses. Although we do not have those data yet for rivalry termination, we now at least have a conceptual grasp on the problem. We hope that some day analyses on rivalry termination—for *all* rivalries, not just enduring ones—will generate the variety of theories of peace that we currently have for war. Perhaps the next edition of the *Handbook of War Studies* will have a companion volume: *Handbook of Peace and Conflict Management.*

Notes

1. In addition, a dispute in an enduring rivalry is more than four times as likely to end in war than one in isolation. Another test is to treat the rivalry as a unit of analysis in order to see if at least one war occurs at some point in the rivalry. The propensity for war grows dramatically as one moves from isolated conflict to the most severe enduring rivalries (almost four times as great in enduring rivalries as in the lowest rivalry category). In enduring rivalries, the chances are better than 58 percent that the two states will go to war at some point in their competition (Diehl and Goertz 2000; Goertz and Diehl 1992a). The only argument against the significance of enduring rivalries is made by Gartzke and Simon (1999). They argue that the distribution of enduring rivalries (unfortunately they do not consider all types of rivalries, a more valid test) across a continuum of dispute frequency is similar to that predicted by a random events model; in effect, they are arguing that repeated militarized disputes might easily occur by chance. Nevertheless, such an argument ignores that conflict patterns, as described earlier, do not occur randomly, and there is a pattern of greater hostility in more enduring rivalries (a random events model would predict no difference in conflict patterns across different kinds of rivalries).
2. Multilateral rivalries are related to what Buzan (1983) refers to as a "security complex." A security complex is "a group of states whose primary security concerns link together sufficiently closely that their national securities cannot realistically be considered apart from one another. Security complexes tend to be durable, but they are neither permanent nor internally rigid" (1983, 106). Although security complexes are broader than rivalries, rivalries and related conflicts are often at the heart of the complex and define its

parameters. Indeed, those who adopt security complexes as a framework for analysis are urged to focus attention on "sets of states whose security problems are closely interconnected" (1983, 113–14). Not surprisingly, Buzan uses the South Asian security complex as an example with the India-Pakistan rivalry as its dominant feature.

3. See Goertz and Diehl (1993) for a discussion of how the enduring rivalry concept differs from that of arms race and crisis.
4. Another set of consequences resulting from the new unit of analysis is a better understanding of the linkage between conflicts. Diffusion research has focused on how war begets war (Most, Starr, and Siverson 1989; Siverson and Starr 1991). Within the rivalry approach this becomes much broader—how rivalries influence each other. The rivalry approach incorporates not only temporal dynamics, but spatial ones as well. For example, alliances are usually thought of as linking states, but alliances are just one of the elements that link dyadic rivalries. The alliance can be a cause of a new rivalry or a consequence of the tighter linking of two existing rivalries. Thus, the rivalry approach can provide a more complex and, probably, more accurate understanding of the effect of alliances on the spread of conflict (and vice versa). The rivalry approach further changes the orientation of traditional diffusion studies. One consequence of replacing war with rivalry in the diffusion framework is that war can arise without a previous war occurring as the initial cause. This is possible because the rivalry continues during times without active hostilities. Thus, there may be no war at time $t - 1$, but there still may be conflict diffusion at time t as long as there was a rivalry at $t - 1$. The rivalry approach is broader in that (1) it accounts for diffusion in the absence of war, and (2) it identifies diffusion involving lower levels of conflict than full-scale war. Another consequence of the rivalry approach is to propose an explanation for the absence of war diffusion (or so-called negative diffusion). The attention and resources that must be devoted to an ongoing rivalry relationship may reduce the ability of individual rivals to engage in conflict with other adversaries. Rivalries (particularly enduring ones) may generate conflict locally (as suggested by the diffusion literature), but at the same time other disputes involving the same protagonists become less likely. Thus, the rivalry approach is more nuanced in that it offers an explanation why some conflicts expand and why others are less likely to occur.

PART III

Structure-Based Theories of War

Interstate Crises and Violence

Twentieth-Century Findings

JONATHAN WILKENFELD and MICHAEL BRECHER

Concepts

The twentieth century, having just exited from human history, was characterized by widespread turmoil. This was often, but not always, accompanied by violence, including the most acute form of hostile interaction among political entities, *war,* as in the two cataclysmic wars of 1914–18 and 1939–45 and many lesser wars in all parts of the world (Small and Singer 1982).

War is closely related to—in fact, it is a subset of—*conflict,* "the overt, coercive interactions of contending collectivities," involving two or more parties using coercion to injure or control their opponents (Gurr 1980, 1–2). Thus conflict encompasses political riot, insurrection, revolution, war, and the most frequent type of disruption in twentieth-century global politics, *interstate military-security crisis.*

Crisis unfolds at two levels, system-interactor and state-actor. At the former, an *international crisis* denotes (1) *a change in type and/or an increase in intensity of disruptive interactions between two or more states, with a heightened (higher-than-normal) probability of military hostilities;* that, in turn, (2) *destabilizes their relationship and challenges the structure of the global system, the dominant system, or a subordinate system.*

An international crisis encompasses, and begins with, an external crisis for one or more states. The trigger to a foreign policy crisis is perceptual; that is, it derives from three interrelated perceptions that are generated by a hostile act, disruptive event, or environmental change:

perceptions of (1) *threat to one or more basic values,* (2) *finite time for response,* and (3) *heightened probability of involvement in military hostilities* before the challenge is overcome.

International crisis and *international conflict* are closely related but they are not synonymous. In essence, every crisis reflects a conflict between two or more adversaries, but not every conflict is reflected in crisis. Moreover, the focus of crisis is (usually) a single issue, a border dispute, economic boycott, alleged mistreatment of a minority group, threat to a political regime, and so on. Even when a crisis is very long it can be distinguished from a conflict, as with the Palestine Partition–Israel Independence crisis of 1947–49 that was part of the Arab/Israel protracted conflict over many issues, tangible and intangible, since the end of the British Mandate in May 1948.

How does one distinguish *protracted conflict (enduring rivalry)* from other types of international turmoil? Protracted conflicts are "hostile interactions which extend over long periods of time with sporadic outbreaks of open warfare fluctuating in frequency and intensity . . . [T]he stakes are very high. . . . [T]hey linger on in time . . . [and] are not specific events or even clusters of events at a point in time; they are processes" (Azar, Jureidini, and McLaurin 1978, 50).

Crisis is also closely linked to war, which has been defined most concretely as a "conflict involving at least one member of [the] interstate system on each side of the war, resulting in a total of 1000 or more battle deaths" (Singer and Small 1972, 381). The crisis-war link is complex. Crisis denotes disruptive interaction among states whether or not accompanied by violence. Many international crises occur without interstate violence, for example, Remilitarization of the Rhineland in 1936, or Munich in 1938. Some are characterized by minor clashes, as in the Beagle Channel II crisis between Chile and Argentina in 1978–79, or serious clashes, as in the Algeria/Morocco crisis in 1963. Others are accompanied by war.

Crises occur not only *before* wars. The outbreak of war can also catalyze a crisis, for example, the German attack on 22 June 1941 ("Barbarossa"), triggering a crisis for the Soviet Union. Crises often escalate to war, as with the India/China crisis of 1960–62. And developments during a war can trigger a crisis for a warring state, an intrawar crisis (IWC), as for Germany following the destruction of its Sixth Army in the Battle of Stalingrad (1942–43). In short, an international crisis can erupt, persist, and terminate without violence. War, in this perspective, does not eliminate or replace crisis. Rather, crisis is accentuated by war. At the actor level, too, perceptions of harm and the consequent stress that decision makers experience in a foreign policy crisis do not require war. Nor do they vanish with war. Rather, they are exacerbated by war.

The conceptual links among conflict, crisis, and war are presented in figure 1. As evident, not all crises escalate to war. Some crises occur within, others outside, protracted conflicts. Some crises within and some outside protracted conflicts are accompanied by war. Other logically possible links are the overlap of (b) and (e), and (b) and (c) in figure 1, that is, the beginning of a protracted conflict in the form of a crisis, which may or may not be accompanied by war; and the emergence of a new international conflict through the eruption of a crisis, with or without war, the overlap between (a) and (d), or (a) and (f).

In the most general sense, all types of turmoil are integral parts of international conflict. They comprise, in descending order of conflict space, protracted conflict, crisis, and war, along with other kinds of transnational or interstate disputes over territory, resources, human rights, and so on.

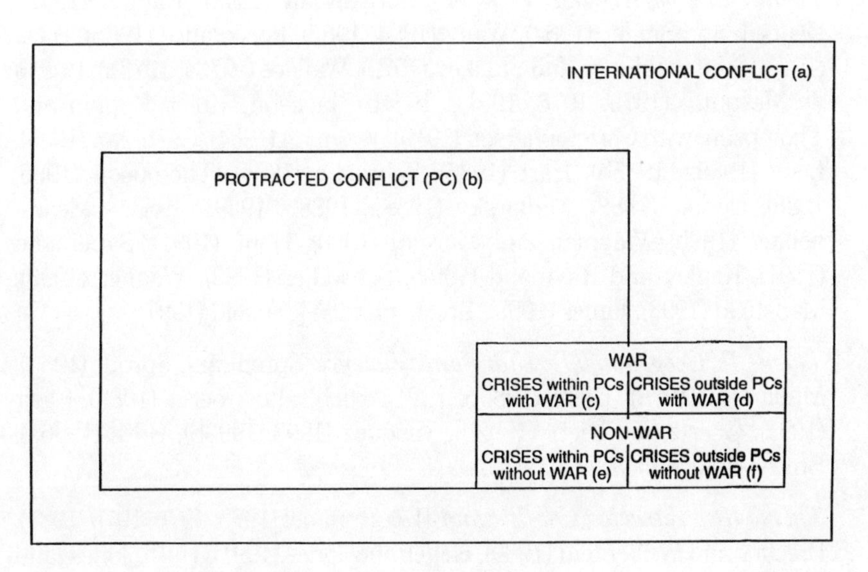

FIGURE 1. Conflict, crisis, war

Literature on Violence (War)

Interstate violence has been an object of inquiry since antiquity, as evident in the works by Thucydides on the Peloponnesian War in classical Greece, Kautilya on war in ancient India, Sun Tzu on war in ancient China, and Machiavelli on war among the city-states of Renaissance Italy. There have also been many studies of specific wars during the past five centuries.

It is not possible, in a single chapter, to survey the contemporary literature on interstate violence. Thus we will confine our attention here to a citation of works on the International Crisis Behavior (ICB) Project's analytical themes as they relate to war, followed by a discussion of two aspects of the crisis-war linkage—*crisis escalation to war* and *de-escalation* or *war termination*.

Overview

Crisis and War. O. R. Holsti (1972), Leng (1980, 1993a, 1993b), Brecher and Wilkenfeld (1988, 1989, 1997), Wilkenfeld and Brecher (1988), Morgan (1994), James (1998).

Theme I: Polarity and Violence. Morgenthau (1948), Kaplan (1957), Deutsch and Singer (1964), Waltz (1964, 1967), Rosecrance (1966), Haas (1970), Singer, Bremer, and Stuckey (1972), Wallace (1973a, 1973b), Bueno de Mesquita (1975, 1978, 1981a, 1981b), Jackson (1977), Rapkin and Thompson, with Christopherson (1979), Wayman (1984), Garnham (1985), Levy (1985a, 1985b), Hart (1985), Sabrosky (1985), Thompson (1986, 1988), Domke (1988), Midlarsky (1988a, 1988b, 1989a, 1989b), Mearsheimer (1990), Wayman and Morgan (1990), Hopf (1991), Saperstein (1991), Kegley and Raymond (1992), Schweller (1993), Wagner (1993), Mansfield (1993), James (1995), Brecher and Wilkenfeld (1997).

Theme II: Geography/Territory and Violence. Sprout and Sprout (1965), Midlarsky (1975), Diehl (1985b, 1991), Diehl and Goertz (1988), Starr (1991), Goertz and Diehl (1992b), Vasquez (1993, 1995b), Huth (1996a), Brecher and Wilkenfeld (1997).

Theme III: Protracted Conflict and War. Rummel (1975, 1976, 1979, 1981), Brecher and Wilkenfeld (1989), Geller and Jones (1991), Huth, Jones, and Maoz (1991), Goertz and Diehl (1992a, 1992b, 1993), Huth and Russett (1993), Maoz and Russett (1993), Maoz and Mor (1996).

Theme IV: Ethnicity and Violence. Gurr (1992, 1993a, 1993b), Midlarsky (1992a, 1992b, 1992c, 1992d), Carment (1993a, 1993b), Carment and James (1995, 1997b), Brecher and Wilkenfeld (1997), Davis, Jaggers, and Moore (1997).

Theme V: Regime Type/Democracy and War. Kant ([1969] 1795), Small and Singer (1976), Rummel (1979, 1983, 1995a, 1995b), Chan (1984, 1993), Weede (1984, 1992), Doyle (1986), Levy (1988, 1994a, 1994b), Maoz and Abdolali (1989), Merritt and Zinnes (1989), Morgan and Campbell (1991), Bremer (1992, 1993), Bueno de Mesquita and Lalman (1992), Ember, Ember, and Russett (1992), Forsythe (1992), Gleditsch (1992, 1995), Lake (1992), Maoz and Russett (1992, 1993), Morgan and Schwebach (1992), Russett and Antholis (1992), Schweller (1992), Sorensen (1992), Starr (1992a, 1992b), Dixon (1993, 1994), Mintz and Geva (1993), Morgan (1993), Ray (1993, 1995), Russett (1993, 1995), Singer and Wildavsky (1993), Cohen (1994), Hagan (1994), Layne (1994), Owen (1994), Raymond (1994), Spiro (1994), Weart (1994), Gowa (1995), Hermann and Kegley (1995), James and Mitchell (1995), Benoit (1996), Hermann and Kegley (1996), Hewitt and Wilkenfeld (1996), Rousseau et al. (1996), Thompson (1996a, 1996b, 1997a, 1997b), Brecher and Wilkenfeld (1997), Chan (1997).

Theme VI: Third-Party Intervention. Young (1967), Haas, Butterworth, and Nye (1972), Touval (1975), Butterworth (1976), Pelcovitz and Kramer (1976), Zacher (1979), Finlayson and Zacher (1980), Bobrow (1981), E. Haas (1983, 1986), Touval and Zartman (1985), Zartman and Touval (1985), Mitchell and Webb (1988), Zartman (1989), Bercovitch (1992), Bercovitch and Rubin (1992), Pricen (1992), Touval (1992), Hewitt (1996), Brecher and Wilkenfeld (1997, 2000).

Escalation

The concept of *escalation* has several meanings: a *prewar* process that leads to war; an *intrawar* process that enlarges the scope, increases the intensity, or crosses a limit of an ongoing war; and a spiral process from nonviolent crisis through conventional war to nuclear war.

The idea of escalation before a war is central to the literature on arms races, pioneered by Richardson's arms race model (1960a, 1960b). Any change in an existing military balance enhances the security of one adversary and the threat perceived by the other, generating the "security dilemma" (see later). Moreover, both are prisoners of self-fulfilling assumptions. A assumes that B will attempt to alter the arms balance in its favor. A's assumption will, in turn, predispose it to increase its arms potential. Such behavior will lead B to perceive threat and to respond in kind. For Richardson, in sum, escalation is a function of the *dynamics of the arms race.*[1]

Crisis escalation to war was also the focus of the "Stanford Studies." Holsti, North, and Brody (1968), Holsti (1972), and Sabrosky (1975), focusing on the crises preceding World War I, found that the *dynamics of mutual perceived hostility* was the key predictor to interstate violence. For Rapoport (1960, 1987), escalation is built into the *dynamics of system instability:* the arms system, like any other, becomes unstable when the rates of change in the military balance, not its level, are not constant. The idea of escalatory steps to war is also embedded in Lebow's (1987) concept of "miscalculated escalation," one of three sequences from crisis to nuclear war (the others are "preemption" and "loss of control").

Leng (1984) and Huth and Russett (1988) found that crisis escalation to war was driven by developments in the international environment and the behavior of one's adversary. And James (1987, 1988) discovered that states were more likely to escalate a military dispute when the dispute coincided with an increase in international turmoil and an opportunity to use force successfully.

The idea of escalation during a war is evident in works on military strategy, nowhere more so than in Clausewitz's *On War* (1832, 1976; Paret, 1985). For him, the essence of war is to compel one's enemy to do one's will. Since victory is the shared yet conflicting goal, the logic of war makes (reciprocal) escalation inevitable: each will raise the stakes and intensity of the contest until one side triumphs. For Clausewitz, in short, escalation is built into the *dynamics of war.*[2]

Escalation is clearly implied in Schelling's *The Strategy of Conflict* (1960). Victory is best achieved through deterrence. However, in the contest over resolve each party will raise the stakes—that is—escalate, to compel the other to yield. For Schelling, then, escalation is built into the *dynamics of bargaining.*[3]

The most explicit formulation of the link between escalation and war was by Smoke (1977, 17): "Escalation is the process by which the previous limits of a war are crossed and new ones established. . . . But limited war is the static term; *escalation* is the dynamic term."

An all-encompassing view of escalation to war was presented by Herman Kahn (1965), who discerned the roots of this process and its early stages in a prewar environment of interstate crisis. Focusing on the "unthinkable," he specified "Six Basic (and Omnipresent) Thermonuclear Threats." The first is "Large Escalation" or "Eruption," defined as "a sudden move up the 'escalation ladder' to very large attacks," which could result in total destruction of the target (139). The second is a "Nuclear Talionic Reprisal", that is, a nuclear tit-for-tat. The third is "Exemplary (and/or Reprisal) Attacks . . ., an equitable response to previous injury or wrong"; this includes all nuclear talionic reprisals, though not all reprisal attacks are talionic (142). The fourth threat is "'Noblesse Oblige' (or Potlach) Response," designed to display how much one cares for a client. The fifth is "Competition in Bearing Costs (or 'Pain')" by the nuclear adversaries. And the sixth is "Competition in Risk-Taking"; that is, "manipulating the risk of war in order to obtain foreign-policy advantages" (145).

When threat becomes operational, the result is escalation. Kahn created an elaborate and complex escalation ladder of 44 rungs, from nonwar to nuclear war. He had no illusions about the possibility of the ultimate horror: "Accidents can happen, staffs can disobey orders, misunderstand, or miscalculate; decision-makers can act wildly, irrationally" (1965, 147–48). For Kahn, then, escalation is built into the *dynamics of interstate conflict.*[4]

Escalation to war is attributed by many to behavior by a single state, designed to achieve one or more of several goals: economic gain; the acquisition or restoration of territory; ideological ends, such as the spread of communism or democracy and market economies; the enhancement of national security or military power in anticipation of future wars; influence; prestige, and so on.

It may be *uncertainty about security of tenure* that leads a regime to escalate a crisis, or *ideological differences* with the adversary (Rosecrance 1963). Some argue that war results from an exponential *growth in military and economic capability* by a state unaccompanied by higher status in the system—that is, "status inconsistency" (Midlarsky 1975; Organski and Kugler 1980). This view was also espoused by Howard (1984, 10, 16). As in the case of Athens and Sparta on the eve of the Peloponnesian War, in 1914 Britain feared German hegemony in Europe, and Germany was determined "to achieve a world status comparable with her latent power."

Another explanatory strand emphasizes *interactive behavior* that generates a spiral of mutually reinforcing hostility culminating in war. This arises from "the 'security dilemma' of men or groups, or their leaders . . . [who, in an anarchic society] must be, and usually are, concerned about their security from being attacked, subjected, dominated, or annihilated. . . . Since none can ever feel entirely secure in such a world of competing units, power competition ensues, and the vicious circle of security and power accumulation is on" (Herz 1950, 157, and 1951; see also Jervis 1976, 67, chap. 3; 1978). And for some (Lenin 1917; Choucri and North 1975), escalation to interstate war may be caused by a conflict over scarce resources.

Escalation to war is attributed by some to *structural factors:* an imbalance in the distribution of power (Morgenthau 1948; Claude 1962) or its obverse, the absence of a preponderant power (Kugler and Organski 1989; Kugler and Lemke 1996); a variant of this theme, namely, unstable military balances resulting from arms races (Brown 1987, Part II); and the notion of acute interstate violence as a disease that exhibits a strong "contagion effect" (Alcock 1972).[5]

A fourth explanation of crisis escalation to war emphasizes the role of threat perception, which may lead to preemptive or preventive war. And misperception—of one's self, intentions and/or capability, and/or of the adversary's intentions and/or capability—is viewed by some as the primary source of escalation to war (Jervis 1976; Lebow 1981; Stoessinger 1985; Vertzberger 1990). This analysis emphasizes the cognitive dimension of behavior: distrust generates countermistrust and a spiraling process of mutual misperception leading to war.

At the other end of the explanatory spectrum is the rational actor/ expected utility explanation of escalation to war. Briefly stated, a state's decision makers who perceive positive expected utility (gain) from war will initiate a war. Escalation will not occur only when state A's positive expected utility from a war with B is less than B's expected loss from a war with A (Bueno de Mesquita 1981b, 86–89; 1985).

What has been learned about the outbreak of war/escalation to war by systematic research? Zinnes (1980b, 360) acknowledged that "the mystery is a long way from being solved. . . . [W]hile we surely do not have laws, the empirical findings . . . appear to be moving us slowly toward lawlike generalizations." Midlarsky (1989b, xviii–xix) concurred: ". . . we have not been considering a general theory of war—we have been considering many different theories that have important areas of convergence but also diverge in essential details. . . . Overall, these studies show that there are many ways to investigate the phenomenon of international warfare, ways that are both analytically rigorous and empirically valid. . . ."

War Termination

For many years scholars seemed indifferent to the winding down of violent conflict. As the reviewer of the first 11 years of the *Journal of Conflict Resolution* observed, "for most *JCR* contributors, once a war happens, it ceases to be interesting" (Converse 1968, 476–77). This attitude is not surprising, for the primary interest of most scholars is to avert an outbreak of war. However, although the literature on de-escalation is much smaller than work on crisis escalation to war, there has been considerable discussion of war termination, especially in the 1960s and 1970s.

Phillipson (1916) first noted three modes of war termination—cease-fire, conquest, and peace treaty; he added a fourth, unilateral declaration. Stone (1954) added a fifth mode, namely, armistice. Then, building on Boulding's (1962) categories, K. J. Holsti (1966, 274–82) specified six modes of conflict outcome: "(1) avoidance or voluntary withdrawal" (e.g., the USSR's withdrawal of its 1960 demand for a "troika"-type UN Secretary-Generalship); "(2) violent conquest"; "(3) forced submission or withdrawal," resulting from a threat to use force; "(4) compromise"; "(5) award," that is, submission of the conflict to arbitration or adjudication; and "(6) passive settlement," that is, acquiescence in a new status quo, without a formal agreement (e.g., the partition of Korea after World War II).

As for how wars end, the dominant view has been that war termination is definitive; that is, wars end in victory or defeat (Calahan 1944, 18; Kecskemeti 1958, 9). Whatever the outcome—victory/defeat, stalemate, or compromise, the alternative outcomes used in the ICB Project—war endings, according to Carroll (1969, 298–99), arose from one of the following: piecemeal conquest of territory; withdrawal of forces by one or more parties; dissolution of a belligerent government; oral agreement; political agreement; and extermination or expulsion of the forces of one side or more. That is, war termination occurs with or without formal or informal agreement.

There are several competing interpretations—implicit hypotheses—on why and under what conditions wars end. Richardson (1948; see also Rapoport 1957, 282–98) attributed de-escalation/termination to changing war moods that spread like an epidemic—that is, irrational mass behavior. Wars, in this view, end when a sufficient proportion (half) of the population becomes infected with war weariness.[6]

Kecskemeti (1958, 1970) invoked two "rational" criteria: the principle of "irreversibility" regarding the military outcome (in ICB terms, a victory/defeat situation); and the principle of "correspondence between effort and stake," that is, a calculus of the relative importance of costs and benefits. Rapoport (1960) distinguished between "gamelike" and "fightlike" wars, whose outcome will depend on rational and irrational considerations, respectively. Wright ([1942] 1965) viewed war termination as a function of calculation, of "costs of . . . hostilities," "world pressures for peace," and "vulnerability (of forces) to destruction."

Fox (1970, 1) cited as factors favoring war termination "world political pressures for peace, constraints [on the full use of] the coercive forces available, competing high-priority domestic policy objectives, the translation of battlefield results into . . . moderated war objectives [and] the continuous calculus of sacrifices still to be made and gains still to be realized." Ikle (1971) argued that decision makers engage in a cost-benefit analysis of military gains versus intolerable destructive activity by the enemy.

Herman Kahn (1970) delineated 11 Types of War Outcome, the counterpart of the 44 steps on his Escalation Ladder. They range from (1) unconditional and total victory, and (2) substantially complete victory, each of which may not be Pyrrhic, to (10) major and/or substantially complete defeat, and (11) unconditional and total surrender, each of which may not be Pyrrhic for the opponent. Among the forms of outcome, he emphasized a cease-fire, ad hoc or conditional, with several possibilities, such as nuclear and conventional cease-fire, and nuclear cease-fire with continued conventional war.

In assessing each of these outcomes, three variables were emphasized by Kahn: political, physical, and social-psychological, measured by élan, morale, and social disruption. A state may succeed on one of these criteria and fail on one or both of the others. Success or failure is measured by: the level of damage to noncombatants; relative costs to the adversaries; comparison with what would have happened in the absence of a war; and the difference between actual and expected outcome. In sum, Kahn treated war termination as the end point of crisis de-escalation.

Stein (1975) noted that war termination, unlike war initiation, is a reciprocal action, except in cases of unilateral withdrawal. More important, war termination was linked to the concept of conflict reduction, which was defined as "that process which facilitates movement toward a relationship of conflict management within cooperation rather than cooperation within conflict. It initiates and reinforces changes in the rules of the game between the participants. . . . The object is not the legal but the political termination of hostilities. . . ." (16–17). And Pilar (1983) analyzed war termination as a bargaining process.

There have been few attempts to employ game theory to explain crisis-war termination. Notable are Brams and Kilgour (1987) who applied two variable-sum games to this problem, a Deterrence Game based upon Chicken, and a New Deterrence Game—Winding-Down. Their main finding was that, "in principle, winding down in either game is possible. Yet in order not to destabilize the cooperative outcomes . . . , the players must upgrade the level of their retaliatory threats against departures by their opponents from these outcomes." Thus "deescalation cannot be safely pursued without strengthening threats of reprisal if cheating is detected" (568, 570).

Research on the duration of wars has generated diverse findings. Wright ([1942] 1965, 226) reported that the 278 wars from 1450 to 1930 averaged 4.4 years, with variations according to type and period. Coser (1961, 347–48) emphasized certain termination "markers," such as the capture of a capital city, that are recognized as salient by both adversaries. Klingberg (1966, 167) concluded that one could not "predict accurately during a war how long the war will last." And Barringer (1972) viewed war termination as one of six phases in a larger conflict: it occurred when the weaker party perceived the negative balance of forces as likely to continue and when great power intervention in support of the adversary was perceived by at least one of the parties as likely if the war escalated.

The evidence on the form of war termination, too, is instructive. According to Wright (1970, 52–53), less than half (137) of the 311 cases of "war in the material sense" from 1480 to 1970 ended formally with a peace treaty. Viewed over the centuries: one-third of the wars in the sixteenth and seventeenth centuries terminated through a peace treaty; half, in the eighteenth century; two-thirds, in the nineteenth; six-sevenths in the first two decades of the twentieth century, declining to half in the inter–World War period, and none thereafter. In sum, a curvilinear pattern is evident for peace treaty outcomes. Focusing on the twentieth century, Carroll (1969, 297) reported that, while all but 1 of the 21 large-scale international wars ended in peace treaties, armistice, truce, or cease-fire agreements, only 2 of 36 civil, revolutionary, and anticolonial wars ended in an armistice or a cease-fire.

How do these findings compare with those of ICB research on interstate crises and violence, including full-scale wars, from the end of World

War I to the end of 1994? These will now be reported in terms of the links between crisis violence and polarity, geography, ethnicity, regime type/ democracy, conflict setting, and third-party intervention.

Findings on Twentieth-Century Crises and Violence

In the pages that follow, we present aggregate findings on the violence dimension of international conflict, drawn from our recent study of crises in the twentieth century (Brecher and Wilkenfeld 1997). The framework for this analysis is provided by seven key attributes of the inter-national system and its member-states. Polarity and geography are fundamental systemic characteristics within which interstate crisis behavior unfolds, while the extent to which events occur within a protracted conflict setting and the choice of crisis management techniques—particularly violence—provide a context for the international community to judge the danger that a crisis poses for the system as a whole or for one of its subsystems. Ethnicity and regime type provide important contexts for decision making in crisis. And all contribute to the extent to which third parties—international or regional organizations, and major powers—will attempt intervention and whether such intervention will prove successful in crisis abatement. These findings will be presented in general terms, and the interested reader is referred to *A Study of Crisis,* Part IV, for an extended discussion of these issues. We begin with a brief overview of violence and interstate crises.

The ICB Project has generated multifaceted data on 412 international crises and 895 crisis actors for the period 1918–94.[7] Among the 152 variables in the data set that explore multiple dimensions of interstate crises, ranging from onset to outcomes, 11 focus specifically on aspects of violence such as crisis trigger, crisis management technique, centrality and severity of violence, and timing of violence in crisis.

Violence is perhaps best viewed initially by examining the frequency of various types of violence in crises. In table 1, we note that, contrary to widespread perceptions, one-fourth of all international crises exhibited no violence at any stage of the crisis. At the other extreme, 22 percent were characterized by full-scale war. In the broadest sense, twentieth-century crises divided almost equally between no/low violence and intense violence. For the crisis actors themselves, the absence of violent

TABLE 1.
Frequency of Violence in International Crises, 1918–94

No violence	105	25%
Minor Clashes	114	28%
Serious Clashes	102	25%
Full-Scale War	91	22%
Total	412	100%

behavior is even more prominent: as evident in table 2, 34 percent of the state participants in crises did not become involved in violence of any kind, while 24 percent became combatants in full-scale wars. These findings highlight an important distinction in the realm of crisis and war: a foreign policy crisis for an individual state, as noted, is marked by a perception of higher-than-normal probability of involvement in military hostilities; in a substantial proportion of these cases no violence materialized.

Appendix 1 lists the 91 ICB crises that were characterized by full-scale war. Appendix 2 lists the major extant sources on conflict and war data, against which the ICB case list was checked. We turn now to a discussion of the major findings on crisis and violence in the twentieth century.

Polarity

An enduring puzzle in international politics concerns the link between systemic structure and international conflict. The debate first crystallized in the aftermath of the Cuban missile crisis, with one school making the case that bipolarity is the more stable system (Waltz 1964), another arguing for multipolarity as the most stable (Deutsch and Singer 1964), while Rosecrance (1966) advocated an intermediate international system, bi-multipolarity.[8] The ICB approach to this question focuses on international crisis as the initial indicator of a conflict of interests among states. For ICB research, three types of international systems characterize the twentieth century: multipolarity (1918–39), signifying a diffusion of military power and political decision making among a group of relatively equal units; bipolarity (1945–62), with a concentration of military power and political decision in two relatively equal preeminent actors;

and polycentrism (1963–89), a hybrid structure with two centers of military power and multiple centers of political decision.[9]

Our central thesis regarding polarity is that international systems vary in terms of the stability that they exhibit. The general proposition is that stability is greatest in a system of two preeminent powers (bipolarity), somewhat weaker in a system with greater dispersion of power (multipolarity), and lowest in a system of two major powers and multiple decisional centers (polycentrism). In this sense, we take a position closer to that of Waltz (1964).

The rationale for this ranking can be stated in terms of the costs of security regimes. Each type of international structure entails different security-related costs to its members: costs of decision making and costs of implementation. The former refers to time spent on bargaining to reach agreement on the components of a security regime for the international system. Clearly, such costs increase with the number of decisions centers. Implementation encompasses fixed and variable costs. Problems arising from collective action would suggest that two power centers (bipolarity) would experience lower fixed costs than three or more power centers. Variable costs, referring to ongoing system management, are expected to be greater when a system has an unequal number of power and decisional centers (polycentrism). Combining these two sets of costs, bipolarity clearly ranks first with regard to stability, while polycentrism is hypothesized to be the most unstable structure. The *Polarity* portion of Model I in figure 2 presents the general thrust of these postulated relationships.

In *A Study of Crisis* (1997) we report an array of findings that point strongly to polycentrism as the most unstable system from the point of

TABLE 2.

Frequency of Violence Employed by Crisis Actors, 1918–94

No Violence	303	34%
Minor Clashes	199	22%
Serious Clashes	181	20%
Full-Scale War	212	24%
Total	895	100%

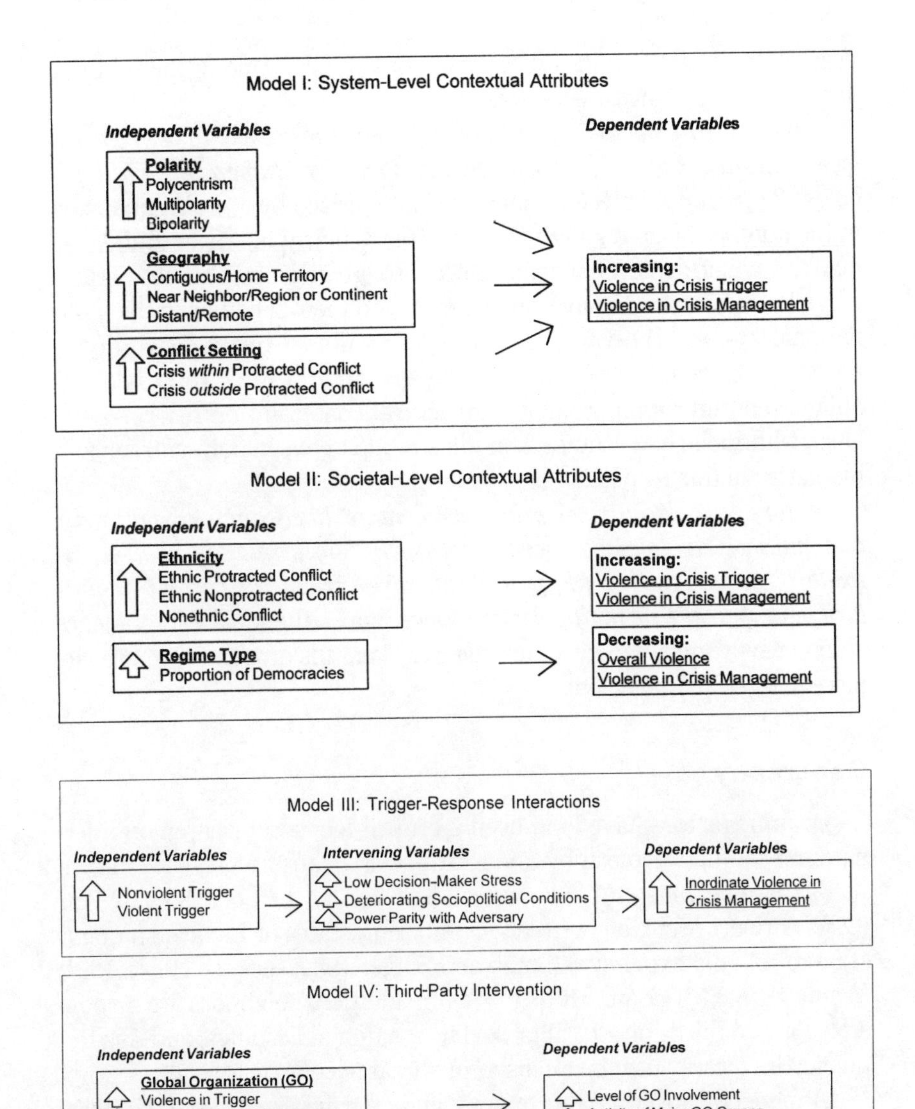

FIGURE 2. Models of violence in international crisis

view of the characteristics of international crisis. Among the findings pertaining to violence are the following.

Crises during polycentrism were by far the most likely to be triggered by violence (53 percent), followed by multipolarity (33 percent) and bipolarity (24 percent). Polycentrism was characterized by a rapid expansion in the number of states in the system (particularly in Africa and Asia), many of which achieved independence through violence, and this pattern of violence appears to have carried over into their behavior in the international system. By contrast, bipolarity exhibited relative stability in terms of the number of states in the system and the tightness of its alliance configuration, a notable structural constraint on resort to violence. Multipolarity occupies a middle ground between polycentrism and bipolarity in this respect.

Actors in polycentrism crises were more likely than in bipolarity and multipolarity to employ severe violence in conflict management—particularly serious clashes (30 percent in polycentrism, 22 percent in bipolarity, 17 percent in multipolarity). Once again, the legacy of violence among newly independent states helps explain this propensity to use violence in crisis management.

Geography

Geographic factors have long been a central focus in research on international conflict. Geography and territory are a strong presence in conflict situations: most interstate wars identified by the Correlates of War (COW) Project occurred between neighboring states or involved a major state in colonial expansion (Small and Singer 1982; see also Holsti 1991; Vasquez 1993, 1996; and Huth 1996a). In addition, neighbors are responsible for two-thirds of all Militarized International Disputes, and this frequency increases with the intensity of threat (Gochman 1990a).

A model of adversarial proximity and crisis violence—see the *Geography* portion of Model I in figure 2—grows out of a series of questions pertaining to the circumstances under which geographic proximity is related to violence in crisis. Does geographic proximity between adversaries affect the likelihood that crisis eruption will be violent? In the event of violence in a crisis, is it likely to be more severe when the crisis adversaries are geographically contiguous? Are crises between near-neighbors more likely to be part of a protracted conflict than crises between adversaries that are geographically distant from each other? Contiguity allows adversaries to undertake military action by moving troops and equipment to a common border, making the resort to violence easier. Distant adversaries can be expected to exhibit a wider range of crisis behavior, since launching military action under such circumstances is a considerably more serious and costly undertaking.

Geographic location, adversarial proximity, and proximity of crisis to the actor serve as the foci for the ICB examination of the interplay of geography and crisis. *A Study of Crisis* (1997) reports the following major findings pertaining to geography and violence in crisis.

Patterns of violence in crisis management vary across regions and, within regions, across systems. Europe accounted for 39 percent of all post–World War I international crises with no violence, largely in the eras of bipolarity and polycentrism, but was the locus of 22 percent of all crises involving war in the international system, largely the by-product of multipolarity and World War II. Two regions—Asia and the Middle East—accounted for an unusually large proportion of wars in the post–World War II era, while Africa accounted for a very high proportion of crises in which violence short of war was employed, virtually all in the polycentric system.

Crises between contiguous or near-neighbor adversaries were more likely to be triggered by violence than were crises between more distant adversaries (44 to 33 to 29 percent). However, among major powers, even more distant crises were often triggered by violent acts, attesting to the global reach of their alliance capabilities and commitments.

The more proximate a crisis was to an actor, that is, occurrence on its home territory or within its subregion rather than in a remote location, the more likely it was to have been triggered by a violent act (37 to 33 to 16 percent). Here again, major powers were often the exception, almost always indicating violence involving a client state.

Conflict Setting

International crises in the twentieth century can be classified according to whether they unfolded in the context of a protracted conflict (enduring rivalry), or occurred as more isolated events. Virtually every key dimension of crisis is affected by this factor. As Azar, Jureidini, and McLaurin (1978) noted, protracted conflicts are "hostile interactions which extend over long periods of time, with sporadic outbreaks of open warfare fluctuating in frequency and intensity." ICB identifies 31 protracted conflicts since the end of World War I, some lasting many decades (Arab/Israel, India/Pakistan, Greece/Turkey), and accounting for 60 percent of all international crises for this period.

The notion that international crises within protracted conflicts are more likely than others to be triggered by violence derives from a protracted conflict's distinctive characteristics: prolonged hostility between the same adversaries creating mutual mistrust and the expectation of violence; the presence of multiple issues within an ongoing conflict; periodic resort to violence in the past; and the importance of the values at stake. Similarly, the tendency toward violence in crisis management derives directly from the dynamics of interaction among adversaries locked in a protracted conflict. These expectations are summarized in the *Conflict Setting* portion of Model I in figure 2.

Our basic argument is that, despite wide variation in their duration, geographic location, number of eruptions, and variety of issues, crises occurring within protracted conflicts exhibit characteristics that clearly differentiate them from crises occurring outside of such a conflict. Key among these differentiating factors is the question of violence.

Actors in protracted conflict crises were more likely to experience violent triggers (51 percent versus 36 percent) and to employ more severe violence in crisis management (55 percent versus 41 percent). Coupled with the finding that threatened values were likely to be more basic in protracted conflict crises, these findings point to the more extreme danger that such crises pose to the international system, by virtue of their propensity to escalate to violence.

Ethnicity

A cursory examination of the international system in the 1990s might lead to the conclusion that the defining characteristic of the current decade is the prominence of conflict with ethnic overtones. A somewhat neglected concept, ethnicity has acquired high visibility only since the end of the cold war. The new forces unleashed by the disintegration of the USSR and the withdrawal of Soviet power from Eastern Europe in 1989–91 cast a fresh light on the role of ethnicity in interstate as well as intrastate politics. ICB's particular vantage point has been the exploration of the relationship between ethnicity and international crisis, arguing that the most dangerous ethnic conflicts from the point of view of system stability are those that spill over into the international system as crises and become part of the existing rivalries among international actors. The significance of this phenomenon is accentuated by the fact that 35 percent of all international crises from the end of World War I to the end of 1994 had an ethnic dimension, although only 24 percent of ICB crises were classified as ethnicity-driven, that is, primarily ethnic in character.

The basic ICB proposition in this domain is that international ethnicity crises will differ from nonethnicity crises along a number of dimensions, from type of trigger and values at stake, through the role of violence in crisis management, and the extent of involvement by the major powers and global organizations, to the type of crisis outcome. A setting of protracted conflict is expected to sharpen the differences between ethnicity and nonethnicity.

The rationale for this proposition is that ethnicity crises are more likely than others to be rooted in mutual mistrust and the expectation of violence from an adversarial ethnic group. Moreover, basic values are more likely to be at stake in an ethnic conflict, creating a predisposition to initiate a crisis by violence, lest the adversary attempt to preempt. Similarly, as long as ethnic adversaries see no end to their glaring differences and disputes and view their conflict in zero-sum terms, the dynamics of their hostile relationship create a disposition to violence in crisis management. A setting of protracted conflict between crisis adversaries will accentuate these tendencies toward the use of violence in ethnicity crises.

These relationships are summarized in the *Ethnicity* portion of Model II in figure 2. Specific findings with relevance to the link between crisis and violence are as follow.

Ethnicity and a protracted conflict (PC) setting generated a much higher frequency of violence in crisis triggers in African crises than for any other region (82 percent in crisis triggers for African cases, compared with 29 percent for the other regions).

Ethnicity and a PC setting also made crises in polycentrism much more likely to exhibit violent triggers than crises in either bipolarity or multipolarity (64 percent for polycentrism, compared with 21 percent for bipolarity and 23 percent for multipolarity). For both of these findings, it appears to be the reinforcing presence of acute ethnic conflict, particularly in Africa during polycentrism, and the protracted nature of African conflicts, which stand out.

Ethnicity and protracted conflict setting together were also associated with more violence in crisis management (51 percent) than was the case for crises in ethnic non-protracted conflicts (45 percent) or in nonethnic conflicts (33 percent). That is, just as violence is more likely to be found among the triggers to crises with an ethnic dimension, such crises are also likely to move quickly to violence in crisis management—the crisis actors tend to resort to violence in such situations. In fact, crises during ethnicity protracted conflicts were likely to exhibit severe violence in crisis management (serious clashes and full-scale war) even if the initial trigger was nonviolent. Thus, the level of existing hostility among the crisis actors in protracted conflicts has a tendency to cause escalation from nonviolence to violence, or from low to severe violence.

Regime Type/Democracy

Among the most widely researched topics in world politics in recent years has been the *theory of democratic peace.* The rarity of wars between democracies has led Levy (1988, 1994a) to refer to peace between democracies as "the closest thing we have to a law in international politics." (For an excellent review of this literature, see Chan 1997.) The basic outline of the theory posits that, although democracies are no less prone than nondemocracies to engage in violence in pursuit of their interests, democracies rarely employ war as a means for resolving conflicts with other democracies.

Both normative and structural models have been proposed to explain this phenomenon (Maoz and Russett 1993; Russett 1993). We find the normative model more persuasive, with the assumption that nation-states externalize the norms of domestic political processes in interstate interactions. The character of interstate behavior is indicative of the norms that guide and shape domestic political institutions. Political behavior in democracies is distinguished by an emphasis on peaceful political competition, with political disputes resolved through negotiation and compromise. These democratic norms contrast sharply with "nondemocratic norms," where the role of violence and coercion is more pronounced (see Hewitt and Wilkenfeld 1996).

ICB has argued that, for states locked in an international crisis, the presence or absence of democratic norms will dictate whether such crises are likely to escalate to violence. The presence of democracies among the crisis actors should have a dampening effect on the propensity to violence. The *Regime Type* portion of Model II in figure 2 presents the ICB view of this relationship. Among the key findings are the following.

As the proportion of democracies among the actors in an international crisis increases, the likelihood of violence decreases. Specifically, when the proportion of democracies among the crisis actors is low, the probability of violence is .52. This probability decreases to .39 for a moderate proportion of democracies, and finally, to a probability of .27 when the proportion of democracies is high.

When crisis actors choose violence as their primary crisis management technique, the severity of violence lessens as the prevalence of democracies in the crisis increases. These findings remain strong even after the introduction of such well-accepted explanatory factors as violence in the crisis trigger, gravity of threat, and protracted conflict setting. These crisis-related findings add a significant new dimension to the theory of democratic peace.

Trigger-Response Interactions

The phenomenon of matching behavior in conflict and crisis situations has attracted considerable attention among International Relations researchers. Matching behavior is defined as a reciprocal relationship between incoming behavior (crisis trigger, in this context) and outgoing behavior (crisis response). In particular, we are interested in the degree to which the crisis management technique, both type and severity, matches the event that triggered a crisis for the state in question. The basic premise is that, exclusive of other factors, there is no intrinsic reason to expect a state to overreact or underreact to incoming stimuli (Wilkenfeld 1975, Wilkenfeld et al. 1980; see also Wilkenfeld 1991).

The ICB analysis of the matching phenomenon in the context of international crisis focuses on the disruptive impact on the trigger-response dynamic of key factors drawn from three different levels of analysis: decision maker stress, sociopolitical conditions, and interstate power relationships. More specifically, our expectation is that low decision maker stress, deteriorating sociopolitical conditions, and relative power parity among the adversaries are conditions that are likely to lead to disruptions in the trigger/response dynamic. With the presence of these factors, we expect disruptions to occur in the trigger-crisis management linkage, such that states would exhibit greater violence in crisis management than would have been predicted, given the level of violence in the trigger. These relationships are summarized in the *Trigger-Response* portion of Model III in figure 2. Among the key ICB findings are the following.

Low decision maker stress, serious deterioration in sociopolitical conditions within a crisis actor at the time of a crisis, and approximate power parity among the crisis actors combine to produce deviations in the nonviolent trigger-to-response mechanism. Nonviolent trigger to nonviolent crisis management matching occurs in about 75 percent of the cases. But in the remaining 25 percent, the presence of some or all of these three factors is likely to lead crisis actors to respond with violence in crises triggered by nonviolent acts. These latter crises pose acute dangers for the international community, because the actors are not interacting based solely on the dynamics of the situation itself but rather on factors seemingly extraneous to the crisis situation.

Third-Party Intervention

The involvement of third parties in the search for peaceful settlement of disputes has been an enduring part of world politics in the twentieth century. This refers to "any action taken by an actor that is not a direct party to the crisis, that is designed to reduce or remove one or more of the problems of the bargaining relationship and, therefore, to facilitate the termination of the crisis itself" (Young 1967, 34). ICB's examination of third-party intervention in international crises focuses on the circumstances in which such intervention is likely to occur, what form it takes, and the conditions under which it is most likely to be effective in crisis management and resolution.

The *Third Party* segments of Model IV in figure 2 summarize the roles of third parties in crises characterized by violence. ICB data reveal that global organizations (the League of Nations and the United Nations) became involved in barely half of the 375 international crises between 1918 and 1994 (the 37 World War II cases were excluded since neither the League nor the UN was functional). Given their mandate in the area of maintaining international peace and security, it is plausible to argue that global organizations are most likely to become involved in crises in which violence is present in the trigger and the crisis management techniques employed by the actors.

Bipolarity (1945–62) and polycentrism (1963–89) exhibited a positive relationship between violent triggers and the propensity for the UN to become involved in crises. As a corollary, these post–World War II crises triggered by violence were more likely than others to have entailed the involvement of high-level UN organs—the General Assembly and Security Council.

For bipolarity and polycentrism, the more severe the violence in a crisis, the more likely it was that the UN would become involved. In addition, for bipolarity, the more intense the violence, the more likely it was that high-level organs would attempt to manage a crisis.

Analysis of major powers as third parties is made more complex by the need to differentiate those crises in which the powers were themselves crisis actors (e.g., the United States and the USSR in the Berlin crises) from those in which they played an intermediary role. With this in mind, we note first that the degree of involvement by great powers as third parties in the international crises of the multipolar system was considerably higher than the comparable rate for superpowers during bipolarity and polycentrism—86 percent for the great powers, compared with 67 percent and 52 percent for the United States and the USSR during the post–World War II international systems. Since major powers as third parties were not specifically evaluated with regard to violence, no results are reported here.

Conclusion

Following a review of the literature on conflict and violence, we have presented an analysis of international crises and violence from the perspective of seven key contextual attributes of the international system and its member-states: polarity, geography, and conflict setting as fundamental structural characteristics; ethnicity and regime type as constraints and influences on decision making in crisis; trigger-response interactions as a criterion that the international community uses to assess the potential danger a crisis poses; and third-party intervention by the system and its actors. It is now our task to explore the significance of these aggregate empirical findings on international crises and violence for the international system as it enters the twenty-first century.

A great deal has been learned about the role of violence in international crises. Polycentrism was particularly susceptible to violence in both triggers and crisis management. Regions differed in terms of the extent and severity of violence. At the same time, regardless of region, contiguity was a strong predictor of violence in crisis. In crises occurring within protracted conflicts, it was more likely for the trigger to be violent and for actors to employ violence in crisis management. Democracies among crisis adversaries dampened the tendency toward the use of violence in crisis management, while ethnicity tended to exacerbate the tendency toward violence in crisis. Decision maker stress, societal unrest, and power discrepancy among adversaries all contribute to the likelihood that violence in crises will escalate. Finally, global organizations had a greater tendency to become involved in crises involving violence, either as the trigger or in crisis management, although their effectiveness in such cases was limited.

Knowledge of twentieth-century crises can be used to discern the general pattern of future crises. First, the phenomenon of military-security crisis is unlikely to disappear; that is, the "end of history," if it has any validity, does not apply to this aspect of world politics. Second, while multistate crises such as the Gulf crisis-war of 1990–91 may recur, the vast majority of international crises will take the form of bilateral conflicts over territory, resources, or status. Third, crises are slightly more likely to be triggered by violence than by nonviolent acts, with the severity of violence escalating over time from minor clashes to serious clashes or full-scale war.

Finally, under what conditions are future international crises likely to erupt in violence? Projecting the findings from an inquiry into twentieth-century crises, the most salient features are (1) geographic contiguity between the adversaries; (2) a military-security-type issue in dispute, notably territory, or several issues combined; (3) the unfolding of the conflict within a subsystem; (4) an international system of fragmented decisional authority, that is, polycentrism, whether accompanied by power bipolarity or unipolarity; (5) considerable heterogeneity; and (6) authoritarian regimes.

Notes

1. The postulated link between an arms race and severe interstate violence (war) was found to be strongly supported by Wallace on the basis of COW evidence from 1816 to 1975, but "the findings do not provide incontrovertible proof of a *causal* link" (1979, 14; also 1982).

   Many have dissented sharply on methodological grounds, notably Weede (1980), Houweling and Siccama (1981), Altfeld (1983), Diehl (1983), Intriligator and Brito (1984), Diehl (1985b), and Diehl and Kingston (1987).

The controversy remains unresolved, perhaps because, as Siverson and Diehl (1989, 32) observed in a review of the debate: "a primary difficulty in arms race studies is their tendency to look at arms races in isolation from the other relevant conditions for war."

2. For other allusions to intrawar escalation in strategic thought during the past two centuries, see Earle (1943) and Paret (1986).
3. For other insightful models of bargaining and escalation in the context of conventional and nuclear crisis-war, see Kahn (1965), Snyder (1972), Snyder and Diesing (1977), Powell (1987, 1988), Morrow (1989), Geller (1990), Zagare (1992), and Carlson (1995).
4. For a severe criticism of Kahn's "escalation ladder" see Beer (1981, 354, n. 43).
5. Many subsequent studies attempted to discover the extent to which the "war virus"—horizontal escalation—spreads among states: Bremer (1982), Levy (1982), Starr and Most (1983, 1985), Siverson and Starr (1991), and, for Houweling and Siccama (1985), the "epidemiology of war."
6. The counterpart to "war weariness" in the literature on conflict is the concept of "ripe for resolution" (Zartman 1989, chap. 6, esp. 267–73; Haass 1990; Stedman 1991).
7. Inter-university Consortium for Political and Social Research (ICPSR) Study #9286.
8. See Brecher, James, and Wilkenfeld (1990) for an extended discussion of this debate.
9. Due to the relatively small number of crises occurring in unipolarity (1990–94), these cases are not included in the current analysis.

APPENDIX 1. INTERNATIONAL CRISIS-WARS 1918–1994*

INTERNATIONAL CRISIS	TRIGGER DATE	TERMINATION DATE	FORM OF OUTCOME
Hungarian War	03/20/1919	03/27/1919	Unilateral act
Third Afghan War	04/15/1919	08/08/1919	Formal agreement
Cilician War	11/--/1919	10/20/1921	Formal agreement
Polish/Russian War	04/25/1920	10/12/1920	Formal agreement
Vilna I	07/12/1920	11/29/1920	Formal agreement
Greece/Turkey War II	01/06/1921	09/12/1921	Unilateral act
Albanian Frontier	07/07/1921	11/18/1921	Imposed agreement
Greece/Turkey War III	08/26/1922	09/15/1922	Unilateral act
Hijaz/Najd War	03/07/1924	12/19/1925	Imposed agreement
Chaco II	06/18/1932	06/12/1935	Formal agreement
Jehol Campaign	02/23/1933	05/31/1933	Imposed agreement
Saudi/Yemen War	12/18/1933	05/20/1934	Imposed agreement
Ethiopian War	12/06/1934	05/05/1936	Unilateral act
Spanish Civil War I	07/17/1936	03/18/1937	Unilateral act
Marco Polo Bridge	07/08/1937	01/16/1938	Unilateral act
Spanish Civil War III	10/30/1938	11/18/1938	Unilateral act
Spanish Civil War IV	12/23/1938	03/31/1939	Unilateral act
Invasion of Albania	03/25/1939	04/13/1939	Unilateral act
Nomonhan	05/28/1939	09/15/1939	Formal agreement
Entry World War II	08/20/1939	09/28/1939	Unilateral act
Finnish War	10/06/1939	03/13/1940	Formal agreement
Invasion of Scandinavia	04/08/1940	06/10/1940	Imposed agreement
Fall of Western Europe	05/10/1940	06/22/1940	Imposed agreement
Battle of Britain	07/10/1940	09/15/1940	Unilateral act
East Africa Campaign	08/19/1940	05/17/1941	Unilateral act
Balkan Invasions	10/28/1940	06/01/1941	Unilateral act
Barbarossa	06/22/1941	12/05/1941	Unilateral act
Pearl Harbor	11/26/1941	06/07/1942	Unilateral act
Stalingrad	06/28/1942	02/02/1943	Unilateral act
El Alamein	10/23/1942	05/13/1943	Unilateral act
Fall of Italy	07/09/1943	09/11/1943	Unilateral act
Soviet Occupation—Eastern Europe	03/26/1944	02/13/1945	Unilateral act
D-Day	06/06/1944	05/07/1945	Unilateral act
Leyte Campaign	10/20/1944	12/26/1944	Unilateral act
Luzon	01/09/1945	03/03/1945	Unilateral act
Final Soviet Offensive	01/11/1945	05/07/1945	Unilateral act
Iwojima	02/19/1945	03/16/1945	Unilateral act
Okinawa	04/01/1945	06/21/1945	Unilateral act
Hiroshima-Nagasaki	08/06/1945	09/02/1945	Unilateral act
Indonesia Independence I	09/29/1945	03/25/1947	Formal agreement
Greek Civil War II	11/13/1946	02/28/1947	Faded
Indonesia Independence II	07/21/1947	01/17/1948	Formal agreement

International Crisis	Trigger Date	Termination Date	Form of Outcome
Kashmir I	10/24/1947	01/01/1949	Formal agreement
Palestine Partitian/ Israel Independence	11/29/1947	07/20/1949	Formal agreement
China Civil War	09/23/1948	12/08/1949	Unilateral act
Indonesia Independence III	12/19/1948	12/27/1949	Unilateral act
Korean War I	06/25/1950	09/30/1950	Unilateral act
Korean War II	09/30/1950	07/10/1951	Semiformal agreement
Dien Bien Phu	03/13/1954	07/21/1954	Imposed agreement
Suez Nationalization-War	07/26/1956	03/12/1957	Unilateral act
China/India Border II	09/08/1962	01/23/1963	Unilateral act
Yemen War I	09/26/1962	04/15/1963	Formal agreement
Yemen War II	05/--/1964	11/08/1964	Formal agreement
Yemen War III	12/03/1964	08/25/1965	Formal agreement
Kashmir II	08/05/1965	01/10/1966	Semiformal agreement
Yemen War IV	10/14/1966	09/26/1967	Formal agreement
Six Day War	05/17/1967	06/11/1967	Imposed agreement
Tet Offensive	01/30/1968	03/31/1968	Unilateral act
War of Attrition	03/08/1969	08/07/1970	Formal agreement
Football War	06/15/1969	07/30/1969	Formal agreement
Invasion of Cambodia	03/13/1970	07/22/1970	Unilateral act
Black September	09/15/1970	09/29/1970	Imposed agreement
Invasion of Laos II	02/08/1971	03/25/1971	Unilateral act
Bangladesh	03/25/1971	12/17/1971	Imposed agreement
Vietnam Ports Mining	03/30/1972	07/19/1972	Semiformal agreement
North/South Yemen I	09/26/1972	11/28/1972	Formal agreement
Christmas Bombing	10/23/1972	01/27/1973	Formal agreement
Oct.-Yom Kippur War	10/05/1973	05/31/1974	Formal agreement
Cyprus III	07/15/1974	02/24/1975	Unilateral act
Final North Vietnam Offensive	12/14/1974	04/30/1975	Unilateral act
War in Angola	07/12/1975	03/27/1976	Unilateral act
Ogaden II	07/22/1977	03/14/1978	Unilateral act
Vietnam Invasion/Cambodia	09/24/1977	01/07/1979	Unilateral act
Chad/Libya II	01/22/1978	03/27/1978	Formal agreement
Chad/Libya III	04/15/1978	08/29/1978	Semiformal agreement
Nicaragua Civil War II	09/10/1978	07/17/1979	Unilateral act
Fall of Amin	10/30/1978	04/10/1979	Unilateral act
Sino/Vietnam War	12/25/1978	03/15/1979	Unilateral act
North/South Yemen II	02/24/1979	03/30/1979	Formal agreement
Chad/Libya IV	04/12/1979	11/10/1979	Unilateral act
Onset Iran/Iraq War	09/17/1980	11/30/1980	Unilateral act
Khorramshahr	03/22/1982	07/30/1982	Unilateral act
Falklands/Malvinas	03/31/1982	06/14/1982	Imposed agreement
War in Lebanon	06/05/1982	05/17/1983	Semiformal agreement
Basra-Kharg Island	02/21/1984	07/11/1984	Semiformal agreement

Capture of Al-Faw	02/09/1986	04/--/1986	Unilateral act
International Crisis	**Trigger Date**	**Termination Date**	**Form of Outcome**
Chad/Libya VIII	12/12/1986	09/11/1987	Semiformal agreement
Iraq Recapture Al-Faw	04/18/1988	08/08/1988	Semiformal agreement
Gulf War	08/02/1990	04/12/1991	Imposed agreement
Yugoslavia I—Croatia/ Slovenia	06/25/1991	01/03/1992	Formal agreement
Yugoslavia II—Bosnia	03/03/1992	11/21/1995	Formal agreement

*Among the 412 international crises in the ICB data set, the level of violence was "war" in 91 cases, "serious clashes" in 102 cases, and "minor clashes" or "no violence" in the remaining 219 cases. Since the primary focus of this book is war, only the war cases are listed here.

As evident, there were many clusters of crisis-wars, notably World War II (20 cases), the Vietnam War (5 cases), and the Yemen War (4 cases).

For the complete ICB list of international crises, see Brecher and Wilkenfeld 1997, 666–737 or in the CD-ROM 2000 version.

APPENDIX 2. Compendia on Violence in International Conflicts

Author	Focus	Period	Cases
Blechman and Kaplan (1978)	U.S. use of military force	1946–75	215
Bouthoul and Carrère (1976)	interstate wars	1920–74	31
		(1740–1974	157)[a]
Butterworth (1976)	interstate security conflicts	1945–74	310
Cusack and Eberwein (1982)	serious international disputes	(1900–76	634)
Deitchman (1964)[b]	military engagements	1945–62	30
Eckhardt and Azar (1978)	international conflicts (COPDAB)	1945–75	144
Gochman and Maoz (1984)	militarized interstate disputes (COW)	(1816–1976	960)
Greaves (1962)[b]	wars, revolts, coups, crises	1945–62	55
Hass (1986)	international disputes	1945–84	319
Holsti (1991)	wars/major armed interventions	1918–41	30
		1945–89	58
		(1648–1989	177)
Kaplan (1981)	Soviet use of military force	1944–79	190
Kellog (n.d.)[b]	wars, coups, crises	1945–64	38
Kende (1971)	local wars	1945–70	95
Kende (1978)	wars	1945–76	120
Leiss and Bloomfield (1967)[b]	local conflicts, limited wars	1945–65	27
Luard (1987)	principal wars	1917–84	161
	international wars in Europe+	(1648–1984	470)
	civil wars in Europe+		
	international wars elsewhere+		
	wars of national independence+		
	civil wars elsewhere+		
	wars of decolonization+		
Maoz (1982)	militarized interstate disputes (COW)	(1815–1976	827)
	serious interstate disputes	1929–76	95[d]
Richardson (1960)[b]	deadly quarrels	1946–54	13
	(armed clashes)	(1820–1954	289)
Singer and Small (1972)	interstate and extrasystemic wars	1919–65	24
	(COW)	(1816–1965	93)
Siverson and Tennefoss (1982)	interstate conflicts	1919–65	152
		(1815–1965	256)

AUTHOR	FOCUS	PERIOD	CASES
Small and Singer (1982)	interstate and extrasystemic wars (COW)	1919–79 (1816–1980	47 118)
Sorokin (1937)	international wars	(1801–1925	189)[c]
Tillema (1991)	wars and military interventions	1945–88	269
Wallensteen and Sollenberg (1995)	armed conflicts	1989–94	94
Wright (1942, [1965])[b]	international, civil, colonial and imperial wars	1919–64 (1480–1964	25 291)
Zacher (1979)	international conflicts	1947–77	116

[a]The number of cases specified within parentheses here and elsewhere in Appendix 2 refers to a period extending beyond the time frame of the ICB data set, 1918–94.

[b]These lists of wars and armed conflicts from 1945 to 1968 are contained in SIPRI (1969).

[c]Wars involving one or more of the following European powers: Austria-Hungary, France, Germany, Great Britain, Italy, Russia, Spain.

[d]A random sample of cases.

Global War and the Political Economy of Structural Change

KAREN RASLER and WILLIAM R. THOMPSON

Many students of war assume that all wars should be explicable in the same theoretical terms. For instance, it is argued that wars are caused by misperceptions, territorial disputes, or arms races gone out of control. We have no doubt that there is ample room in the study of war for a wide variety of causal factors but that does not mean that one model of war, combining a variety of factors, necessarily is the most efficacious way, or the only way, to go in explaining international violence. An alternative path is to focus on theoretically sanctioned, discrete types of wars and their possibly equally distinctive etiologies (Thompson 1990b). Global wars provide a prominent example. These events are wars fought over large expanses of territory, by many actors, for a number of years, and with profound implications for the winners, the losers, and even neutral bystanders. They are also distinctive in the sense that they are instrumental in determining how the world is structured. But we do not focus on them solely because they are big and dramatic events. Rather, we choose to focus on them as constituent elements in ongoing processes of political economy. Global wars are not simply prominent wars although they certainly are that. But they are also significant "cogs" in the political economy "machinery" that structure global politics and economics. And as such, we are able to explain why they occur and, to some degree, with what effect. The rest of this chapter will focus on how structural change generates global wars and, to a lesser extent, how global wars generate structural change.[1]

In this chapter we distinguish between the world economy, which encompasses the aggregation of all economic activities and transactions, and the global economy, which focuses on long-distance commerce and the most technologically advanced industrial production. Within this context, global politics, then, are focused in large part on the management of problems related to the functioning of the global political economy. Global powers are the few states that have the capability and interest in participating in this arena. To do so, they require some minimal capacity for global reach, which has translated historically into maritime and, more recently, aerospace weapons systems. But they also require competitive economic infrastructures to be able to generate and afford global reach. Global wars are intense contests among global and other powers that are fought to determine whose policy preferences are most likely to influence the way, and for whose benefit, the global political economy operates. These contests are neither frequent nor do they erupt randomly. They are geared to the rise and fall of leadership structures and are most probable after an extended period of declining leadership in the global political economy.

By distinguishing between and among such terms as *world, international,* and *global,* we hope to make clear that we are not addressing the sum of all world politics, all international political economy, all military capabilities, or all wars. Only some of these phenomena are pertinent to our focus on the relationship between war and structural change. Put another way, it is quite likely that global structural change impacts have widespread repercussions, but our theoretical interest is focused primarily, and at least initially, on the actors and processes that are most central to the functioning of the global political economy.

We do not assume that nonglobal wars are irrelevant to this story. On the contrary, it is likely that wars in general, as well as conflict and cooperation propensities are linked to structural change—perhaps just as closely as global wars. But we, and others, are only beginning to explore these broader ramifications that include other types of conflicts (Reuveny and Thompson 1997b) but also other processes such as economic growth (Modelski and Thompson 1996), democratization (Modelski and Perry 1991), protectionism (Thompson and Vescera 1992; Reuveny and Thompson 1997a; Thompson and Reuveny 1998), polarity (Thompson 1986; Rasler and Thompson 1994) and rivalry (Thompson 1995b, 1999a; Frederick 1999; Kelly 1999; Modelski 1999; and Goertz and Diehl, this volume).

The factors that are regarded as among the most important to structural change are those forces that contribute to the concentration and deconcentration of global reach capabilities (both economic and military).

Our principal assumption is that things work much differently when global capabilities are highly concentrated than when they are not. High concentration suggests the possibility (but not the guarantee) of relatively strong leadership, less conflict among global powers, and a more facilitative environment for global order. Other things being equal, lower levels of concentration correlate with higher probabilities of conflict, disorder, and leadership succession struggles.[2] Yet it is not so much a matter of identifying which continuum pole (high versus low concentration) is most characteristic of international relations. The problem is that international relations cycle back and forth from high to low and back to high levels of concentration. It is the dynamics of highly uneven, long-term economic growth that drives this cyclical momentum. Global war, ultimately then, is a function of long-term economic growth processes. But long-term economic growth processes are also a function of global war. The relationship is fundamentally reciprocal.

These processes of long-term economic growth and political-military power concentration at the global level are complicated further by the coevolution of regional concentration processes that operate on somewhat different principles and on a differently timed rhythm. These same regional concentration processes have tended to produce the most dangerous challengers to global leaders. Therefore, they are also important to the pace and direction of global capability concentration and deconcentration.

Our model thus encompasses two types of coevolution. One centers on the interaction between economic growth and military/political leadership at the global level. A second focuses on the interaction between the development and decay of global and regional hierarchies. Both sets of coevolutionary dynamics encompass important reciprocal influences on one another. To further explore these relationships, we need to elaborate our model by highlighting two sets of activities: long-term economic growth and global warfare.

Long-Term Economic Growth

Most economists and the theories that they have generated are more concerned about short-term growth prospects and problems. How does one avoid recession and still generate employment and the expansion of income? How does one alleviate balance-of-payments problems? How does one best combine capital and labor endowments to take advantage of comparative advantages? What level of interest rates will discourage inflation without shutting incremental growth down completely? Short-term economic growth concerns certainly are not unimportant, but they do not address structural change. In fact, a focus on short-term economic growth tends to either ignore structural change altogether or else assume that it does not occur.

Long-term economic growth, we assume, is driven primarily by major technological innovations.[3] Innovations encompass the development and application of new ways of doing things—which include pioneering new trade routes, constructing new machines for transporting goods more cheaply or more quickly thereby lowering transportation costs, and finding new ways to manipulate and transfer information (telegraphs, telephones, radios, televisions, and computers). Innovations such as these can be minor or radical but it is the latter that tend to promote major structural changes. Radical technological innovations are also discontinuous in time and space, which means that they have a tendency to appear in clusters and that they tend to emerge first in one economy before diffusing to other economies.

These assertions translate into the observation that major technological innovations generate new commercial and industrial sectors of activity that are likely to lead the rest of the economy in which they appear in terms of growth rates. They are likely to do so at particular times as opposed to being spread out over time, and they are likely to benefit most the pioneering economy in which they first appear. Still, technological innovations have finite trajectories. They are unlikely to generate growth forever. They are instead likely to encounter diminishing returns. Sunrise sectors, with the passage of time, become sunset sectors. If the onetime leading sectors are not replaced by new leading sectors, the long-term growth of the pioneering economy will slow. If another economy (or other economies) picks up the lead in developing radical innovations, the stage is set for major structural change in the global political economy.

Following Modelski and Thompson (1996), we view the modern history of long-term economic growth as being predicated on the schedule described in table 1. Table 1 lists the leading sectors associated with each successive pioneering economy since Sung China. Implicit to this approach is that the pattern described in table 1 first emerged about 1,000 years ago and that it is possible to trace the interconnections and transitions from Sung China through the Italian city-states (especially Genoa and Venice) to Portugal, the Netherlands, Britain, and the United States.

TABLE 1.

Global Lead Economies

Lead Economy	Lead Commodities or Sectors	Approximate Timing
N. Sung	Printing; national market information; rice; iron	10th–11th centuries
S. Sung	Maritime trade	11th–12th centuries
Genoa	Champagne fairs	Early 13th century
	Black Sea trade	Late 13th century
Venice	Galley fleets; pepper	14th–15th centuries
Portugal	African gold	Late 15th century
	Asian spices	Early/mid 16th century
Netherlands	Baltic trade	Late 16th century
	Asian trade	Early/mid 17th century
Britain I	West Indies products	Late 17th century
	Asian-American trade	Early/mid 18th century
Britain II	Cotton textiles; iron	Late 18th century
	Railroads, steam	Early/mid 19th century
United States	Steel; chemicals; electrics	Early 20th century
	Aviation; automobiles; electronics	Mid 20th century

Source: Modelski and Thompson 1996.

Each lead economy, the global political economy's most active or innovative economic zone at particular points in time, enjoys at least two waves of radical innovation. The technological effects of each wave last approximately 40 to 60 years, although the most dramatic impacts are experienced early in the wave called a K-wave (after the Russian economist, Nikolai Kondratieff, who popularized their existence to some extent in the 1920s). The first wave is crucial to the emergence of a new lead economy. It is also crucial to the emergence of a new global leader because it produces a surplus that can be used to finance military capabilities of global reach to protect and enhance its economic lead.

A lead economy and the leading position in military global reach (which has meant naval capabilities over much of the past 500 to 600 or more years) contributes to victory in the period of turmoil and intensive conflict that tends to follow the political-economic disturbances associated with the emergence of new technological trajectories. These periods of turmoil gradually assumed the shape of global wars after conditions conducive to fusing European regional and global problems became sufficiently prominent. A victory in the intense conflict phase then proves critical to the timing and probability of a second burst of innovation and long-term growth.

In describing a pattern that holds over hundreds of years, we do not mean to suggest that each lead economy and global leader has looked exactly alike. Leads have been strong and weak, as well as somewhere in between. The lead may be based on a broad or narrow technological paradigm that links the cluster of innovations into a set of ways of doing things. By and large, though, each successive link in the lead economy sequence has tended to be more impressive than its predecessors. It is also easy to note that the industrial leaders (after the end of the eighteenth century) have generated much more impressive economic foundations for political-military leadership than was even conceivable in earlier centuries.

Nevertheless, it is difficult to remain a pioneer indefinitely. Technology diffuses in spite of attempts to keep its details secret. Some other economies, certainly not all, are capable of emulating the innovations and perhaps even improving upon them. Some will be especially eager to catch up to the front-runner and surpass its lead if possible. Competition escalates. Protectionist instincts rise to the fore as new producers lobby for insulation from external competitors with head starts. The lead economy begins to see its external markets shrinking or at least becoming much more crowded. Access to markets can take on a zero-sum outlook with competitors concerned that rivals will somehow close future access unless one's own side manages to do the same to the competition first.

The problem is compounded by factors internal to the once-pioneering economy. Initial advantages can be transformed into liabilities. For instance, a location that is ideal in one century as a convenient intermediate point between sources of supply and demand may become a hotly contested battleground in the next century. A home market that is large enough in one era may be dwarfed by the development of much larger home markets elsewhere. Similarly, the leading sectors of one era create psychological and financial commitments that sometime must be abandoned in the next era.

Various types of institutional rigidity can be anticipated as a matter of course. As a pioneering economy, its new products initially have no competition. That can generate complacency that is difficult to overcome when the real competition emerges. There is always considerable risk associated with making commitments to new technological trajectories. If old products are still reasonably profitable, the most prudent thing to do may seem to be a matter of staying the course with one's established specializations rather than assuming the high risk of untried lines of production. By the time the apparent risk is reduced substantially, it is too late to maintain a lead in technological innovation. Moreover, strong vested interests in older ways of doing things are created that are also difficult to overcome when it comes time to strike out in new directions.

Finally, there is the possibility of resource exhaustion in areas that are critical to prevailing leading sectors. Maritime states have literally run out of sailors. Mining states have run out of gold and silver. Industrial producers have consumed their local supplies of wood, coal, and petroleum. Resource depletion may of course stimulate innovation, but there is no guarantee that an alternative resource source will be developed in fast enough time to salvage a faltering lead. Nor is there any guarantee that the location of the new resources will not favor somebody else.

Hence, external factors compete with internal factors to increase the probability that an economy that was once willing to assume high risks and to engage in experimentation, as well as embracing innovation, will become less experimental and more conservative in the future. There is really no reason that a technological leader could not maintain its lead status indefinitely. But there are many reasons that suggest the probability of doing so are not high.

The historical pattern has been one of a single innovating economy developing new technologies that bestow the advantages of controlling a monopoly. While that monopoly status can be preserved its lead economy status is assured. The monopolies are never permanent, though. They erode thanks to technological diffusion/emulation, diminishing returns, and internal rigidities that make developing still newer technologies less likely. The lead economy may remain relatively prosperous in the absolute sense, but it is likely to experience decline relative to other economies and competitors.

We should note that one popular approach to explaining relative decline processes conflates, in our opinion, primary and secondary causes. The primary cause is that the pioneering leader loses its ability to be a step ahead of everybody else in terms of developing significant innovations. This occurs because one leading sector or a cluster of related technologies reaches a point of diminishing marginal returns and is not supplanted indigenously (but perhaps elsewhere) by a new set of leading sectors or technological regime. We view consumption trade-offs and strategic overextensions as secondary causes of decline, not primary ones. One argument (Gilpin 1981), for instance, is that leaders overburden themselves by assuming a lion's share of the protection costs for the global political economy. Resources consumed by the world power's military forces leave less for economic investment purposes at the expense of future growth. The burden is certainly real, but we suggest that, for world powers, it at best aggravates a situation in which the long-term engines of growth have already been slowed. Excessive protection costs, in and of themselves, do not retard ongoing growth as much as they may accelerate growth prospects already in decline.[4]

Another secondary cause from our perspective is the argument (Kennedy 1987) that a global leader makes a number of commitments when its resources are maximal. As relative decline sets in and its resource base erodes, a leader must either reduce its commitments or face an overextended strategic situation with more commitments than it can afford. Overcommitment, again, is a very real process (Thompson and Zuk 1986). Our point is that world powers do not experience relative decline because they have become overextended. Rather, they become overcommitted because they are experiencing relative decline.

Global War

We see global war as an outcome of the combination of processes of concentration and deconcentration operating at both the global and key regional levels of analysis. When the two sets of processes become fused intermittently, the probability of a global war breaking out is greatly enhanced.

Global Concentration Processes

From a systemic perspective, the global political economy is characterized by undulating patterns of capability concentration, followed by deconcentration, and then followed again by reconcentration. We attribute this pattern primarily to the emergence and relative decline of lead economies. The linkage to global war is straightforward. When the global political economy is highly concentrated, the outbreak of a global war is unlikely. After the global political economy has experienced considerable deconcentration, the outbreak of a global war becomes more probable because global wars, inherently, can be seen as succession struggles over which economy will replace the incumbent as the global system's military-political center. In fact, we designate as global wars only those intensive conflicts that lead to a new phase of significant reconcentration and global military-political and economic leadership. In this respect, we admit to being more interested in these wars' roles in the concentration-deconcentration process than we are in their identities as increasingly lethal wars among major powers. Put another way, we think global wars merit special attention as a distinctive set of wars that are a critical part of the global political economy's functioning.

The tendency toward concentration, deconcentration, and reconcentration is much older than the "institution" of global war. We can find instances of concentration and deconcentration going back to 3500 B.C. and the Sumerians, but, in our perspective, the concentration-deconcentration-reconcentration sequence only emerged as a continuous process with the advent of Sung Chinese economic and maritime innovations a millennium ago (Modelski and Thompson 1996). In the period roughly between A.D. 1000 and 1500, we can trace early, transitional versions of successive lead economies in the global, transcontinental sense (Northern and Southern Sung, Genoa, Venice, Portugal). Their fluctuations in relative prosperity appear to be associated with periods of intense conflict that intervene between the twin peaks of economic growth described earlier, but they do not take on the form of the global wars with which we have become more familiar in the twentieth century. After A.D. 1500 or, more precisely, 1494, the global war institution begins to emerge. We assume that this emergence reflects an evolving system experiencing environmental change. The global political economy evolved in such a way that it became increasingly susceptible to intermittent fusion with European regional politics. Global wars are one of the consequences of that evolutionary change.

We will return to both the regional dimensions of global war and the implications for system transformation in later sections. For now, we need to focus on further elaborating the global processes that are most important. We identify five global wars: the Italian and Indian Ocean Wars (1494–1516), the Dutch-Spanish Wars (1580–1608), the Wars of the Grand Alliance (1688–1713), the French Revolutionary and Napoleonic Wars (1792–1815), and World Wars I and II (1914–45). These wars are fought by coalitions of global and other types of powers, as identified in table 2.

The pattern is essentially one of the incumbent global system leader and its allies arrayed against a principal challenger and its allies. For reasons to which we will return in the next section, the challenger has never won. On the other hand, the incumbent leader may also lose its status to one of its allies if the most active economic zone has shifted away from the old leader. In both the Dutch-British and British-American transitions, the political-military shifts in relative status took place during the respective global wars. The junior partner going into the war emerged as the senior partner and the new system leader.

In this respect, we should emphasize that the structure of conflict is more complicated than a simple challenger versus incumbent situation. Declining incumbents select, to some extent, which challengers they will fight and with whom they will ally to meet the intensive challenge. Thompson (1997) argues that this selection process is primarily a function of four variables: maritime-commercial orientation, proximity, similarity (regime type, culture, ideology, and race), and innovative nature. The threats that are seen as most dangerous are those associated with explicitly premeditated challenges that come from dissimilar types of states with fundamentally different strategic orientations. States with strategic foci on utilizing land forces to expand territorial control find it difficult to compete with sea powers other than via attempts at direct conquest. Nearby challengers are less easy to ignore than those located farther away. The more "alien" the challenger, the greater is the likely level of suspicion and misperception in divining motivations and intentions. A challenger and incumbent leader are also more likely to fight if their economic competition is based on similar commercial-technological commodities. If the challenger perceives that the leader will thwart any peaceful positional encroachments, a nonpeaceful competition is more probable.

Similarly, potential challengers adopt different strategies of confrontation. The most traditional approach can be referred to as "capture-the-center," in which the challenger attempts to seize control of the lead economy and its commercial networks. An alternative approach is to avoid attacking the leader on its home ground and to instead focus on attacks on its far-flung commercial networks and the development of alternative networks, as demonstrated by warfare among Portugal, Spain, England, France, and the Netherlands in Asian and American waters. A third strategy involves creating a relatively autonomous subsystem within the world economy that excludes economic competition with the system leader. Napoleon's Continental system, German *Mitteleuropa* aspirations, Japan's Co-prosperity Sphere, and the communist international system of the second half of the twentieth century are all illustrations of this third strategy. How threatening this strategy appears will depend on how coercive the subsystem creation and maintenance processes are and who suffers most from the exclusionary policies. Table 3 suggests that the capture-the-center strategy has gradually lost much of its appeal. The flanking, alternative network approach became increasingly popular in the period most focused on long-distance commerce, while the exclusionary subsystemic approach has become more prevalent in the movement toward increased emphasis on industrial production.

Identifying the Elite Actors and the Long Cycle of Global Leadership

In analyzing global political economy processes, some care must be given to identify which actors are most involved at this level. The tradition in

TABLE 2.

Global Wars and Basic Coalitions

Global Wars	Global Power Coalitions		
1494–1516	Portugal/Spain/England	vs.	France
1580–1608	Netherlands/England/France	vs.	Spain
1688-1713	Britain/Netherlands	vs.	France
1792-1815	Britain/Russia	vs.	France
1914-1945	United States/Britain/France/Russia	vs.	Germany/Japan

Source: Based on Modelski and Thompson 1988, 16.

Table 3.

The Evolution of Challenger Strategies

		Challengers by Type		
Iteration	**Active Zone**	**Territorially Based Autocracies**	**Maritime-Commercial Powers**	**Strategies**
1	Northern Sung	Chin		Capture-the-center/imperial expansion
			Southern Sung	
2	Southern Sung	Mongols		Capture-the-center/imperial expansion
3			Genoa	Alternative network development
			Venice	Flanking/skirmishing
4	Genoa		Venice	Alternative network development/flanking/skirmishing
5	Venice	France I		Capture-the-center/imperial expansion
			Portugal	Alternative network development/flanking
6	Portugal	Spain		Capture-the-center/imperial expansion
			Netherlands	Alternative network development/flanking/skirmishing
			England	Alternative network development/flanking/skirmishing
7	Netherlands	France II		Capture-the-center/imperial expansion
			England	Skirmishing/alternative network development/subsystemic protection at home and in colonies
8	Britain I/II	France III		Alternative network development/subsystemic protection and regional/imperial bloc formation (Capture-the-center contemplated)
9	Britain II	Germany I		Industrial competition/alternative network development
			United States	Industrial competition/subsystemic protection and regional expansion
10		Germany II Japan I		Industrial competition/subsystemic protection through regional/imperial bloc formation
11	United States	USSR		Subsystemic protection through withdrawal and regional/imperial bloc formation
			Japan II?	Industrial competition/subsystemic protection at home and regional bloc formation

Source: Thompson 1997b, 307–8.

international relations has been to treat all major powers as if they were similar. We argue that only some major powers are elite players in the global political economy and its global wars. One objective way to identify who is a global player is to require that they expend resources in developing a military capability to participate in, and to protect, long-distance, interregional transactions and leading-sector industrial production. Over the past 500 years (and before) this type of global reach capability has translated most readily into naval and, more recently, aerospace power.

Once the Portuguese circumnavigated Africa, the flow of east-west trade became increasingly maritime in nature. East-west trade, of course, had long preceded the Portuguese entry into the Indian Ocean (by more than 1,500 years), but it had oscillated between overland (Silk Roads) and maritime routes. The overland routes depended on some element of stability and safe passage through the adjacent territories stretching from China to the Mediterranean. When there was stability and relatively safe passage, both overland and maritime routes were utilized. The maritime routes seem to have been utilized more heavily as a fallback when instability on land increased the economic risks and transportation costs of cross-Eurasian caravans. The Portuguese and their other European successors altered these processes by hijacking the maritime routes at a time when the overland routes were characterized by disorder and then ensuring that the maritime routes would persist as the favored path for east-west transactions.

Naval power was necessary to first hijack the east-west maritime routes and then to hold on to them and the initially precarious footholds some Europeans were able to acquire around the maritime rimland of AfroEurasia. Naval power was also necessary to compete with, and to defeat, rival global powers. Mahanian command of the sea, which means protecting one's sea lanes, became a paramount war objective. So too did neutralizing the competition's global reach capabilities. Thus, not only were navies necessary to protect commercial routes and to attack rivals, they were also needed to defend the home country from attacks. Some degree of insularity may have been one of the strongest prerequisites for the ascent to economic and political-military leadership in the global system, but natural defenses and barriers were never sufficient. They had to be assisted by naval force.

Thus we require that global powers demonstrate a minimal naval capability (10 percent of the global capability pool) in specific naval resources that evolve along with technological change in naval weapons systems. Table 4 outlines the criteria employed. We also require that global powers indicate some interest in employing their sea power in more than their immediate neighborhood. Operations in only one sea do not necessarily indicate much involvement in long-distance and transoceanic activities. Regional sea power, therefore, is not sufficient for elite global status. Moreover, we use the same information base to objectively identify when one global power has achieved something approximating a monopoly position (50 percent or more of the global reach capabilities) and thereby earning the designation of "world power" to indicate its distinctive leading position.

The global power elite has remained a small group: Portugal (1494–1580), Spain (1494–1808), England/Britain (1494–1945), France (1494–1945), the Netherlands (1579–1810), Russia/the Soviet Union/

TABLE 4.

Basic Shifts in the Measurement of Global Naval Capability

Period	Indicators
1494–1654	The number of state-owned, armed sailing vessels capable of undertaking oceanic voyages.
1655–1860	The number of ships of the line, subject to an escalating minimal number of guns carried to qualify as frontline fighting vessels (1655–70: 30 guns or more; 1671–90: 40 guns or more; 1691–1756: 50 guns or more; 1757–1860: 60 guns or more).
1816–1945	The level of naval expenditure, which is used to smooth the several abrupt technological changes experienced in the nineteenth and early twentieth centuries and which is given equal weight with the appropriate ship counts in a combined index.
1861–1945	The number of first-class battleships, subject to escalating minimal attributes in ship and gun size after 1910 (distinguishing between pre- and post-Dreadnought battleships).
1946–1993	The number of heavy or attack aircraft carriers and, after 1960, the number of nuclear attack submarines and the number of sea-based nuclear missile warheads weighted according to equivalent megatonnage (EMT) and counter military potential (CMP)—with shares of carriers, attack submarines, EMT, and CMP given equal weight in a combined index.

Source: Modelski and Thompson 1988.

Russia (1714 to the present), the United States (1816 to the present), Germany (1871–1945), and Japan (1875–1945). Of this group, only four global powers have qualified as world powers: Portugal, the Netherlands, Britain, and the United States. Each of the major upward bumps in the naval power concentration series (measured as the world power's share) sketched in figure 1 can be readily identified as a phase of world power leadership. Figure 1 portrays what we refer to as the long cycle of leadership in the global political economy.

It is further possible to break each iteration of the cycle into four phases. In fact, two different set of phases have been proposed (Modelski 1987). Which one is more useful depends on whether one wishes to emphasize the ascent of a world power (agenda setting, coalition building, macrodecision, and execution) or its decline (global war, world power, delegitimation, deconcentration). Table 5 outlines the hypothesized timing of both sets of phases. The utility of the periods is that certain types of behavior are associated with each phase. For instance, the most intensive conflict occurs in the global war/macrodecision phase. The next most conflictual phase is delegitimation/agenda building, which, in some respects, is a response to the erosion of the phase of leadership, order, and peak concentration found in the world power/execution period. These phases also relate to the timing of economic growth fluctuations

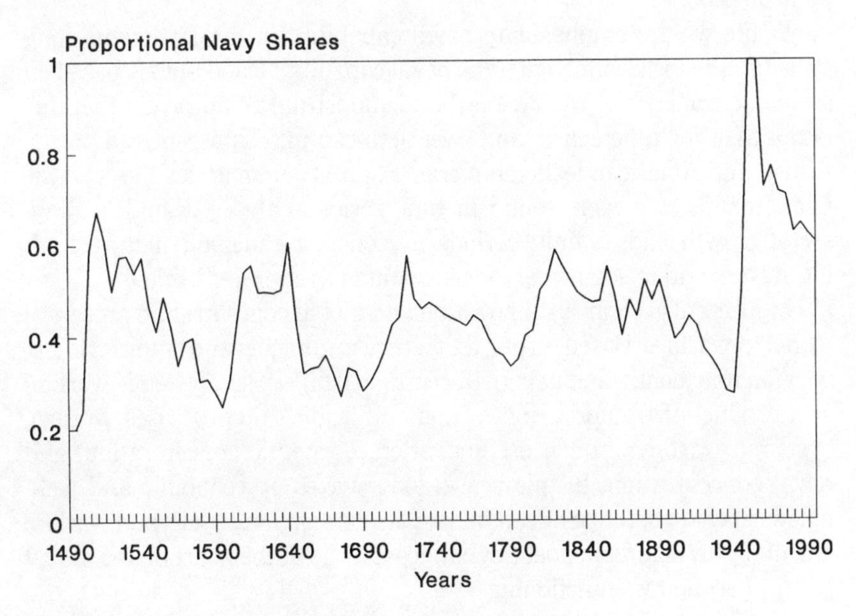

FIGURE 1. The long cycle of global leadership

TABLE 5.

Leadership Long Cycle Phases in the Modern Era

Agenda-Setting/ Delegitimation	Coalition Building/ Deconcentration	Macrodecision/ Global War	Execution/ World Power
1430–1460	1460–1494	1494–1516	1516–1540 (Portugal)
1540–1560	1560–1580	1580–1609	1609–1640 (Netherlands)
1640–1660	1660–1688	1688–1714	1714–1740 (Britain I)
1740–1763	1763–1792	1792–1815	1815–1850 (Britain II)
1850–1873	1873–1914	1914–1945	1945–1973 (United States)
1973–2000	2000–2030	2030–2050	2050–

Source: Based on Modelski and Thompson 1996, 54.

with new leading-sector spurts taking place approximately during the latter portion of a deconcentration/coalition-building phase and during the world power/execution phase. This pattern reflects one of the fundamental coevolutionary processes we have found propelling the global political economy.

While we are emphasizing naval capability in the leadership long cycle figure, it is assumed that the naval capability leadership is based on economic leadership. We have earlier demonstrated empirically that this is the case for nineteenth- and twentieth-century data centered on the British and American leadership eras. Figure 2 summarizes the "causal" relationships that were found in time series analyses. Rapid leading-sector growth leads to finite periods of economic leadership in those leading sectors and to somewhat longer-lasting naval power leads.

Figure 2 also connects innovation and global concentration processes to global warfare. Based on our theoretical arguments and empirical findings (on nineteenth- and twentieth-century data), we see systemic warfare as a product of economic innovation and leadership processes. In turn, systemic warfare influences innovation, economic concentration, and naval concentration. In this sense, long waves of economic and technological change, the political-military leadership long cycle, and warfare are all highly interdependent dynamics that lie at the heart of the global political economy's functioning.[5]

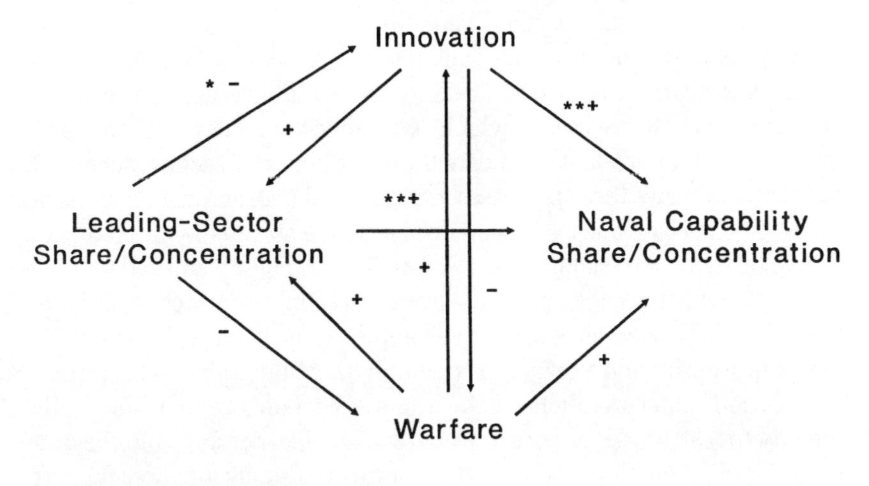

FIGURE 2. Innovation, concentration, and warfare

In terms of general format, this perspective does not differ all that much from alternative interpretations of system dynamics relating political economy and war. Joshua Goldstein's model (1988, 1991a) essentially sees the expansion of the world economy influencing positively the distribution of military power and the severity of war, but in a less than systematic way. Terry Boswell and Michael Sweat's model (1991) also views economic expansion leading positively to the expansion of state resources, and, in turn, the expansion of state resources leads positively and systematically to the size of war. Brian Pollins's (1996; Pollins and Murrin 1997) model, which is more similar to the Goldstein "loose coevolution" perspective, views long-term economic and political-military processes as systematically interrelated but inherently separate processes subject to different dynamics.

Although there is clear overlap in these empirical models, there are also important differences of assumptions and process timing. Our approach emphasizes the system leader's technological innovation as the mainspring of economic growth and contraction that, we contend, has assumed the shape of a twin-peaked kondratieff wave phenomenon with each of the two peaks separated by intensive conflict. The other models are more comfortable beginning with the given of economic expansion and contraction tendencies and generally prefer to make a greater distinction between long waves of economic versus political/military fluctuations. Indeed, there appears to be a fundamental divergence of opinion emerging over the degree to which "economic" and "political-military" processes are interrelated. Goldstein and Pollins represent a school of thought that views these processes as weakly related. For instance, one of the things an economic expansion does is create surplus wealth that can be exploited for war-making purposes. If the war chest is utilized for purposes of systemic violence, subsequent economic contraction is more likely. In this "loose coevolution" interpretation, the linkages between economic prosperity and warfare are certainly there but indirect. In a "tight coevolution" interpretation, such as ours, economic expansion leads directly to a struggle for succession over global leadership, and the outcome of this struggle sets up the appropriate conditions for another spurt of economic expansion.[6]

But there are other differences as well. Other analysts do not make the same distinction between global and world economies that we do. Our approach gives more emphasis to naval concentration than do the other approaches' more general treatment of capability. Nor do we all identify the same wars as the most significant ones. The Boswell/Sweat and Pollins/Murrin models have expanded the core concerns by introducing colonial expansion as a way in which tensions due to economic change have been rechanneled away from war.[7] Pollins's work (see also Bennett 1997) also expands the focus on systemic warfare to interstate conflict. Finally, our approach is the only one to emphasize the fusion of global and regional processes—a subject yet to be discussed.

Two points must be stressed here. One is that the models are overlapping but certainly not identical. A second is that all of these empirical models are fairly recent in origin. Both facts are most encouraging. We are not fighting over "night and day" issues of interpretation in which one group of analysts says the world is round and another says that it is square.[8] We all see processes of economic and military concentration intertwined with warfare. We disagree about what drives economic growth, precisely how and to what extent economic and political-military processes are intertwined, how to measure the processes, and over which actors and wars should receive the most attention. Such disagreements are normal and healthy. They are also encouraging in the sense that the element of convergence, despite different assumptions, suggests that analysis is generally on the right track. Long-term fluctuations in economic growth and capability distributions clearly are linked to the onset and outcomes of the most intensive wars in the system.

The Intermittent Fusion of Global and Regional Processes

An exclusive focus on global politics is inadequate, for the global system is not an autonomous sphere of activity. On occasion, global politics have become fused with regional politics. These fusions can take many forms. Ambitious states in any region may make coercive bids for regional leadership. Vietnam in Southeast Asia or Iraq in the Middle East come to mind as recent examples. Just how dangerous these bids are depends in part on how salient is the region in which they occur. Regional concentration processes in more peripheral regions are apt to be less destabilizing than similar processes in more central regions. The appropriate comparison is between the Third Indochina War and the Gulf War versus, say, World War II. All three events were lethal, but the first two contests were unlikely to become "globalized." The third one spread throughout the planet relatively quickly. They all began as subregional or regional contests. The difference is that World War II emerged in part from a contest over the control of Europe—still one of the most salient or central regions of that time.

It also mattered that the European region was the home base for a number of global powers. It is easier to remain aloof from more distant contests than ones that take place in one's own backyard. Salience and proximity help explain why European regional international relations, on occasion, have been so explosive for the global political economy. We find this intermittent fusion of European regional and global politics absolutely essential to our explanation of structural change and global war. We also acknowledge a strong reliance on Dehio's (1962) interpretation of the history of European international relations, which we have coopted for the purposes of our model.

Unlike other regions of the world, especially eastern Asia, no single power ever established hegemony over Europe for very long. The basic Dehioan insight is that this outcome was due to what appears to be a relatively unique geopolitical pattern. Before a would-be regional hegemon could unify Europe coercively, counterweights emerged from areas immediately adjacent to the region. Introducing extraregional resources, they were repeatedly able to block the creation of European hegemony.

The eastern counterweight supplied brute land force. The western counterweight increasingly specialized in sea power, which was, in turn, predicated on the development of specializations in the role of commercial intermediary among Europe, Asia, and America. When both counterweights were operative, an aspiring regional hegemon was forced to fight a resource-draining war on two fronts that it was likely to lose. The outcome was an intermittently renewed balance of European power that depended on the region remaining open to extraregional resources controlled by flanking states.

The regional motor of the balancing dynamic hinged on an intermittent rise of a hegemonic aspirant and the concentration of regional capabilities. France inaugurated this system in its 1494 attack on Italy. It was resisted by Spain primarily and then for a short time by a unified Hapsburg entity. A Franco-Ottoman coalition thwarted the second bid, this time on the part of the Hapsburgs. Both of these initial efforts preceded the emergence of a western maritime power capable of functioning as a counterweight. With some English assistance, the Netherlands provided the first maritime counterweight to Philip II's bid for supremacy. By the mid–seventeenth century, Spain had surrendered its regional lead to a restrengthened France. Louis XIV's late-seventeenth-century activities came to be perceived as a direct threat to Europe and the global political economy. A second Anglo-Dutch coalition developed the first large-scale maritime blockade of the European continent and defeated the expanding navy of France in 1692. Between 1692 and the next destruction of the French fleet in 1805 at Trafalgar, the generally eroding, relative strength of the French kept the midcentury Anglo-French fighting from turning into a full-fledged struggle over either regional or global supremacy.

Unlike the earlier, more gradual bids for regional hegemony, the third French bid in 1792 emerged abruptly and was unusually successful for a few years before the Napoleonic variant was crushed in 1814 and 1815. After 1815, the main emphasis of global concern shifted away from the European region to the Russo-British sparring along their mutual Eurasian imperial boundaries. The British remained worried about the French potential for causing trouble in Europe for some time after 1815 but a fourth French bid, with hindsight, was increasingly unlikely. One reason was the emergence of a unified Germany.

Whether or not the ascending Germany of the late nineteenth century was merely seeking equality with other leading powers or European domination, a mixture of commercial and naval rivalries combined with geographical proximity increased the probability that Britain would identify Germany as its primary threat. In World War I, Germany then proceeded as if it were indeed seeking regional supremacy. By World War II, which can be seen as a continuation of the first world war, both Germany and Japan had become more overt and ambitious about the extent of their regional aspirations. The end of that war led to the territorial dismemberment of the principal challenger (Germany). The division of the entire region into American and Soviet spheres completed the process of diminishing the regional autonomy of Europe and, presumably, some of its ability to generate local problems that could intrude into the functioning of the global political economy. Although the significance of European economies for the global political economy remains high, a renewed, coercive bid for European regional domination seems unlikely.

From a regional perspective, the principal dynamic of this system has been the movement from a peak in the strength of the leading regional power through a long trough to next peak and so on, as illustrated in figure 3. The long troughs were characterized by leveling process. The regional leader that had peaked earlier was in gradual decline, thereby encouraging and facilitating the emergence of new regional contenders.

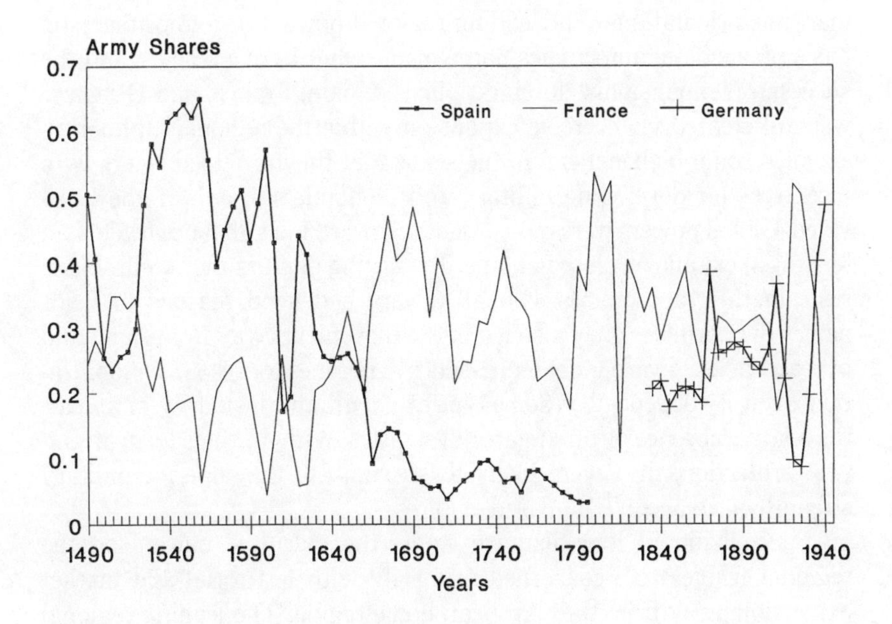

FIGURE 3. Regional leaders in western Europe

During the troughs, relative power relationships and alignments were unstable. The troughs not only provided windows of opportunity for the emergence of new land powers. They also encouraged the upwardly mobile to challenge the regional status quo. At the same time, the strength of the western maritime powers should also be most concentrated during the troughs in regional concentration. The less the threat from adjacent land empires, the more the maritime powers could thrive.

We thus envision the rhythms of two dissynchronized cycles or waves of power concentration, centered on two different types of major powers. On land, the leading regional power waxed and waned. At sea, the leading global power ascended and declined. For the most part, the one declined as the other peaked, but not in a completely dissynchronized fashion. Declining global leaders encouraged would-be regional hegemons. Suppressing would-be regional hegemons galvanized new global leaders to emerge or, in the case of Britain, to reemerge. It is not too much of an exaggeration to say that regional and global powers represent two very different "species" of power. To be sure, there was overlap. Some strong regional powers in Europe were also contenders in the global political economy. But they were never quite as successful as they might have been given their roots in regional/territorial orientations as opposed to maritime orientations. The leading regional powers rose to primacy on basis of absolute autocracies, large armies and bureaucracies, and the success of expansionist foreign policies. Spain, France, and Germany were all created via coercive expansion within the region. Neighboring enemies could be beneficial in the sense that they provided rulers with incentives for developing military and economic strength, if they survived. Global powers were more oriented toward long-distance trade than territorial expansion close to home. To varying degrees they were able to restrain their autocracies. Global powers had good reasons to favor navies over armies. They also led in the movement away from command bureaucracies toward more representative regimes for resource mobilization. Security depended on some type of geographic insularity, or at least the relative absence of proximate adversaries. Without some form of natural protection, they were likely to succumb to the superior military strength of adjacent, land-based empires.

Specializing in long-distance trade, the maritime powers on the regional fringe were concerned primarily with territorial and market expansion away from the European home region. The leading regional powers tended to be overly preoccupied with territorial expansion within their home region. Operating on entirely different strategic vectors, global and regional powers, one might have thought, were not inherently likely to collide often. Their interests pointed in opposite directions.

Nonetheless, conflicting interests and collisions occurred regularly. The problem was that if a regional power was successful in creating European supremacy, it was well situated to take on the global political economy as its next objective. By seeking control over adjacent sources of economic prosperity, which historically meant attacking either northern Italy or the Low Countries, an aspiring hegemon could quickly acquire a platform for a global challenge. Successful expansion into these areas offered quick fixes for wealth imbalances and maritime capability. Therefore, the leading global powers always had strong incentives to prevent a major land power from attaining European supremacy. Not only might they lose access to important markets nearby, the potential for a direct threat to control of the global political economy was not difficult to discern.

Aspiring regional hegemons acted as if they were not always fully aware of the global implications of their local strategies. But this misperception only made conflict with the western maritime flankers all the more likely. When the regional leaders did announce plans for the control of interregional trade, the potential for acute conflict across the regional and global levels was even further accentuated. On the other hand, collisions between an aspiring regional hegemon and the eastern counterweights depended on the less subtle dynamics of mutually timed interests in expansion into the same territories or strategic errors in timing that forced the aspirants to fight on multiple fronts more or less at the same time.

If a would-be regional hegemon appeared to be expanding toward the immediate north/northwest (the Low Countries) or, earlier, the southeast (Italy) as well as toward the east (the Rhine or eastern Europe), the probability of mobilizing resistance on both flanks increased. Would-be regional hegemons in Europe have repeatedly made this same mistake. They made their own victory less likely by encouraging the simultaneous extraregional interventions from different directions that would work toward preserving the European balance of power.

The western flank learned that hegemonic aspirants could be contained by encircling the European peninsula. The maritime containment strategy might be defeated by either breaking through the naval blockade at sea or circumventing it via land if it was possible to avoid antagonizing land forces to the east. Despite repeated tries, the leading regional powers were never able to break through at sea. Nor were they able to avoid becoming bogged down in some type of eastern front fighting. In the pursuit of these goals, the aspiring regional hegemon in Europe tended to overextend itself and exhausted its capability to wage war.

The iterative introduction of extraregional resources could not be repeated an infinite number of times. Drawing in the flanking powers and their resources increasingly reduced the ratio of power that could be mustered within the European region relative to what could be mobilized away from Europe. Eventually, challengers from the European region could no longer expect to compete with stronger states outside Europe.

This finite durability of the classical European regional system may have depended on a unique constellation of geohistorical factors. Would-be regional conquerors found themselves caught between offshore rocks and eastern hard places. Despite repeated attempts, European hegemons could not overcome the western and eastern flanks with much more access to the resources useful for war. Regionally biased strategies to overcome these barriers to supremacy proved to be largely self-defeating. The European subsystem retained its pluralistic structure but, ultimately, at the expense of its onetime autonomy and salience. The Soviet-American cold war subordinated the European region to a global contest after centuries of regional problems diverting global interests and resources.

We contend that it has been the interaction between global and regional structural changes that have generated the contexts for the world's most significant and serious wars. From a regional vantage point, the relationship between concentration and the probability of global war is positive. Greater concentration leads to the greater likelihood of intensive conflict. From the global perspective, though, the relationship is reversed. High concentration leads to a decreased likelihood of intensive conflict. The problem has been that these structural rhythms have been out of sync with one another. Global concentration levels tend to be low when regional concentration levels are on the rise.

Given the intermittent fusion of regional and global political problems, global war has been most probable when the regional and global concentration trends have been most dangerous. There is nothing mystical about these structural trends because they reflect the ascendancy of one or more regional powers and the relative decline of the leading global power. Regional-global structures are in transition and the combined trends in structural change are highly lethal—as demonstrated repeatedly over the past five centuries (and in fig. 4).

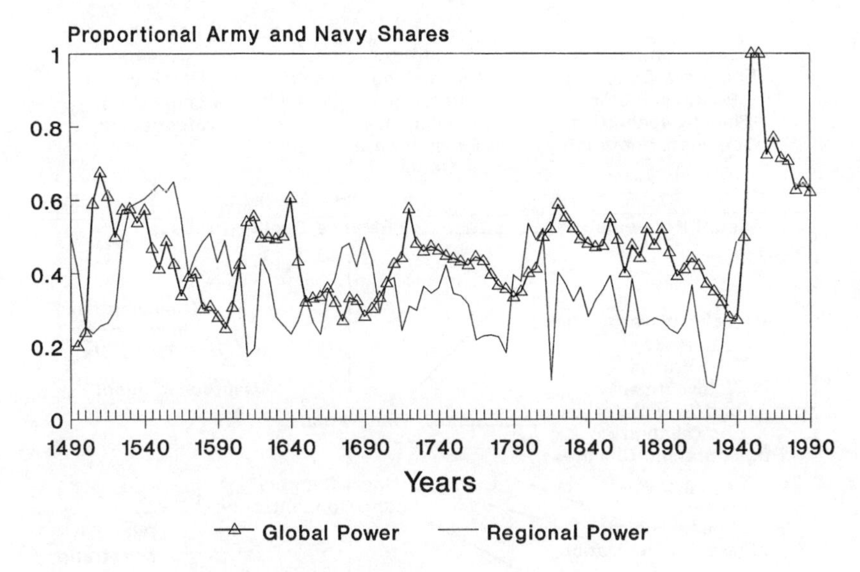

FIGURE 4. Regional and global concentration

Model Summation and Transformation Prospects

Figure 5 summarizes our interpretation of the relationship between global war and the political economy of structural change over the past 500 years. At the core of the model is the tendency for clusters of radical technological innovation to emerge and reemerge. One state is the principal pioneer, beneficiary, and agent of diffusion of these innovations throughout the global political economy based on long-distance commerce and advanced industrial production. But economic change this radical is unsettling and destabilizing. Old leaders are pushed aside. New leaders emerge and fight over whose policy preferences will be predominant in structuring the global political economy.

These global processes have been linked to European concentration processes roughly between 1494 and 1945. The strongest land powers in western Europe have generated periodic challenges of declining global leaders—or, at least, that is the way it has been perceived by the declining global leader. The declining global leader has organized a coalition to suppress the European threat. From that winning coalition, new global leaders have tended to emerge as its predecessor and coalition partner exhausts itself in the ensuing global war.

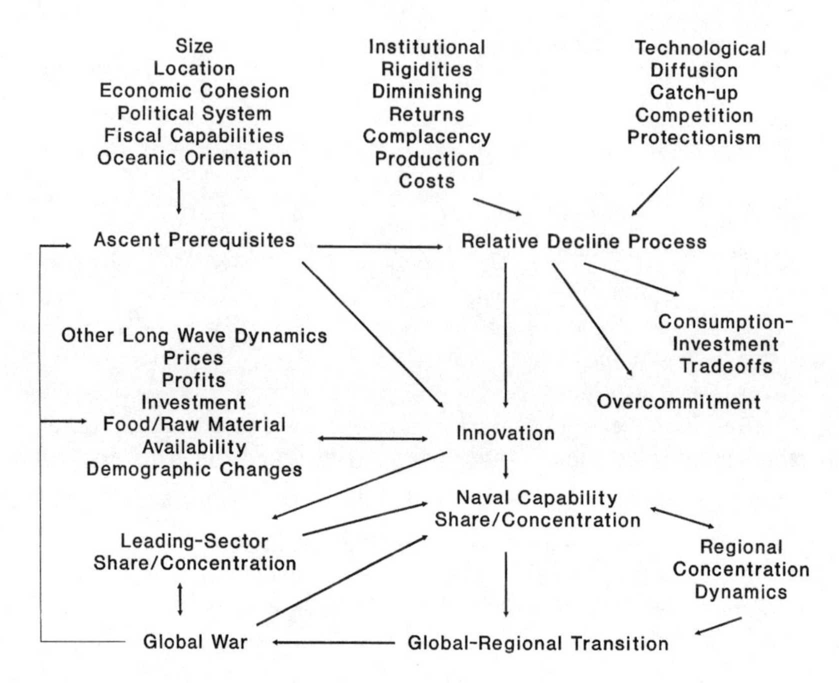

FIGURE 5. Relationship between global war and the political economy of structural change

A variety of processes are linked to the innovation-concentration-warfare core dynamics. There are processes of regional concentration that lead to the fusion of regional and global politics. Another nest of processes is related to the processes of the system leader's ascent and relative decline (internal and external to the system leader as well as consumption tradeoffs and strategic overextension problems). Still another nest of presumably interacting processes are the economic and sociological processes thought to be related to long-term economic growth (such as prices, interest rates, investment, population growth, the development of infrastructure, North-South tensions and debt cycles, generational change, protectionism, and public attitudes). This particular nest has gone undiscussed in this essay because the relationships have yet to be delineated adequately and because it is presumed that they are less close to the global war phenomena than the topics that have been discussed. Another complex that has also gone undiscussed due to the sheer complexity of the subject are the impacts of warfare, and especially global war, on a whole range of phenomena.[9]

Our model-building efforts are ambitious but they are not intended to establish nomothetic laws about international relations and world politics. We would be among the first to acknowledge that international relations have not always worked the way our story suggests. Indeed, the long perspective we adopt makes it very difficult to ignore the significant transformations that the global political economy has undergone. It should not be surprising then if we say that we do not assume that international relations must continue to work the same way in the future as it does now. We have noted at least two quite significant transformations: (1) the emergence of a continuous sequence of concentration-deconcentration-reconcentration beginning around A.D. 1000 and (2) the emergence of global wars beginning around A.D. 1500. Once these processes or dimensions have emerged, it is not carved in stone that they must persist into the indefinite future. Other processes, such as democratization, may emerge and, in doing so, interact with and alter already existing processes in both linear and nonlinear ways.

However, we may not be in a particularly good position to talk about future, long-term transformations of how the system operates. They do not appear to be all that predictable. Even worse, we are only beginning to appreciate just what transformations have taken place already. It is safe to say that an analyst writing some 500 years in the future should have better hindsight on these questions. That still leaves us with some expectation that we say something about the near future, especially in a period of flux in which many observers believe that the past no longer has much to tell us about the present and future.

In the near future, we think four possibilities are most worth contemplating:

1. The nature of technological innovation has been transformed toward the end of the twentieth century such that it is no longer possible for one economy to monopolize innovation rents and/or to provide economic, political, and military leadership.
2. A future global war is too irrational to contemplate.
3. World War II put an end to the intermittent fusion of European and global politics and, as a consequence, made the global political economy less vulnerable to regional disruptions (and global wars).
4. The processes of the global political economy will continue more or less as before, with an increasing vulnerability to eastern Eurasian problems as opposed to the last 500 years of vulnerability to western Eurasian disruptions.

There can be no denying the apparent rapid pace of technological change in the current period. But, minimally, that only means that we are in the midst of another change in technological regimes, one presumably structured around information systems, among other new technologies. If the new leading sectors also prove to have a discernible life cycle in terms of eventual diminishing returns, the likelihood of continuing long wave-like fluctuations in economic growth is high. It is also not abundantly clear who, if anyone, will monopolize the pioneering role and profits in developing the application of information systems. But it is clear that American and Japanese firms and entrepreneurs appear to be well in the lead over the rest of the world. Something similar may have taken place in the late nineteenth century when Germany and the United States were the principal contenders for succession to the British technological lead. Scenario one may yet take place, but there is not much that is going on now to suspect that the processes of technological change with which we are most concerned have undergone substantial transformation.

The second scenario focuses on the irrationality of fighting a third world war that no one could conceivably walk away from as a clear winner. We would like to think that is a very strong scenario. There are, however, at least three problems. One, the stakes involved in deciding policy for the global political economy are very great. The temptation to use coercion may be equally great and as great as it has been in the past. Two, the tendency to fuse regional and global politics complicates the ability of declining global leaders and ascending regional leaders to steer clear of war.[10] It is also never entirely clear to the decision makers that decisions to go to war will ultimately lead to full-scale, global war. Finally, the advent of nuclear weapons at the end of World War II and their contribution to the irrationality of war may have facilitated greatly the ensuing cold war and the avoidance of a war between the United States and the Soviet Union. Yet it did not preclude at least one close call in 1962. For that matter, it has always been irrational for the principal challenger to engage in wars on multiple fronts. That has not stopped challengers from falling into that strategic trap repeatedly over the last several hundred years. Therefore, scenario two may also be right, but it may also be as much wishful thinking as anything else.

The third and fourth scenarios can be treated together since they both focus on global-regional tensions. Scenario 3 seems quite plausible. The regional salience of Europe has certainly diminished. If major European global players reemerge in terms of technological innovation and global reach in the future, it seems more likely that they will represent some type of partial or full unification of Western Europe. That should preclude intra-European contests spilling over into the management of the global political economy. The real question, though, is whether we have truly transcended the potential for regional troublemaking. Without doubt, some potential for these kinds of problems (i.e., coercive attempts at regional hegemony) persist in the Middle East, south Asia, Southeast Asia, and, now, the newly independent Central Eurasian region. But their potentials for creating problems for the global political economy also seem limited.

The same cannot be said for east Asia, which also has a long and continuing history of rivalry, hegemonic schemes, and attempts at power concentration. Moreover, it, or more accurately, parts of it are increasingly one of the foci of technological innovation. The third disturbing element is China. It is not inconceivable that China could break up along lines similar to the disintegration of the Soviet empire. China could also become tightly integrated into a liberal and interdependent global order. But it is also conceivable that Chinese decision makers could decide to pursue foreign policy schemes that resembled those of earlier Hapsburg, French, and German decision makers in a different part of Eurasia. Should this last possibility emerge several decades down the road, the vulnerability of the global political economy to regional disruptions may reassert itself.

Although we would like to be more confident that we know how things will evolve in the future, we are not. If the pattern of the last millennium is maintained into the next one without major modification, we are in for another round of twin-peaked innovation spurts, separated by a period of intensive conflict and possibly the fusion of regional and global processes. These predictions might take place roughly in the middle of the next century (2030–50). But far from being as deterministic as some of our critics suggest, our perspective on the future evolution of the global political economy tells us only that it is likely to combine simultaneously elements of path dependency (history matters) and open-endedness (evolutionary futures are uncertain). That also seems to be the way it has emerged over the past 6,000 years, episodically intermixing substantial elements of continuity and transformation. To avoid another world war or at least another bout of intensive conflict over global policy questions, we will need to see less continuity and more transformation in the next quarter-century than we have seen in the past quarter-century.

Notes

1. The core works in the leadership long cycle perspective are Modelski (1978, 1987, 1996), Modelski and Modelski (1988), Modelski and Thompson (1988, 1989, 1996); Rasler and Thompson (1989, 1994); and Thompson (1988). This chapter follows the approach taken in Rasler and Thompson (1994) most closely. We will not spend much time discussing how our approach differs from a variety of alternative approaches to similar questions. Space considerations argue against such discussion and we have already addressed many of these issues elsewhere (in particular, see Thompson 1983a, 1983b, 1985, 1986, 1988, 1996; Modelski and Thompson 1989; and Rasler and Thompson 1994). We note a number of substantive criticisms that have emerged in the following analyses: Rapkin (1983, 1986, 1987); Zolberg (1983); Levy (1985b, 1991); Rosecrance (1987); Nye (1990a, 1990b); Goldstein and Rapkin (1991); Arquilla (1992); Vasquez (1993); Houweling and Siccama (1993, 1994); Denemark (1997); Frank (1998). We will not be addressing them directly in this chapter either but we do pay attention to these criticisms and have addressed some of them directly (see Modelski 1983a and Thompson and Modelski 1994), just as we continue to modify, extend, and elaborate our theoretical framework—in part due to external feedback. Finally, there is still another literature that debates the cyclical and linear/nonlinear nature of war and economic processes (Conybeare 1990, 1992; Beck 1991; Richards 1993; Sayrs 1993; Mansfield 1994; Williams and Huckfeldt 1996; and S. Bennett 1997) that we will not address here directly either. Our position on the cyclical question is expressed in Thompson and Rasler (1988). Generally, we view the attempt to find strict periodicities misdirected when no one really argues a case for strict periodicity.
2. For an important qualification of this generalization, see Modelski and Thompson (1987), who hypothesize that periods of relatively high conflict alternate with periods of relatively low conflict within each long cycle. The global war phase, of course, is one of high conflict, followed by a world leadership phase (low conflict), an intermediate delegitimization phase in which the world order's status quo comes under attack (high conflict), and then a period of deconcentration (low conflict) just before another phase of global war.
3. Some analysts have tended to characterize our approach as one focusing largely on political-military variables, but the economic emphasis emerged early and, we thought, reasonably consistently. See, in particular, Modelski (1981, 1982) and Thompson (1988, 1990a, 1992a) in addition to Rasler and Thompson (1994) and Modelski and Thompson (1996).
4. For our empirical analyses of these questions, see Rasler and Thompson (1988, 1989, 1991, 1992a, 1994) and Rasler (1990).

5. Rasler and Thompson (1994) were able to demonstrate this empirically with a series of bivariate, Granger causality analyses. Reuveny and Thompson (1997b) take this analysis one step further with a multivariate, VAR examination that essentially confirms and extends the 1994 analysis to include indirect relationships. In both these analyses, the empirical focus is on British and/or U.S. warfare and preparations for warfare—and not on global war per se.
6. A third interpretation is that the coevolutionary pattern is not continuous across time. See Williams, McGinnis, and Thomas (1994).
7. The colonialism angle has actually received considerable empirical attention but usually in isolation of other processes. See, for example, Chase-Dunn and Rubinson (1979), Bergesen and Schoenberg (1980), McGowan (1985), Boswell (1989), Chase-Dunn (1989), and Strang (1991).
8. A pertinent example of a "night and day" debate on these issues of structural change is reviewed in Thompson (1999c).
9. Related war impact analyses are Rasler and Thompson (1983, 1985a, 1985b, 1989, 1992b) and Thompson (1994).
10. Global wars raise special deterrence problems. See Modelski and Morgan (1985) and Thompson (1997/1998).

Confronting the Principles of the Power Cycle

Changing Systems Structure, Expectations, and War

CHARLES F. DORAN

Power cycle theory discloses and elucidates the uniquely international-political "perspective of statecraft." The *power cycle,* the generalized path of a state's relative power change over long time periods, reflects at once the changing structure of the system and the state's rise and decline as a great power. It encompasses each state and the system in a "single dynamic" of changing systemic share. The *principles of the power cycle* explain what sets the cycles in motion and the peculiar nonlinearities of relative power change. For the researcher confronting long-standing puzzles of concept and historical interpretation, the power cycle is a potent analytic device that serves to unify, simplify, clarify, and correct. To attain such an encompassing perspective, however, the analyst must first confront the full complexities of structural dynamics and the greatest paradox of power itself. In the hour of its greatest achievement, the state is driven onto unexpected paths by the bounds of the system. The tides of history have suddenly and unexpectedly shifted against it.

Power cycle analysis seeks both a clear understanding of such structural shifts and insight into the mind-set of contemporaneous statesmen who must contend with them.[1] A systemic construct, the power cycle traces a state's development as a major international-political actor regarding a variety of leadership roles. Both actualized and latent capabilities are necessary to create and sustain its long-term growth in power and role.[2] But this power of statecraft is intrinsically "relative" and hence a conceptual sphere removed from the "absolute" output of interest in economics. A state's international-political behavior is conditioned by how its absolute capability (numerator) compares with the absolute capability of the system (denominator) in the *relative power ratio*—its current ratio and its projected change.[3] A given state power cycle records, at each time point, the state's clearly defined past and the likely trajectory of its yet-to-be-determined future power and role vis-à-vis that system.[4] It reveals at each step how statesmen would perceive the state's past and future evolution as a major player in the system. The power cycle is thus a state "image" in the sense of Kenneth Boulding (1956) and Herbert Kelman (1965, 25), a conception encompassing "specific memories and expectations" as well as perceptions of the present.

With future projections of power and role embedded in the cycle, this uniquely international-political *dynamic* captures the international-political *concerns* of statecraft. It thereby also fosters a concept of general equilibrium to overcome the deficiencies of the balance of power. To confront the principles of the power cycle, the principles driving systemic change, is to discover the *expectations,* and the *unexpected nonlinearities,* of relative power change that so greatly impact state behavior.

Observe that power cycle analysis overcomes the limitations of so-called calculative and perceptual models that, according to Aaron Friedberg (1988, 13–14), divide the assessment of power. It fully integrates calculative and perceptual assessments in a single "estimation" process, seeking a sense of the trend over broad periods of history. A model in which power is a "stock of one or more commodities" and "adaptation to changes [is] continuous" surely does not represent reality. Nor does a model focusing solely on "crises or dramatic events as the most likely agents of attitude change." Perceptions cannot rest on subjective judgment alone (Britain and Germany circa 1908 needed some idea how many Dreadnoughts the other had to develop a naval strategy). Conversely, hard figures that never confront the paradoxes and complexity of perception (let alone the subjective will and perceptual ambiguity surrounding naval engagement) could scarcely be representative of the power relations confronting statesmen. Power cycle analysis does not dichotomize agent and structure, agreeing with David Dessler (1989, 466–67) that structure provides the material conditions that both "enable and constrain" state behavior, behavior that in turn "reproduces and transforms that structure." Models of "bounded rationality" and "prospect theory" likewise probe the interface of structure and decision making.[5] Such a holistic model of power is implicit in all structural theories, which are based on the conviction that the structure of the international system uniquely affects the opportunity, constraints, and behavior of statesmen.[6]

Observe as well that, notwithstanding its focus on the state power cycle dynamic, power cycle analysis is not a state-level theory. On the one hand, the concept of the power cycle has no meaning outside the context of a system (both power and role are necessarily systemic), and causation in the theory lies at the level of interaction among states. The direction of relative power change on the power cycle reflects the state's competitiveness in that system. On the other hand, a system cannot be fully understood outside the context of the power cycle dynamic. A particular international system is a historically determined and structurally specific relationship among individual states. John Ruggie (1986, 153) correctly criticized those who would talk of systems share, or calculate it, without explaining the "underlying principles that govern the patterning of interaction." The principles of the power cycle are the requisite "generative principles" for changing systems structure.

The first section of this chapter assesses the concepts and theoretical arguments of power cycle theory. Aided by three figures, it seeks to clarify the subtleties and idiosyncrasies of systems dynamics that invite confusion and hinder debate. For example, why is the strain between power and role distinct from status inconsistency notions? What is general equilibrium, and how does it overcome the limitations of the balance of power? How do the principles of the power cycle impact on international political economy? The chapter's second section responds to four substantive and empirical challenges to the theory. The principles of the power cycle resolve seeming puzzles of history regarding the causes of World War I. Concerns about the reliability of calculated critical points are shown to be misplaced. Empirical tests demonstrate that critical points do predict the target of aggression. And dyadic analysis attains greater specificity when confronting principles of systemic change.

What Is Power Cycle Theory?

The First Part: Structural Dynamics

Stimulated by "thought experiments" in 1964 about what drives systemic change, the principles of the power cycle explain how absolute power changes in the system create the rise and decline of states. Differing levels and rates of growth in *absolute* capability among the leading states set in motion a particular nonlinear pattern of change on each trajectory of *relative* power. Within this "single dynamic" of changing systemic share, individual states pass through a cycle of relative power in which they become ascendant, mature, and then decline—a cycle that sets the context for the state's foreign policy role (defined later). The relative power changes on those component power cycles together map the changing structure of that system. According to the principles of the power cycle, this single dynamic of changing systems structure (as roughly sketched in fig. 1 for the post-1500 historical state system) will reflect the "trends of history" and "shifting balance of world forces" experienced by statesmen and assessed by economic and diplomatic historians.[7] The "tides of history" follow the paths of ascendancy and demise and the shifting trends on the component state power cycles.

What are these generative principles that set the single dynamic in motion and constrain the contours of the component power cycles? How do differential absolute growth patterns in the system translate into the

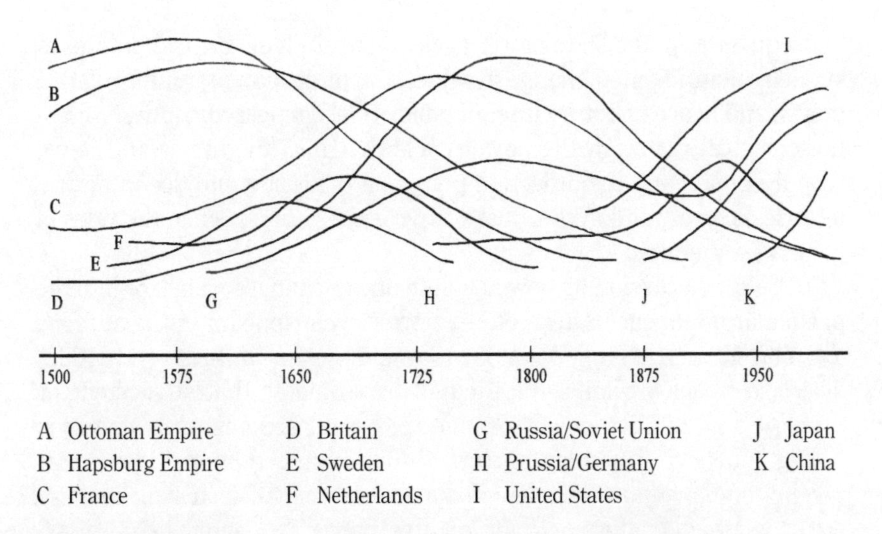

FIGURE 1. Dynamics of changing systems structure: Percent shares of power in the central system for leading states, 1500–1993.
Source: Conceptualized by Doran (1965; updated 1981, 1989, 1993), based on estimations for the period 1500 to 1815, and data for the years 1815–1993.

single dynamic of changing systemic share for the member states? At base, as shown schematically in figure 2, a state's competitiveness in a system, and hence the direction of change on its power cycle, is a function of how its absolute growth rate compares with the absolute growth rate of the system (the systemic norm). Two principles underlie this dynamic:

1. *The First Fundamental Principle of the Power Cycle* is elegant in its simplicity: A state's systemic share will increase when its absolute growth rate is greater than the systemic norm. Moreover, a single state growing faster than the systemic norm will initiate momentum of change on state power cycles throughout the system.
2. According to the *Second Fundamental Principle of the Power Cycle,* even when the differing state absolute growth rates remain unchanged throughout the system, a state's relative power growth will accelerate only for a time and then (at inflection point F) begin a process of deceleration, due to the bounds of the system (finiteness of systemic share), which brings about peaking (Z) and a turn into relative decline. Similarly, accelerating decline will (at inflection point L) begin to decelerate to a minimum level.

Consequently, on the state power cycle, there are four "critical points" of sudden, unanticipated change at which the projection of future relative power, and hence of future foreign policy role, changes abruptly. Each of these critical points in the power cycle dynamic (the upper and lower turning points and the inflection points on the rising and declining trajectories) correspond in the state's experience to times when the tides of history have shifted.

A fuller discussion of how absolute power changes translate into the particular nonlinear pattern of the power cycle appears in the author's *The Politics of Assimilation* (1971, 193), and *Systems in Crisis* (1991, 62).[8] The latter book explains the thought experiments that suggested the principles of relative power change (p. 4) and demonstrates them via seeing-is-believing simulations (pp. 65–68). Its appendix includes proofs for the fundamental principles of the power cycle (of changing systems structure) and "ratio tests" for relative power "convergence or divergence." Its index highlights the variety of equivalent descriptors for the power cycle dynamic, such as "competition for percent share," or "logistic growth in a finite system," or "structural bounds on statecraft." But,

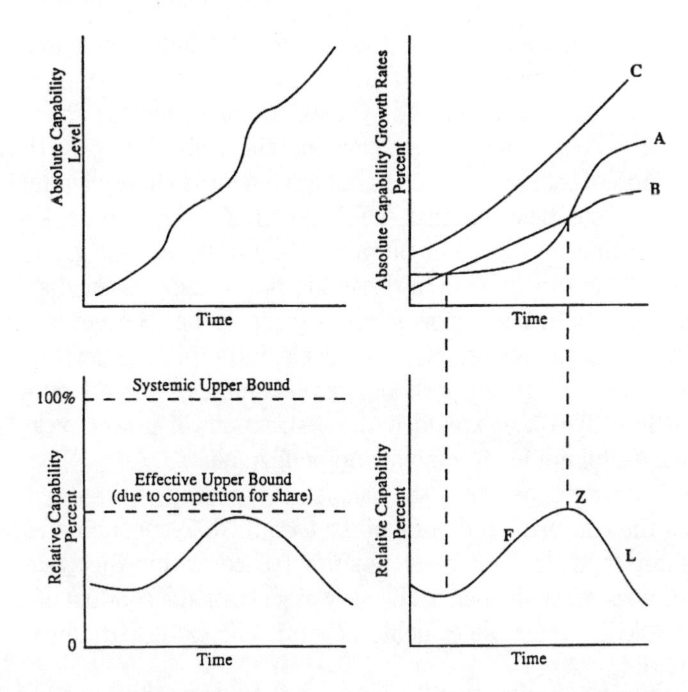

FIGURE 2. The dynamics of absolute and relative capability: Principles of the power cycle (changing systems structure). Curves of absolute growth rate: A: major power system; B: state B; C: entire system. Critical points: F: first inflection point; Z: zenith; L: last inflection point.
Source: On the right is a disaggregation of the figure in Doran, *The Politics of Assimilation: Hegemony and Its Aftermath* (Baltimore: The Johns Hopkins University Press, 1971, 193). This figure appears as figure 3.1 in Doran, *Systems in Crisis: New Imperatives of High Politics at Century's End* (Cambridge: Cambridge University Press, 1991, 63).

most important, chapter 3 undertakes a crucial empirical test (discussed later in this chapter) that validates the theory and underscores the paradigm shift in understanding that it entails. Only from the power cycle perspective do the perceptions and concerns of contemporaneous statesmen look neither distorted nor incongruous.

Confronting the principles of the power cycle reveals that the rise and decline of states is not simple. In fact, as demonstrated in this chapter's second section, relative power change is sometimes insidiously counterintuitive. The shifting tides of history are structural undercurrents that can counter even the largest growth in absolute capability. In every case, states with great, undiminished potential for absolute growth eventually bump against an upper limit to further increase in relative power, constrained by the "bounds of the system." Competition for share comes from other states, perhaps much smaller, whose absolute growth rate is greater. Moreover, a state that has obtained a large share of total power increasingly "competes against itself" more than against other states for share, requiring ever greater output to retain its present growth rate. (This is as true for the firm in the industrial context as for the state in international politics; it is a principle of competition.) Since role expectations are tied to change on the power cycle, incomplete understanding of relative power change supports dangerous fantasies about future power and role. Intuitive once explained, the abstractions of power cycle theory become a useful guide for analyst and policymaker.

While power constitutes the means of statecraft, *foreign policy role* involves the concerns and ends of statecraft. Role encompasses but is much more than state interests, position (place) within the system, and status. It goes much deeper, to the very essence of the conduct of foreign policy.[9] Role is foreign policy achievement itself; status is the award associated with it.

Based in the reality of the push and shove of world politics, foreign policy role indexes the behavior and position of the state manifested in its external relations. Distinct from power, role nonetheless is in the long term affected by the trajectory of power. Like power, role is relative (systemic). Although determined primarily by what a government itself does, a role exists only if the other governments accept its exercise of that role. Strategy and bargaining greatly impact this informal legitimization process. Role is foreign policy behavior that the system has allowed the state to achieve.

A historical example that clearly demonstrates the nuances, and vital significance, of foreign policy role involves Russia, France, and Austria in 1852. Russia traditionally enjoyed the role of protector of the Balkan Slavs (a role it still cherishes). Napoleon III of France pressed claims in the Ottoman as protector of the Latin Christians. When Russia tried to get equal acknowledgment of its position and claims and was rejected by the Sultan, it suspended diplomatic relations with the Ottoman and expanded its territorial claims by occupying Moldavia and Wallachia. These actions led directly to the outbreak of the Crimean War, the first war of consequence since the Congress of Vienna of 1815. France had tried to usurp the Russian role. Other governments whose interests were threatened, especially Austria, were unable to salvage the Russian role, discourage the French acquisition of that role, smooth the transfer of the role or, most seriously, prevent the relatively weakened Russia from expanding its role in a very inappropriate fashion.

Hence, role involves an acknowledged niche in which a country can use its power to obtain additional ends, in particular enhanced security. These behavioral niches change slowly over time in response to state purpose, strategy, capability, and the permissiveness of other actors in the system.

How does foreign policy role change as power changes over broad periods of history? A state's foreign policy expectations are tied to change on its power cycle, but power and role get out of sync because actors and system do not adjust readily to changes in relative power (Doran 1989a; 1991, 100–103).[10] On the upside of the power curve, the increase in power tends to exceed acquisition of role. The system is reluctant to yield role to the ascendant actor, or the rising state may prefer to postpone role gratification and responsibility. On the downside of the curve, there is a tendency for role to exceed power, leading to overextension. Allies and dependent client states do not want the once-ascendant state to step aside, and elites accustomed to the benefits power bestowed do not want to yield role and face a different, more-constricted foreign policy setting. Long in the making, these power-role gaps are shoved to the fore of diplomatic consciousness in crisis intervals when they can no longer be covered up. They then abruptly demand adjustment.

Placed within the dynamic context of power cycle analysis, the tension between power and role attains its fullest meaning and, accordingly, causal specificity regarding the outbreak of major war. Russia and Austria in 1852 were each undergoing critical change on their respective power cycles, signaling an abrupt and unpredictable change in foreign policy outlook: Russia was passing through the second inflection L, and Austria had passed the upper turning point Z within the decade. When France sought to alter the status quo in the Ottoman, it thus unsettled two governments that were already attempting to cope with history's shifting tides. Under these circumstances of massive structural change and foreign policy reorientation for Russia and Austria, a role challenge accompanied by the shock of relative power loss provided the sparks that ignited war.

The strain between power and role goes to the heart of the capacity to act in foreign policy. It is a structural disequilibrium conceptually distinct from the many variants of rank disequilibrium—aspirations/

achievements, power/status, achieved/ascribed power (Midlarsky 1969)—which seek congruence between two coequal goals. The power-role gap involves means (achieved power) versus attained interests or ends (ascribed role), and the adjustment between power and role is necessary to establish systemic equilibrium among all of the members (Doran 1989a; 1991, 134–38). The rank models also lack specificity regarding when a rank disequilibrium is likely to produce a conflict outcome. But the many variants of disequilibrium can be assessed simultaneously in the context of the power cycle dynamic, yielding a more encompassing notion of the requirements for equilibrium (Doran 1974; 1989a; 1991, 34). The aspirations-achievement disparity in Anderson and McKeown (1987) involves the inversion of expectations (trends) occurring at critical points on the power cycle; and the disequilibrium between power and role subsumes the power-status gap.

The Second Part: (Post)-Behavioral Response

Power cycle theory thus is, first, a theory of the changing structure of the international system, and of the particular nonlinear pattern of state rise and decline in relative power that comprises that changing structure. But the unique and peculiar nature of that nonlinear change, of the shifting tides of history, is the foundation for the second part of the theory, which seeks to explain the major wars that historically have accompanied massive structural changes in the system. As Greg Cashman (1993, 269) observed, this second, behavioral component is "a theory of decision-making about war" placed in the context of the rise and decline of states. The theory explores "what statesmen saw and how they reacted" to these unique nonlinearities of relative power change.[11] What is the behavioral response to each of the four critical points involving an abrupt inversion in the power dynamics, and hence in the state's projected future foreign policy role and security?

Lower turning point: birth throes of a major power
First inflection point: trauma of constrained ascendancy
Upper turning point: trauma of expectations foregone
Second inflection point: hopes and illusions of the second wind
Lower turning point: throes of demise as a major power

At no other time in the history of a nation's foreign policy experience is change so unanticipated and yet so massive. Such a sudden shift in future expectations requires difficult adjustments of equilibrium for the state and the system. However, these critical points are seen to bring about exaggerated fear, misperception, and foreign policy overreaction, making adjustment more difficult and major war more likely.

Some analysts have questioned whether governments can make judgments about their position on the power cycle, much less know when they pass through critical points.[12] Over long time periods, change on the power cycle is rather predictable: the state is in stasis, in ascendancy or in decline, and the trajectory is known because it is a linear extrapolation of past experience. Moreover, since statesmen tend to respond to momentum in the series rather than individual fluctuations, the likelihood is low that they would be confused by false critical points.[13] A more telling concern is that the nonlinear change in power at an inflection point is so gradual (invisible)—there is almost no change in the size of the increase—that no contemporary observer or subsequent historian could with confidence determine an inflection point in a power trend. But, although such continuity prevails, something else happens at the inflection point (and at all critical points) that revolutionizes foreign policy cognition. Something happens that transforms understanding of the possible, and the impossible, concerning future foreign policy options.

The Unique Trauma of Critical Change in Expectations. What ensues at a critical point is a profound transformation in foreign policy *expectations,* indeed a complete *inversion in the trend* of expectations. This inversion in thinking marks a sharp break with the past, a discontinuity in how the state views future options. The first inflection and upper turning points trigger doubt as to whether the state can assume all of the foreign policy goals it may have envisioned for generations. This inversion in the trend of expectations comes as a shock to the foreign policy elite, who must suddenly confront both ineluctable limits and monumental uncertainty.

Why has the inversion in expectations come as a shock? Overwhelming evidence from forecasting business cycles shows that a turning point (an inversion in future trend projections) cannot be predicted (Moore 1986). Thus, no discounting of the arrival of a critical point is feasible (Doran 1998). But effective intelligence will soon reveal that change of a profound type has altered the state's future security outlook. To suddenly discover this monumental transformation in its fortunes is unsettling for any government. The more dedicated it is to a larger world role, the more is at stake at the critical point, and the more trying is the task of political adjustment.

The critical point is also a shock because it is an *inversion* from the prior trend. Expectations are based on past experience extrapolated into the future. Since no more complicated model can be justified (an infinite number exist) than the simplest model, linear extrapolation, which is also usually correct, it is used by most decision makers most of the time. In fact, the only time linear extrapolation is wrong in the history of state experience is at the critical points. The critical point is thus a drastic shift in foreign policy cognition. Precisely because it is so apparently subtle, unpredictable, and definitive, and yet so conducive to uncertainty, structural discontinuity at a critical point is so unsettling and potentially devastating.

All of this is represented graphically in the theory (Doran 1991, 98). Expectations are represented by a straight line drawn tangent to the power curve (fig. 3). Between the low point and the first inflection point, the slope of the tangent (the rate of change of relative power) becomes ever steeper, projecting ever greater increases in future power and role. But at the inflection point, the trend of the tangent abruptly inverts. The tangent begins to revolve in the opposite direction, becoming ever less steep, projecting ever declining increments in future role and security position.

Hence, from the perspective of expectations, no more complete sense of discontinuity could transpire than an inversion in the prior trend. No change is more precipitous or more defining. The further the state looks into the future, the larger the disparity between future reality and its prior foreign policy expectations. Ironically, the more foresighted the policy planning, the greater the error of judgment that suddenly confronts the decision maker.

In confronting the principles of the power cycle, the analyst discovers that the "perspective of statecraft"—of relative (systemic structural) change—is indeed idiosyncratic, evoking a paradigm shift in the understanding of foreign policy behavior. Like the statesman, the analyst grasps the most important difference between absolute and relative capability—the nature of their paths over long time periods—and hence the full significance of systemic bounds. At critical points of unexpected nonlinearity, where the tides of history suddenly shift, the expectations induced by absolute trends no longer match the shifted trend in relative power. It is traumatic when a very small change on the state's power curve changes completely the direction of future expectations. It is traumatic when a meteoric rise in relative power suddenly peaks even as absolute capability makes its greatest gains. No theory of international politics can

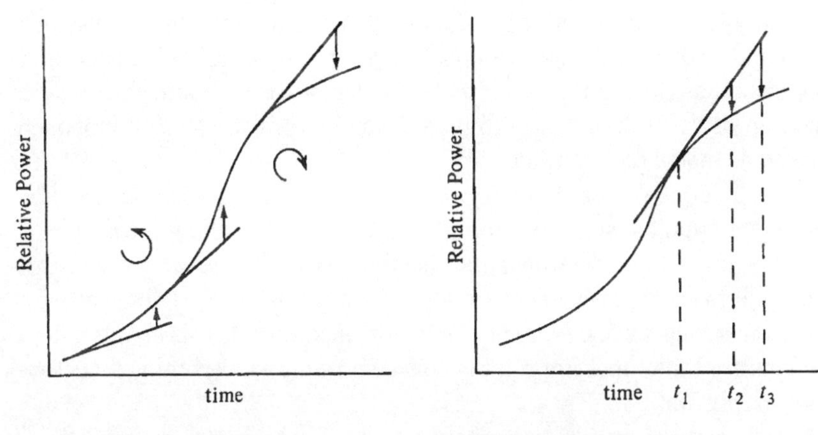

a. Inversion in the Prior Trend of Foreign Policy Expectations

b. Shock of Foreign Policy Reevaluation

FIGURE 3. Crisis of foreign policy expectations at first inflection point

ignore this fundamental difference in trends and expectations, the conflicting messages and shocking surprises. No explanation of major war can dismiss this discordance in perspectives as probable cause.

From Inverted Expectations to Major War. Three processes underlie the impact of the dynamic of the power cycle on the occurrence of major war. First, the cognitive shock of a critical point is itself destabilizing. With the tides of political momentum suddenly shifting, proving the state's future security projections dangerously misguided, the critical point becomes a wrenching invitation to anxiety, belligerence, and overreaction. Second, adjustment to structural change at the critical point is worsened by existing power-role gaps, which are suddenly squeezed to the surface of foreign policy consciousness and appear formidable indeed as the state tries to cope with the shifting tide. Power-role gaps aggravate the tension and uncertainty that already exist at the critical point.

Third, increased inelasticities regarding future role and security lead to an "inversion of force expectations" that accelerates the movement to war. Attitudes and actions rigidify, and rational decision making breaks down.[14] The uncertainties and shocks occurring to foreign policy sensibility cause both potential deterrer and aggressor to find acceptable or even necessary force use previously thought of as "unthinkable." This transmutation of mentality is analogous roughly to the inversion of demand and supply expectations that occurs in so-called inverted markets such as during the stock market collapse of 1929 and the oil price run-up of 1979. Expansion to major war follows the Jervis-Mansbach-Vasquez model of a conflict spiral.[15]

Such a deep sense of political insecurity might also lead to an effort to cope with the insecurity through the formation of alliances. Empirical results now strongly confirm that the high insecurity associated with critical points leads governments to form alliances (Chiu 2000) in an attempt to protect themselves. As explained in the next part of this chapter, these efforts are sometimes improperly conceived, only exacerbating structural disequilibrium.

All of these processes contributing to instability are magnified in a period of systems transformation when a number of major states pass through critical points at about the same time.[16] Long-standing contradictions in the system are exposed, and equilibrium among states may be on the verge of snapping as a backlog of adjustments between interests and power suddenly demand resolution. States throughout the system seek redress of their own perceived condition of internal disequilibrium. Structural uncertainty is monumental and statesmen are unable to assimilate all of these changes without precipitating the violent behavior that in principle they all wish to avoid.

Assisted by figure 1, consider the pattern of abrupt structural change and systemic tension in several historical examples of world war. The tension came not so much from upward or downward mobility in the systemic hierarchy, which occurs at all times, but from a government's sudden discovery that its projected future foreign policy role had dramatically changed.

Contrast the outlooks of Charles V and Philip II of Spain in the sixteenth century, following the Spanish Hapsburg peak in relative power circa 1580.[17] Although the Spanish-Austrian Hapsburgs remained the dominant power in Europe for decades, Philip II suddenly interpreted foreign policy negatively, even arguing that "God had forsaken" Spain, expressing at once both paranoia and belligerence. Long-standing economic and financial policies had undermined Spain's power base from within, accelerating its relative demise as much smaller states began to consolidate power. Sweden and Holland enjoyed a meteoric rise, abruptly demanding a larger role. France under Richelieu began to consolidate its power. Only eight years after this peak, in 1588, Spain struck out against the British fleet, and the fateful "Protestant wind" defeated its Armada. The massive changes in *structure* and *roles* eventually strained the system at its core, resulting in the Thirty Years' War.

Similarly, in the mid–seventeenth century, the passage of Louis XIV's France through a first inflection point, threatening slower growth for the first time in its development as a major power, led to confrontations with Sweden (an erstwhile ally) and Holland, each of whom had discovered that its relative power had peaked, thus creating severe problems of overextension. Meanwhile Prussia was rising in the heart of the central European system, and Britain, reconstituted, was enjoying a renaissance of power growth by the end of the seventeenth century, stimulating it to confront France directly with an army on the Continent. Once again, the wars of Louis XIV resulted from a systemic transformation that saw each of Europe's major players viewing its own foreign policy role in highly altered and more troubling fashion.

French power peaked sometime during the latter eighteenth century in the face of growing British industrial and naval strength. This transformation of the system that came on the heels of startling declines in power in northern and central Europe saw a belligerent France resisting its systemic fortunes under Napoleon. The contrast between the changing foreign policy outlook of the Russians (as expressed by Alexander I) and of the French (under Napoleon) was an acknowledgment of the failure of Europe to assimilate dramatic structural change without major war. In contrast to the eighteenth-century system in which France had played the dominant role, a five-actor concert of shared power, balanced and roughly equilibrated, was emerging.

In these three world wars, the existing system of maintaining order collapsed under the weight of arrangements whose foundations had long since been eroded away (Doran 1971).

Empirical examination of the periods preceding World Wars I and II verified the hypothesis that massive, critical structural change predicts to massive warfare (Thompson 1983a; Doran 1985, 1989a). Between 1885 and 1914, every member of the central system experienced at least one critical point on its power cycle. Hapsburg pretensions lived longer than did Austria-Hungary's capability to be a player in the central system, whereas the United States and Japan emerged as new but as yet uninvolved members. Britain and France passed through the inflection point of declining power and were unwilling to yield systemic role to Germany, which soared to its apex. Russia passed through a minimum, Austria-

Hungary and Italy each passed through two critical points on their downward trajectory, and the United States traversed the inflection point on its upward path. Altogether, nine critical points signifying the most abrupt and wrenching form of change on the power cycle were traversed in the 20 years after 1885. Systemic anxieties and perceptions regarding the German response to its critical point were exacerbated by the types of critical changes occurring on these other power cycles (Doran 1989a). Perhaps few international systems could withstand this degree of structural turmoil in so short an interval. For the analyst of history, the uncertainties and turmoil may often present seeming contradictions.

With the paradigm shift to the unique perspective of statecraft, confronting the full significance of systemic bounds on power and behavior, puzzles of history dissolve. For instance, the perspective and concerns of statesmen prior to World War I, which do not make sense from the traditional paradigm, are seen to be very natural in the context of power cycle analysis. Surprises of history are the essence of all critical changes on the power cycle. With a paradigm shift, reinterpretations of history, new perspectives on the causes of war, and alternative paths to world order become plausible.

When the concerns of statesmen are seen clearly, the so-called dilemma of peaceful change begs reconsideration. The second part of power cycle theory thus takes the theory full circle to the questions that had originally motivated it. What causes systems transformation and the massive war historically associated with it? Why had the balance-of-power mechanism repeatedly failed to preserve order during these times of monumental structural change? Is systems transformation possible without major war?

The Third Part: International Political Equilibrium

At the heart of power cycle theory is what might be labeled its third part, the more general and dynamic concept of international political equilibrium that it proposes to overcome the shortcomings of the balance of power. Power cycle analysis emerged from historical sociological analysis of the first three world wars of the modern state system (the hegemonic onslaughts of Hapsburg Spain, of Louis XIV, and of Napoleon), and the postwar efforts to establish a new world order (Peace of Westphalia, 1648; Treaties of Utrecht, 1713; Congress of Vienna, 1815).[18] These great peace treaties had to focus on static criteria for structures that would allow the new system to evolve and mature. To prevent its own collapse in world war, however, the new system would ultimately have to deal with the long-term relative power changes that inevitably would transform the new structure. The power cycle assessment of peaceful change grew out of the belief that analysis of these long-term changes "might provide a better understanding of the mechanism of systemic adjustment which must *precede* and *complement* any external alliances formed" (Doran 1969, 2). And it recognized that the key issue of systemic adjustment is how to reconcile changing power with legitimate interest.

Was war necessary to restructure world power in the historical periods of systems transformation? If structural change is inevitable, is major war inevitable? Is major war the Machiavellian instrument to coerce a necessary restructuring of world relationships? The thesis that systems transformation is a structural discontinuity caused by major war is at the heart of much international relations theory. According to Liska (1968, 59), "the evolution of a European or any other international system is the story of conflicts which create the system and then later on lead to its destruction." Likewise, Thompson (1988, xii) states that "global war emerged as a systemic mechanism for resolving policy-leadership disputes in the later fifteenth century. Since then, the mechanism continued to evolve." Hegemonic stability (Gilpin 1981), power transition (Organski and Kugler 1980), and long cycle (Modelski 1978) theories also identify major war as the vehicle whereby a new systemic hierarchy is born. The dilemma of peaceful change arises because reluctant governments will not yield privileged power positions except by force.

Power cycle theory argues, on the contrary, that major war can be dissociated from systems transformation. First it shows that historical reality is far more complicated than the inevitable war thesis envisions.

For example, World War I did not cause the relative decline of German power any more than it toppled British dominance within the system. These structural changes were long in the making. British power was declining for decades, and German power peaked a decade prior to the war. Russia, the United States, and Japan were rising on the outskirts of the system. It was the dynamics of intense competition within the central system that caused all of these changes. Thus, the notion that war was necessary to restructure world power in 1914 belies historical fact. Restructuring of power relationships was already occurring. Role adjustment was more dilatory, and the war accelerated role change—but *not in the direction the parties intended.* Role shifted after World War II to the

Soviet Union and United States, not to either the initial belligerents or the defenders of the old order. Major war neither precipitated the fundamental changes in power nor was a reliable purveyor of role.

According to power cycle theory, causation went in exactly the opposite direction, from structural transformation to war. A discontinuity of structure and foreign policy expectations caused the massive warfare. A later section of this paper "confronts the principles of the power cycle" as proof, demonstrating the nature of this discontinuity and how it strained the system to the breaking point. What is at issue in systems transformation, and thus in the massive warfare associated with it, is systemic adjustment. Therein lies the clue to the resolution of peaceful change.

The Problem of Systemic Adjustment. Contained within the dilemma of peaceful change are two strategic problems.[19] For the older declining state, the temptation is to resist yielding role for fear that the newly rising state will want to demand even more in the future, possibly becoming a hegemon dominating all. The logic for the declining state thus becomes, why yield anything now when it will be expected to yield even more in the future? This is the invitation to preemptive attack, to strike now to avoid an ever-worsening situation in the future (Levy and Collis 1985; Levy 1987). But the contradictions are glaring. There is never a "right moment" for preemptive attack since the state is involved in a very long interval of relative decline. Moreover, why should the declining state assume that the rising state has aggressive intent toward it?

The problem for the newly rising state is why it should assume role now instead of later, when it could do so more easily (with greater confidence) and *on its own terms* (with less competition) since it would have more power and other governments less. This is the temptation of deferred gratification. It is also, partially, the mentality of the "free rider," to let others do what they must and to come in under their umbrella since that coverage is collective and cannot be denied. Again, the contradictions are striking. If the rising state waits to assume responsibility, it creates a power-role gap in the system—known traditionally as a political vacuum. This places burdens on other governments incapable of funding the costs of a more extensive foreign policy. Postponing responsibility also postpones the gratification associated with increased status and diplomatic visibility. But deferring gratification carries the risk that it may not be attained. The predicament for the rising state is that it will eventually peak. When that happens it will discover that it has foregone foreign policy opportunity for leadership and visibility that is never likely to return.

Thrasymachus was rightly criticized by Socrates for believing that, internal to the state, justice meant that the strong should "rule" (Plato 1961). Ironically, external to the state, the injustice that has precipitated the most massive wars is more egregious than that of Thrasymachus. It is the injustice of unearned privilege. The decreasingly powerful (capable) want to claim all of the perquisites, status, and influence that they had enjoyed when they were at the top of their power cycle. The increasingly powerful (capable), because they foolishly postponed assuming responsibility until too late, or because the system refused to adjust for them to allow them a timely assumption of rightly earned status and influence, find that they have been denied an appropriate role. Thus Thrasymachus has been gone one better: the no-longer capable, who can no longer "rule" effectively, think they should continue to "rule." The increasingly weak attempt to "rule" at the cost of the increasingly strong. This is a recipe for structural catastrophe.

From Balance of Power to Dynamic Equilibrium. Rapid structural change must be allowed to proceed without increasing the likelihood of major war. Major war cannot, by default, be the arbiter of future systems. Power cycle analysis suggests that collapse of the balance of power and peace twice in this century could have been avoided (Doran 1991, 151–65; 1995b, 186–87, 200–202). The balance of power failed because it is a static and partial conception of equilibrium. While it did preserve stability most of the time, it was a recipe for cataclysmic misjudgment during rapid systems change. Power cycle analysis exposes its flaw.

When a state faces superior power accompanied by suspected hostile intent, the balance of power always prescribes external alliance aggregation or coalition formation. This is both the strength of its prescription and the crux of its greatest weakness. Defenses must always be maintained against aggression, but in the long term rising power cannot be artificially halted and declining power cannot be artificially bolstered. Yet the balance of power promoted precisely these objectives during periods of rapid structural change. External aggregation of power was used to halt the advance of an ascendant state and to shore up the fortunes of a declining state, irrespective of the legitimacy of their respective interests.

Consider the period of Germany's ascendancy in the late nineteenth century. Designed to deter aggression and provide peace and security, the balance of power wrongly conceived ended up precipitating war against the crumbling system it was supposed to protect. The other members of the European system, in severe relative decline, banded together to try to offset the German advances in relative power. Instead of allowing role to shift toward ascendant Germany, the rigidity of the balance of power prevented it. The consequence was intense structural strain within the central system. Increasingly dissatisfied, Germany could "wait" for greater role and status so long as it could anticipate future relative power growth. Its sudden peak in the decade prior to 1914 was one of a confluence of critical changes that exposed and tested the contradictions in the system. War became by default the only apparent instrument available to offset the severe structural strains.

World War I showed that states ignore power-role equilibrium at their peril and that rising power cannot be halted. World War II showed that states ignore the balance of power at their peril and that illegitimate interests must never be appeased. Tragically, the allies tried to correct the wrongs done to Germany prior to World War I by yielding position and role to Hitler; but the situation in 1938 demanded the classical balance-of-power response. So much had changed structurally in three decades that German pretensions in 1938 were far greater than its capacity to assume enlarged diplomatic, economic, and even peacekeeping responsibilities. Moreover, Hitler's territorial demands were inherently aggressive, hence illegitimate, and had to be confronted on these grounds alone. The correct strategic response to Hitler was a firm policy of balance and opposition.

The balance of power is inadequate for peaceful change because it considers power only, leaving out much about which states fight, and it does not distinguish between legitimate and illegitimate interests of the rising and declining states. International political equilibrium requires policies of balance and of accommodation regarding nonvital issues of foreign policy role and status. It seeks systemic adjustment through the transfer of legitimate interests and obligations from the declining to the ascending polity. The territorial sovereignty of the declining state is not affected by the transfer, only its foreign policy role, prestige, and place in the systemic political hierarchy. The strategy must be both appropriate to each state's position on its power cycle and acceptable in terms of the legitimacy of the claims on other states. Thus, international political equilibrium seeks peaceful change through combinations and sequences of strategies, taking the *structural dynamic* and the *legitimacy of claims* into consideration, that will enable each state to bring its power and role in balance prior to the trauma of critical change on its power cycle. Timing strategic response to the dynamics of the power cycle is the key (Doran 1991, 177–86).[20]

Power cycle theory invites a conception of public morality that is complementary to, yet constrains, notions of power. It challenges the very assumptions of Machtpolitik. To understand power is to understand its limits (bounds on relative growth), its issues (systemic role legitimacy and adjustments), its surprises (discontinuous expectations), and hence the shocks and uncertainties and sense of injustice conducive to violence. Vis-à-vis the dilemma of peaceful change, when to accommodate and when to oppose demands for role change, power cycle theory asks, what kinds of international political demands are legitimate, and what is a just response? It proposes a possible solution to that dilemma based on the power cycle dynamic, a solution that puts the burden on decision makers to make adjustments prior to the crisis of critical change. A major task is to assess the limits and possibilities of this proposed solution to the dilemma of peaceful change.[21]

The Fourth Part: International Political Economy and High Politics

A fourth distinct part of power cycle theory involves assessment of future systems change and implications for international political economy.[22]

Debate about U.S. decline versus unilateralism, involving the future path of U.S. power and its foreign policy, is part of the larger scholarly dialogue about the structural dynamics of international politics. The question must be refocused (Doran 1991, 1993): What is the U.S. future power and role in an international system whose structure and modus operandi are changing?

In this transforming world, is the United States "bound to lead," as Joseph Nye (1990a) has argued? Or, as Robert Gilpin (1981) has warned, is it a declining hegemon, whose weakened leadership invites challenge from a rising state planning a new system of rules and benefits? Should the United States accept its "end of empire" and "gracefully retreat" from its leadership role, as Paul Kennedy (1988a, 1988b) has advised? What is an appropriate grand strategy for the United States, appropriate both to

U.S. interests and, since this is what leadership is all about, to the interests of the international system?

At issue is whether the United States is in decline in the same way that Great Britain was at the end of the nineteenth century, and Hapsburg Spain was at the end of its empire. The debate was sparked by provocative titles like "Fin-de-Siecle America" (Kennedy 1990), with all its historical associations regarding level and irreversibility, but none of the historical analogies corresponds to the U.S. situation of the 1990s. Britain at the end of the last century was confronting a system in which Germany was already an equal in both economic and military power, and several other countries were not far behind.

The U.S. power cycle reveals two seemingly divergent empirical findings. First, the United States is the most powerful actor in the system by a large margin only increased by the Soviet collapse. Second, around 1965–70 the United States peaked in relative power, but the process of decline is slow and subject to many possible reforms and policy adjustments by the United States (numerator) and/or other leading states like Japan, the EU, Russia, and China (denominator). A prudent reading of these findings is that, in contrast to exaggerated claims of both "declinist" and unipolar "assume-any-burden" advocates, the United States has a serious role to play as a leader among like-thinking allies, avoiding both isolationist withdrawal and hegemonic unilateralism. Never in the modern state system has a single state been responsible for world order; power has always been pluralistic and shared.[23]

Policy analysts could readily dismiss the exaggerations and dichotomies of the debate, and acknowledge the need for reforms to slow down, halt, or reverse the process of relative decline (Nau 1990; Rosecrance 1990). But they also knew an important fact of statecraft that flawed the thesis of graceful retreat. Inertia in role change is stronger than inertia in the relative power to carry out that role: the United States could well face larger relative burdens of leadership even if its relative power is diminished (Lahneman 1999). Policymakers can assess alternative power relationships and roles. But a clear picture has yet to emerge regarding the larger structural situation in which the United States may find itself—the strategic policy demands it will face, and the strategic policy choices open to it. Future foreign policy roles must evolve amid uncertain change (Doran 1993, 1996, 1997, 1998).

Many counterintuitive aspects of relative change complicate the debate. For instance, a large state whose absolute growth rate is smaller than that of its competitors still so weights the systemic norm that it can long maintain systemic share; this explains the complacence that long attended diminished U.S. economic competitiveness. But once relative decline sets in, the same absolute growth rate differentials will yield accelerating decline, explaining the imperative for U.S. economic resurgence. Similarly, expectations that Japan will continue to rise on its power cycle, replacing U.S. "leadership," are based on extrapolation of absolute trends, reminiscent of the Mastery of Europe expectations regarding Germany in the early century. But the principles of the power cycle show that the expectations induced by absolute trends do not hold. The tiny increments of a faster-growing economic pygmy, such as Russia in relation to Germany circa 1900, and China in relation to Japan today, are sufficient to force the giant toward its peak (Doran 1991, 232–36).

The principles of the power cycle also provide insight into the economic policies of countries on different portions of their power cycles, and trade policies of the system during times of linear versus nonlinear change.

When a country has such predominance of systemic share as did the United States 1950–80 (high noon), managers of many of its principal firms (e.g., IBM, automobiles) find that their industries, like the economy, are bumping against an upper asymptote to further growth in share (Doran 1991, 220–25). The firm (industry), like the state's economy, is competing against itself much more than against others. Not able to expand market share, it seeks to protect that share, or to extract monopoly rents from it. The industries become oligopolistic not so much by choice as by structural circumstance.

In contrast, the objective of countries and their industrial managers lower on the power cycle (like Japan and the NICs) is maximum growth, increase in market share, penetration of foreign markets, and protection of their own sphere. Theirs is an offensive strategy built on aggressive exportation and selective constrained importation. Neomercantilism, augmented by a producer- rather than consumer-oriented set of policies by their home governments, was the strategy of the ascendant economies and their leading industries. These self-interested policies turned the leading actor's strategy further against itself and the open world economy to their great benefit (Doran 1994b).

Linkages between the security imperative and international political economy are the focus of an entire course and book.[24] Systemically, linear structural change provides a rather certain political setting in which firms can make investment and production decisions with comparative trust and confidence and states can relax their relative gains concerns. Government and firms together facilitate a liberalization of trade that is systems-wide and reinforcing. Abrupt nonlinear change unsettles this confidence, causes governments to think increasingly in relative gains and zero-sum terms, and undermines willingness to open borders to trade. Martin Roy (1998) uses a case study, game theory, and regression to study subtleties of this question.

The principles of the power cycle in fact have broad applicability. They are principles of change in any finite system, explaining how absolute growth patterns in the component parts change the structural relations of the whole. To confront the principles of the power cycle is to confront the principles of competition for share. Thus, the shocks and surprises of nonlinear change, the counterintuitive effect of systemic bounds, are likewise experienced by firms, industries, and any entities competing for "market share."

Substantive Challenges and Response

Paradigm Shift: Seeming Puzzles of History Resolved

The power cycles for Germany and Russia (Doran and Parsons 1980) triggered much theoretical discussion among political scientists and historians. Substantively, the debate centers around "the almost universal pre-1914 belief in inexorably increasing Russian power," to quote William Wohlforth (1987, 380). Why did European decision makers foresee great relative gains for Russia? Were the statesmen correct? What were the implications of rising Russian power for Germany, and hence for German behavior?

These curves were provocative because, while they accurately captured the prewar trend (perceived and real) of Russia rising from the low point on its power cycle and Germany near its peak, they show Germany peaking in relative power well *in advance* of the war, counter to accepted historical interpretation and "common sense." The power cycle argument that *expectations,* and hence *behaviors,* are based on an extrapolation of existing trends became a focus of debate. Wohlforth emphasized the need to combine perceptual and structural explanations. But, just as he seemed ready to accept the full implications of his findings—namely, that contemporaneous statesmen realized Germany's leveling out of relative growth—he did a *volte face.* He accepted the arguments put forth by Paul Kennedy (1984) that the contemporaneous perceptions of rising Russian power were "misperceptions" and that Germany was still a rising power prior to the war.

Kennedy supported his argument with the "giant-pygmy" thesis. Germany's power was so much greater than that of Russia, and its yearly increments were so much greater, that surely Germany did not consider Russia a threat. Kennedy examined production data on steel, coal, and other manufactures. So obvious was Germany's superior strength, and so obvious did the continued rise in Germany's relative power seem, that the contemporaneous statesmen must somehow have "misperceived" reality. He thus posed two puzzles that historians must seek to explain. *Puzzle 1:* "Why was Russian power before 1914 so absurdly overrated? . . . Did they not see that Russia, despite its lurch towards industrialization, was a military colossus but an economic pygmy?" *Puzzle 2:* "Which power, Russia or Germany, was *objectively* the most likely to alter the existing order in Europe?" (Kennedy 1984, 28–29).

What were the implications of Russia growing so rapidly, albeit from such a low level? Kennedy's answer was A. J. P. Taylor's "Mastery of Europe" thesis that Germany's fears of Russia "were exaggerated. . . . In fact, peace must have brought Germany the mastery of Europe within a few years" (1984, 29).

Power cycle theory argues that these issues of historical interpretation involve deeper *conceptual* issues: absolute versus relative power, the short-term balance of power versus the long-term trend of relative power, and the static system versus the dynamics of systems change. Moreover, the structural, perceptual, and behavioral aspects of causation must be assessed holistically for a full paradigm shift to the dynamic systemic view. When examined from the perspective of long-term changes in relative power, the giant-pygmy argument and the mastery of Europe thesis are shown to be wrong. From the power cycle perspective, the perceptions of contemporaneous statesmen look neither distorted nor incongruous, but accurately reflect the reality of power trends and the unique concerns of statecraft.

Yet so obvious does the continued rise in German relative power in the European system seem that some analysts have viewed power cycle theory and its empirical findings as suspect.[25] They variously attributed Germany's peaking to supposed flaws or errors in the index, in the choice of a broader system, in the mathematical method, or in the theory of the power cycle itself.

Chapter 3 of *Systems in Crisis* confronts, and eliminates, each of these concerns by anchoring the analysis in the historical puzzles generated by the assumed historical facts. With "seeing-is-believing" simulations, it shows how the pygmy forces the giant into relative decline. It also examines empirically the absolute and relative scores on the production indicators that Kennedy interpreted and that critics used as part of their own complex index for power, using their data source. The empirical tests demonstrate unambiguously that Germany had peaked in relative power terms (1) on a number of individual indicators (the critics' data), (2) within the European subsystem, (3) on data restricted to the period prior to the war, and (4) not as some artifact of curve fitting. The data also show the logistic asymptotic effect.

Taylor (1954, 126) later questioned the war causation aspect of his thesis: "We still have doubts about what the issues were, whether it really was a conscious struggle for the mastery of Europe or of the world." In a study of how wars begin, he concluded that "wars in fact have sprung more from apprehension than from a lust for war or conquest" (1979, 15). Had Taylor realized that German ascendancy itself was not foreordained, that German relative power had already peaked on the eve of the war, he would have had evidence to support his new speculation about the causes of World War I.

Critical Points versus Transitions: Velocity versus Level

Henk Houweling and Jan Siccama (1988) initiated a very important chain of research when they used the data set from power cycle theory to test an alternative theory of war causation, transition theory. Doran (1989a) then used that data (and newly calculated critical points—see later) to compare the two theories empirically, finding that (1) the relation between a critical point and major war is neither spurious nor dependent upon the presence or absence of a transition and (2) the relation between transition and major war is misspecified, for it is dependent upon the presence of a critical point.

Doran (1989a) also includes the author's "challenges for research design" in the field. It examines the interface between power cycle theory and the dynamic decision-making model of interstate war developed by Paul Anderson and Timothy McKeown (1987) as an alternative to explanations based on utility maximization. It shows mathematically that inversions in the trend of slope can approximate critical intervals (the only method used for over a decade). It demonstrates via diagrams of each state's critical change the devastating illusions at the critical points in the years prior to World War I.

Concerns raised about the statistical procedure for calculating the critical points in Doran and Parsons (1980) had prompted reliability tests via a number of approaches. Newly calculated critical points (Doran 1989a; 1991, 8–10, 112–13), based on an improved methodology, yield greater confidence in the statistical technique for calculating them. The only differences arise from changes in constraints or data: (a) constraints in the 1980 study had forced France's High and Britain's Low to fall within the temporal range of the data; (b) the refined technique allowed calculation of Italy's High and Germany's two Lows; (c) using a new estimate of Russia's eighteenth-century share, it showed the 1980 result to be a temporary inversion and determined the true High and Second Inflection for the data; and (d) the post-1950 set of indicators yielded a different U.S. High and no U.S. Second Inflection.

A second article by Houweling and Siccama (1991) issued many criticisms of the comparative empirical test, questioning the reliability of calculated critical points and carrying out additional tests to challenge the validity of the conclusions. The answer to each criticism follows.

1. *Arbitrary Break-Points in Transition Theory's Tests.* Concern about reliability and validity of calculated critical points is eliminated by comparing the earlier "critical points" (1980) with the newly calculated "critical periods" (1991). Recall that the data itself consists of averages over five-year periods. *No change* in the calculation occurred for 9 of the 12 (not 6 of 13 as claimed) critical points under contention (2 are identical, 5 are within two years, and 2 are within seven years). A quick check shows that 2 of the critical points "switch periods" only because of the arbitrary break-point chosen by Houweling and Siccama for their analysis, not because of any error in calculating the critical points—indeed, in each case, they differ by only two years! The remaining 3 critical points that were different are for Russia and the United States, involving a new estimate of pre-1815 data conditions for Russia and new U.S. indicators. These

differences in no way challenge the validity or reliability of calculation of critical points.

The issue throughout is not whether decision makers can discern critical points (they can), but whether researchers can on the basis of historical hindsight replicate the intuitive geopolitical perception of the decision maker. Reliable methodology assists this replication of structural thought.

2. *Tests of Hypotheses That Misrepresent Power Cycle Theory.* Houweling and Siccama's tables 2 and 3, respectively, test the hypotheses that "every state at war is a critical point state," and that "a critical point state will be at war with all other major powers (in all dyads)." Neither of these hypotheses is asserted in power cycle theory, and hence the empirical tests do not challenge the validity of either the critical points or the theory.
3. *One Counting Error in Each Study.* The Doran (1989a) study contained one counting error on the "No" *line* of table 3 testing $H_0(2)$. The correct numbers (5 and 11) are found in table 4. The "Yes" *column* of table 3 should be equivalent to row one of table 4 testing $H_0(3a)$, the "No" *column* equivalent to row three of table 4 testing $H_0(4)$. The Houweling and Siccama (1991) study also contained one counting error. In its table 5, the case "1946–1965, USSR" should be moved from the lower-right to the upper-right quadrant, changing the Q from .75 to .66. Once these corrections are made, it becomes clear that the tests of $H_0(1)$ and $H_0(2)$ in the two studies are completely equivalent.
4. *Findings That Are Completely Equivalent.* As noted by Houweling and Siccama (1991), the tests of $H_0(3b)$ and $H_0(4)$ in Doran (1989a) are completely equivalent to their own. Hence, researchers should consult table 4 in Doran and tables 4.2a and 4.2b in their study for accurate compilations of the data of each study and tests that address hypotheses reflective of each theory.

Other analyses using different data sets and research designs have also replicated aspects of power cycle theory. Anderson and McKeown (1987) and Schampel (1993), exploring subtleties of velocity or slope as cause, Spiezio (1993), examining militarized disputes, and Hebron and James (1997), using both disputes and international crisis behavior data, reinforce the initial findings on war causation and expand the application of the theory to a wider range of international conflict.

Engaged to (with) Whom?

"It is easier to predict that someone will become engaged with anyone than to predict the more interesting case with whom," admonish Houweling and Siccama (1991). They assert that power cycle theory is only capable of doing the former, while transition theory can do the latter as well. We here examine whether power cycle theory is indeed incapable of identifying with whom a nation fights. Out of just such challenges productive research is born.

An intriguing pattern emerges from assessment of several cases. The state that attacks has recently passed through a critical point; the target is the state taking power share from it. Thus, the state that has constrained the belligerent on its power cycle—the state with which competition against it is keenest—is the state against whom the belligerent turns militarily.

In the case of World War I, we have seen that Germany was the giant at the peak of its power curve, and Russia was the pygmy at the bottom of the system that pulled Germany into relative decline. Germany launched its initial attack against Russia, the state German policymakers had long ruminated about in terms of its alleged looming future potential for threat.

Similarly, ongoing research shows that Saddam Hussein attacked Kuwait, one of the two states within the Gulf subsystem (Saudi Arabia was the other) responsible for pulling Iraq into relative decline (Parasiliti 1997).[26]

Prussia on the eve of the Franco-Prussian War had passed through the first inflection point on its power cycle. Which state constrained Prussia's power share the most? We will show that it was France, its main Continental rival and the target of its aggression. A first test uses the same data analyzed by Doran and by Houweling and Siccama. Prussia transisted France in the year of the Franco-Prussian War (1870) and because of the fruits of Prussian victory and French defeat. Transition theory allows that the rising state may go to war prior to transition in order to accelerate the transition. In any case, it was the war that caused the transition, not vice versa.

But did the war likewise "cause" the prewar Prussian inflection point in 1865? Logically, territory and other fruits of victory will have *boosted* Germany's rise on the power cycle, not diminished its rate of increase as occurred at and after the inflection. To look more deeply at the data, we examine four subsystems—the European subsystem (the last four data points omit Japan and the United States) and three dyads (Prussia in turn with Britain, France, and Russia). In about 1865 in each of the subsystems, Prussia experienced an inflection point signifying a slowing down of the rate of increase in its power relative to the respective competitor.

The evidence is clear. Since the rate of increase continued to diminish after the war *despite* acquisition of territory, the war could not have caused the earlier inflection point. But for that very reason, the inflection point occurring just before the war could indeed have caused the war. As the lines tangent to the power curve reveal, the inflection marked a dramatic change in foreign policy expectations. It meant Prussia (Germany) would never again enjoy such heady growth. Bismarck attacked France and acquired new resources but could not stop the declining rate of relative growth.

One issue remains. Was France the state most accountable for taking power share away from Prussia? Its loss of territory logically would give France a worsening dyadic relationship with Germany after the war. But the rate of increase of Prussian (German) power relative to France declined in the year of the war and thereafter, even though the Prussian (German) score reflected the gain of French resources and the French score recorded the loss of a region of increasing importance to its industrial development. In the prior decade, Alsace-Lorraine had quadrupled its output of iron ore, its share of French production growing from about 10 percent to over 30 percent (Landes 1969, 226–27). Clearly Prussia was concerned about the French capacity to outcompete it in relative terms even as its own absolute output continued to soar.

The same pattern appears. A discontinuity in foreign policy expectations precedes a significant war. The target of aggression is not necessarily the largest state, nor a challenger for any kind of political supremacy, but a state that takes power share away. Here Prussia was guilty of "arranged aggression," arranging for France to attack, an act that Prussia planned and manipulated to its own military advantage. But the pattern is identical: first a discontinuity of foreign policy expectations with a loss of power share to another state(s), then attempted military defeat of the state.

A similar empirical exercise demonstrates, in each subsystem, that Germany's relative share of steel production peaked in the decade prior to World War I even though its absolute output continued to increase and far exceeded the output of any other state in the system. Graphs for the dyadic subsystems make unambiguous the states responsible for Germany's peak. Whereas the trend of relative power vis-à-vis Britain continued to rise, albeit more slowly, the trend vis-à-vis France and Russia had flattened and even begun to decline. A critical point once again is associated with *who* (which competing states) causes it and, consequently, will be the target of aggression.

Power cycle theory not only identifies when an act of major aggression is most likely, and why. It also explains who is the likely target of that aggression, and why it is so engaged. Direction of causation is unambiguous.

Dyads in a Systemic World

In conclusion, this section[27] compares the principles of the power cycle, and their predictions, with those of two other structural theories. This chapter argues that the principles of the power cycle reveal the unique perspective of statecraft in the expectations, and unexpected nonlinearities, of relative power change. Figure 4 demonstrates that this perspective is quite in contrast to that of transition theory and hegemonic stability theory.

On the left is a schematic of the pre-1914 absolute trajectories of Britain, Germany, and Russia. Germany experienced very rapid absolute growth in the late nineteenth century, surpassed Britain, and continued its surge with Russia far behind. So great was Germany's absolute economic output that Russia was by comparison a mere pygmy—of the order of one-tenth the size of Germany on most indicators. There were the objective indicators (absolute levels and trends) perceived by statesmen of the period.

On the right are schematics depicting two very different expectations regarding the *relative* power trajectories of these same states. This dual schematic reveals that debate regarding power cycle theory versus transition (and hegemonic stability) theory is not about empirical findings, preferred empirical approaches, different databases, statistical techniques, subtleties of terminology, or confusions of jargon. Nor is it merely about two different points (critical points versus transition points) in relative power change. At heart, the debate concerns theoretical understanding of the dynamics of international politics. Dyadic analysis must confront the principles of the power cycle to escape theoretical misspecification of the causes of major war.

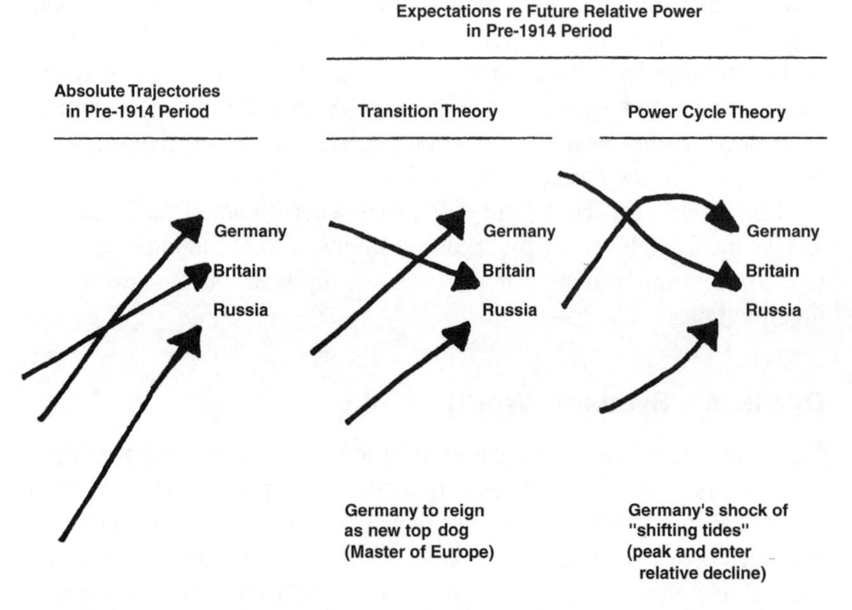

FIGURE 4. Dyads in a systemic world: Confronting the principles of the power cycle

In transition and hegemonic stability theories, expectations about the changing structure of the system (center schematic) precisely match those induced by extrapolation of the absolute power trends (far left). Focusing on the dyadic relation at the top of the system, they assert that the key to systems transformation, and the cause of World War I, was the competition for hegemony between Britain and Germany. The mechanism for the transformation and the war is the "transition" when Germany surpassed Britain in size. These theories conform to the Mastery of Europe thesis: so great was Germany's superiority in the prewar period, and so great were its yearly increases in absolute level, that surely Germany would soon have become Master of Europe if it had not made the strategic error of going to war. In a word, these theories assert that Germany's relative power continued to rise in the prewar period, and only defeat in the war forced it onto a declining relative power path.

In contrast (schematic far right), the principles of the power cycle reveal how the "bounds of the system" suddenly and unexpectedly forced Germany to peak in relative power a decade before the war. Statesmen saw ever greater increments of absolute power growth for Germany; but, they also saw a sudden halt in its previously rapid gain in relative share. Thus, in the power cycle assessment, what most triggered German angst in 1914, and German bellicosity, was the sudden discovery that the tides of history had shifted against it.

Accounts of diplomatic historians support the power cycle assessment. "With no history behind it save forty years of unchallenged success in an undeviating advance to greatness" (Seaman 1963, 143), and "trust[ing] in a current that would carry [them] to [their] goal" (Dehio 1962, 233), the German Foreign Office and General Staff were shocked to discover that German relative power had peaked. Despite its greatest absolute increases ever, its relative power was locked in a structural vise. Germany and all of Europe were aware of the "underwater current," so counterintuitive, that shattered expectations of continued German rise on its power cycle. The tiny absolute increments of Russia, in accelerating economic take-off at the bottom of the system, were sufficient to halt Germany's ascent and force it onto a declining path.

The problem for Germany was not one of misperception of its power level, but of *very clear perception* of a sudden and completely unexpected and even counterintuitive shift in history's prior trend of relative power change in the system. This terrible period of history begins to make some sense when the analyst experiences the conflicting messages and shocking surprises with which statesmen had to contend as Germany suddenly bumped against the upper limit of its relative power growth. At the hour of its greatest achievement, Germany was driven onto unexpected paths by the bounds of the system.

What are the implications for analysis of rival dyads? The transition between Germany and Britain occurs in both schematics for changing systems structure. But in the power cycle schematic, the transition is overwhelmed by the sudden "shifting tides of history" that drove Germany into relative decline. And it is the growth of the pygmy—nowhere near the upper dyad in terms of level—that causes the critical change in Germany's power cycle. That is why the transition hypothesis is said to be misspecified, and why dyads must be examined in the context of the relevant system.

In the context of systems structure, a transition constitutes one point shared by two absolute trajectories, and hence by two intersecting power cycles. A "critical point" is an inversion in the prior trend on a power cycle at which the state's perception of its future relative power and role suddenly changes. The principles of the power cycle show that the expectations induced by absolute trends (transition theory) do not hold, and that it is the shock of the unexpected nonlinearities on the power cycle that cause war.

The schematics also show why power cycle theory rejects the traditional view that systems transformation is a structural discontinuity caused by massive war (that defeat in a massive war forces the faster growing challenger onto a declining path). Power cycle theory shows that the nonlinearities of systems transformation (here the challenger's peak and turn into decline) occurred naturally as shifting tides of history determined by the principles of the power cycle, provoking a discontinuity of perception and expectations that caused the massive war. What is at issue in systems transformation is systemic adjustment. Evaluations by statesmen of their changed future trends ricochet across the system, translating the strains internal to each state to the essence of structural equilibrium for the entire system. Causation goes from continuity of structural change, to inversion in the trend of structural change at a critical point (structural discontinuity), to discontinuity of expectations, to failure of systemic adjustment, to massive war. From state to system and back to state, the discontinuity precipitates tumult.

The hegemonic assumption of world order is based on conditions that arose *after the collapse of world order in massive world war.* It is an assumption arising out of the failure of peaceful change. Power cycle theory, developed during a study of those failures, asserts that the dilemma of peaceful change can have no resolution unless order maintenance is recognized as a shared duty. Only thereby can a just and stable equilibrium prevent a collapse into world war during systems transformation.

There is much complementarity in the field of international relations as analysts work toward a common albeit multifaceted understanding of systems change and major war (Geller and Singer 1998; Pollins 1996). A declining hegemon, a redistribution of capabilities, a scramble for leadership, a power transition, a status disequilibrium—each is an accurate assessment regarding causes of major war, but each also suffers from some degree of incompleteness or misspecification. A hegemon may long be in decline; deconcentration of power, power transition, unfulfilled expectations, and power-interest gaps are so frequent that random effects cannot be discounted. For more accurate specification of cause, all of these perspectives ultimately must confront the principles of the power cycle: the conflicting messages and shocking surprises of relative versus absolute change, the structural bounds on statecraft, the shifting tides of history at points of nonlinearity, the shocks and surprises and uncertainty as statesmen confront the trauma of structural discontinuity. Analysis will thereby approach the "limit point" of understanding, more encompassing and more focused, and thus perhaps more helpful.

Notes

1. According to Collingwood (1956, 282), the analyst of history must "re-enact the past in his own mind." Carr (1964, 26) restates this responsibility to the facts quite strongly: "History cannot be written unless the historian can achieve some kind of contact with the mind of those about whom he is writing."
2. Although power must include national will, strategic skill, and political coherence, it is largely derived from the state's latent resource base, without which there is no power. This capability can be effectively indexed with a bundle of indicators robust across states and, properly qualified, across time. Also, although experts will disagree about the definition of power, they are able to rank states in terms of how powerful they are perceived to be. Without such intuitive *ranking* of perceived power, policymakers could not plan and implement policies rationally. These perceived rankings of "who has power" are also stable across cultures and are *highly correlated* with national capability. See Doran et al. (1974, 1979); Doran (1991, 33–35, 44–58); Singer, Bremer, and Stuckey (1972); Stoll and Ward (1989); and Sullivan (1990).
3. Doran (1991, 265–67) gives equivalent ratios to determine if a state is rising or declining in relative power. The denominator may also be the other states in the system, but that ratio is unbounded; it obscures the effect of the systemic bounds on the dynamic even though it contains the same critical points.
4. Observe that the power cycle thereby consciously preserves causal direction both perceptually and operationally.
5. On bounded rationality, see Anderson and McKeown (1987). On prospect theory, see Kahneman and Tversky (1979) and Levy (1997). Analysts are exploring the interface between power cycle and prospect theories. Hebron and James (1997) use "framing" to classify declining states as defenders of the status quo and rising states as challengers. Cashman (1997) identifies as directly applicable to power cycle theory three conflict hypotheses derived by Levy from prospect theory.
6. Hoffmann (1960), Keohane and Nye (1977), Singer et al. (1972), neorealists including Waltz (1979), Krasner (1985), and Keohane (1984, 1989). Power cycle analysis (Doran 1991, 27–30) answers the objections of Bueno de

Mesquita (1978, 1981a) that no structural change is great enough to so affect behavior. See also McGowan (1989).

7. See, for example, Mowat (1968), Rostow (1971), Dehio (1962), Cipola (1970), and Kindleberger (1996).
8. Doran (1971) is a revision, with annotated bibliography, of Doran (1969).
9. See Doran (1991, 30–33, 180–86), Rosenau (1969), and Holsti (1970). Role involves the extent of leadership or followership; providing or depending upon external security; being an aid giver or recipient, a lender or net debtor; being sought after for counsel or disregarded; being an overachiever or a nonparticipant in systemic affairs. It involves articulation and maintenance of international economic regimes, responsibilities of mediation and peacekeeping, protection of human rights and the environment, and initiative in organizational forums.
10. Disequilibrium on the power-role cycle is examined conceptually with the aid of two models: short-term equilibrium graphs (papers dating from 1970), and a lagging of the two components (since Doran 1974). Doran (1980) compares the inversion of force expectations with a runaway arms race via equilibrium graphs. Doran (1989a) analyzes the lag schema to study movement away from equilibrium in a critical interval. Doran (1991) examines both models fully: chapter 1, short-term disequilibrium graphs; chapter 4, effect of disaggregating the cycle; chapter 7, what each model implies for inter-national political equilibrium. Doran and Marcucci (1990) brings the two schema together in a "power cobweb theorem."
11. The quote refers to a section in Doran (1991, 125–32) that tries to get into the mind of statesmen undergoing the trauma of critical change, 1905 to 1914.
12. For Kupchan (1994, 14, 95–97), policy elite can know if the state is rising or declining but not if a turning point occurs, responding only to short-term shifts in the balance. Yet, if those shifts are not equivalent to the abrupt turning points in the long-term relative power trends, his concept of strategic vulnerability reduces to the familiar mechanics of short-term power balancing. And if German elites were aware of the rising trend of relative power, why would they be less sensitive to the abrupt halt in that rise in the decade prior to 1914, especially since the greatest absolute increases ever were unable to lift the German trajectory back onto a rising path? Evidence that statesmen intuitively know when a turning point occurs is Kissinger's 1968 declaration that "the age of the superpowers is now drawing to a close" (1974, 56).
13. Only one case occurred in our data, namely, Russia's suspected inflection in 1821. This suggests that a suspected critical point may likewise be conducive of major war; indeed, Russia initiated several wars during the next decade.

14. See Snyder and Diesing (1977) and Holsti (1972). The question arises whether diffusion processes are rational or nonrational in origin. See Siverson and Starr (1991).
15. See Jervis (1976) and chapter 6 of Mansbach and Vasquez (1981). Doran (1991, 171–77; 1995, 188–90, 204–5) examines the interface of all three theories. See also Siverson and Diehl (1989) and Siverson and Miller (1993).
16. When a number of states are simultaneously undergoing critical changes, the structural uncertainty contributing to instability is compounded by information uncertainty. Moreover, when opponents become multiple, information overload quickly overwhelms the decision maker. The important relationships between information, structure, and systemic stability, explored theoretically and empirically in Manus Midlarsky (1988), likewise have a bearing here.
17. See Doran (1971). The *Harper Atlas of World History* (1986) gives a precise date for Spain's peak, 1580; most historical accounts give a broader interval.
18. See Doran (1969, 1971). Doran (1995b, 190–97) summarizes the findings on these three assimilative efforts and assesses the two twentieth-century peace treaties.
19. See Doran (1991, chaps. 6–7; 1995, 201–3). Doran (1989b, 106–8) compares as well Midlarsky's hierarchical equilibrium and Rosecrance's notion of equilibrium.
20. Robert Powell (1996b) examines formally strategic problems that arise from expectations tied to changes on state power cycles. In particular, he shows how uncertainty about the intentions and aims of a rising power leads to the classic dilemma of peaceful change for the declining state: either fighting an early unnecessary preemptive war or appeasing an insatiable rising state in a series of concessions. However, the formal analysis of security must also take into account both the full dynamic of the power cycles and the dynamic equilibrium proposed in power cycle theory. In particular, how can the formal model account for the fact that expectations are altered abruptly at the critical points when awareness of decline suddenly dawns, and what are the implications for appeasement in that model?
21. Among the increasing literature on peaceful change, see Holsti (1991), Vasquez et al. (1995), and Kegley and Raymond (1999).
22. Young-Kwan Yoon (1990) examines the relative impact on industrial structure, late in the cycle, of home industry investment migrating abroad to seek greater trade opportunities, comparing the cases of Britain, the United States, Japan, and now possibly the newly industrializing countries like Korea. In the context of Asian power cycles, Sushil Kumar at Nehru University has initiated a long-term project studying the dynamic of these cycles for south Asia in particular.

23. This is one of the contrasts of the multiple state system with the universal empires of ancient Egypt, China, Persia, Alexander the Great, or Rome.
24. Doran, Politics of the International Economy course at Johns Hopkins.
25. See Niou, Ordeshook, and Rose (1989, 301).
26. See Doran and Buck (1991, 189–210) and Doran and Marcucci (1990, 468–71).
27. The arguments in this section were originally presented in Doran (1992).

PART IV

Summary Approaches

Reexamining the Steps to War

New Evidence and Theoretical Insights

JOHN A. VASQUEZ

It has been just over 10 years since the steps-to-war explanation (Vasquez 1987) was first published. That analysis attempted to synthesize the numerous and sometimes disparate findings of the Correlates of War project into a theoretically coherent explanation of the onset of war. A few years later in *The War Puzzle* (Vasquez 1993), the explanation was elaborated by looking at the role of territory and by constructing more detailed analyses of the onset of war and of war expansion. This chapter reviews the theoretical insights the explanation provides and new tests of the steps-to-war explanation, as well as other pertinent quantitative evidence, to provide an initial assessment of its empirical accuracy. It begins by briefly summarizing the explanation. The second section discusses the theoretical insights and how these emphases differ from those that have dominated the scientific study of war. The third section examines recent empirical evidence to see the extent to which it supports the steps-to-war explanation. The concluding section discusses future research.

The Steps to War: Summary of the Explanation

The steps-to-war explanation conceptualizes the onset of war as a process emerging out of the interactions (and foreign policy practices) of states. These interactions in turn are affected by the domestic political situation in which each actor finds itself, as well as being shaped by the existing global institutional context (and norms) of the particular historical era. While the focus is on what actors do to each other that leads them to go to war, this perspective does not ignore domestic politics or systemic factors in shaping foreign policy practices.

The kinds of steps that actors take in dealing with issues will vary depending on their relative capability. Certain policies and practices are more readily available to major states than to minor states. Likewise, states behave differently toward one another depending on whether they are equal. For example, equal states can engage in arms races against one another, while this is not as feasible between major and minor states. For these reasons, the paths to war that nation-states traverse are seen as different. While the steps-to-war explanation assumes that there are several paths by which war can break out, it attempts to delineate the typical path by which the strongest states in the modern global system (1495–present) come to war. It is claimed that in the nation-state system, territorial disputes are more apt to result in wars than other kinds of issues. War is brought about by each side taking a series of steps that increase hostility and make the issues under contention more intractable. This usually involves disputants in a series of crises, one of which escalates to war.

In the modern global system, realist folklore has provided an intellectual culture that guides the foreign policy actions of the strongest states in the system (Vasquez 1993, chap. 3). This realist folklore, which is based on deriving lessons from war and inventing practices and policies to deal with the prospect of war, in effect, tells leaders how to treat various situations they might face in their relations with other states (Morgenthau 1960). For example, if threatened, they should build up their capability. Power, according to realist wisdom, can be increased either by making alliances or by building up one's armaments. In a crisis, states should demonstrate their resolve and act on the basis of their strength. One of the unanticipated consequences of these power politics policies is that when used between equals, instead of increasing security, they result in a security dilemma, and instead of producing peace, they increase the prospects of war. Thus, making an alliance may lead to a counteralliance, and building up one's military may produce an arms race. Demonstrating resolve can lead to a hostile spiral that can escalate out of control.

A review of statistical findings suggests that of all the kinds of actions states can take, the realist practices of power politics—when used among equals—more often end in war (Vasquez 1987). This leads to the hypothesis that states that follow realist advice when dealing with equals often go to war with their rivals. In this way, realism provides an accurate *description* of a road to war. Some scholars take this as evidence of the utility of realism, but to do so is to miss the point that realism, and the logic of power it embodies, is not intended to be a set of practices that leads to war and thereby provide an accurate description of a road to war; it is supposed to provide an understanding of the nature of politics that diplomats can use to avoid war and to win power struggles without necessarily going to war. These findings show that diplomats who engage in the typical realist practices of making alliances, building up their militaries, and employing realpolitik techniques in crises in order to intimidate their opponents do not avoid war, but end up at war.

Table 1 summarizes the typical path by which major states become embroiled in a war. The path is conceptualized as a series of steps that leads to interstate war. The use of power politics practices among equals can be seen as taking a series of steps that eventually result in war; that is, each realist practice (making an alliance, building up one's military,

TABLE 1.

Summary of Steps-to-War Explanation

Summary of Steps-to-War Explanation
Raising Territorial Issues (underlying cause)
Handling them in a power politics fashion by (proximate causes):
Alliance Making
Military Buildups
Repeated Crises
One crisis escalates to war when
—Physical threat to a territorial issue
—Ongoing arms race
—Escalatory bargaining across crises
—Hostile spiral
—Hard-liners on at least one side

engaging in crises, and using realpolitik strategies in those crises) is seen as a step taken along a road to war.

The idea of steps to war is meant to convey that each step in and of itself increases the probability of war. The steps to war, however, need not occur in a particular order, nor is it necessary that each step be taken for war to break out. As a probabilistic explanation, it assumes that the more steps that are taken, the greater the likelihood of war. While none of the steps make war inevitable, the taking of one step increases the probability of taking another, producing a syndrome of behavior (both between the two contenders and within their respective domestic political environments) that makes the avoidance of war increasingly difficult for decision makers. The precise impact of each step on the probability of war cannot be determined a priori, but the interaction of each step with the others produces a dynamic that acts as a causal force to bring about war.

The term *step* refers to the taking of specific actions—disputing territorial claims, adopting realist practices, getting involved in crises. The term is intended to be more metaphorical than highly technical, although as will be discussed, each step or action taken is postulated as resulting in a step-level increase in the amount of hostility between actors. What is important is that observers should find that after each step (listed in table 1) is taken, the overall probability of war increases. Not too much emphasis should be placed on the exact sequence given in the table. Whether states engage in both alliance making and military buildups, let alone in what order, may depend on the specific opportunities with which they are confronted; the only effect posited by the model is that if states engage in both, the probability of war will be greater than if they engage in only one action. Likewise, it would be misleading to think that crises occur at only one point in this sequence; in long rivalries they can be expected to punctuate the relationship. The point of the model is not to specify *when* crises will occur, but their effect on hostility and the probability of war once they do occur. Finally, it is assumed, at least for the strongest states in the system, that "what states fight over" (Diehl 1992) is embodied in their foreign policy goals and that the means (alliance making, etc.) are subsequently selected in light of the preexisting goals. The intensity of interaction and the souring of relations may produce such hostility and insecurity, however, that territorial issues that were latent or nonexistent may suddenly come to the fore, when without the initiation of power politics practices they may have remained latent. Signing an alliance with one's rival, for example, may place a new set of territorial issues on the global agenda or at least move them to the front burner.[1] In such a case, territorial disputes would proceed out of the train of power politics, rather than precede them. Such instances, however, are most likely to be the result of contagion associated with the onset of world wars (see Vasquez 1993, chap. 7; 1996).

Since the twin logics of realist folklore and the security dilemma are not precise enough to specify the order in which steps occur, it is best not to try to derive the order theoretically. This decision is reinforced by the lack of an obvious pattern in cases that come readily to mind. Whether certain dyads or types of actors follow a particular sequence or whether steps can occur simultaneously is best left to an inductive investigation. Similarly, while it is reasonable to expect statistical interactions between the listed factors and to expect that recursive processes will be present, just what these are is best determined empirically. Despite these caveats, certain theoretical expectations can be derived.

Territorial issues are posited as underlying causes of war, and the practices of power politics are seen as the proximate causes of war (see table 1). Territorial issues are seen as underlying causes in that they do not inevitably, nor directly, give rise to war. Depending on how they are handled, they can set off a train of events that will end in war. It is hypothesized that if territorial disputes are handled by power politics, they are more apt to lead to war than other sorts of disputes (e.g., ideological, regime, economic, or policy disputes).

Because territorial issues are often at the root of conflict that may eventually give rise to war, they are seen as the origin of most interstate wars in the modern global system. This holds not only for wars between equals, like France and Germany (1914, 1939), but also for war between unequals, like Germany and Poland (1939). One of the reasons territorial issues serve as an underlying cause of war is that their salience, both in terms of their intrinsic importance and public awareness of them, tends to make disputes recur. The repetition of disputes is one of the main factors most associated with war among equals (see Wayman 1996; Goertz and Diehl 1992a). Presumably this recurrence engenders increasing hostility and a sense of rivalry with all that this entails (see Vasquez 1993, 75–83).

As a security situation arises in which there is a likelihood that force will be threatened or employed, realist folklore recommends that political actors increase their capability by the making of alliances and/or the building up of their military. Both of these, however, frequently produce a counter-response that threatens one's opponent. The empirical evidence shows that alliances, particularly among major states, are not followed by peace as suggested by realists, who see alliances as a way of balancing power and hence preventing war (see Levy 1981, 597–98; Ostrom and Hoole 1978). Clearly, one of the ways in which alliances aggravate a situation is that the making of alliances increases the threat to the other side and can lead to a counteralliance. The end result, in relative terms, is that there has been no increase in power, but in absolute terms both sides now face a greater threat and a greater bloc of capability that must be overcome. Overall, insecurity has increased.

The most fundamental way in which alliances help bring about war is that they increase threat perception, hostility, and general tension. Threat perception gets parties to start thinking about war and defining who their enemies are. In doing so, it generates more hostility. Hostility intensifies rivalry and makes parties define their issue positions more in terms of who is opposing them rather than the specific stakes at issue (see Vasquez 1993, 76–82). General tension promotes war scares and an atmosphere conducive to hard-liners on each side. While the initial formation of an alliance and the formation of a counteralliance are the events that produce these effects, the renewing or tightening of older alliances or the formation of alignments within crises could produce similar effects.

The second way in which alliances increase the probability of war is that they mesh the interests of several different actors, thereby increasing the number of situations and *casus belli* that can give rise to war. On the whole, multiparty disputes are more apt to escalate to war than dyadic disputes (see Cusack and Eberwein 1982; Gochman and Maoz 1984, 601–2; James and Wilkenfeld 1984; Brecher 1993, 1996b). To the extent that alliances bring third parties into a crisis, they make it more difficult for the crisis to be managed and more likely that things might get out of control.

An increase in hostility also results from attempts to build up one's military. Unlike the making of an alliance, this step is both more costly in terms of resources and more time consuming. The building up of one's military frequently leads to an arms race, although such a race may not always take the technical form outlined by Richardson (1960a).

The empirical evidence on the relationship between military buildups and the onset of war is not as clear as the evidence on alliances and war. Suffice it to say here that (at most) military buildups of some kind seem to increase the probability that militarized disputes will escalate to war.

Whether these military buildups need to be mutual ongoing arms races and whether this relationship holds only for arms races of a certain type is still a matter of debate (see Wallace 1979, 1982, 1990 and Diehl 1983, 1985a). Nevertheless, there seems to be at least a statistically significant relationship between the presence of arms races and the escalation of militarized disputes to war. Furthermore, it is clear from the empirical evidence that only a few crises escalate to war in the *absence* of arms races (see Wallace 1982, 1990). In terms of the analysis here, it is also important to note that the relationship between arms racing and war is strongest before world wars (Weede 1980; Diehl 1983).

Overall, the effects of arms racing are not unlike those of alliance making; namely, they tend to increase threat perception, hostility, and general tension. The precise effects of arms racing must await further in-depth case studies, but theoretically it appears that arms racing can be a very important element in generating a rivalry, as was the case in the Anglo-German rivalry, which was brought about in no small part by the German decision to build up a navy (see Kennedy 1982, 251–52, 467). More typically, military buildups may put decision makers (and/or certain bureaucratic actors) under time pressure to act now before the enemy reaps the benefit of a buildup. Such pressures generated by the building of railroads in Russia, for example, seemed to be an element in hard-line arguments in Japan favoring war against Russia in 1904 (see Richardson 1994, 119–20) and in Germany favoring war against Russia in 1914.

Arms races also help identify the enemy and are often related to war scares. The latter are not only an indicator of the high level of tension, but help generate self-amplifying feedback that serves to buttress the arguments of hard-liners in each side and weaken the influence of accommodationists (see Singer 1982). In this manner, arms races promote a domestic political atmosphere for hard-line bargaining, increasing the probability of crises escalating, while making it difficult for accommodationist actions to be taken at crucial junctures within a crisis.

From the preceding analysis, it is postulated that alliances and military buildups constitute two steps toward war among equals. The making of alliances and building up of militaries do not occur in isolation. They are usually punctuated by crises because in an intense rivalry, realism preaches that states test their rivals and demonstrate resolve by relying on threats and coercive tactics (Rummel 1979, 186; Maoz 1983). In a crisis, equal states tend to employ *realpolitik* tactics (Leng 1983). As these crises repeat, the probability of war goes way up, especially if all the other steps to war have already been taken (Wallensteen 1981, 74–75, 84; Leng 1983; Brecher and Wilkenfeld 1989; Brecher 1993).

The repetition of crises is the real engine of war, for it makes it highly likely that eventually a crisis will emerge that escalates to war. This is another way of saying that as crises repeat, actors tend to intensify their bargaining tactics, getting closer and closer to war. This escalation in turn is a function of the increased influence of hard-liners within each side. A crisis is most likely to escalate to war if (1) it is triggered by a physical threat to a territorial issue (Gochman and Leng 1983; Brecher and James 1988), (2) it is one in a series of crises with the same rival (usually resulting in realpolitik tactics becoming more coercive and hostile) (Leng 1983; see also Leng 1993a), (3) a hostile interaction spiral emerges in the crisis (Holsti, North, and Brody 1968), and (4) hard-liners dominate the leadership of at least one side (Vasquez 1993, 155).

Through successive crises, the making of alliances and the building up of their respective militaries, states have engaged in interactions that have taught them that force and war are the best or only ways of handling the situation at hand. The previous steps that have been taken constitute a set of external constraints under which decision makers must act. In the meantime, the interactions also have had important domestic effects on each collectivity, creating a domestic political context that also constrains the choices of decision makers (see Huth 1996a; Roy 1997). In short, each step to war and the threatening reaction it generates in the other side help to create a constituency for hard-liners within a state and reduce the number and influence of those who wish to seek accommodation and avoid war. The balance between hard-liners and accommodationists tips more and more in favor of the former as hostile actions persist and grow.

How long it will take for hard-liners to predominate within a polity depends not only on the external interaction but also on the initial balance between them and the accommodationists. It is hypothesized that the initial balance between the two is a function of the outcome of the last major war. Victory in war that is seen as worth the costs generates hard-liners; whereas defeat that is seen as not worth the costs generates accommodationists, *ceteris paribus.* Victory that is seen as not worth the costs and defeat that is seen as worth the costs produce unstable situations because of cognitive dissonance, with the former favoring accommodationists, and the latter, hard-liners (Vasquez 1993, chap. 6). States that were initially dominated by accommodationists will have a longer fuse than those dominated by hard-liners, but neither will be able to resist the prevailing tendency of interactions (i.e., conflictive actions over the long run increase the influence of hard-liners, and cooperative actions, the influence of accommodationists). The combined effect of hostile external relations and the rise of hard-liners domestically produces a number of psychological effects that help mobilize the society for war and make it difficult to turn the tide to avoid war at the last minute (see Barringer 1972, 102–15; White 1966, 4–5; see also Hagan 1998).

On the basis of the preceding cursory review, it would be expected that the typical dyadic interstate war between equal states in the modern global system would be between neighbors over a territorial dispute. Rivals engaged in a territorial dispute who make alliances against each other and who build up their militaries would be expected to be simultaneously involved in repeated crises.[2] Successive crises result in each side's increasing its escalatory actions, with war becoming more likely.

Territorial issues, however, do not need to be handled by power politics, and if they are not, the probability for war decreases. Whether power politics will be employed depends very much on the extent to which there are clear norms for transferring territory and whether the demands of revisionist states for territorial changes can be easily handled by those norms. Territorial demands that are seen as legitimate are obviously going to require less coercion than those that are not. Nevertheless, the more extensive and complicated the territorial demands, the greater the likelihood existing norms will be unable to handle them. Thus, the norms of the Concert of Europe could resolve minor adjustments to the territorial distribution, but could not have been expected to accommodate the ambitions of nineteenth-century German and Italian nationalists seeking to create new large states for their respective "nations."

Often war will occur because norms and the global institutional order have been put under too much stress or have simply decayed and no longer exist (see Doran 1971). In either instance, revisionist states act unilaterally to bring about territorial changes, thereby initiating a steps-to-war process. If, however, there is an agreement on norms and a rich global institutional context for handling political issues and bringing about peaceful change, then there is a lower probability that revisionist states will (1) resort to unilateral practices like power politics or (2) go to war (see Wallensteen 1984; Kegley and Raymond 1990; Vasquez 1993, chap. 8). The nature of the existing global institutional context, in particular its norms for the transfer of territory, is a crucial factor for explaining the onset of war. It is important therefore to control for this systemic factor.

New Theoretical Insights

The steps-to-war explanation offers several theoretical insights and emphases that make it different from the standard way in which war has been studied, especially prevailing realist approaches. Together these insights provide a different perspective on how war *should* be studied if it is to be understood. Whether these insights are correct will be determined by whether the research guided by them is fruitful. Not all of the following insights are original with the steps-to-war analysis. Nevertheless, they reflect a different way of approaching research than was common in the early years of peace research, and in some cases they are lessons that were not easily learned within the field. While the case on how fruitful these insights are is still open, many have found that ignoring these lessons of inquiry often leads research to be less productive than it could be.

One of the first things that becomes clear to anyone who sifts through the quantitative evidence on war and compares it to the historical record is that various wars are not brought about by the same causal sequence. War among major states seems to be associated with certain foreign policy practices, like alliance making and arms races, that are absent in other wars, like imperial wars between the very strong and the weak.

The idea that war might have multiple causes and that there might be several different paths to war has not been, particularly among scientific researchers, a widely held assumption, although it has gained more credence among those more historically oriented (see Levy 1989a, 227, 279, 281; Thompson 1995b). If this assumption is correct, then researchers need to pay more attention to how different wars might be preceded by different causal sequences. Little of this has been done, especially within the Correlates of War project; instead the tendency has been to assume that all wars are alike and hence a legitimate sample upon which to test a given explanation (for an exception, see Wallace 1990). The closest researchers have come to rejecting the notion that all wars have the same fundamental correlates or causes is when they confine their tests to certain kinds of states; for example, only major states or only interstate as opposed to interstate and extrasystemic wars. In fact, it was the discrepancy between some of the findings on war involving major states on both sides, as opposed to all interstate wars, that first provided the field a clue that there might be different types of war, each with its own set of causes (and correlates).

If one takes this insight seriously, how would it affect the way in which war is studied? If there are different causes for different kinds of wars, then one of the most important things political scientists can do is identify and document the various causal sequences by which war is brought about. The steps-to-war model was an early attempt to uncover one sequence. *The War Puzzle* refined and elaborated that causal sequence and confined its domain to wars among equals that involve the strongest states in the modern global system, 1495 to the present. It further stipulated that while there are numerous causal sequences by which war occurs, the sequence it delineated was seen as the *typical* path by which the strongest states came to war with one another. Ultimately, one would expect from the field a set of documented causal sequences of the paths by which war could come about, along with a list of each of the existing wars that illustrates that path to war. Such an effort would tie the nomothetic efforts of political scientists and the case analyses of neotraditional scholars, as well as historians, together.

Another problem with standard explanations of wars is an ignoring of what role issues play in the onset of war or, as Diehl (1992) put it, "what are they fighting for?" The second theoretical insight provided by the analysis is that territorial issues may be the key to understanding why wars occur and how they can be avoided.[3] The importance of territory is just beginning to receive recognition, as initial research results appear promising. If research shows that territory is an important factor promoting war or an initial step to war, then the inclusion of this variable, which has long been ignored by peace researchers, must be seen as a major contribution to our understanding of war.

A third theoretical insight of the explanation has been the move away from systemic and internal domestic explanations to a focus on dyadic (or interaction) explanations of the onset of war. This was an emphasis already under way in the early 1990s, reaching a very wide audience with Bremer's (1992) publication of "Dangerous Dyads" (see also Vasquez 1983, 57, 85; Bueno de Mesquita and Lalman 1988). Looking at the steps to war means that interactions between political actors, not the structure of the international system (Waltz's [1959] third image) or the characteristics of individual states (the monad) or their decision makers (second and first images) is the most important level of analysis for identifying the factors that appear to be of causal significance. Research on war that has focused on dyads has consistently been more fruitful than that on the other levels, as illustrated most recently by the "democracies do not fight each other" literature (see Maoz and Russett 1993; Ray 1995) (but also see the following earlier dyadic research: Rummel 1972a; Kegley and Skinner 1976, 308–11; see also Singer 1982, 37–38).

A fourth insight is more subtle and has to do with how we think about causality. Typically, this word has been eschewed, but often it is conceived as sufficient and necessary conditions of war (which are frequently but an intellectual euphemism for "cause"). It may be the case, however, that war is such a complex phenomenon that it is misleading to think in terms of sufficient conditions and correlates of war. It may be more useful to think of certain factors as increasing the probability of war. The steps should be seen in this light. Whether they are related to war should be decided not in terms of whether each step is strongly correlated with the onset of war, but whether each step increases the probability of war. In this sense, statistical analyses that compare conditional and unconditional probabilities or use maximum likelihood estimation are much more on the mark than those that employ correlational analyses. A given factor may increase the probability of war, yet may not always be sufficient to bring about war by itself, and hence not appear as a correlate, although at some point enough steps will be taken to produce a sufficient condition.

A fifth insight is to suggest that dynamic models may tell us more about rare occurrences, like war, than static models. The steps to war are a dynamic and not a static condition. Each variable has an effect on other variables in the model, and together they may produce interaction effects. Theoretically, this implies that war is a relationship that evolves from prior interactions (see Mansbach and Vasquez 1981, chaps. 7 and 8). Path dependencies (the burden of history) become relevant. Seeing each step as having an impact on the probability of war permits analysts, in principle, to trace how a relationship changes and how potent each variable is. War results from actors following a causal sequence that gradually increases the probability of war. This is a very different conceptual model from a sufficient conditions model, which sees war more as an explosion occurring when x, y, z are present. The steps-to-war explanation assumes that war is part of a process and not just an "event" (see Bremer 1992, 320) associated with a static set of sufficient or necessary conditions.

A sixth related insight is that peace is not the absence of war, but a *relationship*. It is not something that occurs, but something that must be built (see Vasquez 1993, chap. 8; 1994). Just as war can be learned, so too can peace be learned (Vasquez 1995a). Part of what is involved in explaining war, especially at the system level, may be explaining why an existing peace system (like the Concert of Europe or the Washington Conference System) breaks down. War may emerge not just from an absence of norms but from their decay. In this way, understanding how peace is built and why it works will help us understand why war occurs.

Last, the steps-to-war explanation maintains that power politics is not so much an explanation or body of theory as a type of behavior that must itself be explained (Vasquez 1983, 216; 1998b, 167). Power politics is one way political actors can relate to each other. Among equals, it rarely produces peace, despite various realist analyses about the efficacy of force, coercive diplomacy, and deterrence. Instead, it increases the probability of war by increasing threat perception and hostility, while reducing security. The steps-to-war explanation tries to move analysis away from the exclusive focus on capability and the logic of power. The steps to war provides an explanation that hopes to increase the field's knowledge about other important political variables and their role in bringing about war.

New Evidence

The most important question facing any new explanation is whether it can pass systematic testing. This section presents and reviews tests that have been specifically conducted on the steps-to-war explanation as well as other tests that are directly relevant to its propositions. It begins by examining tests on territory and then looks at tests on alliances and on arms racing.

Territory and War

One of the earliest criticisms of the territorial explanation was that it is tautological. This criticism has two versions. The first says that "Yes, most wars are fought over territory, but this is true only in the descriptive sense." The second is a little more subtle; it suggests that it is easy to define territory in such a broad fashion that some territorial issue can be found prior to most conflict. Both of these criticisms maintain that the territorial explanation is incapable of falsification, a serious charge.

The first criticism misrepresents what the territorial explanation is prepared to predict as an adequate test (see Vasquez 1993, chap. 4; 1995b). The territorial explanation is not referring to the territorial military objectives an army might have when it says wars are fought because of territorial issues. Instead, it maintains that (1) territorial issues (disagreements and/or disputes) clearly precede the outbreak of war; that is, there are explicit political objectives and goals regarding territorial claims that lead one side to become involved in a war and (2) territorial issues are more likely than other types of issues to give rise to war in the modern global system.

The second criticism points out a danger, but this is no more true of territory as a variable than any other somewhat "soft" political variable, like arms races or alignment (as opposed to alliance making). The key to avoiding this criticism is to have reliable and valid operational indicators that exhibit the kind of variance one would normally expect of political variables. The other way of avoiding this danger is to have relevant data collected by at least some who are not tied to the territorial explanation and to have multiple data sets independently collected produce compatible results.

The availability of new Militarized Interstate Dispute (MID) data (Jones, Bremer, and Singer 1996) should put the tautology argument to rest by showing not only that reasonably valid data can be collected on territorial issues but also that these data can be used to construct test designs that are able to falsify propositions in the territorial explanation. One of the codes in the MID data is the revision in the status quo (prior to the dispute) a side is trying to make by its reliance on force. The primary revision sought is coded into one of five types: "(1) making claims to territory, (2) attempting to overthrow a regime, (3) declaring the intention not to abide by another state's policy," (4) all other revisions and (0) nonapplicable (Jones, Bremer, and Singer 1996, 178). If such data, which focus on the threat or use of force, have a certain amount of variance, then this would demonstrate that issues could be defined in a precise and reliable enough fashion to distinguish territorial issues from other types of issues. More important, it would demonstrate that the territorial explanation could be tested and falsified; thereby showing that it is not a tautology.

Table 2 presents the MID data (version MID21) on "revision type" cross-tabbed by "level of hostility"[4] As can be seen from the table, of

TABLE 2.

Percentage of Territorial and Other Types of Disputes within the Militarized Interstate Dispute Data for Each Category of Hostility

Revision Type		Hostility				
	Count Exp Val Row Pct Col Pct Tot Pct	2.00	3.00	4.00	WAR 5.00	Row Total
REVTYP_1						
	.00	12	83	263	5	363
		17.5	79.6	247.7	18.2	17.8%
Nonapplicable		3.3%	22.9%	72.5%	1.4%	
		12.2%	18.6%	18.9%	4.9%	
		.6%	4.1%	12.9%	.2%	
	1.00	16	142	372	53	583
		28.1	127.8	397.8	29.2	28.7%
Territory		2.7%	24.4%	63.8%	9.1%	
		16.3%	31.8%	26.8%	52.0%	
		.8%	7.0%	18.3%	2.6%	
	2.00	64	186	660	31	941
		45.4	206.6	642.1	47.2	46.3%
Policy		6.8%	19.8%	70.1%	3.3%	
		65.3%	41.7%	47.6%	30.4%	
		3.1%	9.1%	32.4%	1.5%	
	3.00	4	22	80	9	115
		5.5	25.2	78.5	5.8	5.7%
Regime		3.5%	19.1%	69.6%	7.8%	
		4.1%	4.9%	5.8%	8.8%	
		.2%	1.1%	3.9%	.4%	
	4.00	2	13	13	4	32
		1.5	7.0	21.8	1.6	1.6%
Other		6.3%	40.6%	40.6%	12.5%	
		2.0%	2.9%	.9%	3.9%	
		.1%	.6%	.6%	.2%	
	Column	98	446	1388	102	2034
	Total	4.8%	21.9%	68.2%	5.0%	100.0%

Source: MID21 data

2,034 militarized disputes occurring from 1815 to 1992, only 28.7 percent (583) are coded as territorial. If the tautological argument were valid, the percentage of territorial disputes should be much higher. Table 2 makes it clear that states are willing to threaten the use of force on a variety of issues. In fact, the most conflict-prone issue in the data set is the "policy dispute," which constitutes 46.3 percent (941) of the militarized confrontations, not territorial disputes. The distribution in table 2 also shows that coders did not have a tendency (conscious or unconscious) to code wars as being fought over territory just because they knew a war was the outcome. Only half of the wars (52 percent) have territory as their primary revision code.

Given these distributions, it should be clear that one of the main claims of the steps-to-war explanation—that territorial disputes are more war prone than other types of disputes—is a testable and falsifiable empirical question. The best and most straightforward test of this claim is to compare the war proneness of territorial disputes with that of other types of disputes.

Table 3 presents the results of such a test based on an analysis by Vasquez and Henehan (forthcoming). It compares the probability of war for each type of dispute (territory, policy, regime, and other).[5] The base or overall probability of war in this sample is .058. Territorial disputes are the only ones that have a significantly higher probability of going to war (.091) than the overall probability of war, with 53 wars occurring where only 33.8 are expected by chance (significance = $\leqslant$ .001). Policy disputes have a lower probability of going to war than the overall probability of war (.033—note the negative Z score; significance = $\leqslant$ .001), with only 31 wars occurring when 55 would be expected by chance. The other two types of dispute show no statistically significant relationship.

Looked at from another perspective, these conditional probabilities mean that even though territorial disputes constitute 34.9 percent (583) of the total number of the 1,671 disputes in this sample, they produce 54.6 percent (53) of the wars. Conversely, policy disputes, which constitute 56.3 percent of the disputes, produce 32 percent (31) of the wars, while regime disputes, constituting 6.9 percent of the sample, produce 9.3 percent (9) of the wars (see Vasquez and Henehan forthcoming, table 1).[6] Vasquez and Henehan also find that territorial issues remain war prone even when controlling for pre-1946 and post-1945 and the status of states (major-major, major-minor, minor-minor).

Table 3 presents clear evidence that territorial disputes are more war prone than other types of dispute, thereby giving support to the territorial explanation of war. Other studies of MID data have produced additional evidence to support that explanation as well. Hensel (1996b, 58–63), analyzing the same data set, finds that territorial disputes (as opposed to nonterritorial disputes) are more likely to produce a response (odds ratio = 3.45), are more likely to recur (odds ratio = 1.85), and are more likely to escalate to war (odds ratio = 3.12).[7] Hensel's findings that territorial disputes are more apt to evoke a response and to recur are precisely what would be expected by the territorial explanation of war, which sees political actors more concerned about their territory than other issues. For them, territorial issues are more salient (in terms of both their intrinsic importance and public awareness of the issue) than other types of issues. Therefore, decision makers are more inclined to respond to any threat or use of force regarding these issues.

Furthermore, once states resort to coercion to resolve these issues, states are not likely to give in but to meet force with force, thereby making these issues more likely to recur and become intractable. Such issues are more apt to be resolved by war. Findings by Hensel (1996a) also support the claim that territorial issues produce rivalries (see Vasquez 1993, 135, 193–94, 311; 1996, 534–36), and these, as is known from other research, have a higher probability of going to war than pairs of states that do not have recurring disputes (Wayman 1996; Goertz and Diehl 1992a). Hensel (1995) finds that even democratic dyads are prone to recurrent conflict if they are contending over territorial issues.

The fact that territorial issues are very important to decision makers and that they are more prepared to incur high costs to get their way on these issues is supported by some findings by Senese (1996). He demonstrates that when territorial issues are at stake, more battle deaths result

TABLE 3.

The Probability of Territorial and Other Types of Disputes Going to War, 1816–1992

Dispute Type	Actual (Wars)	Expected	*N*	*P* conditional (War)	Z	Significance
Territory	53	33.8	583	.091	3.408	<.001
Policy	31	54.6	941	.033	−3.280	<.001
Regime	9	6.7	115	.078	0.918	.1788
Other	4	1.9	32	.125	1.622	.0526
Total	97		1671			

Source: Vasquez and Henehan (forthcoming, table 1).
Note: Base probability of war = 97/1671 = .0580. (Nonapplicable coded cases excluded)

(Senese 1996, 152–53). This indicates that states are more willing to fight for territory and lose life for this kind of issue than they are for nonterritorial issues.

What these findings mean is that states who resort to militarized confrontations to handle territorial issues are more apt to get involved in intractable recurring conflicts, more apt to get involved in wars, and more apt to incur higher battle deaths than states who use or threaten force over nonterritorial issues. One of the reasons for this may be that territorial issues are so salient that they become subject to domestic political pressures. According to the steps-to-war explanation, this would mean that territorial issues have their own hard-line constituencies that put pressure on decision makers if they do not toe the line, although often these leaders themselves may fuel such hard-line tendencies (either because they see this as a way of increasing their power or because they sought power in the first place to do something about the issue).

In two analyses, Paul Huth (1996a, 1996b) argues that domestic political factors determine whether territorial issues will be pursued in a more confrontational manner. In his book, *Standing Your Ground,* Huth (1996a) is concerned with distinguishing why some borders are contested when most are not and why some territorial issues are peacefully resolved, whereas others lead to confrontations and become intractable. Huth's (1996b) article focuses on why some territorial disputes lead to enduring rivalries, whereas other territorial disputes do not. Both studies are based on 129 cases of territorial claims from 1950 to 1990. Because Huth (1996a) collected his own data, his study is also of interest in that it provides a database separate from the MID data to see if the territorial approach can productively guide research. Huth's (1996a) data are also important because they are the only ones to date that look at territorial issues regardless of whether they produce militarized disputes.

Huth (1996a, 1996b) finds that territorial claims involving bordering minority groups that have linguistic or ethnic ties to the challenger or those that involve the unification of the same ethnic group divided into two separate states are more apt to lead to confrontation (Huth 1996a, 108–13, table 9) and an enduring rivalry or repeated confrontations (Huth 1996b, 21, table 2) than territorial claims over purely strategic territory.[8] Davis, Jaggers, and Moore (1997) have a similar finding; examining COPDAB data from 1948 to 1979, they find that an ethnic tie across a border has a significant effect on belligerent foreign policy within a dyad. Huth (1996a, 140) explains the difference between strategic territory and "ethnic" territory by saying that when ethnicity is involved, leaders are apt to face more domestic political pressures.[9]

Huth, however, does not directly measure whether and how these ethnic attributes actually produce domestic political pressures. Here, Bikash Roy's (1997) comparative case studies are interesting. He shows, in detail, that the main reason disputes recur is that domestic hard-liners, usually for ethnic nationalist reasons, will not let decision makers compromise or defuse issues. Instead, these hard-liners constantly push that something be done, and eventually leaders escalate. In his analysis of the Russo-Turkish and India-Pakistan wars, Roy (1997) finds that this lack of caution is directly attributable to domestic political pressure by nonstate actors, who in his two cases actually participate in the communal strife that leads state actors to become more belligerent, even when one side faces strong international constraints against doing so.[10]

Such communal pressures are hardly new, as Midlarsky (1997a) shows in his analysis of the role of communal strife in bringing about World War I and the Yugoslav (civil) wars of the post–cold war era. Both provide illustrations of how, under the right conditions, communal strife can lead to a train of events that results in a systemic war that transforms a system. As with the India-Pakistan case, the two Balkan cases appear prone to war because ethnic and identity issues are tied to specific territorial claims, a point consistent with Midlarsky's (1997a, 73, 77, 79) argument that overlapping conflicts play a crucial role in bringing about systemic war (see also Vasquez 1996).

Huth's analysis provides one database independent of the MID data to support the claim that territory is an important source of war. A third data set that also produces convergent findings is that of the International Crisis Behavior (ICB) project (see Brecher and Wilkenfeld 1997). Unlike the MID data, these data are confined to the most serious and historically visible uses of force. There must be a threat to a basic value, a finite time for response and a heightened probability of military hostilities for a case to be defined as a crisis (Brecher 1996a, 127; see also Brecher 1993). Brecher and Wilkenfeld (1989, chaps. 9 and 10; 1997) and Brecher (1993, 1996b) provide indirect evidence that contention over territorial issues in a crisis increases the probability of a crisis recurring and escalating to full-scale war. While these findings are suggestive, they do not directly measure the presence of territorial issues.

Hemda Ben Yehuda (1997) has conducted a detailed analysis of territorial disputes in the ICB data. She provides explicit tests of several of the territorial propositions in *The War Puzzle.* In terms of the analysis here, what is of most interest is that she finds that crises involving territorial disputes at their core are much more likely to go to war than crises that are nonterritorial. Territorial crises are about twice as likely to result in war than are nonterritorial crises—29.2 percent (61 of 209 territorial crises) versus 14.8 percent (30 of 203 nonterritorial crises).

Nor is it the case that decision makers simply do not resort to armed force (and power politics) when nonterritorial issues are at the core of a crisis. Ben Yehuda (1997, 12–13, table 1a) finds that there is no difference in the propensity of the two different types of crises to be triggered by violence (41.1 percent [of 209] vs. 41.9 percent [of 203]). Also, a large percentage of nonterritorial crises are marked by armed clashes—26.6 percent (of 203) by "serious clashes" and 33 percent (of 203) by "minor clashes" (Ben Yehuda 1997, 16, table 3a). This supports Senese's (1996) contention that what distinguishes territorial from nonterritorial disputes is not that the latter are free of violence, but that territorial disputes are much more likely to escalate to full-scale war and high battle deaths than are nonterritorial disputes. As Brecher (1996b, 223) puts it, "the more basic the value(s) at risk, the higher the cost crisis actors are willing to incur. . . ." Thus, in Ben Yehuda's (1997, table 3a) analysis, the modal category of violence for territorial crises is war (29.2 percent); whereas the modal category for nonterritorial crises is "minor clashes" (33 percent).[11] Overall, Ben Yehuda (1997) finds that crises that center on territorial issues have a distinctly violent profile of behavior associated with them.

All the evidence to this point shows that territorial issues are different, and that, if handled in a power politics fashion, they are much more apt to go to war than other sorts of issues. This evidence, in effect, shows that territorial issues may be a major source of conflict that leads to war. It does not, however, demonstrate anything about the broad claim that territorial issues are an underlying cause of war in that if states can resolve their territorial concerns, the probability of peace goes way up. This claim brings the *causal* force of territorial issues to the forefront: When territorial disputes are present, the probability of war goes up; when territorial issues are resolved, the probability of peace goes up.

Kocs's (1995) analysis provides some evidence that if borders are accepted by both sides, then the probability of war goes down. States that are recognized under international law as having territorial disputes are much more apt to go to war than states who have accepted the legitimacy of their borders. Kocs's findings imply that states at peace are those who do not have territorial disputes or who have resolved their territorial disputes.[12]

Gibler's (1996) analysis provides additional evidence that settling territorial issues will engender long-term peaceful relations among former disputants. He has uncovered a class of alliance that settles territorial questions. According to the territorial explanation of war, it would be expected that such alliances would be followed by peace. Gibler (1996) finds that out of 194 alliances (from 1815 to 1980), 27 settle territorial issues. Of these 27, only 4 result in a war involving an ally within five years.[13] In this sample, the base probability of war is 0.35 (68 alliances out of 194 go to war), but the conditional probability of territorial settlement alliances going to war is only 0.15 (4/27), producing considerably fewer wars than would be expected by chance ($p < .0001$) (Gibler 1996, 85–86, table 1). Conversely, all other alliances (167) have a much higher (conditional) probability of going to war (.38) (64/167).

If it is the case that settling territorial issues has a pacifying effect on the probability of states going to war, then it could be expected that rivals who settle territorial issues might exhibit a tendency to reduce conflict short of war as well. In a highly original analysis, Gibler (1997a) tests this hypothesis. First, he finds that enduring rivals who signed an alliance to settle territorial issues experience a decline in their subsequent average rate of militarized disputes, both in general and for territorial disputes.[14] Second, rivals who have not signed a territorial settlement go to war much faster than those who do. It typically takes three disputes and 9 years for those without a settlement to go to war versus six disputes and 36 years for those with a settlement to go to war (Gibler 1997a, 364, table VIII).[15] A delay in war from 9 years to 36 years shows that the practical impact of territorial settlements can be very significant. Gibler's (1996, 1997a) analyses also show that territorial disputes do not have to go to war but can be resolved peacefully. Although a greater variety of tests than Gibler and Kocs perform will be needed before firm conclusions are reached, their tests show that actually settling territorial issues can have a pacific impact.

The last bit of evidence relevant to the claims on territory made in the steps-to-war explanation deals with the question of why neighbors fight (see Vasquez 1995b). No one doubts that the propensity for neighbors to fight is much higher than the propensity for nonneighbors to fight, but the territorial explanation sees this as an important clue about the source of war, whereas the proximity and interaction explanations see this as a trivial finding. The latter argue that neighbors fight more frequently simply because they have the opportunity to fight and/or they engage in more interactions generally and a certain percentage of these are bound to become conflictive and end in war, whereas more distant states interact less frequently and hence are less likely to have something worth a war to fight over.

Several indirect pieces of evidence exist on this question, and all of them support the territorial explanation rather than the proximity-interaction explanations, although more systematic testing is needed. Gibler (1996, 87) hypothesizes that if the proximity/interactions explanations are correct, then settling territorial disputes should not have the impact on war or on dispute reduction that it has. Instead, since proximate states or those with high interactions still have the opportunity for war, they should still fight at the same rate even if they have settled territorial issues. While Gibler (1996) provides some evidence that the settlement of territorial issues reduces the probability of war, his hypothesis is based on a logical point that still needs to be tested systematically.

Senese (1997b) tests the competing territorial versus proximity-interaction explanations using MID data. He finds that increases in the severity of conflict escalation and the probability of war differ for contiguous states depending on whether they are disputing territorial or nonterritorial issues. The presence of territorial disputes consistently increases the probability of war whether states are contiguous or not. Specifically, he finds that when noncontiguous states are contending over territorial disputes, the probability of war is .093, and when contiguous states are contending over territorial issues, the probability of war is .044. Conversely, when contiguous states are contenders and nonterritorial issues are at stake, the probability of war drops to .033, and when neither contiguous states nor territorial issues are present (but there is at least one dispute between the parties), then the probability of war drops further to .010 (Senese, 1997b, 11–12). Thus, territorial disputes are always more war prone regardless of contiguity.[16]

Hensel (2000, table 5.4), using a different research design and dependent variable, has similar findings. He divides disputes into whether or not they have any fatalities. He then finds that whenever territorial disputes are present, regardless of contiguity, there is a higher probability of disputes ending in battle deaths. Thus, among noncontiguous states, 52.3 percent of the territorial disputes have fatalities, and among contiguous states 41.6 percent of the territorial disputes have fatalities (versus 23.9 percent and

26.3 percent, respectively, for nonterritorial disputes). If contiguity mattered, then contiguous states would consistently have more severe disputes (regardless of issue) than noncontiguous states.[17] Instead, territorial disputes have a tendency to produce fatalities regardless of contiguity.

Both Senese (1997b) and Hensel (2000) provide important evidence that the territorial explanation is much more empirically accurate than the proximity and/or interaction explanation of why neighbors fight. The evidence, as a whole, has demonstrated that territorial disputes are much more war prone than other issues. This proposition has been sustained in three separate databases, something fairly rare in peace research, given that most work has been done on only one database. This adds credence to the territorial aspect of the steps-to-war explanation.

The main area that has not been tested with the use of MID data is the proclivity of territorial issues (that have not yet resulted in disputes) to give rise to the use of force and war. To test this claim, it will be necessary to collect data on territorial claims and compare them with nonterritorial issues. Hensel has started such a project (see Hensel and Reed 1997), and some very preliminary results by Hensel and Tures (1997) based on Latin America look promising.

Additional tests will also be needed on trying to distinguish territorial issues (and disputes) that are resolved peacefully from those that give rise to war. Some evidence already exists that territorial disputes are amenable to a number of nonviolent resolutions (see Ben Yehuda 1997, table 5a; Huth 1996a, chap. 6; Hensel and Tures 1997). The factors associated with these tendencies and what distinguishes these disputes from the more war prone is an area of fruitful inquiry. Two obvious avenues of investigation exist: (1) to control for system norms (Wallensteen 1984; Kegley and Raymond 1990; see also Raymond 1997) and (2) to develop a typology of territorial issues based on various characteristics of issues (e.g., value of territory, ethnic composition, public awareness, historical precedence, etc.) or the actors (see Hensel and Tures 1997).

Alliances

The research on alliances is very extensive and has been conducted over a number of years. Most of this was reviewed in *The War Puzzle* and used to make the claim that alliances (that target opponents), all other factors being equal, are usually a step to war and not a step toward peace.[18] This is because alliances aimed at "deterring" equals tend not to work but instead give rise to a security dilemma that increases threat perception that can set off a train of events that results in war.

The original evidence presented was adduced to make three conclusions. First, alliances are not followed by peace, as would be expected if the realist practice of making alliances to balance opponents worked to prevent attacks. Second, alliances are, with the exception of the nineteenth century, frequently followed by war (not peace), which indicates that they increase the probability of war, although because there is often such a time lag between alliance making and the onset of war, they are probably not a cause of war. Third, alliance making is one of the main mechanisms by which war is diffused. Again, if alliances worked the way they are supposed to in realism, this should not occur. Instead, alliances and alliance polarization are associated with large wars and wars that spread (Siverson and King 1979; Midlarsky 1983, 1988b; Siverson and Starr 1991).

Levy (1981, 597–98) finds that in each century from 1495 on (with the exception of the nineteenth century) 56 percent to 100 percent of alliances are followed by war. Since there is an interval between the making of an alliance and the onset of war, alliances probably do not bring about wars immediately, but they can be seen as aggravating a hostile situation, making war more likely. Ostrom and Hoole (1978) find in an analysis of alliances after 1815 that war is most apt to occur within three years of their signing; thereafter alliances are negatively related to war until an alliance is in its 12th year. After 12 years they find the relationship between alliances and war is random.

Overall, while the evidence indicates that many alliances are followed by war, some are not. In *The War Puzzle* (Vasquez 1993, 171) it was argued that this means that there is a need to create a typology of alliances that will distinguish the alliances that are war prone from those that are not. Gibler (1997b) has worked on this problem extensively by expanding Levy's (1981) alliance data.[19] His analysis of alliances that settle territorial issues is an important step in this direction, by clearly identifying a type of alliance that is followed by peace. He has also, along with Vasquez, tried to identify those characteristics of alliances that are associated with increased threat perception and therefore the eventual outbreak of war. Distinguishing the alliances that are war prone from those that are not makes the steps-to-war explanation more precise and detailed. It also makes it slightly easier to determine whether alliances increase the probability of war.

Gibler and Vasquez (1998, table 1) find that the base probability of war (involving at least one of the signatories to the alliance in a war within five years) is .40, a quite high figure. This finding is consistent with the claim that alliances are a step toward war, not a step toward peace. Joining an alliance seems to result in a step-level increase in the probability of war. Do some alliances increase this probability more than others?

Gibler and Vasquez (1998) show that this is the case. They argue that alliances that are composed solely of major states or states that have been successful in their last war are going to appear more threatening to potential targets than alliances made by minor states or states who have lost their last war.[20] The latter tend to signal that the practice of alliance making is being used to avoid war, whereas the former, by their very nature, tend to signal that capability is being aggregated to make winning a war more likely. As such, it tends to increase threat perception, hostility, and insecurity within those who are targets of the alliance.

Table 4 reports the results of Gibler and Vasquez's (1998) tests of these hypotheses. When parties who have been successful in their last

TABLE 4.

The Probability of Alliance Types Going to War, 1495–1980 (wars involving an ally within five years)

Alliance Characteristic	Actual (Wars)	Expected	*N*	*P* conditional (War)	Z	Significance
Territorial Settlement Alliance						
Resolves Territory	4	(10.78)	27	.15	−2.66**	.0039
No Settlement	85	(78.22)	196	.43	0.99	.1611
Success in War						
All Successful	47	(30.33)	76	.62	3.51**	.0005
Mixed	36	(45.10)	113	.32	−1.79*	.0401
All Unsuccessful	6	(13.57)	34	.18	−1.97**	.0004
Status						
Major-major	43	(27.94)	70	.61	3.68**	.0002
Major-minor	37	(35.53)	89	.42	0.32	.3745
Minor-minor	9	(25.54)	64	.14	−4.22**	.0001
Singer/Small						
I. Defense Pacts	51	(49.89)	125	.41	0.20	.4207
II. Neutrality/ Nonagression	23	(22.35)	56	.41	0.18	.4286
III. Ententes	15	(16.76)	42	.36	−0.56	.2877

Source: Gibler and Vasquez 1998, table 1.
Note: Base probability of war = 89/223 = .40
$*p < .05$
$**p < .01$

war come together to make an alliance, the conditional probability of war increases to .62 (from the base probability of .40). Given that there are 76 such alliances from 1495 to 1980, one would expect that 30 wars involving an ally would occur due to chance alone; instead, 47 occur. Conversely, it can be seen from the table that when states unsuccessful at their last war come into a coalition (either with like states or with states that have been successful in their last war), then the probability of war significantly decreases (.18 and .32 respectively).

Similarly, when major states enter into an exclusive coalition together, the conditional probability of war is .61, a statistically significant increase over the base probability of .40. Conversely, when minor states enter into coalition, this presumably is not seen as threatening, and the base probability decreases considerably to .14, producing many fewer wars (9) than would be expected by chance (26).

Table 4 also examines the data in terms of the conventional correlates-of-war typology of defense pacts, neutrality/nonaggression pacts, and ententes. This serves as a benchmark to see how much improvement a more theoretically oriented typology might produce. As can be seen, the conventional typology is not significantly different from the base probability at the .05 level, whereas looking at the success and status of members is.

The findings on success in the previous war and major state status actually underestimate the war proneness of these alliances because they include territorial settlement pacts. Gibler (1996, 1997b) shows that even when a coalition of major states signs a territorial settlement as part of an alliance, that alliance tends to be followed by peace, not war. In table 5, the territorial settlement alliances are removed to examine the war proneness of coalitions consisting exclusively of major states who have won their previous war. There are only 28 such alliances, and 86 percent of them are followed by a war involving an ally within five years. That is quite an increase in the incidence of war.

This analysis shows that, on the whole, alliances do not seem to work in the way realists have expected. They have tended to be followed by war rather than peace, except in the nineteenth century. Gibler and Vasquez (1998) have made progress in distinguishing those alliances followed by peace (territorial settlements, states who lost the previous war, and minor states) from those that tend to be followed by war (coalitions of major states and those who won their last war).

These findings suggest that alliance making and especially the making of certain kinds of alliances is a factor that increases the probability of war. In themselves, however, these findings do not go beyond that. The presence of socially significant findings always leads to a great deal of discussion and criticism based all too often (unfortunately) on logical possibility than on empirical testing. In this case, two criticisms have been generated.

First, some say that all these findings may show is that states fearing war join alliances and their fears prove correct. If this is the case, it is not alliance making that produces war but the underlying factors that lead states into alliances in the first place. It should be stated initially that such a criticism is not a realist explanation and that although different from the steps-to-war explanation, it shares certain similarities with it. Realists say that alliances, if they balance, should intimidate opponents and prevent war. From this perspective, alliances should not increase the probability of war. The steps-to-war explanation is similar to the criticism offered in that it, too, posits that underlying the decision to enter an alliance is an "unmeasured" factor, in this case threat perception or hostility. But unlike the criticism, it does not see alliance making as simply spurious. Instead, it argues that engaging in the realist practice of making an alliance produces a step-level increase in threat perception and hostility. Alliances are not neutral, but they have an impact on the probability of war. A few reduce the probability, but most (because they increase threat or hostility) increase the probability of war. The findings reported here are consistent with this explanation, even though they have not measured the step-level increase of "the underlying factor." The latter remains a future test, if valid measures can be found for hostility and threat perception.[21]

Second, some dismiss the kinds of findings presented in tables 4 and 5 by arguing that a possible reason for the findings is the presence of selection effects. Specifically, since it is known that major states are prone to war to begin with, the finding on major state alliances may not say

TABLE 5.

Proportion of Alliances Followed by War within Five Years, 16th–20th Centuries

Alliances of only Major/Successful states (excluding Territorial Settlement Treaties)	
86%	$N = 28$

Source: Gibler and Vasquez 1998, table 9.

anything about alliances but only tell us what we already know about major state proclivities. Gibler (1997b) has tested this possibility. He finds that the average war onset per year for all states is .027 from 1648 to 1980. For major states, this increases to .067. Now, if alliances have no impact on the war proneness of major states, there should not be any statistically significant difference between this last rate and the average yearly war onsets of majors in an alliance. The mean yearly war onset of majors in an alliance increases to .106 (which is a statistically significant difference from the .067 for majors as a whole ($p < .01$) (Gibler 1997b, table 5.6). This means that majors in an alliance are more prone to war than majors are normally; thus, the finding on major state alliances is not due primarily to a selection effect related to the difference in war rates between minor and major states.[22] More important, Gibler (1997b, table 5.6) demonstrates precisely the kind of step-level increase in the probability of war that was predicted by the steps-to-war explanation.

Gibler's (1997b, table 5.6) findings are also relevant to another criticism made of the alliance literature that has attracted a certain amount of attention and whose implications support more of a realist orientation. It has been argued that existing evidence cannot count against realism, because it has failed to examine the states without any alliances to see if they have been attacked more frequently than those with allies. This is a good logical point and should be systematically tested. Gibler's (1997b) analysis of selection effects, however, shows that major states outside of alliances have a lower, not a higher, probability of war. The same is true for the more vulnerable minor states—outside of an alliance their mean war onset per year is .012. Once they enter an alliance, it almost doubles to .020 ($p = .012$). Although a proper test would control for presence of a threat and the relative power of the two sides, if this problem were very serious it should leave some trace in Gibler's data analysis. My point here is not that such research is unworthy of being pursued, but that a mere logical possibility (without sustaining research) should not be used to summarily dismiss a body of evidence.[23]

The new findings on alliances and war are very supportive of the steps-to-war explanation. They show that certain types of alliances increase the probability of war. The findings also reflect a progressive increase in knowledge by delineating the characteristics that make alliances war prone and by distinguishing alliances that are followed by peace from those that are followed by war. In this regard, the research on alliances has shown that the steps-to-war explanation can provide a fruitful guide to research that can add to our knowledge and information about processes that lead to war. The next section examines recent work on arms racing.

Arms Racing

The steps-to-war explanation maintains that arms racing and alliance making have similar effects. Both produce a security dilemma and increases in threat perception and hostility. In general, the process by which arms races encourage the escalation of disputes to war is theoretically similar, although the origins of arms racing and the precise consequences are different from those of alliance making. Specifically, most scholars who see arms racing as dangerous in the context of militarized disputes see it as closer (in time) to escalation to war and in that sense a more direct correlate of war (see Wallace 1979).

Firm conclusions about arms racing have been bogged down in measurement and research design questions raised by two of the leading critics of Wallace (1979, 1982)—Diehl (1983) and Weede (1980). These issues and how they might be resolved empirically have been discussed elsewhere (see Vasquez and Henehan, "Editors' Commentary," 1992, 88–92, 103–8). The major new evidence on this question has been provided by Susan G. Sample (1996, 1997) who has resolved much of the Diehl-Wallace debate.

The most important breakthrough she has made is to show that, even when using Diehl's (1983) index of mutual military buildups, most of the cases that do not escalate to war either eventually do so within five years or are cases involving nuclear weapons. As Sample (1997, 16, see also appendix D) puts it: ". . . with the exception of the Cold War, virtually every case in which two countries are both arming at abnormally high levels was at war within five years." Introducing a time lag into her analysis of arms racing and dispute escalation, she finds for the entire period (including the cold war) that 62 percent (32 of 52) of the disputes among arms-racing countries Diehl identifies go to war within five years (Sample 1997, 16). This means that 47 percent of the disputes that did not escalate immediately, eventually do. These are primarily disputes occurring in the interwar period. Using the more restrictive measure of arms races developed by Michael Horn (1987), Sample (1997, 16) finds that 77 percent of the disputes that did not escalate immediately do so within five years. This means that Horn's index, which generally has a stronger relationship between arms racing and dispute escalation, shows that of the 29 disputes involving arms races, 86 percent (25) go to war within five years.

These findings provide strong confirmation of what had been earlier said in *The War Puzzle* (Vasquez 1993, 181–82) and in Vasquez and Henehan (1992, 106); namely, that arms races simply increase the probability of war and do not ensure that war will occur instantly. Instead of war, a series of disputes may occur. As Leng (1983) has shown, among major states it is rare for war to break out after the first crisis—it takes two or three (see Vasquez 1993, 181–82). This also makes sense given the theoretical rationale underlying the steps to war. Sample (1996, 1997), by unpacking the cases that make up the correlation between arms races and war, provides important evidence that this is, in fact, the case. Arms racing in the short run, but not always in the same year, results in war. For this reason, it can be seen as increasing the probability of war.

Sample (1996, chaps. 4 and 7) provides a direct test of this hypothesis. Using first Diehl's (1983) measure of mutual military buildups and then Michael Horn's (1987) measure of arms racing, she compares the probability of dispute escalation to war with and without ongoing arms races. As table 6 shows, the findings are supportive of the steps-to-war explanation. The base probability for war among major states in this sample of 257 disputes (1815–1993) is .12.[24] As can be seen in table 6, using Diehl's index, she finds that the conditional probability of dispute escalation to war is .27, and for Horn's index, the conditional probability of war is .41. Both of these are statistically significant increases (Z scores, $p = .0005$ and $\leqq .0001$, respectively) over the base probability (Sample 1996, 156–57, tables 7.1b, 7.1c). With Diehl's index, she identifies 52 disputes with mutual military buildups; 14 of these escalate to war (within the same year), when only 6.2 should be expected to do by chance. With Horn's index, she identifies 29 arms racing disputes, of which 12 escalate to war, when only 3.5 should by chance.

Sample's (1996) findings show that while arms racing is not always an immediate sufficient condition for dispute escalation to war, it does clearly increase the probability of war in the prenuclear era. Theoretically, this means that arms racing is an additional step to war that states can take. Sometimes this can lead immediately to war, but more typically it does so only after states have had more than one militarized dispute. Sample's (1996, 1997) results suggest that a steps process and dynamic capture what is occurring when major states go to war.

TABLE 6.

Susan Sample's Analysis of Arms Races and the Probability of Dispute Escalation to War, 1816–1992

	Actual (Wars)	Expected	*N*	*p* (War)	Z	Significance
Arms Races						
Diehl index	14	(6.2)	52	.27	3.32	.0005
Arms Races						
Horn index	12	(3.5)	29	.41	4.81	<.0001

Source: Sample 1996, table 4.10.
Note: Base probability of war = 31/257 = .12

Conclusion

The new findings on territory, alliances, and arms racing are very supportive of the steps-to-war explanation. None of the findings have shown the explanation to be inaccurate, but they are primarily bivariate and hence far from complete. Nevertheless, they do show that the steps-to-war explanation can provide a promising research program. Some of the major tasks for future research are outlined in the remainder of this section.

Three bivariate areas of inquiry need to be further investigated: (1) the role repeated crises and the use of realpolitik tactics play as a step to war, (2) the specific characteristics that distinguish the few crises that escalate to war from the many that do not, and (3) the effect of the global institutional context on the steps to war (in particular the norms of a given peace system). While there is a literature on each of these, the new MID data and ICB data provide opportunities for new tests specifically tailored to the steps-to-war explanation.

When bivariate testing is completed, the more complicated task of how the steps are related to one another and how they might interact to increase the probability of war needs to begin. Essentially, this involves not only looking at how a given step to war, say the presence of a territorial dispute, affects the probability of war, but how that probability is further increased by the making of an alliance, then perhaps a counter-alliance and/or a mutual military buildup, and so forth. The highest probability of war would be predicted when all the steps have been taken by each side. Thus, actors who contended over a territorial issue by making alliances against each other, building up their respective militaries, and engaging in repeated confrontation would, given the emergence of a crisis of certain characteristics, be the most likely to go to war.

Once aggregate data analysis is able to document a path to war, the next task will be to use comparative historical case studies to trace out the "causal sequence and process" by which these steps bring about a war. While it can be expected that a number of case studies will be on individual wars, it makes more sense, logically, to study and compare not only wars but long-term relations between politically relevant actors to see whether or not certain steps increase hostility and eventually lead to war. Comparative case studies of relations between states are also useful for assessing whether a given statistical model is overly alarmist, a not uncommon problem in peace research (see Singer 1982).

Case studies of individual wars can help analysts determine just how many given wars are produced by the steps-to-war explanation. Are the steps delineated in this chapter the typical path by which the strongest states in the modern global system come to war? Asking this question implies that there are other paths to war, and these remain to be specified theoretically and researched empirically. A number of propositions in *The War Puzzle* address the question of how the paths to war might differ depending on whether a war is dyadic or complex. Bremer (1992, 320) has been in the forefront of maintaining that researchers separate the question of war onset from war joining. Vasquez (1996) documents that there are two distinct paths to war by which states with and without territorial disputes come to war with each other. States without territorial disputes typically come to war with each other by joining a dyadic war involving neighbors fighting over territorial claims.

Just how many paths to war might exist is an open question. Thompson (1995b) suggests that, in addition to a territorial path to war, there is another path to war whose origin lies in positional issues (i.e., questions of global leadership). Will the diversionary theory of war prove to be another path? Will neo-Marxist theories of imperialism account for the path by which strong and weak actors come to war? Such questions must be examined empirically in a fashion that does not give in to idiographic proclivities. The steps-to-war explanation, then, embodies a research program centered around not only its own propositions but a theoretical framework able to raise new research questions and integrate midrange explanations from other perspectives.

Last, it must be remembered that one of the main insights embodied by the steps-to-war explanation is that there are many exits off the road to war, as Singer says. It is as important for researchers to see what reduces the probability of war as it is to see what increases it. Specifically, an area of research that needs to be investigated in terms of the steps to war is how the dynamic of threat perception and hostility generated by the steps can be defused. With the end of the cold war, there is an increased interest in conflict resolution and management (see Goertz 1997; Vasquez et al. 1995) and concerts of power that can provide governance without government (see Rosecrance 1992). In this sense, there is a pressing need to supplement the Correlates of War project with a correlates of peace(ful) eras (COPE) project. With more peace-centered research, it will become possible some day to supplement the current steps-to-war explanation with an explanation of the steps to peace.

Notes

My thanks to Marie Henehan, Paul Hensel, Manus Midlarsky, and Paul Senese for valuable suggestions and to the University Research Council of Vanderbilt for financial support.

1. The Hitler-Stalin Pact, for instance, permitted the Soviet Union to reassert a number of territorial claims it had not pursued for quite some time in Poland, the Baltic states, and Finland, among others. The territorial claims the USSR asserted, in turn, were in part a function of its fear of Nazi Germany. In this sense, the Russo-Finnish Winter War of 1940 may have had its origin in Soviet fear of a possible alignment between Nazi Germany and Finland, which the Soviets found increasingly threatening. My thanks to Manus Midlarsky for the Winter War example and for suggesting the general theoretical point.
2. Rivalry is defined as: "a relationship characterized by extreme competition, and usually psychological hostility, in which the issue positions of contenders are governed primarily by their attitude toward each other rather than by the stakes at hand" (Vasquez 1996, 532; see also Vasquez 1993, 82–83). One of the advantages of this theoretical definition over the operational definition of rivalry as multiple militarized disputes (see Goertz and Diehl 1993) is that the concept specifies the conditions that will produce disputes, rather than making disputes a defining condition.
3. The work on territory was not incorporated until *The War Puzzle.* The original steps-to-war article, simply put, maintained that power politics, on the whole, resulted in war and not peace when states, especially equals, adopted its foreign policy practices. This did not address whether some issues are more war prone than others; nor did it address whether some issues by their very nature are responsible for war.

4. Level of Hostility is measured in terms of four categories—threat of force, display of force, use of force, and war (Jones, Bremer, and Singer 1996, 170–74)—that are derived from the detailed 22 action codes. I have treated this indicator as "categories of hostility" rather than level because it appears from the distribution that the measure does not reflect a scale (ordinal or interval) (see, e.g., Jones, Bremer, and Singer 1996, 196–97).
5. Disputes whose issues (i.e., revision type) are coded as "nonapplicable" are dropped. These constitute 363 cases of the 2,034.
6. As shown in table 3, the difference between the number of regime disputes in the sample and the number of wars they produce is statistically nonsignificant. However, Vasquez and Henehan (forthcoming) find some evidence to indicate that there might be a greater probability of regime disputes going to war than expected by chance in the post-1945 era, especially when minor states are contending with each other.
7. All the odds ratios are statistically significant at the .001 level. Hensel's (1996b, 59, table 2) evidence that territorial disputes are three times more likely to end in war than nonterritorial disputes is similar to what is reported here in table 3. His test differs with the one presented in table 3 in that (a) he divides disputes into territorial and nonterritorial, (b) he appears to have included the nonapplicable in the nonterritorial category, and (c) he has deleted some of the wars, which are coded for revision type—those involving joiners in an ongoing war.
8. For example, when strategic territory is involved, states are 12 percent more likely to produce a rivalry than when it is not at stake, but when there are ties to bordering minorities or political unification is at question, states are 19.2 percent and 18.0 percent (respectively) more likely to become involved in a rivalry (Huth 1996b, 21, table 2). In terms of escalation to "high levels of diplomatic or military conflict," strategic location is associated with a 15 percent increase in the probability of escalation, ties with bordering minorities a 30 percent increase, and political unification a 28 percent increase (Huth 1996a, 109, table 9).
9. Huth (1996a, 115, 156, table 10, table 15; 1996b, 20, 23–24, table 1) also finds that the stronger the challenger, the more likely an enduring rivalry and the higher the level of conflict, and the weaker the challenger, the less likely an enduring rivalry and the lower the level of conflict. Also, he finds that involvement in more than one dispute reduces the probability of an enduring rivalry; that is, states tend to concentrate on one rival at a time and try to avoid a two-front war, so to speak.
10. From a realist perspective, one of the most serious international constraints is a decline in capability. Such a decline from one dispute to another should lead to more caution, but Leng (1983) finds in his study of recurring crises that this does not always happen. In four of five cases where one side decreases in capability, it still escalates. The four cases all involve Egypt-

Israel and India-Pakistan. The only case that proceeds the way one would expect is the decline in Soviet capability from 1961 to 1962 and its more accommodative strategy in the next crisis. Roy's (1997) analyses would suggest that when increased belligerence in the face of a decline in capability occurs, domestic ethnic pressure is probably at the root (of such an unexpected deviation from the logic of power). Such a pattern is definitely at work in both the India-Pakistan case and the Egypt-Israel case.

11. These findings imply that it is not just the use of realpolitik tactics in a crisis that leads to war, but specifically the use of these tactics on the highly salient territorial issues. It will be interesting to see if this outcome will be found to apply equally well to the use of other power politics practices like alliance making and arms racing. In other words, do states that make alliances against each other or engage in arms races have a more marked proclivity to war if they are disputing territorial issues as opposed to other issues?
12. As Vasquez (1996) has shown quantitatively, this does not preclude that such states might come to war with each other through a contagion process.
13. Of these four wars, only one is really connected to the alliance in question (Gibler 1996, 87).
14. For example, before the territorial settlement alliances, the average dispute rate is .388, and afterward the average dispute rate is .193 (Gibler 1997a, 360, table VII).
15. It should be pointed out that just because a territorial settlement alliance has been signed, this does not mean that all outstanding territorial issues have been resolved. Gibler demonstrates that even if not all territorial issues are settled, they still have a dampening effect on dispute repetition among the states that have been the most dispute prone within the system, that is, rivals.
16. Additional findings on the territorial versus proximity explanation can be found in Vasquez (forthcoming).
17. Ben Yehuda (1997, tables 3a–3b), using ICB data, finds that crises between contiguous states are no more war prone than crises between noncontiguous states (21.4 percent and 23.6 percent, respectively), whereas (as indicated earlier) 29.2 percent of the territorial disputes go to war versus 14.8 percent of the nonterritorial issues. She does not, however, conduct the more controlled tests that Hensel and Senese do.
18. These findings are complicated, but they are not unclear. Subsequent reviews, however, tended to misread this evidence often emphasizing the disparate nature of the findings and their inconclusive nature, although no one says that the research on alliances is any more inconclusive than any other research. In some cases authors have even cited the steps-to-war article in this context, when in fact I reached the opposite conclusion (see Smith 1995, 405–6).

19. See Gibler (1997b) for a replication of Levy (1981). The new data, collected by Gibler, include all states (not just those involving a major state) from 1648 to 1980 and the ententes Levy (1981) dropped.
20. Small and Singer (1982, 44–45) and Levy (1983, 24–43) are used to classify major states. Success is operationalized by whether a state won its last war as coded in Correlates of War data (see Small and Singer 1982, 196–97). For evidence that success in war leads to increased involvement in wars, see Singer and Small (1974, tables 2 and 3) and Nevin (1996).
21. It should be pointed out that, while the steps-to-war explanation has not measured the alleged underlying factor, neither have the advocates of the claim of spuriousness. In *The War Puzzle,* I use one case to show how an alliance seemingly unrelated to a particular war actually created a step-level increase in threat perception and hostility. I analyze the case of NATO and Truman's decision to send troops to Korea (see Vasquez 1993, 173–76). More systematic case studies of this type will help put the argument on spuriousness to rest, especially if they can be coupled with reliable and valid measures of hostility. Last, it must be kept in mind that even if the spuriousness argument proves to be on the mark, that still does not support realism or its prescriptions about alliance making.
22. Gibler (1997b, table 5.6) shows the same thing for states that were successful in their last war. The average war onset per year for those outside an alliance is .07; for those in an alliance, it is .112 ($p < .01$).
23. Likewise, Smith's (1995) formal analysis that states with reliable allies are not attacked by opponents, but states with unreliable allies are more prone to be attacked, illustrates a logical possibility but needs to be tested systematically before it is used to dismiss existing empirical evidence, as Smith (1995, 406) does. Some might say that Smith's analysis implies that the realist position is correct, because coalitions consisting of reliable allies will successfully "deter," but those without will fail. Unfortunately, Smith (1995, 1996b) offers no way of measuring "reliability" before the fact. Without such a measure there is always the danger that alliances followed by war will be presumed to have consisted (or have been perceived as consisting) of unreliable allies and those that are followed by peace will be presumed to have consisted of reliable allies (or perceived as such). This would obviously be an ad hoc explanation that could lead quantitative peace research to exhibit the kind of degenerative research program on alliances that has been exhibited by neotraditional research on alliances (see Vasquez 1997).
24. See Sample (1996, 113, table 4.10). Part of the original controversy is how to disaggregate disputes related to large wars, specifically World War I and World War II. Sample (1996, chap. 4) performs the analysis with and without the controversial dyads, getting the same results overall (see Sample 1997, 13–14). Table 6 includes all 257 dyadic disputes, which she believes is the most historically valid resolution of this question.

Explaining War

Empirical Patterns and Theoretical Mechanisms

DANIEL S. GELLER

Introduction

The systematic quantitative empirical analysis of war has a history traceable to the third decade of the twentieth century in the works of Lewis Fry Richardson and Quincy Wright. Over the following 60 years, however, little effort has been devoted to comparing and integrating the findings of the large number of scientific studies of war produced since the early works of Richardson and Wright. A major development occurred in 1993, when John Vasquez presented an explanation of war between states with relatively equal capabilities that was based on a synthesis of empirical research findings generated over the previous quarter-century. Subsequently, Geller and Singer (1998) identified a series of strong empirical patterns relating to the onset and seriousness of war drawn from a review of more than 500 quantitative data-based studies on international conflict. The volume was constructed around the analytic levels of the state, dyad, region, and international system and identified consistent empirical regularities at each level. Theoretical mechanisms accounting for the regularities were provided in that volume and applied in scientific explanations of specific dyadic and multistate wars. This chapter summarizes the empirical patterns and theoretical mechanisms presented in that work.

Scientific Explanation

A fundamental objective of scientific inquiry is to provide explanations of empirical phenomena. In conventional language, to "explain" a phenomenon is to incorporate it within a "cause and effect" sequence—or, at minimum, to locate it within a pattern of existential regularity. It is a principal ontological assumption of the scientific search for knowledge that the phenomenal universe exhibits certain patterns or regularities and that such patterns are discernible. This position on patterns is consistent with general models of scientific explanation based on either deductive-nomological or inductive-probabilistic forms of reasoning. When an explanation of a phenomenon is provided by reference to a pattern under which the phenomenon is subsumed, this is referred to as a "covering law" explanation. Although there are substantive differences in the epistemologies of empiricist philosophers such as Carl Hempel (1966), Karl Popper (1959), Richard B. Braithwaite (1953), Hans Reichenbach (1951), and Imre Lakatos (1970), all subscribe to the covering law model of explanation in one form or another.

There are two types of covering law explanations: one based on deductive-nomological reasoning and the other based on inductive-probabilistic reasoning. Both models explain events by reference to covering laws. However, the deductive-nomothetic model employs laws of universal form, whereas the inductive model uses laws of probabilistic form. Deductive explanation implies the (internal or logical) truth of the conclusion with absolute certainty; probabilistic (inductive) explanation implies the truth of the conclusion only with a given probability. In both cases, explanations based on covering laws can be supplemented by reference to theoretical mechanisms that underlie the patterns or regularities (Popper 1959, 59; Hempel 1966, 51, 70; Elster 1983, 29). In other words, empirical laws—whether of universal or probabilistic form—may be accounted for by theoretical mechanisms that refer to underlying structures and processes that produce the patterns described in the laws.

The following section summarizes a set of empirical uniformities relating to the onset and seriousness of war that have been identified through quantitative, data-based research and outlines the theoretical mechanisms that are believed to give rise to the patterns. These empirical patterns have been drawn from a review of more than 500 quantitative, data-based studies and are discussed in detail in Geller and Singer (1998). The patterns and theoretical mechanisms are presented on the basis of levels of analysis and identify a set of structural factors associated with the war proneness of states, dyads, regions, and the international system.

Patterns and Mechanisms

Level of Analysis: State

Power Status

> *Empirical Pattern:* The higher the power status of a state, the greater the probability of its war involvement; the higher the power status of a state, the greater the probability of its involvement in severe wars.

The relevance of the power base of a state as a determinant of its involvement in international conflict is a principal component of realist thought. Whether conceptualized as military capabilities alone, or as a broader set of military, economic, and demographic capabilities, the power base of a state has long been considered to be an important factor shaping foreign behavior. While many theories of international conflict and war focus on dyadic- or systemic-level capability distributions, a substantial body of literature deals with state-level capabilities.

There are strong a priori reasons to expect that extant patterns in the onset (occurrence/initiation)[1] of war and the seriousness (magnitude, duration, and severity)[2] of war may be quite dissimilar for major powers and minor powers. For example, major powers may be more likely to engage in war because the hierarchy of which they are a part is structured and restructured primarily through the use of violence. Major powers tend to define their interests more broadly than do minor powers, and the pursuit of those interests may bring them more frequently into violent conflict with other states. Moreover, given the fact that major powers possess greater military capabilities than do minor powers, it is reasonable to assume that their wars will tend to be more destructive than those of minor powers.

The earliest cross-national quantitative research on capabilities and conflict attempted to isolate possible differences in behavior between strong and weak states. Hence, the power status of nations was postulated to be a factor influencing conflict patterns. For example, Wright (1964) reports a positive correlation between state capabilities and belligerency. However, in a subsequent study, Rummel (1968), using the Dimensionality of Nations (DON) database for 77 nations from 1955 to 1957, finds no substantive relationship between national capabilities and foreign conflict. In contradistinction to Rummel, Weede (1970)—also employing the DON data (for a longer time period of 1955–60) and utilizing different operations in measure construction—reports that state capability is positively related to verbal foreign conflict.

Two definitive studies on the subject of power status and war are by Small and Singer (1970, 1982). Using the original (1816–1965) and expanded (1816–1980) Correlates of War (COW) database, Small and Singer demonstrate that major powers are much more likely to engage in wars than are minor powers. Köhler (1975) examines the war behavior of 15 "imperial leaders" at different stages of leadership (COW database) to answer the question of whether dominant nations become less war prone after the loss of hegemony, and he concludes that once-dominant states become more peaceful following the loss of their leadership status. Bremer (1980), also using COW data, contributes to the evidence on power status and conflict by reporting that nations that rank high on a composite index of national capability (CINC) are involved in a greater number of wars and initiate wars with greater frequency than do lower-ranked states. He notes that nations with greater aggregate capabilities also tend to suffer from more severe wars (i.e., battle death totals). Eberwein (1982), in a replication of Bremer's (1980) study, adds the finding that more powerful nations tend to use military force more frequently, and that power status alone accounts for over 60 percent of the variance in "joining" ongoing militarized interstate disputes. Lastly, Geller (1988), using the COW database on wars and battle deaths for the participant, reports that major powers are more likely to fight severe wars (more than 15,000 battle deaths) and less likely to fight moderate wars (between 1,000 and 15,000 battle deaths) than are minor powers, whereas they are equally likely to engage in small wars (less than 1,000 battle deaths).

Power Cycle

> *Empirical Pattern:* Passage through a critical point in the power cycle increases the probability of war involvement for a major power.

Power cycle theory (i.e., Doran 1983, 1989a, 1995a; Doran and Parsons 1980) holds that certain critical points in a major power's cycle of increasing and decreasing capabilities (relative to the major power system's capability pool)[3] are associated probabilistically with both its initiation and involvement in war. The thesis maintains that major powers move through a general, cyclical pattern (i.e., power cycle) of capability growth, maturation, and decline. The pattern itself is a function of differential rates of development among the set of major powers. These differences result from variations in resource distribution, political development, and industrialization.

The power cycle thesis asserts that a state's foreign policy is shaped by its position on this capability cycle. According to Doran and Parsons (1980, 947, 949): "As a nation gains in power relative to others, its capacity to exercise leadership grows; as it falls behind, the capacity to influence international politics wanes. . . . As the cycle evolves and the role changes, significant adjustments are required of the government and the society." Collectively, the evolution of the power cycles of the principal states defines the hierarchy of the international system (Doran 1983, 427).

Doran identifies four critical points on the cycle: the two inflection points occurring on either side of the cycle and the lower and upper turning points. These four points on the evolutionary curve of a state's relative capabilities—termed "critical points"—are important because they represent a disjuncture between a state's interests or aspirations and its actual capabilities. Due to the shift in direction or rate of capability growth, the state's leaders must reevaluate their relative position, capability base, and foreign policy objectives. Doran (1985, 294) maintains that the foreign policy stakes at these critical points are enormous—involving status, security, and power—and are therefore more likely to lead to war involvement. It should be noted that power cycle theory measures time in decades and critical points are not considered to be instantaneous transformations. Similarly, the perceptions of leaders as their states approach critical points may change in a gradual fashion. However, abrupt overreaction to the points is considered more probable (Doran and Parsons 1980, 951). Doran and Parsons (1980, 952) suggest that the critical points most likely to produce the imprudent use of force or the encumbrance of unyielding foreign policy positions are the two inflection points (where the tangents reverse direction).

In short, power cycle theory holds that major power war results from a government's inability to adjust to shifts in its capacity to exercise power and influence. The critical points on the power cycle are especially likely to produce overreaction, misperception, and the aggressive use of force in foreign policy.

For the initial study (Doran and Parsons 1980), capabilities are measured by an index composed of five material indicators, with the population inclusive of all major powers for the years between 1816 and 1975. War data are drawn from the COW database. Doran and Parsons conclude that a major power's point on the power cycle is an important determinant of its probability of initiating war, involvement in war, and of the characteristics of the wars in which it engages. Subsequent studies by Doran (1989a, 1991) reinforce and elaborate the previous results, indicating that 90 percent of major powers passing through a critical point on the power cycle engage in war.[4]

Alliance

> *Empirical Pattern:* The greater the number of a state's alliance ties, the higher the probability of its war involvement.

States enter alliances for many reasons, both defensive and offensive. However, in general, alliances are engaged as a means of increasing a state's capabilities through external ties. Alliances may also stimulate conflict by producing or exacerbating a hostility spiral (e.g., Jervis 1976) or expand conflict by dragging a state into war as a third party. Questions dealing with the conflict effects of opposing alliance systems, characteristics of alliances, and the extent of alliance in the international system will be discussed in sections dealing with higher levels of analysis. In this section, the issue concerns the effects of alliance membership on a state's foreign conflict and war probabilities.

Six analyses provide evidence of alliance effects on state-level conflict. In one of the first quantitative state-level examinations of the relationship between alliances and war, Singer and Small (1966) report that the greater the number of a state's alliance commitments, the greater and more severe its subsequent war involvement (COW database, 1815–1945). Weede (1970) examines the relationship between the number of military treaties in which a state is engaged and its foreign conflict behavior. His analysis employs the DON database of 59 nations for the years 1955 through 1960, and he reports a moderate negative association between the number of a state's military treaties and its verbal foreign conflict behavior. Kemp (1977) analyzes the possible association between state-level alliance patterns and international violence (deaths resulting from violent activity). Using COW data for the years 1925 to 1939, Kemp reports a positive and statistically significant link between state-level military alliance and international violence. Siverson and Sullivan (1984) produce an extensive study including all war participations in the international system from 1815 through 1965 (COW database); their findings indicate no substantive connection between the number of a state's military alliances and its probability of war initiation but do show a positive and significant linkage between the number of alliance ties and the probability of war involvement. Levy (1981) examines evidence regarding a possible connection between great power alliance membership and war over a period that covers five centuries. From the sixteenth through the eighteenth centuries, over two-thirds of major power alliance engagements were followed by war, but in the nineteenth century, very few alliance memberships preceded war involvement. In the twentieth century the earlier pattern is repeated: six of the seven major powers end up in war following alliance engagement.

In a study dealing directly with the war-diffusion effects of alliances, Siverson and Starr (1990) examine whether the presence of a warring alliance partner substantially increases the probability of a nation's joining an ongoing war. Drawing on the COW database (1816–1965), Siverson and Starr analyze 94 cases of war diffusion and conclude that a state with a warring alliance partner has a significantly higher probability of subsequent war involvement than does a state lacking such an external commitment.

Borders

> *Empirical Pattern:* The greater the number of a state's borders, the higher the probability of its war involvement.

Two basic arguments pervade the literature of international politics on the subject of geography as a facilitating condition of war. One thesis holds that proximity provides the physical opportunity for war: wars occur between bordering or proximate states because short distances provide the opportunity for violent conflict (i.e., proximity decreases the requirement of military reach). The second thesis is more complex, suggesting that proximity structures the "context of interaction" in such a way as to increase the probability of conflictual relations. In other words, proximity generates security problems and influences the perception of threats, which may then lead to conflict (Diehl 1991; Starr 1991). A number of quantitative empirical studies have looked at these issues at the level of the monad.

The first perspective—that geographic opportunity (i.e., contact) tends to increase a nation's involvement in foreign conflict—is exemplified by Richardson's (1960b) analysis. He concludes that states tend to engage in wars in proportion to their number of borders. Similarly,

Wright (1964) notes that "geographic frontiers" are often the location of conflict, and that peace may be promoted by the creation of buffer zones. Weede (1970) reports that his analysis, using the DON database of 59 nations for the years between 1955 and 1960, indicates a positive correlation for contiguity (number of borders) and violent foreign conflict. However, Rummel's (1972b) 236-variable factor analysis for the years 1955 to 1957 produces ambiguous results for the contiguity hypothesis. The loading for number of borders on the foreign conflict factor is positive but extremely low.

The second perspective—that proximity establishes a context of interaction that enhances the motivations for war—is exemplified by the work of Starr and Most (1976, 1978, 1983). They argue that proximity increases the perception of threat (e.g., Herz's [1951] security dilemma; Boulding's [1962] loss-of-strength gradient) and that the security context of such interactions is more likely to lead to conflict. In their first study, Starr and Most (1976) analyze war participations over the years 1946 through 1965 and find a moderate positive correlation between contiguous land/water colonial borders and new war participations. Starr and Most (1978) provide additional evidence in support of the hypothesis in their analysis of 34 states over the same period using a different set of statistical techniques. They report that the average number of borders is significantly higher for countries that exhibit a "high" war count than for "low" war-count states. In a similar analysis conducted for the African subsystem, Starr and Most (1983) note statistically significant results indicating that African nations with a "low" border count were less likely to engage in war than African states with a "high" count. A study by Midlarsky (1975) also supports this hypothesis. He argues that a direct relationship exists between the number of borders for a state and its decision maker's level of uncertainty, and that uncertainty is associated with war. In his analysis of wars for the years 1815 to 1945 for COW project central-system states, Midlarsky reports an extremely high correlation between the number of borders and the frequency of war. He concludes that—with a small number of exceptions principally involving common sea borders—almost all wars have begun across contiguous land borders or contiguous colonial extensions.

In the most extensive study on a related subject, Siverson and Starr (1990) explore changes in the probability that nations will enter an ongoing war if they have a warring state on their border. Employing COW data for 1816 through 1965 (and with the nation-year as the basic unit of analysis), Siverson and Starr analyze 3,749 cases—of which 94 involve war diffusion. Their findings indicate that the presence of a warring border nation significantly increases the probability of a nation's subsequent war involvement. Siverson and Starr interpret these results as supportive of a border/war-diffusion hypothesis by means of interaction context (i.e., alterations in environment [violence] affecting the decision calculus).

Summary: State-Level Patterns

There is little evidence reviewed in Geller and Singer (1998) that suggests a broadly based link between national attributes and militarized conflict or war. For example, population pressure, geographic size, economic development, business cycles, national culture, and political system-type appear to be unrelated to state-level involvement in war. The strongest findings relate to capabilities and war—specifically, power status and position on the power cycle affect a nation's probability of involvement in interstate disputes and wars: major powers are much more likely to engage in war than are minor powers, and they are more likely to fight severe (high battle death) wars than are minor powers; and major powers passing through critical points on the power cycle have an increased probability of war involvement. The cumulative evidence also points toward a positive association between both the number of borders and the number of alliances with the frequency of war involvement. Reinforcement of these general patterns can be found in the results on the war-diffusion effects of both warring border states and warring alliance partners on the probability of a nation's joining an ongoing war.

In sum, at the analytic level of the state, national capabilities—whether measured in terms of military capabilities alone[5] or a combination of military, economic, and demographic variables—reveal strong and consistent linkages to foreign conflict. There is also a strong connection between the number of alliances and involvement in war. The evidence on the issue of borders and war is consistent as well. Irrespective of explanatory mechanism—physical opportunity or the context of interactions—there appears to be a substantive linkage between the number of borders and frequency of war at the level of the monad. The additional evidence relating to the presence of warring border states and subsequent war diffusion (involvement) conforms with the general findings on borders.

Level of Analysis: Dyad

Contiguity/Proximity

> *Empirical Pattern:* The presence of a contiguous land or sea (separated by 150 miles of water or less) border increases the probability of war within a dyad.

Research at the monadic level regarding the positive association between the number of state borders and foreign conflict and war was discussed in the previous section. However, as Bremer (1992) notes, these studies permit no strong inference about contiguity and war because they do not examine the identity of the opposing conflict partner. Hence, their evidence on the issue of geographic contiguity and war must be considered, at best, indirect. This section focuses on the results of quantitative empirical studies of both proximity/contiguity and war at the analytic level of the dyad.

The initial dyadic studies of geography and war examine differences in proximity of warring and nonwarring nations. Using the COW database (1816–1965) Gleditsch and Singer (1975) report that the average distance between the capitals of warring states was significantly less than the average intercapital distance of all state-dyads for the period under analysis. Garnham (1976a) examines all dyadic international wars between 1816 and 1965 (COW database) using the distance between state capitals (proximity) as a predictor. His finding coincides with that of Gleditsch and Singer: warring dyads were geographically more proximate than nonwarring dyads.

Weede (1975) examines the question of contiguity and the frequency of military conflict for a population of 3,321 dyads over the period of 1950 to 1969. He reports that contiguous dyads with at least one major power and that had a latent territorial conflict were statistically more war prone than dyads with other characteristics. Mihalka (1976) focuses on military disputes within the European state system for the period between 1816 and 1970 (COW database) and reports that the likelihood of a confrontation escalating to the level of military violence is significantly higher between contiguous nations. Moul (1988) also examines the dispute patterns of European states—however, he limits his analysis to conflicts among great powers. His temporal period covers the years 1815 through 1939, and he uses militarized interstate dispute data[6] (COW database). In an unusual addition, Moul expands the concept of contiguity to include the borders of an alliance partner. Hence, "nonseparated" European great powers are either contiguous or tied to an ally contiguous to another great power (Moul 1985, 252). He reports that of the 22 disputes which occurred between separated European great powers, none escalated to war; however, over 10 percent (6 out of 56) of the disputes between nonseparated great powers escalated to warfare. Moul concludes that contiguity (nonseparation) appears to be a necessary condition for the escalation of disputes to the level of war. Gochman (1990a) adheres to a more conventional definition of contiguity in his study of all interstate disputes occurring between 1816 and 1976. He reports that approximately 65 percent of the militarized conflicts during that period were between contiguous states or between states separated by 150 miles or less of water. Lastly, Bremer's (1992) study of all 202,778 nondirectional dyad-years for the period between 1816 and 1965 provides evidence fully consistent with the previous analyses. Bremer classifies dyads as either land contiguous, sea contiguous (separated by 150 miles or less of water), or noncontiguous. Bremer concludes that the probability of war increases significantly with the presence of either land or sea contiguity. If the categories of land and sea contiguity are combined, then the probability of war between contiguous states is approximately 35 times greater than the likelihood of war between noncontiguous nations.

Political Systems

> *Empirical Pattern:* The absence of joint democratic governments increases the probability of war within a dyad.

A consistent theme in classical liberal political thought holds that democratic institutions reduce the likelihood of violent conflict, both in the domestic and international realms. For example, Kant ([1795] 1939) argues in *Perpetual Peace* that in democratic states the general public will be opposed to war due to the costs the mass population would be compelled to bear. Hence, leaders who make decisions for war will be removed and replaced with more pacifistic individuals. Autocratic leaders, Kant reasons, do not hold power on the basis of elections and therefore are less constrained in pursuing a belligerent or violent foreign policy. Waltz (1959) and Ray (1995) note that similar arguments have been made by such diverse theorists as Jeremy Bentham, Thomas Paine, Georg Wilhelm Friederich Hegel, and Woodrow Wilson. Variations on this theme include the idea that democratic societies inculcate norms for nonviolent conflict resolution and that these carry over into foreign policy. There is also the thesis that democratic political systems place institutional constraints on war decisions requiring the development of a consensus within the population and within a legislature or parliament—a consensus that is frequently difficult to achieve. Autocratic leaders generally do not require either type of consensus before making war decisions and therefore are less constrained in pursuing a violent foreign policy.

The accumulated body of cross-national quantitative evidence at the level of the state suggests that democratic regimes are neither more nor less war prone than other regime types. Studies by Wright (1964), Rummel (1968), Weede (1970, 1984), Chan (1984), Domke (1988), Dixon (1989), and Maoz and Abdolali (1989) all indicate that the proportional frequencies of militarized conflict and war involvement of democracies are approximately the same as for nondemocratic states. However, despite the fact that democracies appear no less war prone than nondemocratic states, recent dyadic-level analyses suggest that democratic nations rarely fight each other. Ray (1993, 1995) demonstrates that large numbers of "exceptions" to this statement may be found, depending on the definition of democracy that is applied, but the strength and consistency of the dyadic-level findings has led both Levy (1988, 662) and Russett (1990, 123) to assert that the absence of war between democratic nations is one of the strongest empirically based generalizations that exists in the field of international politics.

Two early quantitative empirical studies by Babst (1972) and Small and Singer (1976) dealing with the question of democracy and war at the level of the dyad report results strongly supportive of the democratic peace generalization. Six more recent studies provide confirmatory evidence. The first, by Rummel (1979), established the "joint-freedom proposition." Specifically, Rummel hypothesizes that "libertarian systems" will not engage in violence with each other. Examining 50 interstate wars from 1816 to 1965 (COW database) across political system categories of libertarian, authoritarian, and totalitarian, Rummel notes that there were no wars between libertarian states, 14 wars between libertarian and authoritarian states, and 36 wars between nonlibertarian states. He concludes that war does not occur between free societies. In a second study, Rummel (1983) examines both wars and "campaigns of violence" (i.e., patterns of discrete and continuous military actions) for the years 1976 through 1980. Rummel reports findings indicating that violence does not occur within libertarian dyads, and that a necessary condition for interstate conflict between two nations is for one of them to be partially or completely nonlibertarian. Maoz and Abdolali (1989) examine all nation-dyads in the international system for the years between 1816 and 1976 (COW database). Here they include subwar militarized disputes as well as wars, and report that democratic dyads are significantly less likely to engage in militarized conflict or war than are dyads with other regime types. They conclude that the joint-freedom proposition is supported by their results.

Bremer (1992) produces the most extensive evidence on this question. Utilizing the COW database and two collections of regime classifications (Chan 1984 and Polity II by Gurr, Jaggers, and Moore 1989), Bremer examines all dyad-years between 1816 and 1965. With Chan's data, he reports bivariate findings indicating that the occurrence of war for un-democratic dyads (neither state democratic) is approximately 14 times more likely than for democratic dyads. The results with the Polity II data are similar. Bremer also examines six other factors that might impact on this relationship (proximity, power status, alliance, militarization, economic development, and capability differential). Here he reports multivariate findings, which indicate that even after the effects of the other factors have been removed, the negative relationship between democracy and war remains. Although proximity is the strongest predictor of war probability, the absence of democracy (one or both states nondemocratic) in a dyad is second in salience. Bremer (1993) furnishes a second study with the COW database (this time with seven control factors) and reports findings consistent with his earlier analysis. Specifically, the bivariate coefficients indicate that nondemocratic dyads (one or both states nondemocratic) are almost 50 times more likely to engage in war than are democratic pairs. The multivariate results show a 40-fold increase in the probability of war for nondemocratic as opposed to democratic dyads. Lastly, Bremer notes that in a comparison between subwar disputes and wars, democracy is 10 times more potent in suppressing war than in suppressing disputes, and he concludes that this indicates a tendency for democratic dyads to contain conflict at lower levels of intensity rather than to avoid conflict entirely.

In a recent study, Gleditsch (1995) tests the hypothesis that the absence of wars between democratic states might be due to geographical distance between them (i.e., lack of proximity). Using the COW database for the years 1816–1986, Gleditsch produces evidence for rejecting the hypothesis, and he concludes that ". . . double democracy is a near-perfect *sufficient condition* for peace" (Gleditsch 1995, 318).

Economic Development

Empirical Pattern: The absence of joint advanced economic systems increases the probability of war within a dyad.

There exists a long stream of liberal economic thought suggesting a relationship between free trade, market economies, and international peace. For example, theorists as diverse as Richard Cobden, John Stuart Mill, and Henry Thomas Buckle all argued that unfettered free trade and economic development would promote world peace. Basically, it is argued that as free trade creates greater prosperity for all states, growing economic interdependence will increase the costs of war for the entire system. In short, because war would disrupt a market-based international economic system that serves the interests of all states, force as an instrument of foreign policy should decline in utility as free trade and economic development increasingly come to characterize the international economy. A corollary to this logic maintains that wealth and territorial acquisition are unrelated in an international economic system based on trade and development; hence, the need to gain additional territory through war as a means of generating new wealth disappears (Buzan 1984). This thesis has produced two areas of dyadic-level research—one dealing with trade and the other with economic development—and will be discussed in the context of international conflict and war.

Sullivan (1974) examines the dyadic trade flow of states for evidence of conflict patterns over the brief period of 1955 to 1957. Employing trade data generated by the United Nations, he reports that trade flows are negatively correlated with dyadic-level verbal conflict and are positively correlated with the percentage of cooperative interactions. As an indicator of the "social distance" within dyads, Sullivan concludes that trade flows are an important factor in predicting levels of dyadic conflict. Similar results are reported by Gasiorowski and Polachek (1982), who examine the interaction patterns of the U.S. and Warsaw Pact states for the period between 1967 and 1978 (Conflict and Peace Data Bank [COPDAB] and International Monetary Fund [IMF] data sources). As did Sullivan, Gasiorowski and Polachek also report an inverse relationship between trade (imports, exports, total trade) and dyadic-level conflict behavior and note that the results of Granger causality tests indicate that trade affects conflict, rather than conflict levels determining trade patterns.

Oneal et al. (1996) examine the interaction effects of bilateral trade and regime type on interstate conflict. Using the period 1950 through

1984, Oneal et al. focus their study on dyads composed of contiguous states and dyads containing at least one major power, and they introduce controls for income growth rates, alliances, and relative power. Their results indicate that trade is positively associated with peace, and that conflict becomes even less likely when external economic relations are important and the dyad is composed of democratic regimes.

A different finding is reported by Barbieri (1996a). Her analysis entails 14,341 dyad years for the period 1870–1938 and includes 270 militarized disputes and 14 wars. Barbieri concludes that economic linkages have a substantive effect on whether or not dyads engage in militarized disputes, but no effect on the occurrence of wars. However, rather than *inhibiting* militarized conflict, extensive trade interdependence *increases* the probability that dyads will experience militarized disputes. She notes that the relationship holds for both symmetrical and asymmetrical interdependencies.

Regarding the influence of development levels, Wright (1964, 165–66, 302) reports that the system of economic production influences the probability of war. He notes that, at the monadic level, states with economic systems based on commerce and industry have been less war prone than those with economies based on agriculture or animal pasturage, and he goes on to suggest that the interactions of states at advanced levels of economic development are characterized by lower probabilities of conflict:

> The rise of industrialism, capitalism, and freedom of enterprise in Europe was probably both the cause and the effect of that continent's century of relative peace between the battles of Waterloo and the Marne. . . . Wars have occurred during the periods of capitalistic dominance, but they have been least frequent in the areas most completely organized under that system.

Bremer (1992) provides impressive evidence regarding dyadic economic development levels and war. Using four variables from the COW material capabilities data set, he constructs two indices reflecting the demographic and economic dimensions of development and then classifies the dyads as symmetrically developed, asymmetrically developed, or symmetrically underdeveloped over a period totaling 197,922 dyad years. The multivariate results (for the time span between 1816 and 1965) with six additional predictor variables indicate a negative relationship between economic development and war. This association is the third strongest among the set of seven predictors, and Bremer concludes that dyads characterized by the absence of advanced economies or dyads with one advanced and one underdeveloped economy are more war prone than highly developed dyads. In a subsequent study, Bremer (1993) reports that the findings indicate that dyads composed of economically developed states are five times less likely to originate wars than are dyads with only one or no economically developed states.

Capability Balance

> *Empirical Pattern:* The presence of parity in capabilities or shifts toward parity increases the probability of war within a dyad.

The relationship between capability distributions and war is a recurring theme in the literature on international relations. Balance-of-power, long cycle, power transition, hegemonic decline, and world economy theories all focus on the distribution of capabilities and shifts in these distributions as a principal factor associated with interstate conflict. At the level of the dyad, static (stable) and dynamic (unstable) capability balances can be analyzed in terms of static parity and preponderance, or dynamic shifts and transitions.

There is an extensive body of work in international politics involving the connection between static capability balances and war. At the dyadic level of analysis, two opposing theoretical positions have been articulated: "balance of power" and "power preponderance." Balance-of-power theory maintains that an approximately equal distribution of capabilities *reduces* the likelihood of war. This thesis rests on the logic that victory becomes problematic under a condition of relative parity and that the resulting uncertainty enhances deterrence and discourages aggression. A capability imbalance (i.e., preponderance) will tend to support aggression and weaken deterrence by increasing the probability for the successful use of force by the stronger state (e.g., Wright 1964; Waltz 1979).

This logic is rejected by the power preponderance theorists. Their thesis holds that the probability of war *increases* under a condition of relative parity. The reasoning behind this position is that the likelihood of war is greatest when *both* sides see a prospect for victory, and that this condition is met when parity characterizes the balance. With the alternative capability distribution—preponderance—the weaker cannot afford to fight and the stronger usually does not have to in order to achieve its goals (e.g., Blainey 1973).

An interesting corollary to the basic preponderance logic is offered by the power transition theorists who maintain that dynamic as well as static capability distributions are related to war. For example, Organski (1958), Organski and Kugler (1980), Gilpin (1981), Modelski (1983b), and Thompson (1988) all focus on shifting capability distributions as a principal factor in the wars that shape the hierarchy of the international system. The general thesis suggests that great power wars are the result of unstable capability balances: the erosion of a dominant nation's relative capability advantage as a consequence of a challenger's rising power trajectory increases the probability of conflict. This logic appears in the configuration of hegemonic decline (Gilpin), long cycle (Modelski), and power transition (Organski) theories. All of these formulations focus on a mechanism for war in the operation of dynamic capability distributions that lead away from preponderance and toward equality.

Conceptually, dynamic capability balances can be divided into two categories: shifts (capability convergence or divergence) or transitions (a reversal of relative capability position). Intricate explanations as to why dyadic capability shifts may produce conflict can be found in Levy (1987) and Wayman (1996). Most simply, however, either the possibility of advancing national interests or a growing perception of threat to those interests may be generated by closure or transition in relative capabilities among nations.

Balance-of-power theory (e.g., Claude 1962; Wright 1964; Waltz 1979) posits that the likelihood of war increases among disputants if one side possesses preponderant capabilities. Moreover, it is suggested (implicitly or explicitly) that the more powerful state will be the war initiator. At least partial evidence in support of the initiation hypothesis is found in Bueno de Mesquita (1980a), who reports that initiators of interstate wars (COW data 1816–1974) are approximately twice as likely to be stronger than their targets. Although Bueno de Mesquita notes that expected-utility theory produces even more impressive results than a simple comparison of capabilities, he records that the capability balance results are statistically significant. Siverson and Tennefoss (1984) also provide evidence in support of the basic hypothesis. Using data for the years 1815 through 1965, they examine both the initiation and escalation of international conflicts. Their dyadic-level findings suggest support for balance-of-power theory: few disputes among major powers (presumably equal in capabilities) escalate to mutual military action, whereas a much higher proportion of conflicts initiated by major powers against minor powers escalated to reciprocated military action. However, they also note that approximately 19 percent of the total conflicts involved minor power initiation against stronger states, and that over 25 percent of these escalated to the mutual use of force.

A greater number of empirical research studies provide evidence supportive of the parity-leads-to-war hypothesis. An early study by Mihalka (1976), using COW data for the years between 1816 and 1970, indicates that the probability of a confrontation escalating to the level of military violence was significantly lower when the capability differentials between the disputants was high. More evidence supportive of the parity and war hypothesis is provided in a study by Garnham (1976b). Comparing "lethal" with "non-lethal" dyads for the years 1969–73, Garnham reports that relative parity is associated with violence irrespective of whether power is measured by a composite capability index or by separate indicators. Weede (1976), employing COW and Stockholm International Peace Research Institute (SIPRI) data on contiguous Asian dyads for the years 1950–69, concludes that war was much less frequent under a condition of overwhelming preponderance than in its absence. Mandel (1980) examines interstate border disputes for the years between 1945 and 1974 with the Managing Interstate Conflict (MIC) database and reaches a conclusion consistent with those of Mihalka, Garnham, and Weede: violent border disputes were more likely to occur under a condition of relative parity in capabilities. Moul (1988), focusing on patterns of dispute escalation among the European great powers (COW database 1816–1939), reports that over 50 percent of the disputes under a condition of relative parity escalated to war, as opposed to less than a 3 percent escalation rate under an unequal distribution of capabilities. Kim (1991) also examines great power wars (COW database 1816–1975) and reports that the probability of war for major powers whose capabilities were equal is more than double the probability for dyads whose capabilities were unequal. The difference between the two distributions is statistically significant.

In an expanded analysis, Kim (1996) examines the interaction of dyadic capability balances, status quo orientation, and alliance relationships among great powers for the period from the Peace of Westphalia in 1648 to 1975. His findings indicate that basic equality in capabilities between great powers and dissatisfied challengers increases the probability of the onset of war. In the most comprehensive study to date, Bremer (1992) analyzes all dyads in the interstate system present in the COW database (202,778 nondirectional dyad years) for the period between 1816 and 1965. Relative capability was determined by CINC scores using the COW material capabilities data set. Bremer concludes that war is about 33 percent more likely in dyads with small or medium differences in relative capabilities than in dyads with large capability differentials. Lastly, Geller (1993) examines dispute-to-dispute war probabilities for a set of 29 enduring dyadic rivalries (COW database 1816–1986) inclusive of 456 militarized conflicts. This subset of all interstate dyads is the most violence-prone group of nation pairs in the interstate system and is responsible for almost 40 percent of all militarized disputes that occur during the period under examination. The study concludes that static parity (measured by military capability) is roughly twice as likely to be associated with war in these dyads as is static preponderance.

The corollary to the basic parity and war hypothesis involves dynamic capability shifts and transitions as a source of conflict (e.g., Organski 1958; Gilpin 1981; Modelski 1983b; Wallerstein 1984). Organski and Kugler (1980) provide evidence in support of Organski's original power transition theory based on an analysis of dynamic capability balances among selected nations from 1860 to 1975. They report that differential capability growth rates (measured by Gross National Product) that produce transitions in relative position within "contender" dyads are associated with war. In a more comprehensive study, Anderson and McKeown (1987) examine 77 wars (COW database 1816–1980) in terms of capability balances and report that an unstable military balance is associated with war. Houweling and Siccama (1988) provide a reanalysis of the Organski and Kugler power transition test using a more extensive set of nations (all major powers) and a composite indicator of national capabilities (instead of GNP). They conclude that differential growth rates that result in capability transitions are strongly associated with the occurrence of dyadic-level major power war.

In an analysis of differences within dynamic balances for 29 enduring rivalries (COW database 1816–1986), Geller (1993) notes that capability shifts—and particularly shifts toward parity—are associated with higher probabilities of war than are actual transitions. These results are consistent for both composite capability and military capability indices. Lastly, Wayman (1996) analyzes a set of major power rivalries (COW database) and compares their capability and war patterns with nonrival dyads. He reports that the statistical association between capability shifts and war is stronger among rival states than for nonrivals, and that a capability shift within a rival dyad approximately doubles its probability of war—from 14 percent to 31 percent.

The rate of capability convergence has been postulated in some studies (e.g., Levy 1987, 97–98; Schampel 1993, 397–99) as a key factor in the occurrence of war. Rapid approaches (Wayman 1996) and rapid convergence/divergence (Gochman 1990b) have been posited as exacerbating the conflict potential in rival dyads. It is argued that a rapid shift in relative capabilities provides little time for peaceful adjustment and may increase both the sense of threat and opportunity. Alternatively, a gradual change in relative capabilities allows more time for nonviolent adjustment to the shifting power balance. The evidence on the salience of rate of change is mixed: Schampel (1993, 405) and Gochman (1990b, 154–55) report results indicating substantive effects for rapid approaches on the probability of war, whereas Kim (1992, 171) and Kim and Morrow (1992, 917) report the absence of any statistically discernible association between war occurrence and the rate of capability change among major power rivals.

Alliances

> *Empirical Pattern:* Dyads where only one member has an external alliance tie have a higher probability of war than dyads where both members have external ties.

At the level of the dyad, research regarding a possible relationship between alliance and war has coalesced in two areas: (1) alliance within dyads; and (2) alliance external to dyads. With regard to the first area, conventional wisdom has long held that alliance between nations reduces mutual conflict (e.g., Brzezinski and Huntington 1963, 406). Whether based on common or complementary interests and objectives, it has been customarily assumed that allied nations might disagree on joint policy but will rarely engage each other in war, at least for the duration of the alliance. However, using his expected-utility theory of war initiation, Bueno de Mesquita (1981b) deduces the counterintuitive proposition that war is *more likely* between allies than between unallied states.

The second area of research has involved the impact on war of alliance external to dyads. Here, the issues tend to focus on the number of ties to external blocs and their effects on dyadic conflict. For example, if one member of a dyad is allied with a bloc while the other member is unaligned, is war more or less likely than if both members of the dyad possessed external ties? These types of questions generally involve the viability of extended deterrence by superpowers, although some analyses deal explicitly with the aggregate effects of alliance on relative military capabilities for members of a dyad.

Bueno de Mesquita (1981b, 76–78) derives from his expected-utility theory the unsettling hypothesis that allied nations are more likely to engage in war with one another than unallied states, and he presents evidence (1981b, 159–64) in support of this deduction. He reports that of the 76 war initiations that occurred between 1816 and 1974 (COW database), 15 were among nations that had a formal, standing military agreement between them. These 15 wars between allies constitute approximately 20 percent of all wars in his data set, whereas allied dyads represent only about 7 percent of all annual dyads in the data. Bueno de Mesquita concludes that wars between allies are approximately three times more likely than would be expected by chance. Additional evidence in support of this proposition is provided by Ray (1990). Ray tests the hypothesis with more stringent coding rules and a refined COW database and reports that there is evidence of a positive association between alliance within dyads and conflict proneness for the years 1816 to 1974: allied nations have been more likely to engage in both militarized disputes and war among themselves than unallied nations.

However, two studies (Weede 1975 and Bremer 1992) report contrary results. Weede's (1975) analysis of military conflict among 3,321 dyads for 1950 through 1969 shows that common bloc membership (alliance) was negatively associated with war between members of a dyad. In a subsequent analysis, Bremer (1992) codes all dyad-years between 1816 and 1965 into four categories: defense pact, neutrality pact, entente, and no alliance. His bivariate results are similar to those of both Bueno de Mesquita and Ray; the conditional probability of war with the three types of pacts combined compared with no alliance is approximately 4.5 to 1. However, Bremer's multivariate analysis of the data indicates an interaction effect with the level of militarization in the dyad. Specifically, if the dyad is highly militarized, then the alliance coefficient indicates a significant, negative relationship between alliance and war probability. Bremer concludes that the absence of an alliance (in conjunction with other factors) increases the war proneness of a dyad.

Alliance ties that are external to the dyad present a different though related research issue. The question of one alliance tie external to a dyad is examined by Mihalka (1976) and by Siverson and Tennefoss (1984). Mihalka employs the COW database covering the years between 1816 and 1970 for European state-system dyads. He reports that dyads with only one member in an external alliance were most likely to experience dispute escalation to the level of war and that dyads with both members tied to external alliances were least likely to have disputes escalate to war. He concludes that the probability of a confrontation ending in military hostilities is significantly higher if only a single dyad-member has external alliance ties. Siverson and Tennefoss (1984) report a similar finding for dyads in the interstate system over the period between 1815 and 1965. Specifically, they report that disputes were most likely to escalate to war if one dyad-member possessed a major power ally while the other did not. In sum, a dyad with one external alliance tie has a higher war probability than one in which neither party has any external ties.

The issue of two external alliance ties offers some interesting contrasts. Weede (1975) reports that during the period between 1950 and 1969, dyads composed of a U.S. bloc member and Soviet bloc member were less war prone than other dyads. This may be interpreted as reflecting successful mutual extended deterrence. Weede's (1989) results for subwar disputes also indicate conflict reduction for two-alliance dyads. Mihalka (1976), using the COW database for the period between 1816 and 1970 reports that confrontations between dyad-members where each possessed an external alliance were the least likely to escalate to military hostilities. Lastly, Siverson and Tennefoss (1984) report that, for the period between 1815 and 1965, conflicts were least likely to escalate to the level of war where both dyad-members had external alliances with major powers.

Enduring Rivals

> *Empirical Pattern:* The presence of an enduring rivalry increases the probability of war within a dyad.

War is a form of interaction between two or more states. In fact, two-party conflicts have constituted approximately 84 percent of all militarized interstate disputes between 1816 and 1992 (Jones, Bremer, and Singer 1996).

Current empirical work suggests the importance of a subset population of dyads (within the set of all nation-dyads) defined by long-term conflicts. These conflict-prone dyads, or "enduring rivals," account for a disproportionately large amount of the violence that occurs in the interstate system. Two analyses by Goertz and Diehl (1992a, 1993) estimate that long-term rivals are responsible for almost half of the wars, violent territorial changes, and militarized disputes that have occurred in the last two centuries. Accordingly, recent studies have focused on these dispute-prone dyads in an effort to gain a better understanding of the factors associated with a large proportion of interstate conflict (e.g., how arms races, capability balances, and deterrence conditions operate within the rivalry context). For instance, Gochman (1990b, 147) has argued that shifts in relative capability might be expected to have a particularly strong effect on the interaction of rival states with a history of violent conflict.

Multiple definitions of enduring rivals with widely varying criteria have been used in the construction of population sets. For example, Wayman (1982, 1996) includes in his set of major power rivals any dyad that exhibits two or more militarized disputes within a 10-year span; Diehl (1985a) defines a major power enduring rivalry as any dyad exhibiting three or more militarized disputes within a 15-year span; the Gochman and Maoz (1984) rivalry set includes all dyads that have exhibited a minimum of seven militarized disputes during the period from 1816 to 1980. Jones, Huth, and Maoz (Jones 1989) design a database with more elaborate criteria—specifically, they stipulate that for an enduring rivalry to exist, the conditions of "severity," "durability," and "intensity" must be satisfied. These criteria cover, respectively, the minimum number of militarized disputes engaged, the minimum time span between the first and last disputes, and the maximum time span between consecutive disputes.[7] The databases compiled from these criteria sets vary in terms of total rivalries, number of dyads by power status, average number of disputes, average duration of rivalry, and number of wars.[8]

However, Goertz (1994) has argued that enduring rivalries not only provide a context for the analysis of the dynamics of capability balances (e.g., Gochman 1990b; Geller 1993; Wayman 1996) and deterrence conditions (e.g., Huth and Russett 1993) on war but also operate as an independent contributing factor toward war. In other words, a condition of rivalry may increase perceptions of hostility and feed a threat spiral—thereby influencing the onset of war. Employing the Goertz-Diehl (Goertz 1994, 201, 208) definition for enduring rivalry inclusive of (1) a minimum of six militarized disputes; (2) a minimum duration of 20 years; and (3) a 15-year termination rule, Goertz (1994, 208–12) examines the probabilities of conflict within rivalries. His findings indicate that between 1816 and

1976 approximately 40 percent of all non-war militarized disputes occur within enduring rivalries, and that 47 percent of all wars during the same period take place within enduring rivalries. He also calculates that enduring rivals are eight times more likely than nonrival dyads to engage in war.

Summary: Dyadic-Level Patterns

Research based at the analytic level of the dyad has produced some of the most interesting, consistent, and cumulative findings in the area of international conflict and war. For example, a general body of research indicates that both static and dynamic capability balances are associated with the occurrence of war. Specifically, conditions of dyadic military parity and shifts toward parity are consistently and significantly related to the outbreak of war. As Maoz (1993, 37) notes:

> . . . the likelihood of conflict in a dyad is significantly affected by the degree of parity in military capability. . . . This suggests that as states grow more equal in military capabilities, they are more likely to be subject to the kind of calculations that are consistent with the power transition theory (Organski and Kugler 1980). . . . The state losing in relative capabilities invokes the declining power logic (Levy 1987), while the state gaining in capabilities invokes the status inconsistency logic described by East (1972).

This conclusion is reaffirmed by Lemke and Kugler (1996, 14) who note that ". . . a large number of studies linking parity and war at the dyadic level suggest that parity increases the probability of war, and consistently confirm the claim that parity and transitions increase the probability of war." In sum, cumulative evidence has developed, which indicates that parity in military capabilities and convergence toward military parity within dyads are associated with the onset of militarized conflict and war.

Consistency and cumulation also characterize the findings on proximity/contiguity and conflict.[9] At the level of the dyad, the distance between states is inversely related to warfare. Proximate states are more likely to engage in war than are nonproximate states, and war within dyads having a land or narrow water border is much more probable than between noncontiguous states. Explanations for this relationship vary. For example, Wesley (1962) argues that proximity/contiguity provides opportunities for conflict. Starr and Most (1976, 1978) suggest that proximity/contiguity structures the context of interactions (e.g., security and threat perception) and may promote hostile behavior. Vasquez (1993, 1995b) argues that these findings are consistent with an explanation of conflict based on human territoriality.[10] Which theoretical mechanism best accounts for the relationship remains to be established.

The results of analyses on alliance and war are mixed. In the area of alliance within dyads, the findings are inconsistent. However, the results of studies focusing on alliance ties that are external to the dyad present a different picture. Dyads in which only one member has an external alliance tie are more likely to experience war than are dyads where both members have external ties. Explanations for these different relationships may involve military balances as they are affected by the capability additions of allies, estimates of reliability of allies, extended deterrence by nuclear-armed superpowers, or a greater caution on the part of decision makers induced by the potential for a wider war. Additional research is required to choose among these alternatives, but whatever the explanatory mechanism, dyads with one external alliance are more war prone than dyads where both parties have external ties.

The evidence in the area of the joint-freedom proposition is consistent and cumulative.[11] Democratic dyads are less likely to engage in war than are nondemocratic pairs. However, there are two competing explanations for this phenomenon. One explanation focuses on the political culture of democratic states (i.e., nonviolent norms), whereas the other explanation involves democratic political structure (i.e., decision-making constraints). According to the normative or cultural school (e.g., Doyle 1986; Dixon 1993, 1994; Russett 1993), liberal democracies tend to be less violent than autocratic states because democratic societies value and inculcate nonviolent methods of conflict resolution. These preferences for the peaceful resolution of disputes shape policy decisions, and particularly impact on relations with other democratic states that are believed to share the same norms. As a result of these common values, disputes between democracies tend to be settled in a nonviolent manner. Maoz and Russett (1993) attempt to test models representing both the normative and structural explanations for the democratic peace. Although they find that both models are supported by the data, they report that support for the normative model is more robust and consistent.

The alternative explanation for the democratic peace rests on structural or institutional factors (e.g., Bueno de Mesquita and Lalman 1992). This thesis holds that the decision-making units of democracies operate in an environment of divided political power and must gain support or at least acquiescence from legislatures, bureaucracies, interest groups, and the mass public before engagement in war. Creating this consensus is often a long and difficult process. Therefore, the structural explanation posits that democratic dyads tend not to engage in violent conflict due to these constraints on war decisions.[12] Works by Morgan and Campbell (1991) and Morgan and Schwebach (1992) attempt to produce evidence on this issue. Their findings are supportive of the political constraint explanation; however, they suggest that *all* constraining institutional structures—and not just those associated with democracy—may inhibit war.[13]

Evidence on a relationship between dyadic trade patterns and conflict is mixed, but exhaustive analyses by Bremer (1992, 1993) indicate a strong pattern for dyads characterized by highly advanced economies and the absence of war. Goertz (1994) has also provided evidence indicating the independent effect of enduring rivalry as a factor increasing the probability of the onset of war.

In sum, data-based research on conflict and war at the level of the nation-dyad has produced some impressive results. Geographic proximity/contiguity, static parity in capabilities and shifts toward parity, unbalanced external alliance ties, the absence of paired democratic regimes, the absence of joint advanced economies, and the presence of an enduring rivalry are factors substantively and positively associated with the occurrence of both militarized disputes and wars.

Level of Analysis: Region

Contagion/Diffusion

Empirical Pattern: The presence of an ongoing war increases the probability of subsequent war occurrence within the same region.

The possible "contagion" or "diffusion" of international conflict, whether in the form of war or less serious modes of dispute, constitutes an interesting theoretical and empirical question in the study of international politics. The issue of contagion/diffusion processes in various forms of domestic conflict constitutes a closely related area of research (e.g., Spilerman 1970; Lieberson and Silverman 1965; Midlarsky 1970, 1978; Midlarsky, Crenshaw, and Yoshida 1980; and Li and Thompson 1975). These studies—dealing with the spread of domestic violence within national boundaries as well as the spread of domestic violence across national boundaries—treat conflict as both "cause" and "effect." The question at issue is whether something about an act of violence makes the subsequent spread of violence more probable. The metaphors used in these analyses tend to be drawn from medicine (contagion) or from physical processes (diffusion). At the national level, the issue involves the spread of internal violence; at the level of interstate relations it involves the spread of war. Yet another related area of research (at the level of analysis of the state) involves questions of "addiction" or "reinforcement;" specifically, these processes refer to the probability that a war engagement by a nation will lead to another war engagement by the same nation (e.g., Most and Starr 1980; Garnham 1983; Levy and Morgan 1986).

Bremer (1982) examines regional patterns of coercive interstate behavior (involving the threat or use of force [COW database]) for the period between 1900 and 1976 by means of Poisson distribution models. He finds little evidence of inter-regional coercive contagion, but strong evidence that coercive behavior is contagious intra-regionally. In a related study, Faber, Houweling, and Siccama (1984) analyze the spatial and temporal distances between wars (COW database) within five regions of the world for the period extending from 1816 to 1980. In addition to interstate and extrasystemic wars, they also include civil wars in the data analysis. The spatial distance between wars is defined as the geographical distance between locations of successive wars; temporal distance is defined as the time lapse between successive wars. The Faber, Houweling, and Siccama findings indicate that the location and timing of previous conflicts have positive and significant effects on subsequent war location and timing only within each region. They conclude that war outbreaks are not contagious across space (between regions) but are clustered in space and time (within regions). These findings are consistent with Bremer's (1982) conclusions.

Houweling and Siccama (1985) subsequently produce a more detailed analysis of space-time interaction within specific regions. Using the COW database (1816–1980) on interstate, extrasystemic, and civil wars for the five geographic regions of Europe, Western Hemisphere, Middle East, Asia, and Africa, Houweling and Siccama report no evidence of worldwide contagion of interstate war but significant space-time interaction (contagion) in the outbreak of regional war for both Europe and Asia.

Three other analyses relevant to regional contagion focus on Africa. Two of these studies are by Starr and Most (1983, 1985); the third is by

Kirby and Ward (1987). Starr and Most include the factor of "borders" in their examination of contagion/diffusion processes in the African region. The studies cover the temporal periods of 1960 to 1972 and 1960 to 1977 (with five-year lags) and utilize data from Kende (1978) and from COPDAB. Their results indicate that nations with wars on their borders have a higher probability of engaging in war in a subsequent time period than do nations without border wars. Starr and Most conclude that war in Africa tends to diffuse spatially across states through common borders.

Kirby and Ward (1987) also produce a spatial analysis of African conflict. The period covered by their study is from 1948 to 1978 with data drawn from the COPDAB project. Their findings are consistent with those of Starr and Most: specifically, Kirby and Ward note that hostile interactions between African states are significantly affected by existing conflicts among bordering nations.

Summary: Regional-Level Patterns

The results of the six studies summarized in this section suggest that a militarized conflict and war contagion/diffusion process operates at the regional level. The analyses by Bremer (1982), Faber, Houweling, and Siccama (1984), and Houweling and Siccama (1985) explore the probabilities of both inter- and intra-regional contagion—and conclude that conflict spreads within but not across geographical regions. The Starr and Most (1983, 1985) and Kirby and Ward (1987) studies focus on the African region alone. Their conclusions suggest that border contact increases the probability of war contagion.

Hower and Zinnes (1989, 3) express reservations to this apparent consensus. They note that for a "contagion" process to occur, the second conflict event must involve a different nation than the states that were involved in the initial event. Moreover, they argue that some contact must be shown to have existed between the nations through which the contagion process supposedly operated. The studies by Starr and Most and by Kirby and Ward meet the "contact" criterion more closely than the Faber et al. and Bremer research designs, although Hower and Zinnes (1989, 3) allow that nations in the same region may be presumed "to have contact with one another."

The thesis regarding the "contagiousness" of conflict and war on an *intra*-regional basis is supported by the evidence. Despite the apparent absence of such a relationship at the *inter*-regional level, a space-time conflict diffusion or contagion process appears to operate within geographic regions.

Level of Analysis: System

Polarity/Hierarchy

> *Empirical Pattern:* The presence of an unstable hierarchy among the major powers of the international system increases the probabilities of both major power and systemic wars.

The literature of international politics is rife with discussions on the effects of the "polarity" of the international system on war. Unfortunately, due to the ambiguity of the concept of polarity and the multiple ways in which it can be operationalized, confusion rather than clarity has characterized the debate. The essence of this confusion involves the question of whether the polarity of the international system is determined by the number of major states or by the number of distinct clusters of states emerging from the configuration of alliances. For example, should a system with five major states that have coalesced into two opposing alliances be categorized as multipolar or bipolar? For the purposes of classifying data-based studies in this area, the following terminology will be used: the polarity of the international system is determined by the number of major actors. Possible configurations include unipolarity (one dominant state), bipolarity (two major states of approximately equal capabilities), and multipolarity (three or more major states of approximately equal capabilities). As Snyder and Diesing (1977, 420) assert:

> "poles" . . . are *states,* not alliances or "blocs" of states. Alliances and blocs are types of *relations* between states in the system that are influenced by the prevailing structure but do not constitute that structure. Thus the rough equality between the two alliances prior to 1914 did not make the system bipolar, nor did the loosening of the U.S. and Soviet blocs during the 1960s and early 1970s make that system multipolar.

Opposing theoretical schools have developed regarding the war effects of the number of major actors. For example, some analysts argue that unipolar systems should be the least war prone of the various system structures (e.g., Organski 1958; Gilpin 1981; Modelski 1983b; Wallerstein 1984; Thompson 1988), while others maintain that characteristic should inhere in bipolar systems (e.g., Waltz 1979, 174–77) or in multipolar structures (e.g., Morgenthau [1948] 1967, 332–35).[14] Explanations regarding the effects of polarity on war range from the "stable order" imposed by the dominant state in a unipolar system (e.g., Organski 1958; Modelski 1972; Gilpin 1981), to "balanced power" in a bipolar configuration (e.g., Waltz 1979), to "flexibility in alignment" in multipolar systems (e.g., Deutsch and Singer 1964; Morgenthau [1948] 1967). Data-based evidence, however, is mixed.

Mansfield (1988) examines international wars over the period from 1495 to 1980 and reports that the mean number of wars initiated per year was higher during eras when a "hegemonic" state dominated the system (unipolarity) than during eras when hegemony was absent. However, both Thompson (1986) and Spiezio (1990) report opposite results for unipolarity. Thompson's analysis covers a period similar to Mansfield's (1494–1983 [COW database and Modelski and Thompson database]), and specifies categories of bipolarity, multipolarity, and near-unipolarity, in addition to unipolarity. Thompson's evidence suggests that warfare was least likely to occur when the system was unipolar or near-unipolar; he also reports that bipolar and multipolar systems were equally war prone. Spiezio's study covers the more limited temporal period of 1815 to 1939 (COW data) in terms of the rising and falling economic/military capability base of Great Britain relative to that of other major powers. He reports that the relative size of Britain's capability base was negatively and significantly associated with the frequency of war in the international system and concludes that his findings support the unipolar thesis that conflict is inversely related to the capability advantage of the hegemonic state.

Brecher, James, and Wilkenfeld (1990) and Wayman (1984) examine the effects of polarity in terms of international crises and war magnitude (i.e., total nation-months of war). The Brecher et al. analysis covers the temporal span of 1929 to 1985 (International Crisis Behavior [ICB] database) for international crises using system categories of bipolarity and multipolarity. They report that the mean number of international crises per year was higher for the bipolar period (1945–62) than for the multipolar era (1929–39). However, based on an analysis of major power crisis involvement, they conclude that bipolarity is a more "stable" structure than multipolarity. Wayman (1984) examines the dependent variable of major power war magnitude for bipolar and multipolar periods over the years 1815–1965 (COW database). He reports that periods characterized by "power multipolarity" were much more likely to evidence high levels of war magnitude than were periods of "power bipolarity." These differences were statistically significant.

Hopf (1991) and Levy (1984) examine the frequency, magnitude, and severity of wars using polarity (Hopf) and "system size" (Levy) as predictors. Hopf's database includes warfare in the European subsystem for the restricted temporal period of 1495 to 1559. The system is classified as multipolar for the years 1495 to 1520 and as bipolar for the years 1521 to 1559. Hopf reports that the amount of warfare during these two periods was essentially equivalent. He states that polarity has little relationship to patterns of war for the historical period under examination. However, Midlarsky (Midlarsky and Hopf 1993) questions Hopf's conclusions, arguing, instead, that the relationship between polarity and war is contingent on the scarcity of desired international resources.[15] Levy (1984) explores a possible linear association between the number of great powers (system size) and war for the extended temporal span of 1495 to 1975. His findings coincide with those of Hopf. He reports that the frequency, magnitude, and severity of war in the international system is unrelated to the number of major powers in the system.

The cumulative findings in the area of polarity and warfare are mixed. Aside from the evidence of Thompson (1986) and Spiezio (1990) on a relationship between the presence of a hegemonic state (unipolarity) and lower frequencies of warfare, other findings indicate higher numbers of crises during bipolar periods (Brecher, James, and Wilkenfeld 1990) but lower war magnitudes (Wayman 1984) than with multipolar systems. The study with the longest time line and the most extensive set of war variables (Levy 1984) indicates the lack of a substantive linear relationship between the number of great powers and the frequency, magnitude, or severity of warfare.

The results of data-based studies on polarity and warfare indicate no definitive pattern regarding unipolar, bipolar, and multipolar configurations and the occurrence of war. The only polar structure that appears to influence conflict probability is unipolarity. At least part of the difficulty in identifying a stable pattern may result from an interaction effect between factors at multiple analytic levels, as the onset (occurrence/initiation) of major power warfare is determined less by the number of major powers than by the static or dynamic capability distributions among the strongest states themselves. Every international system possesses a hierarchy based on relative capabilities, and the extent of the capability differential between the leading state and potential challengers matters. If the hierarchy is clear, with the leading state in possession of a substantial capability advantage over its nearest potential rival, then the probability of action to rearrange the hierarchical order is likely to be low. However, if the capability advantage of the leading state is small or is eroding, other states may choose to attempt to alter the hierarchy. The challenges may be directed against the leading state or lesser states within an increasingly unstable international order. This logic is found in the works of Organski (1958), Gilpin (1981), Modelski (1983b), Wallerstein (1984), and Thompson (1988). Studies by Doran (1989a, 1991, 1995a), Geller (1992, 1996), and Houweling and Siccama (1993) have presented empirical analyses of these complex cross-level dynamics and indicate that changes in the hierarchical arrangement of major powers are associated statistically with the onset of great power warfare.

In sum, shifts in system-level power structure appear to have an interactive effect with dyadic capability distributions in the onset of both major power and global (or systemic) wars. As the international system moves from a high concentration of resources in the leading state toward multipolarity (power diffusion), lower-order conflict among the set of major states becomes increasingly probable, due to the weakening of the principal defender of the hierarchy. Movement toward power parity within secondary nation-dyads may trigger violent interactions that—though not related to system leadership—are still of considerable consequence. This suggests that the erosion of the system-level power structure links lower-order wars among major powers to system-shaping global wars. In this way, power distributions at both the systemic and dyadic levels of analysis interact synergistically to produce war among the set of major powers. The clarity and stability of the hierarchy rather than the number of major powers is the critical factor affecting the onset of global war.

Number of Borders

> *Empirical Pattern:* The greater the number of total borders in the international system, the higher the number of war participations in the system.

Two studies by Starr and Most (1976, 1978) examine a possible relationship between the total number of borders in the international system and the number of new war participations in the system. Using data from

Richardson (1960b), the COW project, and SIPRI for the years 1946 through 1965, they report that the total number of borders in the international system is positively and significantly correlated with war participations in both the COW and SIPRI data sets.

The findings on the positive relationship between the total number of borders in the interstate system and the frequency of war participations in the system mirror the results on borders/contiguity and war at the monadic and dyadic levels of analysis. Although an explanatory mechanism linking contact with war drawn from lower levels of analysis (i.e., monadic or dyadic) is not necessarily applicable at higher levels (Ray 1997a), King, Keohane, and Verba (1994, 30–31) argue that cross-level inference is a powerful tool in testing the veracity of theory. Therefore, confidence in a mechanism linking contact and conflict is reinforced by the findings that the number of borders or contiguity correlates positively with conflict and war at the state, dyad, and system levels.

Frequency of Civil/Revolutionary Wars

> *Empirical Pattern:* The greater the frequency of civil/revolutionary wars in the international system, the higher the frequencies of interstate disputes and wars in the system.

A number of quantitative empirical studies have examined a possible relationship between the frequencies of civil wars and the frequencies of international disputes and wars. Specifically, both Maoz (1989, 1996) and Hoole and Huang (1989) pose the question of whether the amount of system-level interstate conflict is affected by the amount of civil war or revolution in the international system. Maoz (1989) uses militarized interstate dispute counts (COW database) between 1816 and 1976 as his dependent variable and searches for correlations with the number of revolutionary state formations/transformations. His basic hypothesis—that the number of interstate conflicts in the system will increase when a large number of states are experiencing revolutionary regime changes—is supported statistically. In an expanded analysis for the years between 1816 and 1986, Maoz (1996, 74–77) reports similar findings: the rise of new states in an "evolutionary" (nonviolent) fashion has little effect on the international conflict patterns of the system; however, the rise of revolutionary states is significantly associated with an increase in the number of interstate militarized disputes. Hoole and Huang, using international and civil war data (COW project) for the limited temporal period of 1947 to 1980, report that changes in the amount of system-level international war are significantly affected by changes in the amount of civil war occurring in the interstate system. The results of both the Maoz studies and the Hoole and Huang analysis indicate that international and domestic conflict are part of an interactive global process.

Starr (1994, 482) has moved impressively toward elaborating the theoretical mechanism underpinning such a connection. Specifically, he has argued that:

> . . . we must first differentiate between the ways in which revolution could lead to war and the ways in which war could lead to revolution. Looking at revolution-to-war, two basic relationships emerge—in what ways revolution would lead a state to *attack* another, or in what ways revolution would make a state an attractive *target* for another state. War-to-revolution may be based upon war as an agent of change, as a factor in the growth of domestic discontent, as a factor in the weakening of governmental legitimacy and/or strength, or as a factor in the changing resource base of opposition groups. Whether a war is won or lost also must be factored into the war-to-revolution relationship.

Starr (1994, 495–96) goes on to discuss how the "interaction opportunity" model of conflict diffusion (Most and Starr 1980) can be applied in an explanation of the revolution/war nexus:

> This model proposes that positive spatial diffusion would be enhanced by the presence of violent conflict (either civil war, large-scale collective violence, or interstate war) in neighboring states, based on the heightened salience of conflict in proximate areas. This salience derives from: (1) a newly heightened uncertainty in the neighboring states as to the changing policies of a new government, possible ideological change and its interaction with either a newly strengthened or weakened government and state; (2) a newly heightened uncertainty in the neighboring states as to their own viability or that of their neighbors. The neighbor must discern whether it has a newly strengthened or weakened country on its borders.

Starr (1994, 501) then cites a recent study by Wallensteen and Axell (1993) that identifies 82 armed conflicts for the period 1989–92 and notes that a connection between revolution and war is identifiable in 40 of these conflicts.

Alliances

> *Empirical Pattern:* The presence of polarized alliances increases the probability of the seriousness (magnitude/duration/severity) of war.

Alliance configuration has often been discussed in terms of the polarization of the international system. For example, Kegley and Raymond (1994, 54–55) argue

> . . . whereas polarity pertains to the distribution of power [the number of major states], *polarization* refers to the propensity of countries to cluster in alliance. . . . Thus a system with multiple power centers can be said to be moving toward a greater degree of polarization if its members gradually form two separate blocs whose interactions with others are characterized by increasing levels of conflict while the interactions among themselves become more cooperative.

Alliance configuration, like the distribution of capabilities, is considered to be a factor that affects uncertainty, and therefore the onset of war. In both instances, opposing theoretical schools have developed regarding the war effects of these factors. Specifically, some theorists suggest that alliances deter war by maintaining military equilibrium (e.g., Holsti, Hopmann, and Sullivan 1973), whereas others argue that alliances may increase tension and generate counter-coalitions, thereby raising the probability of war (e.g., Jervis 1976). These explanations maintain that the effects of alliance on the onset (i.e., occurrence or initiation) of war hinge on its role in either enhancing or reducing uncertainty. For example, firm alliances may reduce the level of uncertainty for decision makers,[16] but this may serve either to decrease or to increase the probability of war depending upon the policy objectives of those leaders (Levy 1989a, 235).

Uncertainty and alliance also play a role in Midlarsky's (1986) hierarchical equilibrium theory of war. Midlarsky defines hierarchy in terms of clear capability differentials between states within the same alliance system. He argues that "systemic war" results from the conjunction of an ambiguous internal alliance structure and a disequilibrium in the frequencies of conflicts (disputes and wars) begun and terminated within a given period of time.[17]

Quantitative empirical research in the area of alliances and warfare has produced a set of more consistent results than with system-level polarity and war. Three early studies by Singer and Small (1966, 1968,

1974) defined the problem and established the analytic model. Despite some conceptual ambiguity between alliance formation (aggregation), alliance configuration (polarization), and polarity (number of major states), the results of these analyses have been widely accepted. The basic hypothesis, simply stated, is: "The greater the number of alliance commitments in the system, the more war the system will experience" (Singer and Small 1968, 251). The two early studies cover all nations for the period between 1815 and 1945; the third analysis extends the period to the years between 1815 and 1965 (COW database). Categories of alliance commitments include defense pacts, neutrality pacts, and ententes. The results of all three studies indicate the lack of a substantive statistical correlation between system-level alliance formation (aggregation) and the frequency of war for the entire period under analysis. In a subsequent study, Bueno de Mesquita and Lalman (1988) examine the effects of alliances on the occurrence of major power war in Europe for the period between 1815 and 1965. They conclude that alliance configuration (polarization) among the strongest nations does not appear to affect the probability of warfare in the major power system. Levy's (1981) analysis of great power alliances and warfare for the period between 1495 and 1975 also produces some notable conclusions. He examines a possible connection between the number of great powers engaged in alliances and the "amount" (i.e., frequency, duration, extent, magnitude, severity, intensity, and concentration) of war. With regard to the occurrence of war, Levy (1981, 610) concludes his analysis by noting that ". . . for none of the last five centuries have wars generally been preceded by alliances," and he argues that there is no apparent causal connection between great power alliance formation and the onset of war. In sum, the frequency and occurrence of war is unrelated to system-level alliance formation or configuration.

Other analyses produce generally consistent evidence with regard to alliance effects on the seriousness (magnitude, severity, and duration) of wars. Wallace (1973a) examines war duration (nation-months of war) and war severity (battle deaths) in terms of alliance polarization for the years 1815 to 1964 (COW database). He reports a strong curvilinear relationship between alliance polarization and both war duration and severity: in other words, periods in which alliance clustering in the international system is either extremely high or extremely low are likely to be associated with wars of great duration and severity. Similarly, Bueno de Mesquita (1978) examines war duration as a function of alliance configuration for the years 1816 to 1965 (COW database) and reports a statistically significant positive correlation between alliance polarization and the duration of wars. Lastly, Wayman (1984) provides additional evidence of a connection between alliance configuration and the magnitude of major power war. Wayman's analysis covers the period between 1815 and 1965 for all wars in the major power system (COW database). He defines war magnitude as the total nation-months of major power war involvement and reports that the clustering of major powers into two opposing alliances is significantly correlated with a subsequent increase in the magnitude of war. In sum, alliance polarization appears to be positively associated with the magnitude, severity, and duration of war.

Brecher, James, and Wilkenfeld (1990) provide some insight into the crisis effects of alliance polarization. Using the ICB database for the years 1929 to 1985 and examining the frequency of international crises in periods with and without opposing alliance systems, they report the highest mean number of crises for system-periods characterized by polarized alliances.

The evidence regarding system-level alliances and warfare is clear. The onset (occurrence/initiation) of war is unrelated to either alliance formation (aggregation) or configuration (polarization). However, the magnitude, duration, and severity (or "seriousness") of war does show consistent and significant correlation with the configuration of alliances. This is not surprising since alliance is a principal mechanism by which small wars become big wars—war spreads through alliances. Hence, the greater the extent of alliance polarization in the system, the higher the probability that the wars that do occur will be of greater magnitude, duration, and severity.[18]

Summary: System-Level Patterns

As noted in Geller and Singer (1998), the data-based evidence regarding factors associated with war-prone international systems is mixed. Characteristic of these findings is the evidence on system polarity and war. A principal tenet of realpolitik maintains that the distribution of capabilities is a primary factor in the war proneness of the system. This assumption has led to debates about the relative peacefulness of unipolar, bipolar, and multipolar configurations. However, attempts to answer the question through quantitative empirical analysis have been marred by ambiguity over what characteristics of war (e.g., occurrence, frequency, magnitude, duration, or severity) should be associated with polarity as well as by problems resulting from the misspecification of variables (e.g., incorporating alliances in measures of polarity).

Among the set of empirical patterns noted in this section is a cross-level dynamic affecting the onset of both major power and global (or systemic) wars. Multiple empirical studies have identified an interaction effect between the rising/declining capabilities of the leading state in the international hierarchy relative to those of potential challengers as well as dyadic-level capability balances among lesser major powers as factors influencing the onset of wars among this set of states. This suggests that the erosion of the system-level power structure links lower-order wars among major powers to system-shaping global wars. In this way, power distributions at both the systemic and dyadic levels of analysis interact synergistically to produce war among the set of major powers. The clarity and stability of the hierarchy rather than the number of major powers is the critical factor affecting the onset of global war.[19]

The evidence on alliances and warfare is consistent and cumulative. The frequency and occurrence of war are unrelated to either system-level alliance formation (aggregation) or configuration (polarization). However, the magnitude, duration, and severity (or "seriousness") of war is substantively connected to alliance configuration—for the reason that war spreads through alliances. Therefore, the greater the system-level alliance polarization, the greater the probability that the wars that do occur will engage more states, employ larger amounts of destructive capabilities, last longer, and produce more fatalities. Alliances turn small wars into big wars.

The issue of contiguity and war is raised again—this time at the system level—by an examination of the number of borders and the frequency of war in the interstate arena at different time points. It could be argued that the positive relationship between the number of borders in the international system and the frequency of war in the system is simply the result of an increase in the number of states: as the number of actors increases, the frequency of war increases. However, this system-level evidence also conforms with findings on borders and war at the state and dyadic levels, and therefore cannot be easily dismissed on the basis of the expansion of the number of units within the international system. Borders, contiguity, and war are linked empirically at multiple analytic levels. Which theoretical mechanism—opportunity, context of interaction, or territoriality—best accounts for the relationship remains to be established.

Lastly, the evidence on revolutionary state formations/transformations and system-level warfare is intriguing. Specifically, global counts of civil and revolutionary wars reveal positive associations with global interstate dispute and war frequencies: an apparent nexus between revolution and war has been identified in system-level studies indicating that international and domestic conflict are part of an interactive global process. The Most and Starr (1980) model of the spatial diffusion of conflict has been proposed as an explanatory mechanism for this linkage (Starr 1994).

Conclusion

This chapter has outlined the epistemology and logic of two models of covering law explanations and has described a set of strong empirical patterns relating to both the onset and seriousness of interstate war. The patterns and theoretical mechanisms believed to underlie the uniformities were classified on the basis of levels of analysis and identified a set of structural factors associated with the war proneness of states, dyads, regions, and the international system. Scientific explanations of specific dyadic and multistate wars conforming to the model of inductive covering laws (Hempel [1942] 1959) have been presented in Geller and Singer (1998). Such explanations are inherently probabilistic rather than deterministic, and account for wars in terms of the conjunction of a set of strong empirical patterns and their underlying theoretical mechanisms. It is maintained that the presence or absence of these factors increases the probability of the onset and seriousness of such events. However, the outbreak of war ultimately turns on decisions. Structural forces influence those decisions but do not determine them entirely. In other words, the conditions conducive to war may be present, but due to the element of human choice, the last step remains indeterminate.

Notes

1. The Correlates of War (COW) project defines an international war as a military conflict waged between national entities, at least one of which is a state, and that results in at least 1,000 battle deaths of military personnel. Unless otherwise noted, the following definitions apply to these terms:

   War Occurrence — A dichotomous variable indicating either the presence or absence of war for the unit of observation.

War Initiation	The war initiator is the state that started the actual fighting or first seized territory or property interests of another state.

2. Unless otherwise noted, the following definitions apply to these terms:

War Magnitude	The sum of all participating nations' separate months of active involvement in each war.
War Duration	The length in months from the inception of the war to its termination.
War Severity	Total battle deaths of military personnel in each war.

3. Doran and Parsons (1980, 948, 954) identify critical points in a state's power cycle based on a state's share of the total resource pool available to all major powers at a given point in time. However, as Houweling and Siccama (1991, 643) note: "A critical point on a nation's capability trajectory is an absolute property of the nation concerned." Critical points, therefore, are classified as state-level predictors of warfare.
4. For an application of power cycle theory to subwar crisis involvement, see James and Hebron (1997).
5. Studies dealing with the relationship between the level of militarization of a state and its foreign conflict behavior have produced consistent findings. For example, Feierabend and Feierabend (1969) report a positive correlation between militarization and foreign conflict for the subset of highly developed states. Similarly, Weede (1970), using the DON database for the period from 1955 to 1960 and defining militarization by the twin ratios of military personnel to total population and defense expenditures to GNP, notes a positive association between militarization and both verbal and violent foreign conflict behavior. Kemp (1977), using COW and Stockholm International Peace Research Institute (SIPRI) data for the years between 1925 and 1939, also reports positive and significant links between state-level arms expenditures and international violence.
6. The Militarized Interstate Dispute (MID) data is a component of the Correlates of War (COW) project database. By definition, "[A militarized] interstate dispute is a set of interactions involving the explicit, overt, and government-directed threat, display, or use of force in short temporal intervals" (Maoz 1982, 7). The MID data set also includes a five-level hostility scale with a coded action for both the initiator and target in the dispute. The levels of hostility (LH) are:

LH1	No military confrontation action (target)
LH2	Threat to use force
LH3	Display of force
LH4	Use of force
LH5	War (Small and Singer 1982 criteria)

See Gochman and Maoz (1984) and Jones, Bremer, and Singer (1996) for descriptions of this data set.

7. See Goertz and Diehl (1993) and Goertz (1994) for the definitions and criteria used in constructing these, and other, rivalry data sets, and for discussion of the various populations produced by the criteria.
8. See Thompson (1995b) for a critique of numerically based rivalry identification methods.
9. See Gleditsch (1995) for a review of both the theoretical arguments and empirical findings on proximity/contiguity and war. Also see Lemke (1995a), who provides an interesting approach to the identification of a population of dyads which are proximate enough in terms of distance and terrain to be potential war fighters. He adapts the loss-of-strength gradient concepts of Boulding (1962) and Bueno de Mesquita (1981b) and defines an area in which each state can engage in military action. Lemke argues that potential war dyads are those in which the defined areas overlap.
10. Rummel (1979, 177) asserts unequivocally that: *"It is only attempts to change the territorial status quo by hostile states that risks violence and war."* (Italics in the original.) However, according to Vasquez (1993, 124–25), the issue is less absolute: ". . . a dispute over territorial contiguity is of *causal* significance in that its presence makes war possible and its absence makes war highly unlikely. . . . [O]f all the possible issues that could end in war, issues involving territorial contiguity are indeed the most war prone."
11. Although not indisputable (e.g., Waltz 1993). Ray (1993) demonstrates how definitions of democracy affect the case-set of warring democratic dyads. Spiro (1994) further shows how statistical findings based on this small case-set are sensitive to extremely minor variations in the hypergeometric distributions of all wars and democratic wars (1816–1980) that are produced by different definitions of either democracy or war. His analysis indicates that the absence of wars between democratic states over the last two centuries is not a statistically significant pattern and can be explained on the basis of random chance. In another quantitatively grounded study, Farber and Gowa (1995) report no statistically significant relationship between democracy and war before 1914, and they argue that it is only after 1945 that the probability of war is lower between democratic states than between other dyads. They posit that the Cold War created a strong set of common interests among democracies, and that therefore the post-1945 democratic peace may be more the result of common interests than of common political systems. Using a different method, Layne (1994) attacks the democratic peace thesis by examining four historical cases of confrontations between democracies which failed to escalate to war. He concludes that none of the postulated conflict-dampening factors of democratic peace theory appear to have played any role in the outcomes of the crises. James and Mitchell (1995) take a different

tack. They argue that while war between democratic states may be rare, these dyads do still engage in coercive behavior. James and Mitchell specify a formal model that demonstrates an incentive for powerful democracies to undermine (through covert pressure and subversion) the efforts of weak democratic states to restructure dependent relationships, and they provide a list of cases—all of which involve the United States as one of the participants—that is consistent with their model. See Maoz (1997a) for a response to these critiques.

12. Layne (1994) argues that the structural/institutional explanation is logically inconsistent with the evidence. Democratic monads are as war prone as autocratic monads (e.g., Small and Singer 1976; Chan 1984; Weede 1984; Domke 1988; Dixon 1989). If structural constraints had the effects ascribed to them, democratic states ". . . would be peaceful in their relations with all states, whether democratic or not" (Layne 1994, 12). Also see Gates, Knutsen, and Moses (1996) on this and related points.
13. An analytic framework on political constraints is found in Salmore and Salmore (1978). For early empirical studies on political constraints and foreign conflict, see Geller (1985) and Hagan (1987).
14. Midlarsky (1988b, 44–78) demonstrates both mathematically and historically the multiple issues inherent in these opposing positions.
15. Midlarsky (Midlarsky and Hopf 1993) maintains that if such resources are abundant in the international system, then the occurrence of war in bipolar and multipolar systems should be essentially equivalent. However, under conditions of resource scarcity, a multipolar structure should be more war prone. See also Midlarsky (1988b, 44–78; 1989a).
16. Both Blainey (1973) and Snyder and Diesing (1977) argue that ambiguity in alliance commitments can increase uncertainty. For example, Blainey (1973, 65) describes this situation on the eve of World War I:

    > In every capital city [decision makers] had to predict whether their own allies would support them, whether the allies of the enemy would join in the war, and whether uncommitted nations would fight, give economic aid, or remain aloof.

    Similarly, Snyder and Diesing (1977, 430–31) note:

    > Alliance considerations introduce complications into assessments of relative power by the direct protagonists in a crisis. . . . [B]oth parties must calculate carefully the likely degree of allied support on both sides, since such support will be critical to the outcome. Negotiating positions and threat postures will be heavily affected by expectations about the interests and intentions of allies and other third parties.

17. See also Midlarsky (1988b).
18. See Kim and Morrow (1992) and Vasquez (1993) on alliances and the spread of war.
19. See Thompson (1983a, 1983b), Doran (1983, 1989a, 1991, 1995a), Geller (1992, 1996), Geller and Singer (1998), Houweling and Siccama (1993), and Weede (1994) for a discussion of cross-level dynamics. Vasquez (1993) presents a multilevel explanation for the onset of both World War I and World War II.

Bibliography

Abdollahian, Marc A. 1996. "In Search of Structure: The Nonlinear Dynamics of International Politics." Ph.D. diss., Claremont Graduate School, Claremont, California.

Achen, Christopher H. 1983. "Toward Theories of Data." In *Political Science,* ed. A. W. Finifter. Washington, DC: American Political Science Association.

Achen, Christopher H., and Duncan Snidal. 1989. "Rational Deterrence Theory and Comparative Case Studies." *World Politics* 41:143–69.

Adams, R. M., and H. Nissen. 1972. *The Uruk Countryside.* Chicago: University of Chicago Press.

Adler, Emanuel, and Michael N. Barnett, eds. 1998. *Security Communities in Comparative Perspective.* New York: Cambridge University Press.

Alali, A. Odasuo, and Kenoye Kelvin Eke, eds. 1991. *Media Coverage of Terrorism: Methods of Diffusion.* Newbury Park, CA: Sage.

Alcock, Norman Z. 1972. *The War Disease.* Oakville, Ontario: CPRI Press.

Aldrich, J. 1997. "Does Historical Political Research Pose any Special Methodological Concerns?" *Political Methodologist* 8:17–21.

Algaze, G. 1993. *The Uruk World System.* Chicago: University of Chicago Press.

Allan, Richard. 1990. *Terrorism: Pragmatic International Deterrence and Cooperation.* Institute for East-West Security Studies Occasional Paper No. 19. Boulder, CO: Westview Press.

Almond, Gabriel. 1950. *The American People and Foreign Policy.* New Haven: Yale University Press.

Alsharabati, Carole. 1997. "Dynamics of War Initiation." Ph.D. diss., Claremont Graduate School, Claremont, California.

Alsharabati, Carole, and Jacek Kugler. 1996. "Prospects for Peace After Bilateral Deterrence." Paper presented at the Annual Convention of the International Studies Association, San Diego, California, April 16–20.

Altfeld, Michael F. 1983. "Arms Races?—And Escalation? A Comment on Wallace." *International Studies Quarterly* 27:225–31.

An, Z. 1994. "China during the Neolithic." In *History of Humanity,* ed. S. J. De Laet. New York: Routledge.

Anderson, Benedict. 1991. *Imagined Communities: Reflections on the Origins and Spread of Nationalism,* rev. ed. London: Verso.

Anderson, Paul A., and Timothy J. McKeown. 1987. "Changing Aspirations, Limited Attention, and War." *World Politics* 40:1–29.

Anderson, Scott. 1999. "The Curse of Blood and Vengeance." *New York Times Magazine,* 26 December, 28–57.

Andrews, E. W. 1987. "Spoons and Knuckle-Dusters in Formative Mesoamerica." Texas Symposium on the Olmec, Izapa and the Development of Maya Civilization, Austin.

Anthony, D. W., and N. B. Vinogradov. 1995. "Birth of the Chariot." *Archaeology* 48:36–41.

Apple, R. W. Jr. 1993. "Policing a Global Village: As Peacekeeping Falters in Somalia, Foes of the U.S. Effort in Haiti Are Emboldened." *New York Times,* 13 October, A1, 13.

Arat, Zehra F. 1991. *Democracy and Human Rights in Developing Countries.* Boulder, CO: Lynne Rienner.

Arbetman, Marina. 1996. "The Consequences of the American Civil War." In *Parity and War,* ed. Jacek Kugler and Douglas Lemke. Ann Arbor: University of Michigan Press.

Arkes, H. R., and C. Blumer. 1985. "The Psychology of Sunk Cost." *Organizational Behavior and Human Decision Processes* 35:124–40.

Arquilla, J. 1992. *Dubious Battles: Aggression, Defeat, and the International System.* Washington, DC: Crane Russak.

Ashley, Richard K. 1984. "The Poverty of Neorealism." *International Organization* 38:225–61.

Atkinson, Scott E., and Todd Sandler. 1987. "Terrorism in a Bargaining Framework." *Journal of Law and Economics* 30:1–21.

Avineri, Shlomo. 1994. "Comments on Nationalism and Democracy." In *Nationalism, Ethnic Conflict, and Democracy,* ed. Larry Diamond and Marc F. Plattner. Baltimore: Johns Hopkins University Press.

Azar, Edward. 1972. "Conflict Escalation and Conflict Reduction in an International Crisis: Suez, 1956." *Journal of Conflict Resolution* 16:183–202.

Azar, Edward, Paul Jureidini, and Ronald McLaurin. 1978. "Protracted Social Conflict: Theory and Practice in the Middle East." *Journal of Palestine Studies* 8:41–60.

Babst, Dean V. 1972. "A Force for Peace." *Industrial Research* (April): 55–58.

Bachechi, L., P. F. Fabbri, and F. Mallegni. 1997. "An Arrow-Caused Lesion in a Late Upper Paleolithic Human Pelvis." *Current Anthropology* 38:135–40.

Bachteler, Tobias. 1997. "Explaining the Democratic Peace: The Evidence from Ancient Greece Reviewed." *Journal of Peace Research* 34:315–22.

Badey, Thomas J. 1998. "Defining International Terrorism: A Pragmatic Approach." *Terrorism and Political Violence* 10:90–107.

Banks, Jeffrey S. 1990. "Equilibrium Behavior in Crisis Bargaining Games." *American Journal of Political Science* 34:599–614.

Bar-Adon, P. 1962. "Expedition C-The Cave of the Treasure." *Israel Exploration Journal* 12:215–26.

Barbieri, Katherine. 1996a. "Economic Interdependence: A Path to Peace or a Source of Interstate Conflict?" *Journal of Peace Research* 33:29–49.

Barbieri, Katherine. 1996b. "Explaining Discrepant Findings in the Trade-Conflict Literature." Paper presented at the Annual Convention of the International Studies Association, San Diego, California, April 16–20.

Barringer, Richard E. 1972. *War: Patterns of Conflict.* Cambridge, MA: MIT Press.

Battalio, Raymond C., John H. Kagel, and Komain Jiranyakul. 1990. "Testing between Alternative Models of Choice under Uncertainty: Some Initial Results." *Journal of Risk and Uncertainty* 3:25–50.

Bazerman, Max H. 1983. "Negotiator Judgment." *American Behavioral Scientist* 27:211–28.

Beck, Nathaniel. 1991. "The Illusion of Cycles in International Relations." *International Studies Quarterly* 35:455–76.

Beck, Nathaniel, Jonathan N. Katz, and Richard Tucker. 1998. "Beyond Ordinary Logit: Taking Time Seriously in Binary-Time-Series-Cross-Section Models." *American Journal of Political Science* 42:1260–88.

Beer, Francis. 1981. *Peace against War.* San Francisco: Freeman.

Bennett, D. Scott. 1993. "Security, Economy, and the End of Interstate Rivalry." Ph.D. diss., University of Michigan, Ann Arbor.

Bennett, D. Scott. 1996. "Security, Bargaining, and the End of Interstate Rivalry." *International Studies Quarterly* 40:157–83.

Bennett, D. Scott. 1997a. "Democracy, Regime Change, and Rivalry Termination." *International Interactions* 22:367–97.

Bennett, D. Scott. 1997b. "Testing Alternative Models of Alliance Duration, 1816–1985." *American Journal of Political Science* 41:846–78.

Bennett, D. Scott. 1997c. "Measuring Rivalry Termination." *Journal of Conflict Resolution* 41:227–54.

Bennett, D. Scott. 1998. "Integrating and Testing Models of Rivalry Termination." *American Journal of Political Science* 42:1200–32.

Bennett, D. Scott, and Allan C. Stam III. 1996. "The Duration of Interstate Wars, 1816–1985." *American Political Science Review* 90:239–57.

Bennett, D. Scott, and Allan Stam III. 1998. "A Combined Model of War Outcomes and Duration: Modelling the Declining Advantages of Democracy." *Journal of Conflict Resolution* 42:344–66.

Bennett, Sherry L. 1997. "The Dynamics of Coevolving Systems and Armed Conflicts." Rice University, Department of Political Science.

Benoit, Kenneth. 1996. "Democracies Really Are More Pacific (in General): Reexamining Regime Type and War Involvement." *Journal of Conflict Resolution* 40:636–57.

Benson, Michelle, and Jacek Kugler. 1998. "Power Parity, Democracy, and the Severity of Internal Violence." *Journal of Conflict Resolution* 42:196–209.

Ben Yehuda, Hemda. 1997. "Territoriality, Crisis and War: An Examination of Theory and 20th Century Evidence." Paper presented to the Annual Convention of the International Studies Association, Toronto, Ontario, March 18–22.

Bercovitch, Jacob. 1992. "The Structure and Diversity of Mediation in International Relations." In *Mediation in International Relations: Multiple Approaches to Conflict Management,* ed. Jacob Bercovitch and Jeffrey Z. Rubin. New York: St. Martin's Press.

Bercovitch, Jacob, and Paul F. Diehl. 1997. "Conflict Management of Enduring Rivalries: Frequency, Timing and Short-Term Impact of Mediation." *International Interactions* 22:299–320.

Bercovitch, Jacob, and Jeffrey Langley. 1993. "The Nature of the Dispute and the Effectiveness of International Mediation." *Journal of Conflict Resolution* 37:670–91.

Bercovitch, Jacob, and Patrick Regan. 1997. "Managing Risks in International Relations: The Mediation of Enduring Rivalries." In *Enforcing Cooperation: "Risky" States and the Intergovernmental Management of Conflict,* ed. Gerald Schneider and Patricia Weitsman. London: Macmillan.

Bercovitch, Jacob, and Jeffrey Z. Rubin, eds. 1992. *Mediation in International Relations: Multiple Approaches to Conflict Management.* New York: St. Martin's Press.

Berejikian, Jeffrey. 1997. "The Gains Debate: Framing State Choice." *American Political Science Review* 91:789–805.

Bergesen, Albert. 1985. "Cycles of War in the Reproduction of the World Economy." In *Rhythms in Politics and Economics,* ed. Paul M. Johnson and William R. Thompson. New York: Praeger.

Bergesen, Albert, and R. Schoenberg. 1980. "Long Waves of Colonial Expansion and Contraction, 1415–1969." In *Studies of the Modern World System,* ed. Albert Bergesen. New York: Academic Press.

Betts, Richard K. 1998. "The New Threat of Mass Destruction." *Foreign Affairs* 77:25–41.

Blainey, Geoffrey. 1973. *The Causes of War.* New York: The Free Press.

Blechman, Barry M., and Stephen S. Kaplan. 1978. *Force without War: U.S. Armed Forces as a Political Instrument.* Washington, DC: The Brookings Institution.

Blight, James G., Joseph S. Nye Jr., and David A. Welch. 1987. "The Cuban Missile Crisis Revisited." *Foreign Affairs* 66 (1): 170–88.

Bliss, Harry, and Bruce Russett. 1998. "Democratic Trading Partners: The Liberal Connection." *Journal of Politics* 60:1126–47.

Bobrow, Davis B. 1981. "The Perspective of Great Power Foreign Policy." In *Dynamics of Third Party Intervention: Kissinger and the Middle East,* ed. J. Rubin. New York: Praeger.

Boettcher, William A. III. 1995. "Context, Methods, Numbers, and Words: Evaluating the Applicability of Prospect Theory to International Relations." *Journal of Conflict Resolution* 39:561–83.

Bollen, Kenneth. 1993. "Liberal Democracy: Validity and Method Factors in Cross-National Measures." *American Journal of Political Science* 37:1207–30.

Boswell, Terry. 1989. "Colonial Empires and the Capitalist World Economy: A Time-Series Analysis of Colonization, 1640–1960." *American Sociological Review* 54:180–96.

Boswell, Terry, and J. Brueggemann. 1989. "War in the Core of the World-System: Testing the Goldstein Thesis." In *War and the World-System,* ed. Robert Shaeffer. New York: Greenwood Press.

Boswell, Terry, and Michael Sweat. 1991. "Hegemony, Long Waves and Major Wars." *International Studies Quarterly* 35:123–49.

Boulding, Kenneth E. 1956. *The Image.* Ann Arbor: University of Michigan Press.

Boulding, Kenneth E. 1962. *Conflict and Defense: A General Theory.* New York: Harper.

Bouthoul, Gaston, and René Carrère. 1976. *Le défi de la guerre, 1749–1974.* Paris: Presses Universitaires de France.

Braithwaite, Richard Bevan. 1953. *Scientific Explanation: A Study of the Function of Theory, Probability and Law in Science.* Cambridge: Cambridge University Press.

Brams, Steven J., and D. Marc Kilgour. 1987. "Winding Down If Preemption or Escalation Occurs." *Journal of Conflict Resolution* 31:547–72.

Brandes, M. A. 1979. *Siegelabrollungen aus den archäischen Baus-chichten in Uruk-Warka.* Wiesbaden, Germany: Franz Steiner.

Braumoeller, Bear. 1997. "Deadly Doves: Liberal Nationalism and the Democratic Peace in the Soviet Successor States." *International Studies Quarterly* 41:375–402.

Braumoeller, Bear, and Gary Goertz. 1997. "The Methodology of Necessary Conditions." Paper presented at the Annual Convention of the International Studies Association, Toronto, Ontario, March 18–22.

Brawley, Mark R. 1993. "Regime Types, Markets and War: The Importance of Pervasive Rents in Foreign Policy." *Comparative Political Studies* 36:178–97.

Brecher, Michael. 1984. "International Crises and Protracted Conflicts." *International Interactions* 11:237–98.

Brecher, Michael. 1993. *Crises in World Politics: Theory and Reality.* Oxford: Pergamon Press.

Brecher, Michael. 1996a. "Crisis, Conflict, War—State of the Discipline." *International Political Science Review* 17:127–39.

Brecher, Michael. 1996b. "Crisis Escalation: Model and Findings." *International Political Science Review* 17:215–30.

Brecher, Michael, and Patrick James. 1988. "Patterns of Crisis Management." *Journal of Conflict Resolution* 32:426–56.

Brecher, Michael, Patrick James, and Jonathan Wilkenfeld. 1990. "Polarity and Stability: New Concepts, Indicators and Evidence." *International Interactions* 16:49–80.

Brecher, Michael, and Jonathan Wilkenfeld. 1988. *Crises in the Twentieth Century.* Vol. 1, *Handbook of International Crises.* Oxford: Pergamon Press.

Brecher, Michael, and Jonathan Wilkenfeld. 1989. *Crisis, Conflict and Instability.* Oxford: Pergamon Press.

Brecher, Michael, and Jonathan Wilkenfeld. 1997. *A Study of Crisis.* Ann Arbor: University of Michigan Press. Reprinted in paperback and CD-ROM, 2000.

Bremer, Stuart A. 1980. "National Capabilities and War Proneness." In *The Correlates of War II: Testing Some Realpolitik Models,* ed. J. David Singer. New York: The Free Press.

Bremer, Stuart A. 1982. "The Contagiousness of Coercion: The Spread of Serious International Disputes, 1900–1976." *International Interactions* 9: 29–55.

Bremer, Stuart A. 1992. "Dangerous Dyads: Conditions Affecting the Likelihood of Interstate War, 1816–1965." *Journal of Conflict Resolution* 36:309–41.

Bremer, Stuart A. 1993. "Democracy and Militarized Interstate Conflict, 1816–1965." *International Interactions* 18:231–49.

Bremer, Stuart A. 1996. "Advancing the Scientific Study of War." In *The Process of War,* ed. Stuart A. Bremer and Thomas R. Cusack. Philadelphia: Gordon and Breach.

Breton, Raymond. 1988. "From Ethnic to Civic Nationalism: English Canada and Quebec." *Ethnic and Racial Studies* 11:85–102.

Brilmayer, Lea. 1994. *American Hegemony: Political Morality in a One-Superpower World.* New Haven, CT: Yale University Press.

Brinkman, J. A. 1994. "General Chart of Chronological Periods in Ancient Mesopotamia." Oriental Institute, University of Chicago (typescript).

Brockner, Joel, and Jeffrey Z. Rubin. 1985. *Entrapment in Escalating Conflicts: A Social Psychological Analysis.* New York: Springer-Verlag.

Brodie, Bernard, ed. 1946. *The Absolute Weapon.* New York: Harcourt, Brace.

Brodie, Bernard. 1959. *Strategy in the Missile Age.* Princeton: Princeton University Press.

Bronson, Rachel. 1996. "Cycles of Conflict in the Middle East and North Africa." In *The International Dimensions of Internal Conflict,* ed. Michael E. Brown. Cambridge, MA: MIT Press.

Brophy-Baermann, Bryan, and John A. C. Conybeare. 1994. "Retaliating against Terrorism: Rational Expectations and the Optimality of Rules versus Discretion." *American Journal of Political Science* 38:196–210.

Brown, Michael E. 1996. "The Causes and Regional Dimensions of Internal Conflict." In *The International Dimensions of Internal Conflict,* ed. Michael E. Brown. Cambridge, MA: MIT Press.

Brown, Seyom. 1987. *The Causes and Prevention of War.* New York: St. Martin's Press.

Brummett, Palmira. 1999. "The Ottoman Empire, Venice, and the Question of Enduring Rivalries." In *Great Power Rivalries,* ed. William R. Thompson. Columbia: University of South Carolina Press.

Brzezinski, Zbigniew, and Samuel P. Huntington. 1963. *Political Power: USA/USSR.* New York: Viking.

Buckley, Anthony D., and Mary C. Kenney. 1995. *Negotiating Identity: Rhetoric, Metaphor, and Social Drama in Northern Ireland.* Washington, DC: Smithsonian Institution Press.

Bueno de Mesquita, Bruce. 1975. "Measuring Systemic Polarity." *Journal of Conflict Resolution* 19:187–216.

Bueno de Mesquita, Bruce. 1978. "Systemic Polarization and the Occurrence and Duration of War." *Journal of Conflict Resolution* 22:241–67.

Bueno de Mesquita, Bruce. 1980a. "An Expected Utility Theory of International Conflict." *American Political Science Review* 74:917–32.

Bueno de Mesquita, Bruce. 1980b. "Theories of International Conflict: An Analysis and an Appraisal." In *Handbook of Political Conflict,* ed. Ted R. Gurr. New York: The Free Press.

Bueno de Mesquita, Bruce. 1981a. "Risk, Power Distributions, and the Likelihood of War." *International Studies Quarterly* 25:541–68.

Bueno de Mesquita, Bruce. 1981b. *The War Trap.* New Haven: Yale University Press.

Bueno de Mesquita, Bruce. 1985. "The War Trap Revisited: A Revised Expected Utility Model." *American Political Science Review* 79:156–77.

Bueno de Mesquita, Bruce. 1990. "Pride of Place: The Origins of German Hegemony." *World Politics* 43:28–52.

Bueno de Mesquita, Bruce. 1996. "Counterfactuals and International Affairs: Some Insights from Game Theory." In *Counterfactual Thought Experiments in World Politics,* ed. Philip E. Tetlock and Aaron Belkin. Princeton: Princeton University Press.

Bueno de Mesquita, Bruce, and David Lalman. 1988. "Empirical Support for Systemic and Dyadic Explanations of International Conflict." *World Politics* 41:1–20.

Bueno de Mesquita, Bruce, and David Lalman. 1992. *War and Reason: Domestic and International Imperatives.* New Haven: Yale University Press.

Bueno de Mesquita, Bruce, James D. Morrow, Randolph M. Siverson, and Alastair Smith. 1999. "An Institutional Explanation of the Democratic Peace." *American Political Science Review* 93:791–807.

Bueno de Mesquita, Bruce, and William H. Riker. 1982. "An Assessment of the Merits of Selective Nuclear Proliferation." *Journal of Conflict Resolution* 26:283–306.

Bueno de Mesquita, Bruce, and Randolph M. Siverson. 1995. "War and the Survival of Political Leaders: A Comparative Study of Regime Types and Political Accountability." *American Political Science Review* 89:841–55.

Bueno de Mesquita, Bruce, and Randolph M. Siverson. 1997. "Nasty or Nice: Political Systems, Endogenous Norms, and the Treatment of Adversaries." *Journal of Conflict Resolution* 41:175–99.

Bueno de Mesquita, Bruce, Randolph M. Siverson, and Gary Woller. 1992. "War and the Fate of Regimes: A Comparative Analysis." *American Political Science Review* 86:638–46.

Burger, R. L. 1995. *Chavín and the Origins of Andean Civilization.* London: Thames and Hudson.

Burrin, Philippe. 1994. *Hitler and the Jews: The Genesis of the Holocaust.* Trans. Patsy Southgate. London: Edward Arnold.

Butterworth, Robert L. 1976. *Managing Interstate Conflict, 1945–1974: Data with Synopses.* Pittsburgh: University of Pittsburgh Press.

Buzan, Barry. 1983. *People, States, and Fear.* Boulder, CO: Lynne Rienner.

Buzan, Barry. 1984. "Economic Structure and International Security: The Limits of the Liberal Case." *International Organization* 38:597–624.

Byman, Daniel L., Matthew C. Waxman, and Eric Larson. 1999. *Air Power as a Coercive Instrument.* Santa Monica, CA: Rand.

Calahan, H. A. 1944. *What Makes a War End.* New York: Vanguard Press.

Callamard, Agnès. 1999. "French Policy in Rwanda." In *The Rwanda Crisis from Uganda to Zaire: The Path of a Genocide,* ed. Howard Adelman and Astri Suhrke. New Brunswick, NJ: Transaction Publishers.

Camerer, Colin. 1995. "Individual Decision Making." In *The Handbook of Experimental Economics,* ed. John H. Kagel and Alvin E. Roth. Princeton: Princeton University Press.

Cannizzo, Cynthia A. 1980. "The Costs of Combat: Death, Duration and Defeat." In *The Correlates of War II,* ed. J. David Singer. New York: The Free Press.

Carlson, Lisa J. 1995. "A Theory of Escalation and International Conflict." *Journal of Conflict Resolution* 39:511–34.

Carment, David. 1993a. "The International Dimensions of Ethnic Conflict: Concepts, Indicators, and Theory." *Journal of Peace Research* 30:137–50.

Carment, David. 1993b. "The International Politics of Ethnic Conflict: The Interstate Dimensions of Secession and Irredenta in the Twentieth Century, A Crisis-Based Approach." Ph.D. diss., McGill University, Montreal.

Carment, David, and Patrick James. 1995. "Internal Constraints and Interstate Ethnic Conflict." *Journal of Conflict Resolution* 39:82–109.

Carment, David, and Patrick James. 1997a. "Secession and Irredenta in World Politics: The Neglected Interstate Dimension." In *Wars in the Midst of Peace: The International Politics of Ethnic Conflict,* ed. David Carment and Patrick James. Pittsburgh: University of Pittsburgh Press.

Carment, David, and Patrick James, eds. 1997b. *Wars in the Midst of Peace: The International Politics of Ethnic Conflict.* Pittsburgh: University of Pittsburgh Press.

Carment, David, and Patrick James. 1997c. "The International Politics of Ethnic Conflict: New Perspectives on Theory and Policy." *Global Society* 11:205–32.

Carneiro, R. 1970. "A Theory of the Origin of the State." *Science* 169:733–38.

Carr, Edward Hallett. 1964. *What Is History?* New York: Knopf.

Carroll, Berenice A. 1969. "How Wars End: An Analysis of Some Current Hypotheses." *Journal of Peace Research* 4:295–321.

Carter, Ashton, John Deutch, and Philip Zelikow. 1998. "Combating Catastrophic Terrorism." *Foreign Affairs* 77:80–94.

Cashman, Greg. 1993. *What Causes War? An Introduction to Theories of International Conflict.* New York: Lexington Books.

Cashman, Greg. 1997. "Theoretical Buttresses for Power Cycle Theory." Paper presented at the International Political Science Association XVIIth World Congress, Seoul, Korea, August 17–21.

Cassese, Antonio. 1989. *Terrorism, Politics and Law: The Achille Lauro Affair.* Princeton: Princeton University Press.

Castells, Manuel. 1997. *The Information Age: Economy, Society and Culture, Vol. II: The Power of Identity.* Oxford, England: Blackwell.

Caubet, A. 1994. "Le Levant." In *Les antiquités orientales,* ed. F. Demange. Paris: Réunion des Musées Nationaux.

Cauley, Jon, and Eric Iksoon Im. 1988. "Intervention Policy Analysis of Skyjackings and Other Terrorist Incidents." *AEA Papers and Proceedings* 78: 27–31.

Cauley, Jon, and Todd Sandler. 1988. "Fighting World War III. A Suggested Strategy." *Terrorism* 11:181–95.

Cederman, Lars Erik. 1998. "Back to Kant: Reinterpreting the Democratic Peace as a Collective Learning Process." Paper presented at the Annual Meeting of the American Political Science Association, Boston, September 3–6.

Celmer, Marc A. 1987. *Terrorism, U.S. Strategy, and Reagan Policies.* New York: Greenwood.

Chalk, Peter. 1994. "EU Counter-Terrorism, the Maastricht Third Pillar and Liberal Democratic Acceptability." *Terrorism and Political Violence* 6:103–45.

Chan, Steve. 1984. "Mirror, Mirror on the Wall . . . Are the Freer Countries More Pacific?" *Journal of Conflict Resolution* 28:617–48.

Chan, Steve. 1993. "Democracy and War: Some Thoughts on a Future Research Agenda." *International Interactions* 18:205–13.

Chan, Steve. 1997. "In Search of Democratic Peace: Problems and Promise." *Mershon International Studies Review* 41 (Supplement 1): 59–91.

Chang, K. C. 1986. *The Archaeology of Ancient China,* 4th ed. New Haven: Yale University Press.

Charters, David A., ed. 1991. *Democratic Responses to International Terrorism.* Ardsley-on-Hudson, NY: Transnational Publishers.

Charters, David A., ed. 1994. *The Deadly Sin of Terrorism: Its Effect on Democracy and Civil Liberty in Six Countries.* Westport, CT: Greenwood Press.

Chase-Dunn, Christopher. 1989. *Global Formation: Structures of the World Economy.* New York: Basil Blackwell.

Chase-Dunn, Christopher, and K. O'Reilly. 1989. "Core Wars of the Future." In *War in the World-System,* ed. Robert Schaeffer. New York: Greenwood.

Chase-Dunn, Christopher, and Richard Rubinson. 1979. "Toward a Structural Perspective on the World-System." *Politics and Society* 7:453–76.

Chi, L. 1956. *Ch'eng-tzu-yai.* New Haven: Yale University Publications in Anthropology, 52.

Chiu, Daniel. 2000. "Critical Points on the Power Cycle and Alliance Behavior." Ph.D. diss., Johns Hopkins University, SAIS, Washington, DC.

Choucri, Nazli, and Robert C. North. 1975. *Nations in Conflict: National Growth and International Violence.* San Francisco: W. H. Freeman.

Cioffi-Revilla, Claudio. 1981. "Fuzzy Sets and Models in International Relations." *American Journal of Political Science* 25:129–59.

Cioffi-Revilla, Claudio. 1991. "The Long-Range Analysis of War." *Journal of Interdisciplinary History* 21:603–29.

Cioffi-Revilla, Claudio. 1994. "Martial and Political Items in the Mesopotamian Exhibit of the 'Déparetment des Antiquités Orientales,' Louvre Museum." Long-Range Analysis of War Project, University of Colorado, Boulder, Colorado.

Cioffi-Revilla, Claudio. 1996. "Origins and Evolution of War and Politics." *International Studies Quarterly* 40:1–22.

Cioffi-Revilla, Claudio. 1998a. *Politics and Uncertainty.* Cambridge: Cambridge University Press.

Cioffi-Revilla, Claudio. 1998b. "The Political Uncertainty of Interstate Rivalries: A Punctuated Equilibrium Model." In *The Dynamics of Enduring Rivalries,* ed. Paul F. Diehl. Urbana: University of Illinois Press.

Cioffi-Revilla, Claudio, and David Lai. 1995. "War and Politics in Ancient China, 2700–722 B.C." *Journal of Conflict Resolution* 39:467–94.

Cioffi-Revilla, Claudio, and David Lai. 1999. "Data Set on Chinese Warfare and Politics in the Ancient east Indian International System, ca. 2700 B.C. to 722 B.C." Paper presented at the Annual Convention of the International Studies Association, Washington, DC, February.

Cioffi-Revilla, Claudio, and H. Starr. 1995. "Opportunity, Willingness and Political Uncertainty." *Journal of Theoretical Politics* 7:447–76.

Cipola, Carlo C., ed. 1970. *The Economic Decline of Empires.* London: Methuen.

Claude, Inis L. Jr. 1962. *Power and International Relations.* New York: Random House.

Clausewitz, Karl von. 1976. *On War.* Trans. and ed. Michael Howard and Peter Paret. Princeton: Princeton University Press. (First published in German, 1832.)

Clifford, James. 1988. *The Predicament of Culture: Twentieth-Century Ethnography, Literature, and Art.* Cambridge, MA: Harvard University Press.

Clutterbuck, Richard. 1992. "Negotiating with Terrorists." *Terrorism and Political Violence* 4:263–87.

Coe, M. D. 1968. "San Lorenzo and the Olmec Civilization." In *Dumbarton Oaks Conference on the Olmec,* ed. E. P. Benson. Washington, DC: Dumbarton Oaks Research Library and Collections.

Coe, M. D. 1981. "Gift of the River." In *The Olmec and Their Neighbors,* ed. E. P. Benson. Washington, DC: Dumbarton Oaks Research Library and Collections.

Coe, M. D., and R. A. Diehl, eds. 1980. *In the Land of the Olmec.* Austin: University of Texas Press.

Cohen, M., J. Jaffray, and T. Said. 1987. "Experimental Comparison of Individual Behavior under Risk and under Uncertainty for Gains and for Losses." *Organizational Behavior and Human Decision Processes* 39:1–22.

Cohen, Raymond. 1994. "Pacific Unions. A Reappraisal of the Theory that 'Democracies Do Not Go to War with Each Other.'" *Review of International Studies* 20:207–23.

Collingwood, R. G. 1956. *The Idea of History.* New York: Oxford University Press.

Connor, Walker. 1996. "Beyond Reason: The Nature of the Ethnonational Bond." In *Ethnicity,* eds. John Hutchinson and Anthony D. Smith. New York: Oxford University Press.

Converse, Elizabeth. 1968. "The War of All Against All: A Review of the *Journal of Conflict Resolution,* 1957–1968." *Journal of Conflict Resolution* 12:471–532.

Conybeare, John A. C. 1990. "A Random Walk Down the Road to War: War Cycles, Prices and Causality." *Defense Economics* 1:329–37.

Conybeare, John A. C. 1992. "Weak Cycles, Length and Magnitude of War: Duration Dependence in International Conflict." *Conflict Management and Peace Science* 12:99–116.

Coser, Lewis A. 1956. *The Functions of Social Conflict.* New York: The Free Press.

Coser, Lewis A. 1961. "Termination of Conflict." *Journal of Conflict Resolution* 5:347–53.

Crawford, Vincent P. 1979. "On Compulsory Arbitration Schemes." *Journal of Political Economy* 87:131–59.

Crelinsten, Ronald D. 1991. "Terrorism and the Media: Problems, Solutions, and Counterproblems." In *Democratic Responses to International Terrorism,* ed. David A. Charters. Ardsley-on-Hudson, NY: Transnational Publishers.

Crenshaw, Martha. 1981. "The Causes of Terrorism." *Comparative Politics* 13:379–99.

Crenshaw, Martha. 1989a. "On Terrorism and Counterterrorism." In *Security and Arms Control. Vol. II: A Guide to International Policymaking,* ed. Edward A. Kolodziej and Patrick M. Morgan. New York: Greenwood.

Crenshaw, Martha. 1989b. "Terrorism and International Cooperation." Institute for East-West Security Studies Occasional Paper No. 11. Boulder, CO: Westview.

Crenshaw, Martha. 1992. "Current Research on Terrorism: An Academic Perspective." *Studies in Conflict and Terrorism* 15:1–11.

Crenshaw, Martha. 1994. "Organized Disorder: Terrorism, Politics and Society." In *The Democratic Imagination and the Social Science Persuasion,* ed. Ray C. Rist. New Brunswick, NJ: Transaction Press.

Crenshaw, Martha, ed. 1995. *Terrorism in Context.* University Park: Pennsylvania State University Press.

Crescenzi, Mark, and Andrew Enterline. 1999. "Ripples from the Waves: A Systemic, Time-Series Analysis of Democracy, Democratization, and Interstate War." *Journal of Peace Research* 36:75–94.

Crossette, Barbara. 1998. "Violation: An Old Scourge of War Becomes its Latest Crime." *New York Times,* 14 June, Section 4, pp. 1, 6.

Crossette, Barbara. 1999. "The World Expected Peace. It Found a New Brutality." *New York Times,* 24 January, Section 4, pp. 1, 16.

Cusack, Thomas R., and Wolf-Dieter Eberwein. 1982. "Prelude to War: Incidence, Escalation and Intervention in International Disputes, 1900–1976." *International Interactions* 9:9–28.

Cyphers Guillén, A. 1996. "Reconstructing Olmec Life at San Lorenzo." In *Olmec Art of Ancient Mexico,* ed. E. P. Benson and B. de la Fuente. Washington, DC: National Gallery of Art.

Cyphers Guillén, A. 1997. "Of Earth and Stone." In *Aztec to Olmec,* ed. B. Stark and P. Arnold. Tucson: University of Arizona Press.

Daalder, Ivo H. 1996. "Fear and Loathing in the Former Yugoslavia." In *The International Dimensions of Internal Conflict,* ed. Michael E. Brown. Cambridge, MA: MIT Press.

Dahl, Robert A. 1971. *Polyarchy: Participation and Opposition.* New Haven: Yale University Press.

Danilovic, Vesna. 1996. "Modeling Power Transition: An Extended Version." In *Parity and War,* ed. Jacek Kugler and Douglas Lemke. Ann Arbor: University of Michigan Press.

Danner, Mark. 1997. "Clinton, the UN, and the Bosnian Disaster." *New York Review of Books* 44 (20): 65–81.

Danner, Mark. 1998a. "Bosnia: Breaking the Machine." *New York Review of Books* 45 (3): 41–45.

Danner, Mark. 1998b. "Bosnia: The Turning Point." *New York Review of Books* 45 (2): 34–41.

Dark, K. R. 1998. *The Waves of Time.* London: Pinter.

Davis, David R., Keith Jaggers, and Will H. Moore. 1997. "Ethnicity, Minorities, and International Conflict." In *Wars in the Midst of Peace: The Interna-*

tional Politics of Ethnic Conflict, ed. David Carment and Patrick James. Pittsburgh: University of Pittsburgh Press.

Davis, David R., and Will H. Moore. 1997. "Ethnicity Matters: Transnational Ethnic Alliances and Foreign Policy Behavior." *International Studies Quarterly* 41:171–84.

Davis, James W. 1997. "Selection Effects, Loss Aversion, and Deterrence Failures: Some Preliminary Observations." Paper presented at the Annual Convention of the International Studies Association, Toronto, Ontario, March 18–22.

Davis, Kingsley. 1948. *Human Society.* New York: Macmillan.

De Dreu, Carsten K. W., Ben J. M. Emans, and Evert Van de Vliert. 1992. "Frames of Reference and Cooperative Social Decision-Making." *European Journal of Social Psychology* 22:297–302.

Dehio, Ludwig. 1962. *The Precarious Balance: Four Centuries of the European Power Struggle,* trans. Charles Fullman. New York: Knopf.

Deitchman, Seymour J. 1964. *Limited War and American Defense Policy.* Washington, DC: Institute of Defense Analysis.

Della Porta, Donatella. 1995. *Social Movements, Political Violence, and the State.* Cambridge: Cambridge University Press.

Demange, F., F. Tallon, E. Fontan, A. Benoit, and A. Caubet. 1994. *Les antiquités orientales.* Paris: Réunion des Musées Nationaux.

Denemark, Robert. 1997. "Toward a Social Science of Long-Term Change." *Review of International Political Economy* 4:416–30.

De Nevers, Renée. 1993. "Democratization and Ethnic Conflict." In *Ethnic Conflict and International Security,* ed. Michael E. Brown. Princeton: Princeton University Press.

Der Derian, James. 1992. *Antidiplomacy: Spies, Terror, Speed, and War.* Cambridge: Blackwell.

Des Forges, Alison. 1999. *Leave None to Tell the Story: Genocide in Rwanda.* New York: Human Rights Watch.

De Soysa, Indra, John R. Oneal, and Yong-Hee Park. 1997. "Testing Power Transition Theory Using Alternative Measures of National Capabilities." *Journal of Conflict Resolution* 41:509–28.

Dessler, David. 1989. "What's at Stake in the Agent-Structure Debate?" *International Organization* 43:441–73.

Destexhe, Alain. 1995. *Rwanda and Genocide in the Twentieth Century.* Trans. Alison Marschner. New York: New York University Press.

Deudney, Daniel, and John Ikenberry. 1991–92. "The International Sources of Soviet Change." *International Security* 16 (3): 74–118.

Deutsch, Karl W. 1953. *Nationalism and Social Communication.* Cambridge, MA: MIT Press.

Deutsch, Karl W., et al. 1957. *Political Community and the North Atlantic Area.* Princeton: Princeton University Press.

Deutsch, Karl W., and J. David Singer. 1964. "Multipolar Power Systems and International Stability." *World Politics* 16:390–406.

Diehl, Paul F. 1983. "Arms Races and Escalation: A Closer Look." *Journal of Peace Research* 20:205–12.

Diehl, Paul F. 1985a. "Arms Races to War: Testing Some Empirical Linkages." *Sociological Quarterly* 26:331–49.

Diehl, Paul F. 1985b. "Contiguity and Military Escalation in Major Power Rivalries, 1816–1980." *Journal of Politics* 47:1203–11.

Diehl, Paul F. 1985c. "Armaments without War: An Analysis of Some Underlying Effects." *Journal of Peace Research* 22:249–59.

Diehl, Paul F. 1991. "Geography and War: A Review and Assessment of the Empirical Literature." *International Interactions* 17:11–27.

Diehl, Paul F. 1992. "What Are They Fighting For? The Importance of Issues in International Conflict Research." *Journal of Peace Research* 29:333–44.

Diehl, Paul F. 1994. "Substitutes or Complements? The Effects of Alliances on Military Spending in Major Power Rivalries." *International Interactions* 19:159–76.

Diehl, Paul F., and Gary Goertz. 1988. "Territorial Changes and Militarized Conflict." *Journal of Conflict Resolution* 32:103–22.

Diehl, Paul F., and Gary Goertz. 2000. *War and Peace in International Rivalry.* Ann Arbor: University of Michigan Press.

Diehl, Paul F., and Jean Kingston. 1987. "Messenger or Message?: Military Buildups and the Initiation of Conflict." *Journal of Politics* 49:801–13.

Diehl, Paul F., and Frank W. Wayman. 1994. "Realpolitik: Dead End, Detour, or Road Map?" In *Reconstructing Realpolitik,* ed. Frank W. Wayman and Paul F. Diehl. Ann Arbor: University of Michigan Press.

Dixon, William J. 1989. "Political Democracy and War: A New Look at an Old Problem." Paper presented at the 30th Annual Convention of the International Studies Association, London, England, March 28–April 1.

Dixon, William J. 1993. "Democracy and the Management of International Conflict." *Journal of Conflict Resolution* 37:42–68.

Dixon, William J. 1994. "Democracy and the Peaceful Settlement of International Conflict." *American Political Science Review* 88:14–32.

Dixon, William J. 1997. "Democracy and the Legitimation of Military Intervention." Paper presented at the Annual Convention of the International Studies Association, Toronto, Ontario, March 18–22.

Dixon, William J. 1998. "Dyads, Disputes and the Democratic Peace." In *The Political Economy of War and Peace,* ed. Murray Wolfson. Boston: Kluwer.

Domke, William K. 1988. *War and the Changing Global System.* New Haven: Yale University Press.

Doran, Charles F. 1969. "The Politics of Assimilation: A Comparative Study of the Integration of Defeated Hegemonic States into the International System." Ph.D. diss., Johns Hopkins University, Baltimore, Maryland.

Doran, Charles F. 1971. *The Politics of Assimilation: Hegemony and Its Aftermath.* Baltimore: Johns Hopkins University Press.

Doran, Charles F. 1972. "'Equilibrium' and Rank Equilibrium." Working paper.

Doran, Charles F. 1974. "A Conceptual and Operational Comparison of Frustration-Aggression, Rank Disequilibrium, and Achievement Discrepancy Models: Towards Synthesis Via a General Theory of Conflict Dynamics." Paper presented at the Annual Convention of the International Studies Association, St. Louis, Missouri, March 20–23.

Doran, Charles F. 1980. "Modes, Mechanisms, and Turning Points: Perspectives on the Analysis of the Transformation of the International System." *International Political Science Review* 1:35–61.

Doran, Charles F. 1983. "Power Cycle Theory and the Contemporary State System." In *Contending Approaches to World System Analysis,* ed. William R. Thompson. Beverly Hills, CA: Sage.

Doran, Charles F. 1985. "Power Cycle Theory and Systems Stability." In *Rhythms in Politics and Economics,* ed. Paul M. Johnson and William R. Thompson. New York: Praeger.

Doran, Charles F. 1989a. "Systemic Disequilibrium, Foreign Policy Role, and the Power Cycle: Challenges for Research Design." *Journal of Conflict Resolution* 33:371–401.

Doran, Charles F. 1989b. "Power Cycle Theory of Systems Structure and Stability: Commonalities and Complementarities." In *Handbook of War Studies,* ed. Manus I. Midlarsky. Boston: Unwin Hyman.

Doran, Charles F. 1991. *Systems in Crisis: New Imperatives of High Politics at Century's End.* Cambridge: Cambridge University Press.

Doran, Charles F. 1992. "Dyads in a Systemic World: Confronting the Principles of the Power Cycle (Changing Systems Structure)." Paper presented at the Annual Convention of the International Studies Association, Atlanta, Georgia, April 1–4.

Doran, Charles F. 1993. "Quo Vadis? The United States' Cycle of Power and its Role in a Transforming World." In *Building a New Global Order: Emerging Trends in International Security,* ed. David Dewitt, David Haglund, and John Kirton. New York: Oxford University Press.

Doran, Charles F. 1994a. "Security and Political Economy in US-Asian Relations." *Journal of East Asian Affairs* 8:239–55.

Doran, Charles F. 1994b. "Canada and the United States in the New World of Asian Trade." In *Pacific Partners: Canada and the United States,* ed. Charles F. Doran et al. London: Brassey's, Inc.

Doran, Charles F. 1995a. "The 'Discontinuity Dilemma' of Changing Systems Structure: Confronting the Principles of the Power Cycle." Paper presented at the 36th Annual Convention of the International Studies Association, Chicago, Illinois, February 21–25.

Doran, Charles F. 1995b. "The Power Cycle and Peaceful Change: Assimilation, Equilibrium, and Conflict Resolution." In *Beyond Confrontion: Learning Conflict Resolution in the Post–Cold War Era,* ed. John A. Vasquez, James Turner Johnson, Sanford Jaffe, and Linda Stamato. Ann Arbor: University of Michigan Press.

Doran, Charles F. 1996. "Germany and Japan as Factors in U.S. Global Strategy." In *Amerikas Option fur Deutschland Und Japan,* ed. Gustav Schmidt and Charles F. Doran. Bochum: Brockmeyer.

Doran, Charles F. 1997. "Korea and the Asian Power Cycles." Translated into Korean and published in *Shindonga,* Sept. issue, 468–84.

Doran, Charles F. 1998. "Why Forecasts Fail: The Limits and Potential of Forecasting in International Relations and Economics." Paper presented at the Annual Convention of the International Studies Association, Minneapolis, March 17–21. Forthcoming in special Millennium Volume of *International Studies Review,* ed. Davis B. Bobrow.

Doran, Charles F., and Stephen W. Buck, eds. 1991. *The Gulf, Energy, and Global Security: Political and Economic Issues.* Boulder, CO: Lynne Rienner.

Doran, Charles F., Kim Q. Hill, and Kenneth R. Mladenka. 1979. "Threat, Status Disequilibrium, and National Power." *British Journal of International Studies* 5:37–58.

Doran, Charles F., Kim Q. Hill, Kenneth R. Mladenka, and K. W. Wakata. 1974. "Perceptions of National Power and Threat: Japan, Finland, and the United States." *International Journal of Group Tensions* 4:431–54.

Doran, Charles F., and Edoardo Marcucci. 1990. "International Political Equilibrium in Power Cycle Theory." *Studi Urbanati: Economia Sociologia* 63: 447–71.

Doran, Charles F., and Wes Parsons. 1980. "War and the Cycle of Relative Power." *American Political Science Review* 74:947–65.

Doran, Charles F., and Terrence Ward. 1975. "A General Theory of Power and Conflict." Working paper.

Doyle, Michael W. 1986. "Liberalism and World Politics." *American Political Science Review* 80:1151–69.

Doyle, Michael W. 1995. "Liberalism and World Politics Revisited." In *Controversies in International Relations Theory,* ed. Charles W. Kegley Jr. New York: St. Martin's Press.

Doyle, Michael W. 1997. *Ways of War and Peace.* New York: Norton.

Drake, C. J. M. 1998. "The Role of Ideology in Terrorists' Target Selection." *Terrorism and Political Violence* 10:53–85.

Drennan, R. D. 1991. "Pre-Hispanic Chiefdom Trajectories in Mesoamerica, Central America, and Northern South America." In *Chiefdoms,* ed. T. Earle. Cambridge: Cambridge University Press.

Dupuy, T. N., and E. Dupuy. 1993. *Harper Encyclopaedia of Military History,* 4th ed. New York: HarperCollins.

Earle, Edward M., ed. 1943. *Makers of Modern Strategy: Military Thought from Machiavelli to Hitler.* Princeton: Princeton University Press.

Earle, T. 1991. *Chiefdoms.* Cambridge: Cambridge University Press.

Earle, T. 1997. *How Chiefs Come to Power.* Stanford: Stanford University Press.

East, Maurice A. 1972. "Status Discrepancy and Violence in the International System: An Empirical Analysis." In *The Analysis of International Politics: Essays in Honor of Harold and Margaret Sprout,* ed. James N. Rosenau, Vincent Davis, and Maurice A. East. New York: The Free Press.

Eberwein, Wolf-Dieter. 1982. "The Seduction of Power: Serious International Disputes and the Power Status of Nations, 1900–1976." *International Interactions* 9:57–74.

Eckhardt, William, and Edward E. Azar. 1978. "Major World Conflicts and Interventions, 1945 to 1975." *International Interactions* 5:75–110.

Ehrich, R. W. 1992. *Chronologies in Old World Archaeology,* 3rd ed. Chicago: University of Chicago Press.

Eller, Jack, and Reed Coughlan. 1996. "The Poverty of Primordialism." In *Ethnicity,* ed. John Hutchinson and Anthony D. Smith. New York: Oxford University Press.

Ellingsen, Tanya, and Nils Petter Gleditsch. 1996. "Democracy and Armed Conflict in the Third World." In *Causes of Conflict in the Third World,* ed. Dan Smith and K. Volden. Oslo: North-South Coalition and International Peace Research Institute.

Ellsberg, Daniel. 1960. "The Crude Analysis of Strategic Choices." RAND Monograph P-2183, The RAND Corporation.

Elman, Miriam, ed. 1997. *Paths to Peace: Is Democracy the Answer?* Cambridge, MA: MIT Press.

Elster, Jon. 1983. *Explaining Technical Change: A Case Study in the Philosophy of Science.* Cambridge: Cambridge University Press.

El-Wailly, F., and B. Abu es-Soof. 1965. "The Excavations at Tell es-Sawwan." *Sumer* 21:17–32.

Ember, Carol, Melvin Ember, and Bruce Russett. 1992. "Peace between Participatory Polities: A Cross-Cultural Test of the 'Democracies Rarely Fight Each Other' Hypothesis." *World Politics* 44:573–99.

Ember, Melvin, and Carol R. Ember. 1996. "Identifying, Classifying, and Measuring Armed Conflict within and between Pre-industrial Societies." Paper presented at the Annual Convention of the International Studies Association, San Diego, California, April 16–20.

Emerson, T. E., and R. B. Lewis. 1990. *Cahokia and the Hinterlands.* Urbana: University of Illinois Press.

Enders, Walter, Gerald F. Parise, and Todd Sandler. 1992. "A Time-Series Analysis of Transnational Terrorism: Trends and Cycles." *Defence Economics* 3:305–20.

Enders, Walter, and Todd Sandler. 1993. "The Effectiveness of Anti-Terrorism Policies: A Vector-Autogression-Intervention Analysis." *American Political Science Review* 87:829–44.

Enders, Walter, and Todd Sandler. 1995. "Terrorism: Theory and Applications." *Handbook of Defense Economics,* Vol. 1, ed. Keith Hartley and Todd Sandler. Amsterdam: Elsevier.

Enders, Walter, and Todd Sandler. 1996. "Terrorism and Foreign Direct Investment in Spain and Greece." *Kyklos* 49:331–52.

Enders, Walter, and Todd Sandler. 1999. "Transnational Terrorism in the Post–Cold War Era." *International Studies Quarterly* 43:145–67.

Enders, Walter, Todd Sandler, and Joe Cauley. 1990. "UN Conventions, Technology and Retaliation in the Fight against Terrorism: An Econometric Evaluation." *Terrorism and Political Violence* 2:83–105.

Enders, Walter, Todd Sandler, and Gerald F. Parise. 1992. "An Econometric Analysis of the Impact of Terrorism on Tourism." *Kyklos* 45:531–54.

Enterline, Andrew. 1996. "Driving While Democratizing." *International Security* 20 (4): 183–96.

Enterline, Andrew. 1998a. "Regime Changes and Interstate Conflict, 1816–1992." *Political Research Quarterly* 51:385–409.

Enterline, Andrew. 1998b. "Regime Changes, Neighborhoods, and Interstate Conflict, 1816–1992." *Journal of Conflict Resolution* 42:804–29.

Epstein, Eric J., and Philip Rosen. 1997. *Dictionary of the Holocaust: Biography, Geography, and Terminology.* Westport, CT: Greenwood Press.

Esman, Milton J., and Shibley Telhami, eds. 1995. *International Organizations and Ethnic Conflict.* Ithaca, NY: Cornell University Press.

Esposito, and Voll, John O. 1996. *Islam and Democracy.* New York: Oxford University Press.

Esty, Daniel, Jack Goldstone, Ted Robert Gurr, Barbara Harff, Marc Levy, Gepffreu Dabelko, Pamela Surko, and Alan Unger. 1998. *State Failure Task Force Report: Phase II Findings.* McLean, VA: Science Applications International Corporation.

Eubank, William Lee, and Leonard Weinberg. 1994. "Does Democracy Encourage Terrorism?" *Terrorism and Political Violence* 6:417–35.

Eyerman, Joe, and Robert A. Hart. 1996. "An Empirical Test of the Audience Cost Proposition: Democracy Speaks Louder Than Words." *Journal of Conflict Resolution* 40:597–616.

Faber, Jan, Henk Houweling, and Jan Siccama. 1984. "Diffusion of Wars: Some Theoretical Considerations and Empirical Evidence." *Journal of Peace Research* 21:277–88.

Falconer, S. E., and S. H. Savage. 1995. "Heartlands and Hinterlands." *American Antiquity* 60:37–58.

Falk, Richard. 1988. *Revolutionaries and Functionaries: The Dual Face of Terrorism.* New York: E. P. Dutton.

Falkenrath, Richard A., Robert D. Newman, and Bradley A. Thayer. 1998. *America's Achilles Heel: Nuclear, Biological, and Chemical Terrorism and Covert Attack.* Cambridge, MA: MIT Press.

Fan, Xibo, and Charles F. Doran. 1997. "Foreign Policy Role and the State Power Cycle." International Political Science Association XVIIth World Congress. August 17–21.

Farber, Henry S., and Joanne Gowa. 1995. "Polities and Peace." *International Security* 20 (2): 123–46.

Farber, Henry S., and Joanne Gowa. 1997a. "Common Interests or Common Polities?" *Journal of Politics* 57:393–417.

Farber, Henry S., and Joanne Gowa. 1997b. "Building Bridges Abroad." *Journal of Conflict Resolution* 41:455–56.

Farnham, Barbara. 1994. *Taking Risks/Avoiding Losses.* Ann Arbor: University of Michigan Press.

Fearon, James D. 1994a. "Domestic Political Audiences and the Escalation of International Disputes." *American Political Science Review* 88:577–92.

Fearon, James D. 1994b. "Signaling versus the Balance of Power and Interests: An Empirical Test of a Crisis Bargaining Model." *Journal of Conflict Resolution* 38:236–69.

Fearon, James D. 1998. "Commitment Problems and the Spread of Ethnic Conflict." In *The International Spread of Ethnic Conflict: Fear, Diffusion, and Escalation,* ed. David A. Lake and Donald Rothchild. Princeton: Princeton University Press.

Feierabend, Ivo K., and Rosalind L. Feierabend. 1969. "Level of Development and International Behavior." In *Foreign Policy and the Developing Nation,* ed. R. Butwell. Lexington: University of Kentucky Press.

Fein, Helen. 1979. *Accounting for Genocide: National Responses and Jewish Victimization during the Holocaust.* New York: The Free Press.

Feldman, R. A. 1987. "Architectural Evidence for the Development of Nonegalitarian Social Systems in Coastal Peru." In *The Origins and Development of the Andean State,* ed. Haas J., S. Pozorski, and T. Pozorski. Cambridge: Cambridge University Press.

Feng, Yi. 1997. "Democracy, Political Stability, and Economic Growth." *British Journal of Political Science* 27:391–418.

Ferejohn, John. 1986. "Incumbent Performance and Electoral Control." *Public Choice* 50:5–25.

Ferguson, R. Brian, and Neil L. Whitehead. 1992. *War in the Tribal Zone: Expanding States and Indigenous Warfare.* Santa Fe, NM: School of American Research Press.

Ferguson, Yale H., and Richard W. Mansbach. 1996. "The Past as Prelude to the Future? Identities and Loyalties in Global Politics." In *The Return of Culture and Identity in IR Theory,* ed. Yosef Lapid and Friedrich Kratochwil. Boulder, CO: Lynne Rienner.

Ferrill, Arther. [1985] 1997. *The Origins of War.* Revised ed. Boulder, CO: Westview Press.

Feste, Karen. 1982. "International Enemies: A Review." Paper presented at the Annual Convention of the International Studies Association, Cincinnati.

Fink, Evelyn C., Brian D. Humes, and Valerie L. Schwebach. 1997. "The Size Principle and the Strategic Basis of an Alliance." *International Interactions* 22:279–94.

Finlay, David, Ole Holsti, and Richard Fagen. 1967. *Enemies in Politics.* Chicago: Rand McNally.

Finlayson, J. A., and Mark W. Zacher. 1980. *The United Nations and Collective Security: Retrospect and Prospect.* United Nations Association of America.

Flannery, K. V., and J. Marcus, eds. 1983. *The Cloud People.* New York: Academic Press.

Flemming, Peter A., and Michael Stohl. 1988. "The Theoretical Utility of Typologies of Terrorism: Lessons and Opportunities." *The Politics of Terrorism,* 3rd ed., ed. Michael Stohl. New York: Marcel Dekker.

Fletcher, Roland. 1995. *The Limits of Settlement Growth: A Theoretical Outline.* Cambridge: Cambridge University Press.

Forsythe, David P. 1992. "Democracy, War, and Covert Action." *Journal of Peace Research* 29:385–95.

Fowler, M. L. 1989. *The Cahokia Atlas.* Springfield, IL: Illinois Historic Preservation Agency.

Fox, William T. R. 1970. "The Causes of Peace and Conditions of War." In *How Wars End,* ed. W. T. R. Fox. *The Annals of the American Academy of Political and Social Science (Philadelphia)* 392:1–13.

Frangipane, M. 1996. *La Nascita dello Stato nel Vicino Oriente.* Bari, Italy: Editori Laterza.

Frank, Andre Gunder. 1998. *Reorient.* Berkeley: University of California Press.

Frederick, Suzanne Y. 1999. "Great Power Rivalry: The Anglo-German Case." In *Great Power Rivalries,* ed. William R. Thompson. Columbia: University of South Carolina Press.

Freedman, Lawrence, and Efraim Karsh. 1993. *The Gulf Conflict, 1990–1991: Diplomacy and War in the New World Order.* Princeton: Princeton University Press.

French, Howard W. 1998. "Congo Catches Rwanda's Disease." *New York Times,* 9 August, Section 4.

Frey, R. G., and Christopher W. Morris, eds. 1991. *Violence, Terrorism, and Justice.* Cambridge: Cambridge University Press.

Friedberg, Aaron. 1988. *The Weary Titan: Britain and the Experience of Relative Decline, 1895–1905.* Princeton: Princeton University Press.

Friedländer, Saul. 1994. "Introduction to the English Edition" of *Hitler and the Jews: The Genesis of the Holocaust,* by Philippe Burrin. London: Edward Arnold.

Friedman, George, and Meredith Lebard. 1991. *The Coming War with Japan.* New York: St. Martin's Press.

Gagnon, V. P. Jr. 1994. "Serbia's Road to War." In *Nationalism, Ethnic Conflict and Democracy,* ed. Larry Diamond and Marc F. Plattner. Baltimore: Johns Hopkins University Press.

Gagnon, V. P. Jr. 1995. "Ethnic Nationalism and International Conflict: The Case of Serbia." *International Security* 19 (3): 130–66.

Gal-Or, Noemi. 1985. *International Cooperation to Suppress Terrorism.* New York: St. Martin's.

Ganguly, Sumit. 1996. "Conflict and Crisis in South and Southwest Asia." In *The International Dimensions of Internal Conflict,* ed. Michael E. Brown. Cambridge, MA: MIT Press.

Garfinkel, Michelle R. 1994. "Domestic Politics and International Conflict." *American Economic Review* 84:1294–309.

Garfinkle, Adam. 1997. *Politics and Society in Modern Israel: Myths and Realities.* Armonk, NY: M. E. Sharpe.

Garnham, David. 1976a. "Dyadic International War, 1816–1965: The Role of Power Parity and Geographical Proximity." *Western Political Quarterly* 29:231–42.

Garnham, David. 1976b. "Power Parity and Lethal International Violence, 1969–1973." *Journal of Conflict Resolution* 20:379–94.

Garnham, David. 1983. "Explaining Major Power Bellicosity and Pacifism." Paper presented at the 24th Annual Convention of the International Studies Association, Mexico City, Mexico, April 5–9.

Garnham, David. 1985. "The Causes of War: Systemic Findings." In *Polarity and War,* ed. A. Ned Sabrosky. Boulder, CO: Westview Press.

Garrett, Geoffrey. 1998. "Global Markets and National Politics: Collision Course or Virtuous Circle?" *International Organization* 52:784–824.

Garstang, J. 1953. *Prehistoric Mersin.* Oxford: Clarendon Press.

Gartner, Scott, and Gary Segura. 1998. "War, Casualties, and Public Opinion." *Journal of Conflict Resolution* 42:278–300.

Gartzke, Erik. 1998. "Kant We All Just Get Along? Opportunity, Willingness and the Origins of the Democratic Peace." *American Journal of Political Science* 42:1–27.

Gartzke, Erik, and Michael Simon. 1999. "Hot Hand: A Critical Analysis of Enduring Rivalries." *Journal of Politics* 61:777–98.

Gasiorowski, Mark, and Solomon Polachek. 1982. "Conflict and Interdependence: East-West Trade and Linkages in the Era of Detente." *Journal of Conflict Resolution* 26:709–28.

Gastil, Raymond D. 1988. *Freedom in the World: Political Rights and Civil Liberties.* New York: Freedom House.

Gates, Scott, Torbjørn L. Knutsen, and Jonathan W. Moses. 1996. "Democracy and Peace: A More Skeptical View." *Journal of Peace Research* 33:1–10.

Gaubatz, Kurt T. 1996. "Democratic States and Commitment in International Relations." *International Organization* 50:109–39.

Geertz, Clifford. 1996. "Primordial Ties." In *Ethnicity,* ed. John Hutchinson and Anthony D. Smith. New York: Oxford University Press.

Geller, Daniel S. 1985. *Domestic Factors in Foreign Policy: A Cross-National Statistical Analysis.* Cambridge: Schenkman.

Geller, Daniel S. 1988. "Power System Membership and Patterns of War." *International Political Science Review* 9:365–79.

Geller, Daniel S. 1990. "Nuclear Weapons, Deterrence, and Crisis Escalation." *Journal of Conflict Resolution* 34:291–310.

Geller, Daniel S. 1992. "Capability Concentration, Power Transition, and War." *International Interactions* 17:269–84.

Geller, Daniel S. 1993. "Power Differentials and War in Rival Dyads." *International Studies Quarterly* 37:173–93.

Geller, Daniel S. 1996. "Relative Power, Rationality, and International Conflict." In *Parity and War: Evaluations and Extensions of The War Ledger,* ed. Jacek Kugler and Douglas Lemke. Ann Arbor: University of Michigan Press.

Geller, Daniel S. 1998. "The Stability of the Military Balance and War among Great Power Rivals." In *The Dynamics of Enduring Rivalries,* ed. Paul F. Diehl. Urbana: University of Illinois Press.

Geller, Daniel S., and Daniel M. Jones. 1991. "The Effect of Dynamic and Static Balances on Conflict Escalation in Rival Dyads." Paper presented at the Annual Meeting of the American Political Science Association, Washington, DC, August 29–September 1.

Geller, Daniel S., and J. David Singer. 1998. *Nations at War: A Scientific Study of International Conflict.* Cambridge: Cambridge University Press.

Gelpi, Christopher. 1997. "Democratic Diversions: Governmental Structure and the Externalization of Domestic Conflict." *Journal of Conflict Resolution* 41:255–82.

Gelpi, Christopher, and Michael Griesdorf. 1997. "Winners or Losers: Democracies in International Crisis, 1918–1988." Paper presented at the Annual Meeting of the American Political Science Association, Washington, DC, August 28–31.

George, Alexander L., and Richard Smoke. 1974. *Deterrence in American Foreign Policy.* New York: Columbia University Press.

Geva, Nehemia, Karl DeRouen, and Alex Mintz. 1993. "The Political Incentive Explanation of 'Democratic Peace': Evidence from Experimental Research." *International Interactions* 18:215–29.

Geva, Nehemia, and Alex Mintz. 1994. "Framing the Options for Peace in the Middle East." Paper delivered at ECAAR-Israel Conference, Haifa, Israel, June 20.

Geva, Nehemia, and Alex Mintz, eds. 1997. *Decision-Making on War and Peace: The Cognitive-Rational Debate.* Boulder, CO: Lynne Rienner.

Gibbs, Jack P. 1989. "Conceptualization of Terrorism." *American Sociological Review* 53:329–40.

Gibler, Douglas M. 1996. "Alliances That Never Balance: The Territorial Settlement Treaty." *Conflict Management and Peace Science* 15:75–97.

Gibler, Douglas M. 1997a. "Control the Issues, Control the Conflict: The Effects of Alliances That Settle Territorial Issues on Interstate Rivalries." *International Interactions* 22:341–68.

Gibler, Douglas M. 1997b. "Reconceptualizing the Alliance Variable: An Empirical Typology of Alliances." Ph.D. diss., Vanderbilt University, Nashville, Tennessee.

Gibler, Douglas M., and John A. Vasquez. 1998. "Uncovering the Dangerous Alliances, 1495–1980." *International Studies Quarterly* 42:785–807.

Giddens, Anthony. 1991. *Modernity and Self-identity: Self and Society in the Late Modern Age.* Cambridge: Polity Press.

Gilbert, Martin. 1989. *The Second World War: A Complete History.* New York: Henry Holt.

Gilpin, Robert. 1981. *War and Change in World Politics.* New York: Cambridge University Press.

Gilpin, Robert. 1987. *The Political Economy of International Relations.* Princeton: Princeton University Press.

Ginsberg, H. L. 1958. "Ugaritic Myths and Epics." In *The Ancient Near East,* ed. J. B. Pritchard. Princeton: Princeton University Press.

Gleditsch, Nils Petter. 1992. "Democracy and Peace." *Journal of Peace Research* 29:369–76.

Gleditsch, Nils Petter. 1995. "Geography, Democracy, and Peace." *International Interactions* 20:297–323.

Gleditsch, Nils Petter. 1997. "Environmental Conflict and the Democratic Peace." In *Conflict and the Environment,* ed. Nils Petter Gleditsch. The Hague: Kluwer Academic.

Gleditsch, Nils Petter, and Havard Hegre. 1997. "Peace and Democracy: Three Levels of Analysis." *Journal of Conflict Resolution* 41:283–310.

Gleditsch, Nils Petter, and J. David Singer. 1975. "Distance and International War, 1816–1965." In *Proceedings of the International Peace Research Association, Fifth General Conference,* ed. M. R. Khan. Oslo: International Peace Research Association.

Glenny, Misha. 1996. *The Fall of Yugoslavia: The Third Balkan War,* 3rd ed. New York: Penguin Books.

Gochman, Charles S. 1990a. "The Geography of Conflict: Militarized Interstate Disputes since 1816." Paper presented at the 31st Annual Convention, International Studies Association, Washington, DC, April 10–14.

Gochman, Charles S. 1990b. "Capability-Driven Disputes." In *Prisoners of War? Nation-States in the Modern Era,* ed. Charles S. Gochman and Alan N. Sabrosky. Lexington, MA: Lexington Books.

Gochman, Charles S., and Russell J. Leng. 1983. "Realpolitik and the Road to War." *International Studies Quarterly* 27:97–120.

Gochman, Charles S., and Zeev Maoz. 1984. "Militarized Interstate Disputes, 1816–1976: Procedures, Patterns, and Insights." *Journal of Conflict Resolution* 28:585–616.

Goemans, Hein. 1997. "The Democratic Peace and Civil War." Paper presented at the Annual Meeting of the American Political Science Association, Washington, DC, August 28–31.

Goertz, Gary. 1994. *Contexts of International Politics.* Cambridge: Cambridge University Press.

Goertz, Gary, ed. 1997. "Conflict Management and Termination in International Rivalry." *International Interactions* 22:295–400.

Goertz, Gary, and Paul F. Diehl. 1992a. "The Empirical Importance of Enduring Rivalries." *International Interactions* 18:151–63.

Goertz, Gary, and Paul F. Diehl. 1992b. *Territorial Change and International Conflict.* London: Routledge.

Goertz, Gary, and Paul F. Diehl. 1993. "Enduring Rivalries: Theoretical Constructs and Empirical Patterns." *International Studies Quarterly* 37:145–71.

Goertz, Gary, and Paul F. Diehl. 1995a. "Taking Enduring Out of Enduring Rivalry: The Rivalry Approach to War and Peace." *International Interactions* 21:291–308.

Goertz, Gary, and Paul F. Diehl. 1995b. "The Initiation and Termination of Enduring Rivalries: The Impact of Political Shocks." *American Journal of Political Science* 39:30–52.

Goertz, Gary, and Paul F. Diehl. 1997. "Linking Risky Dyads: An Evaluation of Relations Between Enduring Rivalries." In *Enforcing Cooperation: Risky States and the Intergovernmental Management of Conflict,* ed. Gerald Schneider and Patricia Weitsman. London: Macmillan.

Goertz, Gary, and Paul F. Diehl. 1998. "The Volcano Model and Other Patterns in the Evolution of Enduring Rivalries." In *The Dynamics of Enduring Rivalries,* ed. Paul F. Diehl. Urbana: University of Illinois Press.

Goertz, Gary, and Patrick Regan. 1997. "Conflict Management in Enduring Rivalries." *International Interactions* 22:321–40.

Gold-Biss, Michael. 1994. *The Discourse on Terrorism: Political Violence and the Subcommittee on Security and Terrorism, 1981–1986.* New York: Peter Lang.

Goldstein, Joshua. 1985. "War and the Kondratieff Upswing." *International Studies Quarterly* 29:411–41.

Goldstein, Joshua. 1987. "Long Waves on Production, War and Inflation: New Empirical Evidence." *Journal of Conflict Resolution* 31:573–600.

Goldstein, Joshua. 1988. *Long Cycles: Prosperity and War in the Modern Age.* New Haven: Yale University Press.

Goldstein, Joshua. 1991a. "A War-Economy Theory of the Long Wave." In *Business Cycles: Theories, Evidence and Analysis,* ed. Niels Thygesen, Kumaraswamy Velupillai, and Stefano Zambelli. New York: New York University Press.

Goldstein, Joshua. 1991b. "The Possibility of Cycles in International Relations." *International Studies Quarterly* 35:477–80.

Goldstein, Joshua, and John Freeman. 1991. "US-Soviet-Chinese Relations: Routine, Reciprocity, or Rational Expectations?" *American Political Science Review* 85:17–35.

Goldstein, Joshua, and David P. Rapkin. 1991. "Hegemony and the Future of World Order." *Futures* 23:935–59.

Gordon, Avishag. 1995. "Terrorism and Computerized Databases: An Examination of Multidisciplinary Coverage." *Terrorism and Political Violence* 7:171–77.

Gowa, Joanne. 1995. "Democratic States and International Disputes." *International Organization* 49:511–22.

Graham, Thomas W. 1988. "The Pattern and Importance of Public Awareness and Knowledge in the Nuclear Age." *Journal of Conflict Resolution* 32:319–33.

Greaves, Colonel Fielding V. 1962. "Peace in Our Time—Fact or Fable?" *Military Review* (December): 55–58.

Green, Jerrold D. 1995. "Terrorism and Politics in Iran." In *Terrorism in Context,* ed. Martha Crenshaw. University Park: Pennsylvania State University Press.

Grove, D. C. 1997. "Olmec Archaeology." *Journal of World Prehistory* 11: 51–101.

Guelke, Adrian. 1995. *The Age of Terrorism and the International Political System.* London: I. B. Tauris.

Gurr, Ted R. 1970. *Why Men Rebel.* Princeton: Princeton University Press.

Gurr, Ted R. 1980. "On the Outcomes of Violent Conflict." In *Handbook of Political Conflict,* ed. Ted R. Gurr. New York: The Free Press.

Gurr, Ted R. 1992. "The Internationalization of Protracted Communal Conflicts since 1945." In *The Internationalization of Communal Strife,* ed. Manus I. Midlarsky. London: Routledge.

Gurr, Ted R. 1993a. *Minorities at Risk: Origins and Outcomes of Ethnopolitical Conflicts.* Washington, DC: U.S. Institute of Peace.

Gurr, Ted R. 1993b. "Why Minorities Rebel: A Global Analysis of Communal Mobilization and Conflict since 1945." *International Political Science Review* 14:161–201.

Gurr, Ted R. 1994. "Peoples against States: Ethnopolitical Conflict and the Changing World System." *International Studies Quarterly* 38:347–77.

Gurr, Ted R., and Barbara Harff. 1994. *Ethnic Conflict in World Politics.* Boulder, CO: Westview Press.

Gurr, Ted R., Keith Jaggers, and Will H. Moore. 1989. "Polity II Codebook." Boulder, CO: Department of Political Science, University of Colorado (mimeo).

Haas, Ernst B. 1958. *The Uniting of Europe.* Stanford: Stanford University Press.

Haas, Ernst B. 1983. "Regime Decay: Conflict Management and International Organizations, 1945–1981." *International Organization* 37:189–256.

Haas, Ernst B. 1986. "Why We Still Need the United Nations." University of California Policy Papers in International Affairs, No. 26. Berkeley: Institute of International Studies.

Haas, Ernst B., Robert L. Butterworth, and Joseph S. Nye. 1972. *Conflict Management by International Organizations.* Morristown, NJ: General Learning Press.

Haas, J. 1989. "The Evolution of the Kayenta Regional System." In *The Sociopolitical Structure of Prehistoric Southwestern Societies,* ed. S. Upham and K. G. Lightfoot. Boulder, CO: Westview Press.

Haas, J., S. Pozorski, and T. Pozorski, eds. 1987. *The Origins and Development of the Andean State.* Cambridge: Cambridge University Press.

Haas, Michael. 1970. "International Subsystems: Stability and Polarity." *American Political Science Review* 64:98–123.

Haass, Richard N. 1990. *Conflicts Unending.* New Haven: Yale University Press.

Hagan, Joe D. 1987. "Regimes, Political Oppositions, and the Comparative Analysis of Foreign Policy." In *New Directions in the Study of Foreign Policy,* ed. Charles F. Hermann, Charles W. Kegley Jr., and James N. Rosenau. Boston: Allen & Unwin.

Hagan, Joe D. 1994. "Domestic Political System and War Proneness." *Mershon International Studies Review* 38 (Supplement 2): 183–207.

Hagan, Joe D. 1998. "Unpacking the Democratic Peace: Rulers, Oppositions, and the Wider Political Bases of Great Power Conflict." Paper presented to the Annual Convention of the International Studies Association, Minneapolis, Minnesota, March 17–21.

Hager, Robert P. Jr. 1990. "Latin American Terrorism and the Soviet Connection Revisited." *Terrorism and Political Violence* 2:258–88.

Handler, Richard. 1994. "Is 'Identity' a Useful Cross-Cultural Concept?" In *Commemorations: The Politics of National Identity,* ed. John R. Gillis. Princeton: Princeton University Press.

Hardgrave, Robert L. Jr. 1994. "India: The Dilemmas of Diversity." In *Nationalism, Ethnic Conflict, and Democracy,* ed. Larry Diamond and Marc. F. Plattner. Baltimore: Johns Hopkins University Press.

Hart, Jeffrey A. 1985. "Power and Polarity in the International System." In *Polarity and War,* ed. A. Ned Sabrosky. Boulder, CO: Westview Press.

Hartman, Raymond S., Michael J. Doane, and Chi-Keung Woo. 1991. "Consumer Rationality and the Status Quo." *Quarterly Journal of Economics* 106:141–62.

Hebron, Lui and Patrick James. 1997. "Great Powers, Cycles of Relative Capability and Crises in World Politics." *International Interactions* 23:145–73.

Hegre, Havard, Tanja Ellingsen, Monica Jakobsen, Arvid Raknerud, and Nils Petter Gleditsch. 1997. "Towards a Democratic Civil Peace? Democracy, Democratization and Civil War, 1834–1992." Paper presented at the Annual Convention of the International Studies Association, Toronto, Ontario, March 18–22.

Heldt, Birger. 1997a. "The Dependent Variable of the Domestic-External Conflict Relationship; Anecdotes, Theories, and Systematic Studies." *Journal of Peace Research* 34:101–6.

Heldt, Birger. 1997b. "Reconstructing Kant: Propositions and Methodological Considerations." New Haven, CT: Yale University Political Science Department.

Hempel, Carl G. [1942] 1959. "The Function of General Laws in History." In *Theories of History*, ed. Patrick Gardiner. Glencoe, IL: The Free Press.

Hempel, Carl G. 1966. *Philosophy of Natural Science.* Englewood Cliffs, NJ: Prentice-Hall.

Henderson, Errol. 1998. "The Democratic Peace through the Lens of Culture, 1820–1989." *International Studies Quarterly* 42:461–84.

Henderson, Errol. 1999. "Neoidealism and the Democratic Peace." *Journal of Peace Research* 36:203–31.

Hensel, Paul R. 1995. "Political Democracy and Militarized Conflict in Evolving Interstate Rivalries." Paper presented at the Annual Meeting of the American Political Science Association, Chicago, Illinois, August 31–September 3.

Hensel, Paul R. 1996a. "The Evolution of Interstate Rivalry." Ph.D. diss., University of Illinois at Urbana-Champaign.

Hensel, Paul R. 1996b. "Charting a Course to Conflict: Territorial Issues and Interstate Conflict, 1816–1992." *Conflict Management and Peace Science* 15: 43–73.

Hensel, Paul R. 1997. "What Do They Do When They Are Not Fighting?: Event Data and Non-militarized Dimensions of Interstate Rivalry." Draft manuscript.

Hensel, Paul R. 1998. "Interstate Rivalry and the Study of Militarized Conflict." In *Conflict in World Politics: Advances in the Study of Crisis, War and Peace,* ed. Frank Harvey and Ben Mor. London: Macmillan.

Hensel, Paul R. 2000. "Territory: Theory and Evidence on Geography and Conflict." In *What Do We Know about War?,* ed. John A. Vasquez. Lanham, MD: Rowman & Littlefield.

Hensel, Paul R., Gary Goertz, and Paul F. Diehl. Forthcoming. "The Democratic Peace and Rivalries." *Journal of Politics.*

Hensel, Paul R., and Sara McLaughlin. 1996. "Power Transitions and Dispute Escalation in Evolving Interstate Rivalry." Paper presented at the Annual Meeting of the American Political Science Association, San Francisco, California, August 29–September 1.

Hensel, Paul R., and William Reed. 1997. "Introducing the Issue Correlates of War (ICOW) Project: Territorial Claims and Militarized Interstate Disputes." Paper presented at the Annual Convention of the International Studies Association, Toronto, Ontario, March 18–22.

Hensel, Paul R., and John Tures. 1997. "International Law and the Settlement of Territorial Claims in South America, 1816–1992." Paper presented at the Annual Meeting of the American Political Science Association, Washington, DC, August 28–31.

Hermann, Margaret G., and Charles F. Hermann. 1990. "Hostage Taking, the Presidency, and Stress." In *Origins of Terrorism: Psychologies, Ideologies, Theologies, States of Mind,* ed. Walter Reich. Cambridge: Cambridge University Press.

Hermann, Margaret G., and Charles W. Kegley Jr. 1995. "Rethinking Democracy and International Peace: Perspectives from Political Psychology." *International Studies Quarterly* 39:511–33.

Hermann, Margaret G., and Charles W. Kegley Jr. 1996. "Ballots, a Barrier against the Use of Bullets and Bombs: Democratization and Military Intervention." *Journal of Conflict Resolution* 40 (3): 436–60.

Hermann, Margaret G., and Charles W. Kegley Jr. 1998. "The U.S. Use of Military Intervention to Promote Democracy: Evaluating the Record." *International Interactions* 24:91–114.

Herz, John H. 1950. "Idealist Internationalism and the Security Dilemma." *World Politics* 2:157–80.

Herz, John H. 1951. *Political Realism and Political Idealism: A Study in Theories and Realities.* Chicago: University of Chicago Press.

Hewitt, Christopher. 1994. "Some Skeptical Comments on Large Cross-National Studies." *Terrorism and Political Violence* 6:439–41.

Hewitt, J. Joseph. 1996. "The Strategic Prospects of Mediating International Disputes." Ph.D. diss., University of Maryland, College Park, Maryland.

Hewitt, J. Joseph, and Jonathan Wilkenfeld. 1996. "Democracy and International Crisis." *International Interactions* 22:123–42.

Higgins, Rosalyn, and Maurice Flory, eds. 1997. *Terrorism and International Law.* London: Routledge.

Hill, Stuart, and Donald Rothchild. 1986. "The Contagion of Political Conflict in Africa and the World." *Journal of Conflict Resolution* 30:716–35.

Hill, Stuart, and Donald Rothchild. 1992. "The Impact of Regime on the Diffusion of Political Conflict." In *The Internationalization of Communal Strife,* ed. Manus I. Midlarsky. New York: Routledge.

Hobsbawm, Eric. 1996. "Ethnic Nationalism in the Late Twentieth Century." In *Ethnicity,* eds. John Hutchinson and Anthony D. Smith. New York: Oxford University Press.

Hobsbawm, Eric, and Terence Ranger, eds. 1983. *The Invention of Tradition.* Cambridge: Cambridge University Press.

Hoffman, Bruce. 1989. "The PLO and Israel in Central America: The Geopolitical Dimension." *Terrorism and Political Violence* 1:482–515.

Hoffman, Bruce. 1993. "Terrorist Targeting: Tactics, Trends, and Potentialities." *Terrorism and Political Violence* 5:12–29.

Hoffman, Bruce. 1997. "The Confluence of International and Domestic Trends in Terrorism." *Terrorism and Political Violence* 9:1–15.

Hoffman, Bruce, and Donna Kim Hoffman. 1995. "The RAND-St. Andrews Chronology of International Terrorism, 1994." *Terrorism and Political Violence* 7:178–229.

Hoffman, Bruce, Dennis A. Pluchinsky, and David C. Rapoport. 1997. "Terrorists and Claiming Credit: The Debate." *Terrorism and Political Violence* 9:1–19.

Hoffmann, Stanley. 1960. "International Relations as a Discipline." In *Contemporary Theory in International Relations*, ed. Stanley Hoffman. Englewood Cliffs, NJ: Prentice-Hall.

Hogg, O. F. G. [1968] 1993. *Clubs to Cannon.* New York: Barnes and Noble.

Holsti, Kalevi J. 1966. "Resolving International Conflicts: A Taxonomy of Behavior and Some Figures on Procedures." *Journal of Conflict Resolution* 10:274–82.

Holsti, Kalevi J. 1970. "National Role Conception in the Study of Foreign Policy." *International Studies Quarterly* 14:233–309.

Holsti, Kalevi J. 1991. *Peace and War: Armed Conflicts and International Order 1648–1989*. Cambridge: Cambridge University Press.

Holsti, Ole R. 1972. *Crisis, Escalation, War.* Montreal: McGill-Queen's University Press.

Holsti, Ole R., P. Terrence Hopmann, and John D. Sullivan. 1973. *Unity and Disintegration in International Alliances: Comparative Studies.* New York: Wiley.

Holsti, Ole R., Robert C. North, and Richard A. Brody. 1968. "Perception and Action in the 1914 Crisis." In *Quantitative International Politics,* ed. J. David Singer. New York: The Free Press.

Hoole, Francis W., and Chi Huang. 1989. "The Global Conflict Process." *Journal of Conflict Resolution* 33:142–63.

Hopf, Ted. 1991. "Polarity, the Offense-Defense Balance, and War." *American Political Science Review* 85:475–94.

Horn, Michael D. 1987. "Arms Races and the International System." Ph.D. diss., University of Rochester, Rochester, New York.

Horowitz, Donald L. 1985. *Ethnic Groups in Conflict.* Berkeley: University of California Press.

Horowitz, Donald L. 1994. "Democracy in Divided Societies." In *Nationalism, Ethnic Conflict, and Democracy,* ed. Larry Diamond and Marc F. Plattner. Baltimore: Johns Hopkins University Press.

Houweling, Henk W., and Jan G. Siccama. 1981. "The Arms Race–War Relationships: Why Serious Disputes Matter." *Arms Control* 2:157–97.

Houweling, Henk W., and Jan G. Siccama. 1985. "The Epidemiology of War, 1816–1980." *Journal of Conflict Resolution* 29:641–63.

Houweling, Henk W., and Jan G. Siccama. 1988. "Power Transitions as a Cause of War." *Journal of Conflict Resolution* 32:87–102.

Houweling, Henk W., and Jan G. Siccama. 1991. "Power Transitions and Critical Points as Predictors of Great Power War: Toward a Synthesis." *Journal of Conflict Resolution* 35:642–58.

Houweling, Henk W., and Jan G. Siccama. 1993. "The Neo-functionalist Explanation of World Wars: A Critique and an Alternative." *International Interactions* 18:387–408.

Houweling, Henk W., and Jan G. Siccama. 1994. "Long Cycle Theory: A Further Discussion." *International Interactions* 20:223–26.

Howard, Michael. 1984. *The Causes of War,* 2nd ed. Cambridge, MA: Harvard University Press.

Hower, Gretchen, and Dina A. Zinnes. 1989. "International Political Conflict: A Literature Review." *DDIR-Update* 3:1–14. Merriam Laboratory for Analytic Political Research. University of Illinois at Urbana-Champaign (mimeo).

Hughes, Martin. 1990. "Terror and Negotiation." *Terrorism and Political Violence* 2:72–82.

Huntington, Samuel P. 1993. "The Clash Of Civilizations?" *Foreign Affairs* 72 (3): 22–49.

Huntington, Samuel P. 1996. *The Clash of Civilizations and the Remaking of World Order.* New York: Simon and Schuster.

Huntley, Wade. 1996. "Kant's Third Image: Systemic Sources of the Liberal Peace." *International Studies Quarterly* 40:45–76.

Huot, J. L., J. P. Thalman, D. Valbelle. 1990. *Naissance de cités.* Paris: Éditions Nathan.

Hutchinson, John, and Anthony D. Smith. 1996. "Introduction." In *Ethnicity,* ed. John Hutchinson and Anthony D. Smith. New York: Oxford University Press.

Huth, Paul K. 1988a. "Extended Deterrence and the Outbreak of War." *American Political Science Review* 82:423–43.

Huth, Paul K. 1988b. *Extended Deterrence and the Prevention of War.* New Haven: Yale University Press.

Huth, Paul K. 1996a. *Standing Your Ground: Territorial Disputes and International Conflict.* Ann Arbor: University of Michigan Press.

Huth, Paul K. 1996b. "Enduring Rivalries and Territorial Disputes, 1950–1990." *Conflict Management and Peace Science* 15:7–41.

Huth, Paul K., D. Scott Bennett, and Christopher Gelpi. 1992. "System Uncertainty, Risk Propensity, and International Conflict among the Great Powers." *Journal of Conflict Resolution* 36:478–517.

Huth, Paul K., Daniel M. Jones, and Zeev Maoz. 1991. "Enduring International Rivalries: An Operational Definition and Case Identification Criteria." University of Michigan and Haifa University (mimeo).

Huth, Paul K., and Bruce M. Russett. 1984. "What Makes Deterrence Work?: Cases from 1900 to 1980." *World Politics* 36:496–526.

Huth, Paul K., and Bruce M. Russett. 1988. "Deterrence Failure and Crisis Escalation." *International Studies Quarterly* 31:29–45.

Huth, Paul K., and Bruce M. Russett. 1993. "General Deterrence between Enduring Rivals: Testing Three Competing Models." *American Political Science Review* 87:61–73.

Ikle, Fred C. 1971. *Every War Must End.* New York: Columbia University Press.

Ingram, Edward. 1999. "Enduring Rivalries: Britain and Russia." In *Great Power Rivalries,* ed. William R. Thompson. Columbia: University of South Carolina Press.

Intriligator, Michael D., and Dagobert L. Brito. 1984. "Can Arms Races Lead to the Outbreak of War?" *Journal of Conflict Resolution* 28:63–84.

Iriye, Akira. 1987. *The Origins of the Second World War.* New York: Longman.

Iseminger, W. R. 1996. "Mighty Cahokia." *Archaeology* 49:30–37.

Jackman, Robert. 1993. *Power without Force.* Ann Arbor: University of Michigan Press.

Jackson, Donald. 1994. "Prevention of Terrorism: The United Kingdom Confronts the European Convention on Human Rights." *Terrorism and Political Violence* 6:507–35.

Jackson, William D. 1977. "Polarity in International Systems: A Conceptual Note." *International Interactions* 4:87–96.

Jacobsen, T. 1939. *The Sumerian Kinglist.* Chicago: University of Chicago Press.

Jaggers, Keith, and Ted R. Gurr. 1995. "Tracking Democracy's Third Wave with the Polity III Data." *Journal of Peace Research* 32:469–82.

James, Patrick. 1987. "Conflict and Cohesion: A Review of the Literature and Recommendations for Future Research." *Cooperation and Conflict* 22:21–33.

James, Patrick. 1988. *Crisis and War.* Montreal: McGill-Queen's University Press.

James, Patrick. 1995. "Structural Realism and the Causes of War." *Mershon International Studies Review* 39 (Supplement 2): 181–208.

James, Patrick, and Lui Hebron. 1997. "Great Powers, Cycles of Relative Capability and Crises in World Politics." *International Interactions* 23:145–73.

James, Patrick, and Glenn E. Mitchell II. 1995. "Targets of Covert Pressure: The Hidden Victims of the Democratic Peace." *International Interactions* 21:85–107.

James, Patrick, and Jean Sebastien Rioux. 1998. "International Crises and Linkage Politics: The Experiences of the United States, 1953–1994." *Political Research Quarterly* 51:781–812.

James, Patrick, Eric Solberg, and Murray Wolfson. 1999. "An Identified Systemic Analysis of the Democracy-Peace Nexus." *Defence and Peace Economics* 10:1–37.

James, Patrick, and Jonathan Wilkenfeld. 1984. "Structural Factors and International Crisis Behavior." *Conflict Management and Peace Science* 7:33–53.

Janke, Peter, ed. 1992. *Terrorism and Democracy: Some Contemporary Cases. Report of a Study Group of the David Davies Memorial Institute of International Studies.* New York: St. Martin's.

Jasim, Sabah Abboud. 1985. *The Ubaid Period in Iraq: Recent Excavations in the Hamrin Region.* Oxford, England: B.A.R. [British Archaeological Reports] International Series.

Jervis, Robert. 1976. *Perception and Misperception in International Politics.* Princeton: Princeton University Press.

Jervis, Robert. 1978. "Cooperation under the Security Dilemmas." *World Politics* 30:167–214.

Jervis, Robert. 1991. "Domino Beliefs and Strategic Behavior." In *Dominoes and Bandwagons,* ed. Robert Jervis and Jack Snyder. New York: Oxford University Press.

Jervis, Robert. 1992. "Political Implications of Loss Aversion." *Political Psychology* 13:187–204.

Johnson, James T. 1992. "Religion, Ideology, and Ethnic Identity in the Sri Lankan Conflict." In *The Internationalization of Communal Strife,* ed. Manus I. Midlarsky. New York: Routledge.

Joll, James. 1984. *The Origins of the First World War.* New York: Longman.

Jones, Bruce D. 1999. "The Arusha Peace Process." In *The Rwanda Crisis from Uganda to Zaire: The Path of a Genocide,* ed. Howard Adelman and Astri Suhrke. New Brunswick, NJ: Transaction Publishers.

Jones, Daniel M. 1989. "Enduring Rivalries, Dispute Escalation and Interstate War." Paper presented at the 23rd North American Meeting of the Peace Science Society (International), Columbus, Ohio, November 8.

Jones, Daniel M., Stuart A. Bremer, and J. David Singer. 1996. "Militarized Interstate Disputes, 1816–1992: Rationale, Coding Rules, and Empirical Patterns." *Conflict Management and Peace Science* 15:163–213.

Jongman, A. J. 1992. "Trends in International and Domestic Terrorism in Western Europe, 1968–1988." *Terrorism and Political Violence* 4:26–76.

Judah, Tim. 1997. *The Serbs: History, Myth and the Resurrection of Yugoslavia.* New Haven, CT: Yale University Press.

Kacowicz, Arie M. 1998. *Zones of Peace in the Third World: South America and West Africa in Comparative Perspective.* Albany: State University of New York Press.

Kadera, Kelly. 1996. "The Conditions and Consequences of Dyadic Power Transitions: Deductions from a Dynamic Model." In *Parity and War,* ed. Jacek Kugler and Douglas Lemke. Ann Arbor: University of Michigan Press.

Kagan, Donald. 1995. *On the Origins of War and the Preservation of Peace.* New York: Doubleday.

Kahn, Herman. 1965. *On Escalation: Metaphors and Scenarios.* New York: Praeger.

Kahn, Herman. 1970. "Issues of Thermonuclear War Termination." In *How Wars End,* ed. W. T. R. Fox. *The Annals of the American Academy of Political and Social Science (Philadelphia)* 392:133–72.

Kahneman, Daniel, Jack L. Knetsch, and Richard H. Thaler. 1990. "Experimental Tests of the Endowment Effect and the Coase Theorem." *Journal of Political Economy* 98:1325–48.

Kahneman, Daniel, Jack L. Knetsch, and Richard H. Thaler. 1991. "The Endowment Effect, Loss Aversion, and Status Quo Bias." *Journal of Economic Perspectives* 5:193–206.

Kahneman, Daniel, and Amos Tversky. 1979. "Prospect Theory: An Analysis of Decision under Risk." *Econometrica* 47:263–91.

Kahneman, Daniel, and Amos Tversky. 1984. "Choices, Values, and Frames." *American Psychologist* 39:341–50.

Kant, Immanuel. [1795] 1939. *Perpetual Peace.* Original translation from the first English edition [1796]. New York: Columbia University Press.

Kaplan, Morton A. 1957. *System and Process in International Politics.* New York: John Wiley.

Kaplan, Robert D. 1993. *Balkan Ghosts: A Journey through History.* New York: St. Martin's Press.

Kaplan, Stephen S. 1981. *Diplomacy of Power: Soviet Armed Forces as a Political Instrument.* Washington, DC: The Brookings Institution.

Karmon, Ely. 1998. "Why Iran Starts and Stops Terrorism." *Middle East Quarterly* 5:35–44.

Katzenstein, Peter J. 1993. "Coping with Terrorism: Norms and Internal Security in Germany and Japan." *Ideas and Foreign Policy: Beliefs, Institutions, and Political Change,* ed. Judith Goldstein and Robert O. Keohane. Ithaca, NY: Cornell University Press.

Katzenstein, Peter J., ed. 1996. *The Culture of National Security: Norms and Identity in World Politics.* New York: Columbia University Press.

Kaufman, Stuart J. 1996. "Spiraling to Ethnic War: Elites, Masses, and Moscow in Moldova's Civil War." *International Security* 21 (2): 108–38.

Kaufman, William. 1956. "The Requirements of Deterrence." In *Military Policy and National Security,* ed. William Kaufman. Princeton: Princeton University Press.

Kecskemeti, Paul. 1958. *Strategic Surrender.* Stanford: Stanford University Press.

Kecskemeti, Paul. 1970. "Political Rationality in Ending War." In *How Wars End,* ed. W. T. R. Fox. *The Annals of the American Academy of Political and Social Science (Philadelphia)* 392:105–15.

Keeley, L. H. 1996. *War before Civilization.* Oxford: Oxford University Press.

Kegley, Charles W. Jr., and Margaret Hermann. 1995. "Military Intervention and the Democratic Peace." *International Interactions* 21:1–21.

Kegley, Charles W. Jr., and Margaret Hermann. 1997. "Putting Military Intervention into the Democratic Peace." *Comparative Political Studies* 30:78–107.

Kegley, Charles W. Jr., and Gregory A. Raymond. 1990. *When Trust Breaks Down: Alliance Norms and World Politics.* Columbia: University of South Carolina Press.

Kegley, Charles W. Jr., and Gregory A. Raymond. 1992. "Must We Fear a Post–Cold War Multipolar System?" *Journal of Conflict Resolution* 36: 573–85.

Kegley, Charles W. Jr., and Gregory Raymond. 1994. *A Multipolar Peace?: Great-Power Politics in the Twenty-first Century.* New York: St. Martin's Press.

Kegley, Charles W. Jr., and Gregory A. Raymond. 1999. *How Nations Make Peace.* New York: St. Martin's Press.

Kegley, Charles W. Jr., and Richard J. Skinner. 1976. "The Case-for-Analysis Problem." In *In Search of Global Patterns,* ed. J. Rosenau. New York: The Free Press.

Keightley, D. N. 1978. "The 'Bamboo Annals' and Shang-Chou Chronology." *Harvard Journal of Asiatic Studies* 38:423–38.

Keightley, D. N. 1983. *The Origins of Chinese Civilization.* Berkeley: University of California Press.

Keightley, D. N. 1996. "Warfare and Its Representation in Ancient China." Paper presented at the Annual Convention of the International Studies Association, San Diego, California, April 16–20.

Kellog, James C. n.d. "A Synopsis of Military Conflict 1945–1964." Unpublished paper, Bendix Systems Division, Arms Control Project Office, Ann Arbor, Michigan.

Kelly, David S. 1999. "The Genoese-Venetian Rivalry: Conceptual and Historical Issues." In *Great Power Rivalries,* ed. William R. Thompson. Columbia: University of South Carolina Press.

Kelman, Herbert C. 1965. "Social-Psychological Approaches to the Study of International Relations." In *International Behavior: A Social-Psychological Analysis,* ed. Herbert C. Kelman. New York: Holt, Rinehart.

Kemp, Anita. 1977. "A Path Analytic Model of International Violence." *International Interactions* 4:53–85.

Kende, Istvan. 1971. "Twenty-five Years of Local Wars." *Journal of Peace Research* 1:5–22.

Kende, Istvan. 1978. "Wars of Ten Years, 1967–1976." *Journal of Peace Research* 15:227–41.

Kennedy, Paul. 1982. *The Rise of the Anglo-German Antagonism, 1860–1914.* London: George Allen & Unwin.

Kennedy, Paul. 1984. "The First World War and the International Power System." *International Security* 9 (No. 1)(Summer). Reprinted in *Military Strategy and the Origins of the First World War,* ed. Steven E. Miller. Princeton: Princeton University Press, 1985.

Kennedy, Paul. 1987. *The Rise and Fall of the Great Powers.* New York: Random House.

Kennedy, Paul. 1988a. *The Rise and Fall of the Great Powers: Economic Change and Military Conflict from 1500 to 2000.* New York: Random House.

Kennedy, Paul. 1988b. "The End of Empire: Can We Decline as Gracefully as Great Britain?" *Washington Post,* Outlook section, 24 January.

Kennedy, Paul. 1990. "Fin-de-Siecle America." *New York Review of Books*, 28 June, 31–40.

Kenyon, K. M. 1960 and 1965. *Excavations at Jericho.* Vols. 1, 2. London: British School of Archaeology in Jerusalem.

Kenyon, K. M. 1979. *Archaeology in the Holy Land,* 4th ed. New York: W. W. Norton.

Keohane, Robert. 1980. "The Theory of Hegemonic Stability and Change in International Economic Regimes." In *Change in the International System,* ed. Ole R. Holsti, Randolph Siverson, and Alexander George. Boulder, CO: Westview Press.

Keohane, Robert. 1984. *After Hegemony: Cooperation and Discord in the World Political Economy.* Princeton: Princeton University Press.

Keohane, Robert. 1989. "Theory of World Politics: Structural Realism and Beyond." In *International Institutions and State Power: Essays in International Relations Theory.* Boulder, CO: Westview Press.

Keohane, Robert, and Joseph Nye Jr. 1977. *Power and Interdependence: World Politics in Transition.* Boston: Little, Brown.

Kierman, F. A. Jr., and J. K. Fairbank, eds. 1974. *Chinese Ways in Warfare.* Cambridge, MA: Harvard University Press.

Kilgour, D. Marc and Frank C. Zagare. 1991. "Credibility, Uncertainty, and Deterrence." *American Journal of Political Science* 35:305–34.

Kim, Soo Yeon. 1998. "Ties That Bind: The Role of Trade in International Conflict Processes, 1950–1992." Ph.D. diss., Yale University, New Haven, Connecticut.

Kim, Woosang. 1989. "Power, Alliance, and Major Wars, 1816–1975." *Journal of Conflict Resolution* 33:255–73.

Kim, Woosang. 1991. "Alliance Transitions and Great Power War." *American Journal of Political Science* 35:833–50.

Kim, Woosang. 1992. "Power Transitions and Great Power War from Westphalia to Waterloo." *World Politics* 45:153–72.

Kim, Woosang. 1996. "Power Parity, Alliance, and War from 1648 to 1975." In *Parity and War: Evaluations and Extensions of The War Ledger,* ed. Jacek Kugler and Douglas Lemke. Ann Arbor: University of Michigan Press.

Kim, Woosang, and James D. Morrow. 1992. "When Do Power Shifts Lead to War?" *American Journal of Political Science* 36:896–922.

Kindleberger, Charles P. 1996. *World Economic Primacy, 1500–1990.* New York: Oxford University Press.

King, Gary, Robert O. Keohane, and Sidney Verba. 1994. *Designing Social Inquiry: Scientific Inference in Qualitative Research.* Princeton: Princeton University Press.

Kinsella, David. 1994a. "Conflict in Context: Arms Transfers and Third World Rivalry during the Cold War." *American Journal of Political Science* 38:557–81.

Kinsella, David. 1994b. "The Impact of Superpower Arms Transfers on Conflict in the Middle East." *Defence and Peace Economics* 5:19–36.

Kinsella, David. 1995. "Nested Rivalries: Superpower Competition, Arms Transfers, and Regional Conflict, 1950–1990." *International Interactions* 15:109–25.

Kirby, Andrew, and Michael Ward. 1987. "The Spatial Analysis of War and Peace." *Comparative Political Studies* 20:293–313.

Kissinger, Henry. 1974. *American Foreign Policy.* New York: W. W. Norton.

Kissinger, Henry. 1994. *Diplomacy.* New York: Simon & Schuster.

Klingberg, Frank L. 1966. "Predicting the Termination of War: Battle Casualties and Population Losses." *Journal of Conflict Resolution* 10:129–71.

Knetsch, Jack L., and J. A. Sinden. 1984. "Willingness to Pay and Compensation Demanded: Experimental Evidence of an Unexpected Disparity in Measures of Value." *Quarterly Journal of Economics* 99:507–21.

Kocs, Stephen. 1995. "Territorial Disputes and Interstate War, 1945–1987." *Journal of Politics* 57:159–75.

Köhler, Gernot. 1975. "Imperialism as a Level of Analysis in Correlates of War Research." *Journal of Conflict Resolution* 19:48–62.

Kohn, Hans. 1967. *The Idea of Nationalism: A Study in its Origins and Background.* New York: Collier-Macmillan.

Koshar, Rudy J. 1994. "Building Pasts: Historic Preservation and Identity in Twentieth-Century Germany." In *Commemorations: The Politics of National Identity,* ed. John R. Gillis. Princeton: Princeton University Press.

Kowert, Paul A., and Margaret G. Hermann. 1997. "Who Takes Risks? Daring and Caution in Foreign Policy Making." *Journal of Conflict Resolution* 41:611–37.

Kozhemiakin, Alexander. 1998. *Expanding the Zone of Peace? Democratization and International Security.* Houndsmills: Macmillan.

Krain, Matthew. 1997. "State-Sponsored Mass Murder." *Journal of Conflict Resolution* 41:331–60.

Krain, Matthew, and Marissa Edson Myers. 1997. "Democracy and Civil War: A Note on the Democratic Peace Proposition." *International Interactions* 23:109–18.

Krasner, Stephen D. 1985. *Structural Conflict: The Third World against Global Liberalism.* Berkeley: University of California Press.

Kriesberg, Louis. 1992. *International Conflict Resolution: The US-USSR and Middle East Cases.* New Haven, CT: Yale University Press.

Kuenne, Robert. 1989. "Conflict Management in Mature Rivalry." *Journal of Conflict Resolution* 33:554–66.

Kugler, Jacek. 1984. "Terror without Deterrence." *Journal of Conflict Resolution* 28:470–506.

Kugler, Jacek. 1995. "Stable or Tenuous Deterrence between the Two Koreas?" *The Sejung Review* 3:113–46.

Kugler, Jacek. 1996. "Beyond Deterrence: Structural Conditions for a Lasting Peace." In *Parity and War,* ed. Jacek Kugler and Douglas Lemke. Ann Arbor: University of Michigan Press.

Kugler, Jacek. 1998. "The Policy Implications of Power Parity." *Conflict Management and Peace Science* 16:99–124.

Kugler, Jacek, and Marina Arbetman. 1989. "Exploring the Phoenix Factor with the Collective Goods Perspective." *Journal of Conflict Resolution* 33: 84–112.

Kugler, Jacek, Michelle Benson, Andy Hira, and Dimitry Panasevich. 1997. "Political Capacity and Violence." In *Political Capacity and Economic Behavior,* ed. Marina Arbetman and Jacek Kugler. Boulder, CO: Westview Press.

Kugler, Jacek, and Douglas Lemke. 1996. *Parity and War: Evaluations and Extensions of the War Ledger.* Ann Arbor: University of Michigan Press.

Kugler, Jacek, and A. F. K. Organski. 1989. "The Power Transition: A Retrospective and Prospective Evaluation." In *Handbook of War Studies,* ed. Manus I. Midlarsky. Boston: Unwin Hyman.

Kugler, Jacek, and Frank C. Zagare. 1990. "The Long Term Stability of Deterrence." *International Interactions* 15:113–28.

Kugler, Jacek, and Frank C. Zagare, eds. 1987. *Exploring the Stability of Deterrence.* Boulder, CO: Lynne Rienner.

Kumamoto, Robert. 1999. *International Terrorism and American Foreign Relations 1945–1976.* Boston: Northeastern University Press.

Kupchan, Charles A. 1994. *The Vulnerability of Empire.* Ithaca, NY: Cornell University Press.

Labs, Eric J. 1997. "Beyond Victory: Offensive Realism and the Expansion of War Aims." *Security Studies* 6:1–49.

Lahneman, William. 1999. "Assessing U.S. Power and Foreign Policy Role from the Power Cycle Perspective." Ph.D. diss., The Johns Hopkins University, SAIS, Baltimore, Maryland.

Lakatos, Imre. 1970. "Falsification and the Methodology of Scientific Research Programmes." In *Criticism and the Growth of Knowledge,* ed. Imre Lakatos and Alan Musgrave. Cambridge: Cambridge University Press.

Lakatos, Imre. 1978. *The Methodology of Scientific Research Programmes.* Cambridge: Cambridge University Press.

Lake, David A. 1992. "Powerful Pacifists: Democratic States and War." *American Political Science Review* 86:24–37.

Lake, David A., and Donald Rothchild. 1996. "Containing Fear: The Origins and Management of Ethnic Conflict." *International Security* 21 (2): 41–75.

Lakos, Amos. 1991. *Terrorism, 1980–1990: A Bibliography.* Boulder, CO: Westview Press.

Landes, David S. 1969. *The Unbound Prometheus: Technological Change and Industrial Development in Western Europe from 1750 to the Present.* Cambridge: Cambridge University Press.

Langer, William L. 1969. "The Origin of the Russo-Japanese War." In *Explorations in Crises,* ed. William L. Langer. Cambridge, MA: Harvard University/Belknap Press.

Lapan, Harvey E., and Todd Sandler. 1988. "To Bargain or Not to Bargain: That Is the Question." *AEA Papers and Proceedings* 78:16–21.

Laqueur, Walter. 1996. "Postmodern Terrorism." *Foreign Affairs* 75 (5): 24–36.

Laqueur, Walter. 1999. *The New Terrorism: Fanaticism and the Arms of Mass Destruction.* New York: Oxford University Press.

Larson, Deborah Welch. 1999. "The US-Soviet Rivalry." In *Great Power Rivalries,* ed. William R. Thompson. Columbia: University of South Carolina Press.

Laughhunn, Dan J., John W. Payne, and Roy Crum. 1980. "Managerial Risk Preferences for Below-Target Returns." *Management Science* 26:1238–49.

Lave, Charles A., and James G. March. 1975. *An Introduction to Models in the Social Sciences.* New York: Harper and Row.

Layne, Christopher. 1994. "Kant or Cant: The Myth of the Democratic Peace." *International Security* 19 (2): 5–49.

LeBlanc, Steven A. 1999. *Prehistoric Warfare in the American Southwest.* Salt Lake City, UT: University of Utah Press.

Leblang, David. 1997. "Political Democracy and Economic Growth: Pooled Cross-Sectional and Time Series Evidence." *British Journal of Political Science* 27:453–72.

Lebow, R. Ned. 1981. *Between Peace and War: The Nature of International Crisis.* Baltimore: Johns Hopkins University Press.

Lebow, R. Ned. 1987. *Nuclear Crisis Management: A Dangerous Illusion.* Ithaca, NY: Cornell University Press.

Lebow, Richard Ned. 1994a. "The Long Peace, the End of the Cold War, and the Failure of Realism." *International Organization* 48:249–277.

Lebow, Richard Ned. 1994b. "The Search for Accommodation: Gorbachev in Comparative Perspective." In *International Relations Theory and the End of the Cold War,* ed. Richard Ned Lebow and Thomas Risse-Kappen. New York: Columbia University Press.

Lebow, Richard Ned. 1997. "Transitions and Transformations: Building International Cooperation." *Security Studies* 6:154–79.

Lebow, Richard Ned, and Janice Gross Stein. 1987. "Beyond Deterrence." *Journal of Social Issues* 43:5–71.

Lebow, Richard Ned, and Janice Gross Stein. 1990. "Deterrence: The Elusive Dependent Variable." *World Politics* 42:336–69.

Lee, Dwight R. 1988. "Free Riding and Paid Riding in the Fight against Terrorism." *AEA Papers and Proceedings* 78:22–26.

Lee, Dwight R., and Todd Sandler. 1989. "On the Optimal Retaliation against Terrorists: The Paid-Rider Option." *Public Choice* 61:141–52.

Leeds, Brett Ashley, and David R. Davis. 1997. "Domestic Political Vulnerability and International Disputes." *Journal of Conflict Resolution* 41:814–34.

Leeds, Brett Ashley, and David R. Davis. 1999. "Beneath the Surface: Regime Type and International Interaction, 1953–78." *Journal of Peace Research* 36:5–22.

Leege, D. C., and W. L. Francis. 1974. *Political Research.* New York: Basic Books.

Leiss, Amelia C., Lincoln P. Bloomfield, et al. 1967. *The Control of Local Conflict: A Design for Arms Control and Limited War in the Developing Areas.* Cambridge, MA: Center for International Studies, MIT.

Lemke, Douglas. 1993. "Multiple Hierarchies in World Politics." Ph.D. diss., Vanderbilt University, Nashville, Tennessee.

Lemke, Douglas. 1995a. "The Tyranny of Distance: Redefining Relevant Dyads." *International Interactions* 21:23–38.

Lemke, Douglas. 1995b. "Toward a General Understanding of Parity and War." *Conflict Management and Peace Science* 14:143–62.

Lemke, Douglas. 1995c. "Peace and War in the Middle East: An Application of the Multiple Hierarchy Model." Paper presented at the Annual Meeting of the Peace Science Society.

Lemke, Douglas. 1996. "Small States and War." In *Parity and War: Evaluations and Extensions of "The War Ledger,"* ed. Jacek Kugler and Douglas Lemke. Ann Arbor: University of Michigan Press.

Lemke, Douglas. 1997a. "The Continuation of History: Power Transition Theory and the End of the Cold War." *Journal of Peace Research* 34:23–36.

Lemke, Douglas. 1997b. "Peace and War in the Far East: An Application of the Multiple Hierarchy Model." Paper presented at the Annual Convention of the International Studies Association, Toronto, Ontario, March 18–22.

Lemke, Douglas. 2000. *Regions of War and Peace,* unpublished manuscript.

Lemke, Douglas, and Jacek Kugler. 1996. "The Evolution of the Power Transition Perspective." In *Parity and War: Evaluations and Extensions of The War Ledger,* ed. Jacek Kugler and Douglas Lemke. Ann Arbor: University of Michigan Press.

Lemke, Douglas, and William Reed. 1996. "Regime Types and Status Quo Evaluations: Power Transition Theory and the Democratic Peace." *International Interactions* 22:143–64.

Lemke, Douglas, and William Reed. 1998. "Power Is Not Satisfaction." *Journal of Conflict Resolution* 42:511–16.

Lemke, Douglas, and Suzanne Werner. 1996. "Power Parity, Commitment to Change, and War." *International Studies Quarterly* 40:235–60.

Leng, Russell J. 1980. "Influence Strategies and Interstate Conflict." In *The Correlates of War II, Testing Some Realpolitik Models,* ed. David Singer. New York: The Free Press.

Leng, Russell J. 1983. "When Will They Ever Learn? Coercive Bargaining in Recurrent Crises." *Journal of Conflict Resolution* 27:379–419.

Leng, Russell J. 1984. "Reagan and the Russians: Crisis Bargaining Beliefs and the Historical Record." *American Political Science Review* 78:338–55.

Leng, Russell J. 1993a. *Interstate Crisis Behavior, 1816–1980: Realism versus Reciprocity.* Cambridge: Cambridge University Press.

Leng, Russell J. 1993b. "Reciprocating Influence Strategies in Interstate Crisis Bargaining." *Journal of Conflict Resolution* 37:3–41.

Lenin, V. I. 1939. *Imperialism: The Highest Stage of Capitalism.* New York: International Publishers (first published in 1917).

Lepgold, Joseph. 1998. "Hypotheses on Vulnerability: Are Terrorists and Drug Traffickers Coerceable?" In *Strategic Coercion: Concepts and Cases,* ed. Lawrence Freedman. Oxford: Oxford University Press.

Lesser, Ian O. 1999. "Countering the New Terrorism: Implications for Strategy." In *Countering the New Terrorism,* ed. Ian O. Lesser, Bruce Hoffman, John Arquilla, David Ronfeldt, and Michele Zanini. Santa Monica, CA: Rand.

Lesser, Ian O., Bruce Hoffman, John Arquilla, David Ronfeldt, and Michele Zanini. 1999. *Countering the New Terrorism.* Santa Monica, CA: Rand.

Levi, Ariel S., and Glen Whyte. 1997. "A Cross-Cultural Exploration of the Reference Dependence of Crucial Group Decisions under Risk." *Journal of Conflict Resolution* 41:792–813.

Levitt, Geoffrey M. 1988. *Democracies against Terror: The Western Response to State-Supported Terrorism.* The Washington Papers No. 134, Center for Strategic and International Studies. New York: Praeger.

Levy, Jack S. 1981. "Alliance Formation and War Behavior: An Analysis of the Great Powers, 1495–1975." *Journal of Conflict Resolution* 25:581–613.

Levy, Jack S. 1982. "The Contagion of Great Power War Behavior, 1945–1975." *American Journal of Political Science* 26:562–84.

Levy, Jack S. 1983. *War in the Modern Great Power System, 1495–1975.* Lexington: University Press of Kentucky.

Levy, Jack S. 1984. "Size and Stability in the Modern Great Power System." *International Interactions* 11:341–58.

Levy, Jack S. 1985a. "The Polarity of the System and International Stability: An Empirical Analysis." In *Polarity and War,* ed. A. Ned Sabrosky. Boulder, CO: Westview Press.

Levy, Jack S. 1985b. "Theories of General War." *World Politics* 37:344–74.

Levy, Jack S. 1987. "Declining Power and the Preventive Motivation for War." *World Politics* 40:82–107.

Levy, Jack S. 1988. "Domestic Politics and War." *Journal of Interdisciplinary History* 18:653–73.

Levy, Jack S. 1989a. "The Causes of War: A Review of Theories and Evidence." In *Behavior, Society, and Nuclear War.* Vol. 1, ed. Philip E. Tetlock, Jo L. Husbands, Robert Jervis, Paul C. Stern, and Charles Tilly. New York: Oxford University Press.

Levy, Jack S. 1989b. "The Diversionary Theory of War: A Critique." In *Handbook of War Studies,* ed. Manus I. Midlarsky. Boston: Unwin Hyman.

Levy, Jack S. 1991. "Long Cycles, Hegemonic Transitions and the Long Peace." In *The Long Postwar Peace,* ed. Charles W. Kegley Jr. New York: HarperCollins.

Levy, Jack S. 1992a. "An Introduction to Prospect Theory." *Political Psychology* 13:171–86.

Levy, Jack S. 1992b. "Prospect Theory and International Relations: Theoretical Applications and Analytical Problems." *Political Psychology* 13:283–310.

Levy, Jack S. 1994a. "The Democratic Peace Hypothesis: From Description to Explanation." *Mershon International Studies Review* 38 (Supplement 2): 352–54.

Levy, Jack S. 1994b. "Learning and Foreign Policy: Sweeping a Conceptual Minefield." *International Organization* 48:279–312.

Levy, Jack S. 1996a. "Loss Aversion, Framing, and Bargaining: The Implications of Prospect Theory for International Conflict." *International Political Science Review* 17:177–93.

Levy, Jack S. 1996b. "Hypotheses on the Framing of Decisions." Paper presented at the Annual Convention of the *International Studies Association,* San Diego, California, April 16–20.

Levy, Jack S. 1997. "Prospect Theory, Rational Choice, and International Relations." *International Studies Quarterly* 41:87–112.

Levy, Jack S. 1998. "The Causes of War and the Conditions of Peace." *Annual Review of Political Science* 1:139–66.

Levy, Jack S. 1999. "Economic Competition, Domestic Politics, and System Change: The Rise and Decline of the Anglo-Dutch Rivalry, 1609–1688." In *Great Power Rivalries,* ed. William R. Thompson. Columbia: University of South Carolina Press.

Levy, Jack S., and Salvatore Ali. 1998. "From Commercial Competition to Strategic Rivalry to War: The Evolution of the Anglo-Dutch Rivalry, 1609–1652." In *The Dynamics of Enduring Rivalries,* ed. Paul F. Diehl. Urbana: University of Illinois Press.

Levy, Jack S., and Rick Collis. 1985. "Power Cycle Theory and the Preventive War Motivation: A Preliminary Empirical Investigation." Paper presented at the Annual Meeting of the American Political Science Association, New Orleans, Louisiana, August.

Levy, Jack S., and T. Clifton Morgan. 1986. "The War-Weariness Hypothesis: An Empirical Test." *American Journal of Political Science* 30:26–49.

Levy, Jack S., and Lily I. Vakili. 1992. "Diversionary Action by Authoritarian Regimes: Argentina in the Falklands/Malvinas Case." In *The Internationalization of Communal Strife,* ed. Manus I. Midlarsky. London: Routledge.

Levy, T. E., ed. 1995. *The Archaeology of Society in the Holy Land.* New York: Facts on File.

Lewis, Bernard. 1987. "Introduction." In *Islam, From the Prophet Muhammad to the Capture of Constantinople, Vol. 1: Politics and War,* ed. and trans. Bernard Lewis. New York: Oxford University Press.

Lewis, Bernard. 1993. *Islam and the West.* New York: Oxford University Press.

Li, Richard P. Y., and William R. Thompson. 1975. "The 'Coup Contagion' Hypothesis." *Journal of Conflict Resolution* 19:63–88.

Lian, Bradley, and John Oneal. 1993. "Presidents, the Use of Military Force, and Public Opinion." *Journal of Conflict Resolution* 37:277–300.

Lieberman, Elli. 1994. "The Rational Deterrence Theory Debate: Is the Dependent Variable Elusive?" *Security Studies* 3:384–427.

Lieberman, Elli. 1995. "What Makes Deterrence Work? Lessons from the Egyptian-Israeli Enduring Rivalry." *Security Studies* 4:851–910.

Lieberson, Stanley, and Arnold L. Silverman. 1965. "The Precipitants and Underlying Conditions of Race Riots." *American Sociological Review* 30: 887–89.

Lindley, Dan. 1996. "Collective Security Organizations and Internal Conflict." In *The International Dimensions of Internal Conflict,* ed. Michael E. Brown. Cambridge, MA: MIT Press.

Lippmann, Walter. 1943. *An Inquiry into the Principles of the Good Society.* Boston: Little, Brown.

Lipset, Seymour M. 1959. "Some Social Requisites of Democracy: Economic Development and Political Legitimacy." *American Political Science Review* 53:69–105.

Liska, George. 1968. *War and Order.* Baltimore: Johns Hopkins University Press.

Littauer, M. A., and J. H. Crouwel. 1979. *Wheeled Vehicles and Ridden Animals in the Ancient Near East.* Leiden, Netherlands: E. J. Brill.

Liu, L. 1996. "Settlement Patterns, Chiefdom Variability, and the Development of Early States in North China." *Journal of Anthropological Archaeology* 15:237–88.

Liverani, M. 1988. *Antico Oriente.* Rome: Editori Laterza.

Loehr, M. 1956. *Chinese Bronze Age Weapons.* Ann Arbor: University of Michigan Press.

Luard, Evan. 1987. *War in International Society.* New Haven, CT: Yale University Press.

Lucas, R. 1988. "On the Mechanics of Economic Development." *Journal of Monetary Economics* 21:3–32.

Lustick, Ian S. 1988. *For the Land and the Lord: Jewish Fundamentalism in Israel.* New York: Council on Foreign Relations.

Lustick, Ian S. 1995. "Terrorism in the Arab-Israeli Conflict: Targets and Audiences." *Terrorism in Context,* ed. Martha Crenshaw. University Park: Pennsylvania State University Press.

Lynn, John A. 1999. *The Wars of Louis XIV, 1667–1714.* London: Longman.

MacMillan, John. 1998. *On Liberal Peace: Democracy, War, and the International Order.* London: Tauris.

Mandel, Robert. 1980. "Roots of the Modern Interstate Border Dispute." *Journal of Conflict Resolution* 24:427–54.

Mani, V. S. 1995. "Bilateral Cooperation in Containing Terrorism: Extradition Arrangements." *International Studies* 21:139–50.

Mansbach, Richard W., and John A. Vasquez. 1981. *In Search of Theory: A New Paradigm for Global Politics.* New York: Columbia University Press.

Mansfield, Edward D. 1988. "Distributions of War Over Time." *World Politics* 41:21–51.

Mansfield, Edward D. 1992. "The Concentration of Capabilities and the Onset of Wars." *Journal of Conflict Resolution* 36:3–24.

Mansfield, Edward D. 1993. "Concentration, Polarity, and the Distribution of Power." *International Studies Quarterly* 37:105–28.

Mansfield, Edward D. 1994. *Power, Trade and War.* Princeton: Princeton University Press.

Mansfield, Edward D., Helen Milner, and B. Peter Rosendorff. 1998. "Why Democracies Cooperate More: Electoral Control and International Trade Agreements." Paper presented at the Annual Meeting of the American Political Science Association, Boston, Massachusetts, September 3–6.

Mansfield, Edward D., and Jack Snyder. 1995. "Democratization and the Danger of War." *International Security* 20 (1): 5–38.

Mansfield, Edward D., and Jack Snyder. 1996. "The Effects of Democratization on War." *International Security* 20 (4): 196–207.

Mansfield, Edward D., and Jack Snyder. 1997. "A Reply to Thompson and Tucker." *Journal of Conflict Resolution* 41:457–61.

Maoz, Zeev. 1982. *Paths to Conflict: International Dispute Initiation, 1816–1976.* Boulder, CO: Westview Press.

Maoz, Zeev. 1983. "Resolve, Capabilities, and the Outcomes of Interstate Disputes, 1816–1976." *Journal of Conflict Resolution* 27:195–230.

Maoz, Zeev. 1989. "Joining the Club of Nations: Political Development and International Conflict, 1816–1976." *International Studies Quarterly* 33: 199–231.

Maoz, Zeev. 1990. "Framing the National Interest: The Manipulation of Foreign Policy Decisions in Group Settings." *World Politics* 43:77–110.

Maoz, Zeev. 1993. "The Onset and Initiation of Disputes." *International Interactions* 19:27–47.

Maoz, Zeev. 1996. *Domestic Sources of Global Change.* Ann Arbor: University of Michigan Press.

Maoz, Zeev. 1997a. "The Controversy over the Democratic Peace: Rearguard Action or Cracks in the Wall?" *International Security* 22 (1): 162–98.

Maoz, Zeev. 1997b. "Domestic Political Change and Strategic Response: The Impact of Domestic Conflict on State Behavior, 1816–1986." In *Wars in the Midst of Peace: The International Politics of Ethnic Conflict,* ed. David Carment and Patrick James. Pittsburgh: University of Pittsburgh Press.

Maoz, Zeev. 1998. "Realist and Cultural Critiques of the Democratic Peace: A Theoretical and Empirical Re-Assessment." *International Interactions* 24:3–89.

Maoz, Zeev, and Nasrin Abdolali. 1989. "Regime Types and International Conflict, 1816–1976." *Journal of Conflict Resolution* 33:3–35.

Maoz, Zeev, and Ben Mor. 1996. "Enduring Rivalries: The Early Years." *International Political Science Review* 17:141–60.

Maoz, Zeev, and Ben Mor. 1998. "Learning, Preference Change, and the Evolution of Enduring Rivalries." In *The Dynamics of Enduring Rivalries*, ed. Paul F. Diehl. Urbana: University of Illinois Press.

Maoz, Zeev, and Bruce Russett. 1992. "Alliances, Wealth, Contiguity, and Political Stability: Is the Lack of Conflict between Democracies a Statistical Artifact?" *International Interaction* 17:245–67.

Maoz, Zeev, and Bruce Russett. 1993. "Normative and Structural Causes of Democratic Peace, 1946–1986." *American Political Science Review* 87:624–38.

March, James G., and Zur Shapira. 1987. "Managerial Perspectives on Risk and Risk-Taking." In *Decisions and Organizations,* ed. James G. March. New York: Basil Blackwell.

Marcus, J. 1983. "Aztec Military Campaigns against the Zapotecs." In *The Cloud People,* ed. K. V. Flannery and J. Marcus. New York: Academic Press.

Marcus, J. 1989. "Zapotec Chiefdoms and the Nature of Formative Religions." In *Regional Perspectives on the Olmec,* ed. R. J. Sharer and D. C. Grove. New York: Cambridge University Press.

Marcus, J. 1992a. "Dynamic Cycles of Mesoamerican States." *National Geographic Research and Exploration* 8:392–411.

Marcus, J. 1992b. *Mesoamerican Writing Systems.* Princeton: Princeton University Press.

Marcus, J. 1994. "Introduction." In *Tribal and Chiefly Warfare in South America,* ed. E. M. Redmond. Memoirs of the Museum of Anthropology, University of Michigan, Ann Arbor.

Marcus, J., and K. V. Flannery. 1996. *Zapotec Civilization.* London: Thames and Hudson.

Marshall, J. D., Jack L. Knetsch, and J. A. Sinden. 1986. "Agents' Evaluations and the Disparity in Measures of Economic Loss." *Journal of Economic Behavior and Organization* 7:115–27.

Mazar, A. 1992. *Archaeology of the Land of the Bible.* New York: Doubleday.

McDermott, Rose. 1998. *Risk-Taking in International Politics: Prospect Theory in American Foreign Policy.* Ann Arbor: University of Michigan Press.

McGinnis, Michael. 1990. "A Rational Model of Regional Rivalry." *International Studies Quarterly* 34:111–35.

McGinnis, Michael, and John Williams. 1989. "Change and Stability in Superpower Rivalry." *American Political Science Review* 83:1101–23.

McGowan, Patrick J. 1985. "Pitfalls and Promise in the Quantitative Study of the World-System: A Reanalysis of Bergesen and Schoenberg's 'Long Waves' of Colonialism." *Review* 8:177–200.

McGowan, Patrick J. 1989. "State-agents, International Structures, and Foreign Policy Behavior." *International Affairs Bulletin* (Johannesburg).

McMillan, Susan M. 1997. "Interdependence and Conflict." *Mershon International Studies Review* 41 (Supplement 1): 33–58.

Mead, Margaret. 1940. "Warfare Is Only an Invention—Not a Biological Necessity." *Asia* 40:402–5.

Mearsheimer, John J. 1990. "Back to the Future: Instability in Europe after the Cold War." *International Security* 15 (1): 5–56.

Meernik, James. 1994. "Presidential Decision Making and the Political Use of Force." *International Studies Quarterly* 38:121–38.

Meernik, James. 1996. "United States Military Intervention and the Promotion of Democracy." *Journal of Peace Research* 33:391–402.

Meernik, James, and Peter Waterman. 1996. "The Myth of the Diversionary Use of Force by American Presidents." *Political Research Quarterly* 49:573–90.

Meinecke, Friedrich. 1970. *Cosmopolitanism and the National State.* Princeton, NJ: Princeton University Press.

Mellaart, J. 1960. "Excavations at Haçilar." *Anatolian Studies* 10:83–104.

Merari, Ariel. 1998. "Attacks on Civil Aviation: Trends and Lessons." *Terrorism and Political Violence* 10:9–26.

Merritt, Richard L., and Dina A. Zinnes. 1989. "Democracies and War." In *Measuring Democracy: Its Consequences and Concomitants,* ed. Alex Inkeles. New Brunswick, NJ: Transaction.

Mickolus, Edward F. 1989. "What Constitutes State Support to Terrorists?" *Terrorism and Political Violence* 1:287–93.

Mickolus, Edward F., with Susan L. Simmons. 1997. *Terrorism, 1992–1995: A Chronology of Events and a Selective Annotated Bibliography.* Westport, CT: Greenwood.

Midlarsky, Manus I. 1969. "Status Inconsistency and the Onset of International Warfare." Ph.D. diss., Northwestern University, Evanston, Illinois.

Midlarsky, Manus I. 1970. "Mathematical Models of Instability and a Theory of Diffusion." *International Studies Quarterly* 14:60–84.

Midlarsky, Manus I. 1975. *On War: Political Violence in the International System.* New York: The Free Press.

Midlarsky, Manus I. 1978. "Analyzing Diffusion and Contagion Effects: The Urban Disorders of the 1960s." *American Political Science Review* 72:996–1008.

Midlarsky, Manus I. 1983. "Alliance Behavior and the Approach of World War I: The Use of Bivariate Negative Binomial Distributions." In *Conflict Processes and the Breakdown of International Systems,* ed. Dina Zinnes. University of Denver Monograph Series in World Affairs, Vol. 20, 61–80.

Midlarsky, Manus I. 1984. "Preventing Systemic War: Crisis Decision-Making Amidst a Structure of Conflict Relationships." *Journal of Conflict Resolution* 28:563–84.

Midlarsky, Manus I. 1986. "A Hierarchical Equilibrium Theory of Systemic War." *International Studies Quarterly* 30:77–105.

Midlarsky, Manus I. 1988a. "Rulers and the Ruled: Patterned Inequality and the Onset of Mass Political Violence." *American Political Science Review* 82:491–509.

Midlarsky, Manus I. 1988b. *The Onset of World War.* Boston: Unwin Hyman.

Midlarsky, Manus I. 1989a. "Hierarchical Equilibria and the Long-Run Instability of Multipolar Systems." In *Handbook of War Studies,* ed. Manus I. Midlarsky. Boston: Unwin Hyman.

Midlarsky, Manus I. 1992a. "Communal Strife and the Origins of World War I." In *The Internationalization of Communal Strife,* ed. Manus I. Midlarsky. New York: Routledge.

Midlarsky, Manus I. 1992b. "Reversing the Causal Arrow: Domestic and International Sources of Early Democracy." Paper presented at the Annual Meeting at the American Political Science Association, Chicago, Illinois, September 3–6.

Midlarsky, Manus I. 1992c. "The Origins of Democracy in Agrarian Society: Land Inequality and Political Rights." *Journal of Conflict Resolution* 36: 454–77.

Midlarsky, Manus I. 1995. "Environmental Influences on Democracy: Aridity, Warfare, and a Reversal of the Causal Arrow." *Journal of Conflict Resolution* 39:224–62.

Midlarsky, Manus I. 1996. "Analyzing Political Conflict." *Journal of Politics* 58:863–69.

Midlarsky, Manus I. 1997a. "Systemic War in the Former Yugoslavia." In *Wars in the Midst of Peace: The International Politics of Ethnic Conflict,* ed. David Carment and Patrick James. Pittsburgh: University of Pittsburgh Press.

Midlarsky, Manus I. 1998a. "Causes of Conflict: The Socioeconomic Dimension," *Proceedings of Seminar on Intrastate Conflict and Options for Policy,* Ministry of Foreign Affairs, The Hague, November 16–17.

Midlarsky, Manus I. 1998b. "Democracy and the Environment: An Empirical Assessment." *Journal of Peace Research* 35:341–62.

Midlarsky, Manus I. 1998c. "Democracy and Islam: Implications for Civilizational Conflict and the Democratic Peace." *International Studies Quarterly* 42:485–512.

Midlarsky, Manus I. 1999. *The Evolution of Inequality: War, State Survival, and Democracy in Comparative Perspective.* Stanford: Stanford University Press.

Midlarsky, Manus I. 2000. "Mature Theories, Second Order Properties, and Other Matters." In *What Do We Know about War,* ed. John A. Vasquez. Lanham, MD: Rowman & Littlefield.

Midlarsky, Manus I., ed. 1989b. *Handbook of War Studies.* Boston: Unwin Hyman. Reprint, Ann Arbor: University of Michigan Press, 1993.

Midlarsky, Manus I., ed. 1992d. *The Internationalization of Communal Strife.* London: Routledge.

Midlarsky, Manus I., ed. 1997b. *Inequality, Democracy, and Economic Development.* Cambridge: Cambridge University Press.

Midlarsky, Manus I., and Myron J. Aronoff. 1999. "Security Dilemmas: Changes in State Security and the Onset of Political Violence." Paper presented at the 40th Annual Convention of the International Studies Association, Washington, DC, February 16–20.

Midlarsky, Manus I., Martha Crenshaw, and Fumihiko Yoshida. 1980. "Why Violence Spreads: The Contagion of International Terrorism." *International Studies Quarterly* 24:262–98.

Midlarsky, Manus I., and Ted Hopf. 1993. "Polarity and International Stability." *American Political Science Review* 87:173–79.

Mihalka, Michael. 1976. "Hostilities in the European State System, 1816–1970." *Peace Science Society Papers* 26:100–116.

Miller, Abraham H. 1994. "Comment on 'Terrorism and Democracy.'" *Terrorism and Political Violence* 6:435–39.

Miller, M. 1986. *The Murals of Bonampak.* Princeton: Princeton University Press.

Miller, M., E. Ferorelli, and D. Stern. 1995. "Maya Masterpiece Revealed at Bonampak." *National Geographic* 187:50–69.

Miller, Reuben. 1986. "Acts of International Terrorism: Governments' Responses and Policies." *Comparative Political Studies* 19:385–414.

Miller, Ross A. 1995. "Democratic Structures and the Diversionary Use of Force." *American Journal of Political Science* 39:760–85.

Miller, Ross A. 1999. "Regime Type, Strategic Initiation, and the Diversionary Use of Force." *Journal of Conflict Resolution* 43:388–402.

Mintz, Alex, and Nehemia Geva. 1993. "Why Don't Democracies Fight Each Other? An Experimental Study." *Journal of Conflict Resolution* 37:484–503.

Mishra, Pankaj. 1998. "A New, Nuclear, India?" *New York Review of Books* 45 (11): 55–64.

Mitchell, Christopher R., and K. Webb, eds. 1988. *New Approaches to International Mediation.* Westport, CT: Greenwood Press.

Mitchell, Sara McLauglin, and Brandon Prins. 1999. "Beyond Territorial Contiguity: Issues at Stake in Democratic Militarized Disputes." *International Studies Quarterly* 43:169–83.

Mitchell, Sara McLauglin, Scott Gates, and Havard Hegre. 1999. "Evolution in Democracy-War Dynamics. *Journal of Conflict Resolution* 43:771–92.

Modelski, George. 1972. *Principles of World Politics.* New York: The Free Press.

Modelski, George. 1978. "The Long Cycle of Global Politics and Nation State." *Comparative Studies in Society and History* 20:214–35.

Modelski, George. 1981. "Long Cycles, Kondratieffs and Alternating Innovations: Implications for U.S. Foreign Policy." In *The Political Economy of Foreign Policy Behavior,* ed. Charles W. Kegley Jr. and Patrick J. McGowan. Beverly Hills, CA: Sage.

Modelski, George. 1982. "Long Cycles and the Strategy of U.S. International Political Economy." In *America in a Changing World Political Economy,* ed. William Avery and David P. Rapkin. New York: Longman.

Modelski, George. 1983a. "Of Global Politics, Portugal, and Kindred Issues: A Rejoinder." In *Contending Approaches to World System Analysis,* ed. William R. Thompson. Beverly Hills, CA: Sage.

Modelski, George. 1983b. "Long Cycles of World Leadership." In *Contending Approaches to World System Analysis,* ed. William R. Thompson. Beverly Hills, CA: Sage.

Modelski, George. 1987. *Long Cycles in World Politics.* Seattle: University of Washington Press.

Modelski, George. 1990. "Is World Politics Evolutionary Learning?" *International Organization* 44:1–24.

Modelski, George. 1996. "Evolutionary Paradigm for Global Politics." *International Studies Quarterly* 40:321–42.

Modelski, George. 1999. "Enduring Rivalry in the Democratic Lineage: The Venice-Portugal Case." In *Great Power Rivalries,* ed. William R. Thompson. Columbia: University of South Carolina Press.

Modelski, George, and Sylvia Modelski. 1988. *Documenting Global Leadership.* London: Macmillan.

Modelski, George, and Patrick Morgan. 1985. "Understanding Global War." *Journal of Conflict Resolution* 29:371–419.

Modelski, George, and G. Perry. 1991. "Democratization in Long Perspective." *Technological Forecasting and Social Change* 39:23–34.

Modelski, George, and William R. Thompson. 1987. "Testing Cobweb Models of the Long Cycle." In *Exploring Long Cycles,* ed. George Modelski. Boulder, CO: Lynne Rienner.

Modelski, George, and William R. Thompson. 1988. *Seapower and Global Politics, 1494–1993.* London: Macmillan.

Modelski, George, and William R. Thompson. 1989. "Long Cycles and Global Wars." In *Handbook of War Studies,* ed. Manus I. Midlarsky. Boston: Unwin Hyman.

Modelski, George, and William R. Thompson. 1996. *Leading Sectors and World Powers: The Coevolution of Global Economics and Politics.* Columbia: University of South Carolina Press.

Modelski, George, and William R. Thompson. 1999a. "The Short and Long of Global Politics in the Twenty-first Century: An Evolutionary Approach." *International Studies Review* 1 (Summer): 109–40.

Modelski, George, and William R. Thompson. 1999b. "Pulsations in the World System: Hinterland-to-Center Incursions and Migrations, 4000 BC to 1500 AD." In *Leadership, Product and Exchange: World Systems Theory and Anthropology,* ed. Nicholas Kardulias. Lanham, MD: Rowman and Littlefield.

Molleson, T. 1991. "Cuts on Human Bones Produced by Metal Implements." *Anthropologie* 29:199–204.

Moon, J. Donald. 1975. "The Logic of Political Inquiry: A Synthesis of Opposed Perspectives." In *The Handbook of Political Science.* Vol. 1, ed. Nelson W. Polsby and Fred I. Greenstein. Reading, MA: Addison-Wesley.

Moore, Geoffrey H. 1986. *Business Cycles, Inflation, and Forecasting,* 2nd ed. National Bureau of Economic Research Studies in Business Cycles, no. 24. Cambridge, MA: Ballinger.

Moore, Will H. and David R. Davis. 1998. "Transnational Ethnic Ties and Foreign Policy." In *The International Spread of Ethnic Conflict: Fear, Diffusion, and Escalation,* ed. David A. Lake and Donald Rothchild. Princeton: Princeton University Press.

Moorey, P. R. S. 1986. "The Emergence of the Light, Horse-Drawn Chariot in the Near East, ca. 2000 to 1500 B.C." *World Archaeology* 18:196–215.

Moravcsik, Andrew. 1997. "Taking Preferences Seriously: A Positive Liberal Theory of International Politics." *International Organization* 23:513–53.

Morgan, T. Clifton. 1993. "Democracy and War: Reflections on the Literature." *International Interactions* 18:197–203.

Morgan, T. Clifton. 1994. *Untying the Knot of War.* Ann Arbor: University of Michigan Press.

Morgan, T. Clifton, and Sally Howard Campbell. 1991. "Domestic Structure, Decisional Constraints, and War: So Why Kant Democracies Fight?" *Journal of Conflict Resolution* 35:187–211.

Morgan, T. Clifton, and Valerie L. Schwebach. 1992. "Take Two Democracies and Call Me in the Morning: A Prescription for Peace?" *International Interactions* 17:305–20.

Morgan, T. Clifton, and Rick K. Wilson. 1989. "The Spatial Model of Crisis Bargaining: An Experimental Test." Paper presented at the Annual Convention of the International Studies Association, London, March 28–April 1.

Morgenthau, Hans J. [1948] 1967. *Politics among Nations: The Struggle for Power and Peace,* 4th ed. New York: Knopf.

Morgenthau, Hans J. 1960. *Politics among Nations: The Struggle for Power and Peace,* 3rd ed. New York: Knopf.

Morgenthau, Hans J. 1973. *Politics among Nations,* 5th ed. New York: Knopf. (First ed. 1948).

Morrow, James D. 1988. "Social Choice and System Structure in World Politics." *World Politics* 41:75–97.

Morrow, James D. 1989. "Capabilities, Uncertainty, and Resolve: A Limited Information Model of Crisis Bargaining." *American Journal of Political Science* 33:941–72.

Morrow, James D. 1994. *Game Theory for Political Scientists.* Princeton: Princeton University Press.

Morrow, James D. 1997. "A Rational Choice Approach to International Conflict." In *Decision-Making on War and Peace: The Cognitive-Rational Debate,* ed. Nehemia Geva and Alex Mintz. Boulder, CO: Lynne Rienner.

Morrow, James D. 1999. "The Strategic Setting of Choices: Signaling, Commitment, and Negotiation in International Politics." In *Strategic Choice and*

International Relations, ed. David A. Lake and Robert Powell. Princeton: Princeton University Press.

Morrow, James D., Randolph Siverson, and Tressa Tabares. 1998. "The Political Determinants of International Trade: The Major Powers 1907–90." *American Political Science Review* 92:649–61.

Most, Benjamin A., and Harvey Starr. 1980. "Diffusion, Reinforcement, Geopolitics and the Spread of War." *American Political Science Review* 74:932–46.

Most, Benjamin A., and Harvey Starr. 1989. *Inquiry, Logic, and International Politics.* Columbia: University of South Carolina Press.

Most, Benjamin A., Harvey Starr, and Randolph Siverson. 1989. "The Logic and Study of the Diffusion of International Conflict." In *Handbook of War Studies,* ed. Manus I. Midlarsky. Boston: Unwin Hyman.

Moul, William B. 1985. "Balances of Power and European Great Power War, 1815–1939: A Suggestion and Some Evidence." *Canadian Journal of Political Science* 43:481–528.

Moul, William B. 1988. "Balance of Power and the Escalation of Serious Disputes among European Great Powers, 1815–1939: Some Evidence." *American Journal of Political Science* 32:241–75.

Mousseau, Michael. 1997. "Democracy and Militarized Interstate Collaboration." *Journal of Peace Research* 34:73–87.

Mousseau, Michael. 1998. "Democracy and Compromise in Militarized Interstate Conflicts, 1816–1992." *Journal of Conflict Resolution* 42:210–30.

Mowat, Charles L., ed. 1968. *Shifting Balance of World Forces 1898–1945.* Cambridge: Cambridge University Press.

Moynihan, Daniel P. 1993. *Pandaemonium: Ethnicity in International Politics.* New York: Oxford University Press.

Mueller, John E. 1973. *War, Presidents, and Public Opinion.* New York: Wiley.

Muller, Edward N., and Erich Weede. 1990. "Cross National Variation in Political Violence: A Rational Action Approach." *Journal of Conflict Resolution* 34:624–51.

Muncaster, Robert, and Dina Zinnes. 1993. "The Phenomenology of Enduring Rivalries." Paper presented at the Workshop on Processes of Enduring Rivalries, Bloomington, Indiana, April.

Nacos, Brigitte L. 1994. *Terrorism and the Media: From the Iran Hostage Crisis to the World Trade Center Bombing.* New York: Columbia University Press.

Nau, Henry R. 1990. *The Myth of America's Decline: Leading the World Economy into the 1990s.* Oxford: Oxford University Press.

Neale, Margaret A., and Max H. Bazerman. 1985. "The Effects of Framing and Negotiator Overconfidence on Bargaining Behaviors and Outcomes." *Academy of Management Journal* 28:34–49.

Nevin, John A. 1996. "War Initiation and Selection by Consequences." *Journal of Peace Research* 33:99–108.

Nie, Norman H., Jane Junn, and Kenneth Stehlik-Barry. 1996. *Education and Democratic Citizenship in America.* Chicago: University of Chicago Press.

Nincic, Donna J., and Miroslav Nincic. 1995. "Commitment to Military Intervention: The Democratic Government as Economic Investor." *Journal of Peace Research* 32:413–26.

Nincic, Miroslav. 1992. *Democracy and Foreign Policy: The Fallacy of Political Realism.* New York: Columbia University Press.

Nincic, Miroslav. 1997. "Loss Aversion and the Domestic Context of Military Intervention." *Political Research Quarterly* 50:97–120.

Niou, Emerson M. S., and Peter C. Ordeshook. 1990. "Stability in Anarchic International Systems." *American Political Science Review* 84:1207–34.

Niou, Emerson M. S., Peter C. Ordeshook, and Gregory F. Rose. 1989. *The Balance of Power: Stability in International Systems.* Cambridge: Cambridge University Press.

Nissen, Hans J. 1990. *Protostoria del Vicino Oriente.* Bari, Italy: Editori Laterza.

Nivison, D. S. 1998. "The Riddle of the *Bamboo Annals.*" Paper presented at the Annual Meeting of the American Oriental Society, Western Branch, Boulder, Colorado.

Nodia, Ghia. 1994. "Nationalism and Democracy." In *Nationalism, Ethnic Conflict, and Democracy,* ed. Larry Diamond and Marc F. Plattner. Baltimore: Johns Hopkins University Press.

Nye, Joseph S. 1990a. *Bound to Lead: The Changing Nature of American Power.* New York: Basic Books.

Nye, Joseph S. 1990b. "The Changing Nature of World Powers." *Political Science Quarterly* 105:177–92.

O'Brien, Kevin A. 1998. "The Use of Assassination as a Tool of State Policy: South Africa's Counter-Revolutionary Strategy 1979–1992." *Terrorism and Political Violence* 10:86–105.

O'Brien, Sean P. 1996. "Foreign Policy Crises and the Resort to Terrorism: A Time-Series Analysis of Conflict Linkages." *Journal of Conflict Resolution* 40:320–35.

O'Connell, R. L. 1991. "The Mace." *Military History Quarterly* 3:92–93.

Olick, Jeffrey K., and Daniel Levy. 1997. "Collective Memory and Cultural Constraint: Holocaust Myth and Rationality in German Politics." *American Sociological Review* 62:921–36.

Olson, Mancur. 1993. "Dictatorship, Democracy, and Development." *American Political Science Review* 87:567–76.

Oneal, John R., and Annal Lillian Bryan. 1995. "The 'Rally Round the Flag' Effect in U.S. Foreign Policy Crises, 1950–1985." *Political Behavior* 17:379–401.

Oneal, John R., Indra de Soysa, and Yong-Hee Park. 1998. "But Power and Wealth Are Satisfying." *Journal of Conflict Resolution* 42:517–20.

Oneal, John R., Bradley Lian, and James Joyner. 1996. "Are the American People 'Pretty Prudent'? Public Responses to U.S. Use of Force." *International Studies Quarterly* 40:261–80.

Oneal, John R., Frances H. Oneal, Zeev Maoz, and Bruce Russett. 1996. "The Liberal Peace: Interdependence, Democracy, and International Conflict, 1950–85." *Journal of Peace Research* 33:11–28.

Oneal, John R., and James Lee Ray. 1997. "New Tests of the Democratic Peace Controlling for Economic Interdependence." *Political Research Quarterly* 50:751–75.

Oneal, John R., and Bruce M. Russett. 1997. "The Classical Liberals Were Right: Democracy, Interdependence and Conflict, 1950–1985." *International Studies Quarterly* 41:267–94.

Oneal, John R., and Bruce Russett. 1999a. "Assessing the Liberal Peace with Alternative Specifications: Trade Still Reduces Conflict." *Journal of Peace Research* 36:423–42.

Oneal, John R., and Bruce Russett. 1999b. "The Kantian Peace: The Pacific Benefits of Democracy, Interdependence, and International Organizations, 1885–1992." *World Politics* 52:1–37.

Oneal, John R., and Bruce Russett. 1999c. "Is the Liberal Peace Just an Artifact of Cold War Interests? Assessing Recent Critiques." *International Interactions* 25:213–41.

Oneal, John R., and Bruce Russett. 2000. "Why 'An Identified Systemic Analysis of the Democracy-Peace Nexus' Does Not Persuade." *Defence and Peace Economics* 11:1–17.

Onuf, Nicholas G., and Thomas J. Johnson. 1995. "Peace in the Liberal World: Does Democracy Matter?" In *Controversies in International Relations Theory,* ed. Charles W. Kegley Jr. New York: St. Martin's Press.

Oren, Ido. 1995. "The Subjectivity of the 'Democratic' Peace." *International Security* 20 (2): 147–84.

Organski, A. F. K. 1958. *World Politics.* New York: Knopf.

Organski, A. F. K. 1965. *The Stages of Political Development.* New York: Knopf.

Organski, A. F. K. 1968. *World Politics,* 2nd ed. New York: Knopf.

Organski, A. F. K., and Jacek Kugler. 1977. "The Costs of Major Wars: The Phoenix Factor." *American Political Science Review* 71:1347–66.

Organski, A. F. K., and Jacek Kugler. 1980. *The War Ledger.* Chicago: University of Chicago Press.

Organski, A. F. K., and Jacek Kugler. 1988. *The War Ledger.* Chicago: University of Chicago Press.

Organski, A. F. K., Jacek Kugler, Timothy Johnson, and Youssef Cohen. 1984. *Births, Deaths, and Taxes: The Demographic and Political Transitions.* Chicago: University of Chicago Press.

Organski, Katherine, and A. F. K. Organski. 1961. *Population and World Power.* New York: Alfred A. Knopf.

Ortiz, M. A., and A. Cyphers G. In press. "La geomorfología y las evidencias arqueológicas en la region de San Lorenzo Tenochtitlán, Veracruz." In *Población, Subsistencia y Medio Ambiente en San Lorenzo Tenochtitlán.,* ed. A. Cyphers G. México: UNAM.

Ostrom, Charles W. Jr., and Francis W. Hoole. 1978. "Alliances and War Revisited." *International Studies Quarterly* 22:215–36.

Ostrom, Vincent. 1997. *The Meaning of Democracy and the Vulnerability of Democracies.* Ann Arbor: University of Michigan Press.

Owen, John M. 1994. "How Liberalism Produces Democratic Peace." *International Security* 19 (2): 87–125.

Owen, John M. 1997. *Liberal Peace, Liberal War: American Politics and International Security.* Ithaca, NY: Cornell University Press.

Page, Benjamin, and Robert Shapiro. 1992. *The Rational Public: Fifty Years of Trends in Americans' Policy Preferences.* Chicago: University of Chicago Press.

Paletz, David L., and Alex P. Schmid, eds. 1992. *Terrorism and the Media: How Researchers, Terrorists, Government, Press, Public, Victims View and Use the Media.* Newbury Park, CA: Sage.

Parasiliti, Andrew T. 1997. "Iraq's War Decisions, 1978–1991." Paper presented at the Annual Convention of the International Studies Association, Toronto, Ontario, March 18–22. (A chapter from Ph.D. diss., Johns Hopkins University, SAIS, Baltimore, Maryland, 1998).

Paret, Peter, ed. 1985. *Clausewitz and the State: The Man, His Theories, and His Times.* Princeton: Princeton University Press.

Paret, Peter, ed. 1986. *Makers of Modern Strategy: From Machiavelli to the Nuclear Age.* Princeton: Princeton University Press.

Payne, John. W., Dan J. Laughhunn, and Roy Crum. 1981. "Translation of Gambles and Aspiration Level Effects in Risky Choice Behavior." *Management Science* 27:953–59.

Peceny, Mark. 1997. "A Constructivist Interpretation of the Liberal Peace: The Ambiguous Case of the Spanish-American War." *Journal of Peace Research* 34:415–30.

Peceny, Mark. 1999. "Forcing Them to Be Free." *Political Research Quarterly* 52:549–582.

Pelcovitz, Nathan A., and Kevin L. Kramer. 1976. "Local Conflict and UN Peacekeeping: The Uses of Computerized Data." *International Studies Quarterly* 20:533–52.

Peterson, Steven A., and Robert Lawson. 1989. "Risky Business: Prospect Theory and Politics." *Political Psychology* 10:325–39.

Phillipson, Coleman. 1916. *Termination of War and Treaties of Peace.* London: T. F. Unwin.

Picard, Robert G. 1993. *Media Portrayals of Terrorism: Functions and Meaning of News Coverage.* Ames: Iowa State University Press.

Piggott, S. 1983. *The Earliest Wheeled Transport.* Ithaca, NY: Cornell University Press.

Pilar, Paul R. 1983. *Negotiating Peace: War Termination as a Bargaining Process.* Princeton: Princeton University Press.

Plato. 1961. *The Republic.* In *The Great Political Theories,* ed. Michael Curtis. 2 vols. New York: Avon Discuss Books.

Poe, Steven C., and C. Neal Tate. 1994. "Repression of Human Rights to Personal Integrity in the 1980s: A Global Analysis." *American Political Science Review* 88:853–72.

Polachek, Solomon. 1997. "Why Do Democracies Cooperate More and Fight Less: The Relationship Between Trade and International Cooperation." *Review of International Economics* 5:295–309.

Polanyi, Karl. 1944. *The Great Transformation.* Boston: Beacon Press.

Pollins, Brian M. 1996. "Global Political Order, Economic Change, and Armed Conflict: Coevolving Systems and the Use of Force." *American Political Science Review* 90:103–17.

Pollins, Brian M., and Kevin P. Murrin. 1997. "Where Hobbes Meets Hobson: Core Conflict and Colonialism, 1495–1995." Paper presented at the Annual Convention of the International Studies Association, Toronto, Ontario, March 18–22.

Popper, Karl R. 1959. *The Logic of Scientific Discovery.* New York: Basic Books.

Posen, Barry R. 1984. *The Sources of Military Doctrine.* Ithaca, NY: Cornell University Press.

Posen, Barry R. 1993. "The Security Dilemma and Ethnic Conflict." *Survival* 35:27–47.

Postgate, N., T. Wang, and T. Wilkinson. 1995. "The Evidence for Early Writing." *Antiquity* 69:459–80.

Powell, G. Bingham. 1982. *Contemporary Democracies: Participation, Stability and Violence.* Cambridge, MA: Harvard University Press.

Powell, Robert. 1987. "Crisis Bargaining, Escalation, and MAD." *American Political Science Review* 81:717–35.

Powell, Robert. 1988. "Nuclear Brinkmanship with Two-Sided Incomplete Information." *American Political Science Review* 82:155–78.

Powell, Robert. 1990. *Nuclear Deterrence Theory: The Search for Credibility.* New York: Cambridge University Press.

Powell, Robert. 1996a. "Stability and the Distribution of Power." *World Politics* 48:239–67.

Powell, Robert. 1996b. "Uncertainty, Shifting Power, and Appeasement." *American Political Science Review* 90:749–64.

Pozorski, S. 1987. "Theocracy vs. Militarism." In *The Origins and Development of the Andean State,* ed. J. Haas, S. Pozorski, and T. Pozorski. Cambridge: Cambridge University Press.

Pozorski, S., and T. Pozorski. 1990. "Reexamining the Critical Preceramic/Ceramic Period Transition." *American Anthropologist* 92:481–91.

Pricen, Thomas. 1992. *Intermediaries in International Conflict.* Princeton: Princeton University Press.

Pritchard, J. B. 1958. *The Ancient Near East.* Princeton: Princeton University Press.

Prunier, Gérard. 1995. *The Rwanda Crisis: History of a Genocide.* New York: Columbia University Press.

Przeworski, Adam, Michael Alvarez, Jose Antonio Chebub and Fernando Limongi. 1996. "What Makes Democracies Endure?" *Journal of Democracy* 7:39–55.

Przeworski, Adam, and Fernando Limongi. 1997. "Modernization: Theories and Facts." *World Politics* 49:155–83.

Purkitt, Helen. 1984. "Dealing with Terrorism: Deterrence and the Search for an Alternative Model." *Conflict in World Society: A New Perspective on International Relations,* ed. Michael Banks. New York: St. Martin's.

Putnam, Robert D. 1988. "Diplomacy and Domestic Politics: The Logic of Two-Level Games." *International Organization* 42:427–60.

Putnam, Robert D. 1993. *Making Democracy Work: Civic Traditions in Modern Italy.* Princeton: Princeton University Press.

Rabushka, Alvin, and Kenneth Shepsle. 1972. *Politics in Plural Societies: A Theory of Democratic Instability.* Columbus, OH: Charles E. Merrill.

Ragnerud, Arvid, and Havard Hegre. 1997. "The Hazard of War: Reassessing the Evidence for the Democratic Peace." *Journal of Peace Research* 34:385–404.

Ranstorp, Magnus, and Gus Xhudo. 1994. "A Threat to Europe? Middle East Ties with the Balkans and their Impact upon Terrorist Activity Throughout the Region." *Terrorism and Political Violence* 6:196–223.

Rapkin, David P. 1983. "The Inadequacy of a Single Logic: Integrating Political and Material Approaches to the World System." In *Contending Approaches to World System Analysis,* ed. William R. Thompson. Beverly Hills, CA: Sage.

Rapkin, David P. 1986. "World Leadership." In *Exploring Long Cycles,* ed. George Modelski. Boulder, CO: Lynne Rienner.

Rapkin, David P. 1987. "The Contested Concept of Hegemonic Leadership." In *World Leadership and Hegemony,* ed. David P. Rapkin. Boulder, CO: Lynne Rienner.

Rapkin, David P., and William R. Thompson, with Jon A. Christopherson. 1979. "Bipolarity and Bipolarization in the Cold War Era." *Journal of Conflict Resolution* 23:261–95.

Rapoport, Anatol. 1957. "Lewis F. Richardson's Mathematical Theory of War." *Journal of Conflict Resolution* 1:282–98.

Rapoport, Anatol. 1960. *Fights, Games and Debates.* Ann Arbor: University of Michigan Press.

Rapoport, Anatol. 1987. "Conflict Escalation and Conflict Dynamics." In *The Quest for Peace,* ed. Raimo Vayrynen. Beverly Hills, CA: Sage.

Rapoport, David C. 1992. "Terrorism." *Encyclopedia of Government and Politics,* ed. Mary Hawkesworth and Maurice Kogan. London: Routledge.

Rasler, Karen. 1990. "Spending, Deficits and Welfare: Investment Tradeoffs: Cause or Effect of Leadership Decline?" In *World Leadership and Hegemony,* ed. David P. Rapkin. Boulder, CO: Lynne Rienner.

Rasler, Karen. 1992. "International Influences on the Origins and Outcomes of Internal War: A Comparative Analysis of the 1958 and 1975–6 Lebanese Civil Wars." In *The Internationalization of Communal Strife,* ed. Manus I. Midlarsky. New York: Routledge.

Rasler, Karen, and William R. Thompson. 1983. "Global Wars, Public Debts and the Long Cycle." *World Politics* 35:489–516.

Rasler, Karen, and William R. Thompson. 1985a. "War Making and State Making: Governmental Expenditures, Tax Revenues and Global Wars." *American Political Science Review* 79:491–507.

Rasler, Karen, and William R. Thompson. 1985b. "War and the Economic Growth of Major Powers." *American Journal of Political Science* 29:513–38.

Rasler, Karen, and William R. Thompson. 1988. "Defense Burdens, Capital Formation and Economic Growth: The Systemic Leader Case." *Journal of Conflict Resolution* 32:61–86.

Rasler, Karen, and William R. Thompson. 1989. *War and State Making: The Shaping of the Global Powers.* Boston: Unwin Hyman.

Rasler, Karen, and William R. Thompson. 1991. "Relative Decline and the Overconsumption-Underinvestment Hypothesis." *International Studies Quarterly* 35:273–94.

Rasler, Karen, and William R. Thompson. 1992a. "Politico-Economic Tradeoffs and British Relative Decline." In *Defense, Welfare and Growth: Perspectives and Evidence,* ed. Alex Mintz and Steve Chan. London: Routledge.

Rasler, Karen, and William R. Thompson. 1992b. "Assessing the Costs of War: A Preliminary Cut." In *The Effects of War on Society,* ed. Georgio Ausenda. Republic of San Marino: Center for Interdisciplinary Research on Societal Stress.

Rasler, Karen, and William R. Thompson. 1994. *The Great Powers and Global Struggle, 1490–1990.* Lexington: University Press of Kentucky.

Ray, James Lee. 1974. "Status Inconsistency and War Involvement in Europe, 1816–1970." *Papers of the Peace Science Society (International)* 23:69–80.

Ray, James Lee. 1990. "Friends as Foes: International Conflict and Wars between Formal Allies." In *Prisoners of War? Nation-States in the Modern Era,* ed. Charles S. Gochman and Alan N. Sabrosky. Lexington, MA: Lexington Books.

Ray, James Lee. 1993. "Wars between Democracies: Rare, or Nonexistent?" *International Interactions* 18:251–76.

Ray, James Lee. 1995. *Democracy and International Conflict: An Evaluation of the Democratic Peace Proposition.* Columbia: University of South Carolina Press.

Ray, James Lee. 1997a. "On the Level(s): Does Democracy Correlate with Peace?" Paper presented at the Conference on "Scientific Knowledge of War: Identifying Patterns, Constructing Explanations," Vanderbilt University, Nashville, Tennessee, March 14–16.

Ray, James Lee. 1997b. "The Democratic Path to Peace." *Journal of Democracy* 8:49–64.

Ray, James Lee. 1998. "Does Democracy Cause Peace?" In *Annual Review of Political Science,* ed. Nelson W. Polsby. Palo Alto, CA: Annual Reviews, Inc.

Raymond, Gregory A. 1994. "Democracies, Disputes, and Third Party Intermediaries." *Journal of Conflict Resolution* 38:24–42.

Raymond, Gregory A. 1996. "Demosthenes and Democracies: Regime-Types and Arbitration Outcomes." *International Interactions* 22:1–20.

Raymond, Gregory A. 1997. "The Place of International Norms in the War Puzzle." Paper presented at the Conference on "Scientific Knowledge of War: Identifying Patterns, Constructing Explanations," Vanderbilt University, Nashville, Tennessee, March 14–16.

Reed, William. 1997. "Alliance Duration and Democracy: An Extension and Cross-Validation of 'Democratic States and Commitment in International Relations.'" *American Journal of Political Science* 41:1072–78.

Regan, Patrick. 1994. *Organizing Societies for War: The Process and Consequences of Societal Mobilization.* Westport, CT: Praeger.

Reich, Walter, ed. 1990. *Origins of Terrorism: Psychologies, Ideologies, Theologies, States of Mind.* Cambridge: Cambridge University Press.

Reichenbach, Hans. 1951. *The Rise of Scientific Philosophy.* Berkeley: University of California Press.

Reiter, Dan. 1995a. "Exploding the Powder Myth Keg: Preemptive Wars almost Never Happen." *International Security* 20 (2): 5–34.

Reiter, Dan. 1995b. "Political Structure and Foreign Policy Learning: Are Democracies More Likely to Act on the Lessons of History?" *International Interactions* 21:39–62.

Reiter, Dan, and Curtis Meek. 1999. "Determinants of Military Strategy, 1903–1994: A Quantitative Empirical Test." *International Studies Quarterly* 43:363–87.

Reiter, Dan, and Allan Stam III. 1997. "The Soldier's Decision to Surrender: Prisoners of War and World Politics." Paper presented at the Annual Meeting of the American Political Science Association, Washington, DC, August 28–31.

Reiter, Dan, and Allan Stam III. 1998a. "Democracy, War Initiation and Victory." *American Political Science Review* 92:377–90.

Reiter, Dan, and Allan Stam III. 1998b. "Democracy and Battlefield Effectiveness." *Journal of Conflict Resolution* 42:359–77.

Reiter, Dan, and Allan Stam III. 1998c. "In Defense of a Rationalist Model of Domestic Politics and War." Paper presented at the Annual Meeting of the American Political Science Association, Boston, Massachusetts, September 3–6.

Renfrew, Colin. 1972. *The Emergence of Civilization: The Cyclades and the Aegean in the Third Millennium* B.C. London: Methuen.

Renfrew, Colin, and P. Bahn. 1996. *Archaeology,* 2nd ed. London: Thames and Hudson.

Reuveny, Rafael, and Heejoon Kang. 1996. "International Trade, Political Conflict/Cooperation, and Granger Causality." *American Journal of Political Science* 40:943–70.

Reuveny, Rafael, and William R. Thompson. 1997a. "The Timing of Protectionism." *Review of International Political Economy* 4:179–213.

Reuveny, Rafael, and William R. Thompson. 1997b. "War, Systemic Leadership, and Economic Growth: The United States Case." Paper presented at the Annual Meeting of the Peace Science Society (International), Indianapolis, Indiana, November.

Richards, Cara. 1975. "Comment" on M. K. Roper "Evidence of Warfare in the Near East from 10,000–4,300 B.C." In *War, Its Causes and Correlates,* ed. M. A. Nettleship, R. D. Givens, and A. Nettleship. The Hague, Netherlands: Mouton.

Richards, Diana. 1993. "A Chaotic Model of Power Concentration in the International System." *International Studies Quarterly* 37:55–72.

Richardson, James L. 1994. *Crisis Diplomacy.* Cambridge: Cambridge University Press.

Richardson, Lewis F. 1948. "War Moods." *Psychometrika* 13:147–74, 197–232.

Richardson, Lewis F. 1960a. *Arms and Insecurity.* Pittsburgh, PA: Boxwood Press.

Richardson, Lewis F. 1960b. *Statistics of Deadly Quarrels.* Pittsburgh, PA: Boxwood Press.

Rieff, David. 1995. *Slaughterhouse: Bosnia and the Failure of the West.* New York: Simon and Schuster.

Riker, William H. 1962. *The Theory of Political Coalitions.* New Haven: Yale University Press.

Rioux, Jean-Sebastien. 1998. "A Crisis-Based Evaluation of the Democratic Peace Proposition." *Canadian Journal of Political Science* 31:263–83.

Risse-Kappen, Thomas. 1995. *Cooperation among Democracies: The European Influence on U.S. Foreign Policy.* Princeton: Princeton University Press.

Risse-Kappen, Thomas. 1996. "Collective Identity in a Democratic Community: The Case of NATO." In *The Culture of National Security: Norms and Identity in World Politics,* ed. Peter Katzenstein. New York: Columbia University Press.

Ritov, Ilana, and Jonathan Baron. 1990. "Reluctance to Vaccinate: Omission Bias and Ambiguity." *Journal of Behavioral Decision Making* 3:263–77.

Roberts, Brad, ed. 1997. *Terrorism with Chemical and Biological Weapons: Calibrating Risks and Responses.* Alexandria, VA: The Chemical and Biological Arms Control Institute.

Robinson, W. S. 1950. "Ecological Correlates and the Behavior of Individuals." *American Sociological Review* 15:351–57.

Rollefson, G. O., Z. A. Kafafi, and A. H. Simmons. 1990. "The Neolithic Village of cAin Ghoazal, Jordan." *Bulletin of the American Schools of Oriental Research. Supplement* 27:95–116.

Romanov, Valentin A. 1990. "The United Nations and the Problem of Combatting International Terrorism." *Terrorism and Political Violence* 2:289–304.

Romer, Paul. 1986. "Increasing Returns and Long-Run Growth." *Journal of Political Economy* 94:1002–37.

Roper, M. K. 1969. "A Survey of the Evidence for Intrahuman Killing in the Pleistocene." *Current Anthropology* 10:427–59.

Roper, M. K. 1975. "Evidence of Warfare in the Near East from 10,000–4,300 B.C." In *War, Its Causes and Correlates,* ed. M. A. Nettleship, R. D. Givens, and A. Nettleship. The Hague, Netherlands: Mouton.

Rosecrance, Richard N. 1963. *Action and Reaction in World Politics.* Boston: Little, Brown.

Rosecrance, Richard N. 1966. "Bipolarity, Multipolarity, and the Future." *Journal of Conflict Resolution* 10:314–27.

Rosecrance, Richard N. 1987. "Long Cycle Theory and International Relations." *International Organization* 41:283–301.

Rosecrance, Richard N. 1990. *America's Economic Resurgence: A Bold New Strategy.* New York: Harper & Row.

Rosecrance, Richard N. 1992. "A New Concert of Powers." *Foreign Affairs* 71 (spring): 64–82.

Rosen, Steven J. 1977. "A Stable System of Mutual Nuclear Deterrence in the Arab-Israeli Conflict." *American Political Science Review* 71:1367–83.

Rosenau, James N. 1969. *Linkage Politics: Essays on the Convergence of National and International Systems.* New York: The Free Press.

Rosenberg, Gerald N. 1991. *The Hollow Hope: Can Courts Bring About Social Change?* Chicago: University of Chicago Press.

Ross, Dennis. 1984. "Risk Aversion in Soviet Decisionmaking." In *Soviet Decisionmaking for National Security,* ed. Jiri Valenta and William Potter. London: Allen & Unwin.

Ross, Jeffrey Ian. 1991. "The Nature of Contemporary International Terrorism." In *Democratic Responses to International Terrorism,* ed. David A. Charters. Ardsley-on-Hudson, NY: Transnational Publishers.

Ross, Jeffrey Ian. 1992. "Attacking Terrorist Attacks: Initial Tests of the Contagion between Domestic and International Terrorism in Canada." *Low Intensity Conflict and Law Enforcement* 1:163–82.

Ross, Jeffrey Ian. 1993. "Structural Causes of Oppositional Political Terrorism: Towards a Causal Model." *Journal of Peace Research* 30:317–29.

Ross, Jeffrey Ian. 1994. "The Psychological Causes of Oppositional Political Terrorism: Toward an Integration of Findings." *International Journal of Group Tensions* 24:157–85.

Ross, Marc H. 1997. "Culture and Identity in Comparative Political Analysis." In *Comparative Politics: Rationality, Culture, and Structure,* ed. Mark I. Lichbach and Alan S. Zuckerman. Cambridge: Cambridge University Press.

Rostow, Walt W. 1971. *Politics and the Stages of Growth.* New York: Cambridge University Press.

Roth, Alvin E. 1995. "Introduction to Experimental Economics." In *The Handbook of Experimental Economics,* ed. J. H. Kagel and A. E. Roth. Princeton: Princeton University Press.

Rothman, M., ed. 2000. *Mesopotamia in the Era of State Formation.* Santa Fe, NM: School of American Research Press.

Rousseau, David. 1996. "Domestic Institutions and the Evolution of International Conflict." Ph.D. diss., University of Michigan, Ann Arbor.

Rousseau, David. 1997. "Regime Change and International Conflict: Is Democratization Really So Dangerous?" Paper presented at the Annual Meeting of the American Political Science Association, Washington DC, August 28–31.

Rousseau, David L., Christopher Gelpi, Dan Reiter, and Paul Huth. 1996. "Assessing the Dyadic Nature of the Democratic Peace, 1918–88." *American Political Science Review* 90:512–33.

Roy, A. Bikash. 1997. "Intervention across Bisecting Borders." *Journal of Peace Research* 34:3–14.

Roy, Martin. 1998. "Change in World Politics and International Trading Systems." Ph.D. diss., The Johns Hopkins University, SAIS, Baltimore, Maryland.

Rubin, Barry, ed. 1990. *The Politics of Counterterrorism: The Ordeal of Democratic States.* Washington: The Johns Hopkins Foreign Policy Institute.

Ruggie, John Gerard. 1986. "Continuity and Transformation in the World Polity: Toward a Neorealist Synthesis." In *Neorealism and Its Critics,* ed. Robert Keohane. New York: Columbia University Press.

Ruggie, John Gerard. 1982. "International Regimes, Transactions, and Change: Embedded Liberalism in the Postwar Economic Order." *International Organization* 36:379–416.

Rule, John. 1999. "The Rivalry between France and Spain during the Years 1460 to 1720." In *Great Power Rivalries,* ed. William R. Thompson. Columbia: University of South Carolina Press.

Rummel, Rudolph J. 1968. "The Relationship between National Attributes and Foreign Conflict Behavior." In *Quantitative International Politics: Insights and Evidence,* ed. J. David Singer. New York: The Free Press.

Rummel, Rudolph J. 1972a. "U.S. Foreign Relations: Conflict, Cooperation, and Attribute Distances." In *Peace, War, and Numbers,* ed. Bruce Russett. Beverly Hills, CA: Sage.

Rummel, Rudolph J. 1972b. *The Dimensions of Nations.* Beverly Hills, CA: Sage.

Rummel, Rudolph J. 1975. *Understanding Conflict and War.* Beverly Hills, CA: Sage.

Rummel, Rudolph J. 1976. *Understanding Conflict and War.* Vol. 2, *The Conflict Helix.* Beverly Hills, CA: Sage.

Rummel, Rudolph J. 1979. *Understanding Conflict and War.* Vol. 4, *War, Power, Peace.* Beverly Hills, CA: Sage.

Rummel, Rudolph J. 1981. *Understanding Conflict and War.* Vol. 5, *The Just Peace.* Beverly Hills, CA: Sage.

Rummel, Rudolph J. 1983. "Libertarianism and International Violence." *Journal of Conflict Resolution* 27:27–71.

Rummel, Rudolph J. 1985. "Libertarian Propositions on Violence within and between Nations: A Test against Published Research Results." *Journal of Conflict Resolution* 29:419–55.

Rummel, Rudolph J. 1994. *Death By Government.* New Brunswick, NJ: Transaction.

Rummel, Rudolph J. 1995a. "Democracy, Power, Genocide, and Mass Murder." *Journal of Conflict Resolution* 39:3–26.

Rummel, Rudolph J. 1995b. "Democracies ARE Less Warlike Than Other Regimes." *European Journal of International Relations* 1:457–79.

Rummel, Rudolph J. 1997. *Power Kills: Democracy as a Method of Nonviolence.* New Brunswick, NJ: Transaction.

Russett, Bruce M. 1963a. "The Calculus of Deterrence." *Journal of Conflict Resolution* 7:97–109.

Russett, Bruce M. 1963b. *Community and Contention: Britain and the United States in the Twentieth Century*. Cambridge, MA: MIT Press.

Russett, Bruce M. 1972. *No Clear and Present Danger.* New York: Harper Torchbacks.

Russett, Bruce M. 1985. "The Mysterious Case of Vanishing Hegemony." *International Organization* 39:207–31.

Russett, Bruce M. 1990. *Controlling the Sword: The Democratic Governance of National Security.* Cambridge: Harvard University Press.

Russett, Bruce M. 1993. *Grasping the Democratic Peace: Principles for a Post–Cold War World.* Princeton: Princeton University Press.

Russett, Bruce M. 1995. "The Democratic Peace: 'And Yet It Moves.' " *International Security* 19 (4): 164–75.

Russett, Bruce M. 1996. "Counterfactuals about War and Its Absence." In *Counterfactual Thought Experiments in World Politics: Logical, Methodological, and Psychological Perspectives,* ed. Philip Tetlock and Aaron Belkin. Princeton: Princeton University Press.

Russett, Bruce M. 1998. "A Neo-Kantian Perspective: Democracy, Interdependence, and International Organizations in Building Security Communities." In *Security Communities in Comparative and Historical Perspective,* ed. Emanuel Adler and Michael Barnett. New York: Cambridge University Press.

Russett, Bruce M., and William Antholis. 1992. "Do Democracies Fight Each Other? Evidence from the Peloponnesian War." *Journal of Peace Research* 29:415–34.

Russett, Bruce M., John R. Oneal, and David R. Davis. 1998. "The Third Leg of the Kantian Tripod for Peace: International Organizations and Militarized Disputes, 1950–1980." *International Organization* 52:441–67.

Sabrosky, A. Ned. 1975. "From Bosnia to Sarajevo: A Comparative Discussion of Interstate Crises." *Journal of Conflict Resolution* 19:3–24.

Sabrosky, A. Ned. 1985. "Alliance Aggregation, Capability Distribution, and the Expansion of Interstate War." In *Polarity and War,* ed. A. Ned Sabrosky. Boulder, CO: Westview Press.

St. John, Peter. 1998. "The Politics of Aviation Terrorism." *Terrorism and Political Violence* 10:27–49.

Salmore, Barbara G., and Stephen A. Salmore. 1978. "Political Regimes and Foreign Policy." In *Why Nations Act: Theoretical Perspectives for Comparative Foreign Policy Studies,* ed. Maurice A. East, Stephen A. Salmore, and Charles F. Hermann. Beverly Hills, CA: Sage.

Sample, Susan G. 1996. *Arms Races and the Escalation of Disputes to War.* Ph.D. diss., Vanderbilt University, Nashville, Tennessee.

Sample, Susan G. 1997. "Arms Races and Dispute Escalation: Resolving the Debate." *Journal of Peace Research* 34:7–22.

Samuelson, William, and Richard Zeckhauser. 1988. "Status Quo Bias in Decision Making." *Journal of Risk and Uncertainty* 1:7–59.

Sandler, Todd. 1995. "On the Relationship between Democracy and Terrorism." *Terrorism and Political Violence* 7:1–9.

Sandler, Todd, and Harvey E. Lapan. 1988. "The Calculus of Dissent: An Analysis of Terrorists' Choice of Targets." *Synthese* 76:245–61.

Saperstein, Alvin M. 1991. "The 'Long Peace'—Result of a Bipolar Competitive World?" *Journal of Conflict Resolution* 35:68–79.

Sawyer, R. D., ed. 1993. *The Seven Military Classics of Ancient China.* Boulder, CO: Westview.

Sayrs, Lois W. 1993. "The Long Cycle in International Relations: A Markov Specification." *International Studies Quarterly* 37:127–52.

Schampel, James H. 1993. "Change in Material Capabilities and the Onset of War: A Dyadic Approach." *International Studies Quarterly* 37:395–408.

Schelling, Thomas C. 1960. *The Strategy of Conflict.* New York: Oxford University Press.

Schelling, Thomas C. 1966. *Arms and Influence.* New Haven: Yale University Press.

Schelling, Thomas C. 1991. "What Purposes Can 'International Terrorism' Serve?" In *Violence, Terrorism, and Justice,* ed. R. G. Frey and Christopher W. Morris. Cambridge: Cambridge University Press.

Schmid, Alex P. 1992. "Terrorism and Democracy." *Terrorism and Political Violence* 4:14–25.

Schmid, Alex P., and Ronald D. Crelinsten, eds. 1992. "Western Responses to Terrorism." Special Issue. *Terrorism and Political Violence* 4:1–356.

Schmid, Alex P., and Janny de Graaf. 1982. *Violence as Communication: Insurgent Terrorism and the Western News Media*. Beverly Hills and London: Sage.

Schmid, Alex P., and Albert J. Jongman, et al. 1988. *Political Terrorism: A New Guide to Actors, Authors, Concepts, Data Bases, Theories and Literature*. New Brunswick, NJ: Transaction Books.

Schmitt, Bernadotte. 1958. *The Origins of the First World War.* London: Routledge and Kegan Paul.

Schmookler, Andrew B. 1984. *The Parable of the Tribes: The Problem of Power in Social Evolution.* Berkeley: University of California Press.

Schoemaker, P. J. H., and H. C. Kunreuther. 1979. "An Experimental Study of Insurance Decisions." *Journal of Risk and Insurance* 46:603–18.

Schroeder, Paul. 1999. "The Enduring Rivalry between France and the Hapsburg Monarchy, 1715–1918." In *Great Power Rivalries,* ed. William R. Thompson. Columbia: University of South Carolina Press.

Schultz, Kenneth A. 1998. "Domestic Opposition and Signalling in International Crises." *American Political Science Review* 92:829–44.

Schultz, Kenneth A., and Barry Weingast. 1997. "Limited Governments, Powerful States." In *Strategic Politicians, Institutions, and Foreign Policy,* ed. Randolph Siverson. Ann Arbor: University of Michigan Press.

Schweller, Randall L. 1992. "Domestic Structure and Preventive War: Are Democracies More Pacific?" *World Politics* 44:235–69.

Schweller, Randall L. 1993. "Tripolarity and the Second World War." *International Studies Quarterly* 37:73–103.

Schweller, Randall L. 1996. "Neorealism's Status Quo Bias: What Security Dilemma?" *Security Studies* 5:90–121.

Seaman, L. C. B. 1963. *From Vienna to Versailles.* New York: Harper & Row.

Sells, Michael. 1996. *The Bridge Betrayed: Religion and Genocide in Bosnia.* Berkeley: University of California Press.

Sen, Amartya. 1981. *Poverty and Famine.* New York: Oxford University Press.

Senese, Paul D. 1996. "Geographical Proximity and Issue Salience: Their Effects on the Escalation of Militarized Interstate Conflict." *Conflict Management and Peace Science* 15:133–61.

Senese, Paul D. 1997a. "Between Disputes and War: The Effect of Joint Democracy on Interstate Conflict Escalation." *Journal of Politics* 59:1–27.

Senese, Paul D. 1997b. "Dispute to War: The Conditional Importance of Territorial Issue Stakes and Geographic Proximity." Paper presented to the Annual Convention of the International Studies Association meeting, Toronto, Ontario, March 18–22.

Shaikh, Ayaz R. 1992. "A Theoretic Approach to Transnational Terrorism." *The Georgetown Law Journal* 80:2131–74.

Sharer, R., and D. Grove. 1989. *Regional Perspectives on the Olmec.* New York: Cambridge University Press.

Shaughnessy, E. L. 1988. "Historical Perspectives on the Introduction of the Chariot into China." *Harvard Journal of Asiatic Studies* 48:189–237.

Sick, Gary. 1990. "Taking Vows: The Domestication of Policy-Making in Hostage Incidents." In *Origins of Terrorism: Psychologies, Ideologies, Theologies, States of Mind,* ed. Walter Reich. Cambridge: Cambridge University Press.

Sidahmed, Abdel S., and Anoushiravan Ehteshami, eds. 1996. *Islamic Fundamentalism.* Boulder, CO: Westview Press.

Signorino, Curtis S., and Jeffrey M. Ritter. 1999. "Tau-b or Not Tau-b: Measuring the Similarity of Foreign Policy Positions." *International Studies Quarterly* 43:115–44.

Silber, Laura, and Allan Little. 1996. *Yugoslavia: Death of a Nation.* New York: Penguin.

Simmel, Georg. 1955. *Conflict.* Trans. Kurt H. Wolff. New York: The Free Press.

Simon, Jeffrey D. 1994. *The Terrorist Trap: America's Experience with Terrorism.* Bloomington: Indiana University Press.

Simon, Marc V., and Harvey Starr. 1995. "Two-Level Security Management and the Prospects for New Democracies: A Simulation Analysis." Paper presented at the Annual Meeting of the American Political Science Association, Chicago, Illinois, August 31–September 3.

Simon, Michael W., and Erik Gartzke. 1996. "Political System Similarity and the Choice of Allies." *Journal of Conflict Resolution* 40:617–35.

Singer, Eric H. 1989. "Terrorist Attacks on Nationals: The Lawful Use of Force Against Terrorist Bases on Foreign Soil." *Terrorism and Political Violence* 1:435–65.

Singer, J. David. 1982. "Confrontational Behavior and Escalation to War, 1816–1980: A Research Plan." *Journal of Peace Research* 19:37–48.

Singer, J. David, ed. 1979. *The Correlates of War: I.* New York: The Free Press.

Singer, J. David, Stuart Bremer, and John Stuckey. 1972. "Capability Distribution, Uncertainty, and Major Power War, 1820–1965." In *Peace, War, and Numbers,* ed. Bruce M. Russett. Beverly Hills, CA: Sage.

Singer, J. David, and Melvin Small. 1966. "National Alliance Commitments and War Involvement, 1815–1945." *Peace Research Society (International) Papers* 5:109–40.

Singer, J. David, and Melvin Small. 1968. "Alliance Aggregation and the Onset of War, 1815–1945." In *Quantitative International Politics: Insights and Evidence,* ed. J. David Singer. New York: The Free Press.

Singer, J. David, and Melvin Small. 1972. *The Wages of War 1816–1965: A Statistical Handbook.* New York: John Wiley.

Singer, J. David, and Melvin Small. 1974. "Foreign Policy Indicators: Predictors of War in History and in the State of the World Message." *Policy Sciences* 5:271–96.

Singer, Max, and Aaron Wildavsky. 1993. *The Real World Order: Zones of Peace/Zones of Turmoil.* Chatham, NJ: Chatham House Publishers.

Singh, K. R. 1995. "International Terrorism as an Instrument of State Policy." *International Studies* 32:119–37.

Siverson, Randolph M. 1995. "Democracies and War Participation: In Defense of the Institutional Constraints Argument." *European Journal of International Relations* 1:481–89.

Siverson, Randolph M., and Paul F. Diehl. 1989. "Arms Races, the Conflict Spiral, and the Onset of War." In *Handbook of War Studies,* ed. Manus I. Midlarsky. Boston: Unwin Hyman.

Siverson, Randolph M., and Juliann Emmons. 1991. "Birds of a Feather: Democratic Political Systems and Alliance Choices." *Journal of Conflict Resolution* 35:285–306.

Siverson, Randolph M., and Joel King. 1979. "Allliances and the Expansion of War." In *To Augur Well,* ed. J. D. Singer and M. Wallace. Beverly Hills, CA: Sage.

Siverson, Randolph M., and Ross A. Miller. 1993. "The Escalation of Disputes to War." *International Interactions* 19:77–97.

Siverson, Randolph M., and Harvey Starr. 1990. "Opportunity, Willingness, and the Diffusion of War." *American Political Science Review* 84:47–67.

Siverson, Randolph M., and Harvey Starr. 1991. *The Diffusion of War: A Study of Opportunity and Willingness.* Ann Arbor: University of Michigan Press.

Siverson, Randolph M., and Harvey Starr. 1994. "Regime Change and the Restructuring of Alliances." *American Journal of Political Science* 38:145–61.

Siverson, Randolph M., and Michael P. Sullivan. 1983. "The Distribution of Power and the Onset of War." *Journal of Conflict Resolution* 27:473–94.

Siverson, Randolph M., and Michael P. Sullivan. 1984. "Alliances and War: A New Examination of an Old Problem." *Conflict Management and Peace Science* 8:1–15.

Siverson, Randolph M., and Michael R. Tennefoss. 1982. "Interstate Conflicts: 1815–1965." *International Interactions* 9:147–78.

Siverson, Randolph M., and Michael R. Tennefoss. 1984. "Power, Alliance, and the Escalation of International Conflict, 1815–1965." *American Political Science Review* 78:1057–69.

Skrentny, John D. 1998. "The Effect of the Cold War on African-American Civil Rights: America and the World Audience, 1945–1968." *Theory and Society* 27:237–85.

Sloan, Stephen. 1993. "US Anti-Terrorism Policies: Lessons to Be Learned to Meet an Enduring and Changing Threat." *Terrorism and Political Violence* 5:106–31.

Slovic, Paul, Baruch Fischoff, and Sarah Lichtenstein. 1982. "Facts versus Fears: Understanding Perceived Risk." In *Judgment under Uncertainty: Heuristics and Biases,* eds. Daniel Kahneman, Paul Slovic, and Amos Tversky. Cambridge: Cambridge University Press.

Small, Melvin, and J. David Singer. 1970. "Patterns in International Warfare, 1816–1965." *Annals* 391:145–55.

Small, Melvin, and J. David Singer. 1976. "The War-Proneness of Democratic Regimes, 1816–1965." *Jerusalem Journal of International Relations* 1:50–69.

Small, Melvin, and J. David Singer. 1982. *Resort to Arms: International and Civil Wars, 1816–1980.* Beverly Hills, CA: Sage.

Smith, Alastair. 1995. "Alliance Formation and War." *International Studies Quarterly* 39:405–26.

Smith, Alastair. 1996a. "Diversionary Foreign Policy in Democratic Systems." *International Studies Quarterly* 40:133–53.

Smith, Alastair. 1996b. "To Intervene or Not to Intervene: A Biased Decision." *Journal of Conflict Resolution* 40:16–40.

Smith, Anthony D. 1993. "The Ethnic Sources of Nationalism." In *Ethnic Conflict and International Security,* ed. Michael E. Brown. Princeton: Princeton University Press.

Smith, G. Davidson. 1989. "Military Options in Response to State-Sponsored Terrorism." *Terrorism and Political Violence* 1:294–323.

Smoke, Richard. 1977. *War: Controlling Escalation.* Cambridge, MA: Harvard University Press, 17.

Snyder, Glenn H. 1972. "Crisis Bargaining." In *International Crises: Insights from Behavioral Research,* ed. Charles F. Hermann. New York: The Free Press.

Snyder, Glenn H., and Paul Diesing. 1977. *Conflict Among Nations: Bargaining, Decision Making, and System Structure in International Crises.* Princeton: Princeton University Press.

Snyder, Jack L. 1985. "Perceptions of the Security Dilemma in 1914." In *Psychology and Deterrence,* ed. Robert Jervis, Richard Ned Lebow, and Janice Stein. Baltimore: Johns Hopkins University Press.

Snyder, Jack L. 1991. *Myths of Empire: Domestic Politics and International Ambition.* Ithaca, NY: Cornell University Press.

Solingen, Etel. 1996. "Democracy, Economic Reform and Regional Cooperation." *Journal of Theoretical Politics* 8:79–114.

Sommer, Henrik. 1997. "Rivals at Risk?: Democratisation and Interstate Rivalry." In *Enforcing Cooperation: "Risky" States and the Intergovernmental Management of Conflict,* ed. Gerald Schneider and Patricia Weitsman. London: Macmillan.

Sorensen, George. 1992. "Kant and Processes of Democratization: Consequences for Neorealist Thought." *Journal of Peace Research* 29:397–414.

Sorokin, Gerald. 1994. "Arms, Alliances, and Security Tradeoffs in Enduring Rivalries." *International Studies Quarterly* 38:421–46.

Sorokin, Pitirim A. 1937. *Social and Cultural Dynamics.* Vol. III, *Fluctuation of Social Relationships, War, and Revolution.* New York: American Book Co.

Spencer, C. S. 1990. "Human Agency, Biased Transmission, and the Cultural Evolution of Chiefly Authority." *Journal of Anthropological Archaeology* 12:41–74.

Spiezio, K. Edward. 1990. "British Hegemony and Major Power War, 1815–1939: An Empirical Test of Gilpin's Model of Hegemonic Governance." *International Studies Quarterly* 34:165–81.

Spiezio, K. Edward. 1993. "Power Cycle Theory and State Involvement in Militarized Interstate Disputes, 1816–1976." *Conflict Management and Peace Science* 13:87–100.

Spilerman, Seymour. 1970. "The Causes of Racial Disturbances: A Comparison of Alternative Explanations." *American Sociological Review* 35:627–49.

Spiro, David E. 1994. "The Insignificance of the Liberal Peace." *International Security* 19 (2): 50–86.

Sprinzak, Ehud. 1991. "The Process of Delegitimation: Towards a Linkage Theory of Political Terrorism." In *Terrorism Research and Public Policy,* ed. Clark McCauley. London: Frank Cass.

Sprinzak, Ehud. 1998. "The Great Superterrorism Scare." *Foreign Policy* 112: 110-24.

Sprout, Harold, and Margaret Sprout. 1965. *The Ecological Perspective on Human Affairs.* Princeton: Princeton University Press.

Stam, Allan III. 1996. *Win, Lose, or Draw: Domestic Politics and the Crucible of War.* Ann Arbor: University of Michigan Press.

Stark, B., and P. Arnold, eds. 1997. *Aztec to Olmec.* Tucson: University of Arizona Press.

Starr, Harvey. 1991. "Joining Political and Geographic Perspectives: Geopolitics and International Relations." *International Interactions* 17:1–9.

Starr, Harvey. 1992a. "Democracy and War: Choice, Learning and Security Communities." *Journal of Peace Research* 29:207–13.

Starr, Harvey. 1992b. "Why Don't Democracies Fight One Another? Evaluating the Theory-Findings Research Loop." *Jerusalem Journal of International Relations* 14:41–59.

Starr, Harvey. 1994. "Revolution and War: Rethinking the Linkage between Internal and External Conflict." *Political Research Quarterly* 47:481–507.

Starr, Harvey. 1995. "D2: The Diffusion of Democracy Revisited." Paper presented at the Annual Convention of the International Studies Association, Chicago, Illinois, February 21–25.

Starr, Harvey. 1997a. *Anarchy, Order, and Integration: How to Manage Interdependence.* Ann Arbor: University of Michigan Press.

Starr, Harvey. 1997b. "Democracy and Integration: Why Democracies Don't Fight Each Other." *Journal of Peace Research* 34:153–62.

Starr, Harvey., ed. 1999. *The Understanding and Management of Global Violence: New Approaches to Theory and Research on Protracted Conflict.* New York: Macmillan.

Starr, Harvey, and Benjamin A. Most. 1976. "The Substance and Study of Borders in International Relations Research." *International Studies Quarterly* 20:581–620.

Starr, Harvey, and Benjamin A. Most. 1978. "A Return Journey: Richardson, 'Frontiers,' and Wars in the 1946–1965 Era." *Journal of Conflict Resolution* 22:441–67.

Starr, Harvey, and Benjamin A. Most. 1983. "Contagion and Border Effects on Contemporary African Conflict." *Comparative Political Studies* 16:92–117.

Starr, Harvey, and Benjamin A. Most. 1985. "The Forms and Processes of War Diffusion: Research Update on Contagion in African Conflict." *Comparative Political Studies* 18:206–29.

Stedman, Stephen J. 1991. *Peacemaking in Civil War: International Mediation in Zimbabwe, 1974–1980.* Boulder, CO: Lynne Rienner.

Stein, G., and M. S. Rothman. 1994. *Chiefdoms and Early States in the Near East.* Madison, WI: Prehistory Press.

Stein, Janice G. 1975. "War Termination and Conflict Reduction or, How Wars Should End." *Jerusalem Journal of International Relations* 1:1–27.

Stein, Janice G., and Louis Pauly. 1992. *Choosing to Cooperate: How States Avoid Loss.* Baltimore: Johns Hopkins University Press.

Stern, Jessica. 1999. *The Ultimate Terrorists.* Cambridge, MA: Harvard University Press.

Stoessinger, John G. 1985. *Why Nations Go to War,* 4th ed. New York: St. Martin's Press.

Stohl, Michael. 1988a. "National Interests and State Terrorism in International Affairs." In *The Politics of Terrorism,* 3rd ed., ed. Michael Stohl. New York: Marcel Dekker.

Stohl, Michael, ed. 1988b. *The Politics of Terrorism,* 3rd ed. New York: Marcel Dekker.

Stoll, Richard, and Michael Ward, eds. 1989. *Power in the International System.* Boulder, CO: Lynne Rienner.

Stone, Julius. 1954. *Legal Controls of International Conflict.* New York: Rinehart.

Strang, David. 1991. "Global Patterns of Decolonization." *International Studies Quarterly* 35:429–54.

Sullivan, Michael. 1974. "Escalatory and Non-escalatory Systems." *American Journal of Political Science* 18:549–58.

Sullivan, Michael. 1990. *Power in Contemporary International Politics.* Columbia: University of South Carolina Press.

Taçon, P., and C. Chippindale. 1994. "Australia's Ancient Warriors." *Cambridge Archaeological Journal* 4:211–48.

Taliaferro, Jeffrey W. 1994. "Analogical Reasoning and Prospect Theory: Hypotheses on Framing." Paper presented at the Annual Convention of the International Studies Association, Washington, DC, March 29–April 2.

Taliaferro, Jeffrey W. 1995. "Gambling with the 'House Money' in International Relations: The Truman Administration and the Korean War Decision of 1950." Paper presented at the Annual Meeting of the International Society of Political Psychology, Washington, DC, July 5–8.

Taliaferro, Jeffrey W. 1997. "Quagmires in the Periphery: Foreign Wars and Escalating Commitment to Recover Sunk Costs." Paper presented at the Annual Convention of the International Studies Association, Toronto, Ontario, March 18–22.

Tammen, Ronald, Jacek Kugler, Douglas Lemke, Allan Stam, Mark Abdollahian, Carole Alsharabati, Brian Efird, and A. F. K. Organski. 2000. *Power Transitions: Strategies for the Twenty-first Century.* New York: Chatham House Publishers.

Taubman, Geoffry L. 1997. "Nationalism, Loss-Gain Framing and the Confederate States of America." *Nations and Nationalism* 3:251–71.

Taylor, A. J. P. 1954. *The Struggle for Mastery in Europe, 1848–1919.* Oxford: Clarendon Press.

Taylor, A. J. P. 1979. *How Wars Begin.* New York: Atheneum.

Taylor, Michael. 1982. *Community, Anarchy, and Liberty.* New York: Cambridge University Press.

Taylor, Michael, and Sara Singleton. 1993. "The Communal Resource: Transaction Costs and the Solution of Collective Action Problems." In *Proceedings of a Conference on Linking Local and Global Commons,* ed. Robert O. Keohane, Michael D. McGinnis, and Elinor Ostrom. Cambridge, MA: Harvard University Center for International Affairs.

Tellis, Ashley J., Thomas S. Szayna, and James A. Winnefeld. 1997. *Anticipating Ethnic Conflict.* Santa Monica, CA: RAND.

Thaler, Richard. 1980. "Toward a Positive Theory of Consumer Choice." *Journal of Economic Behavior and Organization* 1:39–60.

Thaler, Richard H., and E. J. Johnson. 1990. "Gambling with the House Money and Trying to Break Even: The Effects of Prior Outcomes on Risky Choice." *Management Science* 36:643–60.

Thompson, William R. 1983a. "Cycles, Capabilities, and War: An Ecumenical View." In *Contending Approaches to World System Analysis,* ed. William R. Thompson. Beverly Hills, CA: Sage.

Thompson, William R. 1983b. "Succession Crises in the Global Political System: A Test of the Transition Model." In *Crises in the World-System,* ed. Albert Bergesen. Beverly Hills, CA: Sage.

Thompson, William R. 1985. "Cycles of General, Hegemonic and Global War." In *Dynamic Models of International Conflict,* ed. Urs Luterbacher and Michael D. Ward. Boulder, CO: Lynne Rienner.

Thompson, William R. 1986. "Polarity, the Long Cycle, and Global Power Warfare." *Journal of Conflict Resolution* 30:587–615.

Thompson, William R. 1988. *On Global War: Historical-Structural Approaches to World Politics.* Columbia: University of South Carolina Press.

Thompson, William R. 1990a. "Long Waves, Technological Innovation and Relative Decline." *International Organization* 44:201–33.

Thompson, William R. 1990b. "The Size of War, Structural and Geopolitical Contexts, and Theory Building/Testing." *International Interactions* 16:183–99.

Thompson, William R. 1992a. "Long Cycles and the Geohistorical Context of Structural Transitions." *World Politics* 43:127–52.

Thompson, William R. 1992b. "Systemic Leadership and Growth Waves in the Long Run." *International Studies Quarterly* 36:25–48.

Thompson, William R. 1994. "The Consequences of War." In *The Process of War,* ed. Stuart Bremer and Thomas Cusack. New York: Gordon and Breach.

Thompson, William R. 1995a. "Comparing World Systems: Systemic Leadership Succession and the Peloponnesian War Case." In *The Historical Evolution of International Political Economies.* Vol. 1, ed. Christopher Chase-Dunn. London: Edward Elgar.

Thompson, William R. 1995b. "Principal Rivalries." *Journal of Conflict Resolution* 39:195–223.

Thompson, William R. 1996a. "Balances of Power, Transitions, and Long Cycles." In *Parity and War,* ed. Jacek Kugler and Douglas Lemke. Ann Arbor: University of Michigan Press.

Thompson, William R. 1996b. "Democracy and Peace: Putting the Cart before the Horse?" *International Organization* 50:141–74.

Thompson, William R. 1997a. "Intermittent Republics and Democratic Peace Puzzles." *Review of International Studies* 23:93–114.

Thompson, William R. 1997b. "The Evolution of Political-Commercial Challenges in the Active Zone." *Review of International Political Economy* 4:286–318.

Thompson, William R. 1997/98. "The Anglo-German Rivalry and the 1939 Failure-of-Deterrence Problem." *Security Studies* 7:58–89.

Thompson, William R., ed. 1999a. *Great Power Rivalries.* Columbia: University of South Carolina Press.

Thompson, William R. 1999b. "Martian and Venusian Perspectives on International Relations: The Evolution of World Politics." In *International History and International Relations Theory: Bridges and Boundaries,* ed. Colin Elman and Miriam Elman. Cambridge, MA: MIT Press.

Thompson, William R. 1999c. "The Evolution of a Great Power Rivalry" In *Great Power Rivalries,* ed. William R. Thompson. Columbia: University of South Carolina Press.

Thompson, William R. 1999d. "The Military Superiority Thesis and the Ascendancy of Western Eurasia in the World System." *Journal of World History* 10:143–78.

Thompson, William R., and George Modelski. 1994. "Long Cycle Critiques and Deja Vu All Over Again: A Rejoinder to Houweling and Siccama." *International Interactions* 20:209–22.

Thompson, William R., and Karen Rasler. 1988. "War and Systemic Capability Reconcentration." *Journal of Conflict Resolution* 32:335–66.

Thompson, William R., and Rafael Reuveny. 1998. "Tariffs and Trade Fluctuations: Does Protectionism Matter As Much As We Think?" *International Organization* 52:421–40.

Thompson, William R., and Richard Tucker. 1997a. "A Tale of Two Democratic Peace Critiques." *Journal of Conflict Resolution* 41:428–54.

Thompson, William R., and Richard Tucker. 1997b. "Bewitched, Bothered, and Bewildered: A Reply to Farber and Gowa and to Mansfield and Snyder." *Journal of Conflict Resolution* 41:462–77.

Thompson, William R., and Lawrence Vescera. 1992. "Growth Waves, Systemic Openness and Protectionism." *International Organization* 46:493–532.

Thompson, William R., and Gary Zuk. 1982. "War, Inflation and Kondratieff Long Waves." *Journal of Conflict Resolution* 26:621–44.

Thompson, William R., and Gary Zuk. 1986. "World Power and the Strategic Trap of Territorial Commitments." *International Studies Quarterly* 30:249–67.

Thomson, Janice E. 1994. *Mercenaries, Pirates, and Sovereigns: State-Building and Extraterritorial Violence in Early Modern Europe.* Princeton: Princeton University Press.

Tillema, Herbert K. 1991. *International Armed Conflict since 1945: A Bibliographic Handbook of Wars and Military Interventions.* Boulder, CO: Westview Press.

Topic, J. R. 1989. "The Ostra Site." In *Cultures in Conflict. Proceedings of the Twentieth Annual Chacmool Conference,* ed. D. C. Tkaczuk and B. C. Vivian. Calgary, Alberta, Canada.

Topic, J. R., and T. L. Topic. 1987. "The Archaeological Investigation of Andean Militarism." In *The Origins and Development of the Andean State,* ed. J. Haas, S. Pozorski, and T. Pozorski. Cambridge: Cambridge University Press.

Topic, J. R., and T. L. Topic. 1997. "Toward a Conceptual Understanding of Andean Warfare." In *Arqueología, Antropología, e Historia en los Andes,* ed. R. V. Gabai and J. F. Espinoza. Lima, Peru: Instituto Nacional de Cultura y Banco Central de Reserva del Perú.

Touval, Saadia. 1975. "Biased Intermediaries: Theoretical and Historical Considerations." *Jerusalem Journal of International Relations* 1:51–70.

Touval, Saadia. 1992. "The Superpowers as Mediators." In *Mediation in International Relations: Multiple Approaches to Conflict Management,* ed. Jacob Bercovitch and Jeffrey Z. Rubin. New York: St. Martin's Press.

Touval, Saadia, and I. William Zartman. 1985. *International Mediation in Theory and Practice.* Boulder, CO: Westview Press.

Tucker, David. 1997. *Skirmishes at the Edge of Empire: The United States and International Terrorism.* Westport, CT: Praeger.

Tversky, Amos, and Daniel Kahneman. 1986. "Rational Choice and the Framing of Decisions." *Journal of Business* 59:S251–78.

Tversky, Amos, and Daniel Kahneman. 1991. "Loss Aversion in Riskless Choice: A Reference Dependent Model." *Quarterly Journal of Economics* 41: 1039–61.

Underhill, A. 1989. "Warfare During the Chinese Neolithic Period." In *Cultures in Conflict. Proceedings of the Twentieth Annual Chacmool Conference,* ed. D. C. Tkaczuk and B. C. Vivian. Calgary, Alberta, Canada.

Underhill, A. 1994. "Variations in Settlements during the Longshan Period of Northern China." *Asian Perspectives* 33:197–228.

Vachudová, Milada A. 1996. "Peaceful Transformations in East-Central Europe." In *The International Dimensions of Internal Conflict,* ed. Michael E. Brown. Cambridge, MA: MIT Press.

Van Belle, Douglas. 1997. "Press Freedom and the Democratic Peace." *Journal of Peace Research* 34:405–14.

Van Evera, Stephen. 1999. *Causes of War: Power and the Roots of Conflict.* Ithaca, NY: Cornell University Press.

Vanhanen, Tatu. 1984. *The Emergence of Democracy: A Comparative Study of 119 States, 1850–1979.* Helsinki: Finnish Society of Sciences and Letters.

Vanhanen, Tatu. 1990. *The Process of Democratization: A Comparative Study of 147 States, 1980–88.* New York: Crane Russak.

Vasquez, John A. 1983. *The Power of Power Politics: A Critique.* New Brunswick: Rutgers University Press.

Vasquez, John A. 1987. "The Steps to War: Toward a Scientific Explanation of Correlates of War Findings." *World Politics* 40:108–45.

Vasquez, John A. 1992. "Factors Related to the Contagion and Diffusion of International Violence." In *The Internationalization of Communal Strife,* ed. Manus I. Midlarsky. New York: Routledge.

Vasquez, John A. 1993. *The War Puzzle.* Cambridge: Cambridge University Press.

Vasquez, John A. 1994. "Building Peace in the Post–Cold War Era." In *From Rivalry to Cooperation: Russian and American Perspectives on the Post–Cold War Era,* ed. M. Midlarsky, J. Vasquez, and P. Gladkov. New York: HarperCollins.

Vasquez, John A. 1995a. "The Learning of Peace: Lessons from a Multidisciplinary Inquiry." In *Beyond Confrontation: Learning Conflict Resolution in the Post–Cold War Era,* ed. John A. Vasquez, James Turner Johnson, Sanford Jaffe, and Linda Stamato. Ann Arbor: University of Michigan Press.

Vasquez, John A. 1995b. "Why Do Neighbors Fight? Proximity, Interaction, or Territoriality." *Journal of Peace Research* 32:277–93.

Vasquez, John A. 1996. "Distinguishing Rivals That Go to War from Those That Do Not: A Quantitative Comparative Case Study of the Two Paths to War." *International Studies Quarterly* 40:531–58.

Vasquez, John A. 1997. "The Realist Paradigm and Degenerative versus Progressive Research Programs: An Appraisal of Neotraditional Research on Waltz's Balancing Proposition." *American Political Science Review* 91: 899–912.

Vasquez, John A. 1998a. "The Evolution of Multiple Rivalries Prior to the Second World War in the Pacific." In *The Dynamics of Enduring Rivalries,* ed. Paul F. Diehl. Urbana: University of Illinois Press.

Vasquez, John A. 1998b. *The Power of Power Politics: From Classical Realism to Neotraditionalism.* Cambridge: Cambridge University Press.

Vasquez, John A. Forthcoming. "Mapping the Probability of War and Analyzing the Possibility of Peace: The Role of Territorial Disputes." Presidential Address to the Peace Science Society. *Conflict Management and Peace Science.*

Vasquez, John A., and Marie T. Henehan, eds. 1992. *The Scientific Study of Peace and War: A Text Reader.* New York: Lexington Books.

Vasquez, John A., and Marie T. Henehan. 2000. "Territorial Issues and the Probability of War, 1816–1992." Unpublished manuscript.

Vasquez, John A., James Turner Johnson, Sanford Jaffe, and Linda Stamato, eds. 1995. *Beyond Confrontation: Learning Conflict Resolution in the Post–Cold War Era.* Ann Arbor: University of Michigan Press.

Vayrynen, Raimo. 1983. "Economic Cycles, Power Transitions, Political Management and War between the Major Powers." *International Studies Quarterly* 27:389–418.

Vencl, S. 1984. "War and Warfare in Archaeology." *Journal of Anthropological Archaeology* 3:116–32.

Verdier, Daniel. 1994. *Democracy and International Trade: Britain, France, and the United States, 1860–1990.* Princeton: Princeton University Press.

Vertzberger, Yaacov Y. I. 1990. *The World in Their Minds: Information Processing, Cognition, and Perception in Foreign Policy Decision-Making.* Stanford: Stanford University Press.

Vertzberger, Yaacov Y. I. 1995. "Rethinking and Reconceptualizing Risk in Foreign Policy Decision Making: A Sociological Approach." *Political Psychology* 16:347–80.

Vertzberger, Yaacov Y. I. 1998. *Risk Taking and Decisionmaking: Foreign Military Intervention Decisions.* Stanford: Stanford University Press.

Viertl, R. 1996. *Statistical Methods for Non-Precise Data.* New York: CRC Press.

Vojnić, Dragomir. 1995. "Disparity and Disintegration: The Dimension of Yugoslavia's Demise." In *Yugoslavia, the Former and Future,* ed. Payam Akhnavan and Robert Howse. Washington, DC: The Brookings Institution.

Volgy, Thomas J., and Lawrence E. Imwalle. 1995. "Hegemonic and Bipolar Perspectives on the New World Order." *American Journal of Political Science* 39:819–34.

Volgy, Thomas J., and John E. Schwarz. 1997. "Free Trade, Economic Inequality, and the Stability of Democracies in the Democratic Core of Peace." *European Journal of International Relations* 3:239–53.

Wagner, R. Harrison. 1993. "What Was Bipolarity?" *International Organization* 47:77–106.

Wagner, R. Harrison. 1994. "Peace and the Balance of Power in a Three-State World." Paper presented at the Annual Meeting of the American Political Science Association, New York, New York, September 1–4.

Wallace, Michael D. 1973a. "Alliance Polarization, Cross-Cutting, and International War, 1815–1964: A Measurement Procedure and Some Preliminary Evidence." *Journal of Conflict Resolution* 17:575–604.

Wallace, Michael D. 1973b. *War and Rank among Nations.* Lexington, MA: D. C. Heath.

Wallace, Michael D. 1979. "Arms Races and Escalation: Some New Evidence." *Journal of Conflict Resolution* 23:3–16.

Wallace, Michael D. 1982. "Armaments and Escalation: Two Competing Hypotheses." *International Studies Quarterly* 26:37–51.

Wallace, Michael D. 1990. "Racing Redux: The Arms Race-Escalation Debate Revisited." In *Prisoners of War,* ed. C. Gochman and A. Sabrosky. Lexington, MA: Lexington Books.

Wallensteen, Peter. 1981. "Incompatibility, Confrontation, and War: Four Models and Three Historical Systems, 1816–1976." *Journal of Peace Research* 18:57–90.

Wallensteen, Peter. 1984. "Universalism vs. Particularism: On the Limits of Major Power Order." *Journal of Peace Research* 21:243–57.

Wallensteen, Peter, and Karin Axell. 1993. "Armed Conflict at the End of the Cold War, 1989–92." *Journal of Peace Research* 30:331–46.

Wallensteen, Peter, and Margareta Sollenberg. 1995. "After the Cold War: Emerging Patterns of Armed Conflict, 1989–94." *Journal of Peace Research* 32:345–60.

Wallerstein, Immanuel. 1984. *The Politics of the World-Economy.* Cambridge: Cambridge University Press.

Walt, Stephen M. 1987. *The Origins of Alliances.* Ithaca, NY: Cornell University Press.

Waltz, Kenneth N. 1959. *Man, the State, and War.* New York: Columbia University Press.

Waltz, Kenneth N. 1964. "The Stability of a Bipolar World." *Daedalus* 93:881–909.

Waltz, Kenneth N. 1967. "International Structure, National Force, and the Balance of World Power." *Journal of International Affairs* 11:215–31.

Waltz, Kenneth N. 1979. *Theory of International Politics.* Reading, MA: Addison-Wesley.

Waltz, Kenneth N. 1981. "The Spread of Nuclear Weapons: More May Be Better." *Adelphi Paper #171.* London: International Institute of Strategic Studies.

Waltz, Kenneth N. 1993. "The Emerging Structure of International Politics." *International Security* 18 (2): 44–79.

Wang, Kevin. 1996. "Presidential Responses to Foreign Policy Crises: Rational Choice and Domestic Politics." *Journal of Conflict Resolution* 40:68–97.

Ward, Michael D., and Kristian S. Gleditsch. 1998. "Democratizing for Peace." *American Political Science Review* 92:51–62.

Warlimont, Walter. 1964. *Inside Hitler's Headquarters: 1939–45.* Trans. R. H. Barry. London: Weidenfeld and Nicolson.

Way, Christopher. 1997. "Manchester Revisited: A Theoretical and Empirical Evaluation of Commercial Liberalism." Ph.D. diss., Stanford University, Stanford, California.

Wayman, Frank W. 1982. "Power Transitions, Rivalries, and War, 1816–1970." Paper presented at the Institute for the Study of Conflict Theory and International Security Meeting, Urbana-Champaign, Illinois, September 22–24. Correlates of War Project (mimeo).

Wayman, Frank W. 1984. "Bipolarity and War: The Role of Capability Concentration and Alliance Patterns among Major Powers, 1816–1965." *Journal of Peace Research* 21:61–78.

Wayman, Frank W. 1996. "Power Shifts and the Onset of War." In *Parity and War: Evaluations and Extensions of* The War Ledger, ed. Jacek Kugler and Douglas Lemke. Ann Arbor: University of Michigan Press.

Wayman, Frank W., and Daniel Jones. 1991. "Evolution of Conflict in Enduring Rivalries." Paper presented at the Annual Convention of the International Studies Association, Vancouver, British Columbia, March 19–23.

Wayman, Frank W., and T. Clifton Morgan. 1990. "Measuring Polarity in the International System." In *Measuring the Correlates of War,* ed. J. David Singer and Paul F. Diehl. Ann Arbor: University of Michigan Press.

Weart, Spencer R. 1994. "Peace among Democratic and Oligarchic Republics." *Journal of Peace Research* 31:299–316.

Weart, Spencer R. 1998. *Never at War: Why Democracies Will Not Fight One Another.* New Haven, CT: Yale University Press.

Weber, Eugen J. 1976. *Peasants into Frenchmen: The Modernization of Rural France, 1870–1914.* Stanford: Stanford University Press.

Webster, D. 1976. *Defensive Earthworks at Becán, México.* New Orleans: Tulane University, Middle American Research Institute.

Weede, Erich. 1970. "Conflict Behavior of Nation-States." *Journal of Peace Research* 7:229–37.

Weede, Erich. 1975. "World Order in the Fifties and Sixties: Dependence, Deterrence and Limited Peace." *Peace Science Society Papers* 24:49–80.

Weede, Erich. 1976. "Overwhelming Preponderance as a Pacifying Condition among Contiguous Asian Dyads, 1950–1969." *Journal of Conflict Resolution* 20:395–411.

Weede, Erich. 1980. "Arms Races and Escalation: Some Persisting Doubts." *Journal of Conflict Resolution* 24:285–87.

Weede, Erich. 1984. "Democracy and War Involvement." *Journal of Conflict Resolution* 28:649–64.

Weede, Erich. 1989. "Extended Deterrence, Superpower Control, and Militarized Interstate Disputes, 1962–1976." *Journal of Peace Research* 26:7–17.

Weede, Erich. 1992. "Some Simple Calculations on Democracy and War Involvement." *Journal of Peace Research* 29:377–83.

Weede, Erich. 1994. "Constraints, States, and Wars." *European Journal of Political Research* 26:171–92.

Weede, Erich. 1996. *Economic Development, Social Order, and World Politics.* Boulder, CO: Lynne Rienner.

Weinberg, Leonard. 1991. "Turning to Terror: The Conditions under Which Political Parties Turn to Terrorist Activities." *Comparative Politics* 23:423–38.

Weinberg, Leonard B., and William L. Eubank. 1998. "Terrorism and Democracy: What Recent Events Disclose." *Terrorism and Political Violence* 10: 108–18.

Welch, David A. 1993. *Justice and the Genesis of War.* New York: Cambridge University Press.

Wendt, Alexander. 1994. "Collective Identity Formation and the International State." *American Political Science Review* 88:384–98.

Werner, Suzanne. 1996. "Absolute and Limited War: The Possibilities of a Foreign Imposed Regime Change." *International Interactions* 22:67–88.

Werner, Suzanne, and Jacek Kugler. 1996. "Power Transitions and Military Buildups." In *Parity and War,* ed. Jacek Kugler and Douglas Lemke. Ann Arbor: University of Michigan Press.

Werner, Suzanne, and Douglas Lemke. 1997. "Opposites Do Not Attract: The Impact of Domestic Institutions, Power, and Prior Commitments on Alignment Choices." *International Studies Quarterly* 41:529–46.

Werner, Suzanne, and Douglas Lemke. 1998. "The Consequences of Anarchy: Security Dilemmas and Security Communities." Unpublished manuscript.

Wesley, James Paul. 1962. "Frequency of Wars and Geographical Opportunity." *Journal of Conflict Resolution* 6:387–89.

Weyland, Kurt. 1996. "Risk Taking in Latin American Economic Restructuring: Lessons from Prospect Theory." *International Studies Quarterly* 40:185–208.

White, Ralph K. 1966. "Misperception and the Vietnam War." *Journal of Social Issues* 22:1–164.

White, Ralph K. 1970. *Nobody Wanted War: Misperception in Vietnam and Other Wars.* New York: Doubleday.

Whyte, Glen, and Ariel S. Levi. 1994. "The Origins and Function of the Reference Point in Risky Group Decision Making: The Case of the Cuban Missile Crisis." *Journal of Behavioral Decision Making* 7:243–60.

Wieviorka, Michel. 1993. *The Making of Terrorism.* Chicago: University of Chicago Press. (*Societes et terrorism.* 1988. Paris: Fayard.)

Wilkenfeld, Jonathan. 1975. "A Time-Series Perspective on Conflict Behavior in the Middle East." In *Sage International Yearbook of Foreign Policy Studies.* Vol. 3, ed. Patrick J. McGowan. Beverly Hills, CA: Sage.

Wilkenfeld, Jonathan. 1991. "Trigger-Response Transitions in Foreign Policy Crises, 1929–1985." *Journal of Conflict Resolution* 35:143–69.

Wilkenfeld, Jonathan, and Michael Brecher. 1988. *Crises in the Twentieth Century.* Vol. 2, *Handbook of Foreign Policy Crises.* Oxford: Pergamon Press.

Wilkenfeld, Jonathan, Gerald W. Hopple, Paul J. Rossa, and Stephen J. Andriole. 1980. *Foreign Policy Behavior.* Beverly Hills, CA: Sage.

Williams, John. 1993. "Dynamic Change, Specification Uncertainty, and Bayesian Vector Autoregression Analyses." *Political Analysis* 4:97–125.

Williams, John, and Robert Huckfeldt. 1996. "Empirically Discriminating between Chaotic and Stochastic Time Series." *Political Analysis* 6:125–49.

Williams, John, Michael D. McGinnis, and John C. Thomas. 1994. "Breaking the War-Economy Link." *International Interactions* 20:169–88.

Wilson, D. J. 1988. *Prehistoric Settlement Patterns in the Lower Santa Valley, Peru.* Washington, DC: Smithsonian Institution Press.

Wilson, Edward O. 1998. *Consilience: The Unity of Knowledge.* New York: Knopf.

Wilson, J. Brent. 1994. "The United States' Response to International Terrorism." In *The Deadly Sin of Terrorism: Its Effect on Democracy and Civil Liberty in Six Countries*, ed. David A. Charters. Westport, CT: Greenwood Press.

Winkates, James E. 1991. "Towards a Western Counter-terrorist Policy." In *Global Policy Studies: International Interaction toward Improving Public Policy,* ed. Stuart S. Nagel. Houndmills, Basingstoke: Macmillan.

Wohlforth, William C. 1987. "The Perception of Power: Russia in the Pre-1914 Balance." *World Politics* 39:353–81.

Wohlstetter, Albert. 1959. "The Delicate Balance of Terror." *Foreign Affairs* 37 (2): 211–34.

Woodward, Susan L. 1995. *Balkan Tragedy: Chaos and Dissolution After the Cold War.* Washington, DC: The Brookings Institution.

Woolley, S. L. 1963. *Excavations at Ur.* New York: Barnes and Noble.

Wright, H. T. 1977. "Recent Research on the Origin of the State." *Annual Review of Anthropology* 6:379–97.

Wright, Quincy. 1964. *Study of War.* Abridged ed. Chicago: University of Chicago Press.

Wright, Quincy. [1942] 1965. *A Study of War.* 2 vols., rev. ed. Chicago: University of Chicago Press.

Wright, Quincy. 1970. "How Hostilities Have Ended: Peace Treaties and Alternatives." In *How Wars End,* ed. W. T. R. Fox, *The Annals of the American Academy of Political and Social Science (Philadelphia)* 392:51–61.

Yadin, Yigael. 1963. *The Art of Warfare in Biblical Lands.* New York: McGraw-Hill.

Yaniv, Avner. 1994. *Politics and Strategy in Israel.* Tel-Aviv: Po'a'lim.

Yasin, W. 1970. "Excavations at Tell es-Sawwan," 1969. *Sumer* 26:3–20.

Yates, R. D. S. 1988. "New Light on Ancient Chinese Military Texts." *T'oung Pao* 74:211–48.

Yoon, Young-Kwan. 1990. "The Political Economy of Transition: Japanese Foreign Direct Investments in the 1980s." *World Politics* 43:1–27.

Young, Oran R. 1967. *The Intermediaries: Third Parties in International Crises.* Princeton: Princeton University Press.

Zacher, Mark W. 1979. *International Conflicts and Collective Security,* 1946–77. New York: Praeger.

Zagare, Frank C. 1987. *The Dynamics of Deterrence.* Chicago: University of Chicago Press.

Zagare, Frank C. 1992. "NATO, Rational Escalation and Flexible Response." *Journal of Peace Research* 29:435–54.

Zartman, I. William. 1989. *Ripe for Resolution: Conflict and Intervention in Africa.* New York: Oxford University Press.

Zartman, I. William. 1990. "Negotiating Effectively with Terrorists." In *The Politics of Counterterrorism: The Ordeal of Democratic States.,* ed. Barry Rubin. Washington, DC: The Johns Hopkins Foreign Policy Institute.

Zartman, I. William. 1998. "Putting Humpty-Dumpty Together Again." In *The International Spread of Ethnic Conflict: Fear, Diffusion and Escalation,* ed. David A. Lake and Donald Rothchild. Princeton: Princeton University Press.

Zartman, I. William, and Saadia Touval. 1985. "International Mediation: Conflict Resolution and Power Politics." *Journal of Social Issues* 41:27–45.

Zimmermann, Tim. 1994. "Coercive Diplomacy and Libya." In *The Limits of Coercive Diplomacy*, 2nd ed., ed. Alexander L. George and William E. Simons. Boulder, CO: Westview Press.

Zinnes, Dina A. 1980a. "Three Puzzles in Search of a Researcher." *International Studies Quarterly* 24:315–42.

Zinnes, Dina A. 1980b. "Why War? Evidence on the Outbreak of International Conflict." In *Handbook of Political Conflict: Theory and Research,* ed. Ted R. Gurr. New York: The Free Press.

Zolberg, Aristide R. 1983. "'World' and 'System': A Misalliance." In *Contending Approaches to World System Analysis,* ed. William R. Thompson. Beverly Hills, CA: Sage.

Zulaika, Joseba, and William A. Douglass. 1996. *Terror and Taboo: The Follies, Fables, and Faces of Terrorism.* New York: Routledge.

Index